THE INVENTION OF

SIMPLICITY

PUBLISHED BY 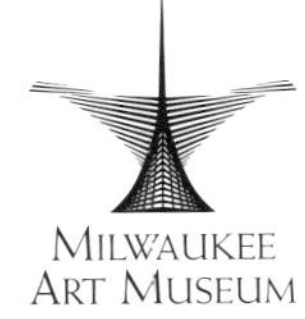 MILWAUKEE ART MUSEUM 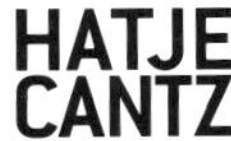 HATJE CANTZ

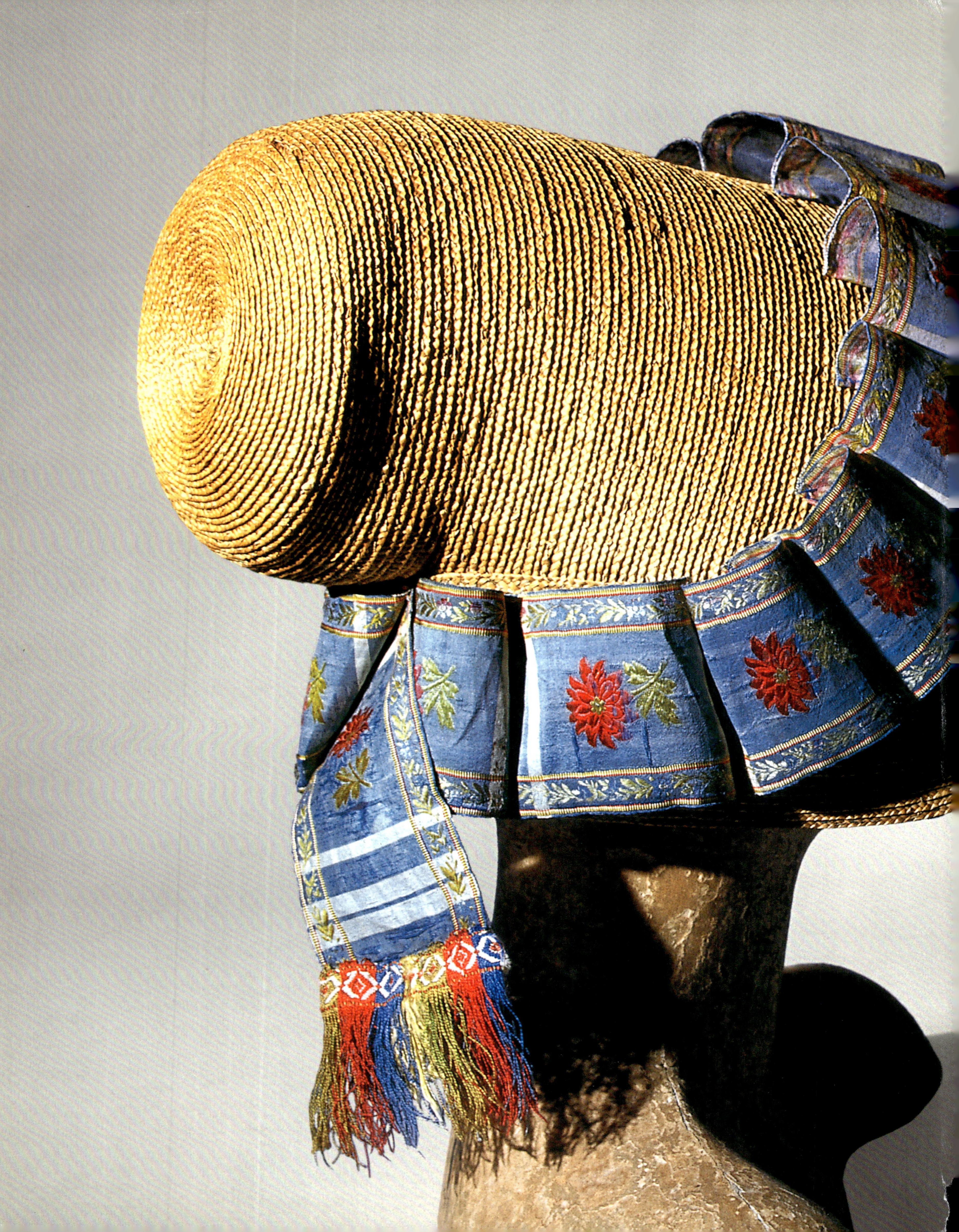

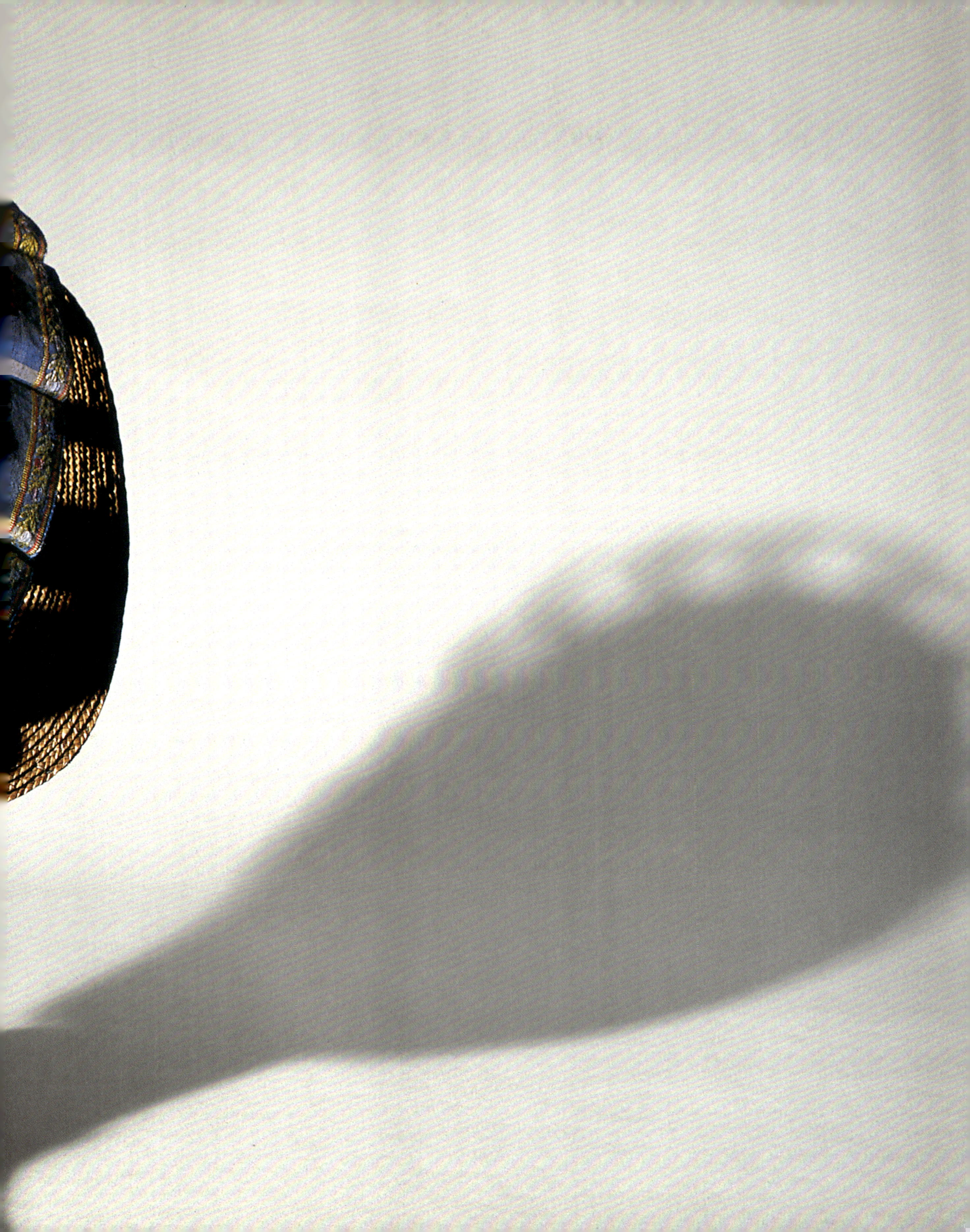

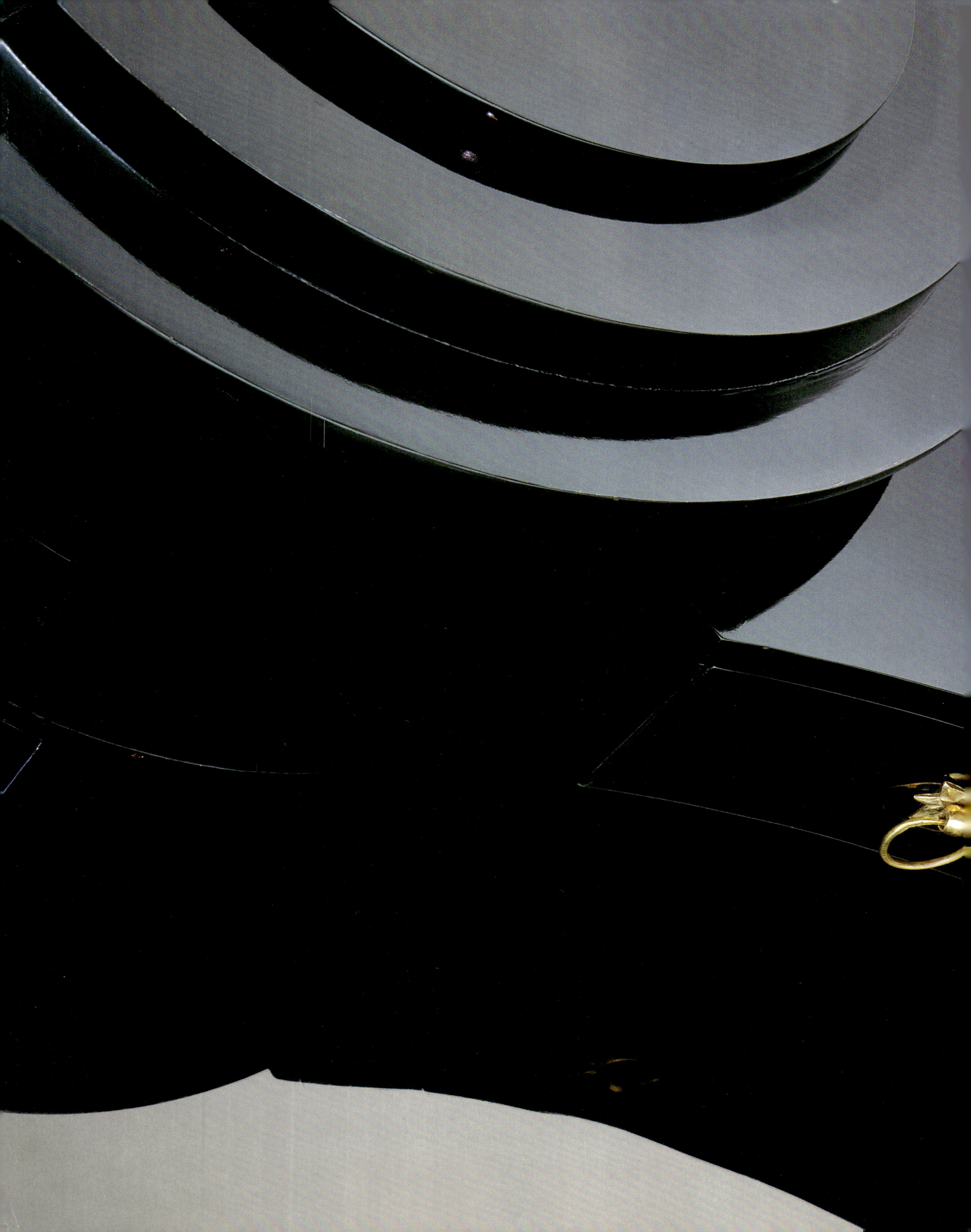

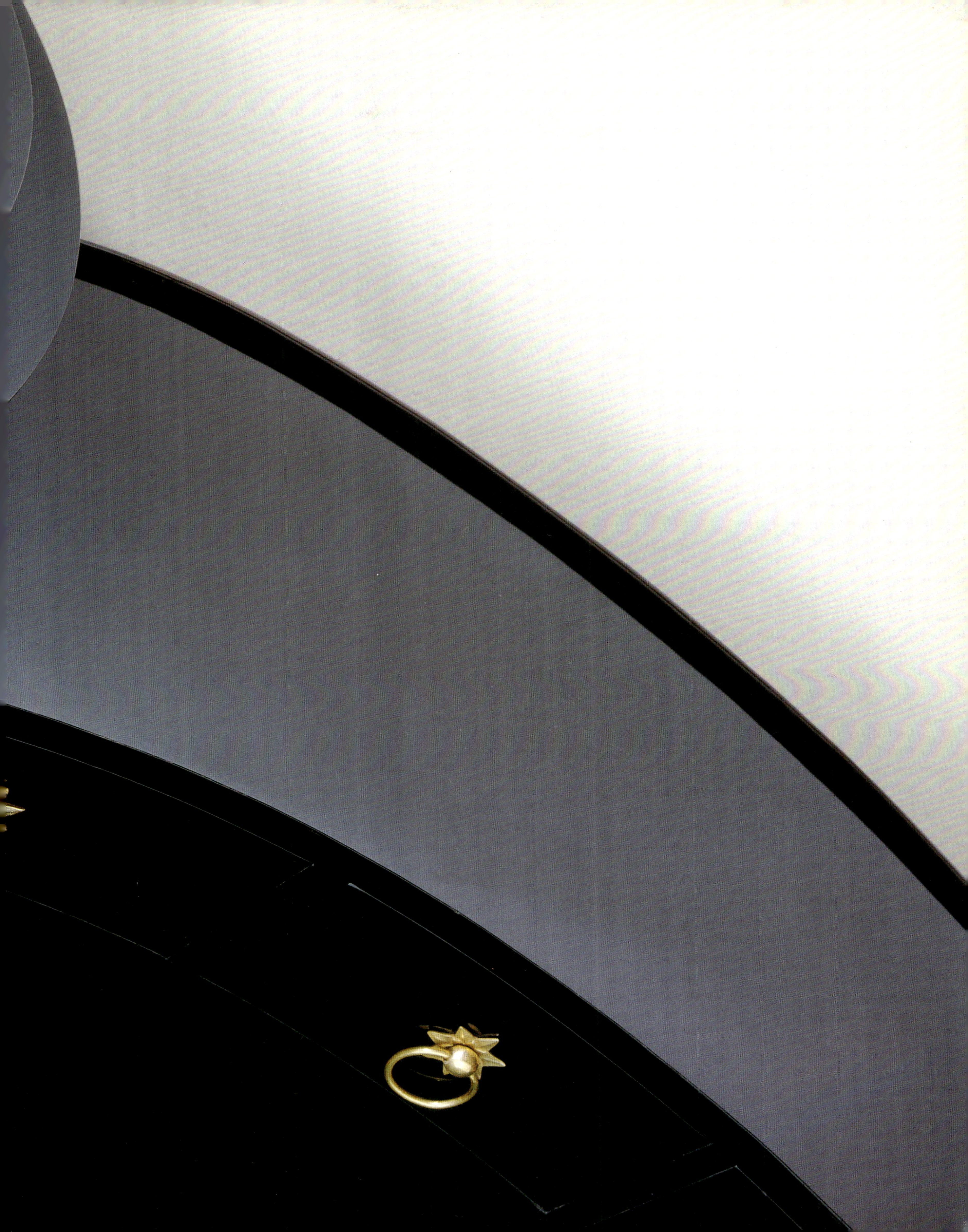

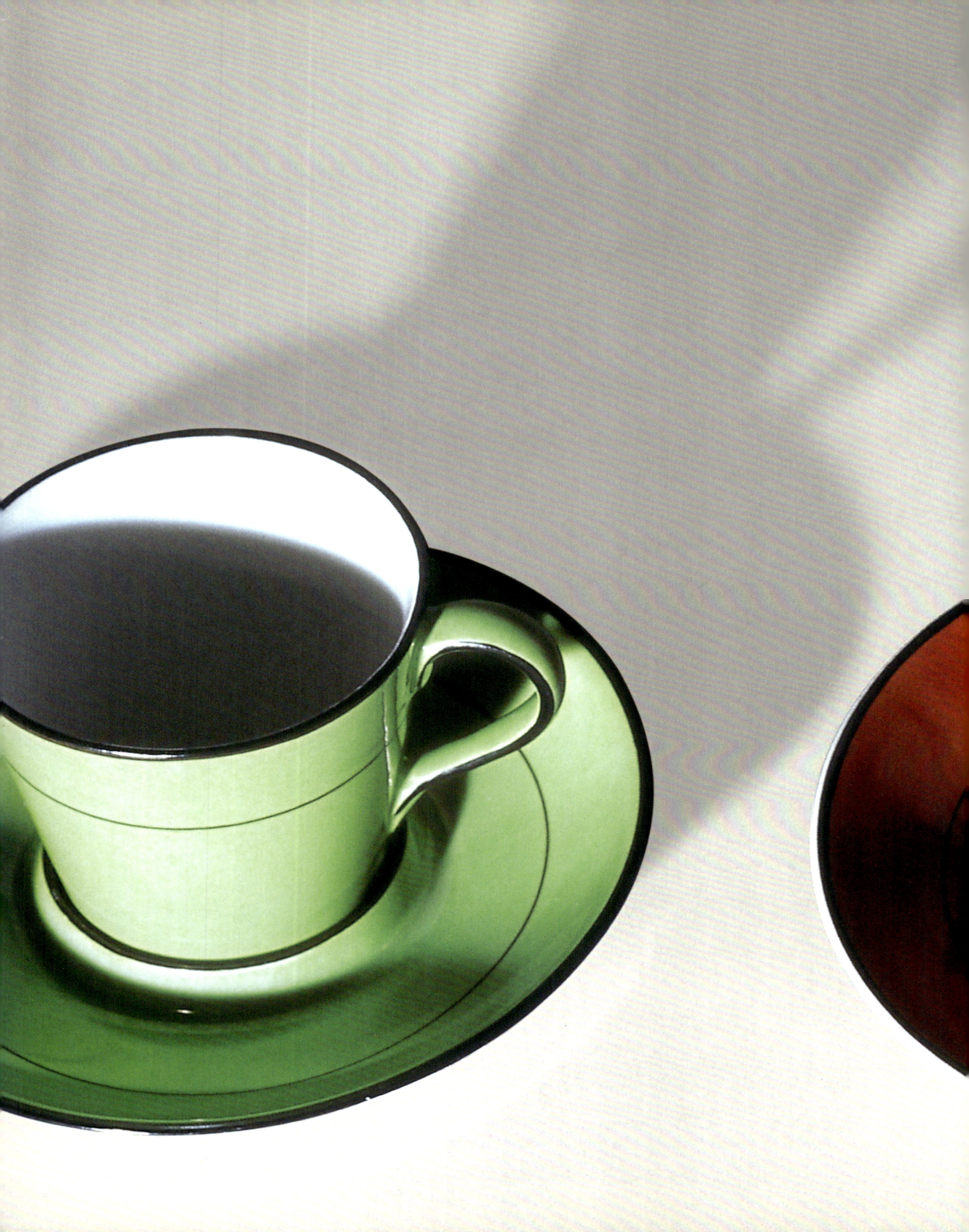

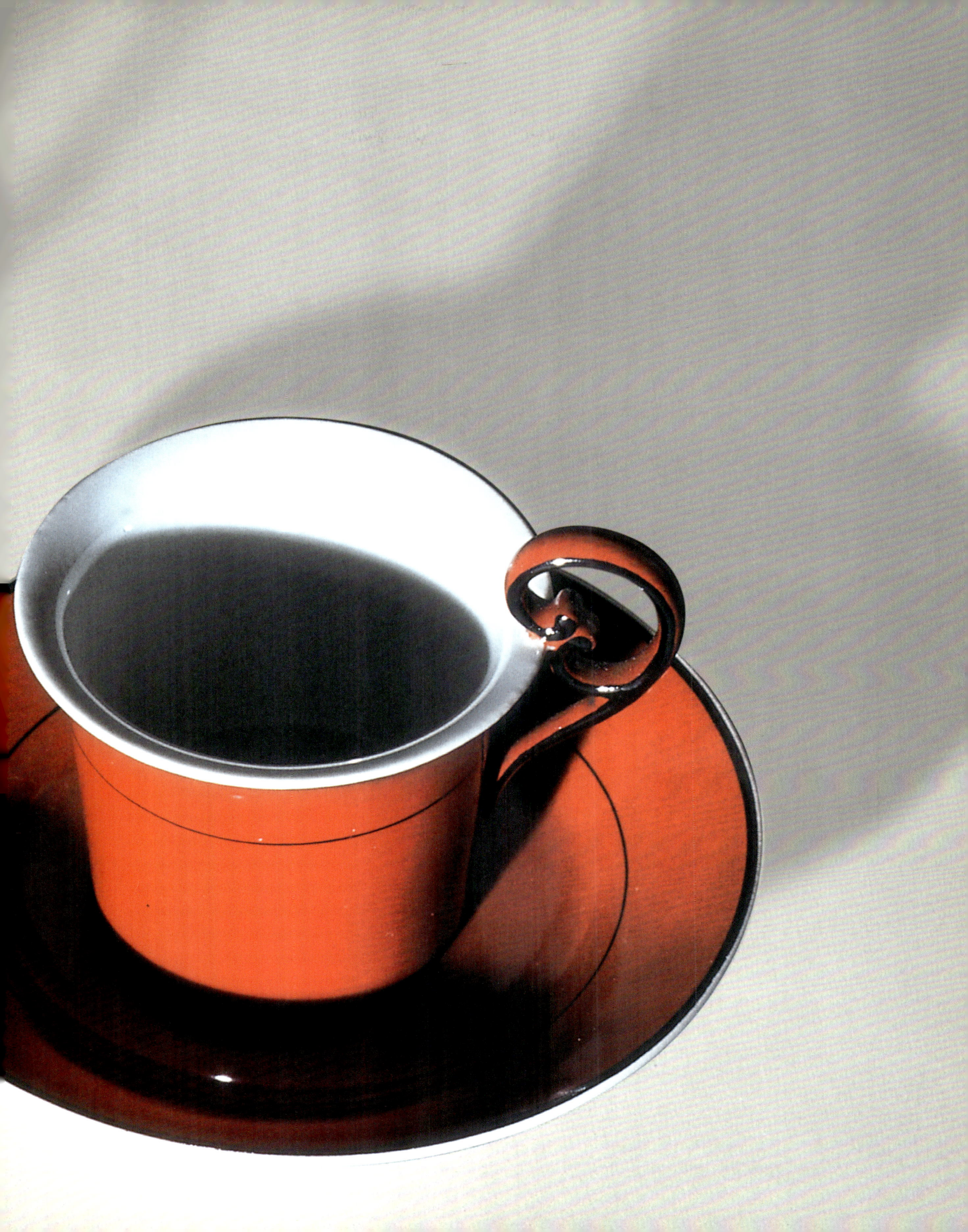

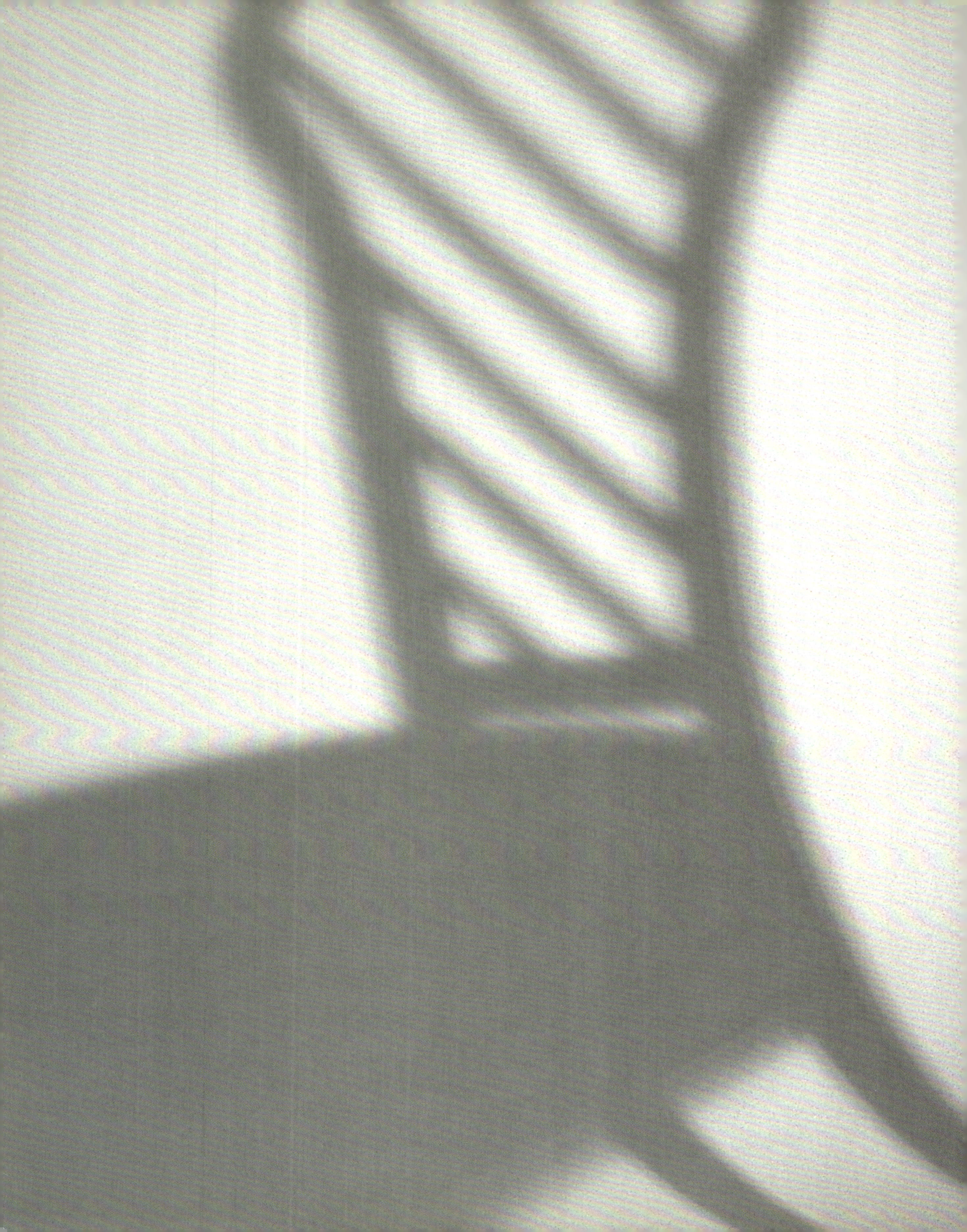

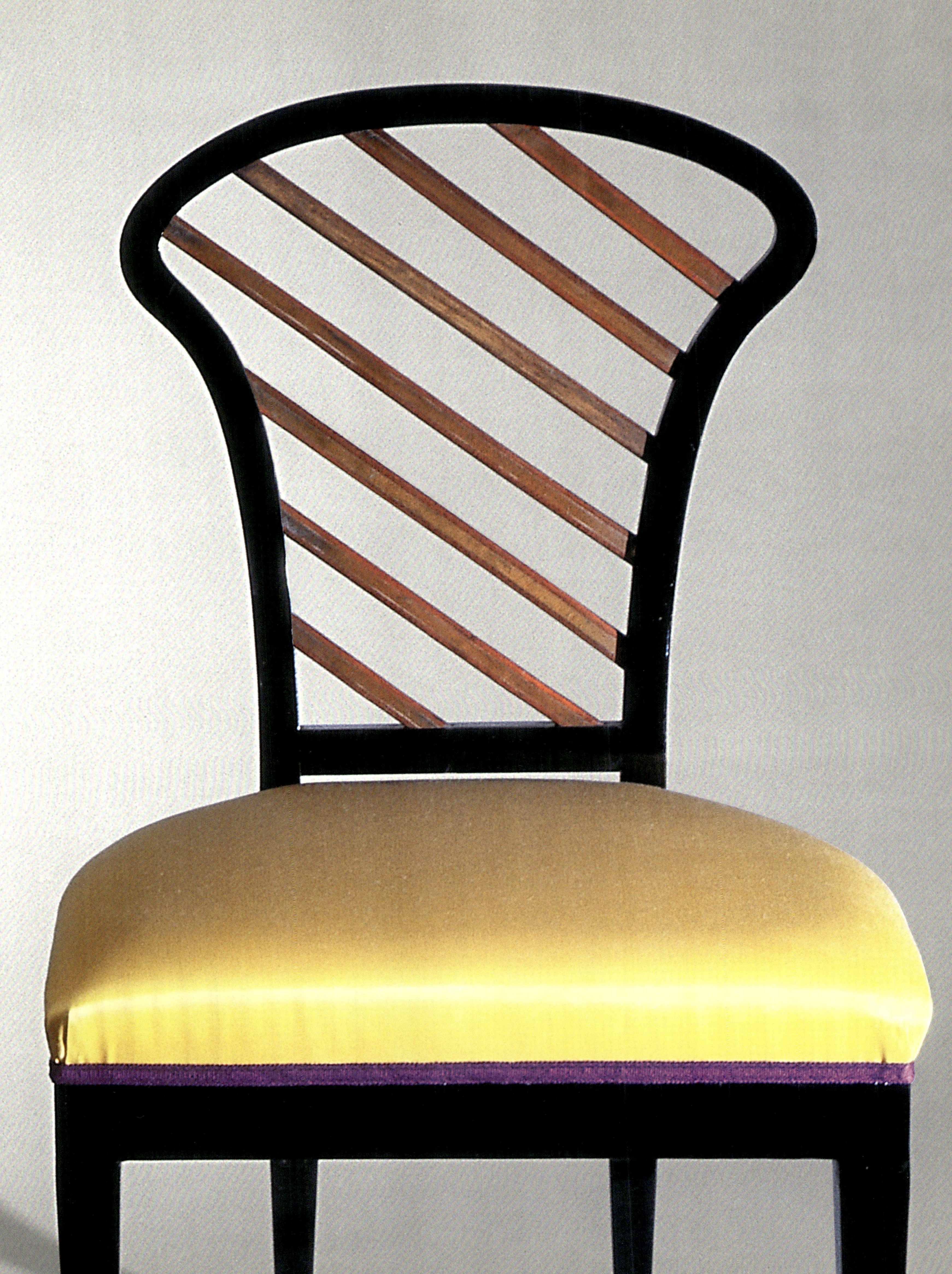

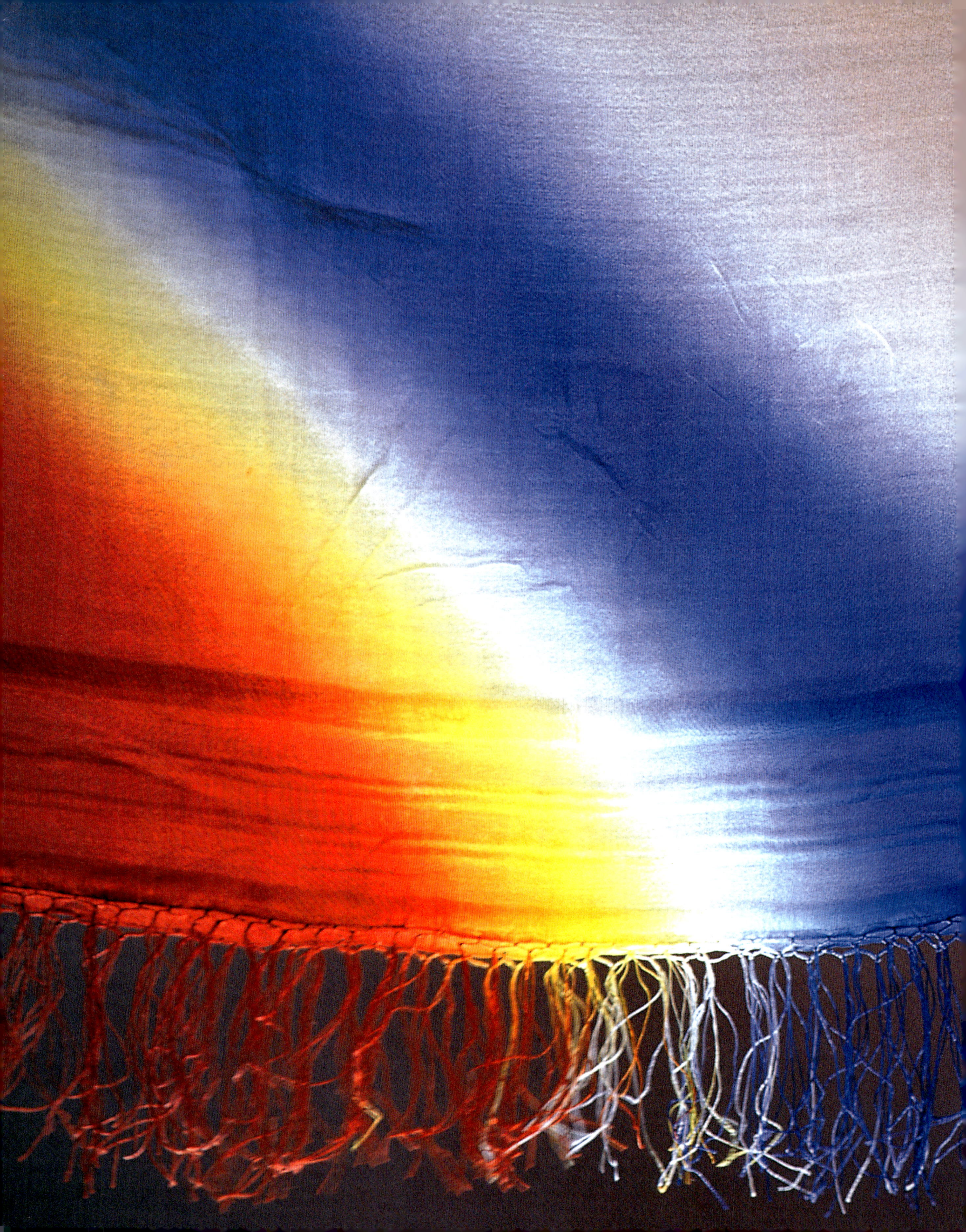

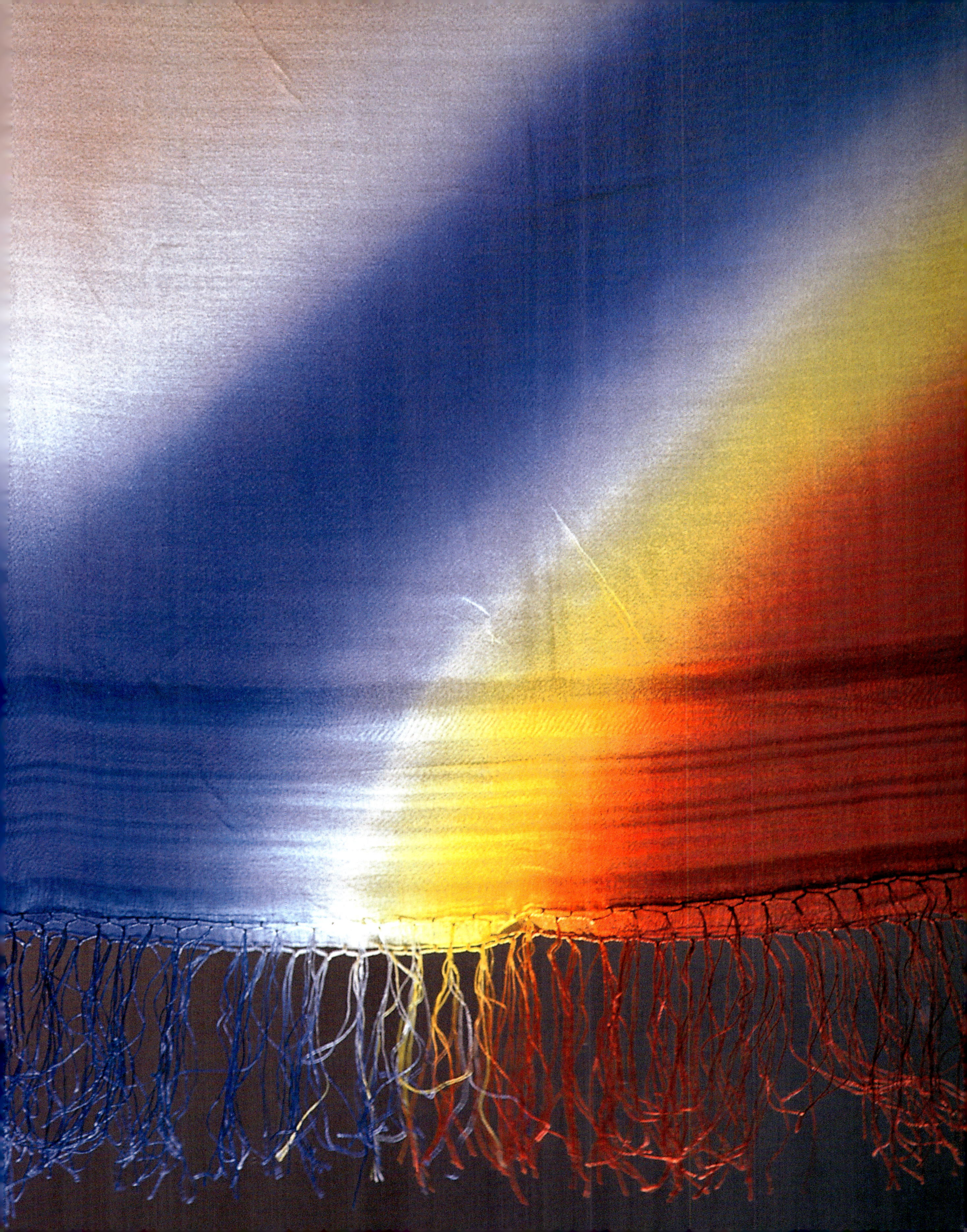

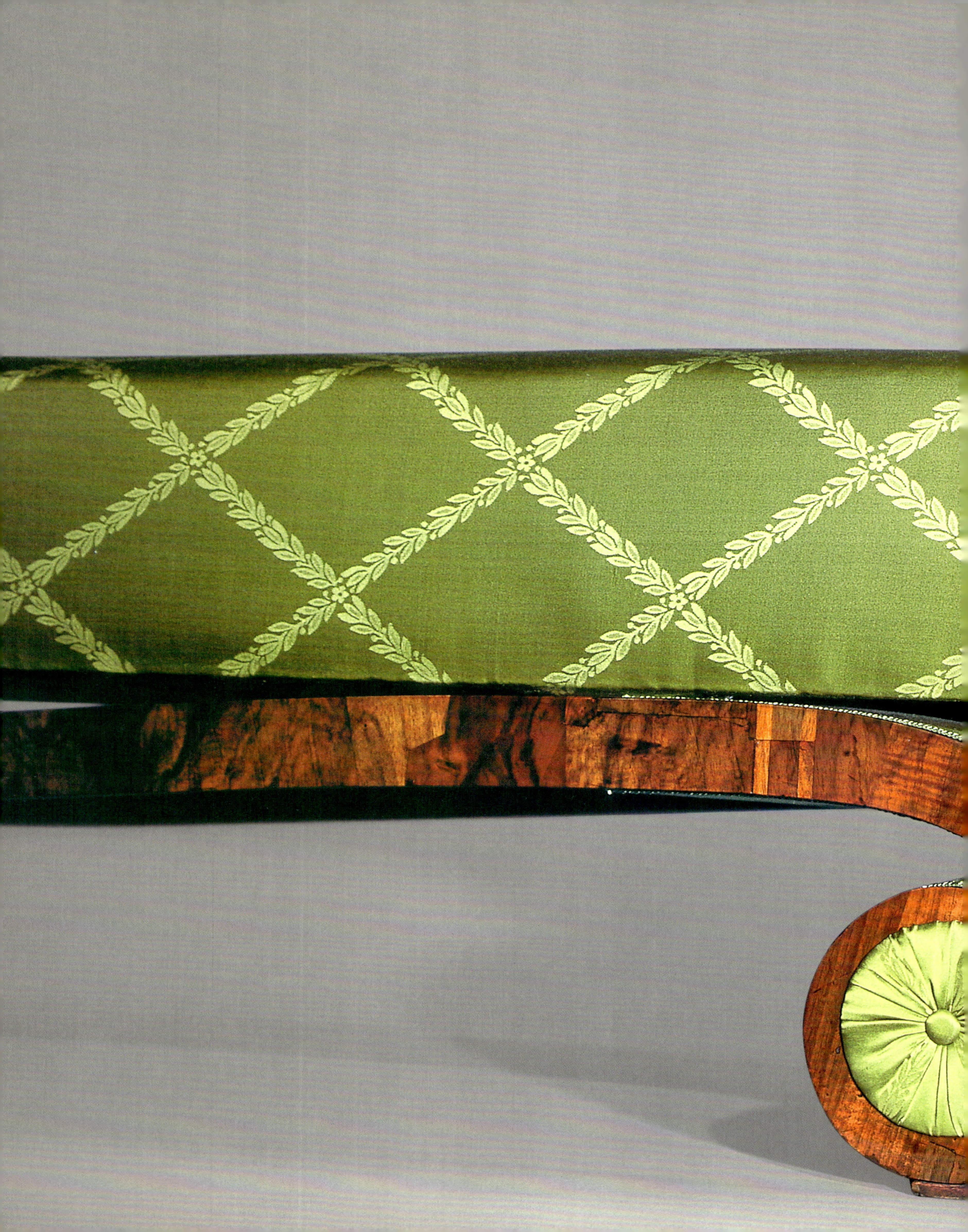

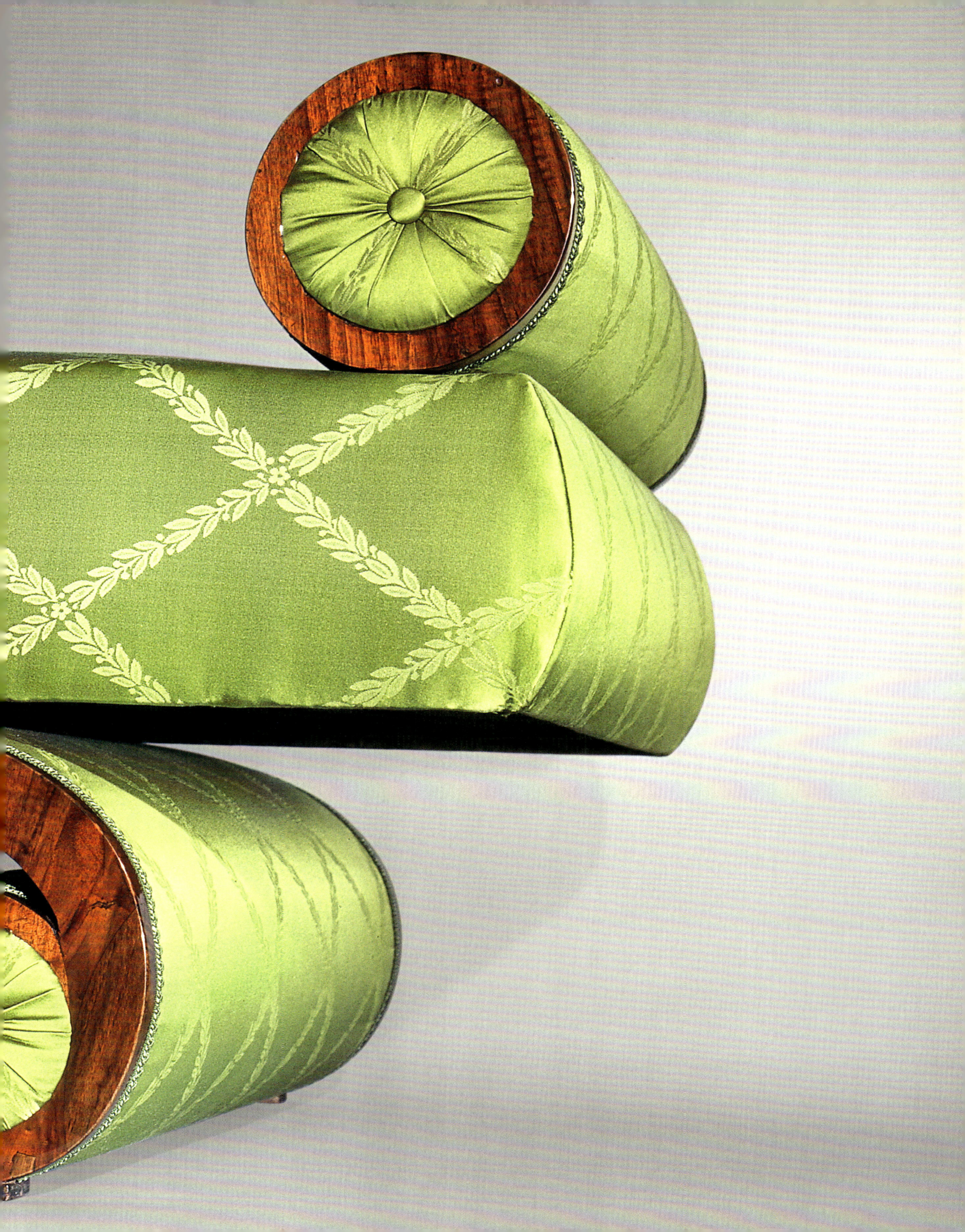

BIEDER

THE INVENTION OF SIMPLICITY

HANS OTTOMEYER, KLAUS ALBRECHT SCHRÖDER, AND LAURIE WINTERS

MEIER

CONTRIBUTIONS BY ALBRECHT PYRITZ AND MARIA LUISE STERNATH-SCHUPPANZ
Paul Asenbaum, Regina Karner, Gisela Maul, Jutta Annette Page, Cornelia Reiter, Laurie A. Stein, Sabine Thümmler, and Christian Witt-Dörring

MILWAUKEE ART MUSEUM ALBERTINA DEUTSCHES HISTORISCHES MUSEUM
MILWAUKEE VIENNA BERLIN

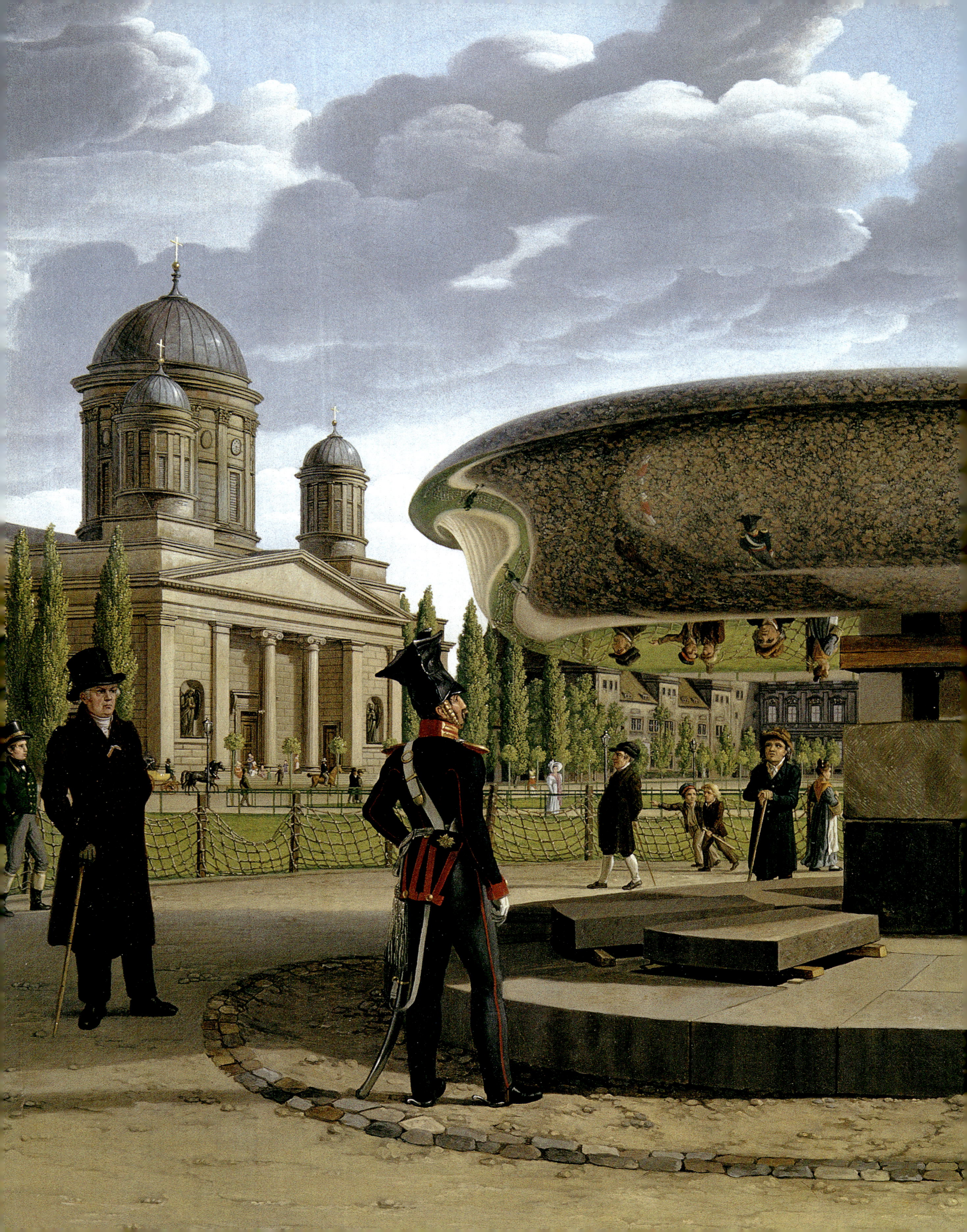

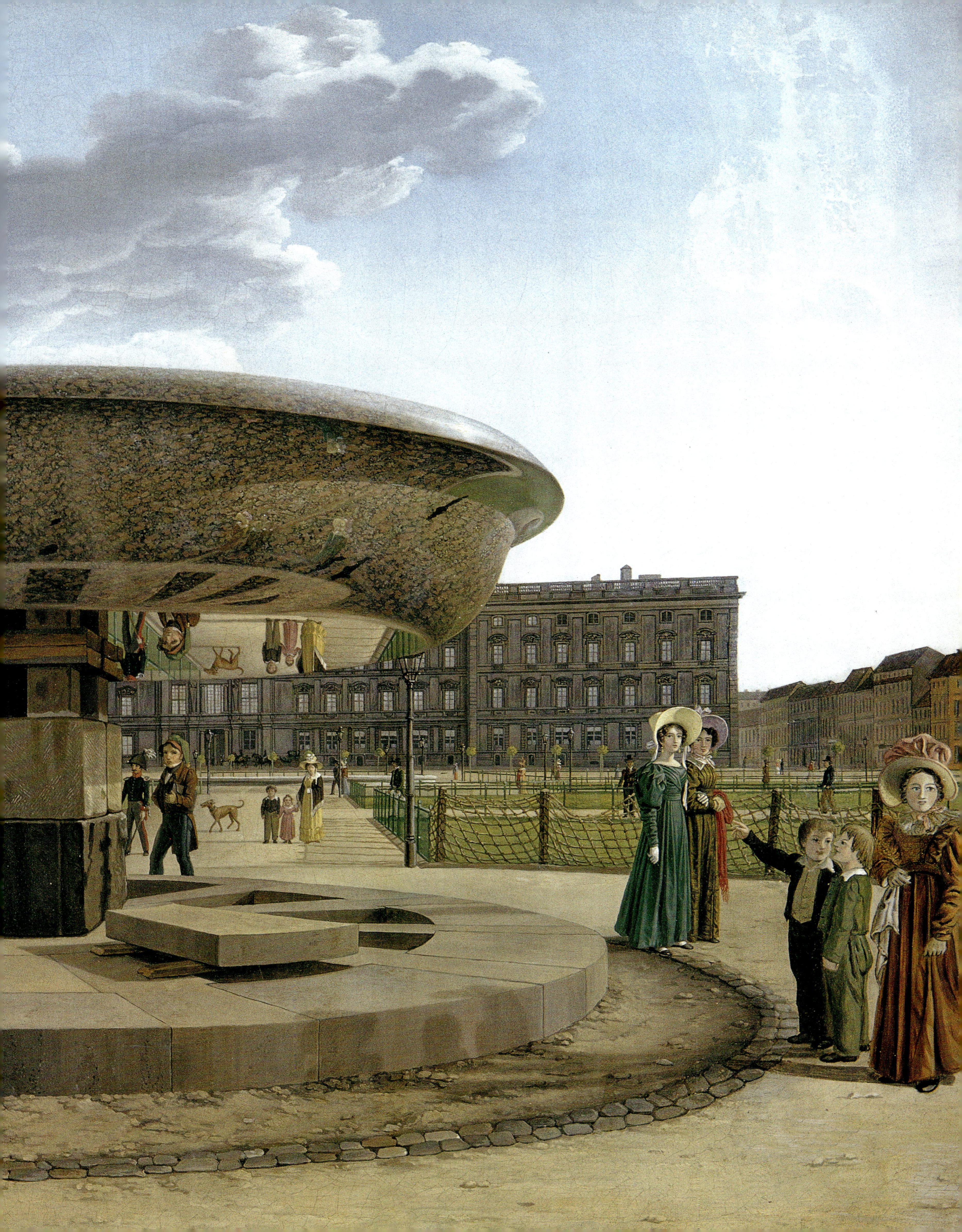

CONTENTS

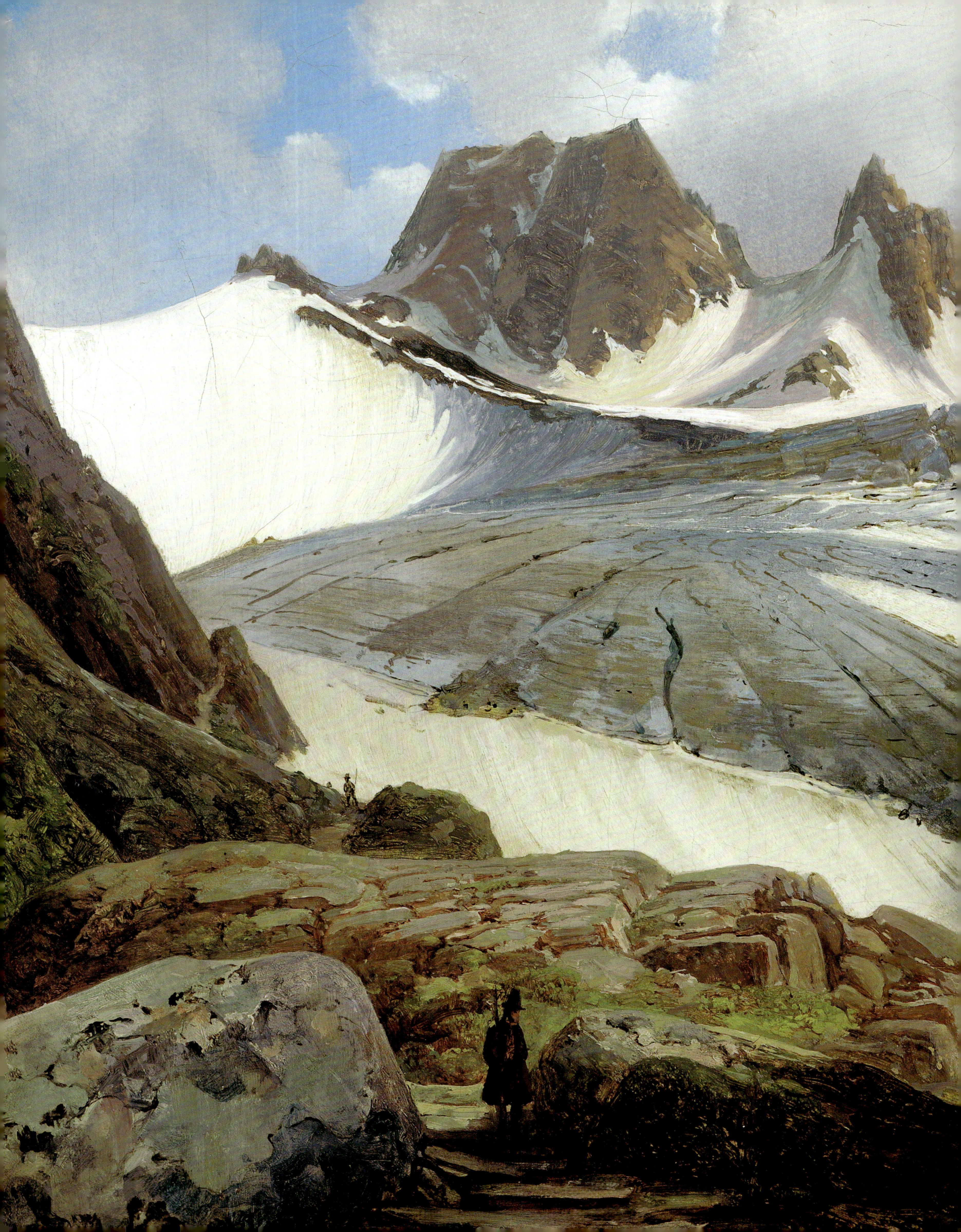

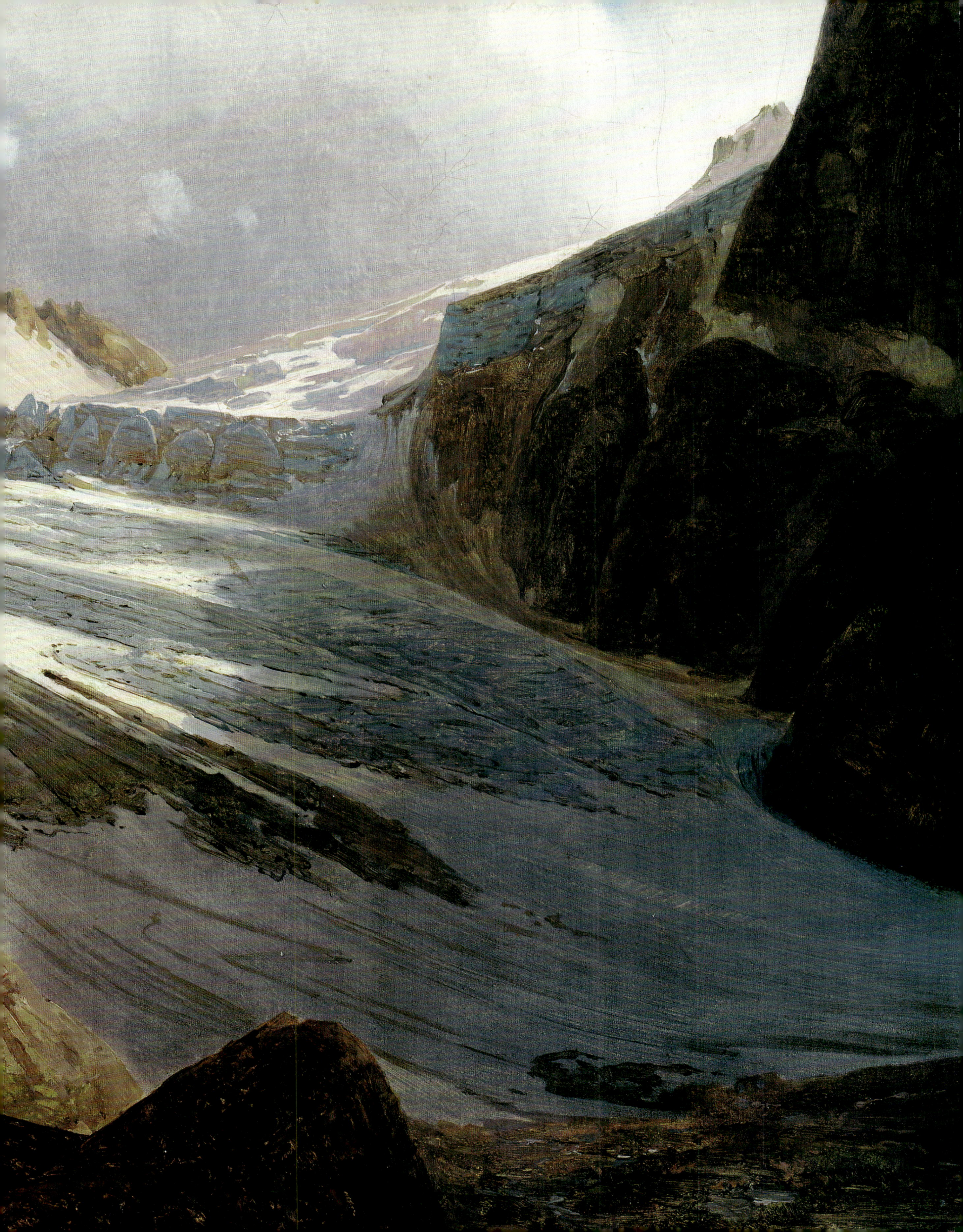

DAVID GORDON
Director and CEO, Milwaukee Art Museum, Milwaukee

HANS OTTOMEYER
General Director, Deutsches Historisches Museum, Berlin

KLAUS ALBRECHT SCHRÖDER
Director, Albertina, Vienna

FOREWORD

Biedermeier: The Invention of Simplicity is not only a deeply rewarding exhibition, it also represents an enriching international collaboration among leading institutions from three different nations and traveling to a fourth. The exhibition and accompanying catalogue contain many of the greatest works of arts produced during the Biedermeier period. Striking in their simplicity and modern design, these works are certain to resonate with museum audiences today. The exhibition appears substantially the same in Milwaukee, Vienna, and Berlin, with changes only to light-sensitive objects. Due to space limitations, a truncated version will be shown at the final venue in Paris.

Biedermeier: The Invention of Simplicity is the first exhibition in Europe to focus on Biedermeier around 1820 and the very first exhibition on any aspect of the period in North America. Also unprecedented is the combined presentation of furniture, decorative arts, paintings, and drawings in an effort to define the core aesthetics of the period. Earlier exhibitions have aimed at identifying generally the nature of the period or at a cultural interpretation that has mistakenly grounded the objects in the taste of the emerging bourgeois class. The present exhibition's unconventional emphasis on aesthetics is intended to provide a fresh perspective. Many of the more than 400 works of art are on view for the first time. Offering an exhibition on this scale to the public and the scholarly community has been a challenging but gratifying feat of coordination.

Our greatest debt is to the lenders – institutions as well as private individuals – who graciously consented to part with cherished artworks for almost a year. All lenders have been identified in the catalogue, but we would like to single out Ilsebill Barta, Director of the Bundesmobilienverwaltung, Hofmobiliendepot, Möbel Museum Wien and Silberkammer Wien, for kindly agreeing to lend more than sixty works; the essential themes developed in the exhibition would not have been possible without this important loan.

We owe special thanks to the respective curators at our institutions – Laurie Winters at the Milwaukee Art Museum, Albrecht Pyritz at Berlin's Deutsches Historisches Museum, and Maria Luise Sternath-Schuppanz at the Albertina, Vienna – for shaping the content of the project and articulating that vision in the catalogue. We are very grateful to Henri Loyrette, Director of the Musée du Louvre, for his enthusiasm and support in mounting a version of the exhibition in Paris, and we thank Louvre Curator Marc Bascou for his participation in the selection of objects. The combined efforts and cooperation among these institutions have resulted in an exhibition of the highest standards.

We are also deeply grateful to the American, Austrian, and German embassies and to local consulates for their enthusiastic support and assistance throughout the entire project.

To our colleagues in Europe and the United States and to all of the sponsors who have generously enabled this exhibition to travel, we offer our sincere appreciation. We are confident that our gratitude will be echoed by the tens of thousands of visitors on both sides of the Atlantic who will be able to discover and enjoy one of the great periods of European art.

LENDERS TO THE EXHIBITION

Asenbaum Collection
Basel, Kunstmuseum Basel
Berlin, Collection of Manfred Ludewig
Berlin, Deutsches Historisches Museum
Berlin, Humboldt-Universität zu Berlin, Museum für Naturkunde
Berlin, Schloss Tegel Verwaltungs GmbH
Berlin, Staatliche Museen zu Berlin, Kunstbibliothek
Berlin, Staatliche Museen zu Berlin, Nationalgalerie
Berlin, Staatliche Museen zu Berlin, Kupferstichkabinett
Berlin, Stiftung Preussische Schlösser und Gärten Berlin-Brandenburg, KPM-Porzellansammlung des Landes Berlin
Berlin, Stiftung Stadtmuseum Berlin
Braunschweig, Richard Borek Stiftung
Bruchsal, Staatliche Schlösser und Gärten Baden-Württemberg
Chicago, The Art Institute of Chicago
Chicago, Rita Bucheit
Cleveland, The Cleveland Museum of Art
Coburg, Kunstsammlungen der Veste Coburg
Cologne, Wallraf-Richartz-Museum
Copenhagen, The Danish Museum of Decorative Art
Copenhagen, The David Collection
Copenhagen, The Hirschsprung Collection
Copenhagen, Ny Carlsberg Glyptotek
Copenhagen, Statens Museum for Kunst
Dresden, Staatliche Kunstsammlungen Dresden, Galerie Neue Meister
Frankfurt am Main, Städelsches Kunstinstitut
Graz, Neue Galerie am Landesmuseum Joanneum
Halle (Saale), Stiftung Moritzburg, Kunstmuseum des Landes Sachsen–Anhalt
Hanover, Niedersächsisches Landesmuseum Hannover
Innsbruck, Tiroler Landesmuseum Ferdinandeum
Kassel, Staatliche Museen Kassel
Kassel, Stadtmuseum Kassel
Kiel, Kunsthalle zu Kiel
Kronberg, Hessische Hausstiftung
Linz, Lentos Kunstmuseum Linz
London, Hildegard Fritz-Denneville Fine Arts, Ltd.
Lübeck, Museen für Kunst und Kulturgeschichte der Hansestadt Lübeck
Milwaukee, Milwaukee Art Museum
Munich, Bayerisches Nationalmuseum
Munich, Bayerische Verwaltung der staatlichen Schlösser, Gärten und Seen
Munich, Deutsches Museum
Munich, Kunstkammer Georg Laue München
Munich, Münchner Stadtmuseum
Munich, Schlapka KG, Axel Schlapka
Munster, Museum für Lackkunst
New York, Barry Friedman, Ltd.

New York, Collection of Christopher Forbes
New York, Collection of Ellen and Bill Taubman
New York, Daniel Romualdez Collection
New York, Eugene V. Thaw Collection
New York, Iliad Antik
New York, The Metropolitan Museum of Art
New York, Private Collection, Courtesy Iliad Antik, New York
Nuremberg, Germanisches Nationalmuseum
Paris, Musée du Louvre
Paris and New York, Didier Aaron, Inc.
Paris, Private Collection, Courtesy Didier Aaron & Cie
Potsdam, Stiftung Preussische Schlösser und Gärten Berlin-Brandenburg
Prague, Fürst Karl zu Schwarzenberg
Prague, Galerie Zlatá Husa
Prague, Museum of Decorative Arts
Prague, National Gallery
Prague, National Heritage Institute
Salzburg, Salzburger Museum Carolino Augusteum
St. Petersburg, The State Museum Reserve
St. Pölten, Niederösterreichisches Landesmuseum
Toledo, Ohio, Toledo Museum of Art
Vaduz/Vienna, Sammlungen des Fürsten von und zu Liechtenstein
Vienna, Akademie der bildenden Künste, Kupferstichkabinett
Vienna, Albertina
Vienna, Bundesmobilienverwaltung, Hofmobiliendepot, Möbel Museum Wien
Vienna, Bundesmobilienverwaltung, Silberkammer Wien
Vienna, C. Bednarczyk
Vienna, Collection of Christian Witt-Dörring
Vienna, Collection of Irmagard Müller-Mezin
Vienna, D & S Antiques
Vienna, Galerie und Auktionshaus Hassfurther
Vienna, Kovacek Spiegelgasse Glas
Vienna, Leopold Museum
Vienna, Michael Huey
Vienna, Österreichische Galerie Belvedere
Vienna, Österreichische Nationalbibliothek, Bildarchiv und Porträtsammlung
Vienna, Technisches Museum Wien
Vienna, Wien Museum
Warsaw, National Museum in Warsaw
Weimar, Stiftung Weimarer Klassik, Goethe-Nationalmuseum
Windsor, Windsor Castle, The Royal Library
Zurich, Uhrenmuseum Beyer Zürich
And private collectors who wish to remain anonymous

SPONSOR'S STATEMENT

Chris Abele, Chief Executive Officer
Argosy Foundation

This is the sixth exhibition the Argosy Foundation has supported at the Milwaukee Art Museum, and it is certainly one of the most ambitious. *Biedermeier: The Invention of Simplicity* is not about a particular artist, school, or medium. It is about new aesthetic ideas blossoming in Central and Northern Europe in the early 1800s and the expression they found in art and design. This exhibition brings you the very best examples, gathered from museums and private collections throughout Europe and the United States.

Crisp, uncluttered, and concise. Biedermeier is always about refined forms, and its greatest contribution lies in its concept of simplicity. Its affection for natural materials, clean lines, graceful curves, and careful craftsmanship anticipates the Wiener Werkstätte by more than a century. While Biedermeier style is most closely associated in the United States with furniture, its expression of simplicity, purity of form, and brilliant color can also be found in painting and drawing of the period. The exhibition's unconventional emphasis on aesthetics and the idea of beauty is to be praised. The Biedermeier style offers something elemental, simple, enduring, and sure. Its beauty reaches across the centuries and touches us today.

The exhibition joins four important museums in an international collaboration that links Milwaukee with Berlin, Vienna, and Paris. Building on the Milwaukee Art Museum's impressive record of exhibitions of earlier European art, *Biedermeier: The Invention of Simplicity* is an outstanding example of what can be accomplished when strong partners join hands. The Argosy Foundation is very proud to help bring this wonderful exhibition to life.

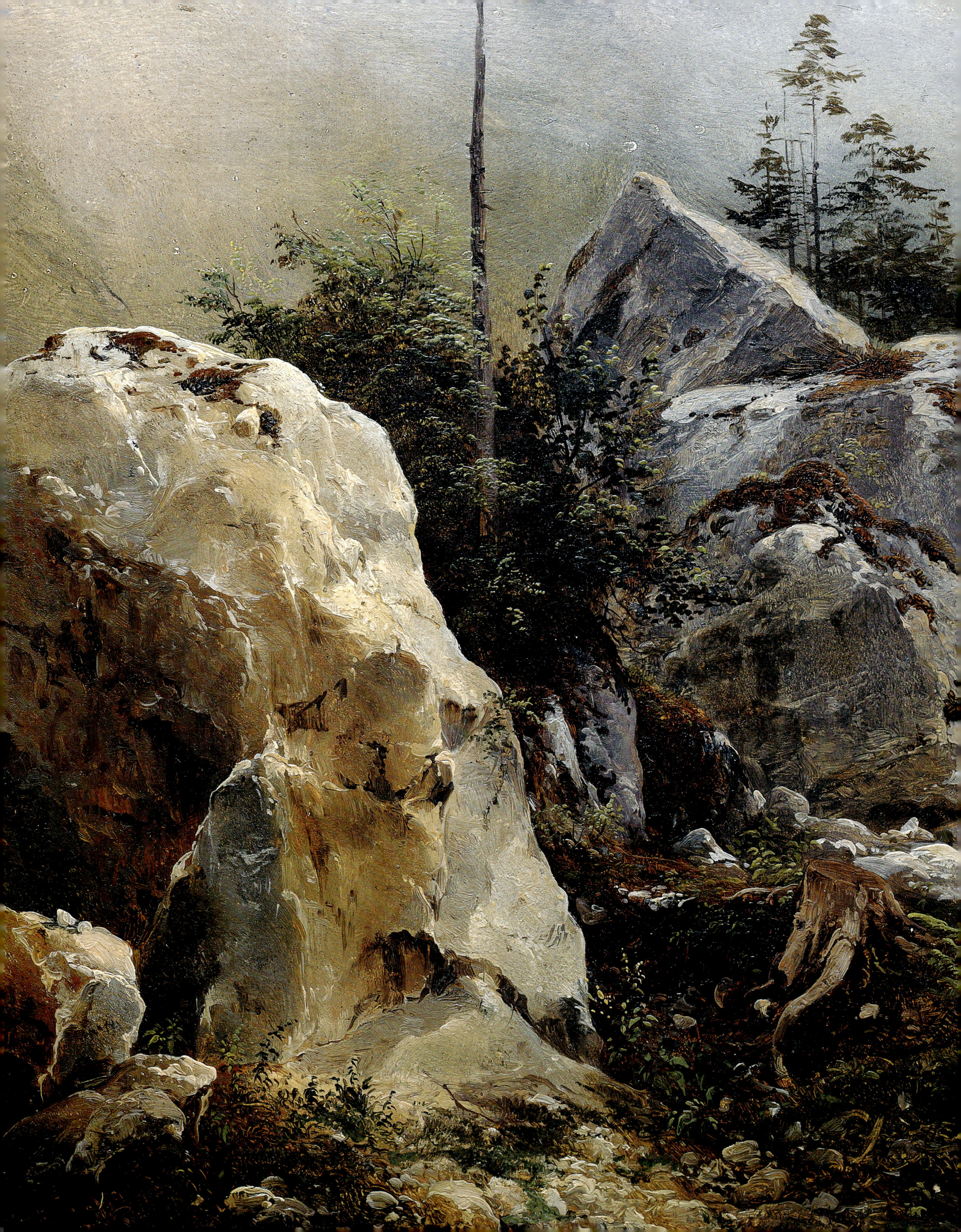

ACKNOWLEDGMENTS

Laurie Winters, Milwaukee Art Museum, Milwaukee
Albrecht Pyritz, Deutsches Historisches Museum, Berlin
Maria Luise Sternath-Schuppanz, Albertina, Vienna

Biedermeier: The Invention of Simplicity was originally conceived as an exhibition proposal at the Milwaukee Art Museum and enthusiastically supported by its Director and CEO David Gordon. Hans Ottomeyer, General Director of the Deutsches Historisches Museum in Berlin, and Klaus Albrecht Schröder, Director of the Albertina in Vienna, who have published widely on Biedermeier topics, immediately embraced the potential of an international exhibition on the subject. They joined the project not only as museum directors but as partners in the formation of the exhibition. Christian Witt-Dörring, Paul Asenbaum, both independent consultants in Vienna, and Marc Bascou, Senior Curator and Head of the Département des Objets d'Art at the Louvre, soon joined the group and the exhibition was well under way. We would like to offer our sincere thanks to all the members of the team, and to Laurie A. Stein, independent consultant, Chicago, who helped with the early conceptualization of the exhibition.

A project of this magnitude would not have been possible without the collaboration of individuals from around the world who brought their knowledge and expertise to the exhibition and catalogue. The catalogue bears eloquent testimony to the degree of collaboration and shared enthusiasm for the exhibition. For their essays, we would like to thank Hans Ottomeyer, Christian Witt-Dörring, and Laurie A. Stein. We would also like to offer a special note of gratitude to the authors who contributed the introductions that precede the plate sections: Paul Asenbaum; Regina Karner, Curator, Wien Museum; Gisela Maul, Curator, Stiftung Weimarer Klassik, Goethe-Nationalmuseum, Weimar; Jutta Annette Page, Curator of Glass, Toledo Museum of Art; Cornelia Reiter, Akademie der bildenden Künste, Kupferstichkabinett, Vienna; Laurie A. Stein; and Sabine Thümmler, Curator, Hessisches Landesmuseum, Deutsches Tapetenmuseum, Kassel.

Colleagues in every department at the organizing institutions have contributed immeasurably to bringing the project to fruition. We are particularly grateful to curatorial assistants Stefanie Chaloupek in Vienna and Catherine Sawinski in Milwaukee, and to Mary Weaver Chapin, Assistant Curator of Earlier European Art at the Milwaukee Art Museum, who helped with the bibliography and countless other details. For exhibition management, we thank Margarete Heck and Lisa Kreil in Vienna and Ulrike Kretzschmar and Nicole Schmidt in Berlin. We also thank the many departments in our mutual museums – conservation, education, development, marketing, and exhibition design – for their tireless work behind the scenes.

For his commitment to copublishing the beautiful catalogue that accompanies this exhibition in both English and German editions, we want to acknowledge Markus Hartmann of Hatje Cantz. We are also extremely grateful to the designers of the book, Kathy Fredrickson and Garrett Niksch of Studio Blue, whose sensitivity and clear-sightedness have produced a volume of exceptional elegance. Lois Lammerhuber must also be recognized for his photography that has created a book not only of great beauty but one of unconventional design. The translators are also to be commended for their careful work at every stage of the book's development. Our greatest debt is in many ways to the English and German editors, Terry Ann R. Neff and Karin Osbahr, who brought the catalogue to completion under daunting time pressures without any sacrifice to the quality of the book.

We also offer our sincere thanks to Sotheby's and to Furthermore: A Program of the J. M. Kaplan Fund for helping to fund the exhibition catalogue.

For their help in many ways, it is a pleasure to thank the following: Tine Blicher-Moritz, Bruce Boucher, Adam Brown, Michelle Bucheit, Rita Bucheit, Bodil Büsk Laursen, Isabella Croy, Gudrun Danzer, John Dienhart, Elke Doppler, Stephanie Ellis, Marianne Feiler, Helyn Goldenberg, Sabine Grabner, Maren Gröning, Andreas Gugler, Eleonore Gürtler, Robert and Eileen Kalupa, Karl Kemp, Bonnie Kirschstein, Helena Koenigsmarkova, Leonore Koschnick, Monika Knofler, Wolfgang Krug, Susan Kurek, Manfred Ludewig, Jan Gorm Madsen, Kasper Monrad, Elisabeth Novak-Thaller, Eva-Maria Orosz, Sabine Puppe, Nina del Rio, Lea Ross, Lauren Schadford, John Schaefer, Nikolaus Schaffer, Eugene Edward Schlepp, Uwe Schögl, Jutta Schütt, Sabine Schulze, Michael Schweller, Niall Smith, Achim Stiegel, Stephen Szczepanek, Patricia Tang, Carolle Thibaut-Pomerantz, Charles Venable, Radim Vondracek, Clair Watson, Hubert Weitensfelder, Heinz Widauer, Angus Wilkie, Samuel Wittwer, Ghenette Zelleke, and Alfred Ziffer. To all who have made this enterprise possible, we extend our most sincere thanks.

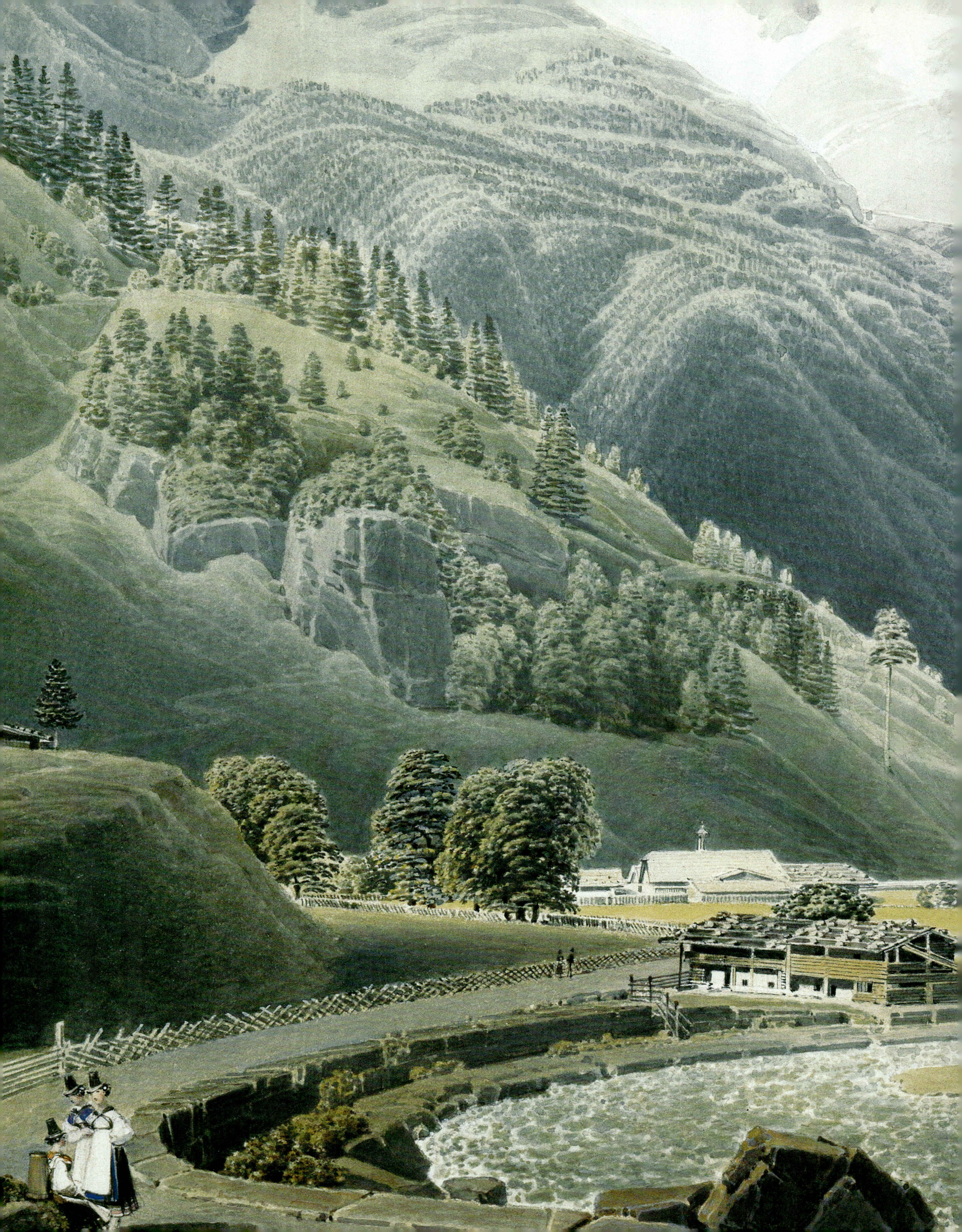

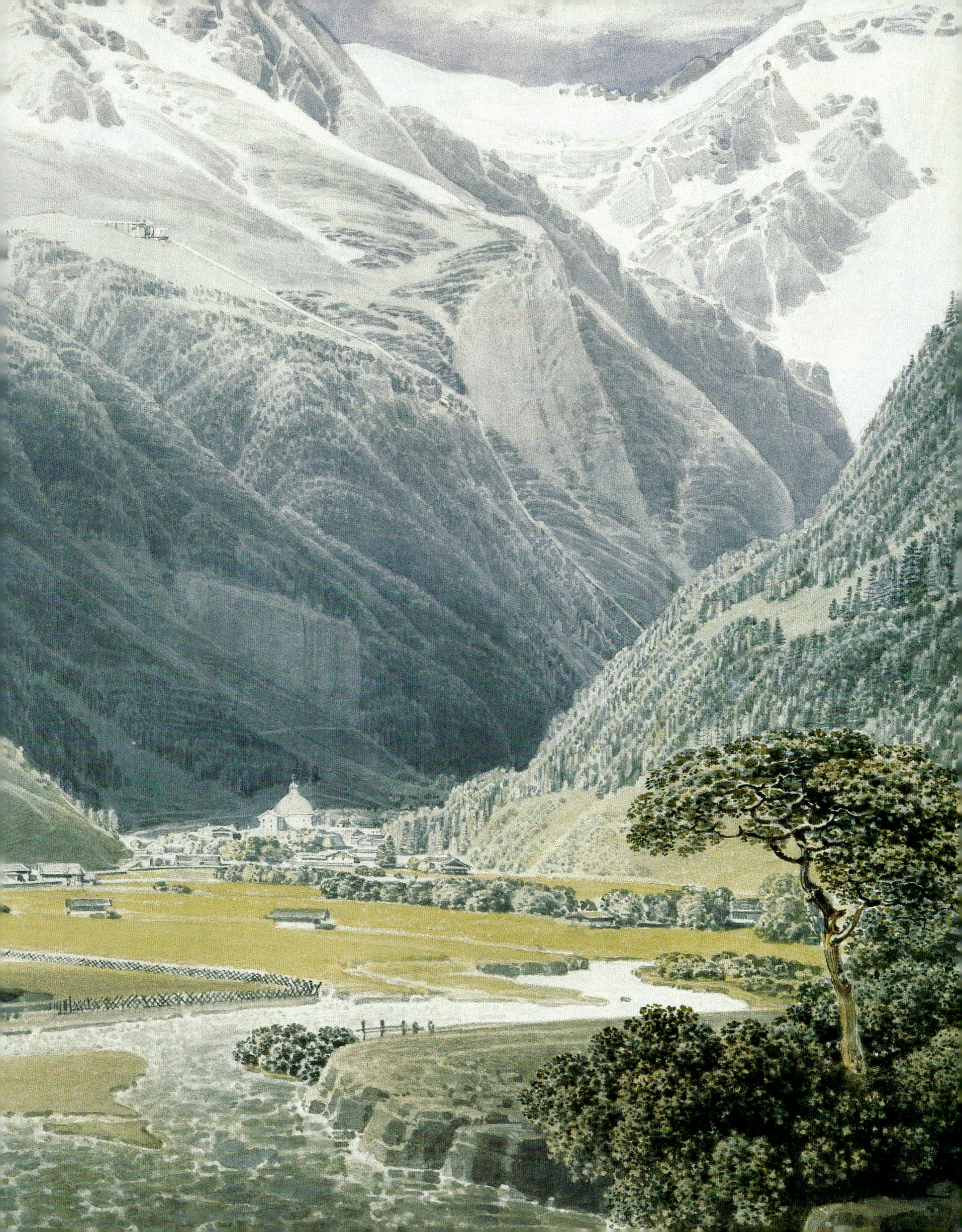

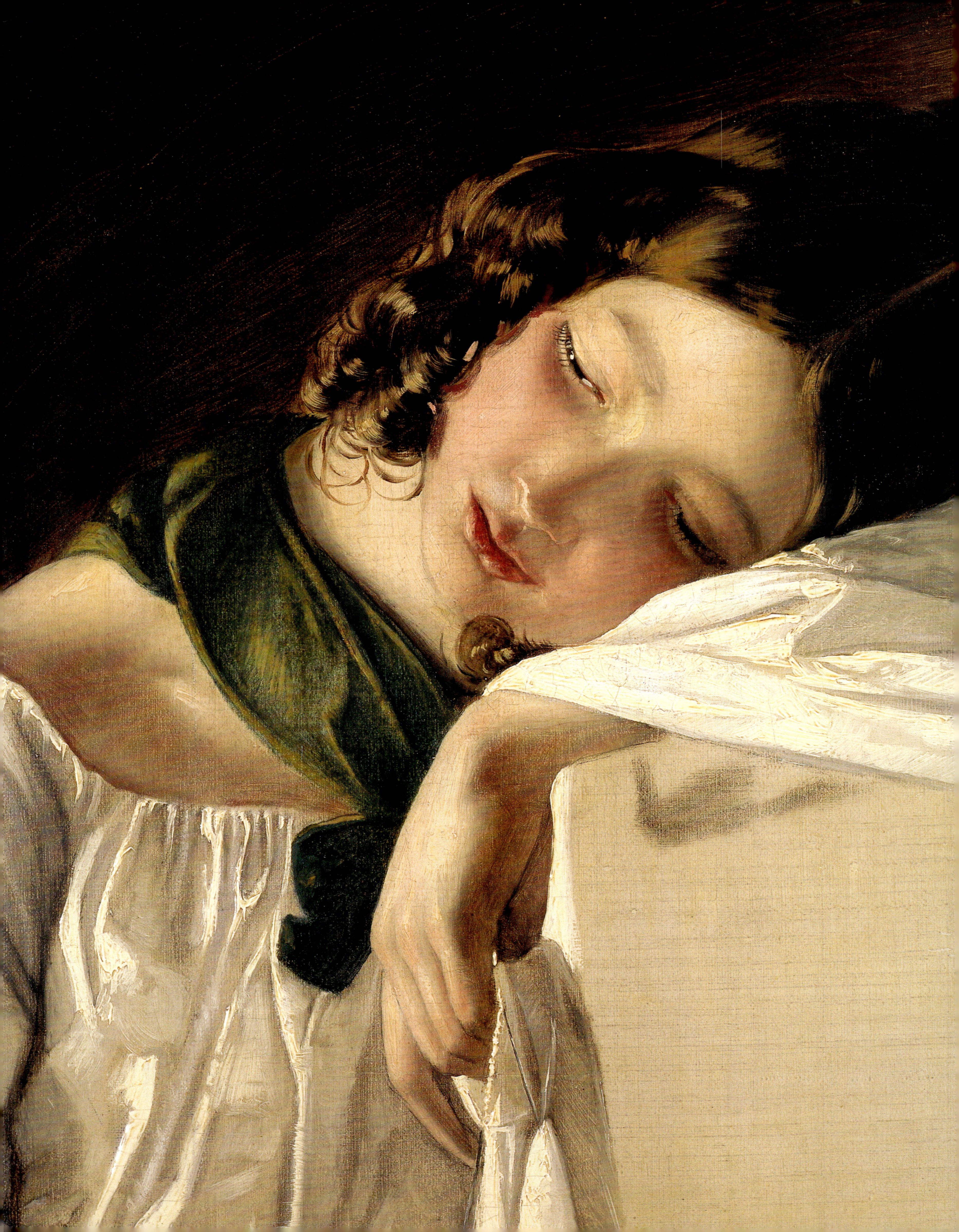

THE

REDISCOVERY

OF THE BIEDERMEIER PERIOD

LAURIE WINTERS

Between the end of the Napoleonic Wars in 1815 and the revolutions of 1848, there was a period of relative stability and peace in Central and Northern Europe. The art associated with this period, and the culture that gave rise to it, have come to be known by the name "Biedermeier." Although much has been written in the last quarter-century on the subject, the Biedermeier style and era have eluded clear definition. In contrast to the neoclassical period that preceded it and Romanticism that to some extent overlapped with it, the term "Biedermeier" evolved without any strict logic: Biedermeier has variously been identified as a branch of Romanticism, as a late manifestation of Romanticism, as a completely independent, self-contained period distinct from Romanticism, and as a prelude to mid-century realism. Dates for the Biedermeier period are similarly problematic. Some art historians end the period in 1835 with the death of Austrian Emperor Franz I, others with the outbreak of revolution in 1848. However, characteristics typical of the period appear well before 1815 and as late as the 1860s.

Biedermeier art is problematic not only because of the stylistic lines of demarcation, but because the period is so closely associated with the political landscape of the "restoration" following the Napoleonic Wars. Exhibitions and publications in the twentieth century, with two important exceptions, have interpreted the works within the framework of the period's emerging bourgeoisie, leading to grossly exaggerated interpretations of Biedermeier as a middle-class art made quickly, cheaply, and with middle-class interests in mind. New understanding has shown it to be a misconception to believe that the new middle class was the only patron of this art and that the spare, simple designs were a reflection of bourgeois modesty in taste and exhausted postwar economies. The classification of artists and objects has been equally fluid: the Dresden painter Georg Friedrich Kersting has just as often been identified as a principal exponent of the Biedermeier style as of German Romanticism.

Biedermeier: The Invention of Simplicity addresses these issues through the unconventional perspective of the aesthetics. Biedermeier is here identified as a term for an artistic era characterized by an emphasis on functionality and natural beauty. The style is marked by a considered balance of opposites in the ideal of nature and the simplicity of design. In its pure form, Biedermeier is characterized by an overall abstraction and geometry, brilliant color, and a lack of superficial ornamentation. Intentionally excluded from the exhibition are the many revivalist and historical forms of design and style that developed parallel to Biedermeier, as well as formal blends that were backward-looking, such as the ornamental antique, the Empire style, a literature-based Romanticism, neo-Gothic, neo-Renaissance, and neo-Baroque styles.[1]

The over 400 works seen here encompass all branches of the decorative arts as well as paintings and drawings. They have been carefully selected for their shared characteristics of simplicity, purity of form, and artistic intention. Many have startling affinities with designs of the twentieth century, although the exhibition eschews any attempt to discuss Biedermeier's anticipation of a corresponding modernity.

The exhibition further illustrates the interconnections among the great cities of Central and Northern Europe following the Congress of Vienna. Twentieth-century publications and exhibitions have generally focused on the artistic heritage of individual cities, creating the impression that during the early nineteenth century, centers were isolated and disconnected rather than part of a larger cultural phenomenon. However, as the political map of this period suggests, Central and Northern Europe participated in a common culture, and the availability of artistic training at public drawing schools and the extensive travel of many artists contributed to an international style and culture.

POLITICAL MAP OF EUROPE

The geographic scope of the Biedermeier style is generally taken to include the former Austrian Empire, Germany, and Denmark. After the defeat of Napoleon, European rulers met in 1815 at the Congress of Vienna to determine the governance of territories conquered by Napoleon. With the restoration of traditional hegemonies, it was natural for Emperor Franz I to become the first president and resume the leadership of the Germanic states.[2] A German Confederation was created, with thirty-nine original members, ranging from the powerful kingdom of Prussia to the smaller city-states of Frankfurt, Bremen, Hamburg, and Lübeck. The ruling federal body or Diet met in Frankfurt am Main and functioned more or less as a permanent congress of ambassadors. England, Holland, and Denmark were represented because they controlled Hanover, Luxembourg, and Holstein respectively. Their membership thus strengthened an existing link between Denmark and the German states, and from as early as the late 1790s, a lively exchange took place between artists located on the north and south shores of the western end of the Baltic Sea.[3]

The realignment of Europe in the aftermath of the Napoleonic Wars gave Vienna, Berlin, and Copenhagen, three of the most powerful capitals in the new European order, political and cultural prominence. The first art academy in Northern Europe was established in Copenhagen in 1738. Offering free classes and situated near Dresden and Berlin, it attracted many German artists, including Caspar David Friedrich and Kersting.[4] Around 1830, there was as much German as Danish spoken in the academy. The exchange was mutual: Danish artists gravitated to Dresden, Berlin, and even Munich.

Berlin and Vienna were especially important artistic centers. Berlin was the capital of Prussia and the second largest city in the German Confederation after Vienna. It had a formal court around Prussian King Friedrich Wilhelm III, and the Berlin University, founded in 1810, attracted some of the best minds on the continent.[5] Vienna was the capital of the Austrian Empire and the most important city of the German-speaking world. Emperor Franz I had hosted the Congress of Vienna, which lasted for more than a year and reshaped Europe.[6] Vienna had also long been the artistic center of the Hapsburg Empire and its rich traditions and collections were well known. Its fine art academies attracted artists from all over Europe. The many and diverse cross references of the period were further enhanced by artists traveling south through Vienna to Rome where they convened with the Nazarenes, Joseph Anton Koch, or the Danish sculptor Bertel Thorvaldsen.

BIEDERMAIER TO BIEDERMEIER

The interconnectedness within Central and Northern Europe was ignored in the earliest writings on the Biedermeier period, distorting all later interpretations of the era and the art. An overview of the changing reactions to Biedermeier art sheds light on the present understanding. As is often the case with stylistic terms, "Biedermeier" was coined at a later date and is both nostalgic and critical in nature. In 1855-57, the physician Adolf Kussmaul and the lawyer Ludwig Eichrodt created for the Munich satirical weekly *Fliegende Blätter* the fictional character Weiland Gottlieb Biedermaier, a recently deceased schoolteacher and poet from a village in Swabia.[7] Biedermaier's name can be translated as "common man," and his uneventful daily life and naïve poems were paraded in issue after issue for the entertainment of the paper's bourgeois readers. Only in the last decade of the nineteenth century was the character's name used to describe the artistic and cultural period preceding the revolutions of 1848. Thus a naïve and perhaps even disparaging perception of Biedermeier was formed at the end of the nineteenth century, looking back upon a fictional figure that even in the 1850s had functioned as a parody of prerevolutionary Europe.

In the Viennese review *Hohe Warte*, Joseph August Lux offered an analysis of the Biedermeier period in a 1904-1905 article entitled "Biedermeier as Educator."[8] Offering a positive reassessment, Lux asserted that "the interiors of all classes, from the emperor and the prime minister down to the petty bourgeoisie, share the same characteristic features."[9] Without examining the veracity of this statement, Lux lamented that the art of his own time, at the beginning of the century, had no such broad acceptance. Lux's assessment of the Biedermeier period as one that had enjoyed a leveling of the social classes through the decorative arts was something that he had himself hoped to encourage as part of the arts and crafts movement. In using words such as "native" and "rooted" to describe the period, Lux gave the impression that everything had been home grown; the notion that Biedermeier was a bourgeois art concentrated in particular regions was thus well launched.[10]

A lexicon of nationalism in the history of art soon enveloped the interpretation of Biedermeier. A 1901 Copenhagen retrospective of artists of the Danish Golden Age increased public awareness of these artists and placed them prominently under the umbrella of Danish nationalism.[11] The 1906 Centennial Exhibition in Berlin, the famous *Jahrhundertausstellung 1775-1875*, was a landmark in the reassessment of German realist painting, which gradually became known as Biedermeier realism.[12] The exhibition introduced to the public such artists as Friedrich and Johann Erdmann Hummel, who had long been absent from the historical consciousness of the nineteenth century. In early publications, the same nationalistic approach characterizes Ludwig Hevesi's treatment of Austrian art in *Österreichische Kunst im 19. Jahrhundert* (1903) and Richard Muther's 1909 publication *Geschichte der Malerie*, which identifies Biedermeier art as "treu deutsch" and "a style that genuinely and sincerely expressed the signature of an age."

In the first publication devoted entirely to Biedermeier art, Paul Ferdinand Schmidt in 1923 identified it as primarily realist, bourgeois, and concentrated in city centers that reflected the city-state framework of the nineteenth-century German

Confederation; the art of Vienna was given only six pages in the book and Prague and Copenhagen were completely ignored. Similar emphases on nationalism are found in Austria in Bruno Grimschitz's 1928 *Die österreichische Zeichnung im 19. Jahrhundert.* Paul Weiglin followed the same city-center format and nationalistic identification in his 1941 *Berliner Biedermeier. Leben, Kunst und Kultur in Alt-Berlin zwischen 1815 und 1848.* The focus of the interwar years throughout Europe was on cataloguing and regional identification, which was continued in the postwar era by Herbert von Einems's survey of German painting and by Helmut Börsch-Supan's *Die deutsche Malerei* (1988), considered the culmination of the encyclopedic approach to the association of different schools of painting with German cities.

Monographs on individual artists began to appear at about the same time and may also be linked to nation building and efforts to emphasize national identity that occurred in the early twentieth century. The Danish art critic Emil Hannover prepared some of the earliest, on Christen Købke (1893) and Christoffer Wilhelm Eckersberg (1898), thus furthering awareness of Danish culture.[13] With the exception of Schinkel in Berlin, who received public and scholarly attention from the beginning, and the 1954 book on Hummel, major monographs emerged in Germany at a relatively late date.[14] Significant work on Friedrich occurred only in the 1970s and the first major comprehensive exhibition and catalogue on Eduard Gaertner took place as recently as 2001.[15] The year 1930 in Vienna saw one of the first major monographs and exhibitions devoted to Ferdinand Georg Waldmüller, whose work has now been linked to the *Neue Sachlichkeit* (New Objectivity) movement of the interwar wars.[16] Walter Koschatsky, Director of the Albertina from 1964 to 1986, and the present director, Klaus Albrecht Schröder, have helped establish the place of nineteenth-century artists through the publication of collection catalogues and exhibitions.[17]

UNDER THE UMBRELLA OF ROMANTICISM AND NEOCLASSICISM

In the 1960s, there was a growing recognition that Romanticism, Neoclassicism, realism, and Biedermeier were separate stylistic entities. Fritz Novotny's 1960 overview of European painting identified larger classicist and naturalist movements in the early nineteenth century to which the entire family of European artists belonged. His thesis generated a flurry of books and exhibitions that separated the art of the period into two distinct categories, Romanticism and Neoclassicism, with the consequent development that Biedermeier became the awkward sidekick of both movements. International recognition of German Romanticism began only in 1959 with the London exhibition *The Romantic Movement.* This exhibition took place under the aegis of the Council of Europe and an international organizing committee. Its influence was far-reaching, affecting museum acquisitions, publications, and international exhibitions. This was followed in 1969 by a Vienna exhibition, *Wien 1800–1850: Empire und Biedermeier,* organized by the Historisches Museum der Stadt Wien, and in 1972 by the landmark *Age of Neo-Classicism* in London, again organized by the Council of Europe.

German Romanticism became the darling of international exhibitions. Kermit Champa's exhibition *German Painting of the Nineteenth Century* traveled widely in 1970, engendering the first international symposium on the topic in the United States.[18] Robert Rosenblum's groundbreaking 1975 book on northern painting of the nineteenth and twentieth centuries redressed the earlier neglect of the Danish and

German landscape painters, connecting them to an international movement of "plein-air" painting. William Vaughan's 1980 *German Romantic Painting*, also a seminal publication on the subject, brought artists such as Kersting and Hummel under the spreading umbrella of German Romanticism. Notable among the popular exhibitions on these popular themes throughout the 1980s and the 1990s was the exhibition and accompanying catalogue *The Romantic Spirit in German Art, 1790-1990*.[19] Religious views of nature starting with Friedrich and Carl Gustav Carus gave shape to the catalogue's thesis.

Attempts to align Biedermeier with Romanticism and Neoclassicism gradually proved misleading. In 1981, *German Masters of the Nineteenth Century* at The Metropolitan Museum of Art avoided the issue entirely by omitting Biedermeier artists from the exhibition program, with the exception of Kersting's *Caspar David Friedrich in His Studio*, likely included only because it depicted the great Romantic painter.[20] No mention was made of Kersting's role as a Biedermeier painter.

THE LIMITATIONS OF BOURGEOIS TASTE

In 1963, Rupert Feuchtmüller and Wilhelm Mrazek's *Biedermeier in Österreich* marked a resurgence of interest in Biedermeier. The book broke new ground in its comprehensive treatment of media and in its efforts to distinguish and categorize the styles of the many Viennese painters. Willi Geismeier's 1979 book *Biedermeier* elaborated on the connection between Biedermeier the period and the fictional character Biedermaier, and enlarged the geographic scope of the period to include German, Austrian, and Danish painting, though his emphasis was clearly on German painting. Both publications continued to define the period conventionally within the context of the bourgeoisie. The most important publication on the social and political context of the Biedermeier period – in many ways the culminating text – was Robert Waissenberger's *Wien 1815-1848: Zeit des Biedermeier* (1986). The wide circulation of the book in German and English editions stimulated interest among new international audiences.

At roughly the same time, new publications devoted specifically to the decorative arts helped establish the significance of the Biedermeier period. In 1979, the first international exhibition on the decorative arts of the period – *Vienna in the Age of Schubert: The Biedermeier Interior 1815-1848* – took place outside Paris at the Palais Trianon in Versailles, and in London at the Victoria and Albert Museum. Although the exhibition and the accompanying catalogue were small in scale and conventional in approach by today's standards, they constituted important scholarship on the topic in the French- and English-speaking worlds. Two years later, in 1981, Christian Witt-Dörring and Paul and Stefan Asenbaum organized the seminal exhibition *Moderne Vergangenheit 1800-1900* for the Künstlerhaus in Vienna. This was the first exhibition to establish a connection between the simple, unadorned designs of the Biedermeier period and modern movements of design in the early twentieth century.

Although scholarship on the decorative arts of the Biedermeier period had generally been slower to develop, it was in this area that a radical new approach to the period first emerged.[21] Two exhibitions in 1987 altered scholarly understanding of the period. In Vienna, Waissenberger and Gunter Duriegl spearheaded the enormous exhibition for the Historisches Museum der Stadt Wien, *Bürgersinn und Aufbegehren: Biedermeier und Vormärz in Wien 1815-1848*, selecting more than 2,000 objects to illustrate the cultural life of the period. Although the catalogue makes an important and comprehensive contribution to our understanding of the period, the ideas were largely a recapitulation of the themes developed in Waissenberger's 1986 publication. A notable exception to this was Christian Witt-Dörring's essay on furniture, which was to prove important to new thinking on the role of the bourgeoisie in the Biedermeier period. The other exhibition in 1987 was organized by Hans Ottomeyer at the Münchner Stadtmuseum, *Biedermeiers Glück und Ende: die gestörte Idylle*. In that seminal exhibition devoted entirely to the decorative arts, Ottomeyer, like Witt-Dörring, defined an entirely new way of thinking about the Biedermeier period.

Witt-Dörring and Ottomeyer, working independently of each other in Vienna and Munich, both refuted the well-entrenched notion that Biedemeier art was made cheaply and quickly for the middle classes. Their careful research demonstrated for the first time that the best and simplest examples of furniture were commissioned for the courts and the aristocracy. They also explored the basic historical and social underpinnings of the period in their respective cities but they did not address core aesthetic principles of the art. Achim Stiegel, influenced in his dissertation by the work of Ottomeyer, has recently published a book on Berlin furniture that similarly repositions its patronage and places its development ten to fifteen years earlier than previously thought.[22]

Outside the European decorative arts community, the groundbreaking reassessments of Witt-Dörring and Ottomeyer had little impact. In her 1987 publication on Biedermeier painting, English scholar Geraldine Norman continued to view the period as a reflection of middle-class taste, but her innovative determination to see Biedermeier as an art of Central and Northern Europe emphasized Copenhagen as an important center of artistic production. In the same year, Angus Wilkie, unaware at the time of Ottomeyer's and Witt-Dorring's new ideas concerning patronage, published what is still regarded in many circles as the best text in the English language on the decorative arts of the Biedermeier period. In late December 1987, Georg Himmelheber organized a large, comprehensive exhibition in Munich on the Biedermeier period, combining painting and decorative arts in a synthetic approach to the material. Narrowing the period to 1815–35, he avoided politicization and brought together for the first time works by German, Austrian, Czech, and Danish artists. Although his work was innovative in many ways, Himmelheber's neglect of the research published by Ottomeyer and Witt-Dörring contributed to a lingering, overarching assessment of the Biedermeier period as a product of middle-class values.

Despite the lack of an international reconsideration of Biedermeier as an artistic style and era, interest in the period flourished during the 1990s and beyond. Klaus Albrecht Schröder and Gerbert Frodl broke new ground in their 1993 exhibition *Wiener Biedermeier: Malerei zwischen Wiener Kongress und Revolution* by insisting on a completely new evaluation of Viennese painters that removed the pejorative taint associated with the Biedermeier period. Artists such as Erasmus von Engert and Franz Ebyl were elevated to a place of new prominence among European painters of the early nineteenth century. The 2005 exhibition organized around the Liechtenstein collection of Biedermeier is another example of important scholarship concentrating on the Biedermeier period in Vienna.[23]

Two internationally traveling exhibitions in 1993 and 2001 of paintings from the Oskar Reinhardt Collection in Winterthur and the Nationalgalerie Berlin

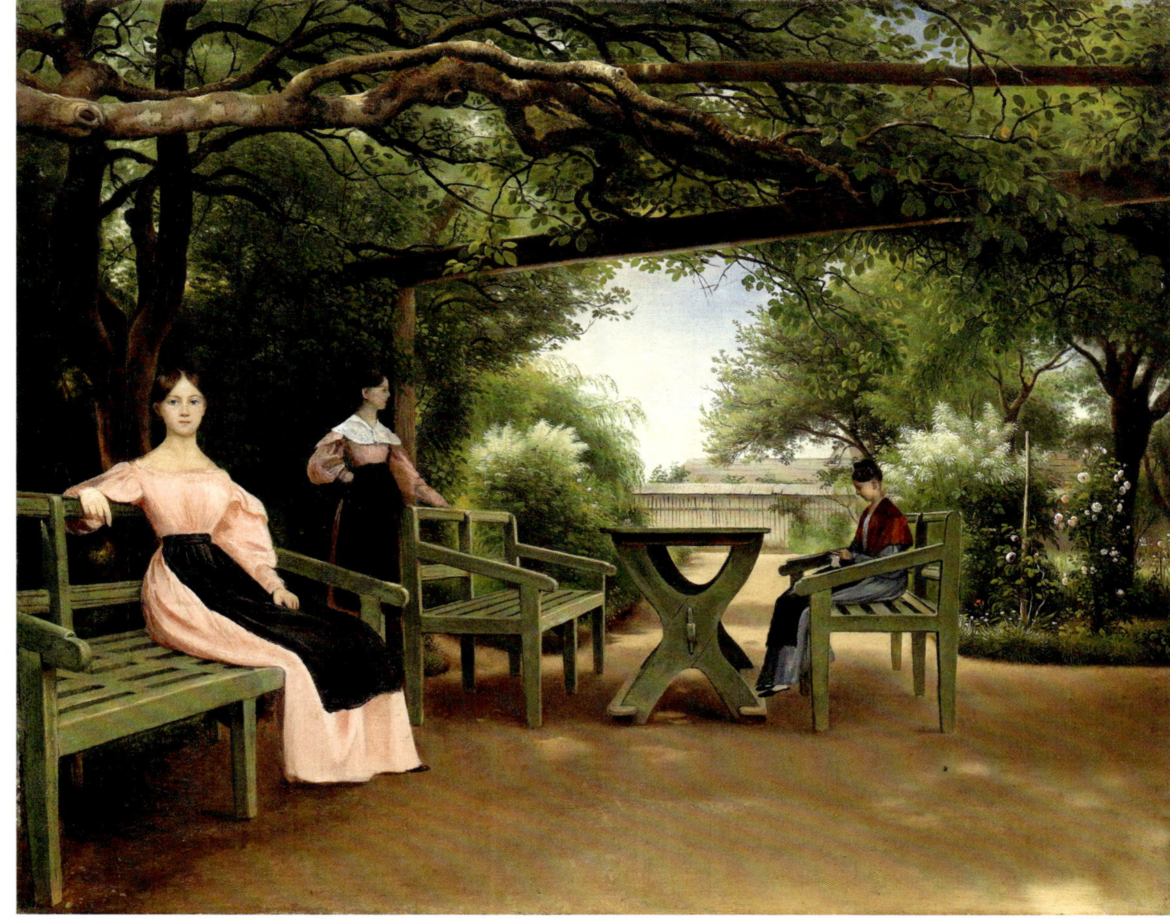

Figure 1
Erasmus von Engert
Girl in an Arbor
ca. 1828
Cat. XIII-29

included such artists as Hummel, Kersting, Gaertner, and Wilhelm von Kobell, identifying them as important representatives of the Biedermeier period and giving them pride of place among the Romantics of the early nineteenth century and the later German Impressionists and Symbolists.[24] The 1993 exhibition went under the lingering populist title of *Caspar David Friedrich to Ferdinand Hodler: A Romantic Tradition*, while the 2001 exhibition sought a more comprehensive scope with the title *Spirit of an Age*. In the world of furniture and decorative arts, the most important recent contribution to the field has been the publication of the *World of Biedermeier* by Karl Kemp, Linda Chase, and Lois Lammerhuber. The book's exquisite photography encouraged fresh perspectives and connections with the art of the early twentieth century, stimulating greater public awareness of Biedermeier art and a surge in the collecting market in the United States.

EXHIBITION THESIS

Forged from the lessons of the past, *Biedermeier: The Invention of Simplicity* takes the unconventional approach of aesthetics to reassess the Biedermeier period and its art. With the research of Ottomeyer and Witt-Dörring as the starting point, Biedermeier is here interpreted not as a lowly product of bourgeois taste but rather as a highly cultivated and refined quest for simplicity and purity of form that has its roots in the late eighteenth century. The provenances for many of the most important works clearly indicate that the patrons were members of the courts or the aristocracy. As Ottomeyer summarized clearly in 1994: "The cult of simplicity developed itself as a principle of beauty in contrast to the luxurious style of the close of the eighteenth century. Whoever could afford to pay for it acquired new decoration in the new style of unpretentiousness."[25]

The Biedermeier style is also recognized as occurring in all media throughout Central and Northern Europe. The objects present the hallmarks of the style: a purity and abstraction of form, brilliant color, lack of superficial ornamentation, and a sensitive appreciation for and reliance on nature. The best examples date from the narrow period of 1815–25. The generation of artists working after 1835 was already producing something dramatically different in style and conception. The present exhibition thus excludes the many revivalist and historical styles that ran parallel to and should now be seen as separate from the purest and most cohesive form of Biedermeier. This exhibition seeks to present the very best of Biedermeier. The choice of artworks and their installation are intended to underscore the essential Biedermeier style.

Furniture comprises one of the largest and most significant categories of the exhibition with almost one hundred examples. Wood veneer was the primary decorative element of this furniture and often determined the shape, size, and contour of the piece. The same refined sensibility and purity of form occur in the related decorative arts. Important works of porcelain from Berlin and Vienna demonstrate a new emphasis on streamlined floral motifs and vibrant color. The brilliant hues and patterns that are so characteristic of the period are explored through a judicious selection of clothing, textiles, and wallpapers. Equally important are examples of glass from Prague and Vienna that show not only new colors but new approaches to materials with the invention of red and black hyalith and stained hyalith in imitation of stonework. The silver and metalwork, with their strikingly modern forms, further underscore fundamental aesthetic principles of the period.

Paintings and drawings are a significant component of the exhibition. Not well known in the United States, and often thought of more broadly in Europe, Biedermeier painting and drawing are represented by a carefully selected group of artists with similar aesthetic aims. Important examples by Austrian, German, and Danish artists demonstrate the interconnectedness of style around 1820 that distinguishes them from contemporaneous romantic and neoclassical painters and from the generation of painters working in the 1840s and 1850s. Artists of the "Pre-March" generation working in Vienna – Peter Fendi, Albert Schindler, and the late works of Waldmüller and Friedrich von Amerling – although most often referred to as Biedermeier painters, are intentionally excluded from the exhibition.[26] Their works' pronounced sentimentality, nostalgia, and painterly bravura mark them as the product of a later generation driven by dramatically different aesthetic principles.

It is our hope that this unique exhibition will offer new insight into the Biedermeier period. The objects speak for themselves through their beauty and simplicity, manifesting as a group a consistency and coherency of vision. Following few established traditions, the exhibition has brought together an extraordinary assembly of works for the first time, many of which have never before been on view in the United States.

NOTES

1   I would like to offer a special note of thanks to Hans Ottomeyer and Christian Witt-Dörring for contributing their expertise to the formation of this introduction.

2   Norman 1987, p. 12.

3   Ottawa 2000, pp. 16–23. Helmut Börsch-Supan's excellent essay entitled "Between Copenhagen and Dresden: Berlin" examines the political and artistic relationship between these northern territories in the late eighteenth and early nineteenth centuries.

4   Norman 1987, p. 12.

5   Ibid., p. 62. For a thorough discussion of the cultural life in Northern Europe and Berlin, see Sheehan 1994, pp. 324–88.

6   There is a great deal of general information on this topic in Waissenberger 1986, pp. 9–50.

7   The best summary of the name's origins appears in Sheehan 1994, p. 536.

8   Lux 1904–1905, pp. 145ff.

9   Quoted in Waissenberger 1986, p. 161.

10   Ibid.

11   Catherine Johnston provides an excellent summary of the cultural perception of Danish art in the twentieth century, in Ottawa 2000, esp. p. 31. This portion of the text is greatly indebted to her work.

12   Norman 1987, p. 8.

13   Ottawa 2000, p. 31. I would like to thank Catherine Johnston for her important work on this topic.

14   See Hummel 1954, which was written by his grandson Georg Hummel.

15   Berlin 2001B. There are earlier books and articles on Gaertner, but this was the first important exhibition and accompanying catalogue of note.

16   Waissenberger 1986, pp. 162–63.

17   Important exhibitions and catalogues on nineteenth-century Austrian art include Vienna 1973, Vienna 1978, Vienna 1997, and Vienna 2005.

18   New Haven 1970.

19   Edinburgh 1994.

20   New York 1981.

21   For some of the earliest literature on Biedermeier decorative arts, see Folnesics 1903A, and from the 1920s, Luthmer and Schmidt 1922, Schmitz 1920, and Schmidt 1923. It is interesting that these publications overlap with the European Arts and Crafts Movement and the Wiener Werkstätte in Vienna.

22   Stiegel 2003.

23   Vaduz 2005.

24   London 2001 and Los Angeles 1993.

25   Ottomeyer 1994, p. 83.

26   "Pre-March" refers to the period preceeding the 1848 revolution in Vienna.

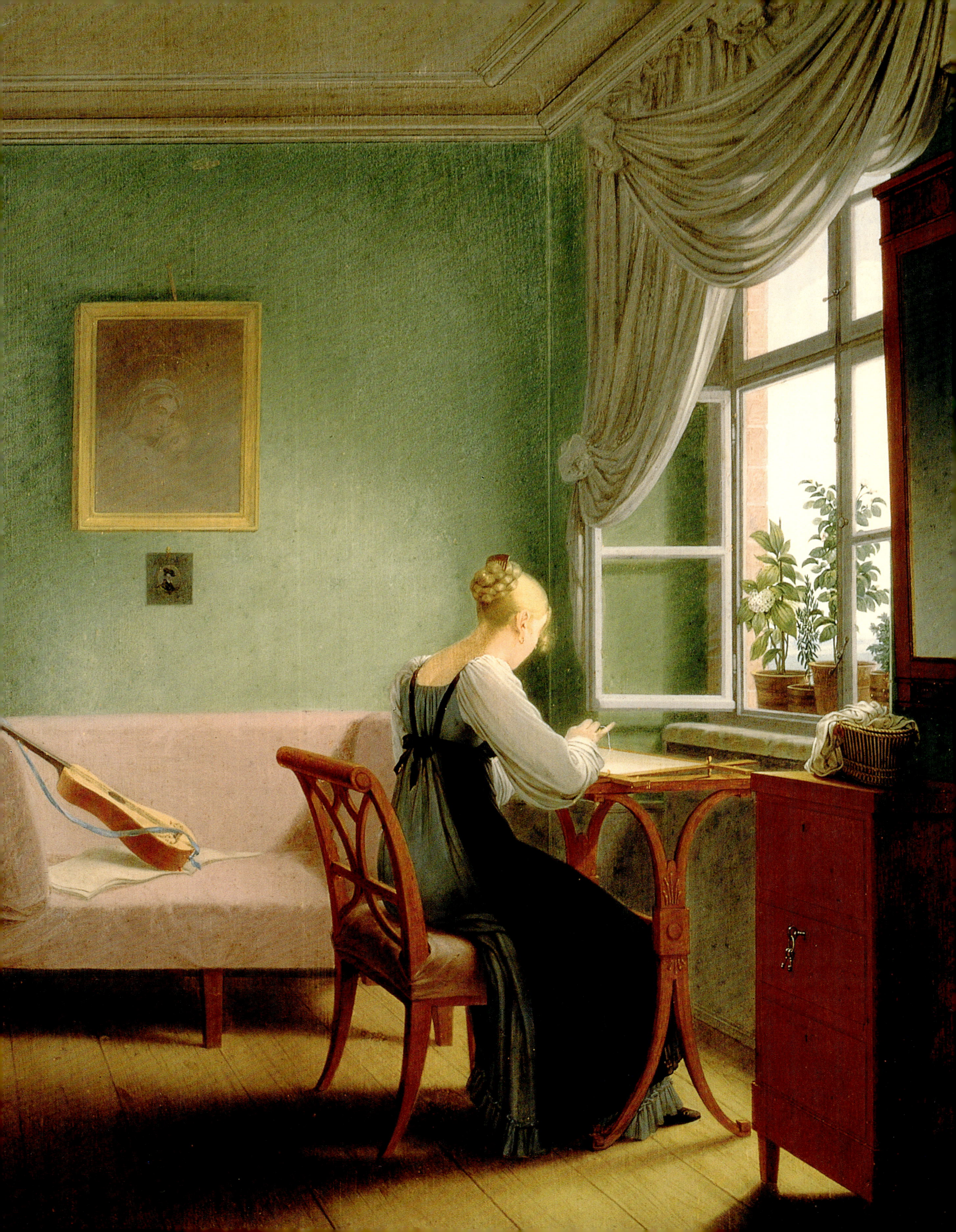

SIMPLICITY

HANS OTTOMEYER

ALL THINGS ARE SIMPLE AND PLAIN; AND NEITHER CARVING NOR GILDING
NOW ARE EMPLOY'D, AND FOREIGN TIMBER IS NOW ALL THE FASHION.
I SHOULD BE ONLY TOO PLEASED TO POSSESS SOME NOVELTY ALSO,
SO AS TO MARCH WITH THE TIMES, AND MY HOUSEHOLD FURNITURE ALTER.
BUT WE ALL ARE AFRAID TO MAKE THE LEAST ALTERATION,
FOR WHO IS ABLE TO PAY THE PRESENT CHARGES OF WORKMEN?

Johann Wolfgang von Goethe, 1798[1]

THE ERA AND THE STYLE

Biedermeier: The Invention of Simplicity approaches Biedermeier as an epoch in Germanic art and culture as well as a particular aesthetic characterized by functionality, rationality, and material beauty. It focuses on aspects of Biedermeier in which principles associated with Neoclassicism and ideals of nature found expression alongside new emphases on simplicity, scale, abstraction, and geometric forms. When these principles were distilled to their essence, what emerged was the "Invention of Simplicity," a state that was appropriate to its time and place in the early nineteenth century, but also evinced proto-abstract and proto-modern tendencies. By illuminating these principles in Biedermeier, traditional understanding of the concept of Biedermeier can be redefined.

In the past, there have been significant misconceptions about the origins and development of Biedermeier. The term was usually applied as a nonspecific and overarching designation for the entire period from 1815 to 1848, connoting the cliché of a new bourgeois style, embraced by a stronger middle class in a time of social and political upheaval. Biedermeier was seen as synonymous with virtues of solidity, simplicity, stability, and frugality, and encompassed the concept of a bourgeois idyll. Simultaneously, historians of decorative arts have generally eschewed the broad definition of Biedermeier, employing the term narrowly as a descriptive reference for furniture from 1815 to 1830.

Stylistically, Biedermeier has always been a chimera. It has defied specific stylistic uniformity or designation, and has denoted a plurality of prevailing styles that coexisted throughout the era. The term was attached to categorizations that served the associations of a host of preconceived ideas, and this engendered a general understanding of Biedermeier that has little to do with its essential concept or its specific historical and material circumstances. In response to such prevailing misconceptions, the current exhibition reconsiders basic assumptions of Biedermeier, and discards overly broad or overly narrow definitions.

There is sufficient evidence of Biedermeier's popularity in royal residences and courts long before 1815, so the long-held notion of the style as a purely bourgeois development must be dismissed. Biedermeier should be accepted as a style that originated in commissions for private domestic interiors by aristocratic and royal patrons. It evolved initially from the court and thereafter spread into more broad-based usage among the new moneyed social classes.[2]

For a true understanding of Biedermeier, it is also essential to recognize the parallel and intertwined styles of the period, and to explore the complex interplay of reciprocal influence and distance among them. Biedermeier shared broad popularity and duration with prevailing styles of late representative Neoclassicism or "Empire style," as well as with historicist variations of neo-Renaissance, Gothic Revival, and early neo-Baroque for courtly public interiors. All efforts to describe Biedermeier in relation to a linear development of style obscures the reality of simultaneous and contrary aesthetic expressions during the era. For this exhibition, the stylistic variations of the period are reassessed in light of the commonalities or coexisting impulses that informed their aesthetic developments. What ensues is new understanding of the relationship between parallel and interacting neoclassical and historical styles that both influenced and contradicted one another at that time.

The expressive aesthetic voice of a work of architecture or an interior is generally viewed as legitimizing the design relationship to its era and style. But for the Biedermeier epoch, descriptions of the differing parallel styles often hindered a comprehensible picture of the era and its intense struggles for social and political models. Even contemporary individuals were painfully aware of the rivalry and lack of clarity among competing heterogeneous styles, observing: "Our capitals bloom in all conceivable styles, and thus we tend to forget in pleasant disappointment to which century we belong in the end."[3]

The current exhibition exposes Biedermeier as a style grounded in reason or rationally determined conventions amidst a tense field of oppositional styles and relationships. The exhibition presents the fundamental positions of Biedermeier as it emerged and gained definition within the pluralistic stylistic environment of the evolving nineteenth-century German and Austrian culture.

A BATTLE OF STYLES

The first fifty years of the nineteenth century were strongly influenced by the pluralism of coexisting forms and mixed styles, although the architects of this period relied primarily on neoclassical forms for specific – usually state or cultural – building projects. Neoclassical principles were propagated by academies of architecture, thereby ensuring the continuity of representational Neoclassicism. Simultaneously, though, writers and decorators promoted progressive and changing fashions. The conflict among styles was referred to in England as a "battle of styles," a phrase that emphasizes the deep-seated antipathies between advocates of Neoclassicism, Gothic architecture, and Romanticism. The matter was taken less seriously in France, where people observed the rapid progression of changing fashions and furnishing styles as an amusing spectacle and enjoyed the spirited dialogue it engendered.

In contrast to Biedermeier, Empire remained true to its origins throughout the period. The grotesque style practiced in 1770–96, as the "goût étrusque" or "goût arabesque," drew inspiration from antique Roman models and the Renaissance and not only incorporated architectural structuring elements such as pedestal profiles, ledges, columns, pilasters, and herms, but also processed the repertory of linear motifs from grotesque painting. The "Empire style," which must be regarded as the consistent, self-sufficient form of state representation, gave rise to an idiosyncratic ornamentation. The filigree, flat, consistently stylized decorative motifs of the older grotesque style influenced by painting were replaced after 1815 by increasingly naturalistic plant motifs until ponderous, fundamentally architectural, forms and elaborately sculptural decorations oriented toward Roman architecture and Roman marble furnishings of the Empire period assumed a dominant role for this style between 1820 and 1830.

What differentiates Empire from Biedermeier? The art of the Biedermeier period is characterized by abstraction in form, ornamentation, and color. In terms of basic aspects of design, the style drew from a wide variety of proto-abstract and modern elements. It was oriented toward a reduction of ornament, so redolent in Empire style, and to the two-dimensional surface. It was not concerned with the powerful volumes and massive proportions of Empire that are known as "pathetic materialism."[4] It dispensed with the obviously costly materials and requisite appliqués, exotic veneers, rare marbles, luxurious gilding, and elaborately carved elements that served as representational manifestations of sovereignty in the grand reception rooms and halls of power.

Empire was not a personal style, nor was it a home furnishing style. Most of the monarchs of the nineteenth century had been raised and educated in the spirit of Jean-Jacques Rousseau and taught to prefer simplicity, plainness, and personal unpretentiousness. It was in this realm that Biedermeier emerged, manifested most clearly in the royal studies or offices – new types of rooms in which rulers spent most of their time. The French-influenced style of palaces found its corollary in French courtly language, and the more elegant bourgeois circles adopted this vernacular as well. Official and everyday clothing met the needs of the same people and the same social classes. This was an officially prescribed ostentation. It was only in the "elegant modesty" ascribed to the personal sphere where one would encounter the circles in which one would expect to find Biedermeier furnishings – namely the court, in the broadest sense of the term, which included civil servants, high-ranking clerics, the upper ranks of the military, and both the affluent and the educated bourgeoisie.

Alongside Empire and Biedermeier, a concurrent style throughout the era was Gothic Revival. With its reliance on historicist motifs, decorative ideas, and archaeologically exact feudal and medieval sources, it represented an alternative to the prevailing neoclassical architectural currents. By the late Biedermeier period in Germanic culture, the influence of Gothic Revival had increased, and the style began to evince many of the characteristics of the Historicism that succeeded it. A growing sense of disorientation in the present spawned increasing interest in relics of the past, which people now eagerly began to collect. In search of renewal, the era looked to styles of the past for models.

IDEALS AND ELEMENTS OF STYLE

We have grown accustomed to calling the simple cabinetmaker's furniture of the period "Biedermeier," and although there are some elements of interrelationship with Neoclassicism, such work can be interpreted independently. The forms of early Neoclassicism, which developed as "goût grec" in France in 1755–75 and in Germany from 1770 to around 1800, differ from those of Biedermeier utilitarian furniture by virtue of the use of carved, abstract architectural ornaments that force the flat surface into serving as a mere backdrop for sculptural elements. Gilt elements contrast accordingly with the white or pastel-colored wood. The emphasis on ornamentation achieved through metal appliqués and sculptured elements is also characteristic of the Empire style. In contrast, so-called Biedermeier furniture was created from available material, namely the flat board. The rectangle provided the basic form: "furnishings are the relatives of architecture, its grandchildren or great-grandchildren, so to speak, and have emerged from them …. Our rooms are like hollow cubes or boxes, and rectangular, flat-surfaced furniture fits well in them."[5]

During the Biedermeier period, in which the negative effects of fifteen years of war had not been overcome and technical inventions had not yet impacted on the economy, many concessions were needed to realize this ideal and make it affordable. It was not the profligate excess of luxury art that dominated during those years but rather honest contentment with what was available. An aesthetic of waste gave way to an aesthetic involving the economical use of resources. Polytechnic journals and accounts clearly indicate that people preferred the color and material characteristics of mahogany and other exotic woods but they were usually not available. The sustained boycott on trade between England and France, the continental blockade between 1806 and 1814, brought imports to a standstill and impaired economic relations for many years afterward. There was no choice but to be satisfied with native or indigenous woods. Mercantilist, nationalist-oriented attitudes devoted to the promotion of commerce expressed in these publications frequently emphasize the need to use local wood in order to achieve independence from expensive imports, which would have a negative impact on the balance of trade.

COLOR SYSTEMS

The dominant color system of the era was based on complementary coloration. Color harmonies begin to appear as an empirical principle starting in the late eighteenth century. Around 1800, palettes of two complementary colors became a norm. For example, this is found in the rare combination of yellow and purple found in the widely acclaimed showcase bedroom of Madame de Recamier.[6] Johann Wolfgang von Goethe articulated the philosophical experience of artistic color combinations as a principle in his *Theory of Colors* of 1810. "The three primary colors are red, blue, and yellow. The eye is not satisfied by one such color alone but demands, when it has seen one, the others as well, which then appear in their mixed forms …. Thus the principal formula is: yellow requires reddish-blue, blue requires reddish-yellow, purple requires green, and vice-versa. In order to grasp this totality, to satisfy itself, the eye searches next to every colored field a colorless one in which to bring out the required color. And herein lies the fundamental natural law of all color harmony …." So reads the paraphrase of Goethe offered to interested readers of the *Schorn'sches Kunstblatt*.[7] The acceptance of this color theory is reflected in its application: "Two complementary primary colors are accompanied by the noncolor white, which, as a neutral element, makes the perception of color possible in the first place. In the color scheme typical of Biedermeier rooms, the two colors that appear on the walls are also used in the other furnishings as well, appearing repeatedly in the colors of veneer and wood, of coverings and curtains, with the intent to preserve the uniformity, consistency, and integrity of the room."

"This world [of Roman antiquities] must exert an extraordinary influence on the study of the arts and the entire genius of Europe. Surely the love of the beautiful, simple, and true will be applied to the imitation of nature."[8]

The point of departure for the development of neoclassical art is simplification based upon principles of classical antiquity, the use of plain Attic Greek contours and basic designs that during about 1790–1804 resulted in a reductive approach to forms and contours. As the fruits of eighteenth-century knowledge, these ideas follow the principle of primal forms and archetypes as the source of all art. The reduction to basic geometric forms and the theory of archetypes were modeled on examples, such as the Attic stele, which underlies the structure of much cabinet furniture, or on Greek vases and the *Klismos Chair*, which provide inspiration for primal forms of glass, ceramics, and seating furniture (plate 32). As the eighteenth century gave way to the nineteenth, these principles were applied through the imposition of simplicity and reduction to utilitarian function.

The French Enlightenment expanded the discussion by introducing to art history the concept of development reflected in insights regarding evolution and ontogenesis. In art, the rigorous development of basic functions and archetypes was observed and incorporated into principles of evolution, principally by Johann Joachim Winckelmann and David Le Roy. Le Roy noted that all buildings since antiquity have their roots in refinements and combinations of a few basic types, most notably the archetype of the columned temple, the basilica, and the domed cruciform church. In order to design and build well, he contended, it was necessary to recognize this and follow the lines of formal development. The progress of history validates form.

This historical approach to design was recognized during the ancien régime as a strategy and transposed by architect and designer Charles Percier into the Empire style. In the preface to the 1812 edition of his *Recueil des Arts décoratifs*, he postulated that beautiful and perfect design can be achieved only if the archetype is clearly recognized and brought into harmony with the modern era and current requirements without altering or concealing the fundamental form. In his view, a form can be preserved only by pursuing progressive development of the historical line of success. Furthermore, he was the first to articulate the principles of modern design: emphasis on the beauty of simple materials, rigorous renunciation of supposed surface refinement achieved through handcrafting techniques, and total adherence to the laws of symmetry and order. *Recueil des Arts décoratifs* was first published in 1801 and appeared in four successive editions. The book became the "Bible of Empire" and the most influential source of models for arts-and-crafts and commercial production. Percier's principles go further than the designs, which he presented as two-dimensional outline drawings. They formed the basis for the subsequent theories of Gottfried Semper and John Ruskin and were still recognized as valid principles of good design in the early years of the twentieth century. In this context, the outline drawing and the outline sketch became a medium for the preservation and development of form in Europe and influenced the reduction of form to surface configuration and essential contours.

THE FRENCH INFLUENCE

In France in 1755–70, artists and writers of the Enlightenment promoted the development of a new, straightforward ornamental style derived from classical traditions and architectural models in an effort to revive centuries-old laws of an architecture based on antique models. Architects began using ancient Greek and Roman ornaments: acanthus leaves, laurel leaves, garlands, cymas, Ionic friezes, and medallions formed the vocabulary of the revived style. With the return to classical motifs, the terms "grandeur" and "simplicité" were linked together as aesthetic ideals that also assumed moral connotations. The early neoclassical style, or "goût grec," as it was called in France, comprises additive combinations of ornamental elements that accompany and emphasize the deliberately heavy, simple tectonic construction. The ornamental motifs trace their roots to the architectural adornments of Greek temples, yet in their free, unconstrained arrangements, their huge scale relative to the entire structure, and their often contradictory juxtaposition, these elements reveal their long journey through history. A persistent characteristic is the replacement of the natural model with almost abstract, reductive, stylized decorative forms. In the German-speaking region, this style is often referred to as the "Zopfstil" (braid style) in reference to the frequently recurring leitmotifs of the braided band frieze or vertically hanging leaf garlands.[9] The term is appropriate, as the reformists of the early nineteenth century referred to the waning years of the eighteenth century, which were characterized by a pompous system of small principalities, as the "Zopfzeit," in allusion to the mandatory courtly hairstyle.

While artists, connoisseurs, and critics became bored with this style and turned away from it soon after 1770 in France, it began to receive critical attention in the German-speaking region about the same time. Particularly significant in this context were the publications of Jean-Charles Delafosse, who published his *Nouvelle Iconologie Historique* in 1768, and supplemented it in revised and expanded editions in 1773, 1776, and 1785. Delafosse's often passionate convictions are characterized by a striking aesthetic appeal; they led to both direct and indirect applications. The ornamental style attracted attention in Germany through model drawings, engravings, and designs by other Frenchmen, such as Jean-François de Neufforge and François Blondel. As a rule, this aesthetic involved graphic simplification, which was then further simplified in drawings configured for artisans and in furniture adorned with carvings and pressed fittings. This process of projecting the ornament onto furniture was performed totally apart from the tectonic configuration. Originally conceived as three-dimensional, these forms derived from Greco-Roman architectural ornamentation were applied to smooth furniture surfaces, where they appear as optical illusions, seemingly sculptural trompes l'oeil. Traces of Zopfstil forms exhibiting the architecturally influenced yet highly restrained syntax of an additive structure are still evident around 1800. Eventually, the additive style resulted in displacement of the style of simplicity.

THE ENGLISH INFLUENCE

In the first issue of his *Journal des Luxus und der Moden*, published in Weimar in 1786, Justin Bertuch expressed the following sentiments in a programmatic introduction: "Furniture must be simple and beautiful in form, comfortable and practical to use, durable and built with precision, and of good material if it is to be regarded as perfect. Almost all English furniture has a solid, practical character; the French is lighter in form, more thoroughly composed, and more eye-catching … but England will surely remain the legislator of good taste in this field for Europe as a whole for many years to come."[10]

England's role as a model is attributable less to the influence of furniture imported to the continent than to the impact of publications that rapidly gained widespread attention and acceptance. The engravings of furniture designer George Hepplewhite (d. 1786) and Thomas Sheraton (1751–1806) left an impression of structural simplicity and technical refinement of invention in convertible furniture that endured well into the nineteenth century. These designs were repeatedly copied and distributed as re-engravings, which resulted in an increasing linear simplification of furniture structure. The so-called "English" furniture style of the late eighteenth century, which was also produced in France during a wave of anglophile fashion in the 1790s, is characterized by straight lines, flat forms, and frugal ornamentation. Mahogany or "satin-wood" veneer was allowed to unfold its full effect, and only a few molding elements and fittings of fire-gilt bronze were added as distinctive features or to emphasize the architectural configuration. We often see similar types and forms as outgrowths of these nailed-on appliqués in the basic structure of Biedermeier furniture.

The persistent influence of the prerevolutionary "English style" was evident in several places in Germany around 1800 – at Schlösschen Paretz near Berlin, for example, which was built for Queen Luise according to plans drafted by Friedrich Gilly, or furnishings designed by Gentz for the Weimar court, furniture made for Duke Wilhelm von Birkenfeld-Zweibrücken for his residence in Landshut, and the Wilhelms-Palais in Munich. On the whole, these furnishings and furniture made for German courts express a new attitude. Instead of the French "bon cher," the ostentatious use of recognizably rare, precious, and expensive materials, we find in this transitional style from early Neoclassicism, which was very popular in Germany, and Biedermeier a deliberate departure from representational forms of expression and expensive, difficult-to-obtain materials. For the most part, this simple style appears within the context of a culture influenced by England and characterized by landscape gardens, the cult of emotion, and quotations from English art and culture. The cult of souvenirs, tea in Wedgwood china, full-length portraits in the park, sentimental novels, top hats and tails were the paraphernalia that captivated all of Europe as elements of a new style of unpretentious, natural simplicity.

These models rarely came direct from England, however, but rather via circuitous routes between Spain and St. Petersburg, Stockholm and Naples. In the years preceding the devastating wave of nationalism, European society was more mobile and international than it had been for some time. The wars between England and France and its allies between 1799 and 1815 divided Europe and spawned nationalist tendencies which nonetheless retained the seeds of that fruitful era immediately preceding the French Revolution and adopted, conserved, or refined the styles of the years around 1785.

All types of Biedermeier furniture, along with certain aspects of manners and social life, originated in the "English style." We find eloquent evidence of this in writing cabinets, settees, round sofa tables, dumb waiters, open-backed chairs, cabinet furniture and tables without marble tops, mahogany furniture, unadorned veneered furniture, and so on. The era of grand, pompous, self-contained furniture suites was over. Small groups or islands of matching furniture were much more in tune with the new spirit. Instead of large, hierarchically organized social settings, people now gathered in smaller, more intimate circles of friends and kindred spirits. What began as a style born of need and imposed modesty and that was oriented to the positions of the waning eighteenth century now evolved through a process of introspection and increasing identification with external circumstances into a deliberately articulated and propagated ideal of modesty and sober objectivity; these principles came to be seen as aesthetic and moral virtues.

THE IDEAL OF NATURE

The idealization of nature as God's creation played a very important role in Biedermeier art. As the crowning achievement of Christianity's view of Creation, the human being gave nature a recognizable form of expression through art: the beauty of Creation as reflected in its growth patterns, the natural forms of wood and woodworking processes (sanding and polishing), marble and stone, prismatic primary colors, coloration using natural elements (glass), advanced forms of naturalism (landscape painting), insights into the microcosm – the laws of growth in nature as reflected in still-life painting and floral painting on porcelain.

The Age of Enlightenment (1740–1850) was a period of intensive exploration of nature and its laws. Charles Darwin's theory of evolution through mutation and selection had not yet been accepted as a fundamental law of nature. Prior to the publication of his *On the Origin of Species* in 1859, prevailing belief was in the concept of a universe created by God in a single act and governed as a whole and in all of its parts by divine order. This fundamental view of nature underlay the entire early nineteenth century: the Creator was present in his creatures, each perfect in itself.

Near the end of the eighteenth century, the Swedish naturalist Carl Linnaeus proposed a system of classification through which all living organisms – the Flora and Fauna – could be compared and grouped together or distinguished from one another. Observation of fine distinctions between organisms became the means by which to establish their uniqueness and identify their place within the system. This concept was based upon a perspective of universal order. In this investigation of nature, using observation as the source of scientific knowledge, the written word was seldom sufficient to describe the forms observed; colored drawings were also used as scientific aids. Artists became indispensable to botanists. Everyone who aimed to describe and categorize organisms also made drawings of them, and no expedition was undertaken without the accompaniment of a professional draftsman to capture the state of organisms in nature.

Precise drawings for purposes of classification and distinction were indispensable for an understanding of nature. The artist's objective was not to render the peculiarities of the specific unique example but to emphasize the fundamental characteristics of a flower, for example, as an ideal type, to convey an understanding of the basic form of the species. The task was to record color and form, which were always subject to change, and transpose them into universally valid images. This explains the strange state of suspension between surrealistic precision and idealized typology that characterizes the flower paintings of the early nineteenth century.

Every blossom was regarded as an expression of the law of Creation. "It was an ordinary small flower; what naturalists need several lectures to explain, it expressed in a minute; it told of its birth and of the power of the sunlight that opened the delicate leaves and prompted them to give off their fragrance," wrote Hans Christian Andersen. This principle, according to which the laws of the great are expressed in the small and the laws of the microcosm are reflected in the macrocosm, was recognized not only by those who accepted the Christian concept of Creation. Goethe held a similar view of nature. In his *Metamorphosis of Plants,* he observed analogous structures in the large and the small, described the laws of dynamic growth, and employed observations of nature as a means of attaining knowledge of higher truths. The key objective in this process was to cultivate an objective style that was capable of identifying distinctive aspects.

SIMPLICITY AND SCALE

The basic design of primary and elementary forms began to rely on reduction of the surface to clear contours. The cult of simplicity or plainness evolved as an ideal of beauty in opposition to the luxurious, highly decorated style of the waning eighteenth century. This new aesthetic emerged in Germany roughly between 1798 and 1804 and was embodied in furniture built between about 1818 and 1830. Here, as well, it is evident that quality was valued most highly when it was rooted in material beauty not material luxury. These principles of simplicity characterize not only Biedermeier furniture but also the smooth surface designs and unpretentious forms of glass, silver, porcelain, and ceramic objects of the period.

A trend in architectural theory as it related to the aesthetic appeal of architectonic structures that emerged toward the end of the eighteenth century dictated that such objects should not be composed of subdivided or additive parts, but rather should be conceived as solid forms, and were never to be decorated with molding or sculptural elements, the intent being to preserve the pure essential scale. One of the most noteworthy exponents of this view was David Le Roy, a longtime professor at the Académie Royale d'Architecture in Paris, whose courses in architectural systems were mandatory for students. Le Roy contended in his preface to the second edition of his pioneering work *Les Ruines des plus beaux monuments de la Grèce* (1770), that only that which is undivided, solid, and smooth appears truly grand. In the debate on aesthetics waged in Rome, Paris, and Europe at large, he sided with the "Greeks" against the "Romans" or "Etruscans" represented by Piranesi, Clerisseau, Adam, and Bélanger, all staunch advocates of the high-minded grotesque element.[11]

Analogous to the demand for scale and simplicity, which Le Roy defended with great success – as evidenced in so-called French "revolutionary architecture" – Winckelmann proposed similar principles for art, sculpture in particular. His writings were eagerly received and intensively reviewed in the German-speaking region. As early as 1764, he noted on the basis of his studies of Roman architecture, that "Unity and simplicity make all beauty sublime, as it does everything we do and say: for what is great in itself becomes sublime when executed and presented with simplicity." He adds, "The harmony that delights our spirit does not consist in an endless array of broken, divided, isolated tones but in simple, sustained features."[12]

This appeal for simplicity, expressed in such words as simplicity, plainness, or unity, became the fundamental premise of the aesthetic that provided the basic guidelines for good design in the early nineteenth century. The classicist authors of Weimar placed particular emphasis on simplicity and plainness. At the same time, they advocated the application of acquired insights: "In Italy, most notably in Rome and Naples, where people live closer to the noble and beautiful relics of the art of the ancients and are more familiar with their purified tastes, this spirit of the noble simplicity of antiquity has also conquered the world of modern furniture."[13]

The principles that evolved during the philosophical age prior to 1800 were applied during the first decades of the age of pragmatism. We should not be irritated by the fact that the primary requirement of simplicity and plainness was concealed behind an abundance of terms with similar meanings, which was intended to give greater emphasis to the matter through repetition. The standard German encyclopedia of 1844 provides a definitive explanation of the similarities of meaning shared by these terms and definitions:

Simple is what has either no or very few components or what is restricted to the essential and thus equates to plain, or finite, whereby no combination or mixture with others occurs or is perceivable, and thus one speaks in this sense of the simplicity or plainness of an object. Plainness is originally synonymous with simplicity; but this word is also used in both a positive and a pejorative sense …. Aesthetic simplicity consists in the artless interplay of all individual elements of a work of art to form a whole. Dismissing all means through which constant consideration of the aspect of appeal seeks to call attention to itself, as if governed by alien laws, and still paying tribute to the spirit of the time, aesthetic simplicity expresses its innermost soul without posing demands. It gives no more than its purpose requires; its artistic resources are the very simplest; its arrangement and relationships are the most natural and comprehensible; it is far removed from all ambition, all splendor, and all overburdening. It is not rich and does not deceive; but it is certain, virtuously true, true and intimate. It proceeds in a strong, straight line to its goal; and a certain childlike sincerity is evident throughout.[14]

Shortly after this final hymn of praise to simplicity was written in such strong overtones, a wave of criticism and ironic commentary regarding the faded idyll of this naïve simplicity was unleashed. Writing in the Munich journal *Fliegende Blätter*, Adolf Kussmaul and Ludwig Eichrodt railed at

a naïve view of the simplest circumstances of life which the refined, modern citizen of the world cannot possibly recognize, an attitude of devotion to authority and order that we have unfortunately lost in the course of the confusing developments of recent years. A pity that our great Schiller was not acquainted with our brave countryman. He surely would not have forgotten in his treatise on the naïve to develop the relationship through modest conservatism to an idea of the beautiful, and he would not have forgotten the concepts of modest beauty and Biedermaier, which are now left to us to present.[15]

Thus was the first retrospective concept and the first definition of the Biedermeier period born and defined in the spirit of parody as an idyll of naïve simplicity and moralistic credulity.

GEOMETRIC FORMS AND ABSTRACTION

Beyond the desire to design orthogonal surfaces and focus on the unlimited beauty of simple, natural materials, one of the first obvious tendencies in Biedermeier is a striving for interesting composite geometric forms. Fear of monotony made designers wary of simplicity and reduction to basic forms:

It pained me to have to work with these stark, straight-edged forms, which looked as if they had been cast from ore and iron and which are regarded as all the more appealing, the straighter and more austere their lines …. And then that mournfully monotonous mahogany, in which veins of gold or a shimmer appear only at second glance but whose overall effect is quite dreary. [16]

This trend in favor of geometric forms went hand in hand with the use of vivid, pure elementary colors and was characteristic of developments after 1820. Geometric arrangements of primary colors in kaleidoscope style became a leitmotif in design after that time, and a system of primal formal and color configurations reflected the consistent and deliberate pursuit of simplicity as an aesthetic goal. Development progressed from the flat surface to the solid body to the simple elements of spatial order.

Reduction to geometric simplicity then shifted from overall form, and was followed by the increasing geometricization of the design of elements (circles and squares) applied as ornamentation. Geometry now provided not only the basic form but also the principles applied to the design of detail motifs as well. As these ideas developed, the process of reduction to elementary forms (cubes, rectangles, and cylinders) was completed, although it remained a basic prerequisite for the design of matching surfaces, bringing out the beauty of the material and the clarity of the elements.

The last tendency to emerge from this style of objectivity and simplicity was an approach to design in which cubic forms played an increasingly important role. Pure geometric lines and volumes were concentrated into highly expressive compositions. Additional ornamentation, figuration, and details composed of plant motifs were eliminated in order to preserve the coherency of the linear, surface-oriented designs. This brought forth the first abstract furniture designs, some of which were revived again around 1900. This was a kind of delayed reaction, as the style of simplicity disappeared for the most part around 1827 from the Central European world of design and ceased to play a significant part in subsequent developments. As noted by Semper, "a surplus of resources is the first real danger art must struggle to overcome."[17]

NOTES

1   Goethe 1900 (1798), pp. 211f.
2   Since Germany lags decades behind the English and French with respect to research based on inventories of royal and aristocratic collections, previous knowledge of the coexistence in a courtly household of both private styles in the Biedermeier aesthetic and public spaces decorated in representational styles such as Neoclassicism or Gothic Revival was likely hindered.
3   Semper 1834, p. 6.
4   Heine 2000 (1835), pp. 126ff.
5   Stifter 2000 (1857), p. 115.
6   See the color descriptions in the text in Krafft and Ransonnette 1801–12, pp. 16ff.
7   *Schorn'sches Kunstblatt* 76 (September 21, 1820), p. 301.
8   Quatremère de Quincy 1998 (1796), p. 13.
9   Cf. Munich 1991, pp. 12ff.
10   Bertuch 1786, vol. 1, pp. 29f.
11   Ottomeyer 1976, p. 23.
12   Winckelmann 1764, p. 150.
13   Bertuch 1786, vol. 5, p. 522.
14   Brockhaus 1844, pp. 609f.
15   *Fliegende Blätter*, 1855, p. 103.
16   Tieck 1836, pp. 247f.
17   Semper 1852, p. 12.

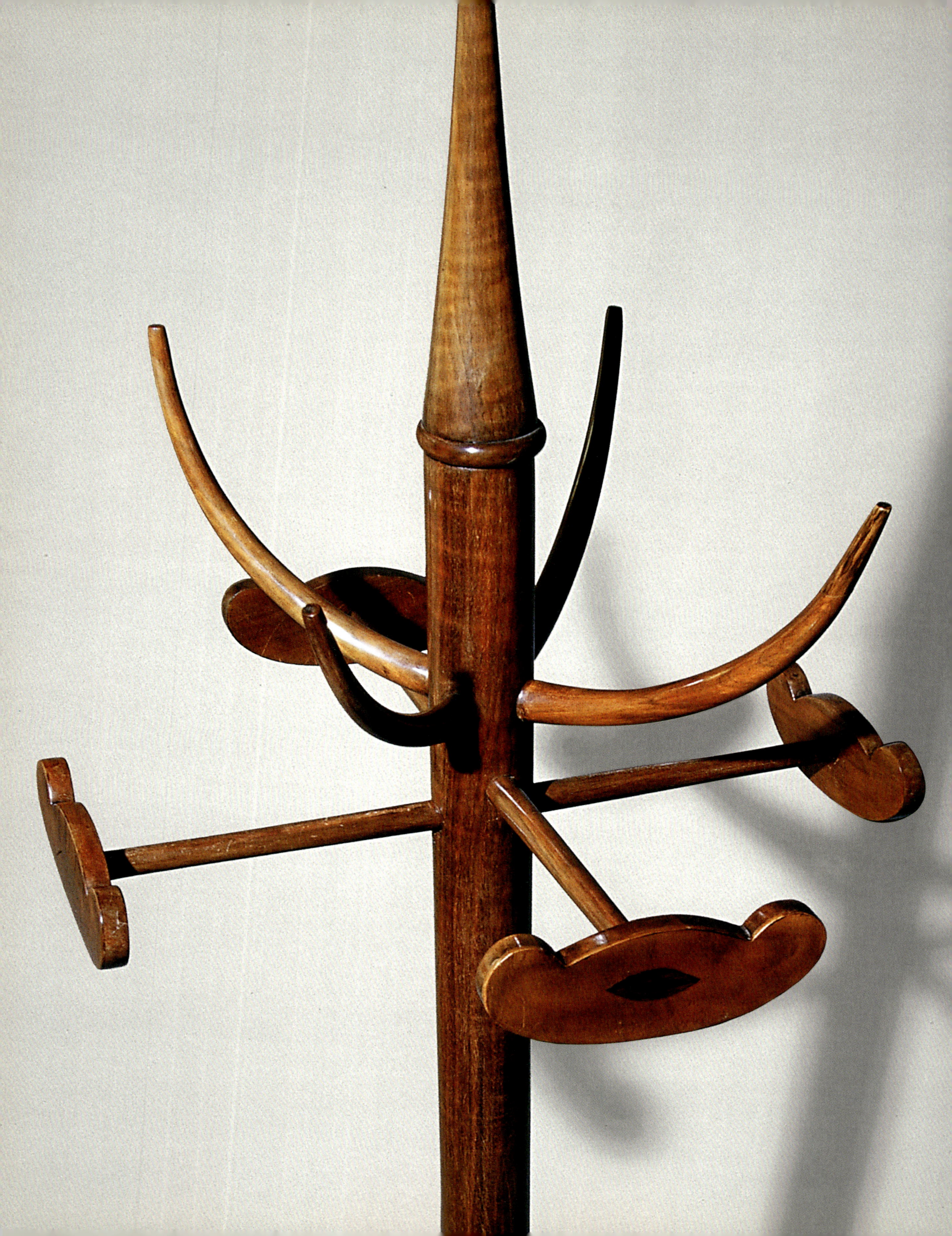

THE

AESTHETICS

OF BIEDERMEIER FURNITURE

CHRISTIAN WITT-DÖRRING

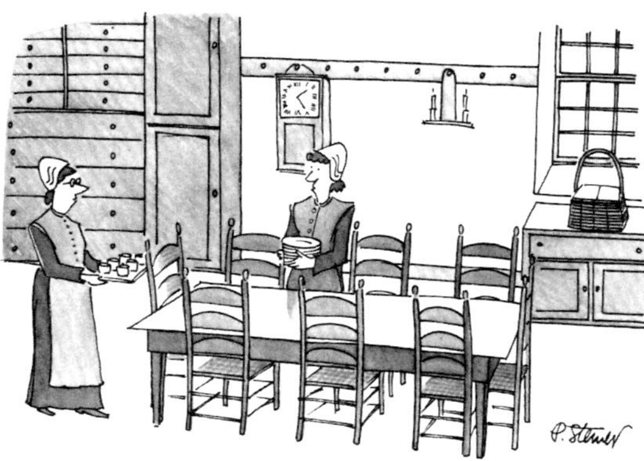

Figure 1
Peter Steiner
cartoon, *The New Yorker*
March 5, 1990
© The New Yorker Collection
1990 Peter Steiner from
cartoonbank.com
All Rights Reserved

"If the truth be told, I prefer Biedermeier," states the caption beneath a cartoon by Peter Steiner in *The New Yorker* (fig. 1).[1] The drawing shows two female members of the Shaker community in a dining room designed and furnished in keeping with Shaker aesthetics. In this little joke, two different worlds – that of Biedermeier and that of the Shakers – appear to collide. Both worlds set specific aesthetic standards for functional objects and both reentered the public consciousness at a moment when the world of objects was being subjected once again to a process of purification in the quest for modern form. During periods of significant social change, the longing for authenticity, for things cleansed of the superficial trappings of representation, has prompted people to look back to an era whose cultural achievements supposedly exemplify these qualities. In America, the Shaker culture[2] assumed this role during the 1920s, whereas at the end of the nineteenth century, the German-speaking countries of Europe looked back to the Biedermeier era. The focus was not on the purely formal revival of the two different aesthetics but on a renewal of the spirit they embodied.[3] In attributing the imaginary value judgment cited above to a Shaker woman, the cartoonist turned Shaker philosophy on its head, while at the same time calling our attention to the essential difference between the two cultures. The Shakers were not concerned primarily with the role of the individual in the creation of a beautiful object but rather with the elimination of all personal factors in the attempt to achieve the absolute. Beauty per se was not the issue; rather, it was believed to be the result of the abandonment of all striving to attain it.

What are the qualities we still admire so much today in furniture from the Biedermeier period? Where did the criteria through which our eyes have been schooled originate? Do they reflect historical facts or are they the product of a kind of wishful thinking in response to a very specific challenge? This challenge was broadly posed in the field of art at the turn of the nineteenth century in the quest for a contemporary, modern, national[4] mode of formal expression. It sought to vanquish Historicism, which had come to be regarded as internationally interchangeable, inappropriate to cultural progress, and essentially dishonest. The formal use of historical solutions did not reflect the realities of the everyday world. It supported an attitude of the parvenu, in that modern middle-class people made use of an outdated aristocratic language of form and representation that had nothing to do with their actual needs. The question arose as to when everything man-made had last embodied a uniform aesthetic concept and been united in a harmonious whole.[5] To restore a link to this ideal and thereby create a tradition of quality was the chief aim of the Viennese avant-garde around 1900. It was not a battle between old and new art but a battle for art itself.[6]

THE BIEDERMEIER REVIVAL IN VIENNA AROUND 1900

The situation in Vienna is representative of the debate on artistic style at the turn of the century. It is particularly interesting in this context because it took place within the multinational context of the Austro-Hungarian monarchy precisely at a time when the conflict of nationalities had come to a head. In 1898, Adolf Loos published the article "Die potemkin'sche Stadt" (The Potemkin City) in the first volume of *Ver Sacrum,* the monthly journal of the Vienna Secession.[7] Basing his argument on direct relationships between the aesthetic practices of Historicism and the concurrent patterns of social behavior, he developed his critique of prevailing social value judgments and their misguided application to matters of aesthetics. Guided by the urge to represent more than to be, people, he noted, tended to resort to affordable material and formal substitutes. This involved the use of ersatz materials and techniques developed during the Industrial Revolution, and the appropriation of aristocratic forms of representation in the absence of corresponding social standing, thereby elevating the world of illusion to the status of a standard. Believing this wholly dishonest and thus immoral, Loos appealed for a new way of thinking – later realized to a certain extent in the ideas propagated by the Secession. However, Loos soon took a position that was diametrically opposed to that of the Secessionists, who sought to develop a modern formal language through individual artistic expression, as articulated by Otto Wagner, the father of the modern movement in Vienna. Wagner's appointment as Professor of Architecture at the Akademie der bildenden Künste in Vienna in 1894 heralded the break with Historicism that Jakob von Falke[8] had called for in 1883. For Wagner, who was a generation younger than Loos, individual artistic creativity was the logical opposite of the predominantly scientific Historicism. Individual artistic creativity and the early Italian Renaissance revival that had begun in Vienna in the 1860s were two starting points for Wagner's early architectural theory. In 1889, he proposed the so-called "free Renaissance embraced by our *genius loci*" as the best contemporary formal-aesthetic approach to overcoming the twenty-year dominance of historical styles.[9] At the same time, however, he contended that the future lay not in the identification of a stylistic movement but must rather develop from a natural urge, which must necessarily lead to his own concept of "utilitarian style." Thus Wagner's concept of style was based not on formal definitions but on aspects of function and purpose. Because he was not seeking a new mode of formal expression in the tradition of historical styles, he may be regarded as a precursor of modernism. He was not concerned with traditionalizing new subject matter in new form but with a fundamental reevaluation of contemporary needs. And that qualified him in Loos's eyes as a person who exemplified the opposition to the development of style through individual artistic expression. While Wagner regarded this as a necessary point of departure in the struggle to overcome Historicism, he also saw it as a means of ensuring the quality of contemporary expression.[10]

THE LOST IDENTITY OF THE CRAFTS

As a symbol of reverence for local tradition, the *genius loci* cited by Wagner as the source of creative inspiration represented an important coefficient in the Vienna style debate that was to come, a discussion dominated by nationalist ideas. It not only served the ostensible purpose of developing style in the sense of individual, local artistic expression but also became a determining factor in imbuing Viennese products with a unique, internationally competitive character rather than international Historicism. As early as the 1860s, proposals for achieving independence from the qualitatively superior French and English products and thus supplying even these markets with goods are a continuous thread in the theoretical discussion.[11]

In addition to Wagner's reformist activities, ideas from the Anglo-Saxon cultural sphere also had a significant impact on the artistic revival in Vienna. When Arthus von Scala was appointed Director of the Kaiserlich-Konigliches Österreichisches Museum für Kunst und Industrie in 1897, that institution, which had been instrumental in attempts to reform Austrian arts and crafts since its founding in 1864, was placed in the hands of a certified anglophile. In his very first exhibition, the Winter Exhibition of 1897, Scala departed from the museum's traditional propagation of historical Viennese "art furniture," presenting in its place simple English utilitarian furniture as the model for the future. His selection included copies based on designs from the latter half of the eighteenth century[12] as well as plain cabinetmakers' pieces, among other things. Yet the show was criticized not only by local furniture producers but by the Vienna avant-garde as well.[13] The former regarded Scala as a traitor to local economic interests, the latter as an advocate of the old-style copy and thus as an opponent of individual, contemporary artistic expression. Only Loos supported Scala's reform efforts.[14] Scala's efforts were focused on the integrity of the artisan (cabinetmaker) who, without regard for the pronouncements of the architect (artistic expression), placed his traditional skills in the service of comfort, of solid material, and precise workmanship. In Loos's view, the cabinetmaker should no longer be forced to speak the language of another person (prescribed design), a different culture, or an unfamiliar age (historicist), but rather his own original German tongue. Loos credited only Wagner with the capacity to speak the language of the individual craftsman when it came to designing a utilitarian object.[15] A return to a time in which design and execution were not separated by distribution of labor in production, in which the craftsman did not depend upon the approval of an artist or architect, was the only guarantee of honest, modern expression. In his opinion, the English still maintained the tradition of an independent local quality that the Viennese had lost. England, unlike France, did not traditionally cater to the international luxury market but rather primarily to the needs of the common people, thereby giving her products a character shaped by function more than representation. Therefore, English furniture from 1790 to 1830 was regarded around 1900 as the source and origin of true modern furniture.[16] "Modern" was what conformed to the needs of the middle class and thus represented a democratic attitude. Wagner articulated his guiding principle regarding the education of architects: "Every modern creation must conform to the new materials and the requirements of the present if it is to meet the needs of modern people. It must reflect our own better, democratic, self-confident, yet critically thoughtful essence and reflect both the colossal technical and scientific achievements and the consistently practical considerations of humanity – that goes without saying!"[17] In Vienna, the goal of exploring this bourgeois tradition within the local cultural sphere became one of the most important criteria in the rediscovery of the culture of Biedermeier.

In 1898, in describing the new Viennese mode as an "English" style that must be sought in honest construction, art historian Franz Wickhoff in his article on the future of the Kunstgewerbemuseum[18] brought the quest for a modern, national style to a head.[19] He not only affirmed Scala's reorientation toward England but also echoed Wagner's and Loos's appeals for rediscovery of the *genius loci* or the "German" mode of expression. He asked when Vienna had had a signature mode of formal expression that was not merely a response to that of the world's national cultural leaders. When had the correspondence between form and everyday life come to an end in Vienna? When had local producers last served the needs of the people and not primarily the dictates of aristocratic representation?

THE GRANDCHILDREN OF BIEDERMEIER
Some believed that these principles had been embodied in the time of their grandparents, a formal world that had until then been regarded as a period of decline in aesthetic quality and craftsmanship. Art historians gave the period a name: Biedermeier.[20] In 1898, Karl Rosner included the Biedermeier era in his history of the decorative arts, with an extremely negative assessment of its contribution: "It was an age … in which the voice of beauty was never heard above the din of efforts to produce the cheap and the practical. From the standpoint of art history, this style, which posed virtually no aesthetic requirements on the artisan, had a far-reaching impact, and there is practically no other example in the entire history of arts and crafts in which the rapid, unstoppable deterioration of technical skill, accompanied by lack of interest, is more frighteningly evident than here."[21] Nothing better illlustrates the tremendous shift in values that took place in the younger generation around 1900 than this judgment that denied the practical claim to beauty. Viewed within the context of the generation of the children of the Biedermeier period, that judgment is easily understandable: history is full of examples of the rejection by children of the aesthetics of their parents and their revival in the generation of the grandchildren.[22] Wagner's pronouncement that "what is impractical cannot be beautiful"[23] is only one such example.

In 1898, Adolf Bartels was among those attempting to define art that is in tune with the times. He framed two requirements in the form of questions: "1. Does it correspond to the national character? And 2., Does it have the right temporal character, i.e., can one find in it the particular mode of seeing and feeling of the time?"[24] Vienna's artistic avant-garde found that Viennese Biedermeier met these conditions, both from the viewpoint of formal aesthetic criteria and in a broader cultural sense.[25] In his 1903 lecture "Our Relationship to the Biedermeier Style," Josef Folnesics pointed out that

In Vienna, this style coincided with a very important period in the history of the city, an era in which the prevailing taste in art was revealed in its purest and most perfect form in music; Schubert, Lanner, and Strauss had reached their zenith; it was the period we refer to as Old Vienna and which epitomizes the inner quality of poetry for our local patriotic sensibilities. It was also the era of competence, strength, and bloom in the bourgeoisie, which we find all the more pleasing in that it appeared as something self-evident and had none of the trappings of tasteless self-glorification.[26]

Vienna did indeed develop a cultural language of its own between about 1815 and 1820. In the arts and crafts, in particular, an independent aesthetic mode of expression emerged uninfluenced by France or England, the most important sources of inspiration at the time. This is most clearly and distinctively manifested in the furniture of the period, which is characterized above all by a clear, simple, material-conscious, functional approach to form. This furniture prompted Folnesics to express the (no longer accepted) opinion that it confronted us with "a new social order." In his view, it did not represent "the era of gallant courtly custom and aristocratic regimen; it was rather the era of labor and the ascendancy of the bourgeoisie."[27] Such opinions may be seen as representative of the views of an entire generation of historians of art and culture who created the myth of bourgeois Biedermeier. Thus W. Fred, for example, as archival research and the study of countless surviving depictions of the interiors of courtly and aristocratic provenance confirm,[28] arrived at the following mistaken conclusion: "Untouched by the stabilization of the bourgeois Biedermaier [sic] style, with its angular or subtly curving lines, its stolid forms, its colorful cotton fabrics, and the odor of restrictiveness, the interiors of the upper ten thousand and their imitators remain archaic masks."[29] Hartwig Fischel succumbed to similar wishful thinking – for that is what it was – that inspired the grandchildren's generation of "Homo" Biedermeier to seek the roots of local bourgeois culture: "and thus local art derived its impulses much less from the upper levels of society, as in the preceding eras and in other places, but instead exhibited a primarily bourgeois character."[30] The fact is that although the bourgeoisie gained strength in Vienna during the first half of the nineteenth century, the court and the aristocracy still set the dominant tone in both social and cultural life.[31] While Biedermeier furniture and interiors may conform to our notions of bourgeois values, their forms and configurations were the product of the shift in values in the courtly, aristocratic world that had abandoned the original unity of public and private spheres even in Germany near the end of the eighteenth century and developed two distinct and separate ways of life. They culminated in the simultaneous formal coexistence of the public, representational, and decorative Empire style and the private, simple, practical, unadorned Biedermeier.[32] It was in this spirit, for example, that Emperor Franz I ordered the strict distinction between public and private rooms in his court and decreed that only furniture made with expensive, exotic woods should be placed in the former, while those with cheaper, native varieties could be used in the latter. Only Ludwig Hevesi, the Positivist-Humanist chronicler of Vienna's artistic spring, recognized the leading role of the aristocracy in shaping the culture of the period of the Congress of Vienna in his first history of Austrian art in the nineteenth century – a publication conceived as a nationalist monument[33] – although he went on to examine the bourgeois roots of Biedermeier culture as well. "That was not Empire but rather an outgrowth of

Empire, in a bourgeois-practical variant, for a populace steeped in comfortable customs. Yet it was not small-townish but emerged instead from an exaggerated refinement of everyday comfort of the kind enjoyed by people who have always been in touch with the 'world.'"[34] He was referring to arts and crafts shown at the exhibition on the Congress of Vienna presented at the Österreichisches Museum für Kunst und Industrie in 1896,[35] an exhibition he identified as the true source of inspiration for the reawakened appreciation of the people of Vienna for the culture of their grandparents.

WIENER WERKSTÄTTE

Aside from the purely formal orientation toward English models from the late eighteenth and early nineteenth centuries, it was above all the moral dimension of the English Arts and Crafts Movement that pointed the way for the artistic renewal in Vienna around 1900. At the root of this trend was the fundamental issue of the dignity of human life and labor, with regard to laborers and consumers alike. From this concern emerged the appeal for the elimination of the traditional distinction between high (fine or creative) art and low (applied) art in order to enable everyone to experience artistic expression in everyday life. With respect to the production of a utilitarian object, the logical consequence was the reintroduction of manual methods of production. This unity of the arts, to which the Vienna Secession gave highest priority,[36] is nothing other than a different way of expressing the question posed at the outset: when had everything created by human beings last embodied a single, consistent concept of art? Thus it is only logical that Josef Hoffmann and Koloman Moser, the founders of the Wiener Werkstätte (Vienna Workshop), came from the Secessionist camp. In their program for the Wiener Werkstätte, they openly addressed the artistic responsibility of the bourgeois client.

Only the parvenu will be satisfied with surrogates. The burghers of our time, like the working people, must be proud and fully aware of their importance, and they must not seek to compete with other classes whose cultural functions are fulfilled and who rightly look back upon a glorious artistic past. Our bourgeoisie has by no means fulfilled its artistic function. It is now its turn to do full justice to the progress of our age.[37]

Their ideas were devoted only to reservations concerning art and material. Programmatic emphasis was placed on the development of contemporary style and on the quality of workmanship. They continued to place the bourgeoisie in the tradition of the aristocratic desire for representation with luxurious, handcrafted individual objects. Renewal was pursued through form, rather than content, and was thus in diametric opposition to Adolf Loos and did not point toward modernism, which placed the human being, not things, at the center of its world. The human being's sense of beauty was defined through function, as Wagner had proposed. "The modern mind demands above all that the utilitarian object be practical. It regards beauty as the embodiment of the highest perfection. And because the impractical is never perfect, it cannot be beautiful, either."[38]

FURNITURE OF SIMPLICITY

Thus a subjective, functionally oriented concept of Biedermeier furniture composed of a wide variety of components emerged around 1900. Dictated by considerations of art and cultural history as well as by aesthetic ideas, its primary goal was to foster the

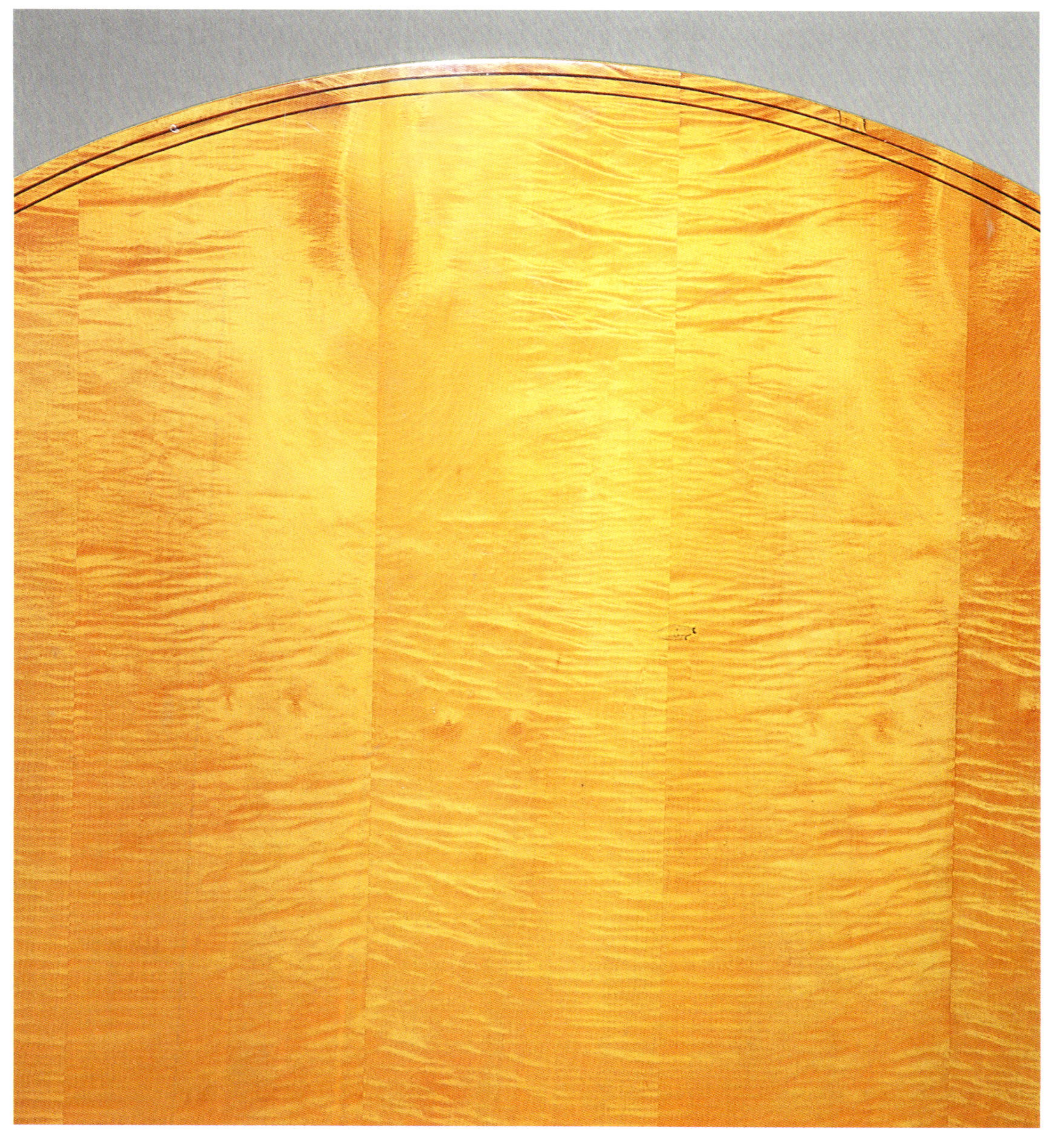

Figure 2
Tea Table
Vienna, ca. 1825
Cat. 1-16 (detail)

development of a genuine bourgeois form of expression that regarded the practical or functional aspect of an object, rather than its representational character, as the ideal of beauty. To that was added the motivating force of the individual character of a national, formal mode of expression no longer defined in terms of class hierarchy. This was the basis after the Congress of Vienna for the construction of a simple, honest kind of bourgeois furniture that served the needs of the emotions and not of public representation. The equation of simplicity and practicality with the bourgeoisie and the tendency to date this development to the years following the Congress of Vienna is not a correct interpretation.

For the most part, the selection of "simple" furniture that represents the theme of this exhibition is a deliberately chosen alternative to a public, representational ambience. Mostly without the classicist decorative features of the Empire style that was popular at the same time, its quality lies in its rich and formally varied abstract language based on proportions, the interplay of surface and volume, and material qualities, which are highlighted by pure, undecorated form. Born of a classicist spirit, it emphasizes tectonic features. Loads and supporting elements are usually clearly defined and permit an inventive approach to the combination of very different volumes. Although created in the German-speaking region or within its sphere of influence, the furniture exhibits striking regional differences that mark fundamental distinctions between North and South. The northern region (Prussia, Saxony-Weimar, Hamburg, and Lübeck) is more firmly anchored in the English sphere of influence, while the southern region (Austrian Empire, Bavaria, Württemberg, and Baden) is more closely oriented toward Vienna.

Despite the restrictions on the autonomy of the guilds by the heads of state beginning in the second quarter of the eighteenth century, furniture production in the German states and the Austrian Empire, unlike in France and England, was still based largely on the traditional guild system. This involved the strict separation of individual crafts required to build a piece of furniture. Thus a cabinetmaker was permitted to perform only woodworking tasks; carving, gilding, or upholstery had to be done in the corresponding workshops. Only in slowly emerging furnishing houses granted special privileges could the performance of the various handcrafting techniques be under a single roof. The guild system still operated on the assumption that the market was limited, and therefore local. Rules governing admission of journeymen to master status were accordingly protectionist and restrictive. Only legitimately born applicants with proper references, proper religious affiliation, and citizenship in a given city or town were accepted. New, additional master positions were approved only after a rigorous assessment of the ability of the local market to assimilate them. Such positions usually became available only when a master died. The best guarantee of advancement was to marry the widow of a master cabinetmaker. Normally, the number of apprentices and journeymen trained in a given trade was also limited in order to prevent the emergence of unwelcome competition. Alongside this tightly regimented guild system, larger groups of unaffiliated or unauthorized master cabinetmakers were formed. Although their training was not significantly different, they were not required to be citizens and thus often brought fresh, foreign energy to local markets. Yet, in every case, there arose a self-contained urban environment that produced formally homogeneous products. Generally speaking, Berlin's regulations were less stringent than Vienna's and Berlin offered more favorable opportunities for economic advancement.[39] While freedom of trade and commerce was not officially sanctioned in Vienna until 1859, it had become a reality in Prussia, which also abolished customs restrictions at the same time, as early as 1818.

Despite significant local differences in specific aspects of cabinetmaker training within the German-speaking region and the countries under Austrian dominion, a three-year apprenticeship appears to have been the rule. Apprenticeship was followed by training for qualification as a journeyman under different master cabinetmakers for an unspecified period of time. Candidates could acquire some of the requisite skills and knowledge in their home towns or during a period of "Wanderschaft" (traveling as "wandering" craftsmen) abroad. The master's examination was usually administered in the candidate's home town, as citizenship was a customary prerequisite for admission. Candidates had to complete a master project and submit a corresponding technical drawing. Accordingly, craftsmen were required to take drawing instruction at local fine arts academies beginning in the 1770s. Copenhagen offered the first such courses in 1771, followed by Vienna in 1775 and Berlin in 1787. This instruction was intended to acquaint future masters not only with fundamental drawing techniques but also with the various architectural and contemporary decorative systems. This heightened emphasis on draftsmanship as part of a cabinetmaker's training coincided with the first manifestations of individualization in furniture design. For good reason, it had progressed farthest in the Viennese sphere of influence, where drawing instruction was promoted vehemently by the state.[40] In the residential city of the Holy Roman Empire, which naturally attracted numerous foreign cabinetmakers during their years of Wanderschaft, they were confronted with drawing instruction for the first time and later returned home with significant new inspirations. Traces of training in Vienna are evident throughout the German states and as far beyond as Denmark. Such pieces, despite their place of origin, can be regarded as an item of Viennese furniture.[41] While it strengthened the unity of design and execution – that is, the independent role of the cabinetmaker as designer that was the rule in the guild system – the establishment of drawing instruction as an integral part of the training also anticipated the distribution of tasks that characterized the newly emerging age of industrialization. Beginning in the 1840s, many drawing schools became schools for model draftsmen who later supplied designs to industry.

Regardless of whether they originated around 1795, 1810, 1820, or 1830, and thus from the era of the late Louis XVI, Empire, or Biedermeier styles, the items of furniture exhibited here are classicist. They are all products of a fundamental shift in values that credited the practical with aesthetic quality. As different as they may be in formal terms, they all reflect the same attitude, which placed a higher premium on personal needs than on public representation. This is evident not only in a reduced use of decorative elements but also in a very deliberate approach to materials. On the one hand, most notably in the case of wood, this represented creativity untainted by civilization and thus noble simplicity; on the other, it possessed a quantifiable material value that shifted economic reality to the center of focus. What emerged between these two parameters was an extremely subtle atmospheric image that in its time spoke a clearly readable material language. Oriented toward what was actually available in the market and toward individual affordability, it created a differentiated, graduated cost system. Not only the different varieties of wood and textile elements but all aspects of interior design had their place within this order. A sophisticated system of ersatz materials and ersatz techniques emerged to make such luxury affordable. And it is interesting to note that no negative or embarrassing connotations of the kind opposed by the Arts and Crafts Movement of the latter half of the nineteenth century were attached to this method of substitution. It was inspired instead by a pioneering spirit of innovation that evokes a feeling of sensitive craftsmanship. Everything was possible. Walnut could be stained to look like mahogany. Cheap, simple walnut could be varnished to resemble expensive, grained walnut. American walnut was grafted to native walnut so that it would form knots, which in turn produced an immensely popular grain pattern. Wood inlay gave way to ink pen work, paste decoration replaced gilt-bronze, and "verde-antico" coatings imitated the greenish patina of bronze.

The key to this materialistic albeit sensitive world lies in the blending of the useful with the beautiful. Sensitivity appears frozen beneath the lustrous surface of the furniture. With its visually hard, glassy coating, shellac, which had begun to replace wax polish in the late eighteenth century, hastened the process of alienation between the viewer and the material. In this way, by casting off their natural qualities, the genuine natural forms exhibited by wood grain patterns became abstract notions of nature.

The simple form of the furniture built between the late eighteenth century and around 1830 appears in a wide range of variations. Born of the tectonic qualities of classicism, the straight line took precedence over the curved. If a line was curved, it exhibited clear, sharp contours that extended into the flat plane rather than into three-dimensional space and thus emphasized frontality (plates 31, 44). This same attitude is evident in the consistent use of veneer: it was possible to draw the grain of the wood vertically over front surfaces, regardless of their horizontal structural details (plate 7). Although this counteracted the tectonics of the furniture, it emphasized the face of an item of furniture as a single, unbroken surface. In chronological terms, between the 1790s and the 1830s, there was a progressive development from intricate designs that generated lightness and transparency toward a more uniform style that favored monumentality. As in the painting of the same period, the external appearance of furniture shifted from a graphic, linear, permeable presence to one that is more painterly and tends to emphasize volume (plate 60). Approaches to the integration of furniture into interior space also changed accordingly. Until about 1815, interior designers sought primarily to achieve strong contrasts between the shell of the walls and the individual pieces of furniture. Dark furniture stood out against light-colored walls, light furniture from dark walls. The pieces of furniture themselves exhibited strong color contrasts that set off their contours against their basic shapes (plate 1). Popular combinations included black-stained surfaces framed with light maple or a body of mahogany outlined by dark, stained maple. Seating furniture upholstery exhibited the same types of interplay. The usually monochrome upholstered surfaces were often framed with braids and cords in contrasting colors (plate 57). Equally important was the emphasis of the seat edges through sewn-on gimps or galloons which also underscored the tectonics of the individual upholstered elements. In furniture from about 1820 to 1825, however, there was a gradual tendency to deemphasize contrasts between furniture and walls. Individual volumes are no longer sharply outlined. Most furniture is covered with a single type of wood veneer, accentuating the impression of a solid uniform body. The increasingly popular patterns of wall and furniture fabrics now appear in less linear alignment (horizontal, vertical, or diagonal) but are instead distributed uniformly and without structure over the surface. Thus braids and cords stand out less prominently in terms of color and tectonics in seating furniture. Draperies laid over the arms and backs of seating furniture or affixed below the seat frame had become outdated by 1820. At this point, there was an explosion of myriad playful formal features in seating furniture, particularly in the Viennese sphere of influence. This is manifested primarily in furniture backs, which often exhibit whimsical elements.

By virtue of the manner in which the furniture described above blends material, function, and feeling to form a harmonious whole, it serves as a mediator between individualism and anonymity. In this sense, the cartoon cited in the introduction is particularly apt, in that Peter Steiner opposes the Shakers' rejection of design with the modest formal individualism of Biedermeier furniture.

NOTES

1   *The New Yorker*, March 5, 1990, p. 35.

2   Andrews and Andrews 1928, pp. 132-36.

3   "It can be produced again, never as the inevitable expression of time and circumstance, yet still as something to satisfy the mind which is surfeited with over-ornamentation and mere display." Andrews and Andrews 1937, p. 63.

4   Bahr 1898, p. 5.

5   Folnesics 1903B, esp. p. 3.

6   Bahr 1898, pp. 8-10.

7   Loos 1898, pp. 15ff.

8   Nearly twenty years after the first initiatives toward reform in arts and crafts appeared in Vienna following the poor reception of Austrian products at the 1862 London World's Fair, Jakob von Falke called attention to the limited role of historical models in the quest for a contemporary style in his *Ästhetik des Kunstgewerbes* (Stuttgart, 1883), p. 54. In his view, the revival of a once existing but now lost quality via the circuitous route through the arts (design and execution) of the past could be only a makeshift transitional phase that must necessarily lead to creative freedom.

9   Wagner 1987 (1889), p. 17.

10   Wagner 1896, p. 31.

11   Zuckerkandl 1898, pp. 4-6, esp. p. 6.

12   It is interesting to note in this context that Loos tended to furnish his own home with reproductions of eighteenth-century English seating furniture, some based upon models presented by Scala. This conforms to Loos's belief that it made no sense to redesign a model that had proven its worth merely for the sake of modernity. He regarded that as a waste of creative talent that did nothing to enhance functional value.

13   Bahr 1898, pp. 3f.; Zuckerkandl 1908, pp. 1-6, esp. pp. 4f.; Schölermann 1898, p. 25.

14   Loos 1962, vol. 1, pp. 33ff.

15   Ibid., p. 47.

16   Lichtwark 1899, esp. p. 123.

17   Wagner 1979 (1914), p. 39.

18   For museums of arts and crafts, outdated Historicism also implied the need to reassess their traditional role as providers of historical models for designers, craftsmen, and consumers.

19   Zuckerkandl 1898, pp. 4-6, esp. p. 5.

20   *Kunst und Kunsthandwerk* 5 (1902), pp. 212f.

21   Rosner 1898, p. 39.

22   Lux 1906-1907, pp. 1-2.

23   Wagner 1979 (1914), p. 44.

24   Bartels 1898, pp. 19-22, esp. p. 20.

25   Zuckerkandl 1908, pp. 1-6, esp. pp. 4f.

26   Folnesics 1903B, p. 12.

27   Ibid., p. 10.

28   One of the most important photographic source works on Austrian furniture and interior design of the Empire and Biedermeier periods. Folnesics 1903A presents a number of examples from the context of the upper Austrian aristocracy. Munich 1987, pp. 91-128; Witt-Dörring in Vienna 1987A, pp. 367-87.

29   Fred 1903, p. 61.

30   Fischel 1900, p. 102.

31   Godsey 2003.

32   Witt-Dörring 1991; Witt-Dörring 1998.

33   Sármány-Parsons 2001.

34   Hevesi 1902, vol. 2, p. 106.

35   Hevesi 1906; Hevesi 1909, pp. 8-53.

36   Schölermann 1898, pp. 5-7, esp. p. 6.

37   Hoffmann, Moser, and Wärndorfer 1905, pp. 12ff.

38   Loos 1962, vol. 1, p. 152.

39   Stiegel 2003; Zatschek 1958.

40   Vienna 1996.

41   Graf and Sangl 2004, pp. 80-81.

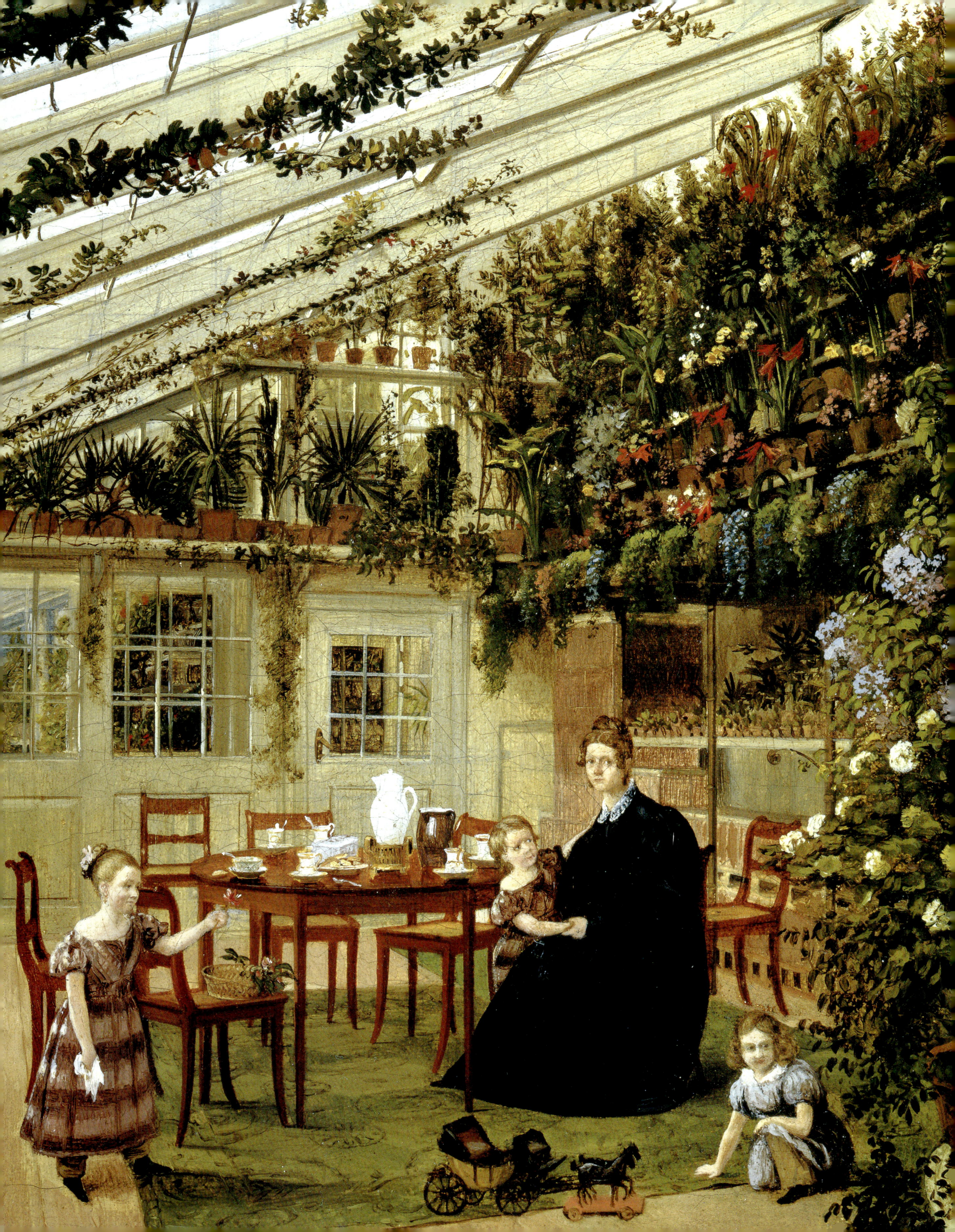

A CULTURE OF
HARMONY
AND MEMORY
LAURIE A. STEIN

HOW HEAVENLY IT WAS IN THAT ROOM. "SEE, CHILDREN," DECLARED AUNT PAULA, "THIS IS AN AUTHENTIC OLD BIEDERMEIER ROOM. EVEN THE EMBROIDERY ON THE CHAIRS, THE BELL PULL. EVERYTHING. THE FURNITURE, THE WARDROBE, THE CUPS. EVERYTHING. PLEASE TAKE NOTE OF THIS WORD: BIEDERMEIER."

Charlotte Berend-Corinth, "Als ich ein Kind war," 1950[1]

THE DREAM OF A HARMONIOUS ENVIRONMENT

In 1834, the young poet/writer Adalbert Stifter wrote about his ideal domestic living space, explaining:

I want to have an apartment with two large rooms, with well-polished floors, upon which no dust lays; soft green and pearl gray walls, near which stand new furniture, nobly massive, with antique simplicity, sharp-edged and glossy; gray silk window draperies, stretched like frosted cut glass in small folds and which can be drawn sideways from the middle.[2]

Stifter's description can be understood as the musings of an individual about how to shape a domestic interior based on his specific personal stylistic preferences for simplified lines, highly polished finishes, and a serene palette. From another perspective, however, Stifter's ambition for classically inspired furniture forms, glossy wood surfaces, and taut curtains seems to go beyond the parameters of simple interest in modern interior decoration. His wishes indicate a keen awareness of the larger ideological concerns of his time, and, as a member of literary society, he would undoubtedly have been knowledgeable about philosophical ideas such as Johann Wolfgang von Goethe's theories of color or Immanuel Kant's concept of beauty.[3]

Stifter's model of an ideal domestic environment can be understood as a reflection of a deep-rooted urge for order and clarity – a dream that transcends the particularity of a desire for an individualized personal space to encompass a larger vision of a harmonious environment in a universal societal sense. Such complex interpenetration of ideals about the relationships between personal space, aesthetic evolution, and cultural representation infused the historical moment we know today as the Biedermeier era.

THE ARISTOCRACY AND THE CULTURE OF DOMESTICITY

In Austria and in the German states after 1815, the post-Enlightenment, post-French Revolution, and post-Napoleonic era was punctuated by economic and social upheaval.[4] As prosperity slowly returned, first for the aristocratic elite beginning around 1820 and then subsequently for a burgeoning bourgeois class, there arose a culture of domesticity. Sheltered domestic environments were seen as places of refuge in which personal interests and social culture could be nurtured. Domestic space became revered as the central site for harmonious personal and family life, a place in which individual definition – in spatial, aesthetic, formal, and functional terms – became tied to the comfort, security, and informality of the home environment.

Until relatively recently, traditional art history viewed Biedermeier culture as the first significant bourgeois style, based in part on the emphasis during the period on clean formal lines and unornamented surfaces in furniture and decorative arts, as well as the centrality of focus on home and hearth.[5] Newer literature has challenged these assumptions, and recognized and acknowledged the importance of royal and aristocratic commissions for Biedermeier culture.[6]

This was a period of transition in imperial domestic life, as power was being consolidated among members of the conservative Hapsburg-Metternich system in the Austrian Empire and among the newly realigned ruling classes in Germany. The phenomenon of Biedermeier developed as part of a larger cultural redefinition and flourished in the royal residence towns such as Vienna, Berlin, Munich, Darmstadt, and Dresden, and in the sites of summer palaces such as Brandenburg and Silesia.[7]

Indeed, the blossoming of Biedermeier culture was spawned through the interconnection of familial relationships among the ruling and politically powerful families in Germany and Austria.[8] A circle of young royals and aristocrats came into their own in the early years of the nineteenth century. For them, the culture of domesticity became a form of retreat, in both the positive and negative senses of that concept. Members of this circle, and of a select group of the cultural and political elite, began to undertake radical redecoration projects in private rooms of their official palaces, summer retreats, and stately homes. They chose for their domestic familial spaces the less formal furnishing style and new aesthetic expression that evolved as Biedermeier. For some, this choice may have been rooted in a reactionary conservatism – burrowing behind safe doors – but for the majority, this embrace of a "modern," alternative style reflected "something more, a readiness among nobles to appreciate artistic innovation, a surprising degree of support for what was new and even challenging in contemporary culture."[9]

BIEDERMEIER AND PAST STYLES: LAYOUTS, SPATIAL ARRANGEMENTS,
AND TYPES OF FURNISHINGS

It is important to note that these same families continued to choose more formal and highly ornamented aesthetic styles of French Empire or neoclassicist "Zopfstil" for the emblematic and representational public interiors in their households. Biedermeier flourished and coexisted continuously alongside other major aesthetic tendencies, such as Empire, Romanticism, and neo-Gothicism, until the onset of Historicism in the 1840s.[10] And not all Biedermeier interiors are pure in their aesthetic; one finds subtle traces of former aesthetic choices – the inclusion of a beloved piece of Empire furniture or a gilt decorative object placed on a shelf. Biedermeier was never a sole option; it was a conscious choice.

As divisions emerged between taste for domestic and public spaces, new layouts and flow of communication between rooms were developed in residential designs.[11] For example, many apartments indicate a clear separation of design choice for the official and the private areas.[12] A remarkable series of memorializing "Zimmerbilder," or room portraits, from the late 1820s and later, detail the domestic interiors of royals such as Princess Marianne and Prince Wilhelm of Prussia or Princess Marie and Princess Mathilde of Bavaria. These designs elucidate that the aesthetic concept for classicist opulence and strict furnishing arrangement was still common in rooms used for official occasions (fig. 1), in stark contrast with the more reserved private Biedermeier plans for informal familial spaces. In some cases, the disjuncture was eased by a spatial separation within the layout, with public rooms in one axis and the private behind; in other instances, the issue was solved architecturally through the building of new communication axes.

The overall ideal of a Biedermeier room was based on the "Raumbild," or aesthetic room concept, and was supported by decoration and arrangement that were appropriate to the functions and uses of the space by the entire family, from children to adults. Spaces were defined by unique coloration and pattern choices and by individualized spatial organization.

The development of the "Wohnzimmer," or living room, as opposed to the traditional formal salon, was an important innovation of the Biedermeier era; such rooms reflected the new informality of domesticity. Furnishings were moved out from strict placement against the walls. It became common practice in the Wohnzimmer to have a multiplicity of "Wohninseln," or activity areas, decorated with objects suited to the specific activities for which they would be used (plate 96).[13] Following 1815, particular forms of furniture, such as writing desks, sewing tables, étagères, and baluster tables, underwent refinement. A broad range of seating furniture was developed. Rather than ornate gilding and applied decoration, new furniture relied for ornament on the pure quality of the wood surfaces, the natural patterns of the veneers, and the architectonic clarity of line and form. The aesthetic for such works was one that "would be distinguished by freedom from superfluous ornament, through simplicity, regularity, beauty and solidity."[14] Technical virtuosity was highly prized in all designs, including those for silver, glass, and ceramics. Creativity was fostered in upholstery, wall coverings, and draperies; a broad array of patterns and types of textiles and wallpapers was invented to meet increased demand and taste.

Biedermeier interiors illuminate the personal interests of the period: smaller rooms, or cabinets, were often dedicated to specific domestic activities, such as music, reading, sewing, or dressing. Function dictated the placement of pieces: for example, toilette tables and sewing tables were usually placed near windows to take advantage of the light. A typical suite of rooms for the upper classes was "a magnified image of Biedermeier domesticity, crammed full of the splendours of former times and gleaming showcase articles, with proportions and an environment designed for people, with bastions and fortifications within whose walls security, peace and comfort and the leisure to enjoy life could unfold themselves."[15]

Figure 1
Artist Unknown
*Red Room in the Apartment
of Princess Marianne and
Prince Wilhelm of Prussia,
Berlin Palace*
ca. 1830
Kronberg, Hessische
Hausstiftung

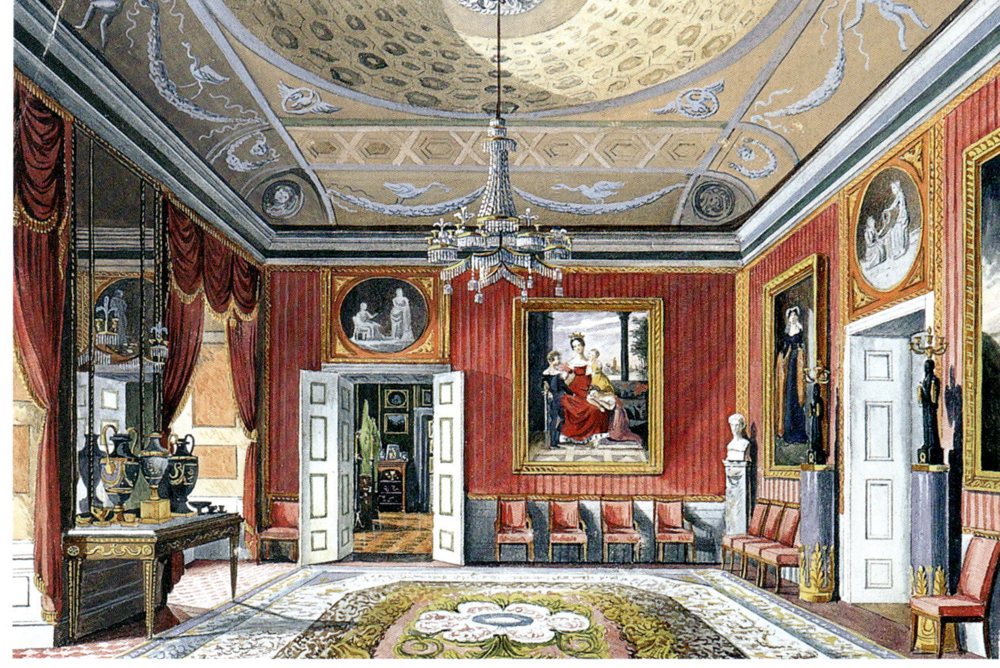

Figure 2
Eduard Gaertner
*Study in the Apartment
of Princess Marianne
and Prince Wilhelm of
Prussia, Berlin Palace*
1852
Kronberg, Hessische
Hausstiftung

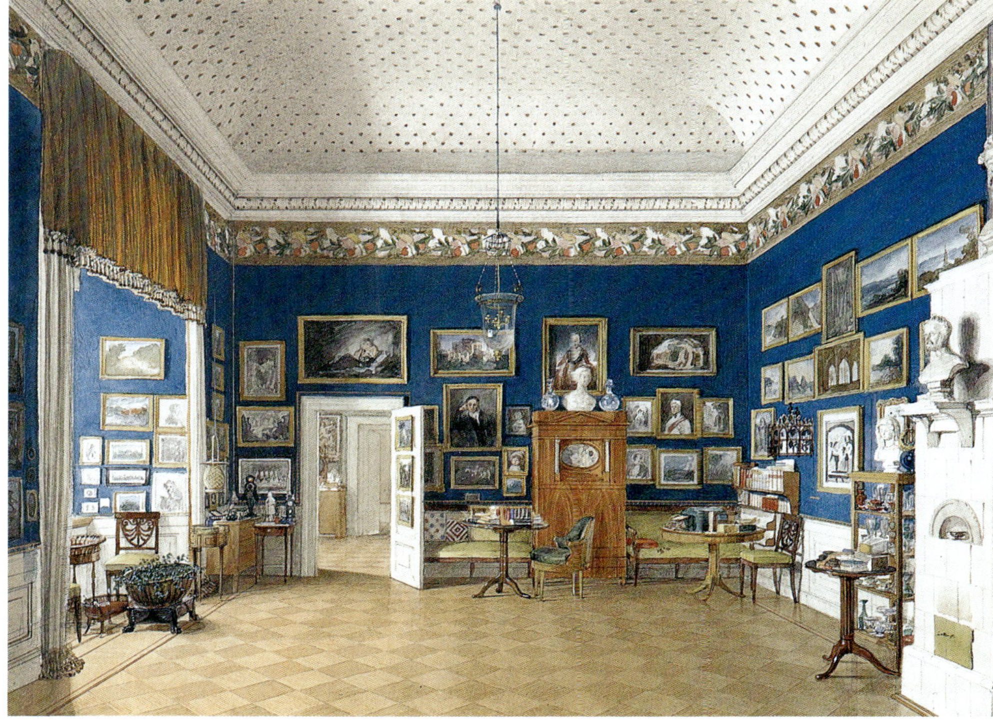

SOUVENIR CULTURE AND THE AESTHETIC BOURGEOISIE

The standard aesthetic profile for Biedermeier as a style of uncluttered simplicity is a myth. Simplicity in Biedermeier meant simplicity of lifestyle rather than simplicity of decorative aesthetic. It was actually common to cover the surfaces of tables, shelves, and étagères with a profusion of small objects and souvenirs, often decorated with landscape and architectural views or floral and animal images. Birds, plants, and all manner of natural items were even brought into the interiors, and an entire genre of furnishings, such as birdcages and jardinières, developed in response to this fashion. With walls hung densely with artworks and smaller decorated objects and plants scattered about, the interiors were quite full, in both aesthetic and real terms (fig. 2). Rooms were replete with collections of "Nippes," or memorabilia:

the wedding and godparent gifts, the jugs and cups, the tiny bits of embroidery and the small decorative objects which have to be protected from breakage and dust, the memorabilia of friendship and love. Particularly numerous and beloved were the painted cups, with which a true luxury was propelled.[16]

Often, there were also personal albums, or "Stammbücher," filled with letters, poetry, and watercolors, through which to leaf at leisure and recall fond memories. Biedermeier is infused with the culture of memory, of longing for an idealized past and the return to universal harmony.[17]

The philosopher Goethe's reflections on harmony and on clarity in the order of things are usually associated with Romanticism, but they also strongly permeated Biedermeier aesthetic and ideals. In domestic interiors, Goethe's color theories were embraced to appeal to the temperament as well as the eye. In his *Farbenlehre* (*Theory of Colors*), published in 1810, Goethe had urged, "Therefore for rooms, in which one would regularly find oneself, the color green should be chosen for the wallpapers."[18]

By 1834, Adalbert Stifter was perhaps influenced by Goethe in advocating green and gray walls for his ideal apartment. By this point, the clientele for Biedermeier design had slowly begun to expand beyond the aristocracy. The personal domestic goals of private imperial life had intersected with those of the new moneyed cultural and commercial classes, and the longing for domestic security and familial informality that had spurred Biedermeier innovations in interior arrangements and stylistic expression had radiated to the intellectual, cultural, and middle classes. The resultant overarching Biedermeier domestic aesthetic eventually became accessible to multiple layers of society and applicable to a variety of domestic environments.

For example, in 1837, a young official at the imperial Bavarian embassy in Berlin, Alexander von Fahnenberg, sent his sister an exhaustive description of the living room of his new apartment,[19] for which a remarkably detailed "Zimmerbild" in watercolor exists (plate 84). Fahnenberg praised the functionality of his room for reading, entertaining, and other activities. He detailed its contents, including everything from wall coverings to furniture to the small decorative objects and personal memorabilia, and even discussed the items in the drawers and the names of his neighbors. Such specificity provided his sister with a "photographic" inventory of his space, and evoked for her a mirrored image of himself as a participant in his personal environment. The hallmarks of Biedermeier culture, such as embrace of individualism, practicality, domesticity, and familial informality, were equally functional for a palace suite, the main living area of a bourgeois family, or even for the small rooms of a culti-vated individual such as Fahnenberg.

MARKETING AND DISSEMINATING OF BIEDERMEIER CULTURE

Biedermeier's accessibility broadened through the establishment of "Möbelmagazine," or furniture warehouses.[20] In a development similar to those of British upholsterers and French "marchands-merciers," such premises were established around 1800 in the major design centers to showcase examples of work that could be bought or ordered by clients. Soon, warehouses such as Josef Danhauser in Vienna and A. Bembé in Mainz began to focus on "Fertigmöbel," or ready-made furniture, which could appeal to a larger market. Around 1830, most clients still came from the upper classes, but by the 1840s, many came as well from the bourgeoisie.[21]

The firm Josef Danhauser, "kaiserlich königlich privilegierte Möbel-Fabrik" was granted a permit in 1814 to manufacture all manner of furniture. They soon were creating unified garnitures, or sets, which could be ordered as shown or produced in a choice of woods and with individualized detailing and upholstery. [22] The firm devel-oped standardized norms and types, a practical marketing decision in light of the fact that many interiors were completed over extended periods of time, and clients often returned to purchase supplementary pieces.[23] Often, objects were purchased and installed in interiors as pairs or pendants.

Soon after the establishment of Danhauser's firm, the Congress of Vienna brought a stream of royalty and political figures to the Austrian capital. Duke Ernst II of Saxony-Coburg-Saalfeld (later Ernst I, Duke of Saxony-Coburg and Gotha, and father of Queen Victoria's husband, Prince Albert), stayed in Vienna from September 1814 to May 1915 to attend the congress. While there, he also "made connections with artists and craftsmen," as part of his ongoing effort to redesign and decorate his home, Rosenau Palace in Coburg.[24] Duke Ernst sought interiors in a simplified aes-thetic "of the best quality ... namely beautifully decorated and tastefully worked."[25] In Vienna, he became acquainted with Biedermeier aesthetics. He commissioned some ninety-five pieces, comprising eight suites, from the furniture maker Ferdinand Hasselbrinck, choosing designs distinguished by clean lines and highly polished ebon-ized surfaces. He also ordered numerous individual pieces from Danhauser. Much of the upholstery for the seating furniture was undertaken by Viennese craftsman Georg Tscheppe (plate 99).[26]

Documentation details the path of Ernst's furnishing campaign. He him-self made purchases in Vienna, then ordered through catalogues after his return to Coburg. He remained informed about changing design developments through his brother and sister, who came to live in Vienna. He even retained an artistic advisor to search for pieces, and his political representative in Vienna dealt with contracts and shipping.[27] The level of Ernst's personal involvement in the creation of his individu-alized domestic environments is a strong indication of the importance of personal choice and decision for some of the clientele for Biedermeier design.

Numerous periodicals disseminated taste during the late eighteenth and early nineteenth centuries, including, for example, *Magazin für Freunde des guten Geschmacks* and *Journal des Luxus und der Moden*.[28] With wide distribution, such magazines had a profound impact on the styles and preferences in decorative interiors. Their articles had a broad range and, as was noted aptly in one article in the *Journal des Luxus und der Moden*, "One can easily determine the characteristics of a person, if you see the place where he customarily lives."[29]

The periodicals also communicated traditions outside of Germany, such as those of French Empire and English Sheraton and Hepplewhite. English taste was a particularly strong influence on Biedermeier in Germany, and many of the types of objects that we think of as classically Biedermeier, such as round baluster tables, and preferences such as mahogany for furniture, can be traced back to English precedents. At the same time, the elegance of line and the geometricizing classicism of Biedermeier derived from French antecedents such as Charles Percier and the high style of Empire.[30] There was never a true rejection of non-German sources in this most Germanic of aesthetic moments.

BIEDERMEIER AS CULTURAL MEMORY

The term "Biedermeier" made its first appearance only in 1855, long after the era that it came to denote had already passed into history.[31] The application of the name to the cultural epoch of 1815–40 was retroactively applied to that style of decorative arts and furniture and the lifestyle. For decades, the term Biedermeier was plagued by negative connotations and by "Nachträglichkeit," or belated meaning, that encoded the aesthetic as the scorned legacy of the small-minded bourgeoisie – a culture of "forget-me-not" trinkets and thrifty grandparents, associated with evocatively condescending phrases such as:

A Sense of Security. Peace. Roasted Apples in the Oven …. Modesty. The Writing Desk. The Cherry Commode. Brooms …. Impeccably Clean Floors … Happy Children at Play, the Industrious Housewife, the Good Father … the Loving Grandparents … Knitting and Breadbaking.[32]

Around 1900, this "tea-cosy view of an era" was called into question.[33] Reformist artists, writers, and philosophers of the late 1800s sought to define a new modern style for Austria and Germany that would be antihistoricist and more appropriate to the national characters. In their view, the Historicism of the post-Biedermeier world had led to a riotous and discordant jumble of sources and aesthetic expressions, and relied on inauthentic materials to produce imitative and deceptive objects. Through the generational lenses of those rejecting the historicist era, the goal emerged to reconnect with the creative roots of earlier Germanic progressive design, and to situate a new aesthetic in relation to a specific meaningful framework of prior national tendencies. In a 1905–1906 article, Joseph August Lux, an influential Viennese writer, asked, "What do we know of our country's own artistic and cultural past?"[34]

The response was a widespread reappraisal of standard assumptions about Biedermeier, seeing it not as a negative historical occurrence but as the last cultural moment in which pure and honest design had been valued. Lux stated, "If we want to achieve a new style, we must annex ourselves to the last historical style which was suitable. And that was the style before 1830, a German style."[35]

Critics of "Biederkeit," "Biederschönen," "Biedermeier," and "Biedermänner" began to reconsider their grandparents' taste in domestic interiors. They reassessed the abstracted lines and classicized geometry of Biedermeier forms, the natural decoration based on the material patterns of the veneers, and the functionality of object design. The expressive formal and ideological language of Biedermeier, with its reliance on indigenous materials and craftsmanship, on an aesthetic of economy and conscious simplicity, and its grounding in Germanic lifestyles, was reclaimed as a valuable inheritance. By 1904, the German modernist reform architect Hermann Muthesius argued:

If here a sense of conviction is set in place, to only choose the simplest and the noblest, to avoid snobbery and to turn away completely from every appearance of deception, we would have already won greatly. We would have an unpretentious household furnishing of elevated manner and true distinction, and indeed from true distinction, not the pseudo-aristocratic type of today. A furnishing of such unaffectedness and love of truth, as was had by our grandfathers and great-grandfathers.[36]

The same traits and aesthetics that had been scorned in the pages of the *Fliegende Blätter* had become transformed through a mirror of retrograde cohesiveness to become the positive virtues of the Germanic aesthetic past. They became a critical link between early nineteenth-century modernism and early twentieth-century modernism.

NOTES

Author's Note: All translations from the German are by the author.

1   Quoted in Berlin 1970, p. 20.

2   Quoted in Munich 1991, p. 29.

3   Goethe 1984 (1805-10); Kant 1790.

4   Godsey 2003, pp. 375-77; London 1979, pp. 18-19.

5   Munich 1988; Berlin 1970; Boehmer 1968, n. p.

6   Munich 1987; Godsey 2003.

7   Munich 1991; Munich 1987.

8   Eichenzell 2004, pp. 9-16.

9   Jonathan Dewald, *The European Nobility, 1400-1800* (Cambridge, 1996), n.p., quoted in Godsey 2003, p. 377.

10   Ottomeyer discusses this in a number of articles and books, with one of the best being Simpson and Ottomeyer 1994, p. 79. For an excellent discussion in English, see Wilk in New York 2003, pp. 363-67.

11   Ottomeyer 1979.

12   Eichenzell 2004.

13   Waissenberger 1986, p. 110.

14   W. C. W. Blumenbach, *Wiener Kunst- und Gewerbsfreund* (Vienna, 1825), vol. 1, p. 2, quoted in Munich 1991, p. 28.

15   London 1979, p. 23.

16   Munich 1991, p. 29.

17   Simson and Ottomeyer 1994, pp. 78, 83.

18   Goethe 1984 (1805-10), p. 284.

19   Nuremberg 1995, p. 11.

20   Hamburg 2002; Ottomeyer 1994, pp. 77-85; Munich 1991.

21   Heidrun Zinnkann of Frankfurt has done excellent research on the late arrival of commissions for Biedermeier interiors by the middle classes at the major Mainz factories of Knussmann, Bembe, and Kimbel. See Zinnkann 1985.

22   Witt-Dörring 1987, pp. 54-67.

23   Concerning the example of continued purchases by the Coburg dukes, see Seelig 1981, pp. 2-10.

24   Heym 1990, p. 24.

25   Ibid, p. 15.

26   For detailed descriptions of the commissions, see Seelig 1981 and ibid., p. 24.

27   See Seelig 1981.

28   Huey in New York 2003, p. 52.

29   Quoted in Nuremberg 1995, p. 23.

30   Munich 1991; Simson and Ottomeyer 1994.

31   Ottomeyer and Schlapka 2000, pp. 12-14.

32   Boehmer 1968, p. 7.

33   Huey in New York 2003, p. 100.

34   Joseph August Lux, "Wien und die kuenstlerischen Gemeinde-Aufgaben," *Hohe Warte* 1, 2 (1905-1906), quoted in ibid., p. 100.

35   Simpson and Ottomeyer 1994, pp. 86-87.

36   Hermann Muthesius, in *Kunstwart* 17, 23 (1904), p. 473, quoted in Munich 1991, p. 39. For an analysis of Muthesius's search for modern sources in British precedents, see also Stein 2002.

PLATES

CABINET FURNITURE AND TABLES

SECTION I

Christian Witt-Dörring and Hans Ottomeyer

CABINET FURNITURE AND TABLES

Christian Witt-Dörring

In the Biedermeier period, new types of cabinet furniture and tables that reflected changing tastes in home furnishings began to appear alongside established forms. The most intricately designed furniture item was the writing cabinet, which served both functional and representational purposes. Like a conversation piece, it was frequently used by its owner as an object of impressive display. Journeyman cabinetmakers chose the writing cabinet for their master projects to mark the beginning of their careers. Master craftsmen exhibited their versions in public and demonstrated hidden functions to paying viewers. Furnished with an unprecedented number of sophisticated secret drawers, which satisfied the need for security as well as a certain playful urge, the writing cabinet exemplified the new desire for privacy. The contrast between inner and outer life could scarcely be more striking: its outward appearance is calm, self-enclosed, and indicative of public uprightness, while its interior embodies the intimacy of emotional diversity.

A completely new type of living-room furniture – the showcase – offers a glimpse into the personal sphere of homes during the period. Objects that had been mute were now allowed into society, providing new channels for human communication. Formerly utilitarian items now became used as focal points of everyday life. Once mere tools used to perform daily chores, suddenly they were everywhere; people surrounded themselves with them, like old friends. Coffee and tea cups, books, plates, portraits, souvenirs, and miniature sculptures gained visual prominence, exhibited on or in specially designed open shelves and enclosed glass showcases in the living room. The mode of presentation catered to two basic needs: personal feelings and personal comfort. To the extent that a utilitarian object had become the public signifier of individual spheres of emotions, it was used preferably without the help of a servant. No longer accessible through the mediation of others, it was permanently at hand and guaranteed and signaled the newly acquired privacy.

Tea and coffee tables were in widespread use in Northern Germany during the first half of the eighteenth century but did not become a standard furnishing item in Central Europe until the early nineteenth century. Usually round in shape, they were no longer surrounded by seats in hierarchical arrangement. The table, however, was always part of a seating group and occupied a fixed position in the room, thus no longer exhibiting the lightness and flexibility of the eighteenth century. In contrast, the work table, as the setting for women's activities, retained its flexibility and became an important part of the diversity of furniture design. It appears in its most artistic form as the globe table.

FURNITURE VENEERS

Hans Ottomeyer

In Biedermeier furniture, the most essential and characteristic element, the veneered surface, dominated all other aspects of design, such as shape, construction, and ornamentation. Its sheen, color, and structure were viewed as autonomous qualities in their own right. As much as possible, cabinetmakers dispensed with ornaments that would disturb the beauty of the large, patterned wood surfaces, eliminating decorative appliqués, handle and lock hardware, carvings, and even inlays. The surface art of veneer, which reveals the unique character of the wood like a microscopic section, defined the structure of a piece of furniture and determined its quality. Cabinetmakers created only surfaces that could be suitably covered with veneer, which was available only in certain sizes and thicknesses. In later years, when machine-cut and eventually even thinner shaved veneers became available, standard methods were developed for drawing the fine layer of wood over the blank wood core, which could then exhibit more pronounced rounded and bulging forms. Developed deliberately and systematically, these new techniques opened the way for the striking swollen, curved pieces that emerged after 1830. In most cases, the blank wood structure comprised a complex system of boards cut for frames and fillings and braced against one another – a stable, expansion-resistant substructure that prevented the veneer from shifting.

The shape of Biedermeier furniture was not developed from its internal structure. Instead, the veneered surface, with its own unique qualities, intervened as a medium between inner construction and outward appearance. The veneered surface is analogous to a precious, colorful dress with an appealing material structure that is drawn over the body, concealing more than it reveals. Truth to material was reflected instead in the surface appearance of the fine woods, which revealed their hidden qualities only when cut, sanded, and polished. Light showed the color and structure of the wood fibers as grain pattern, which was admired for its unique natural character.

The care used in working with veneer also indicates the importance attached to these grained surfaces. The finest Biedermeier furniture exhibits a wide range of methods. In most cases, the wood sheets were positioned to cover the piece in a vertical pattern and form mirror images along the central axis, creating what looks like a symmetrical fold. Depending on the configuration of the colors and fiber structures of the grain of each tree trunk chosen, cabinetmakers created very distinctive and characteristic patterns. Homogeneous surfaces were achieved with fine-grained wood, such as slow-growing cherry, intricately structured pear (also in black-stained versions), or – for those who could afford it – mahogany. Expressive, symmetrical "pyramids" or "fountains" stand out against the grain like sculptures – the result of using long-fibered wood with marked striping or undulating grain patterns, such as mahogany, cherry, ash, and, later, walnut. Where irregular, rounded knots were incorporated, dark "figures" form on the surface, the result of the light-and-dark contrast. These fantastical forms rendered in folded symmetry, with knots often appearing as eyes, were designed intentionally.

In the 1820s and 1830s, walnut was often enhanced with black stain to achieve a particularly interesting and expressive pattern. Another popular look was obtained with prominently structured veneers that exhibited either shimmering waves and spots of light, as in the case of birch, maple, or ash, or the intricate flame pattern of grained root wood. The use of this extremely hard wood from the root, which was very difficult to saw into sheets of veneer, took on the character of a cult. Whereas in the eighteenth century only small pieces and strips could be used for inlays, now the new water- and steam-powered mechanical circular and band saws facilitated larger sections of veneer from this tough wood. When the highly prized roots became scarce, trees were "crippled" for the purpose of obtaining the coveted raw material. The most elaborate furniture was often made entirely of root wood.

Cabinetmakers sought to give native woods the luster and intense grain structure of exotic varieties by letting oil penetrate deep into the surface. Shellac polishes, used increasingly from the early nineteenth century onward, created a light browning effect. Because the colors and oil have faded and evaporated over time, it is likely that many pieces of furniture that today appear light in color were once much darker. Dark, polished walnut holds the mahogany tone the longest and often bears a deceptively close resemblance to actual mahogany.

Local substitutions also were a solution for the extremely expensive fire-gilt fittings imported from Paris, which ordinarily cost more than the furniture itself. Nevertheless, a cabinetmaker's specially made gilt-bronze piece was often only slightly cheaper than the imported article, which explains why ungilt cast-bronze and later oil-gilt, cast-tin items became options. A frequent alternative involved gilt or patina-coated carved wood or hardened papier-mâché; mechanically pressed fittings made of ultra-thin brass or hand-molded items were another choice. The most common solution, however, was to eliminate hardware entirely, leaving the surface undisturbed. Drawers and doors often could be opened only by pulling the inserted key or the lower edge of the drawer. However, this intended look was often later altered by affixing handles, knobs, and lock plates with nails or screws in order to create the impression of a more practical, elaborate item of furniture.

The gradual trend toward anonymity in the production and sale of furniture had an even greater impact on traditional structures in the manual trades than these technical advances. Most Biedermeier furniture was prefabricated and sold either by cabinetmakers themselves or, more rarely, by privileged merchants and the new furniture stores, which also distributed catalogues. This mode of producing for inventory and the new sales channels resulted in a trend toward standardization in external form. This is not furniture that reflects the wishes or peculiarities of a client. Given the prevailing aesthetic sensibilities and social conventions, which demanded uniform furnishings, it became necessary to establish standards of quality in order to enable customers to purchase pieces or groups that could be placed alongside furniture they already owned without producing a clash of styles. Producers had to confine themselves to basic patterns and a limited range of woods. The result was a uniformity of appearance that amounted to classicism beyond the reach of stylistic developments. The accepted standardized forms and the "canonized" woods – cherry, walnut, and mahogany – remained unchanged for many years.

1
Writing Cabinet
Vienna, ca. 1810
Cat. 1-3

2
Writing Cabinet
Vienna, 1810/15
Cat. 1-2

1

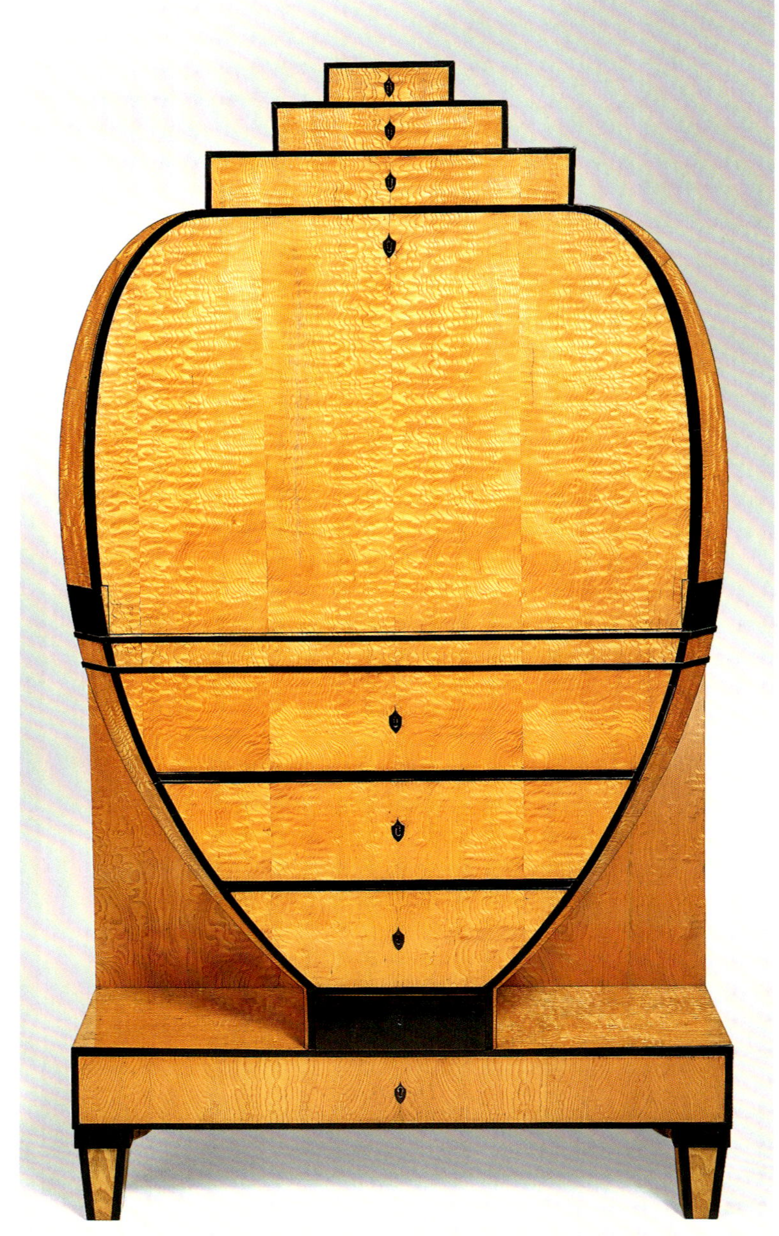

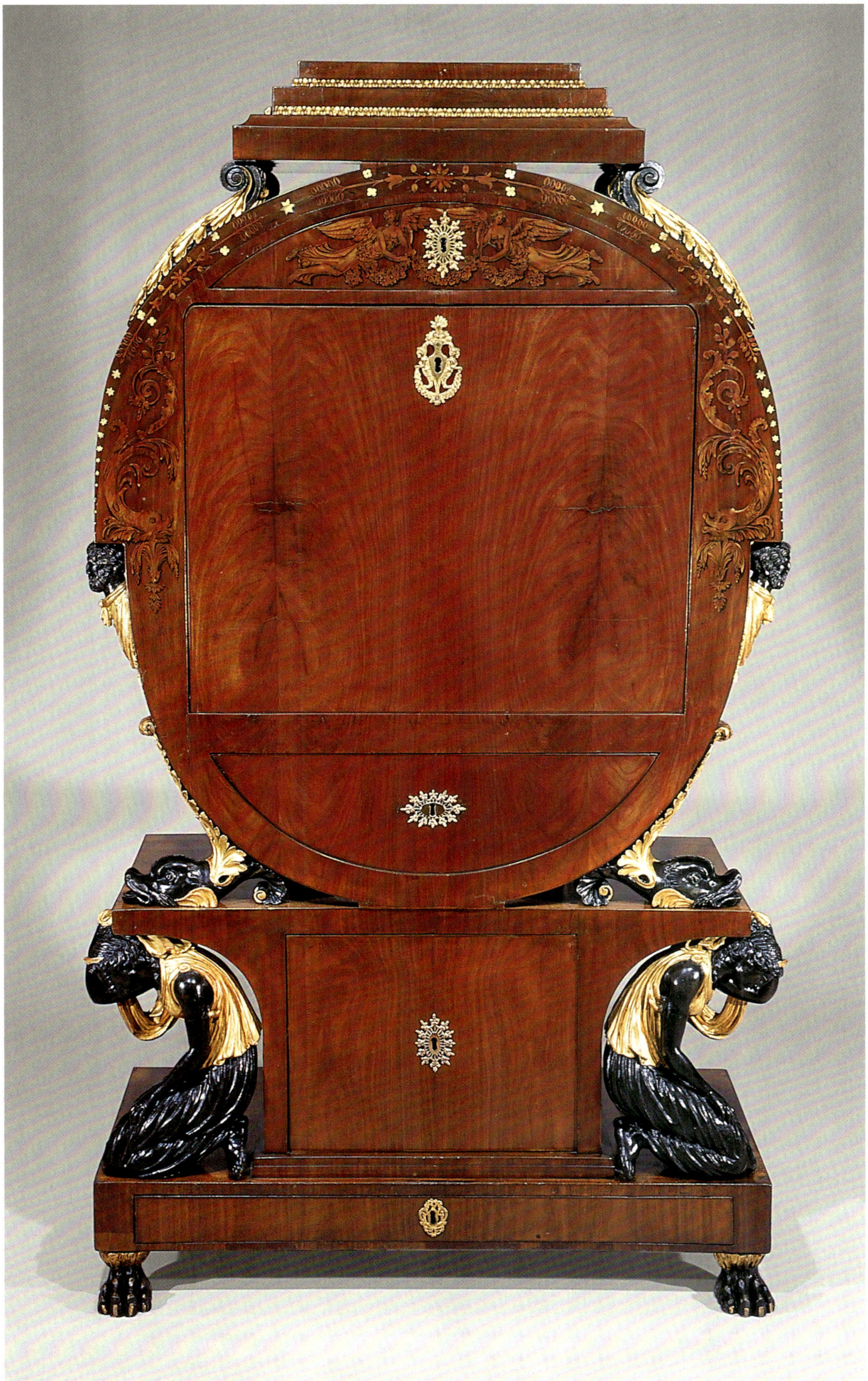

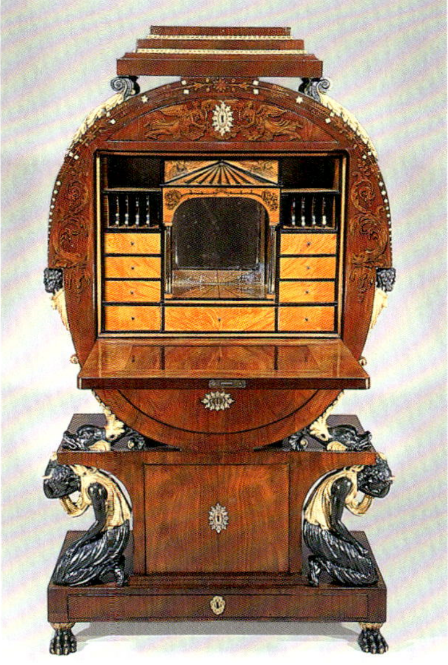

3

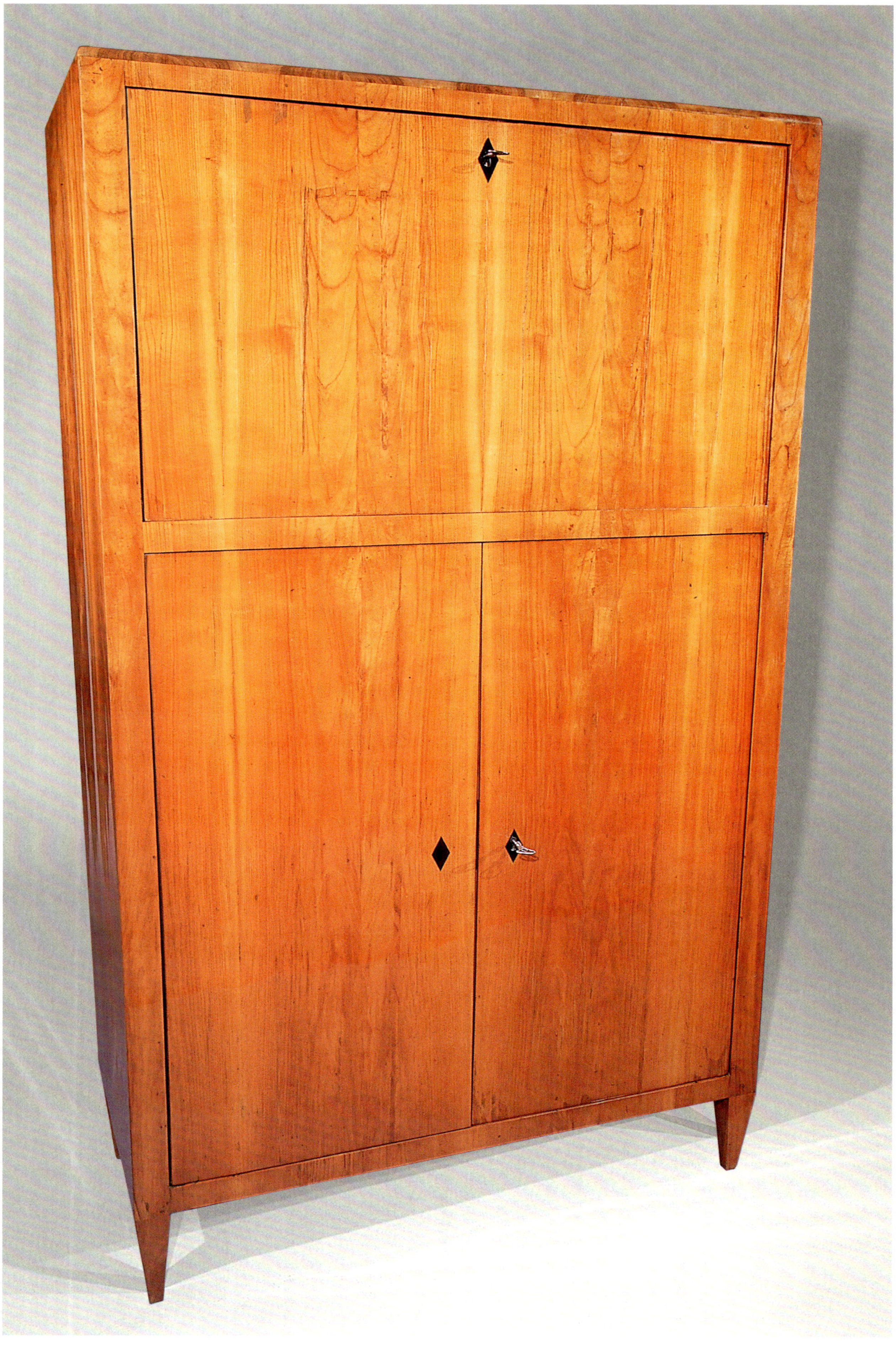

3
Writing Cabinet
Munich, ca. 1810
Cat. 1-1

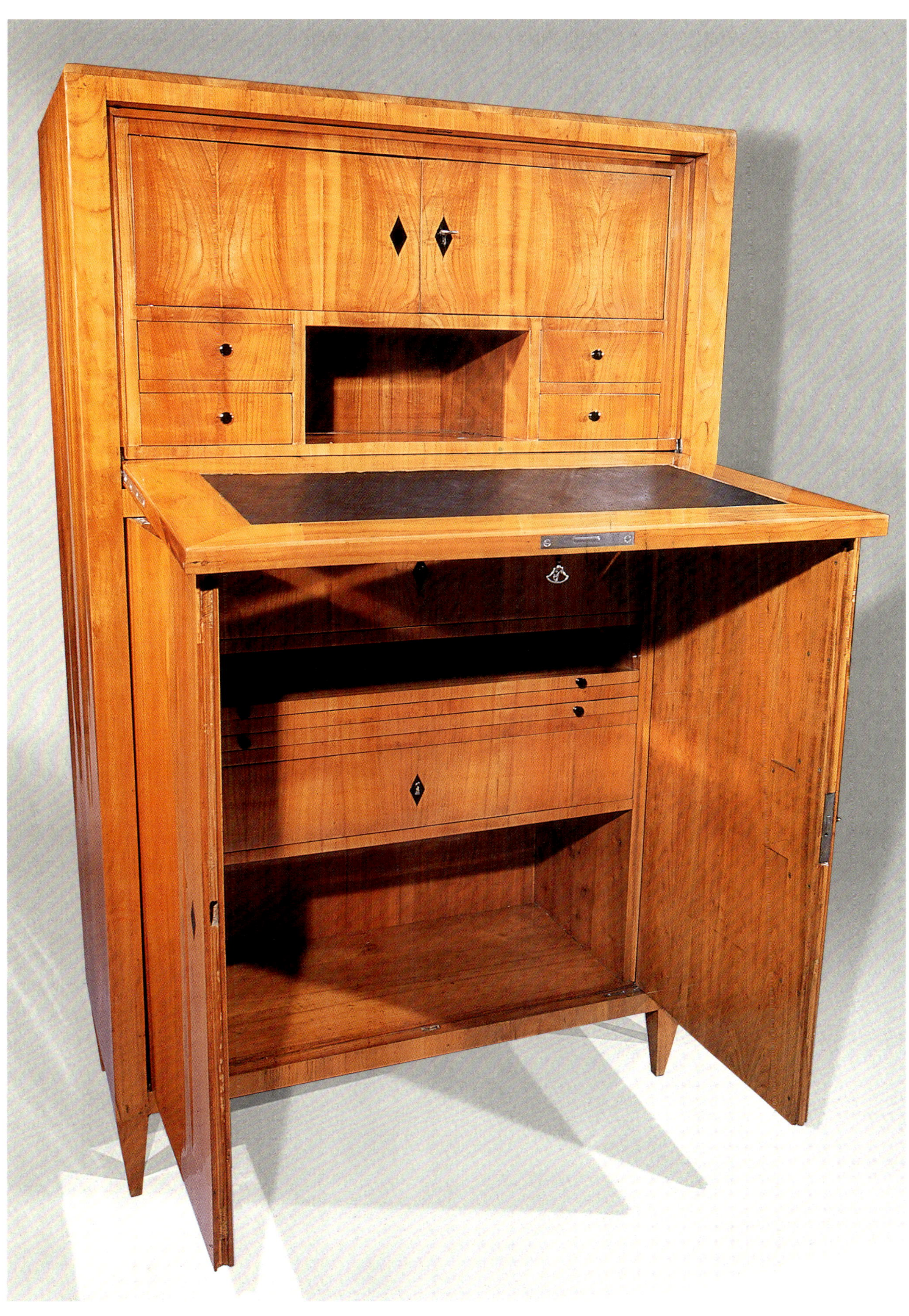

4
Chiffonier
Munich, ca. 1810
Cat. 1-6

5
(Opposite)
Cabinet with Drawers
Vienna, 1815/20
Cat. 1-8

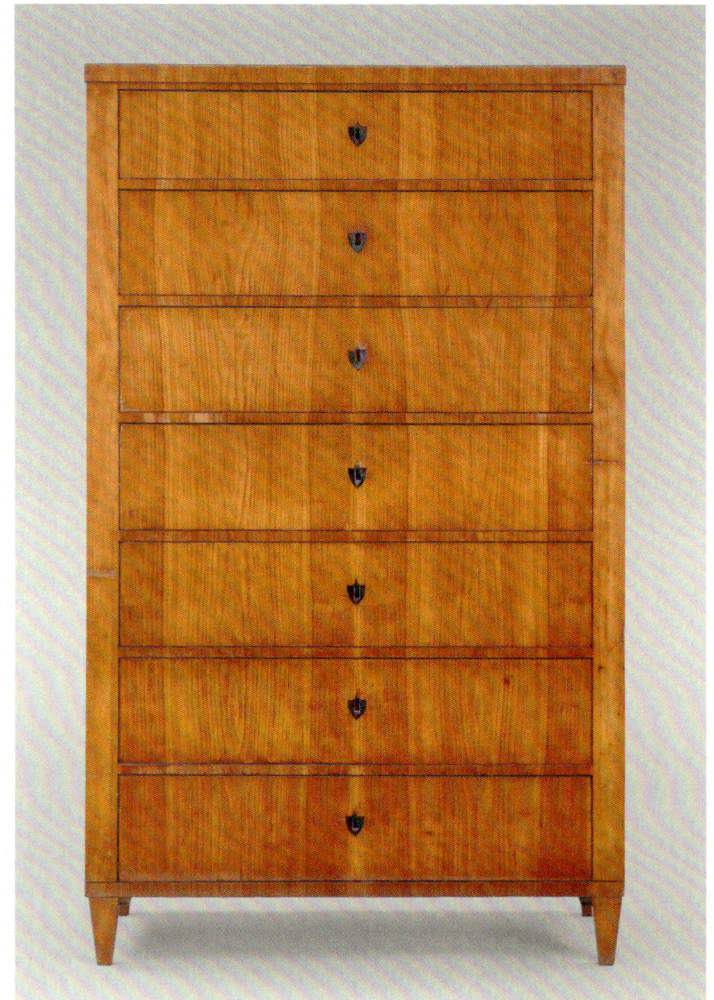
4

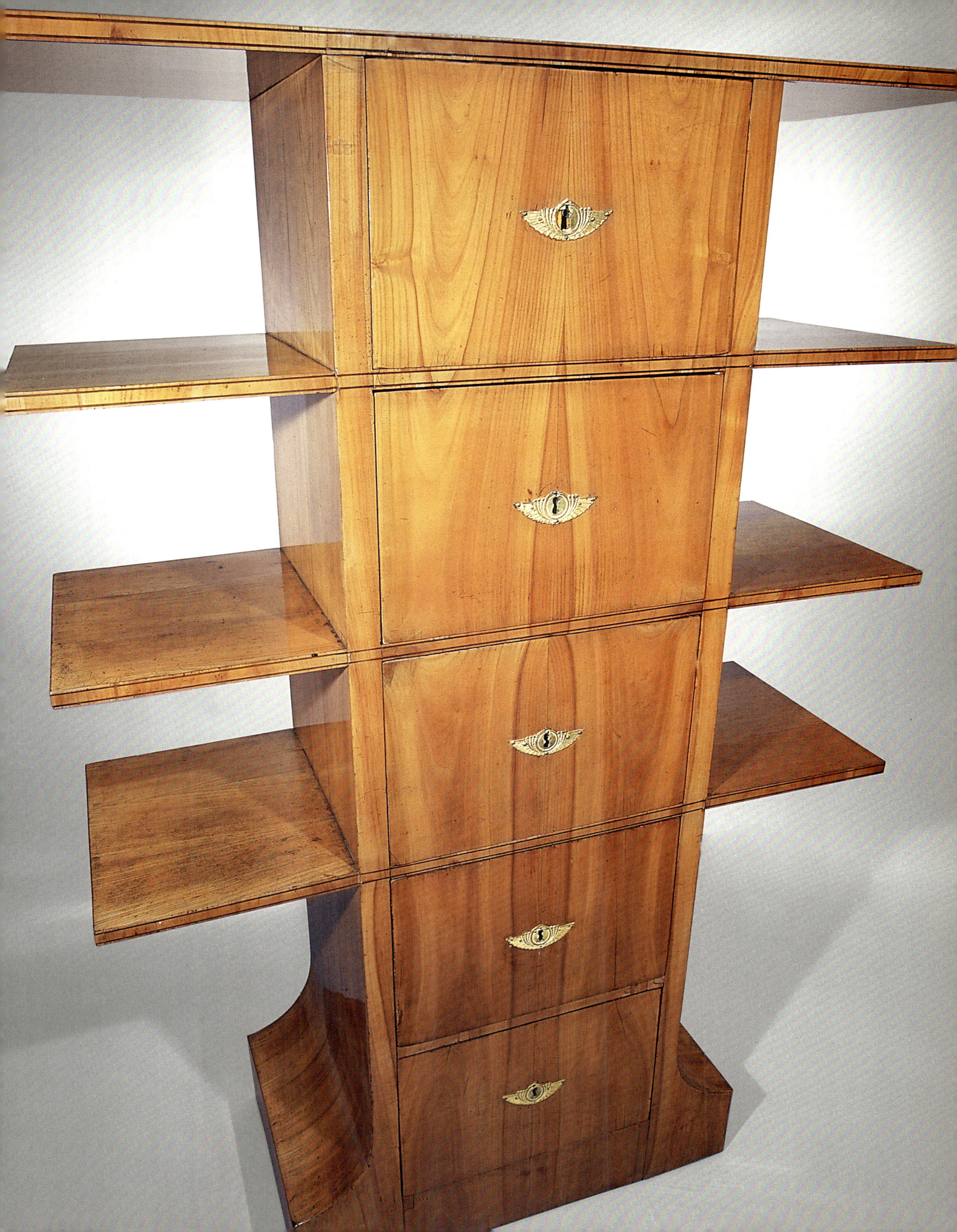

6

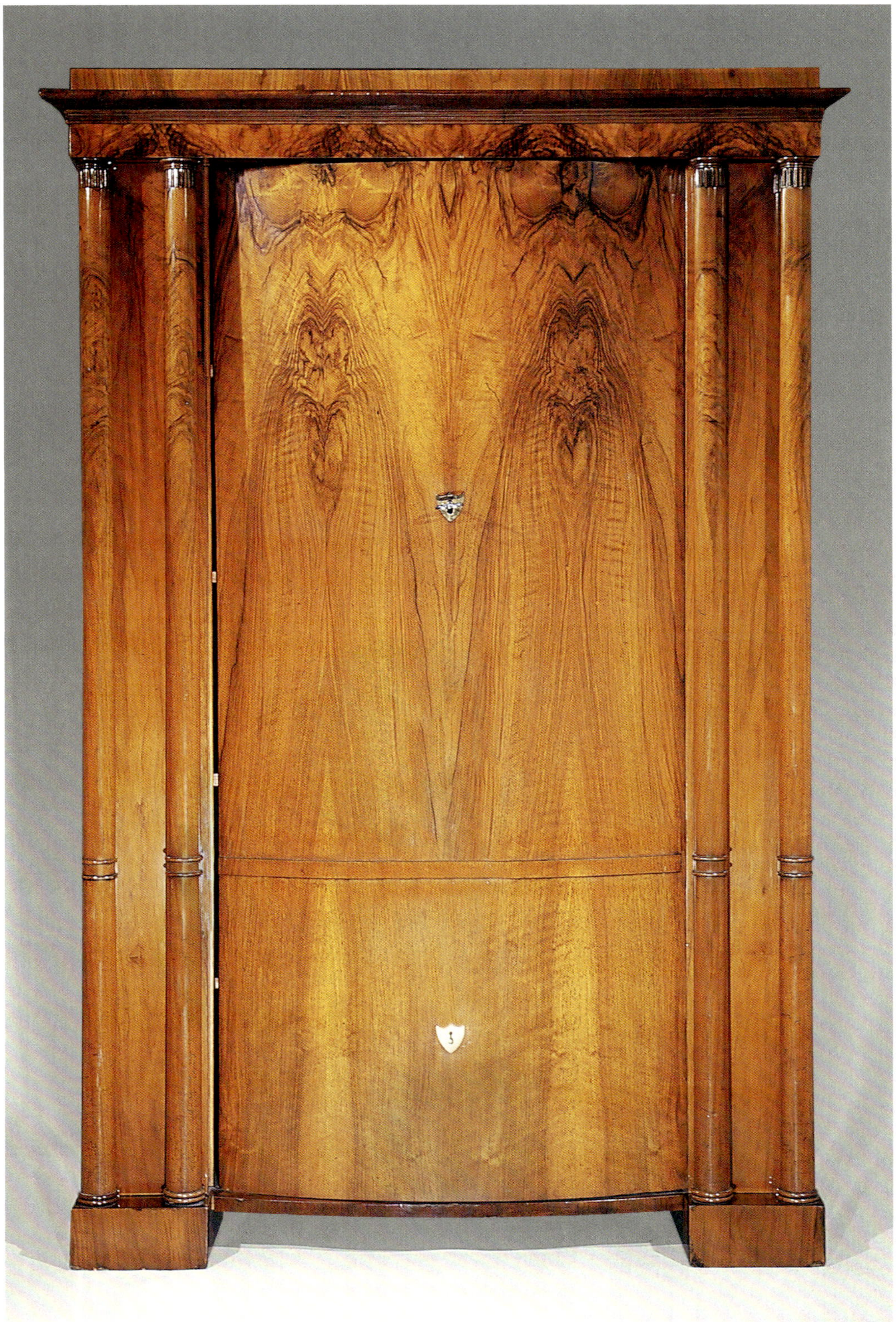

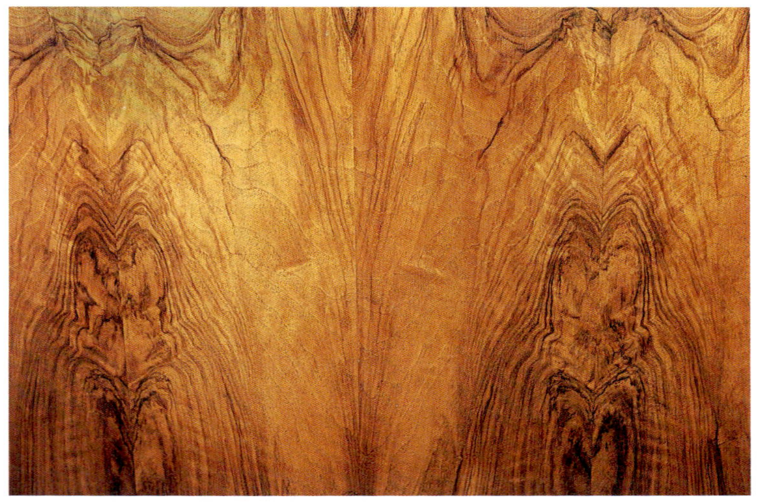

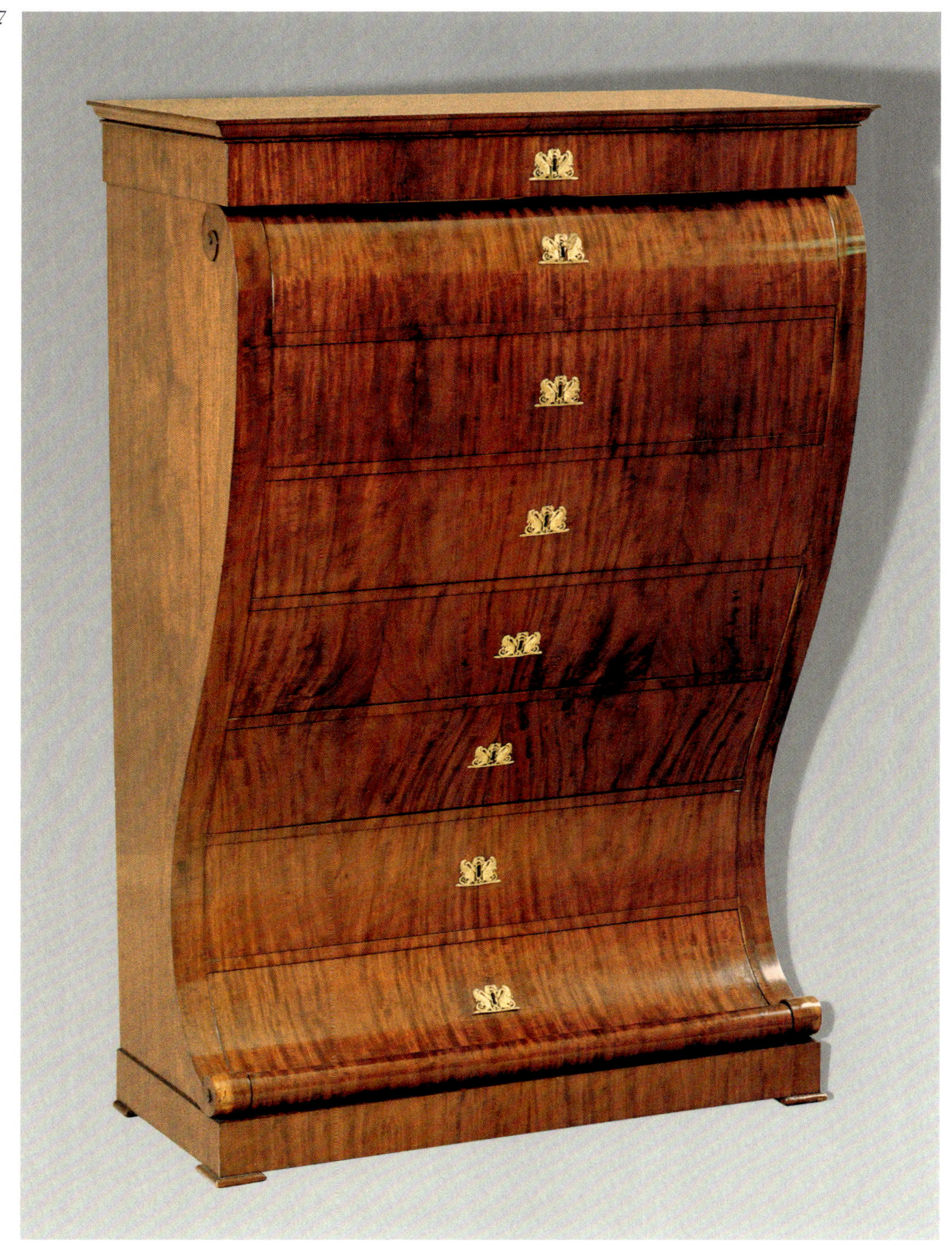

7

6
Pair of Cabinets
Vienna, 1825/30
Cat. 1-4 (detail)

7
Chiffonier
Vienna, ca. 1820
Cat. 1-7

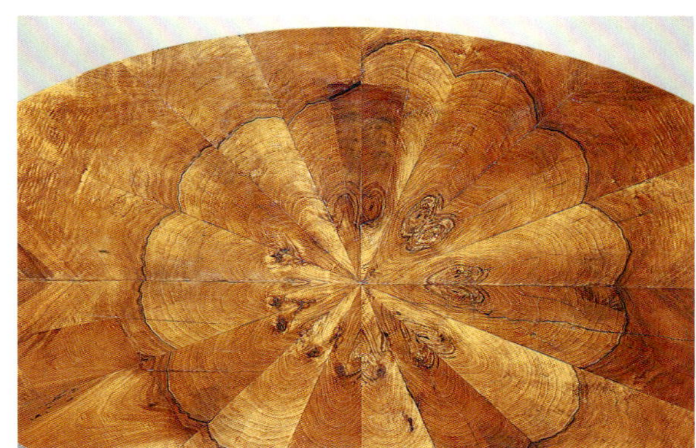

8

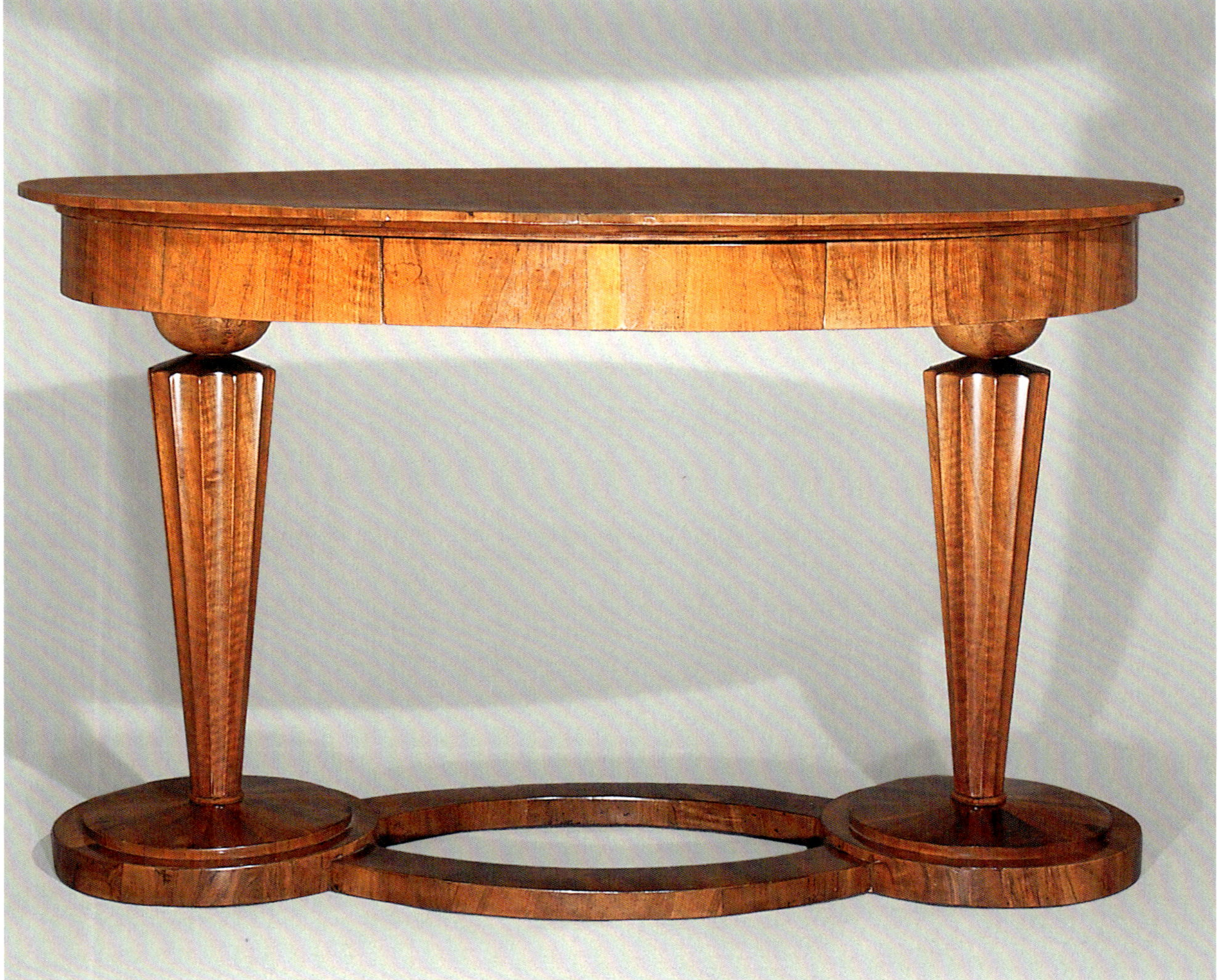

8
Writing Desk
Vienna, 1820/30
Cat. 1-9

9
Column Desk
Vienna, ca. 1825
Cat. 1-10

9

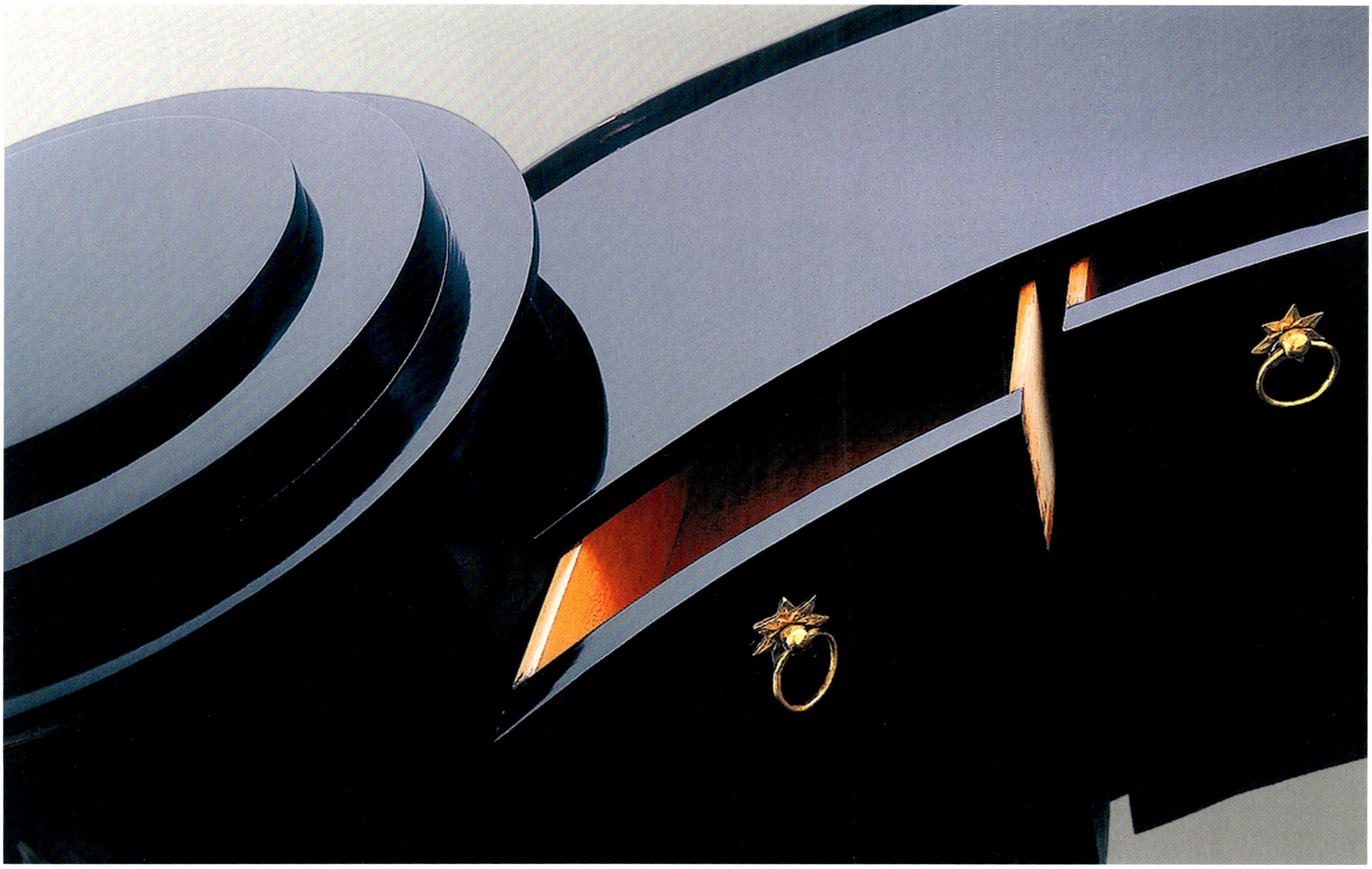

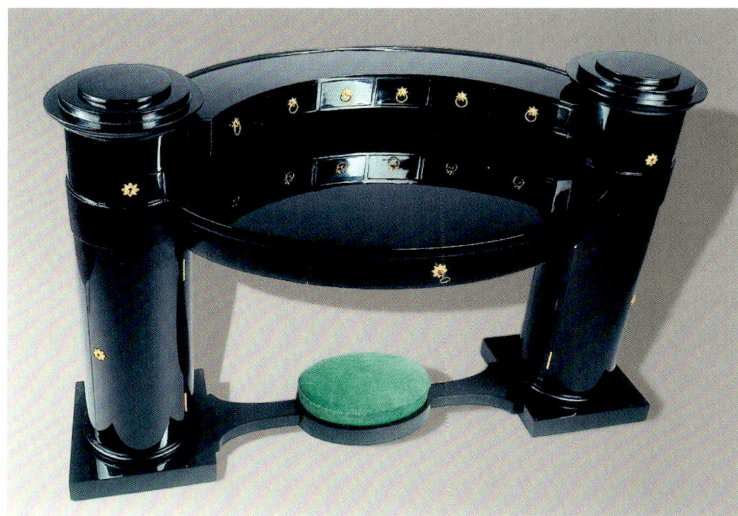

10
Patent Writing Cabinet
Vienna, ca. 1820
Cat. I-11

11
Standing Desk
Vienna, 1825/30
Cat. I-12

10

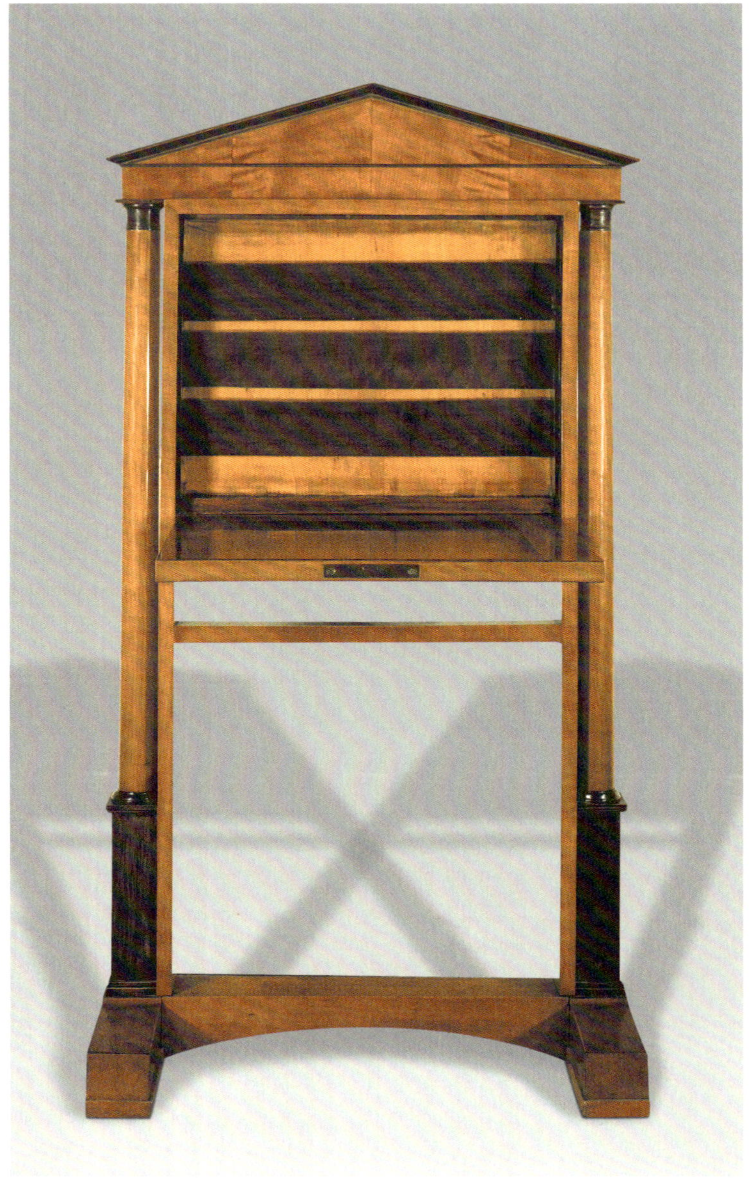

11

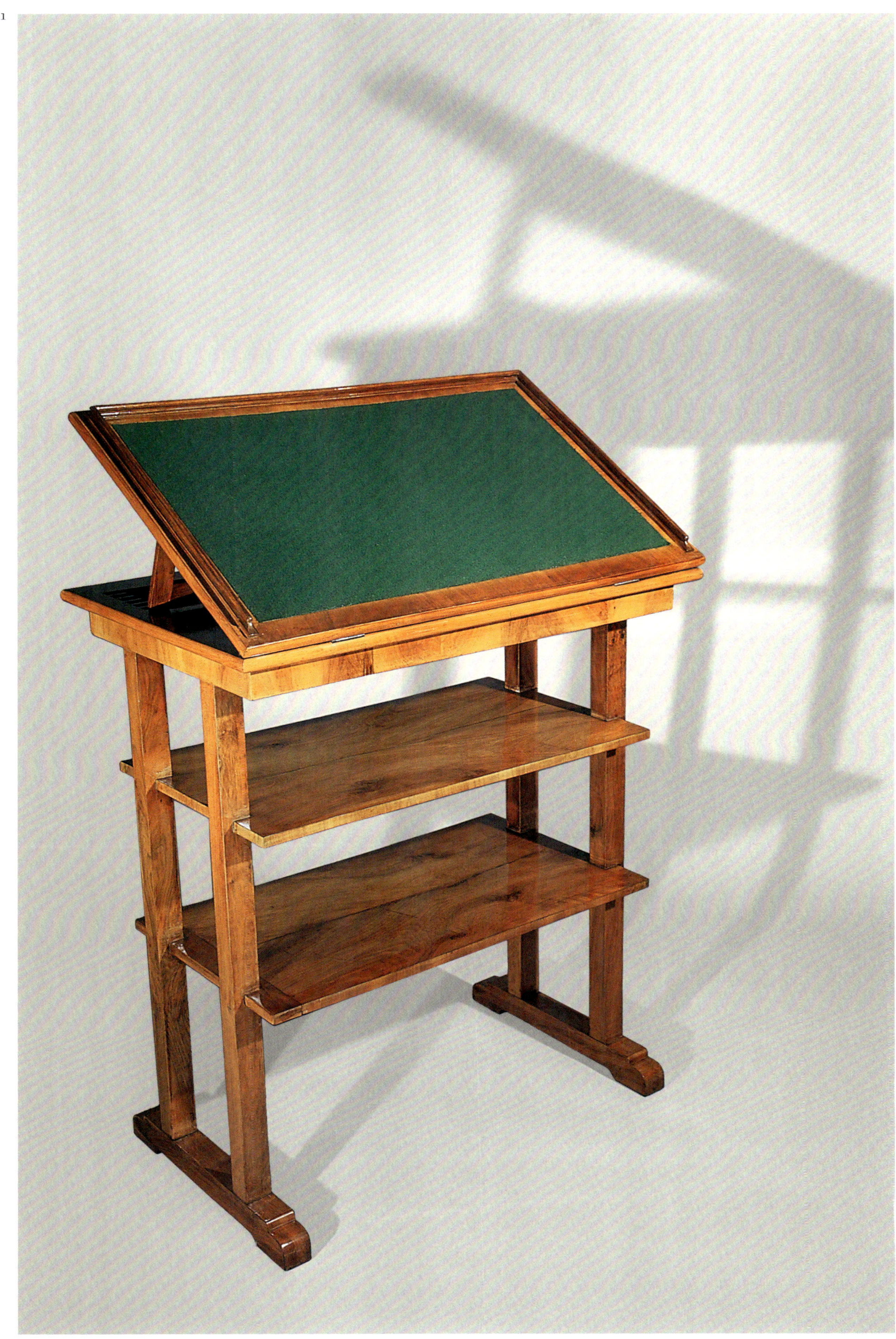

12
Table
Vienna, ca. 1825
Cat. I-13

13
Table
Vienna, 1826
Cat. I-14

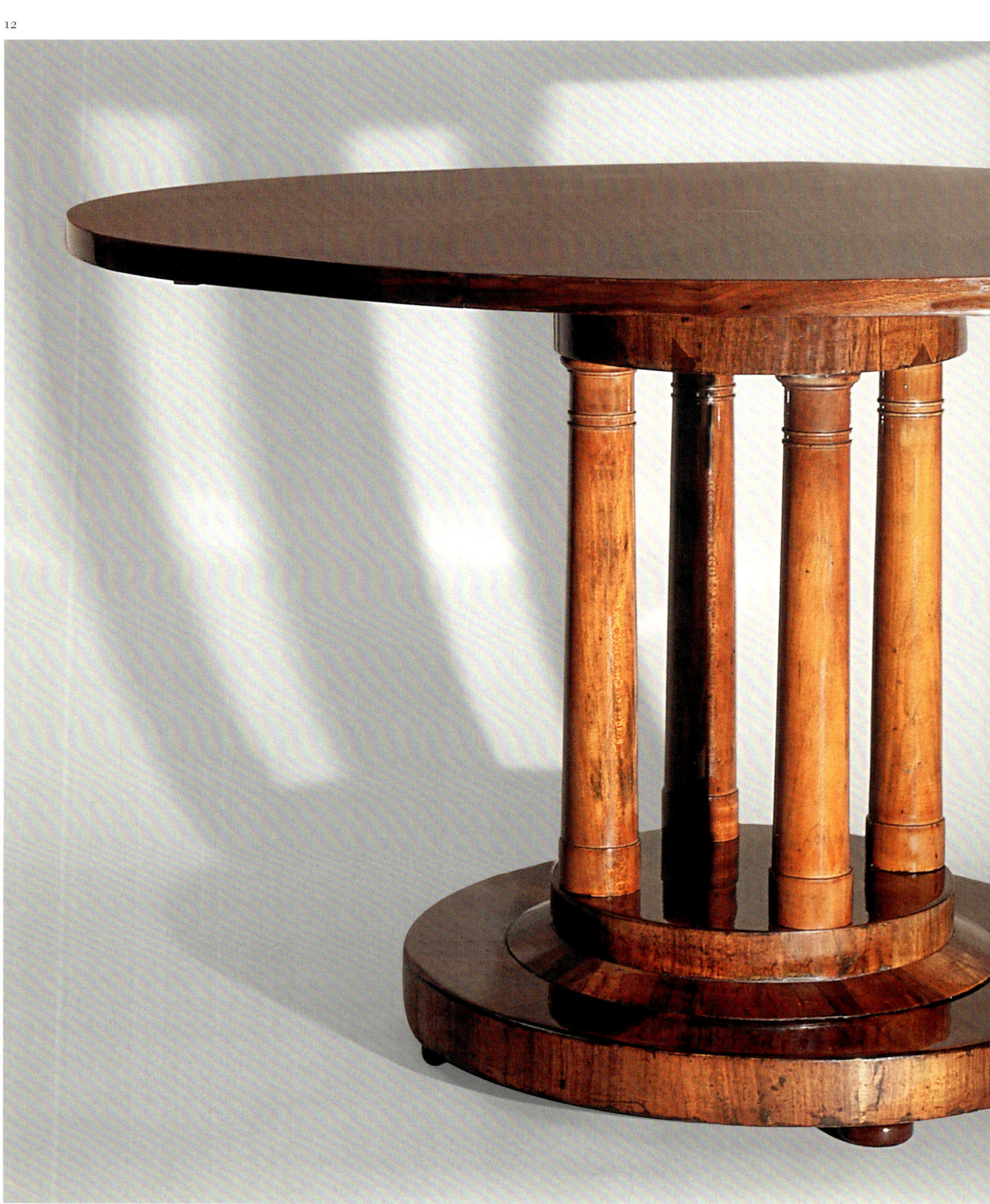

12

13

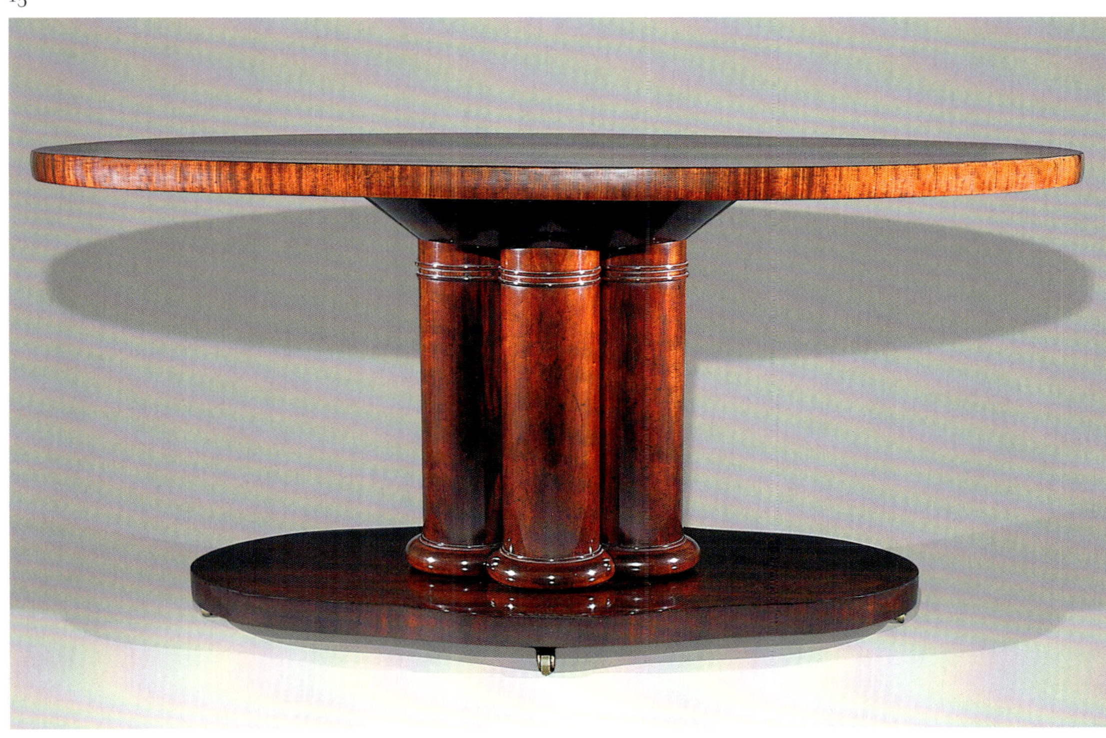

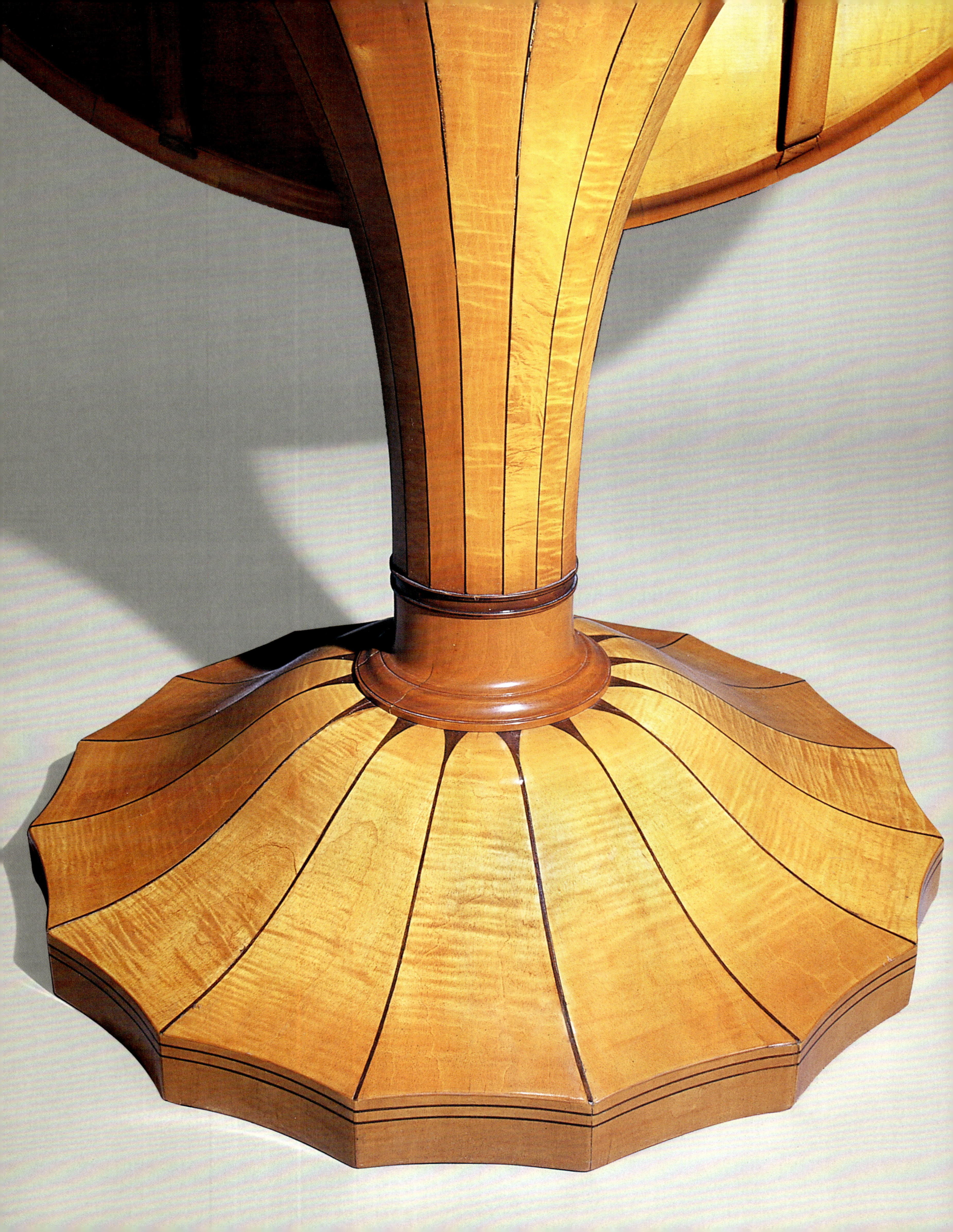

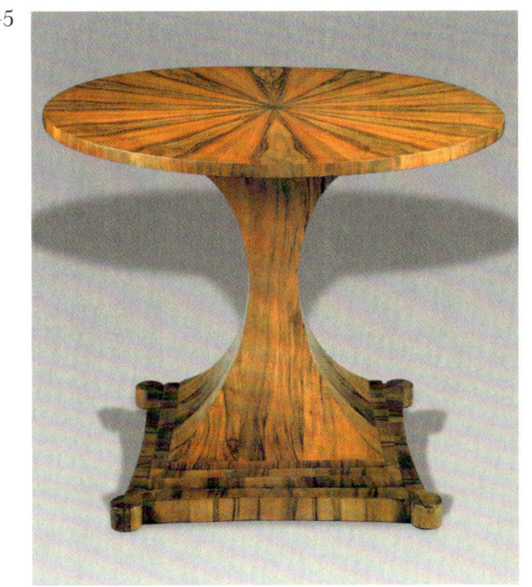

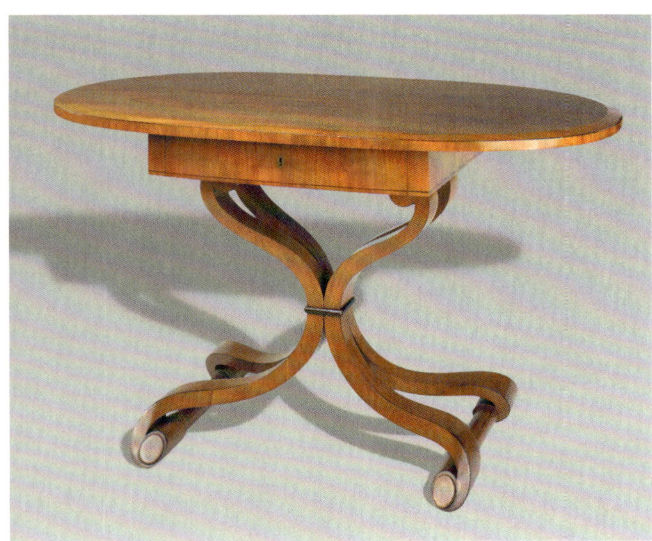

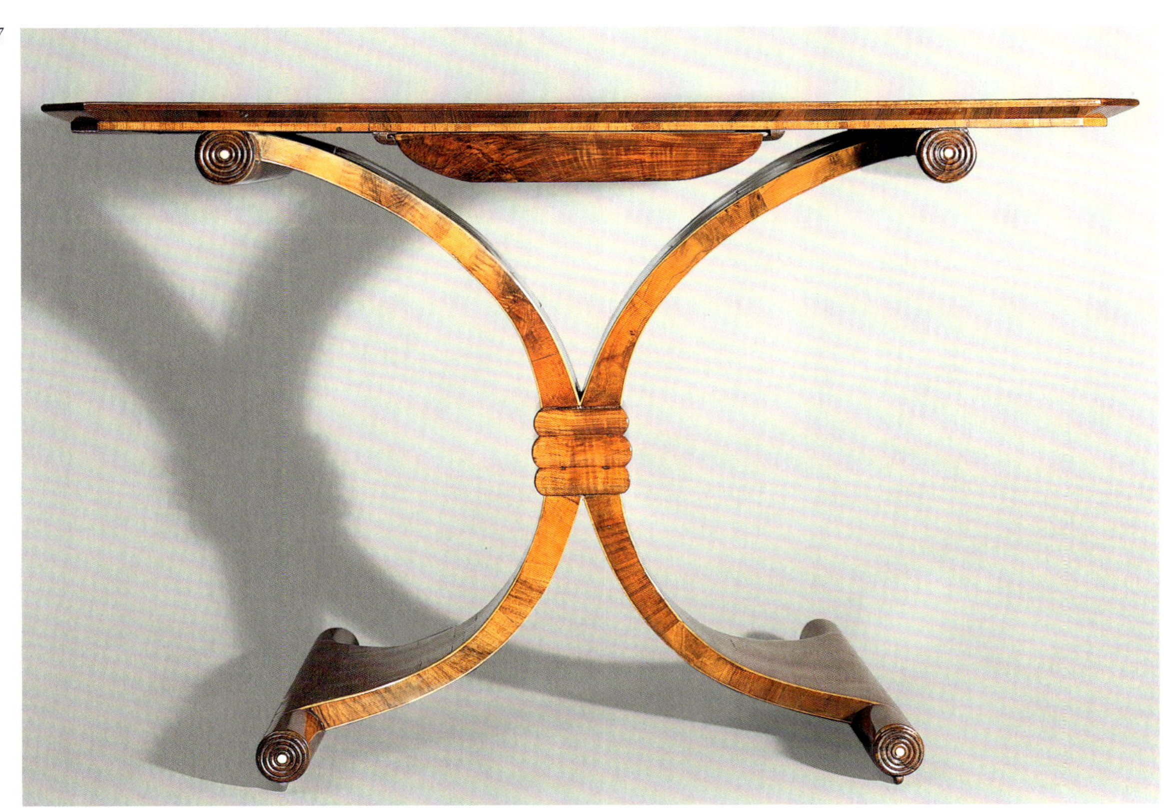

14
(Opposite)
Tea Table
Vienna, ca. 1825
Cat. I-16 (detail)

15
Center Table
Austria, 1825/30
Cat. I-17

16
Tea Table
Vienna, ca. 1825/30
Cat. I-19

17
Table
Vienna, ca. 1820
Cat. I-18

18
Pair of Night Stands
(Column Cabinets)
Vienna, ca. 1820
Cat. I-21

19
Dumb Waiter
Vienna, 1815/20
Cat. I-22

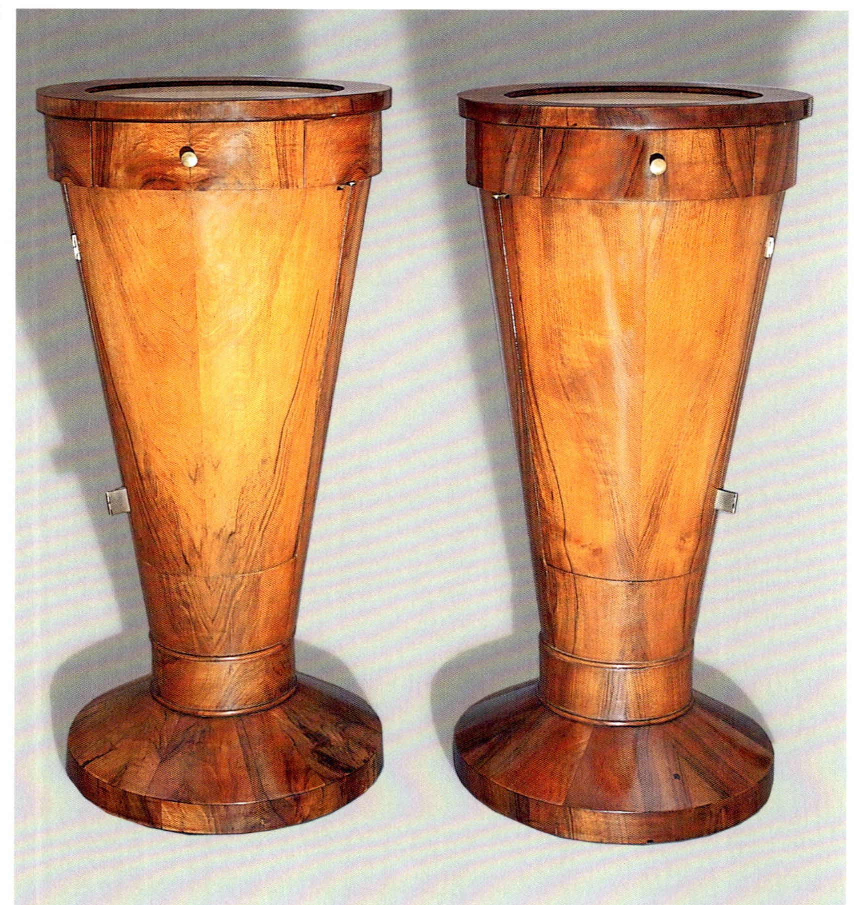

18

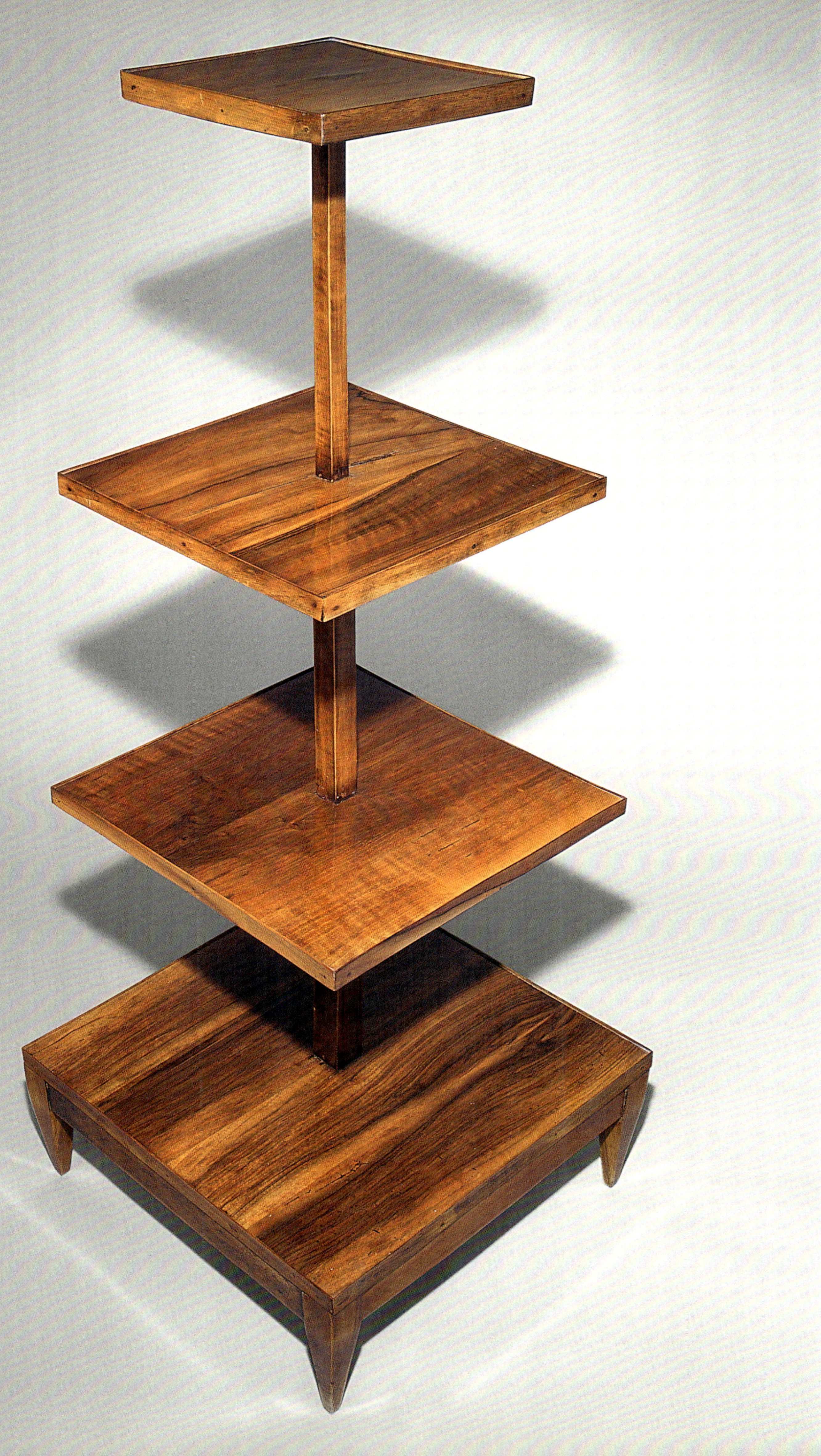

20
Etagère (Music Stand)
Vienna, ca. 1820
Cat. I-23

21
Pair of Dumb Waiters
Vienna, ca. 1822/23
Cat. I-24

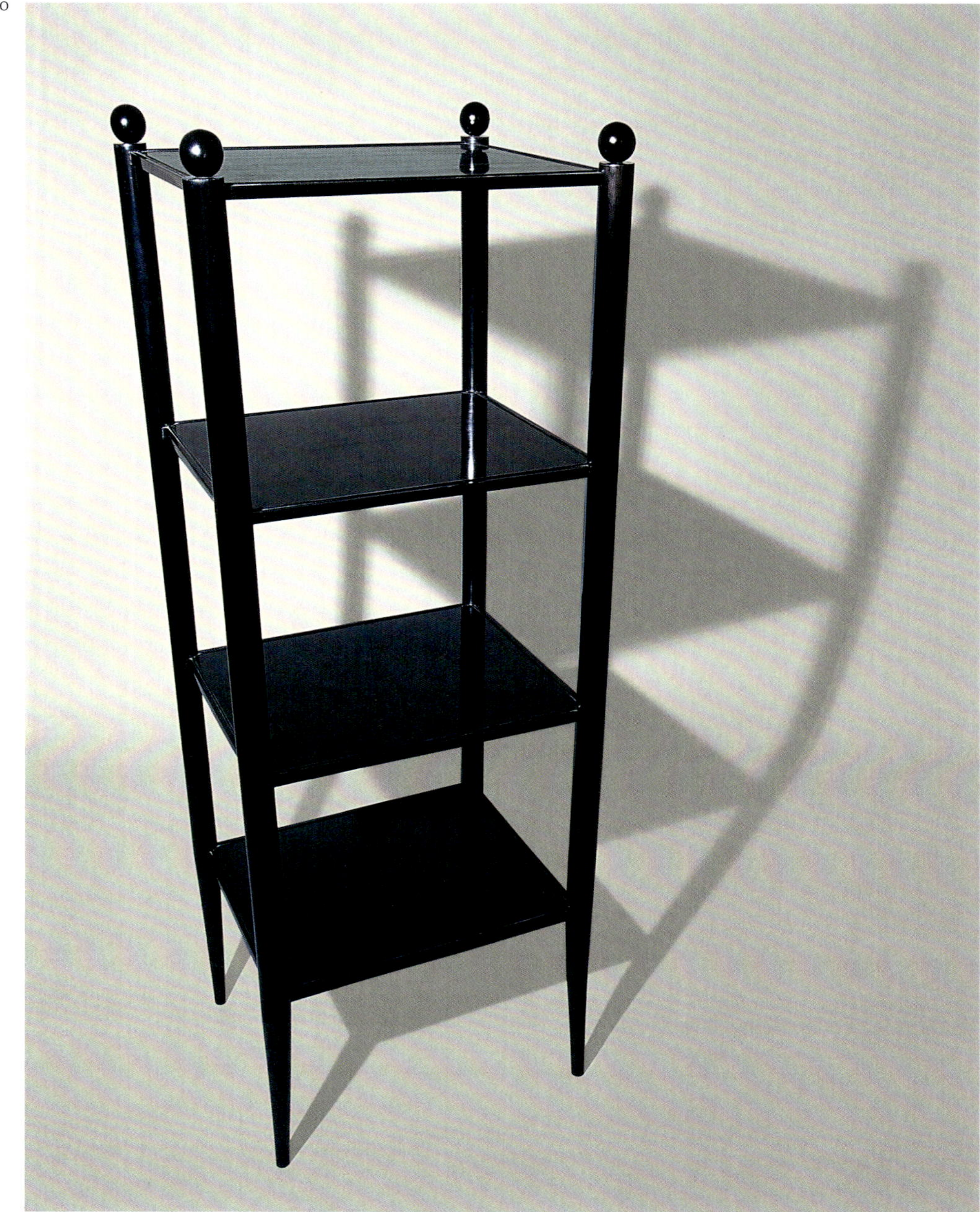

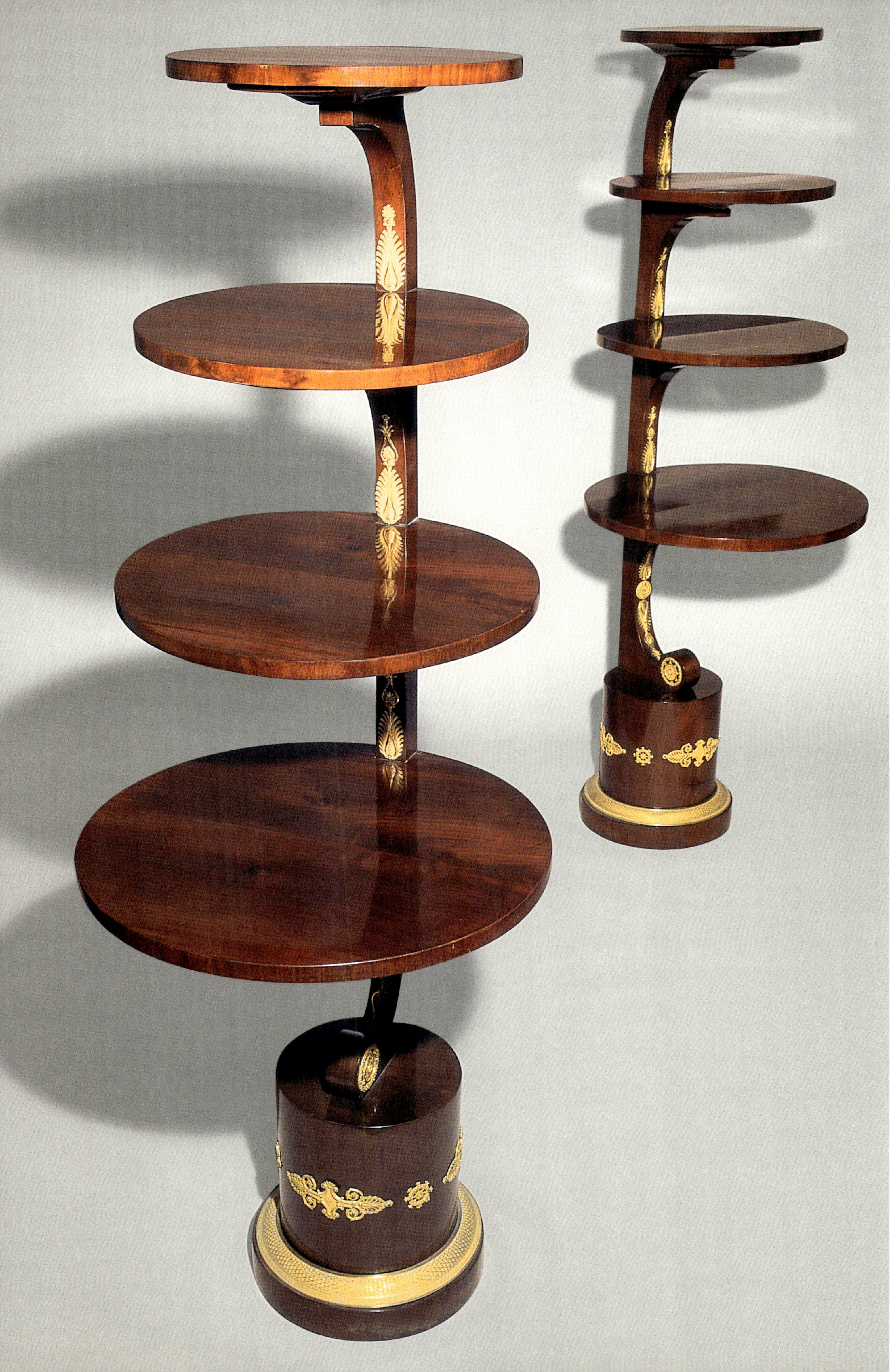

22
Spittoon
Vienna, 1825/30
Cat. 1-29

Spittoon
Vienna, 1825/30
Cat. 1-30

Spittoon
Vienna, 1825/30
Cat. 1-31

Spittoon
Vienna, 1825/30
Cat. 1-32

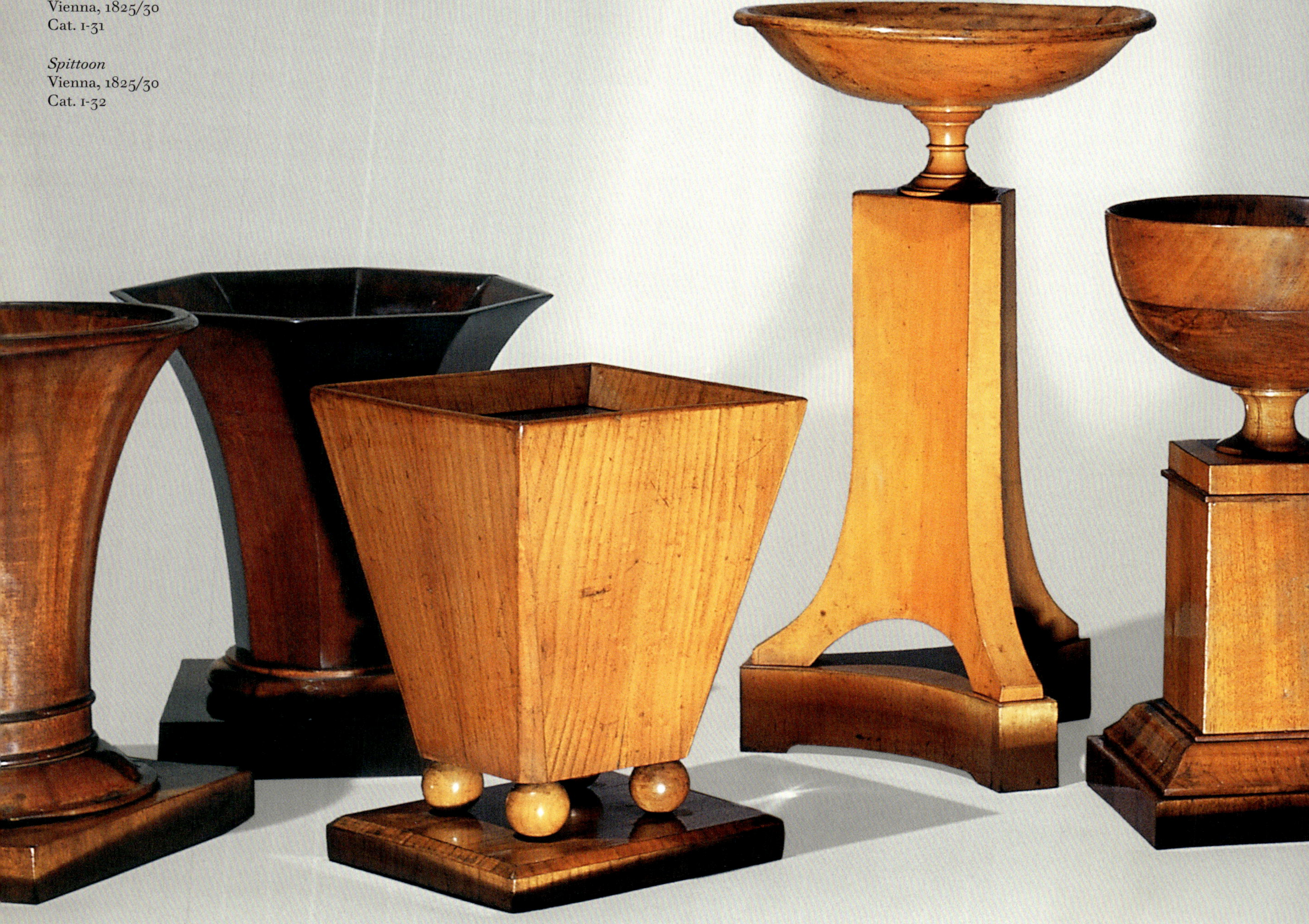

Spittoon
Vienna, 1825/30
Cat. 1-33

Spittoon
Vienna, 1825/30
Cat. 1-34

Spittoon
Vienna, ca. 1825/30
Cat. 1-35

Spittoon
Vienna, 1825/30
Cat. 1-36

Spittoon
Vienna, ca. 1828
Cat. 1-37

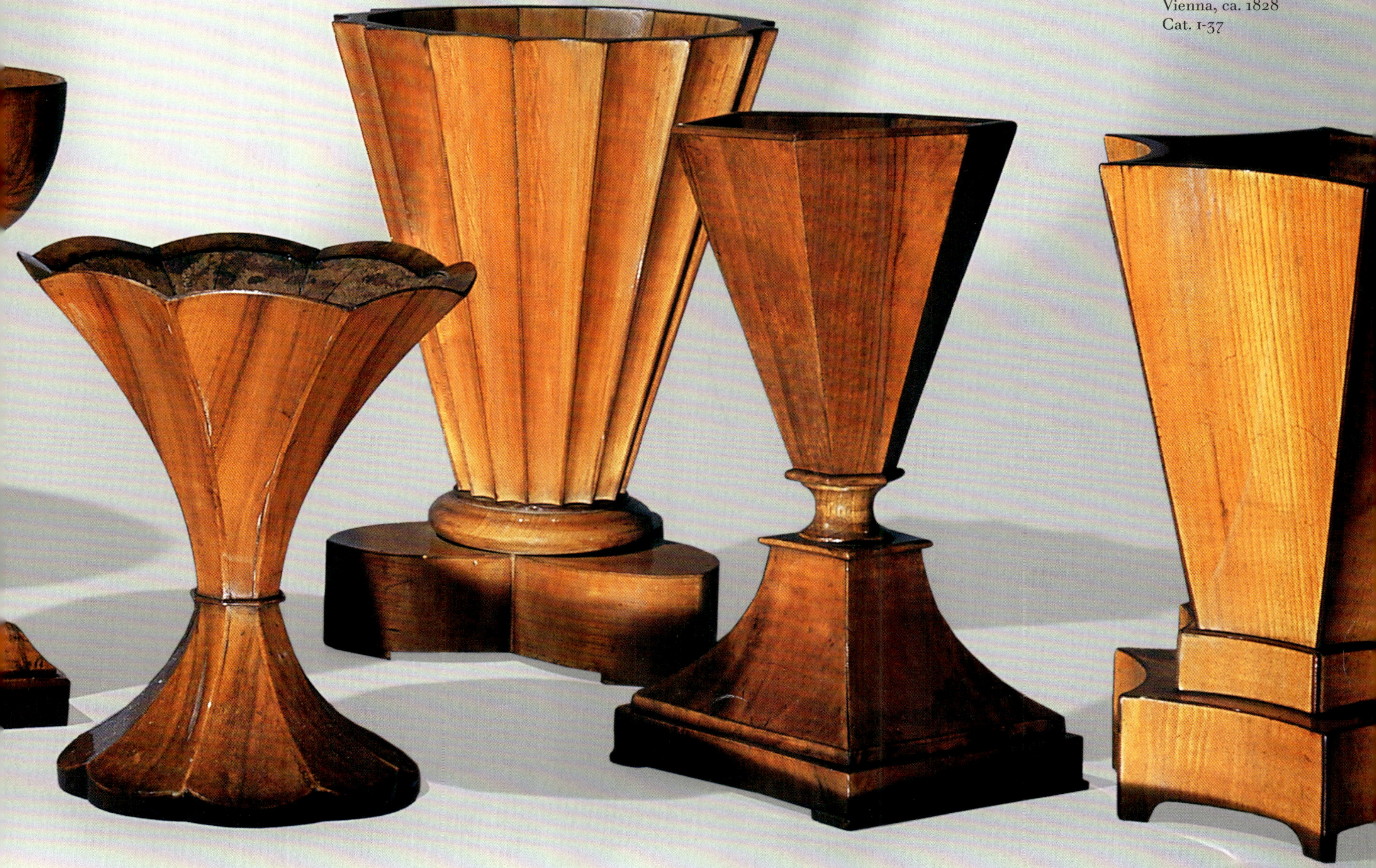

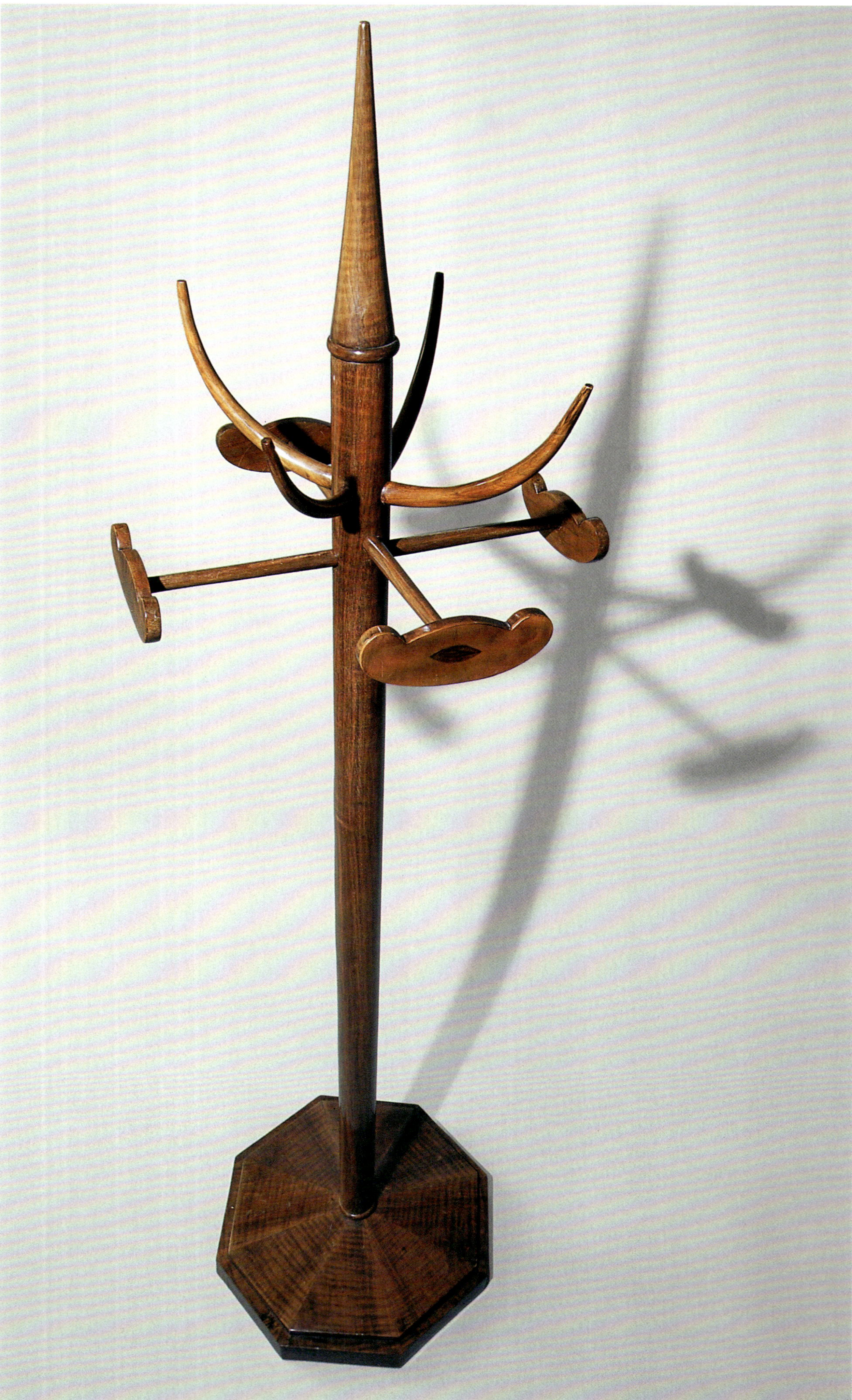

23
Coat Rack
Vienna, ca. 1825
Cat. 1-27

24
Tilt Mirror
Vienna, 1825
Cat. 1-26

24

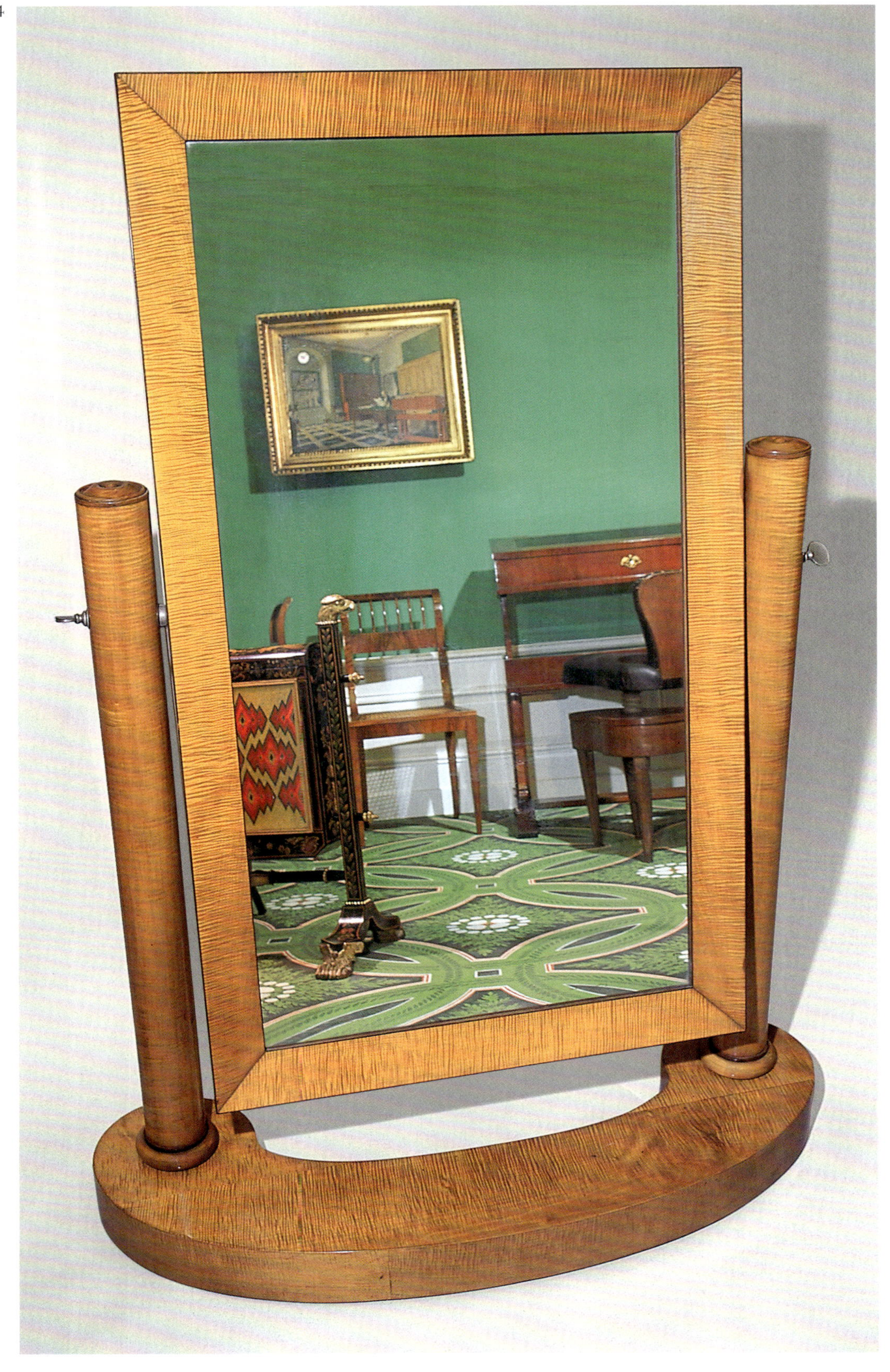

25
Picture Clock, Emperor Franz I in His Study
Vienna, 1829
Cat. 1-40

26
Long Case Clock
Germany, ca. 1790
Cat. 1-38

27
Long Case Clock
Berlin, ca. 1820
Cat. 1-39

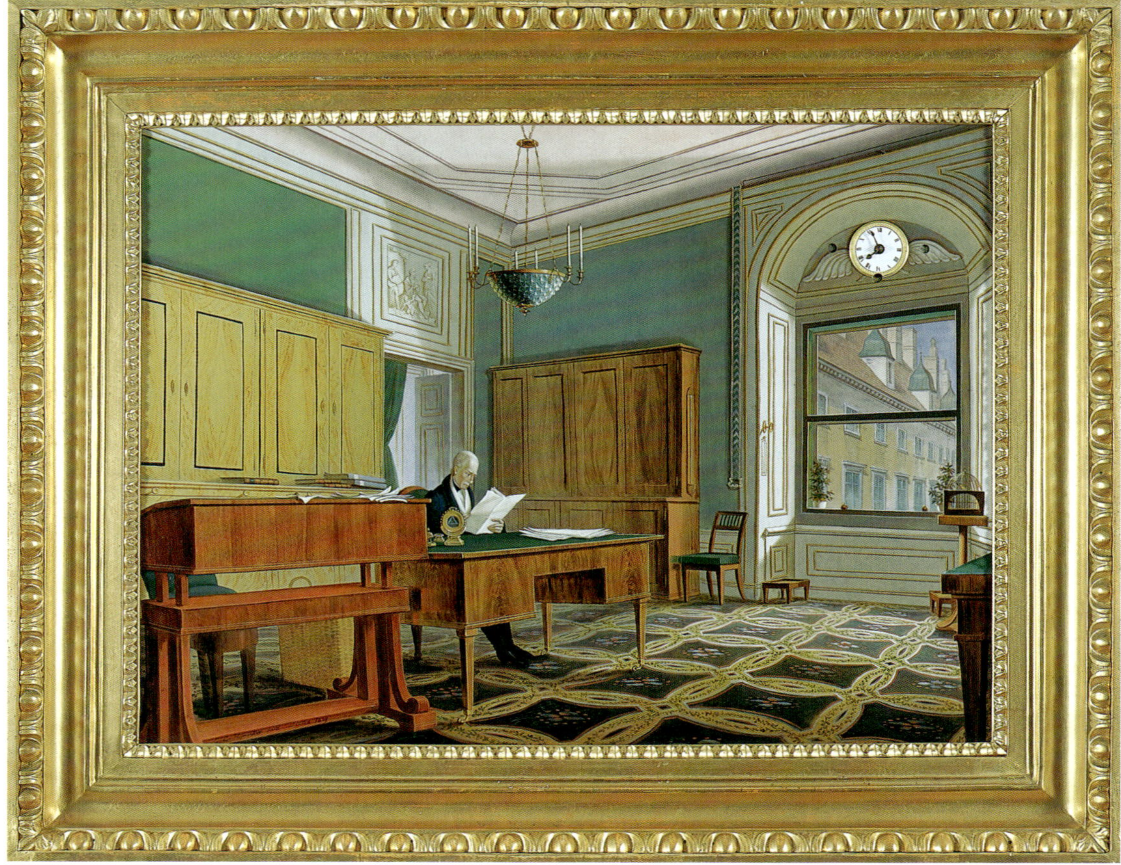

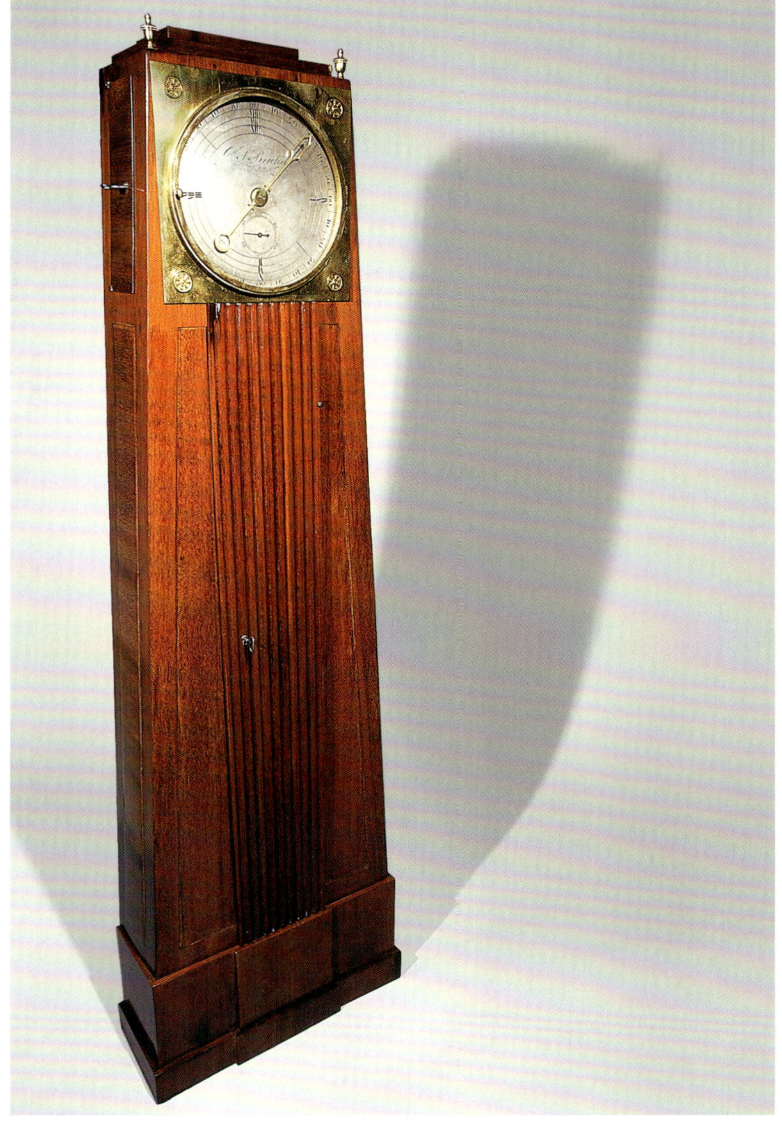

26

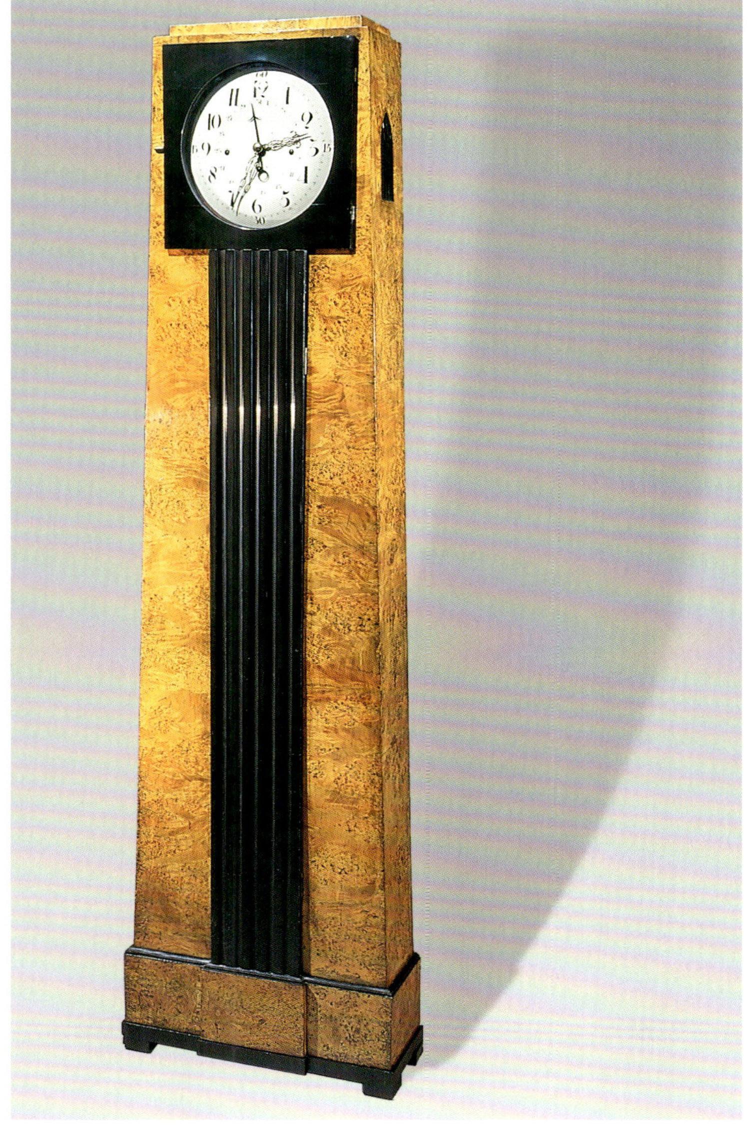

27

SEATING FURNITURE

SECTION II

Christian Witt-Dörring

The Biedermeier period witnessed the development of new types of seating furniture for the first time since the years of the Rococo. The innovations were a reflection of changing patterns of social behavior and a concurrent trend toward emphasis on the private household sphere. Although the old Baroque tradition of the visual representation of social status through seating furniture persisted, a newly emerging private domestic context weakened the existing hierarchy and sought to counteract it. The increasing popularity in Germany and Central Europe of round tea and settee tables, at which all chairs and seating positions were equal, offers persuasive evidence of this trend, which developed much later than in the English-speaking cultural sphere. The new styles involved an improvement in seating comfort as well as technical advances in upholstery. Influenced by English models, upholsterers in Vienna began using metal box springs to achieve maximum elasticity in the seating surface. As a trend in favor of the Turkish styles of the Rococo progressed, introducing to Europe the divan composed of individual cushions, fully upholstered, multiseat furniture became the new visual accent in living rooms. It marked the beginning of increasingly strong competition between cabinetmakers and upholsterers, which intensified during the nineteenth century.

The most obvious result of the new importance attached to private living space was the unification of various different functions within a single room. People lived, slept, and ate in the same room. The necessary articles of furniture were grouped together in individual living or functional islands that occupied the middle of the room, moving in from the walls. Seating furniture assumed a leading role, defining the different furniture groups and shaping the dialogue among them. Thus, new types of seating furniture began to appear, such as the corner divan, the "dos à dos," or the cube, which mediated between the furniture islands and no longer faced the room frontally but rather in two or more different directions. The arrangement adopted from the ancien régime composed of "fixed" pieces ("chaises meublantes") that corresponded architecturally to the wall, and "mobile" pieces ("chaises courantes") that could be positioned around the room as needed, was preserved in the courtly aristocratic social circles of the nineteenth century. Yet a lighter type of chair known as the "Laufsessel" also began to appear. Its novelty lay in the fact that it no longer matched the seating furniture of the room and was instead distributed throughout the house as a standard, formally autonomous type of chair. It was a "mass product" that denied individuality. The best-known example of this chair came from Chiavari in Liguria and could be found all over Europe. Beginning in the 1840s, it was replaced primarily in Central Europe by the Thonet bentwood chair.

A veritable tidal wave of new chair-back designs spread through the cultural region of Southern Germany from Vienna. They became the medium of formal individualism and diversity and a kind of leitmotif for the era. Previously unknown fantasy creations appeared on fully upholstered seating furniture modeled on the divan, the settee, or the "causeuse." In this furniture, fabric assumed the role of the load-bearing framework. Upholsterers and cabinetmakers joined in creative union, thereby making it impossible to attribute exclusive authorship to one or the other craft. One influenced the other in both a functional and a formal sense: the cabinetmaker's frame explains the upholstery, and vice-versa. Thus, despite the apparent fantastical quality of this seating furniture, it represents a logical whole in which the tectonic character of the furniture is never neglected. An integral component of this quality and a useful aid in achieving it was the thoughtful arrangement of borders and draperies.

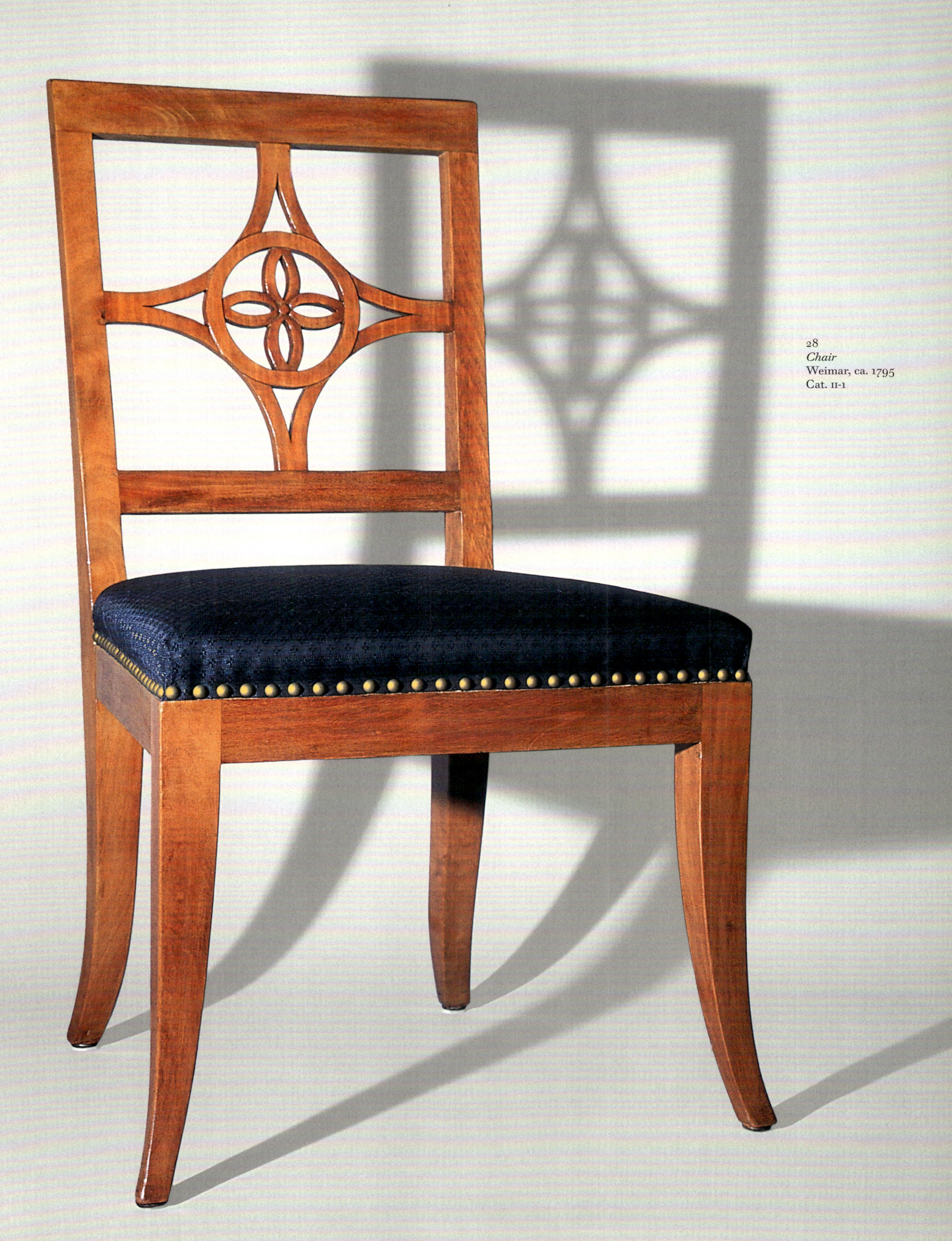

28
Chair
Weimar, ca. 1795
Cat. II-1

29

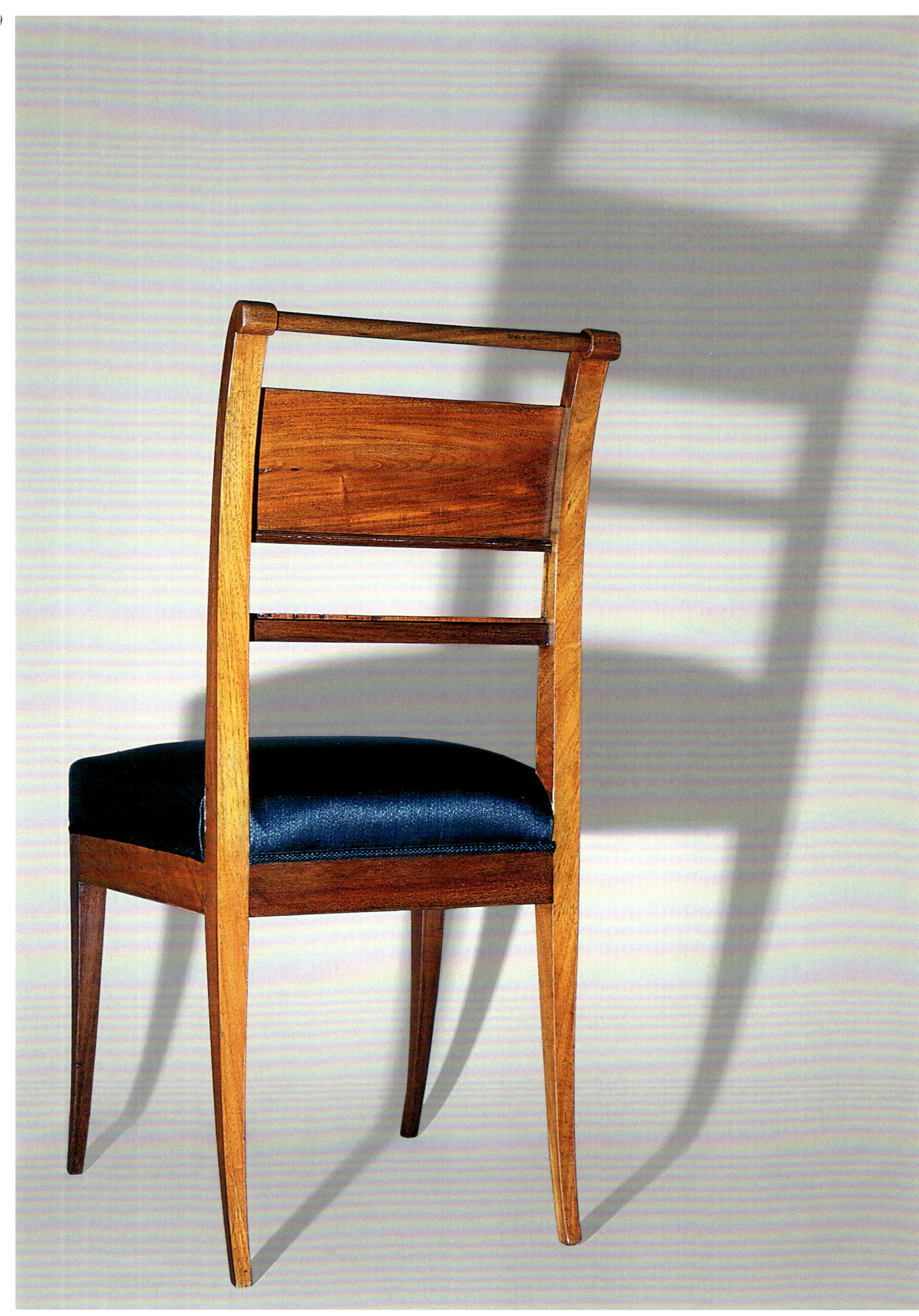

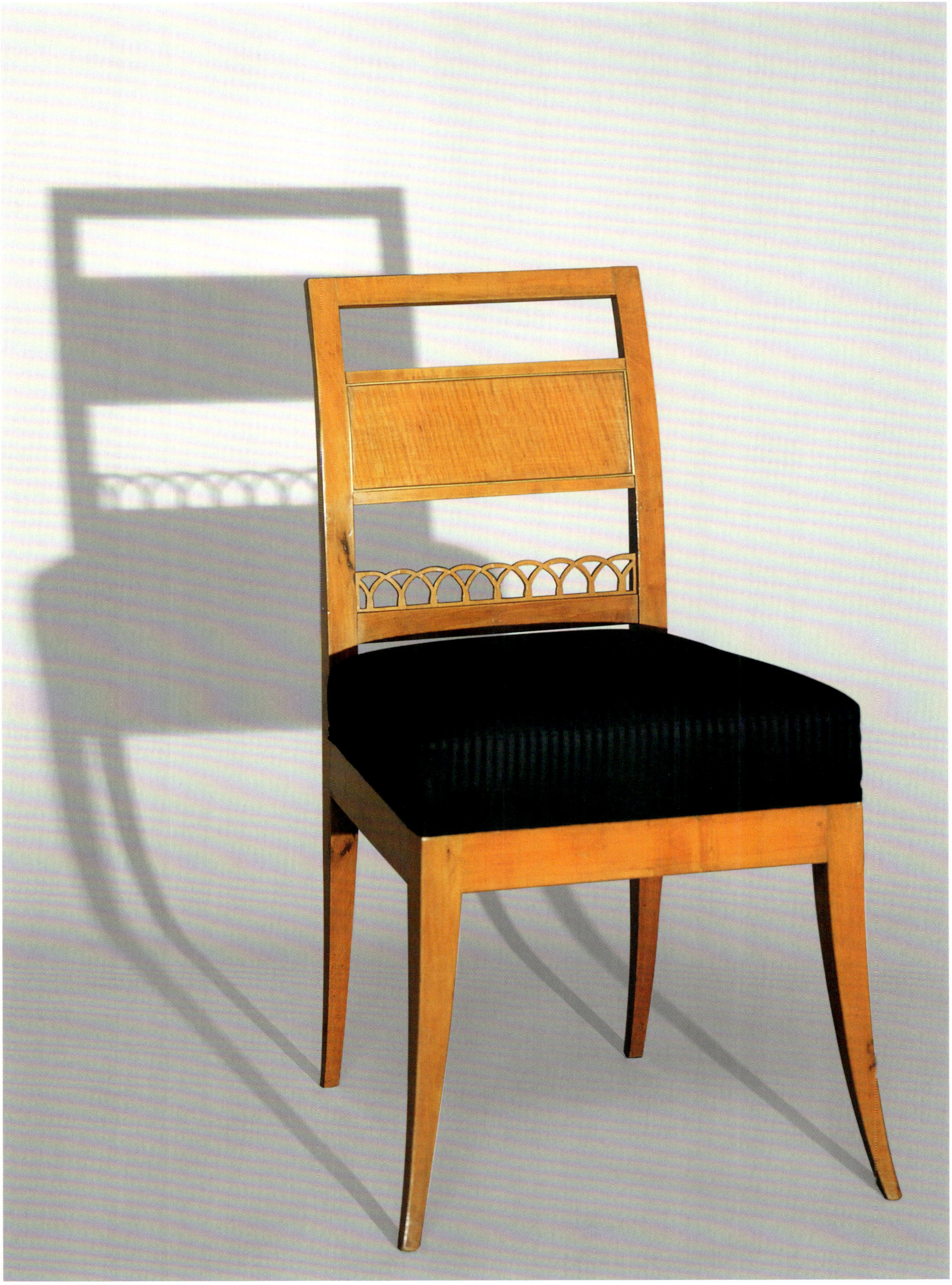

29
Chair
Weimar, 1810/20
Cat. II-2

30
Chair
South Germany,
ca. 1804/1805
Cat. II-3

31

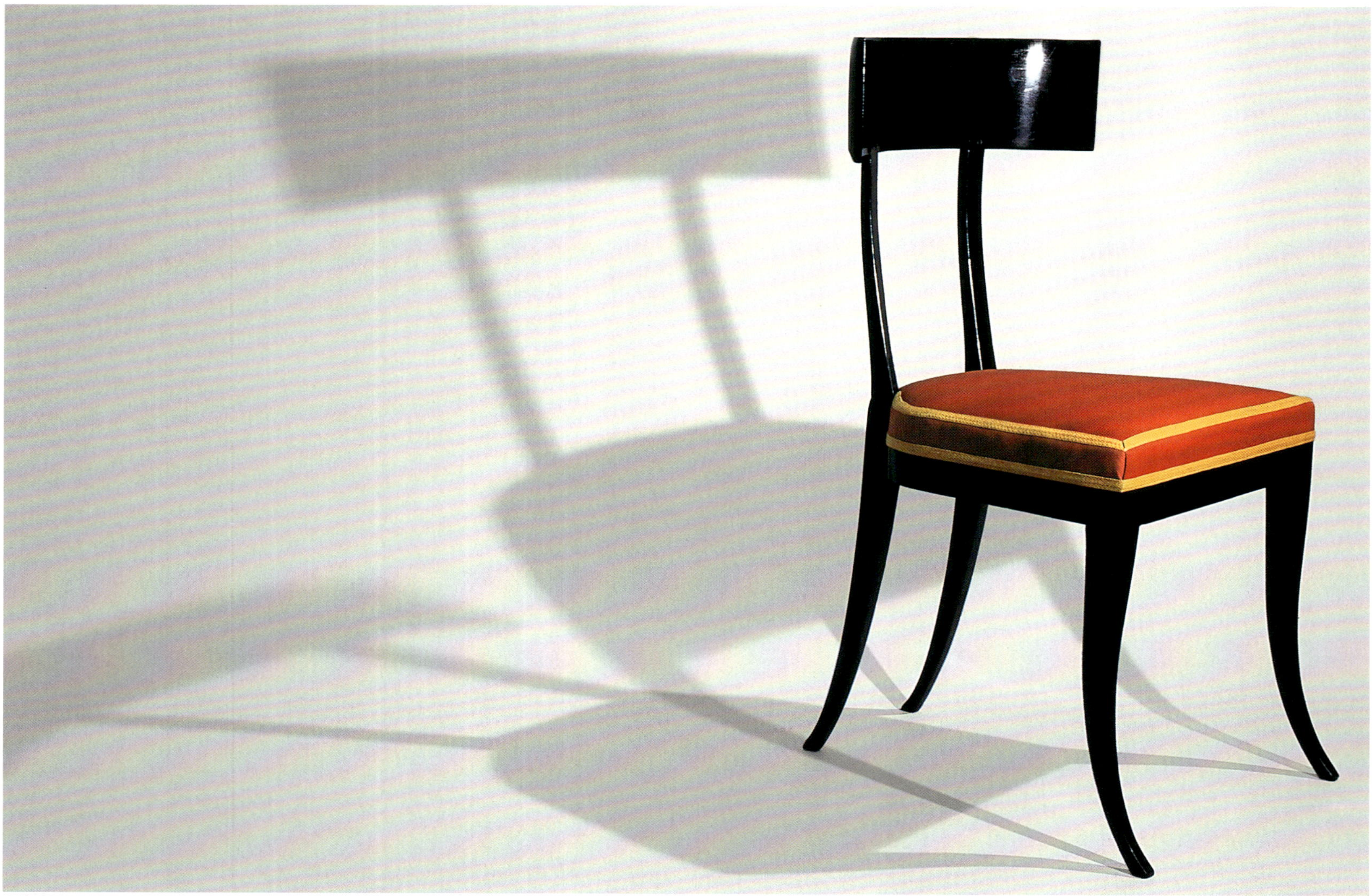

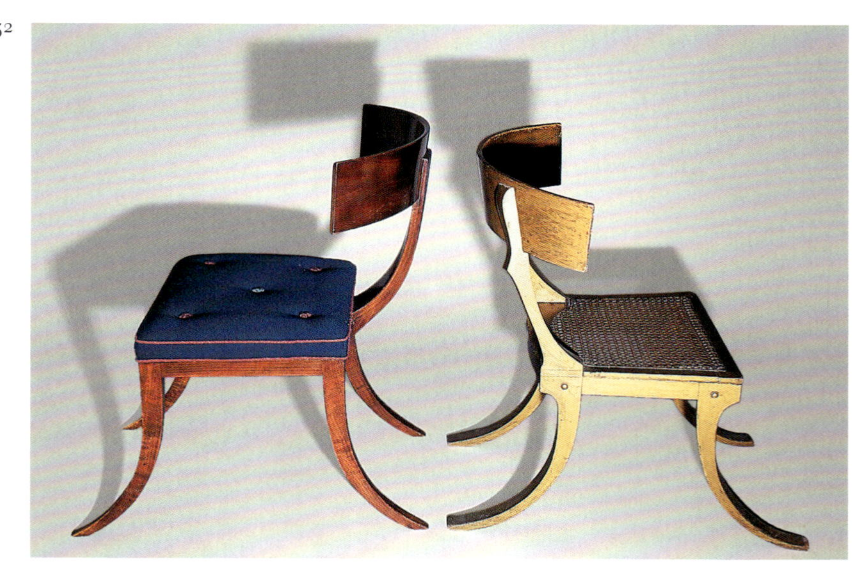

32

33

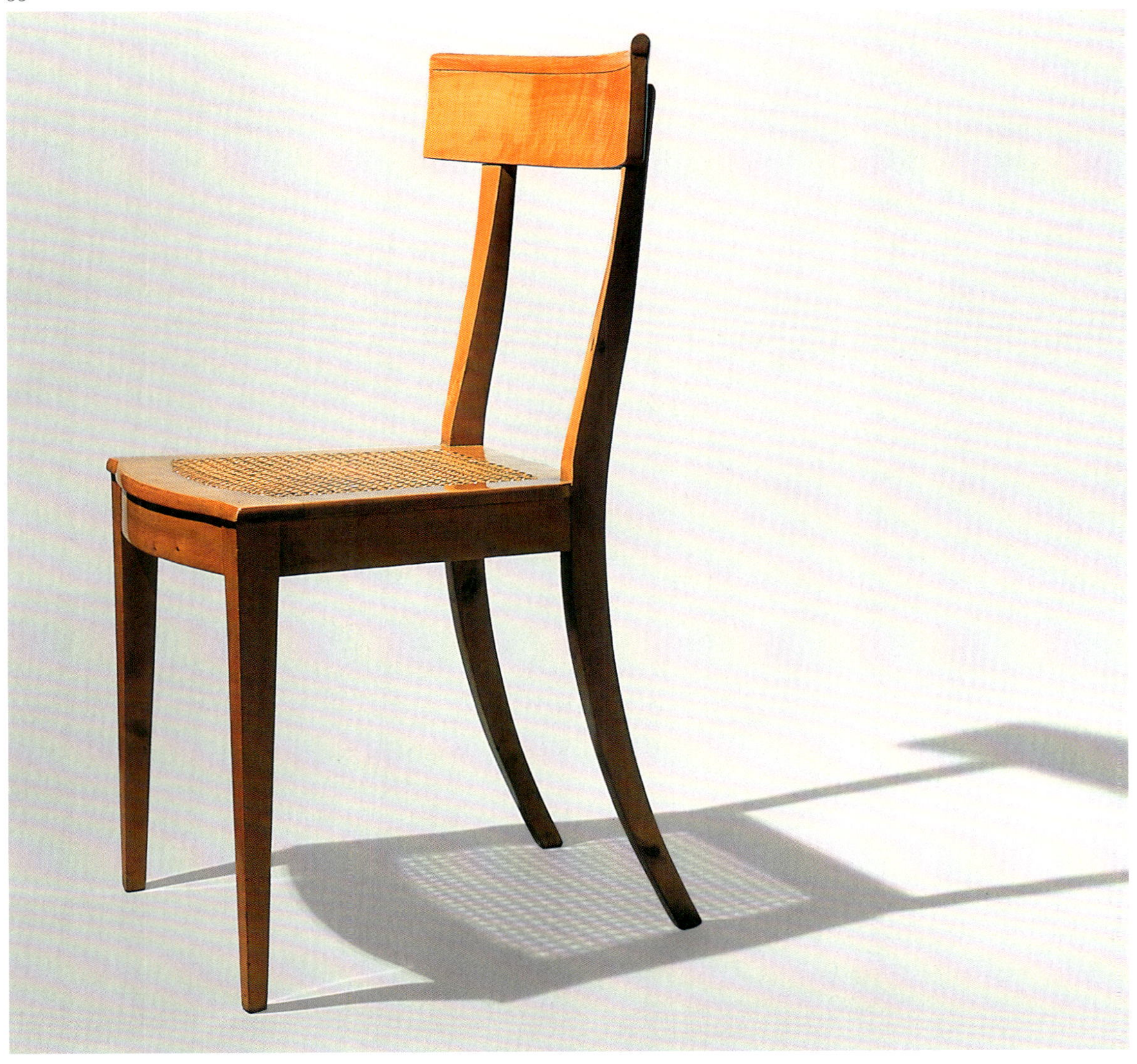

31
Chair
Berlin, 1805/10
Cat. II-7

32
Klismos Chair
Copenhagen, ca. 1840
Cat. II-5

Klismos Chair
Copenhagen, early 1790s
Cat. II-4

33
Chair
Berlin, ca. 1825
Cat. II-8

34

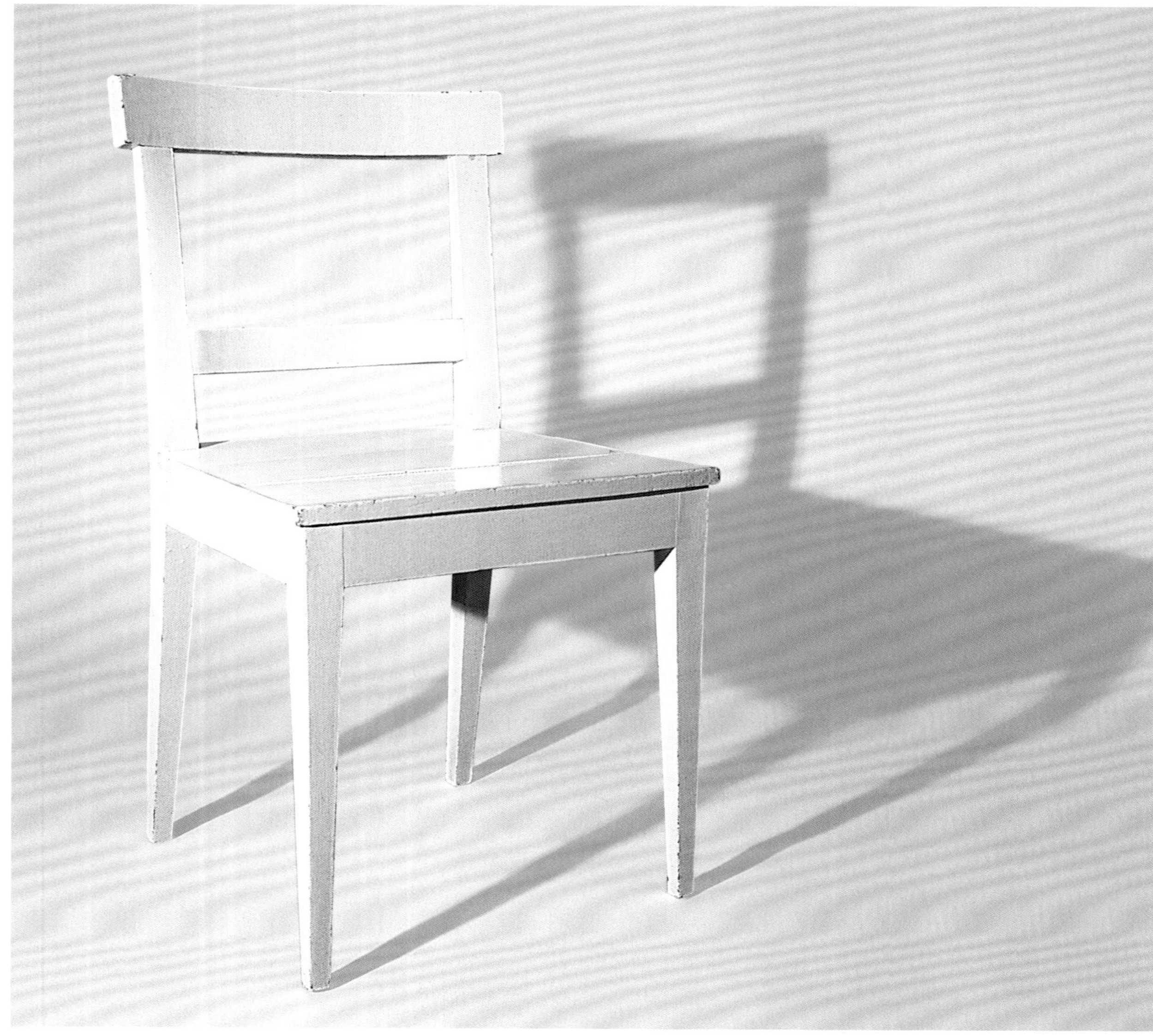

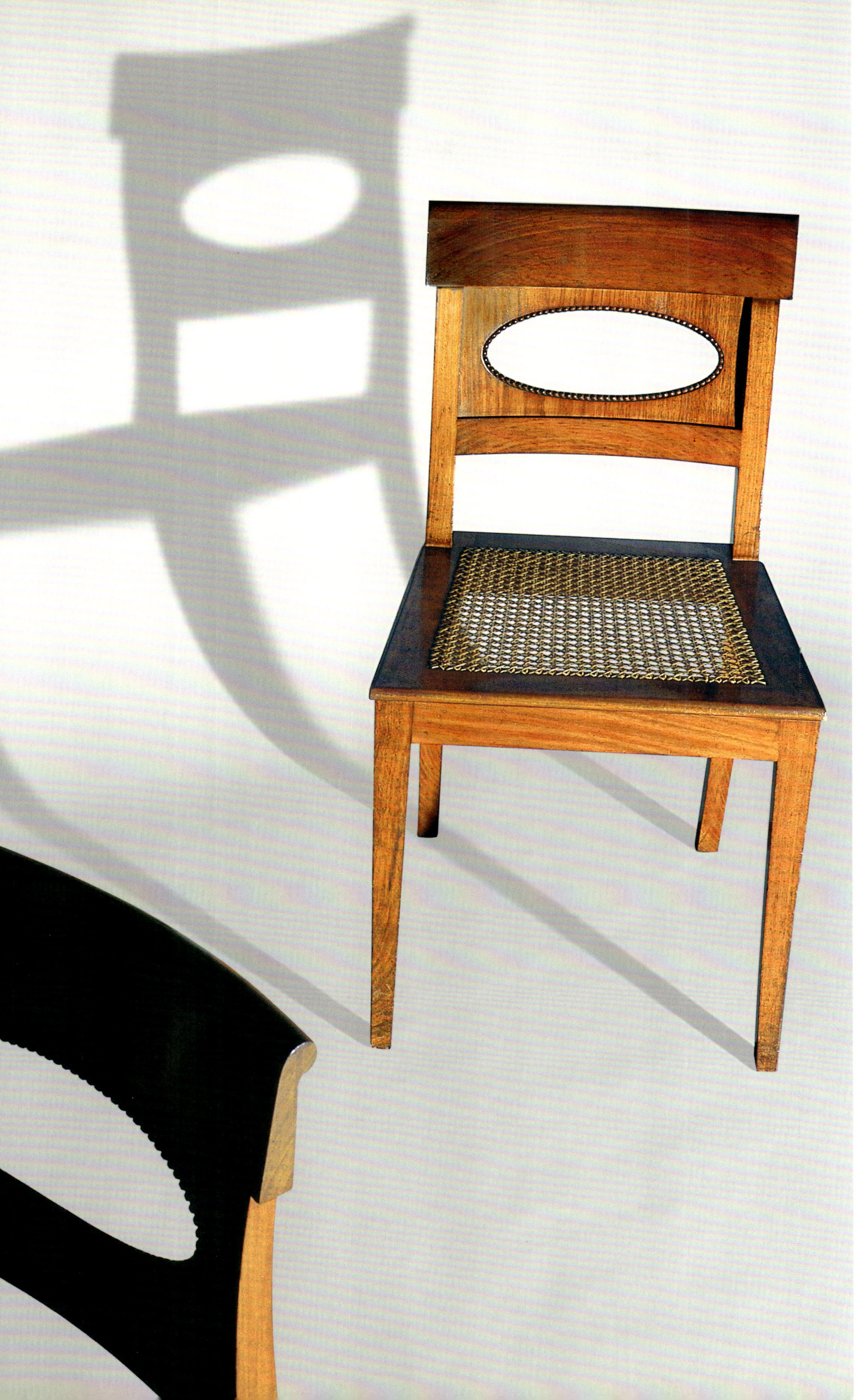

34
Kitchen Chair
Berlin, ca. 1820
Cat. II-9

35
Chair
Berlin, ca. 1820
Cat. II-10

36
*Garden or
Terrace Chair*
Vienna, ca. 1825
Cat. II-11

*Garden or
Terrace Chair*
Vienna, ca. 1825
Cat. II-12

37
Chair
Lavagna, ca. 1830
Cat. II-13

38
Bentwood Chair
Boppard am Rhein,
1835/40
Cat. II-14

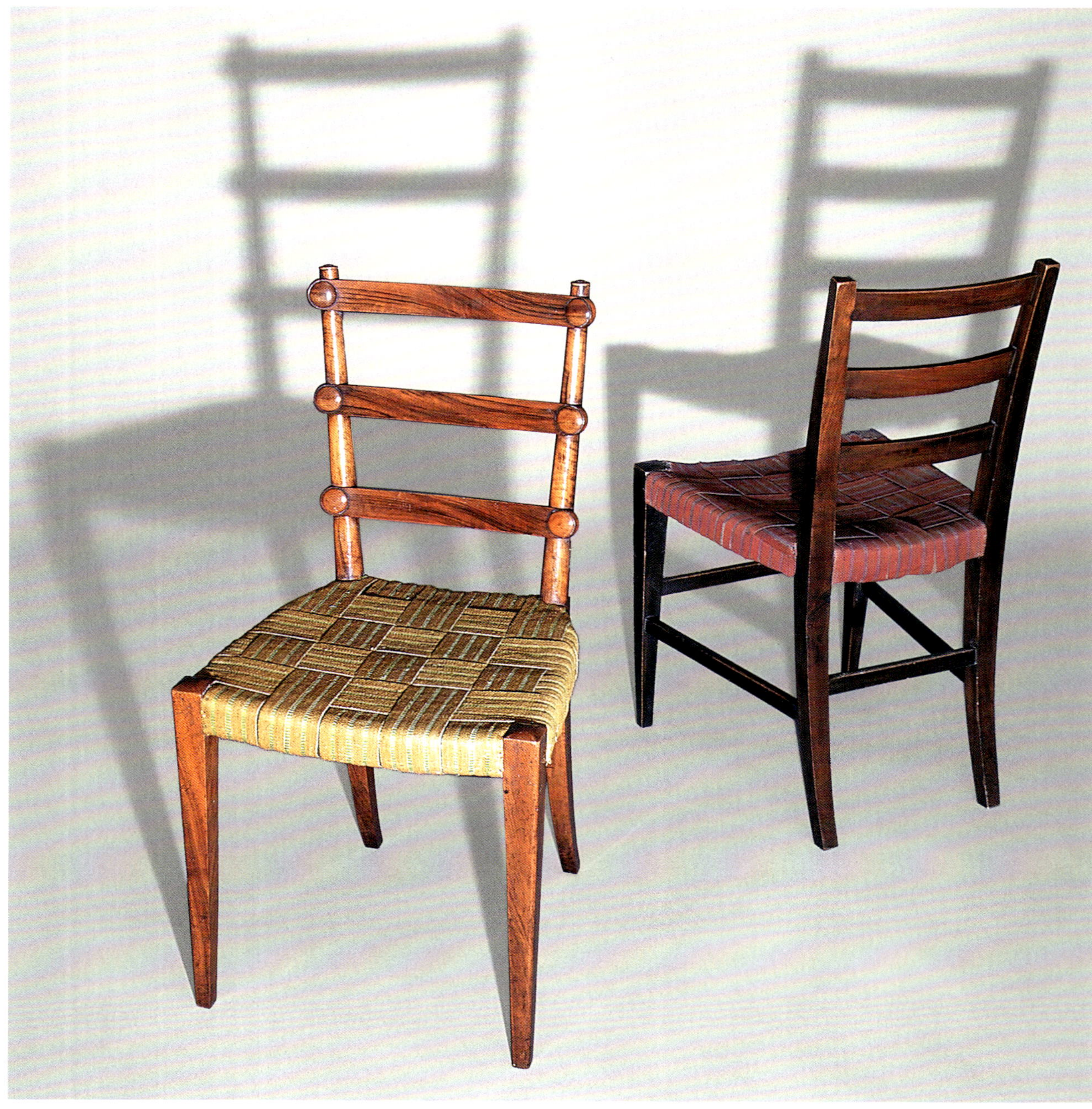
36

37

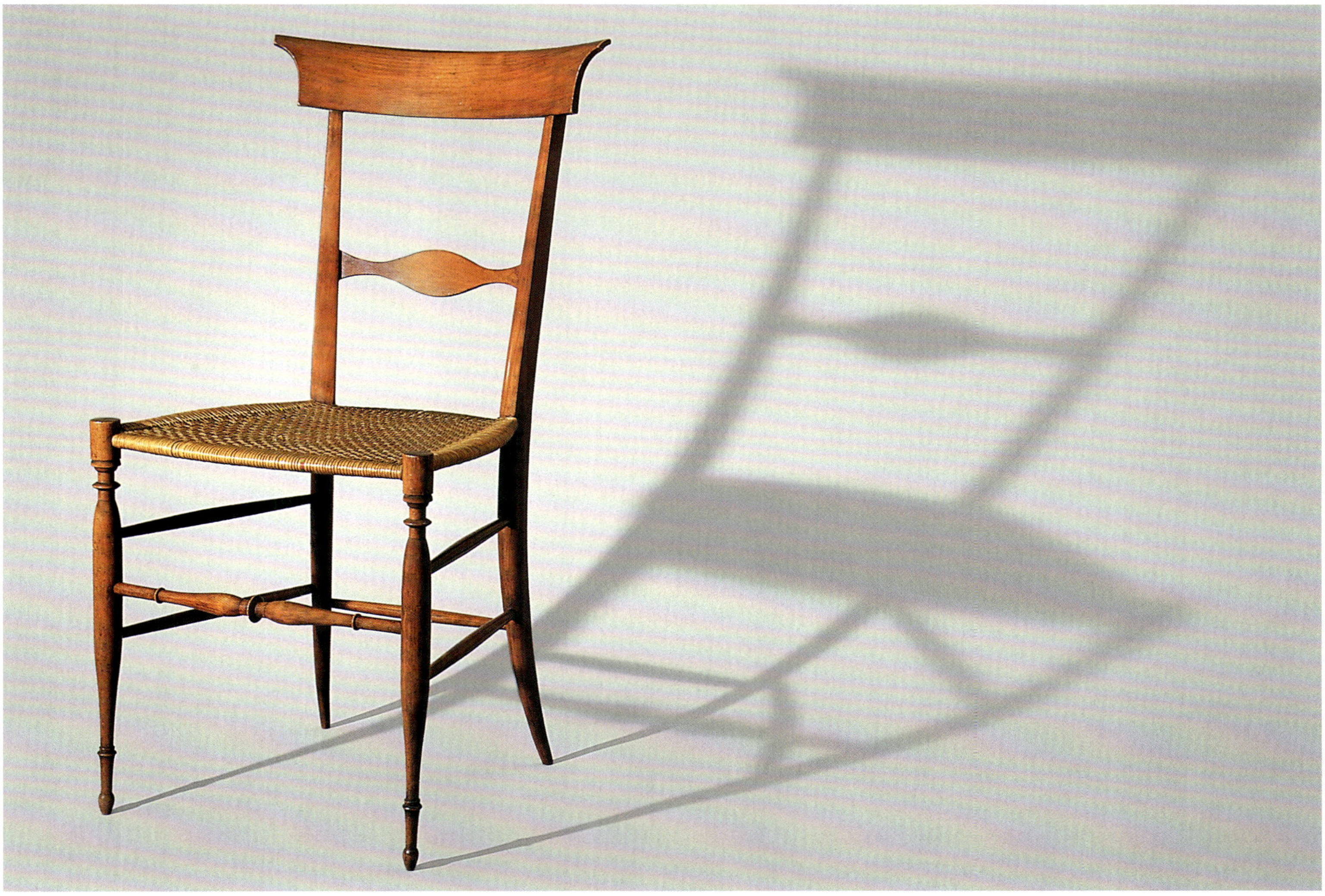

38

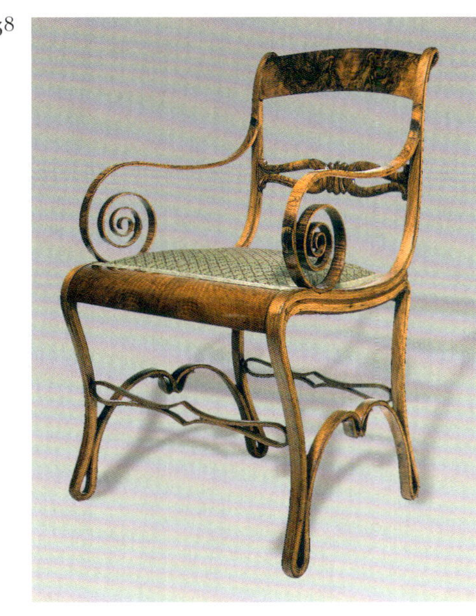

39
Chair
Vienna, ca. 1826
Cat. II-16

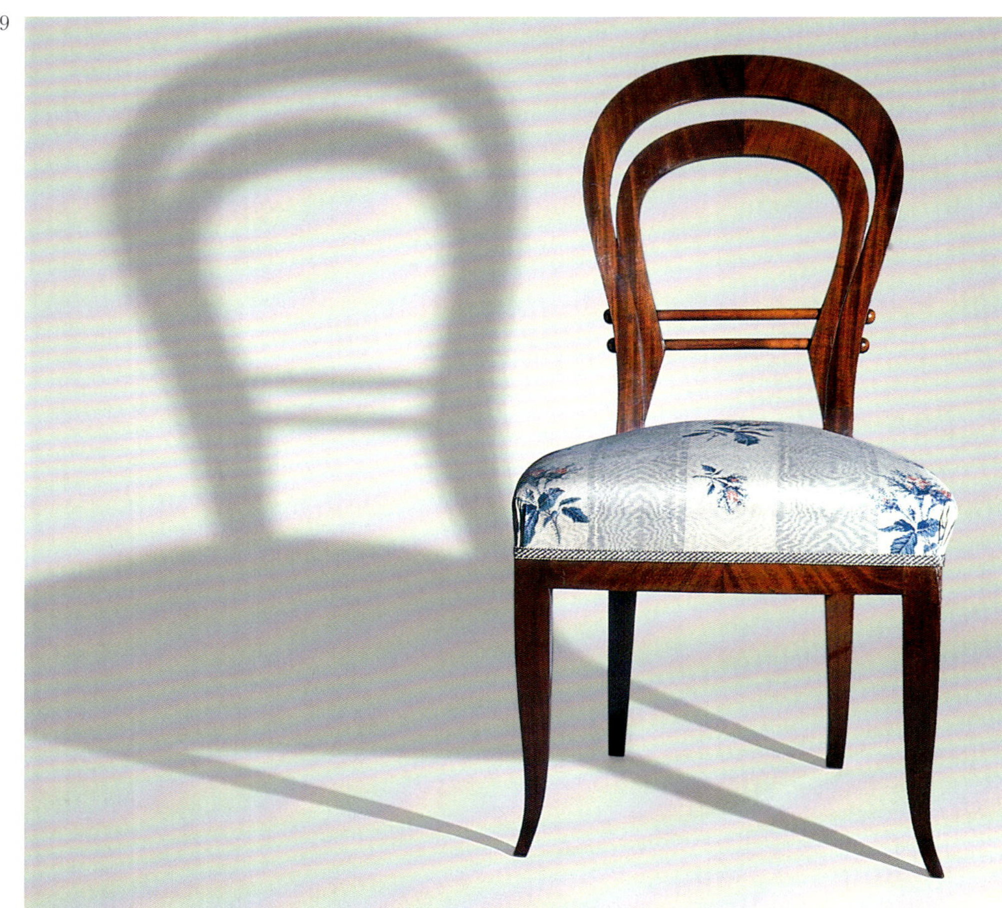

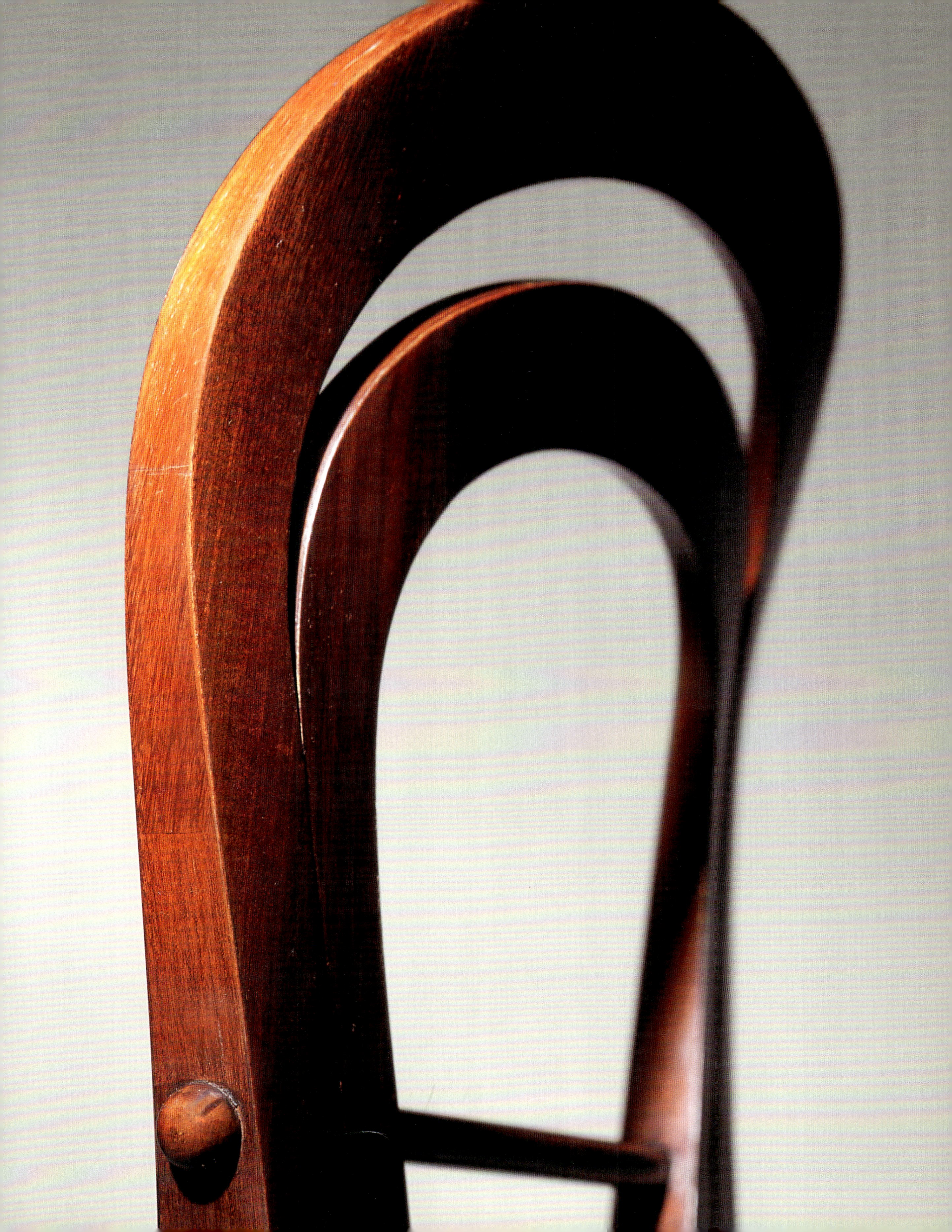

40
Chair
Vienna, ca. 1825
Cat. II-17 (detail)

41
(Opposite)
Chair
Vienna, ca. 1825
Cat. II-18

42
Chair
Vienna, 1826
Cat. II-19 (detail)

43
Chair
Vienna, 1830/35
Cat. II-22 (detail)

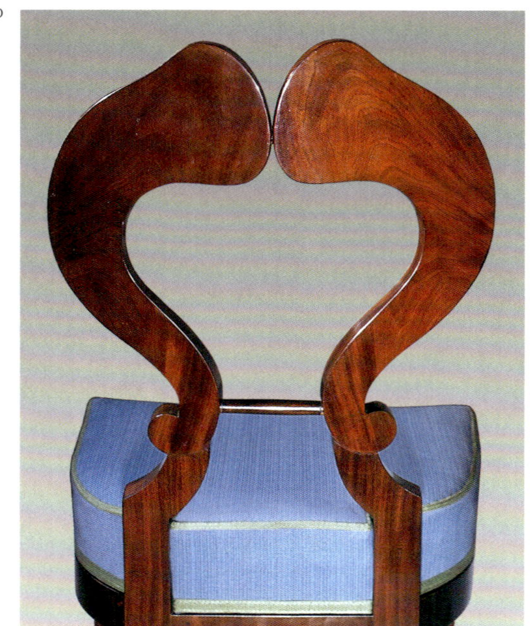

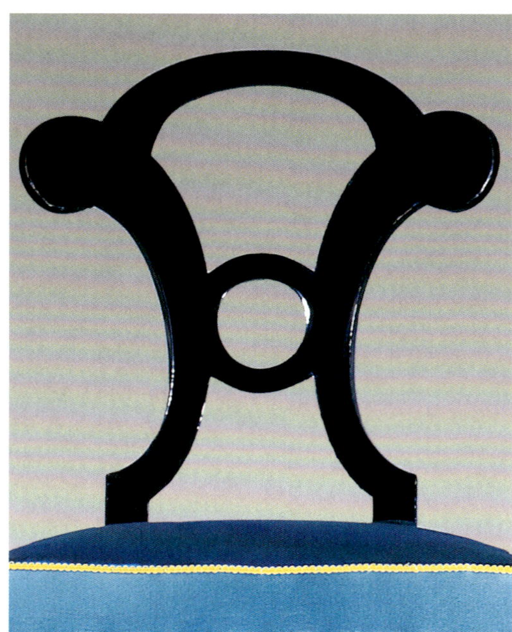

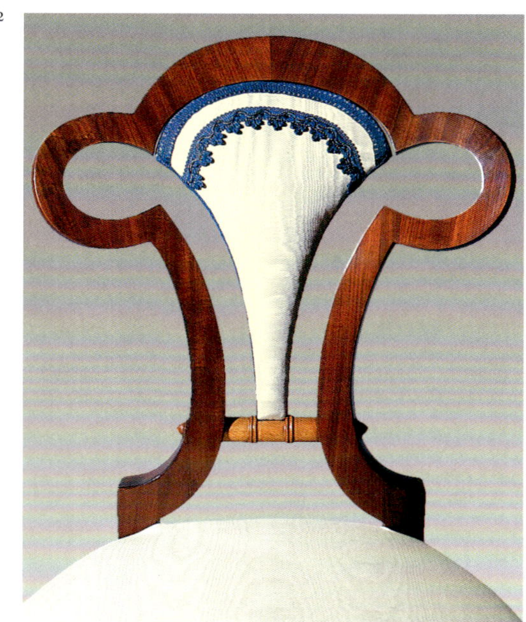

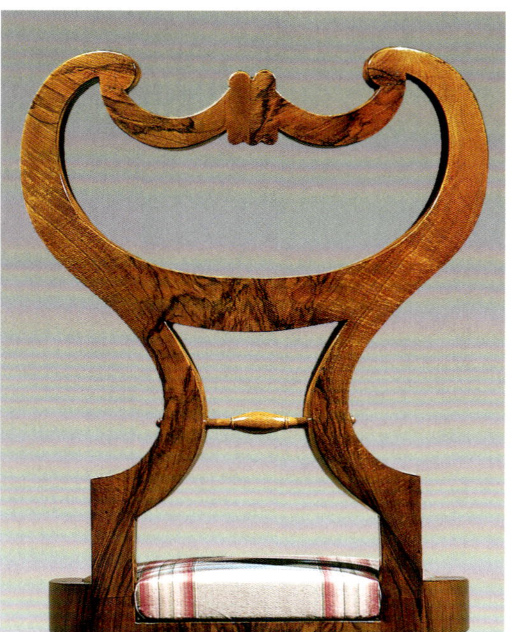

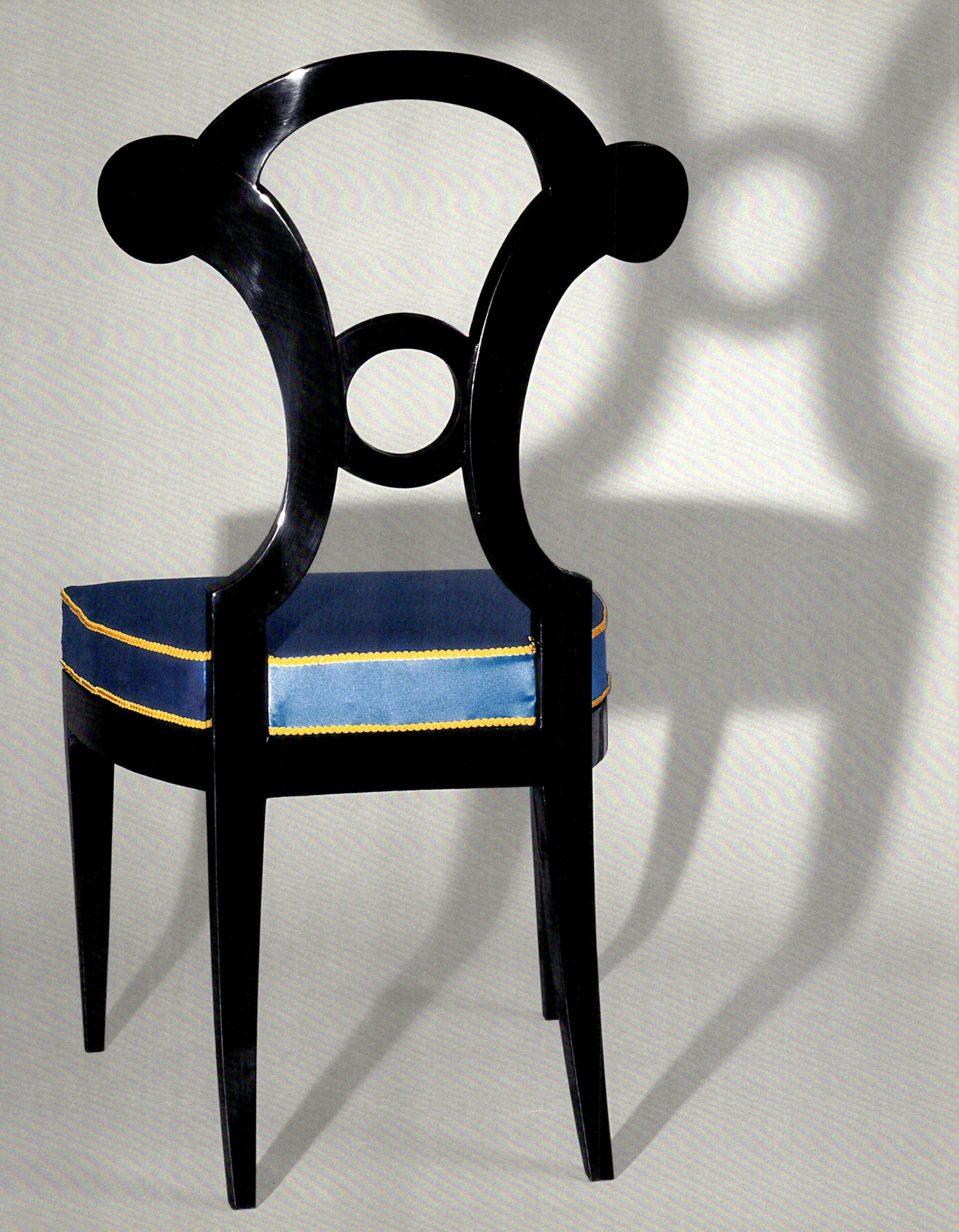

44
Chair
Vienna, ca. 1820
Cat. II-20

45
Chair
Vienna, ca. 1825
Cat. II-24 (detail)

46
Chair
Vienna, ca. 1825
Cat. II-26 (detail)

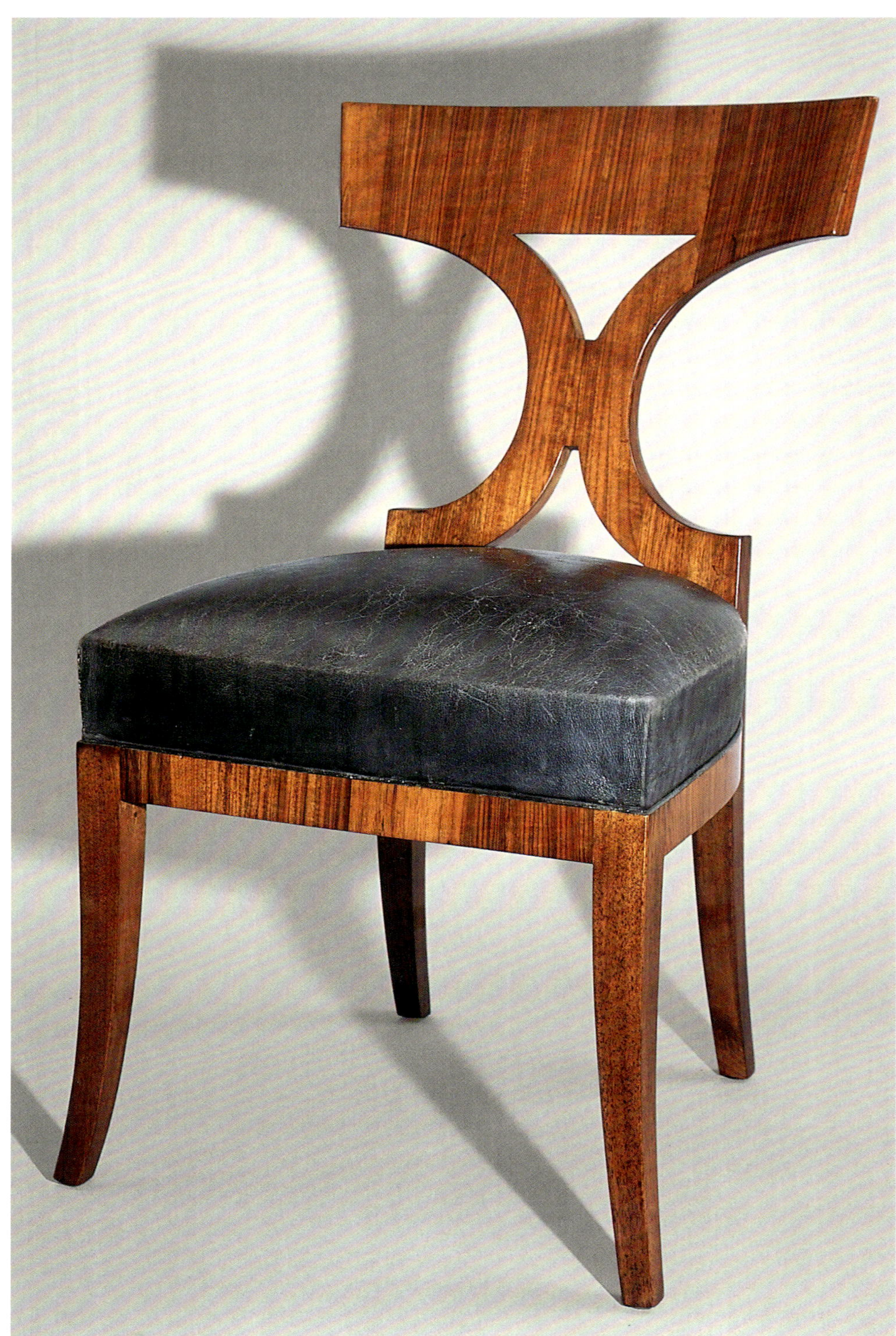

44

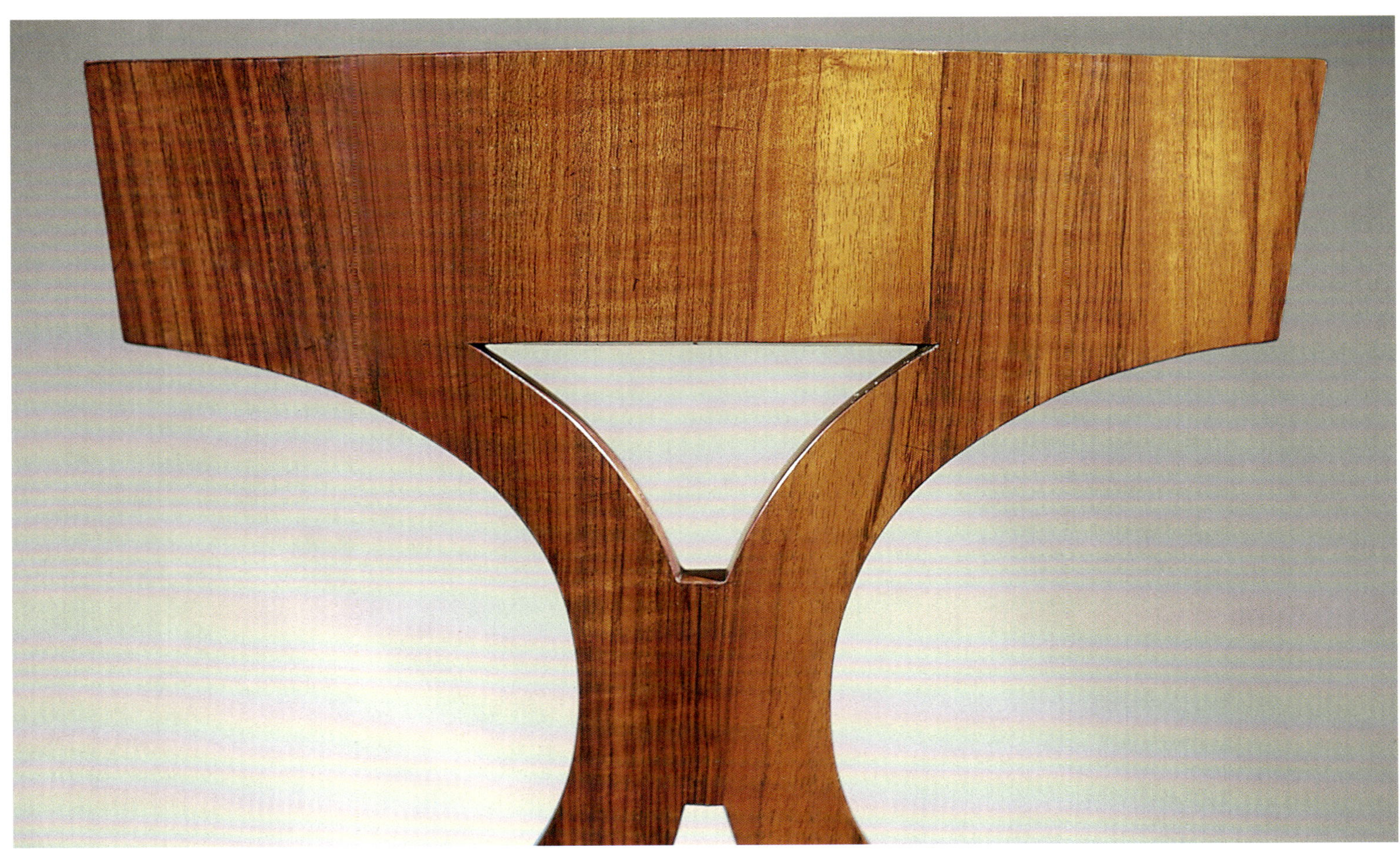

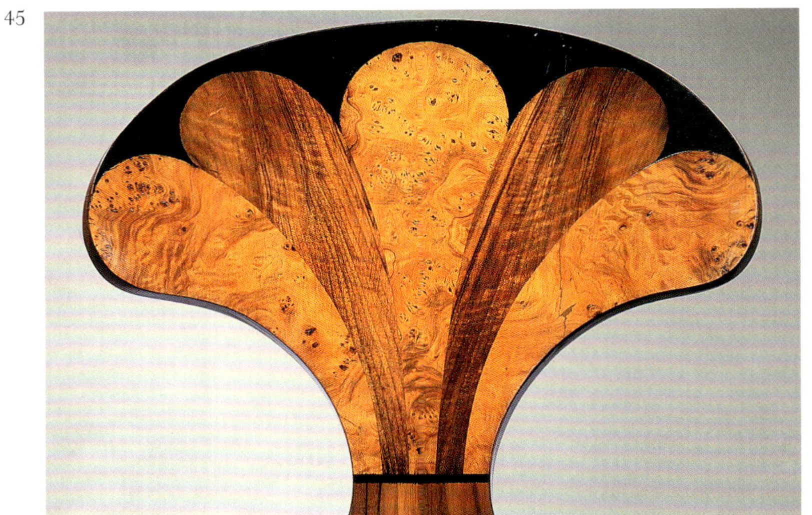

45

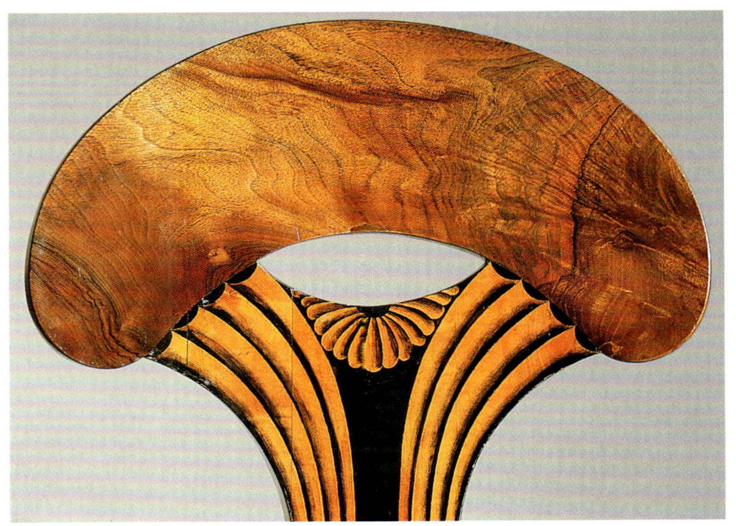

46

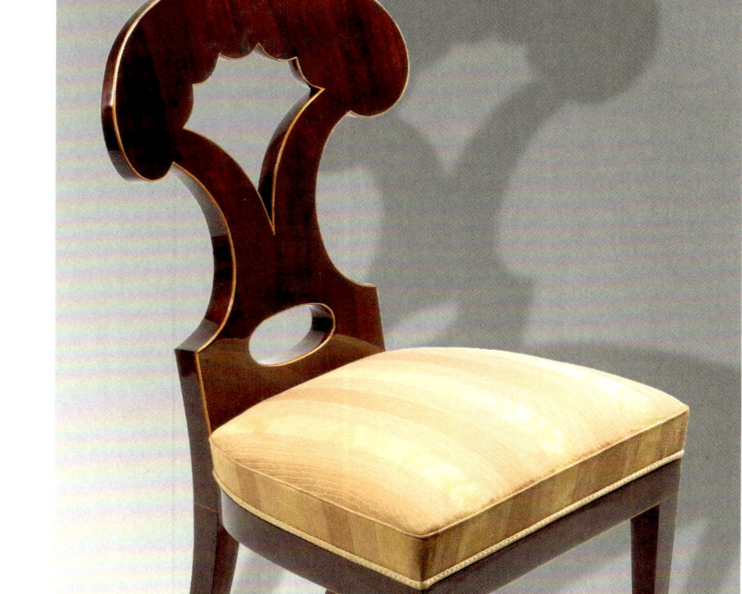

47

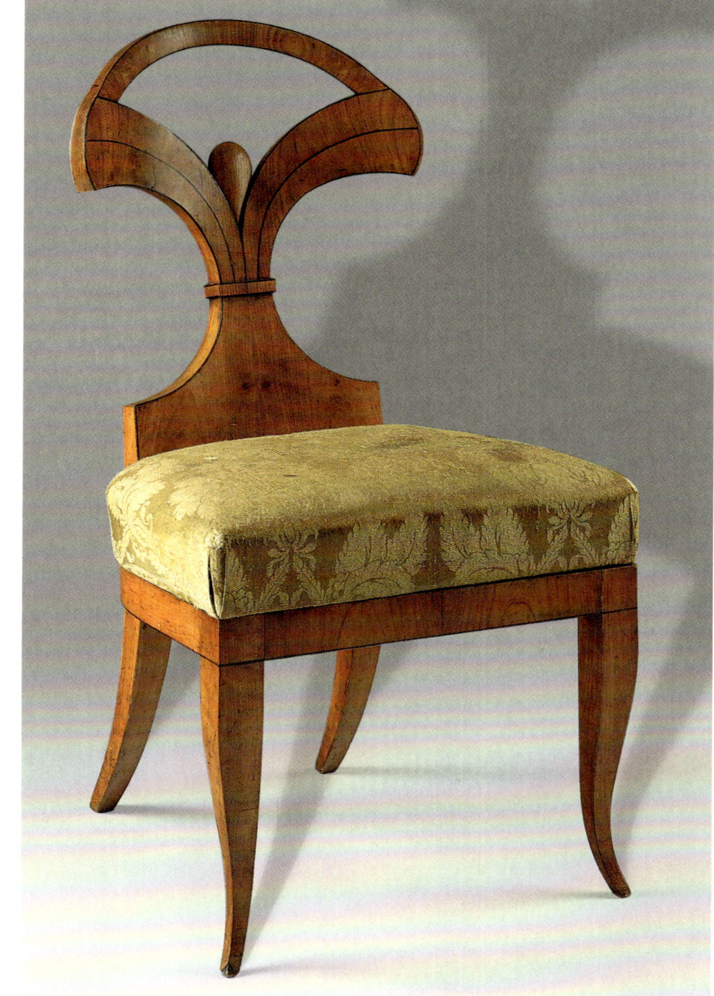

48

49

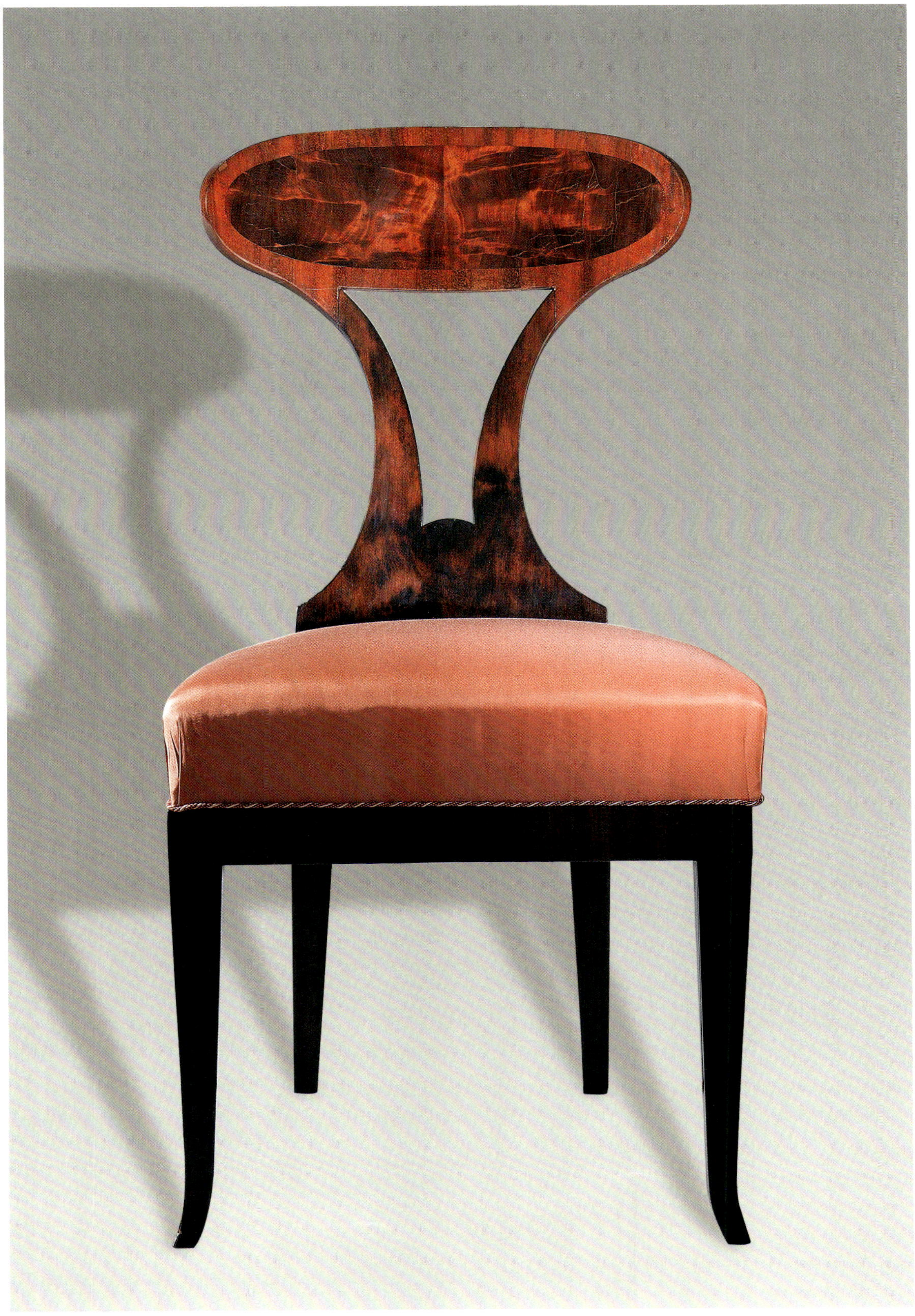

47
Chair
Vienna, ca. 1825
Cat. II-25

48
Chair
Vienna, 1815/20
Cat. II-21

49
Chair
Vienna, 1815/20
Cat. II-27

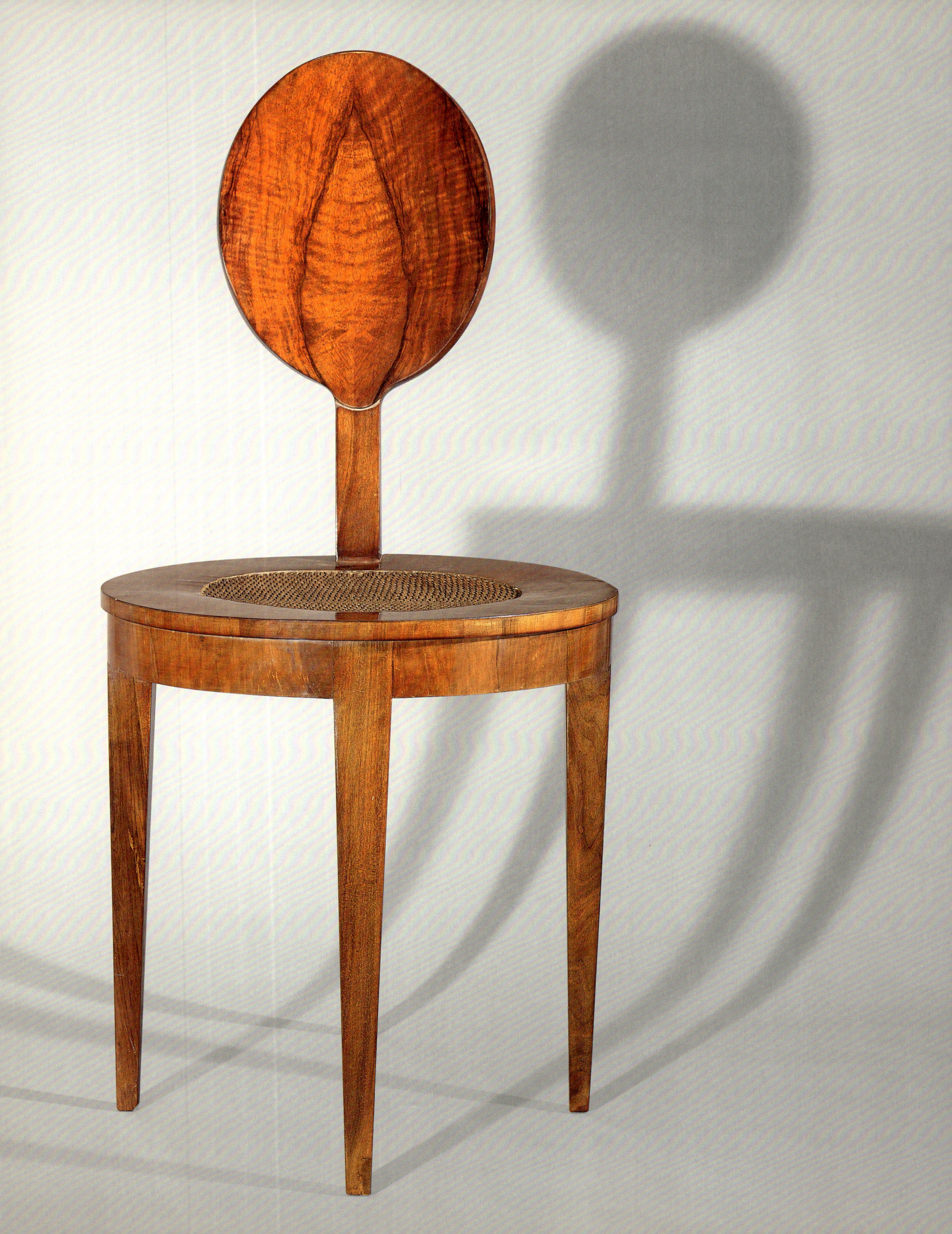

51

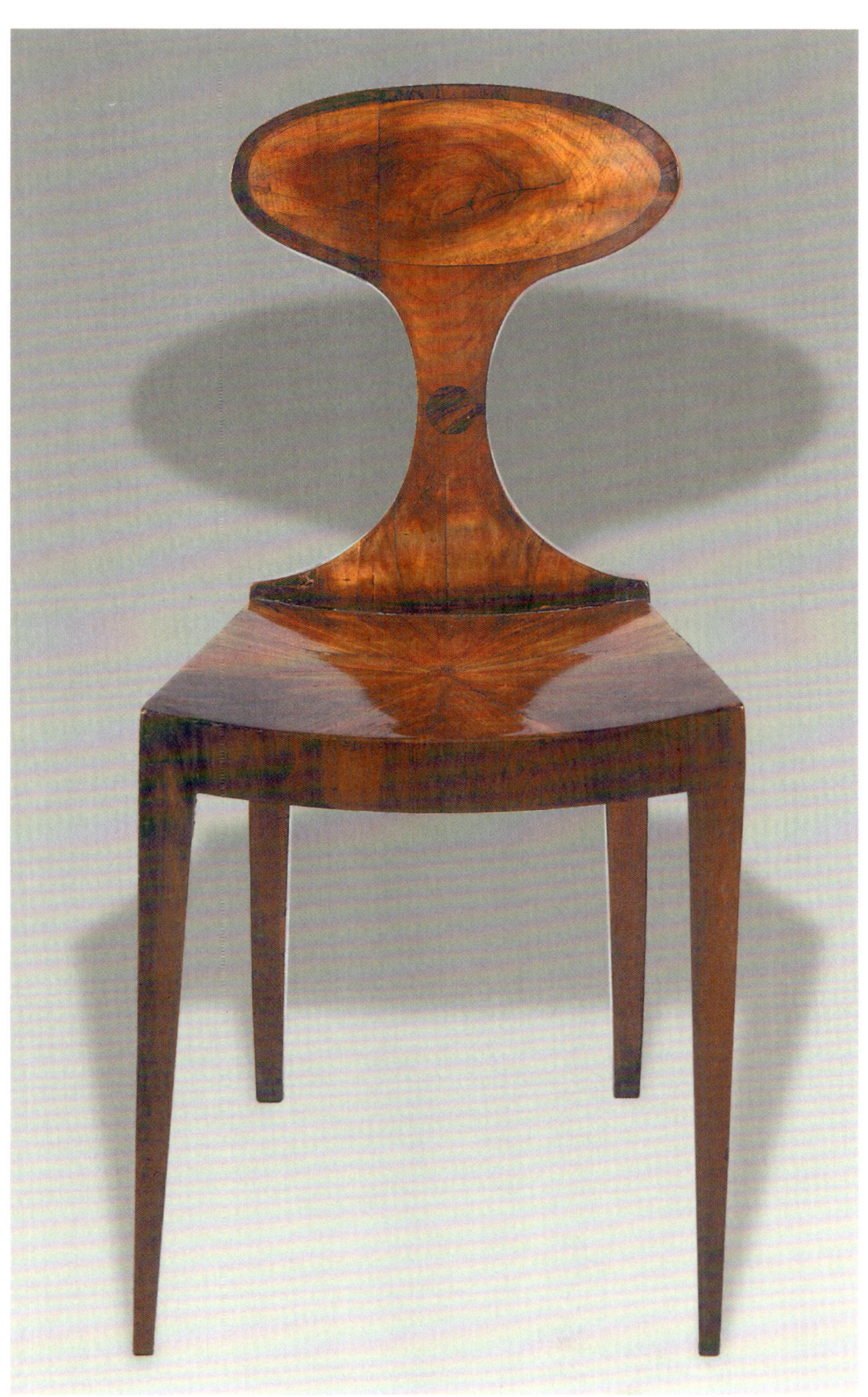

50
(Opposite)
Chair
Austria, ca. 1820
Cat. II-29

51
Chair
Bohemia, 1815/20
Cat. II-28

52
Chair
Vienna, 1815/20
Cat. II-31

53
Armchair
Vienna, ca. 1825
Cat. II-32

52

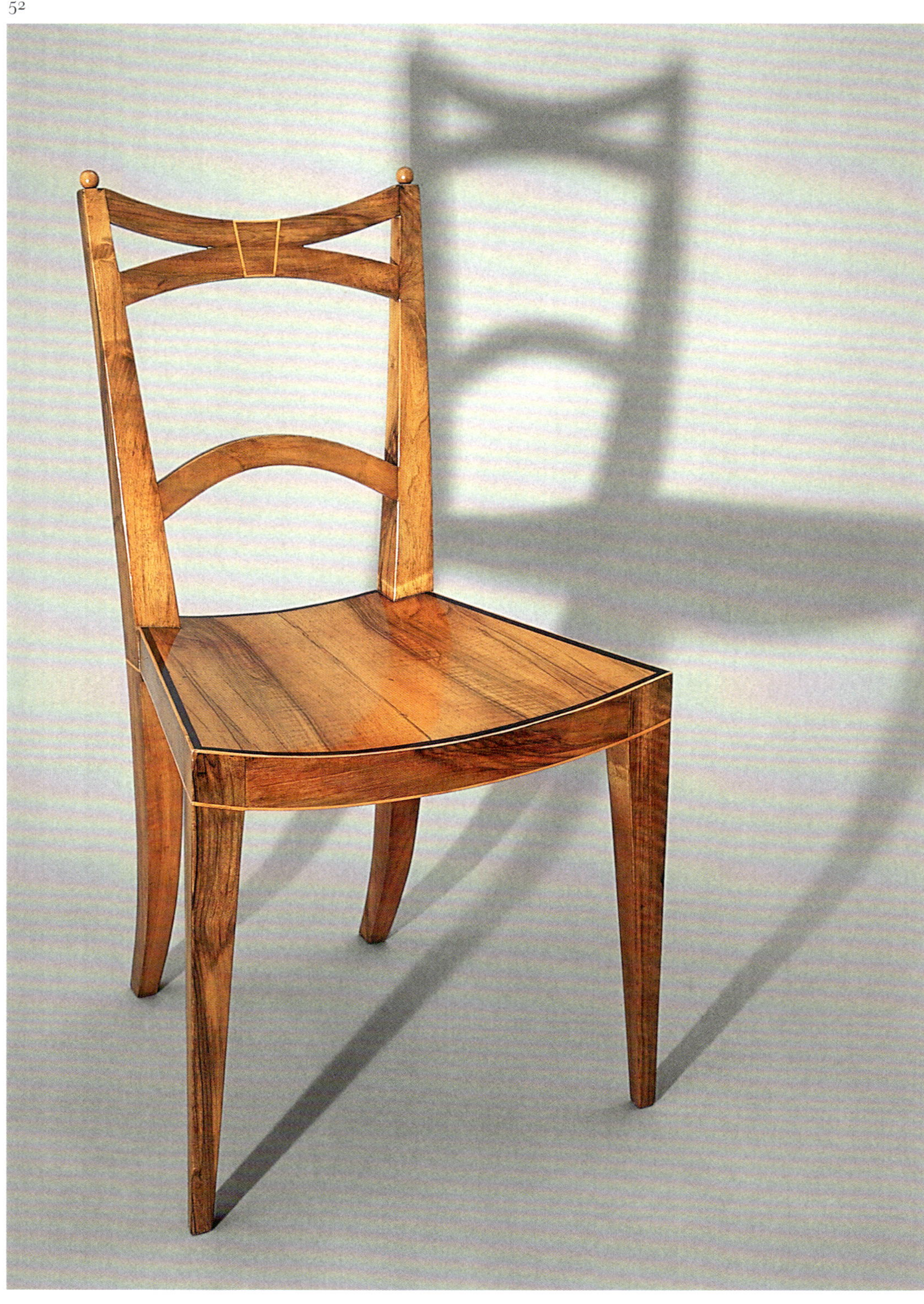

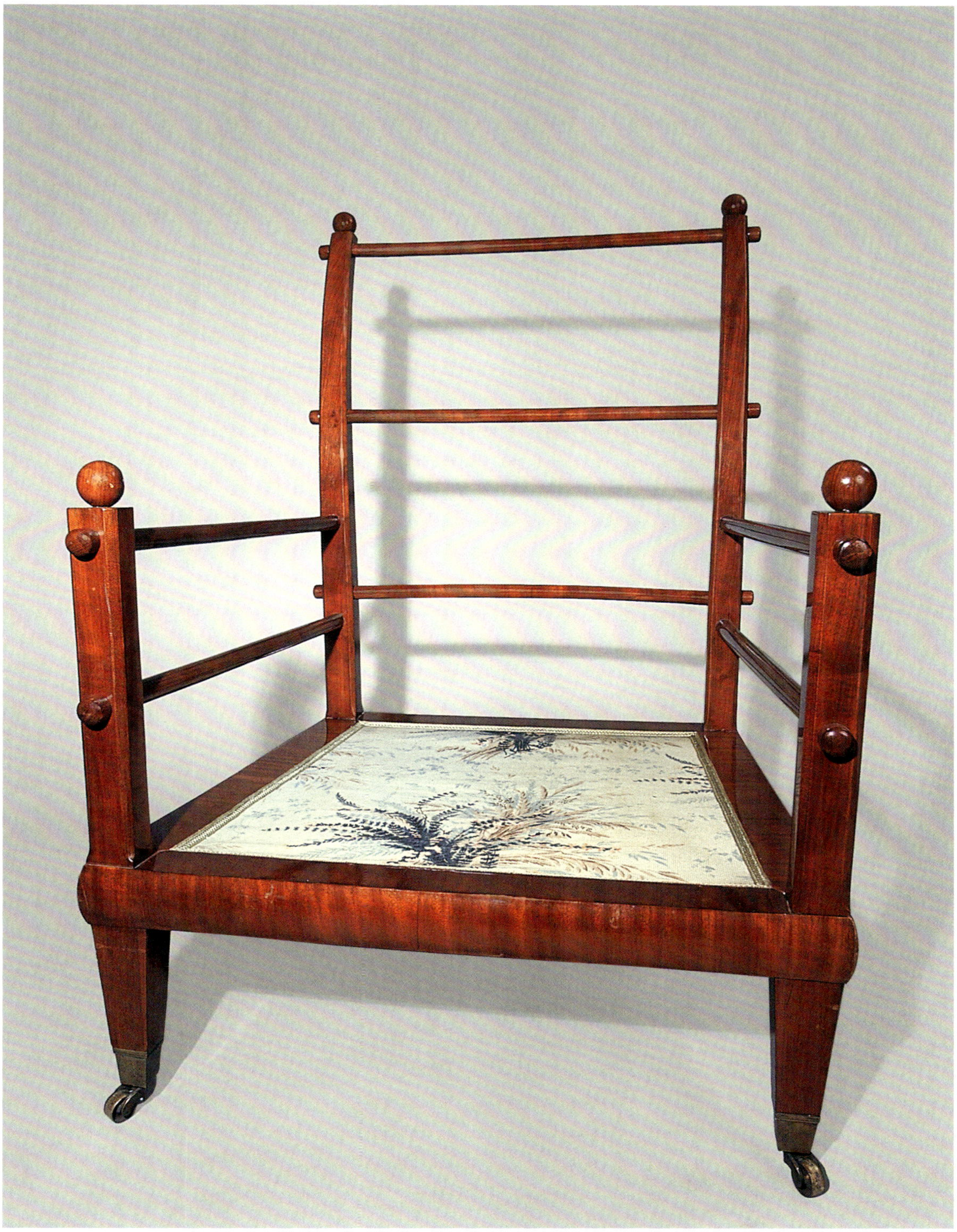

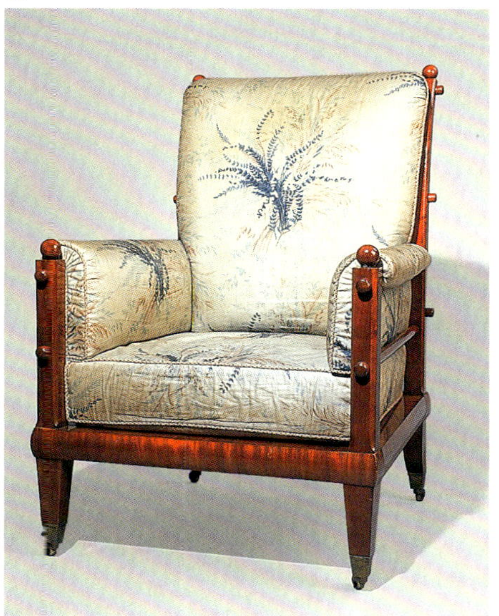

53

54
Pair of Armchairs
Austria, ca. 1830
Cat. II-34

55
Pair of Armchairs
Austria (?), 1825/30
Cat. II-33 (one of pair)

56
Settee
Austria, ca. 1820
Cat. II-36

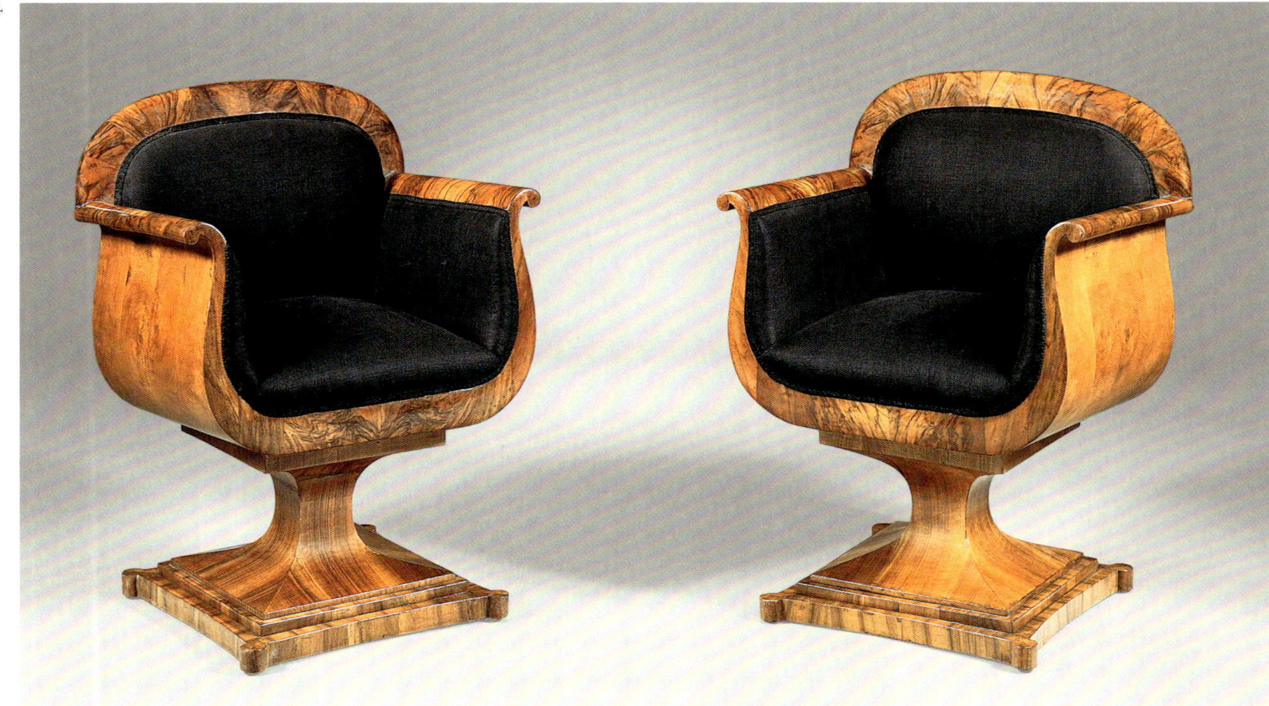

54

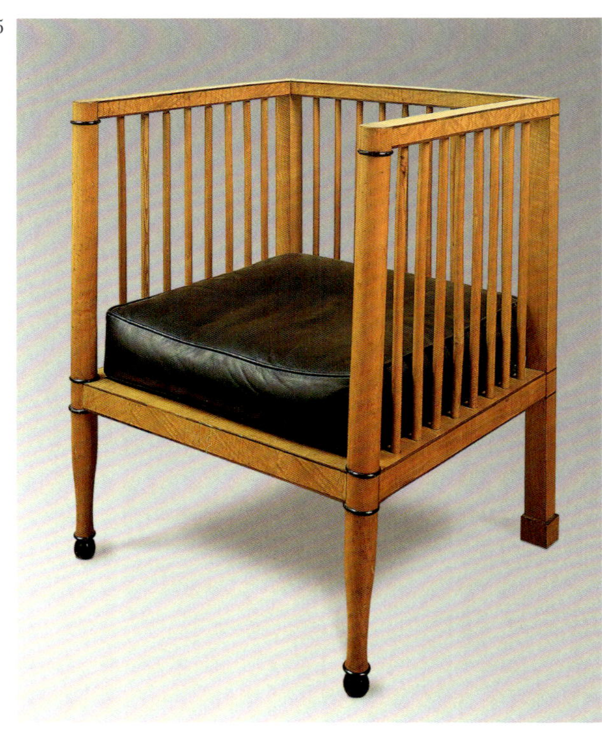

55

56

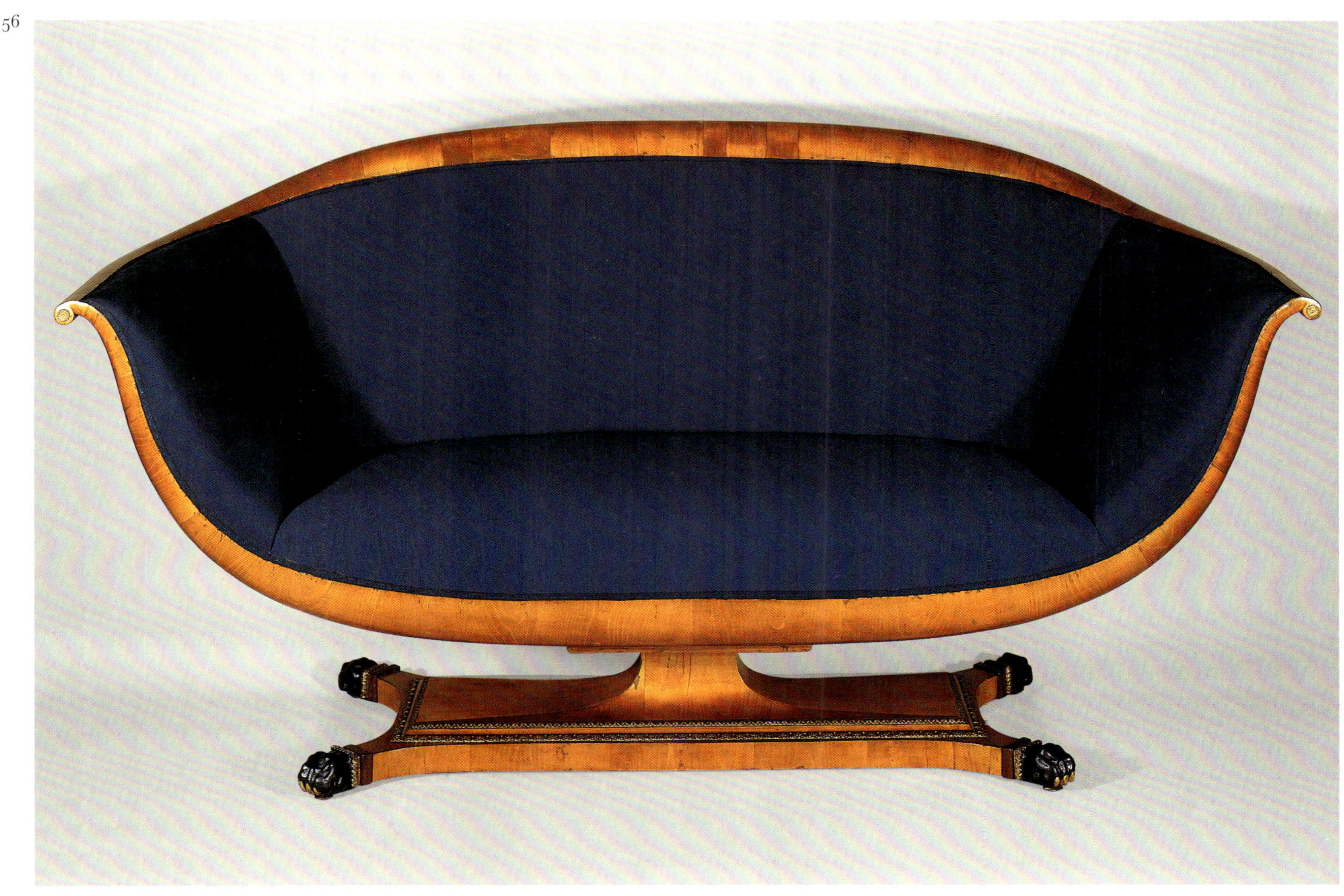

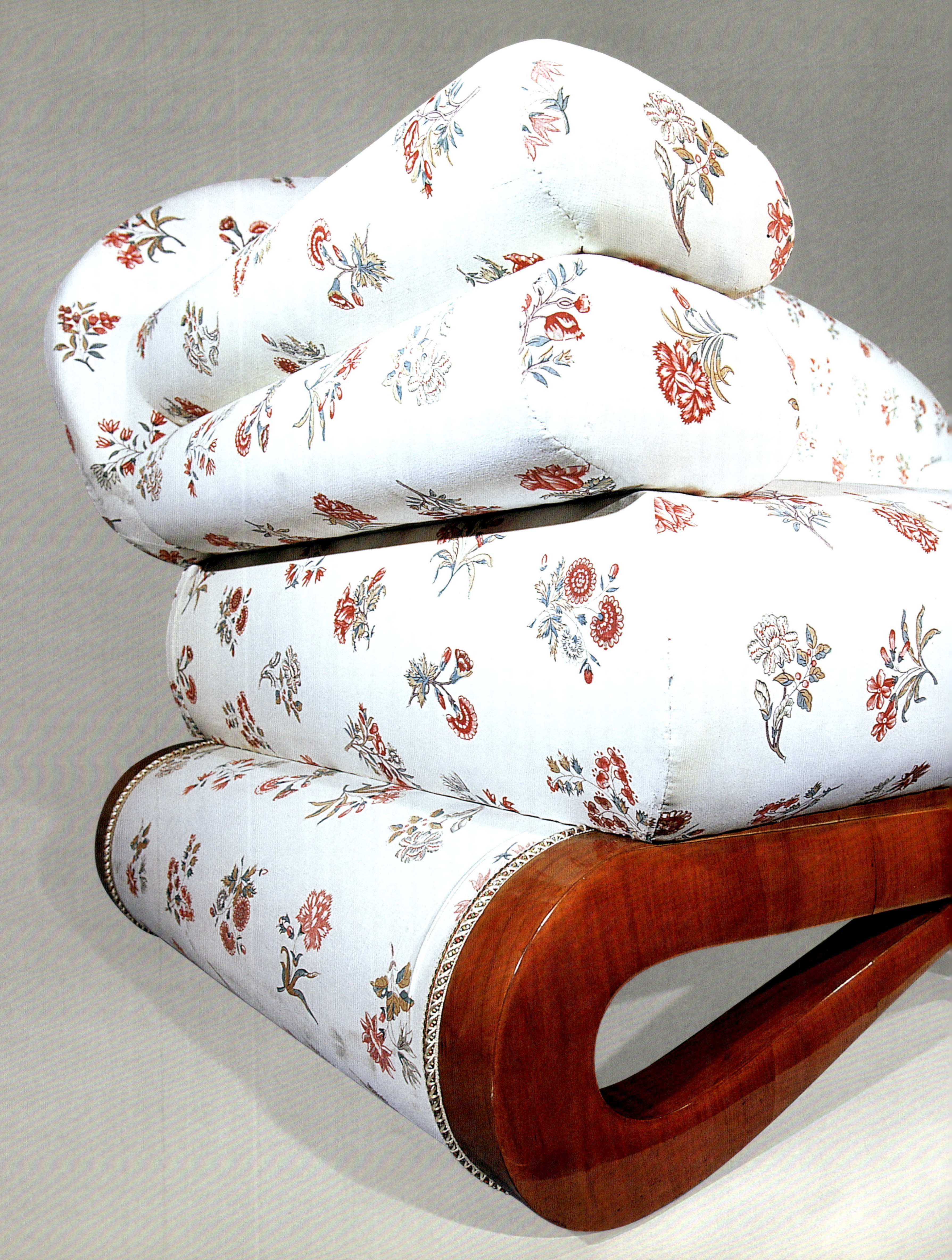

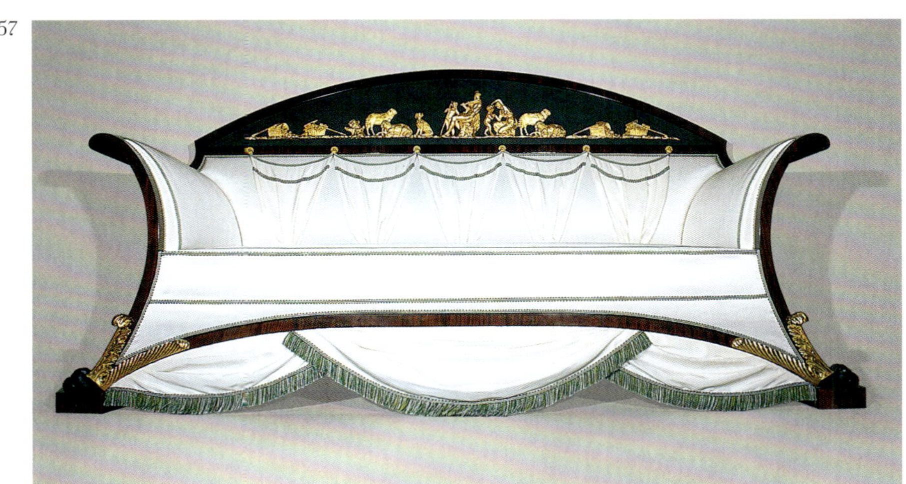

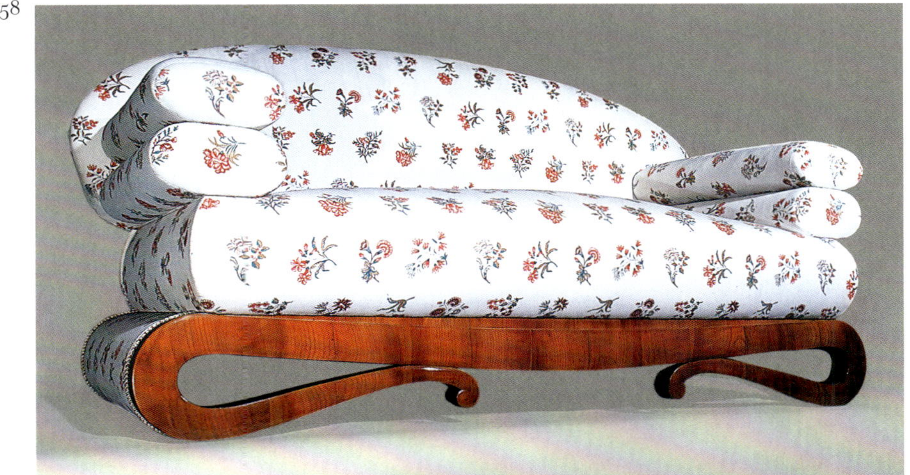

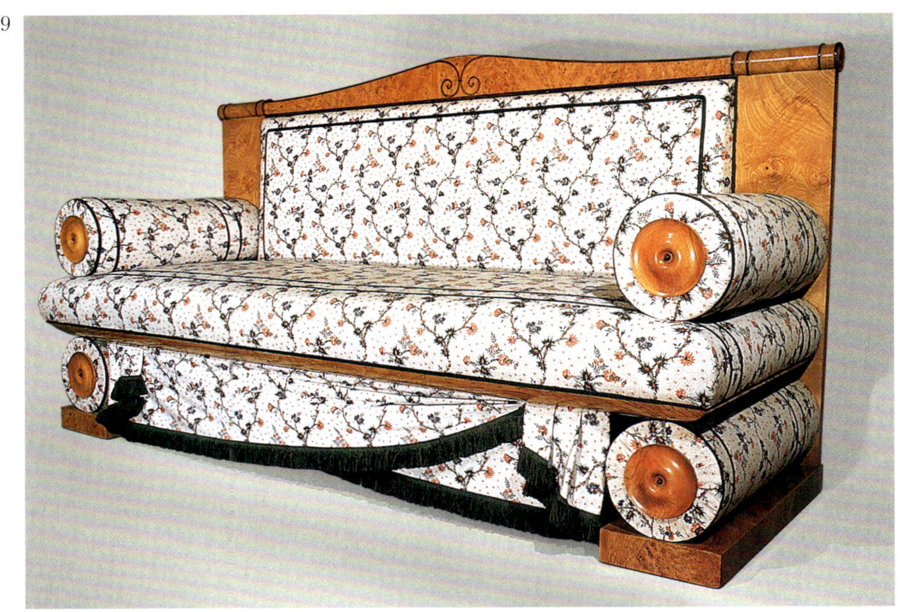

57
Settee
Vienna, ca. 1815
Cat. II-35

58
Settee
Vienna, 1825/30
Cat. II-37

59
Settee
Vienna, 1825/30
Cat. II-38

60
Settee
Vienna, 1825/30
Cat. II-39

61
Settee
Vienna, 1825/30
Cat. II-40

62
Settee
Vienna, ca. 1830
Cat. II-41

60

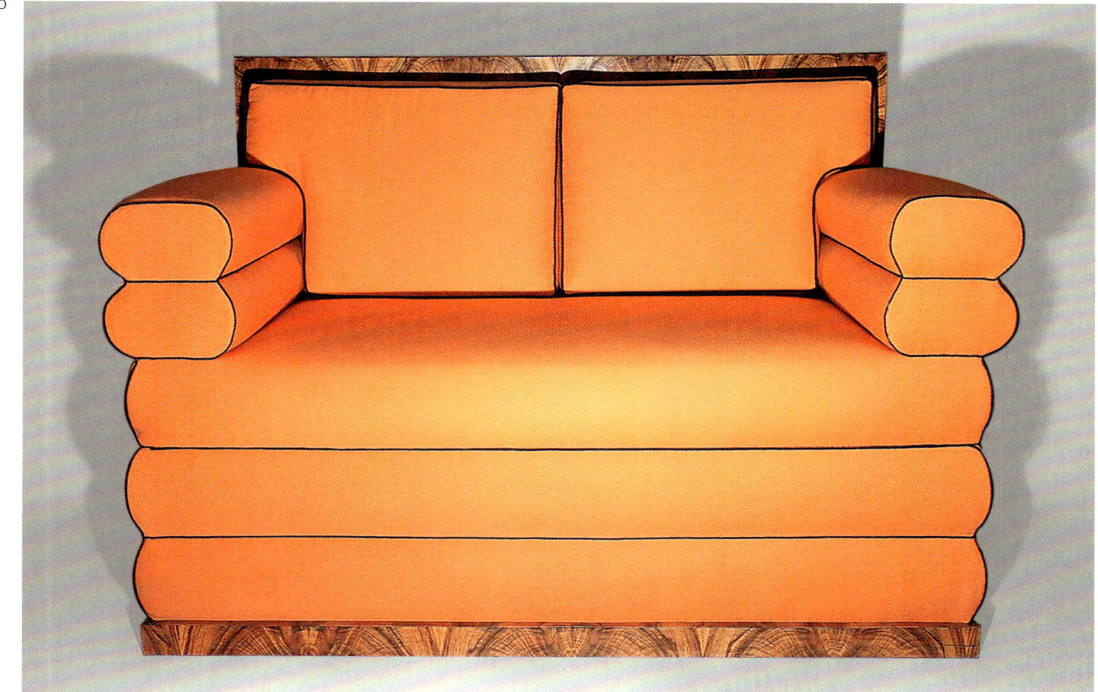

61

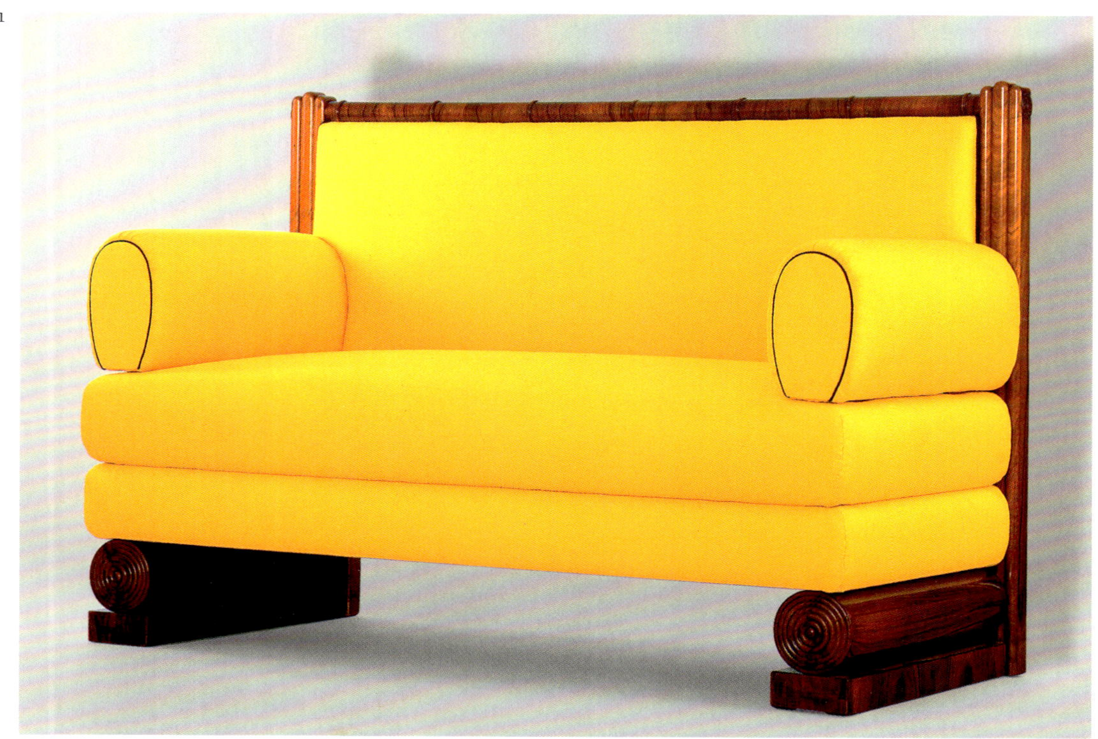

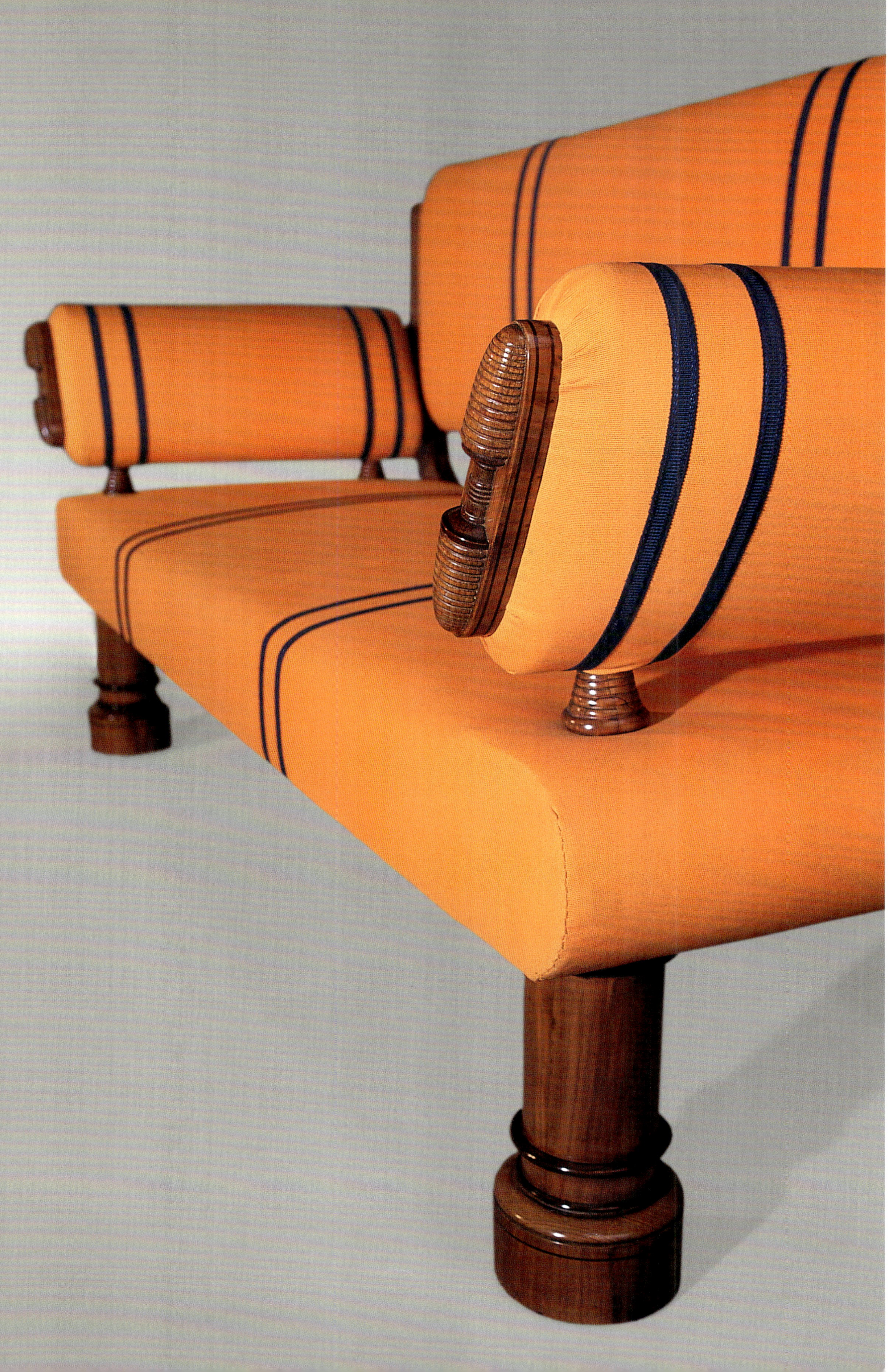

63
Daybed
Vienna, 1825/30
Cat. II-42

63

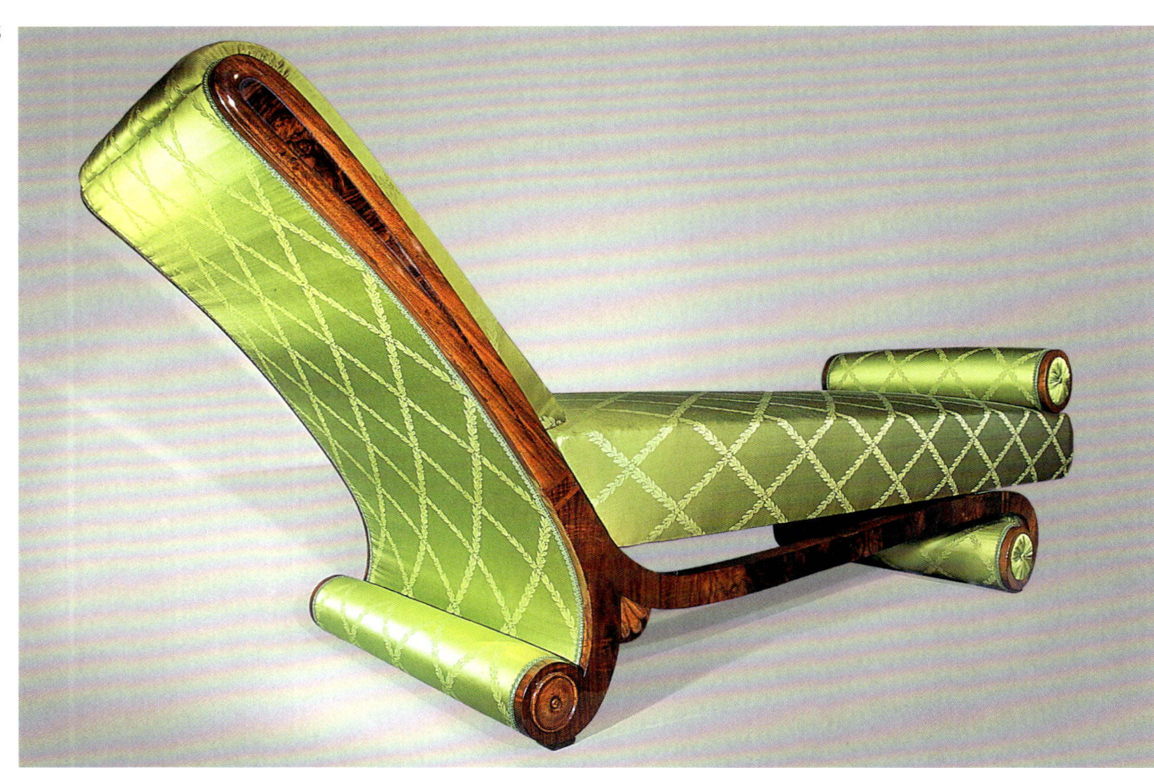

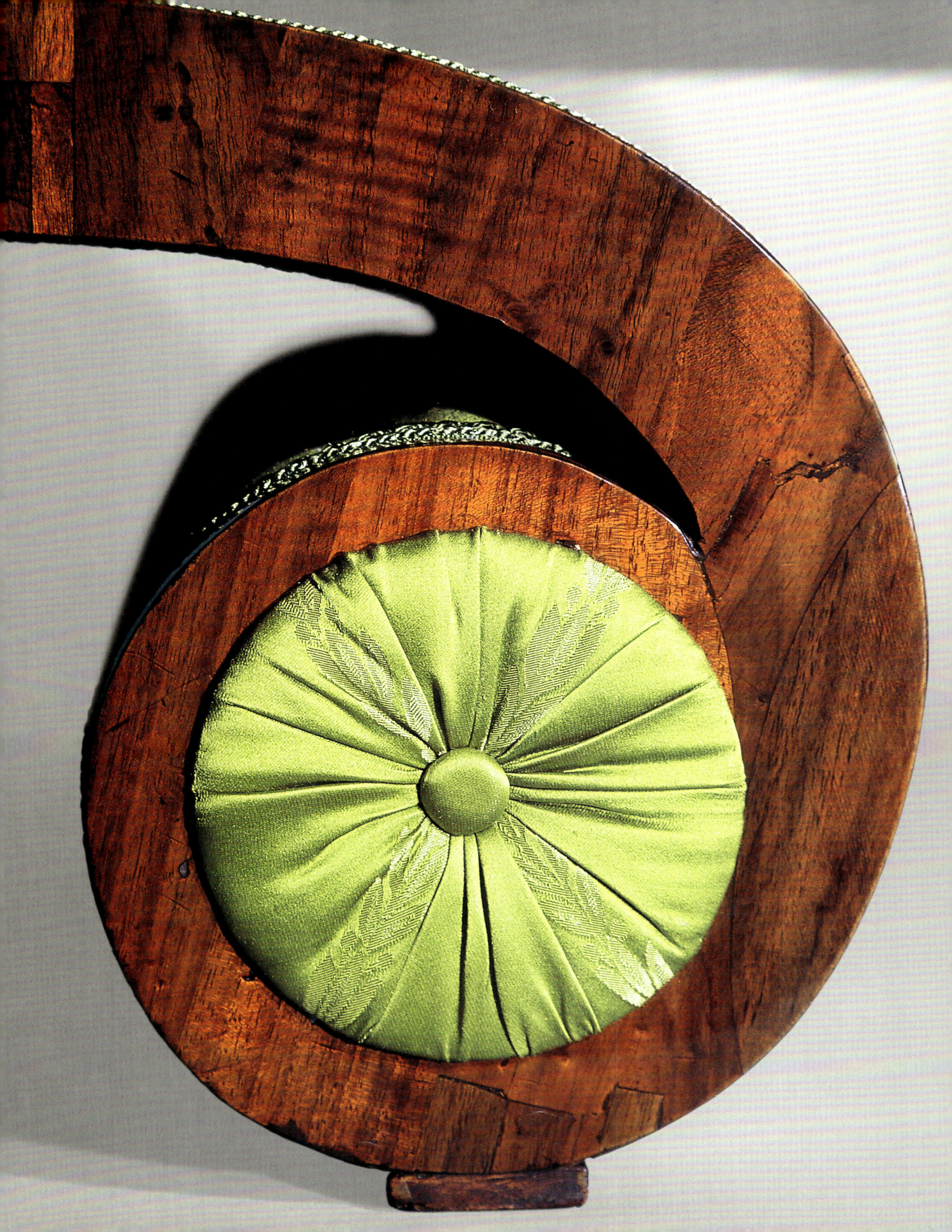

CABINETMAKERS' DRAWINGS

SECTION III

Christian Witt-Dörring

Furniture drawings prepared in drawing classes for cabinetmakers, known as master's drafts, and drawings of completed items of furniture are an indispensable source of information on the furniture culture of the first half of the nineteenth century. Since German and Austrian furniture was seldom signed or dated, these drawings represent one of the few sources of reliable dates of origin and provenance and thus provide insight into shifting trends in furniture fashion.

In drawing classes for cabinetmakers, young craftsmen not only learned the technical principles of drawing and illustration in perspective but were also familiarized with the most important forms of classicist ornamentation and classical column configuration. City academies and guilds placed a high premium on the ability of cabinetmakers to express their ideas in drawings. Therefore, the submission of a drawing of a candidate's master project was a prerequisite for admission to the master's examination. This requirement was meant to ensure that a master cabinetmaker could communicate his ideas to his clients.

One of the most significant collections of furniture drawings is the group of some 2,000 sheets from the Danhauser'sche Möbelfabrik (1814–42) in Vienna. The group also served as the company's catalogue and contains not only furniture but other elements of interior design as well, including designs for curtains, lamps, and furniture decorations. Particularly interesting are the seating furniture illustrations, which represent one of the few extant reliable sources of materials on upholstery design. Few examples of upholstery from the period have been preserved, largely because of the fragility of the materials and the fact that tastes were constantly changing. As a consequence, fully upholstered, fabric-covered, multiseat furniture, in particular, has survived for the most part only in the form of drawings.

64
*Patterns for
Small Tables*
Copenhagen, 1826
Cat. III-3

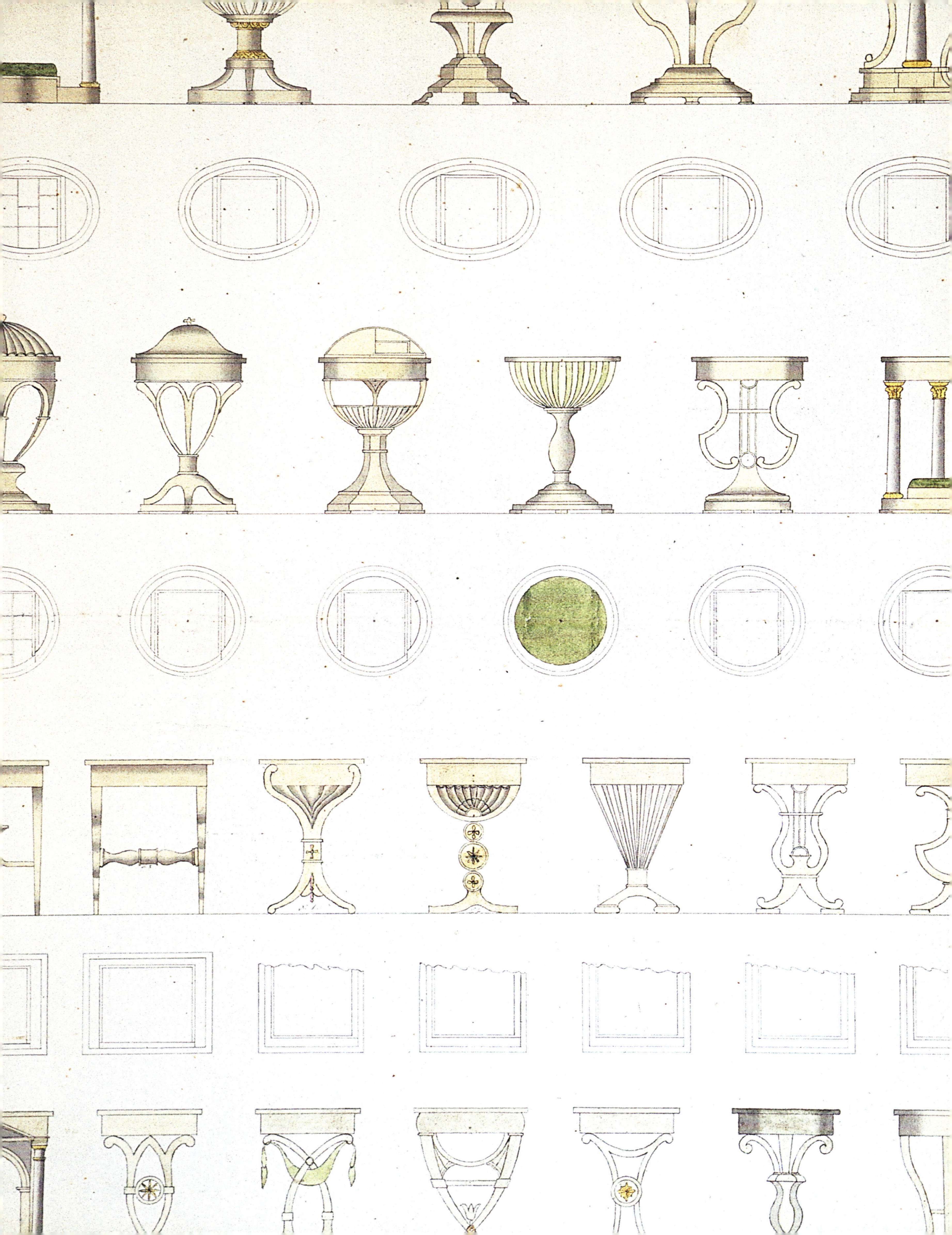

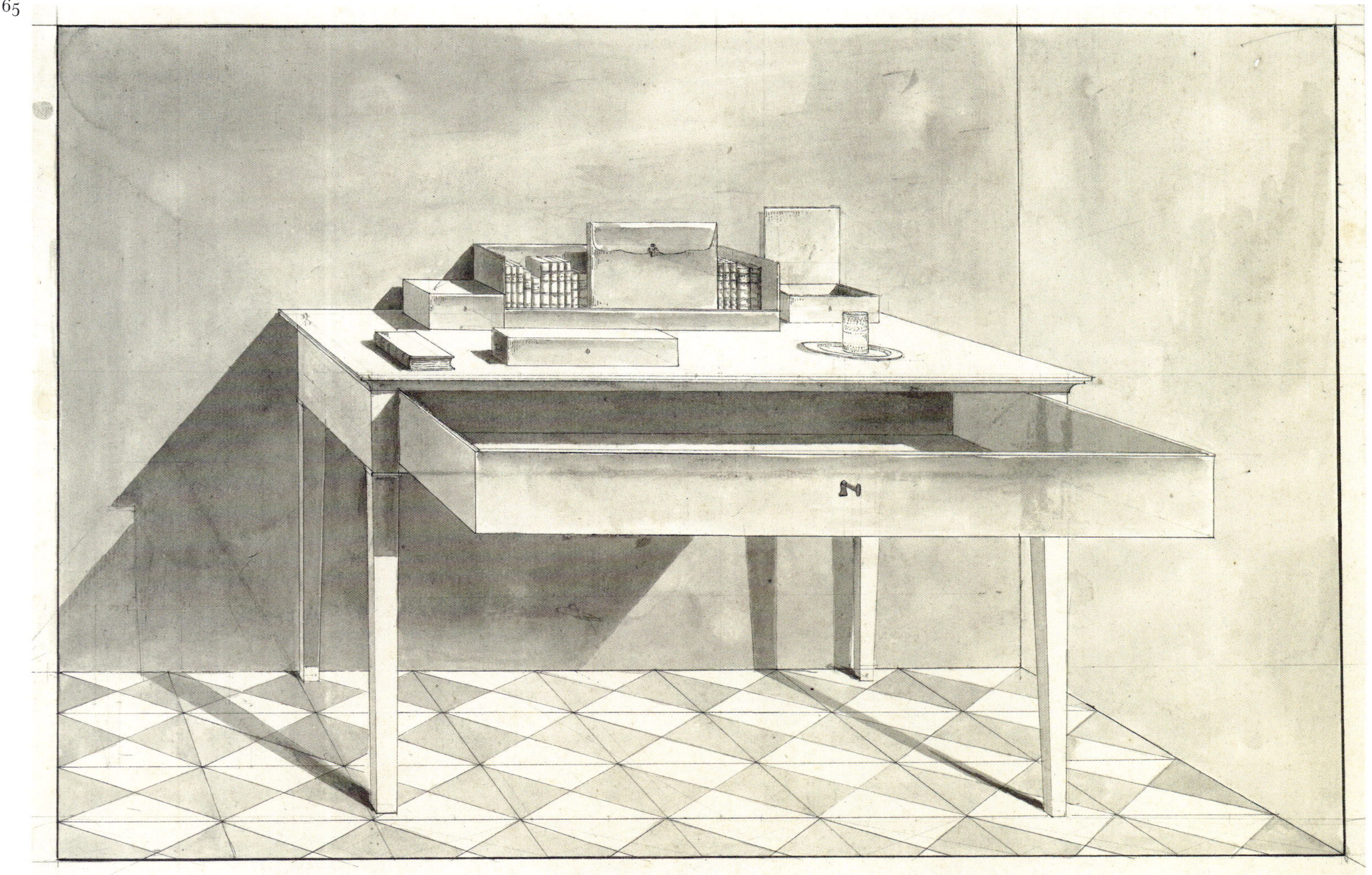
65

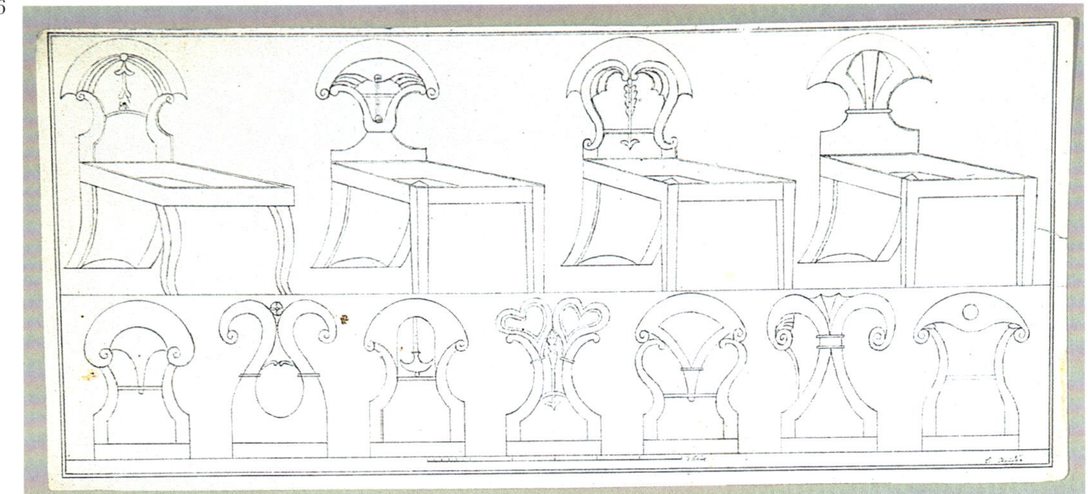

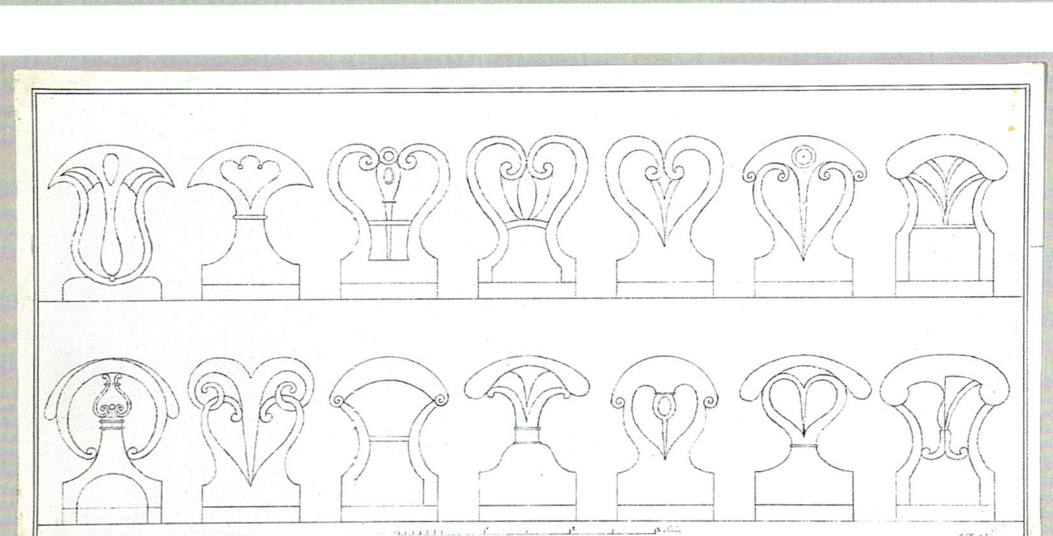

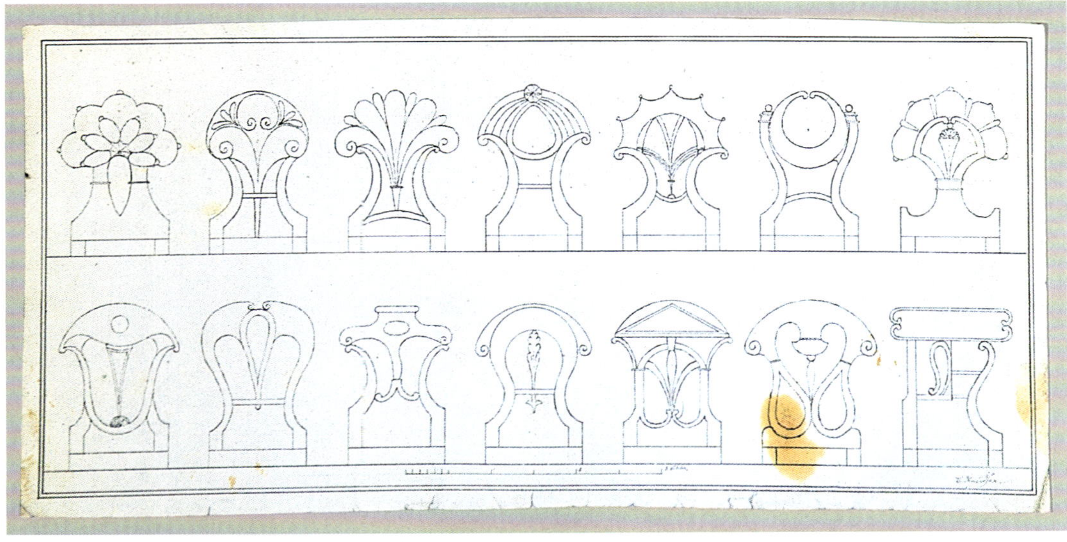

65
*Drawing for
a Simple Table*
Vienna, ca. 1815
Cat. III-1

66
Patterns for Chairs
Copenhagen, 1826
Cat. III-2

67
*Design Drawing for
Two Writing Cabinets:
Elevation, Cross
Section, Groundplan*
Copenhagen, ca. 1820
Cat. III-5

68
*Design for a Writing
Cabinet: Elevation,
Cross Section,
Groundplan*
Copenhagen, 1810/25
Cat. III-4

69
*Design Drawing for a
Writing Cabinet: Cross
Section, Oblique View
(open), Groundplan*
Austria, 1825
Cat. III-6

70
*Drawing for a Settee or
Tea Table: Front View,
Side View with Part of
Cross Section, Top View
of the Pedestal with
Groundplan*
Vienna, 1819
Cat. III-7

67

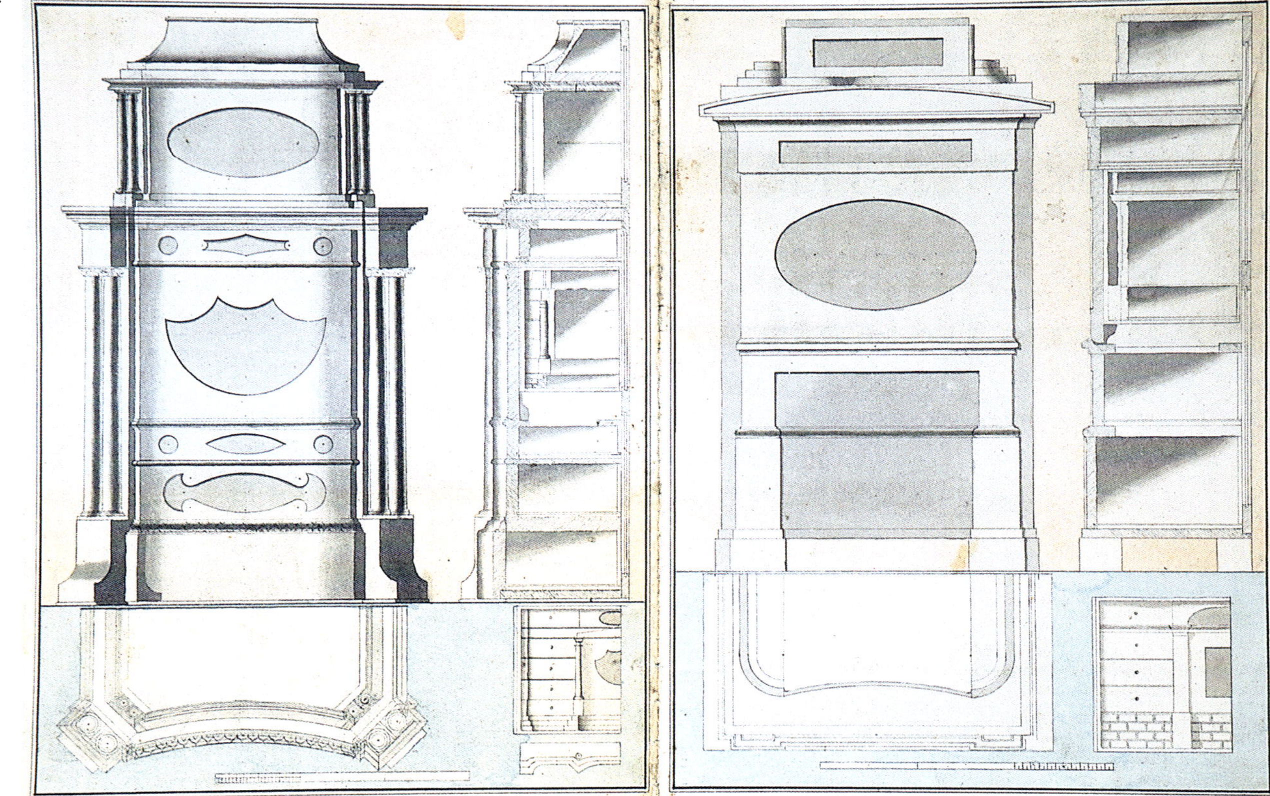

68

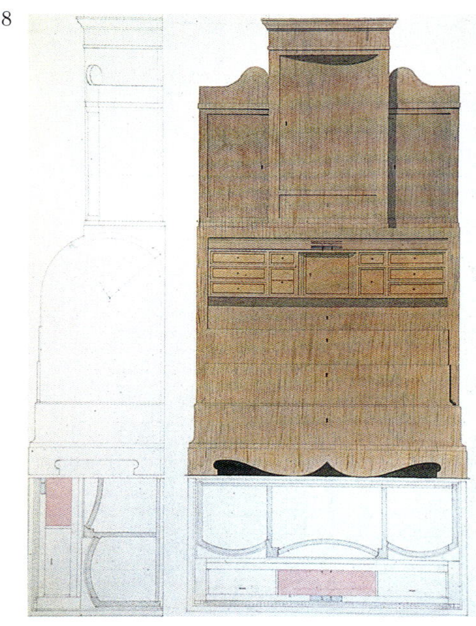

69

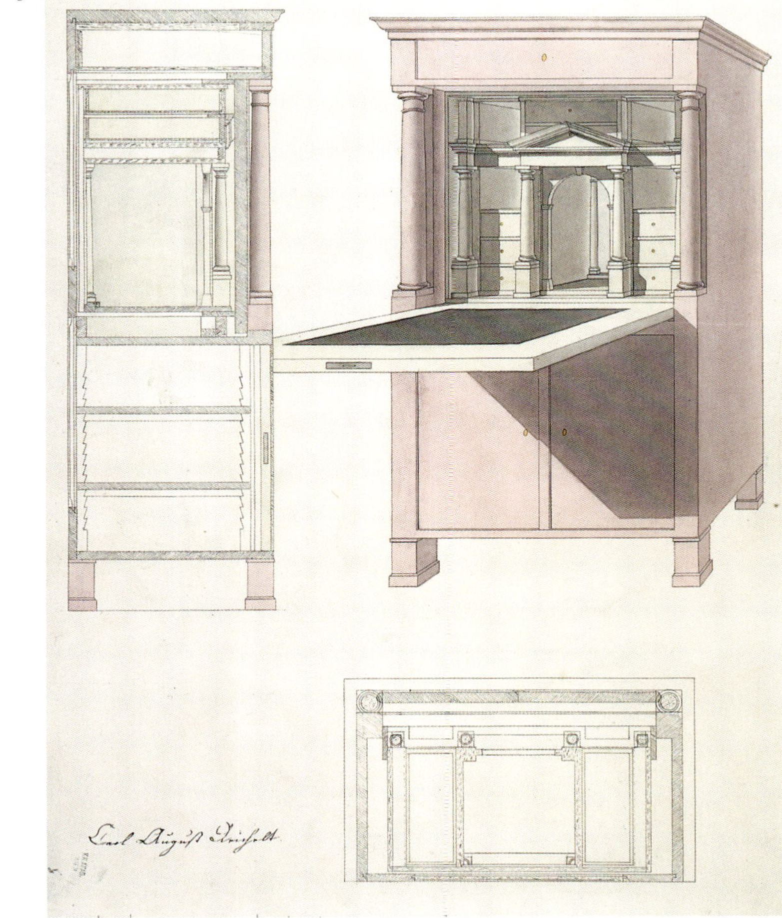

70

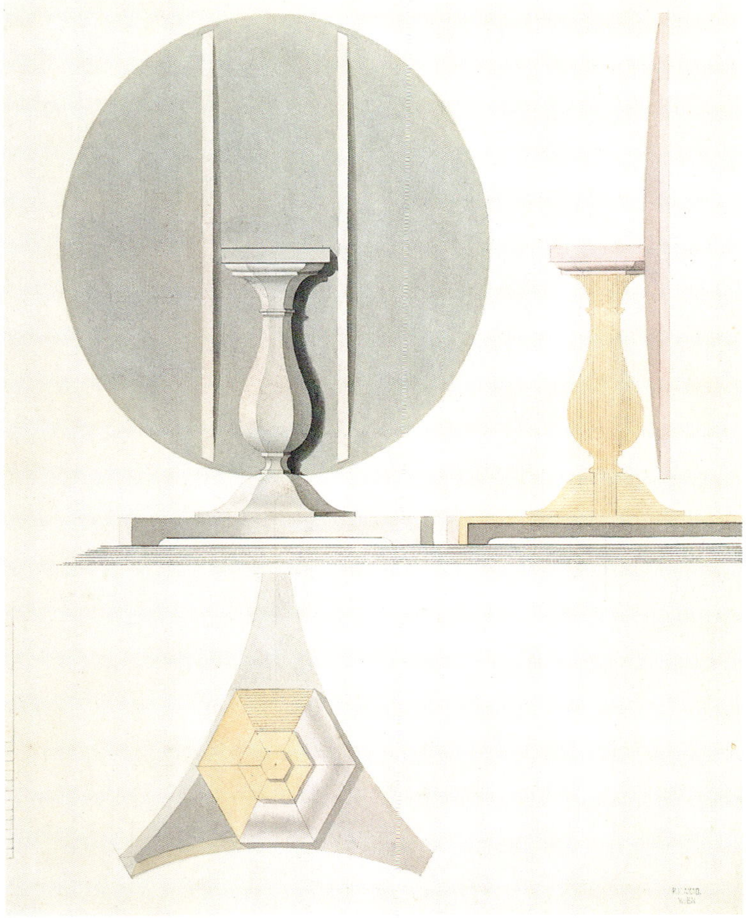

71

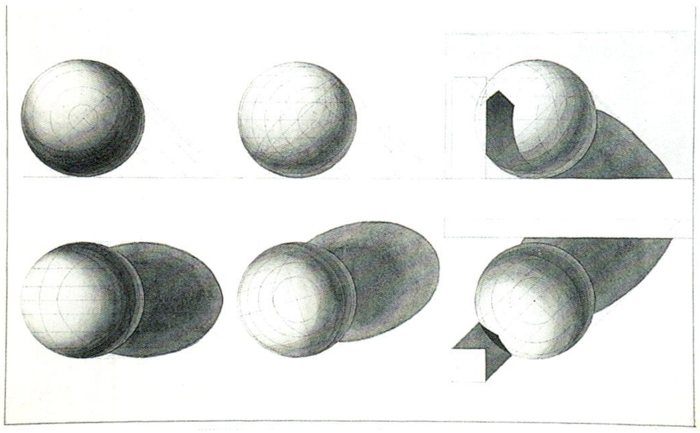

72

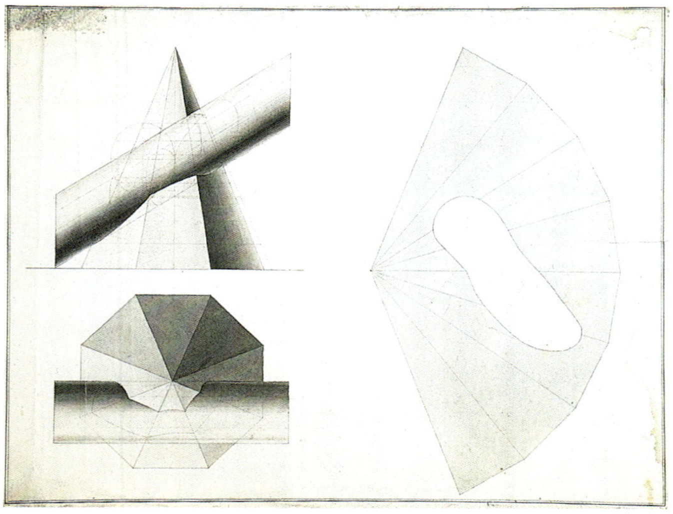

73

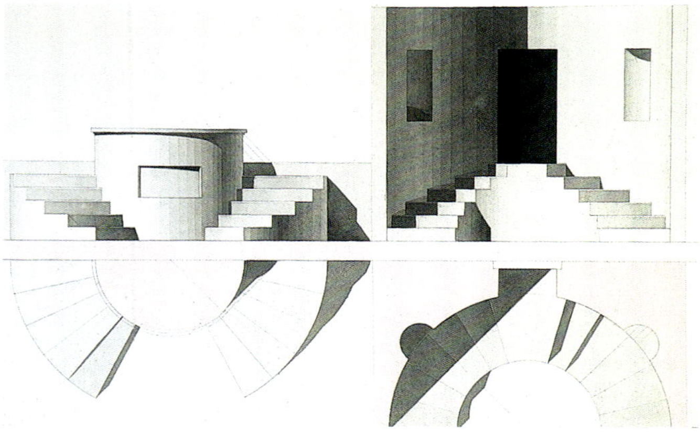

74

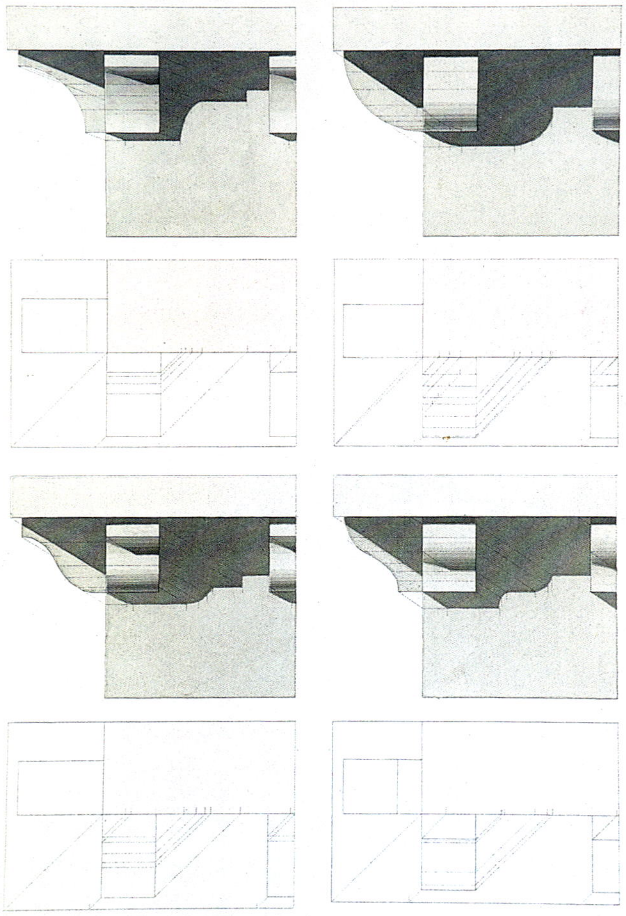

75

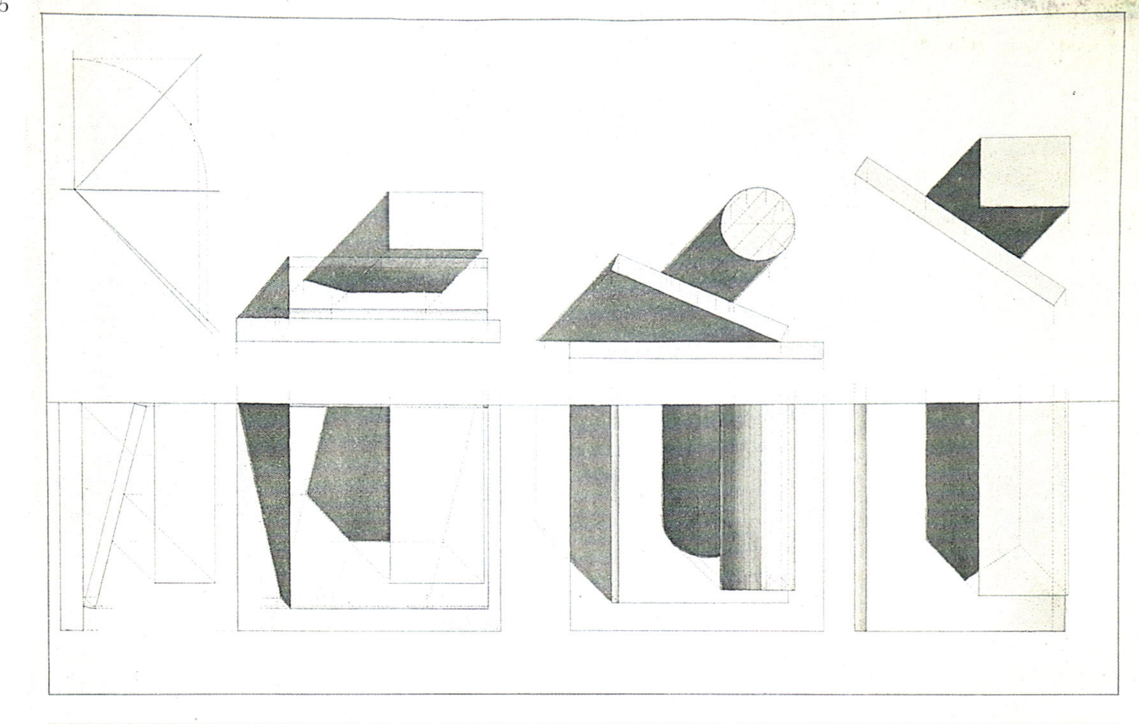

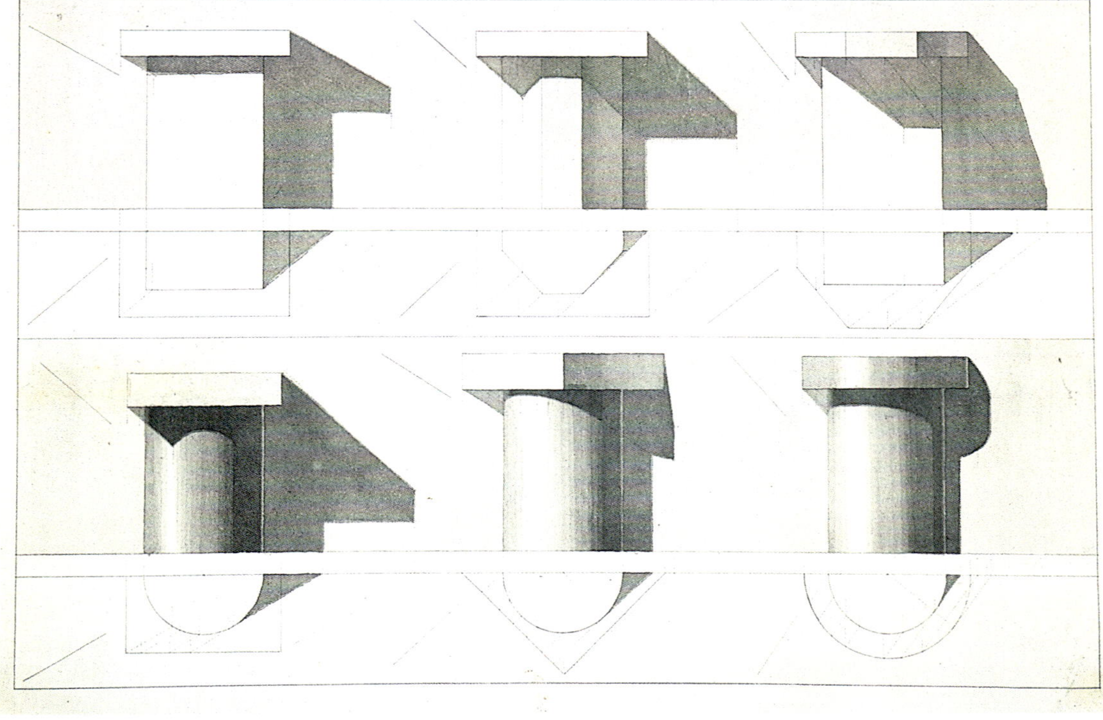

71
*Six Views of the Linear
Light-Dark Gradation of
a Ball with Shadowing*
Copenhagen, 1820
Cat. III-8

72
*Three Views of the
Interface of Roll
Molding and
Octahedron: Elevation,
Cross Section,
Groundplan*
Copenhagen, ca. 1820
Cat. III-9

73
*Two Views of a
Stepped Gradation of a
Crowning Ornament*
Copenhagen, ca. 1820
Cat. III-10

74
*Four Views of Moldings:
Elevation, Groundplan*
Copenhagen, ca. 1820
Cat. III-11

75
*Six Views of Pilaster
Moldings with Plinths:
Elevation, Groundplan*
Copenhagen, ca. 1820
Cat. III-12

INTERIOR VIEWS

SECTION IV

Laurie A. Stein

"The interior is not just the universe but also the container of the private individual. To dwell means to leave traces. In the interior, these are accentuated" (Walter Benjamin, 1935, in Benjamin 1999, pp. 8-9).

From the perspective of the present day, the term "Biedermeier" conjures thoughts about an aesthetic of the past based on beauty of materials, simplicity of forms, modest sensibilities, and an atmosphere of informal domesticity. These notions have been shaped by the surviving traces of Biedermeier found in furniture, glassware, metalwork, and ceramics, and, most profoundly, by a group of surviving interior watercolors, known as "Zimmerbilder," or room images. The Zimmerbilder provide a remarkable body of memorialized visual information. They serve as mirrors into the world of the Biedermeier culture, and "bear witness to the degree of involvement with which the people of the period fashioned their personal surroundings and to their desire to document it" (Waissenberger 1986, p. 109).

The Zimmerbilder were usually commissioned as private gifts and have been preserved chiefly in European royal collections, including the Wittelsbacher Ausgleichsfonds in Munich, the Hessische Hausstiftung in Darmstadt and Eichenzell, and the Royal Collection at Windsor Castle. They have been kept as albums and passed down through royal inheritance. Additionally, individual sheets of aristocratic and bourgeois interiors can be found in the collections of historical museums such as the Germanisches Nationalmuseum Nürnberg, the Stiftung Stadtmuseum Berlin, and the Historisches Museum der Stadt Wien.

The genre of the Zimmerbilder blossomed during the first half of the nineteenth century. The earliest examples are from Vienna and Munich and date from around 1815-20, and thereafter from 1828 in Berlin. Their genealogy can be traced to precedents such as Dutch still lifes and French interior drawings and architectural designs, but as an independent genre, the Zimmerbilder are most uniquely associated with Germanic Biedermeier culture.

Zimmerbilder can be understood as visual evidence, almost in the tradition of written documentary inventories. A Biedermeier Zimmerbild, such as *My Room in Vienna*, 1837/42, is a room portrait, detailing with remarkable objectivity the furnishings and decoration of a particular interior at a particular time, and providing a glimpse of furniture types and arrangements, styles and choices of wallpapers, carpets, upholstery, and even the kinds of souvenirs and works of art that serve as decorations. The subject matter of most Zimmerbilder is the private domestic interior, attesting to the place of the individual within the social community and to his or her taste and lifestyle. The works can be read as self-representations, as bridges between "Sein und Schein" (being and appearance) (Börsch-Supan 1976, pp. 9-10).

Beauty came to be judged based on simplicity and on the quality of individual objects rather than on abundant luxury or gilded style. For the wealthy commercial and cultural classes, "The cult of simplicity developed itself as a principle of beauty in contrast to the luxurious style of the close of the eighteenth century. Whoever could afford to pay for it, acquired new decoration in the new style of unpretentiousness"(Ottomeyer 1994, p. 83). And what better embodiment of social and material acquisition could there be than a portrait of one's private realm?

Beyond the intelligibility of the Zimmerbilder as status indicators or documentary inventories, the interior images are replete with further layers of symbolic function and intention. A Zimmerbild was intended to evoke in the recipient either memory or expectation, and was generally commissioned at a moment of life transition, for example, to memorialize a family member who had died, to serve as a souvenir for a child who had married and moved away, or as a form of personal letter or diary entry. Sometimes, numerous copies were prepared and gifted to different recipients.

The user of an interior is always present in the traces of his domestic space; thus, a Zimmerbild can be understood as an abstracted portrait of the inhabitant. For example, a watercolor *Study of Grand Duke Ludwig II of Darmstadt* shows the grand duke's books and papers strewn about as if he had just left the room. Several versions of this image are known, dating variously to around 1846-49. Since Ludwig passed away in 1848, the choice to commission the image posthumously takes on added meaning, evoking his lingering presence in the empty space. In a

contrasting manner, the exceptionally beautiful gouache *Room in the Apartment of Princess
Elisabeth*, ca. 1840, was a gift from the princess'
parents after she had moved to her new marital
home in Darmstadt. It gives a glimpse of her child-
hood home in the Berlin Palace, and is powerfully
expressive through the stillness of the image, the
lack of personal clutter, and the absence of figural
representation. It was intended as a catalyst for
fond memory – a reminder to the young married
woman of her treasured early home.

Princess Elisabeth's drawing room had actually been furnished around 1825, when she was
eleven years old, which was fifteen years before
this watercolor was prepared. Another watercolor,
*Toilette Room in the Apartment of Prince Wilhelm
and Princess Marianne in the Royal Palace*, dated
1849, depicts that couple's bedroom in a state of
furnishings also from a much earlier time. The
practice of depicting an interior as a retrospective
moment was common in the Zimmerbilder genre.
These are souvenirs of mirrored memory, of life
lived in the past, and they encapsulate a struggle
against the transitory nature of existence and
the inevitability of change. One infers through
these Zimmerbilder an existence that can no longer be experienced.

In other cases, there exist multiple images
of the same interior, each showing the room with
different furnishings or arrangements. For
example, there are three extant images of one
interior, *Interior with Three Mirrors*, by Johann
Erdmann Hummel, each with differing furnishings
and figures. As exemplified by *A Room in Schönbrunn Palace*, ca. 1818, the figures in a Zimmerbild
are usually engaged in activities typical for the
room, such as embroidery, reading, or child's play.

Some painters of Zimmerbilder, such as
Eduard Gaertner and Johann Stephan Decker,
were respected court artists, but there were also
specialized "Zimmermaler." The format of most
Zimmerbilder is that of a "Guckkastenbühne," or
peep-hole theater. The overall image was usually
oriented through a perspective view into the room
from a point outside and on an axis shifted to the
left. Legibility is based on the Western norm of
reading from left to right; through the beholder's
reading, he satisfies his curiosity and his voyeurism,
and also becomes a participant in an exchange with
the depicted interior (Nuremberg 1995, p. 25).

The genre of the Zimmerbilder was essentially
a self-reflexive and hermetic one, and this aspect
hindered the expansion of the tradition beyond
the era of Biedermeier culture. The watercolors
were neither exhibited nor sold, but rather were
pasted into albums or souvenir collections, a
gendered pastime and one that made the works
inaccessible to outsiders. The albums themselves
became "mirror images of their owners: they
show their artistic sensibility, their educational
level and their relationship with relatives and
friends and beyond these are an instrument of self-
memory" (Eichenzell 2004, p. 27). Following the
Biedermeier era, the Zimmerbilder were relegated
to a rejected aesthetic past before the advent of
photography. But the memory of these cherished
domestic environments never quite expired. The
Zimmerbilder survived as visual reminders, passed
down through generations.

76

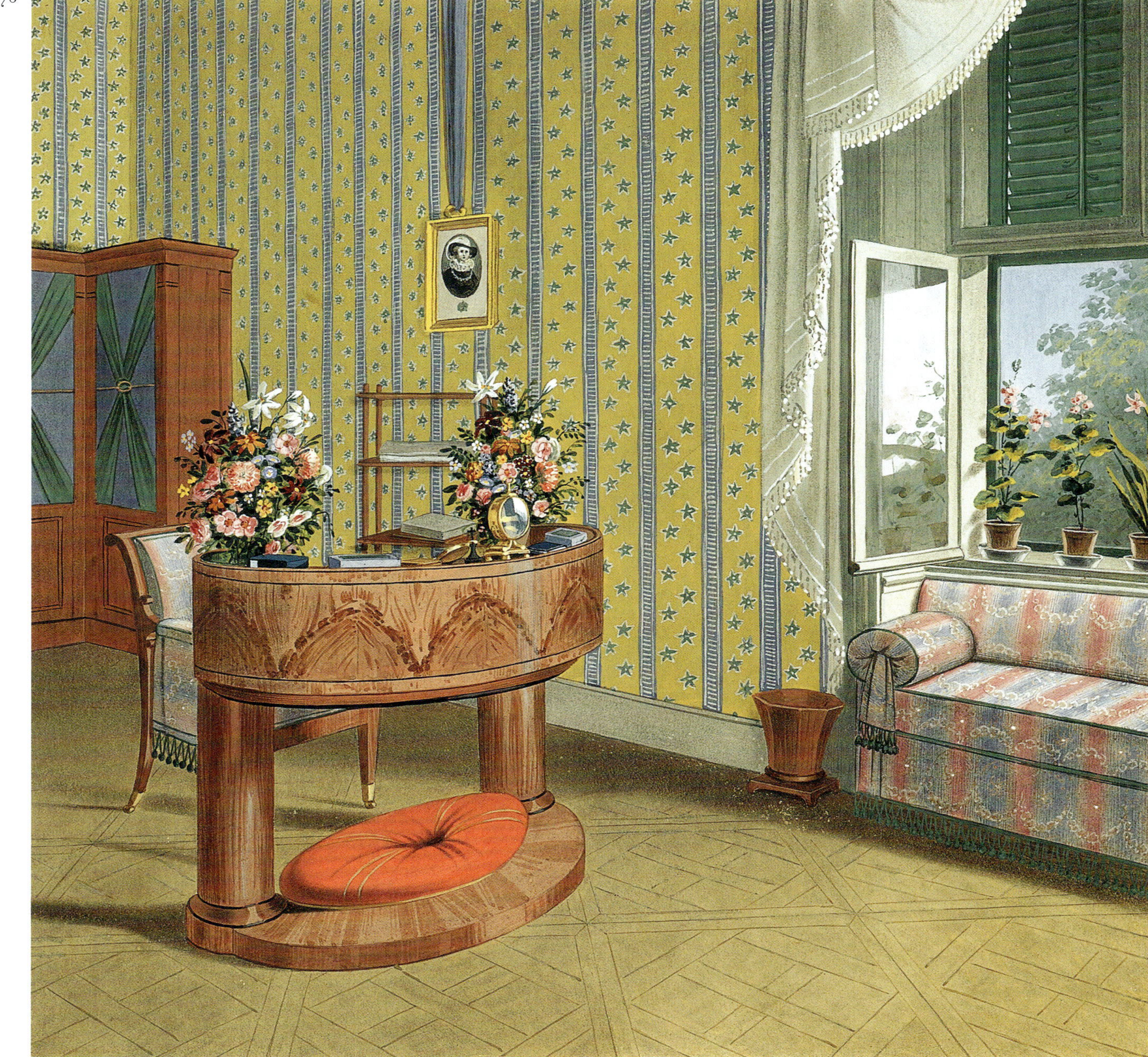

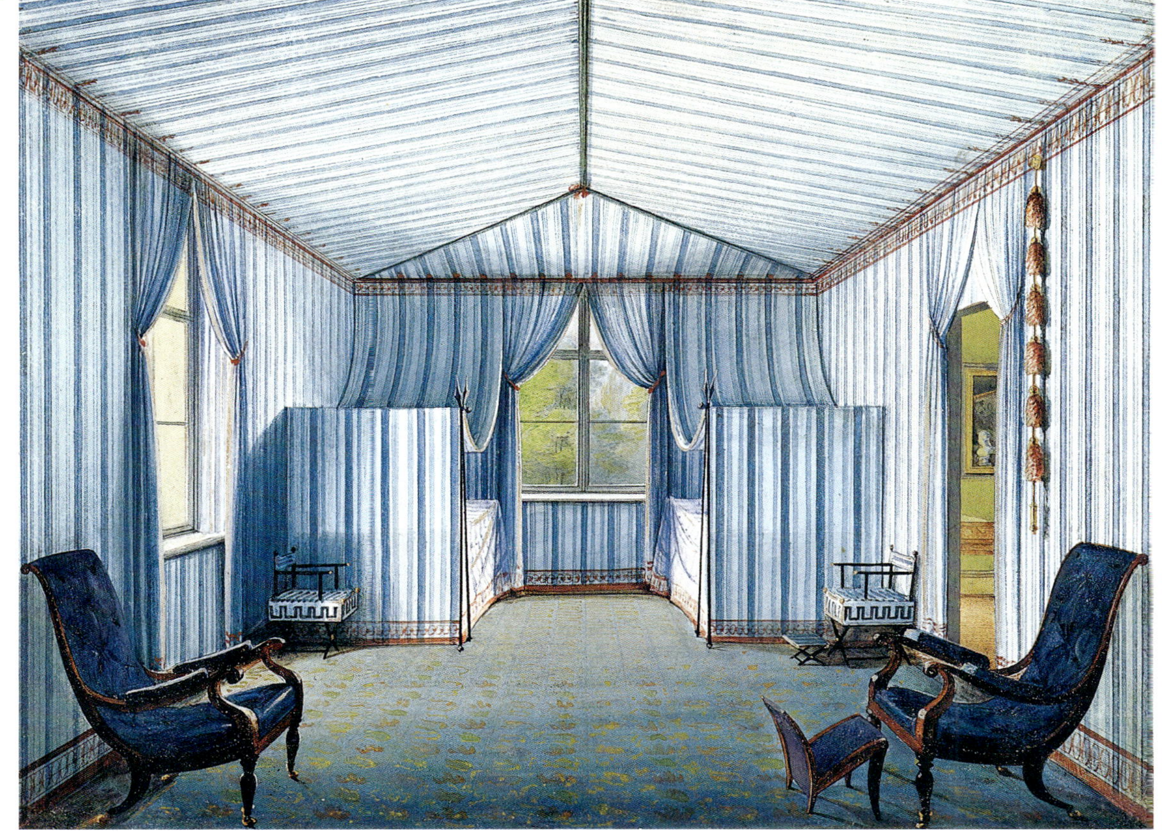

76
Johann Stephan Decker
*Room in the apartment
of Duchess Sophie in
Blauer Hof in Laxenburg*
Vienna, 1826
Cat. IV-1

77
Artist Unknown
*Tent Room,
Charlottenhof Palace*
Potsdam, after 1830
Cat. IV-2

78
Johann Erdmann
Hummel
*Interior with
Three Mirrors*
Berlin, ca. 1820
Cat. IV-3

79
Leopold Zielcke
*Erdmann Hummel
Teaching Perspective
at the Königliche
Akademie der Künste*
Berlin, ca. 1830
Cat. IV-4

80
Artist Unknown
*Living Room with
Laid Table*
Berlin, ca. 1830
Cat. IV-5

81
Artist Unknown
*Dining Room with
Laid Table*
Berlin, ca. 1840
Cat. IV-6

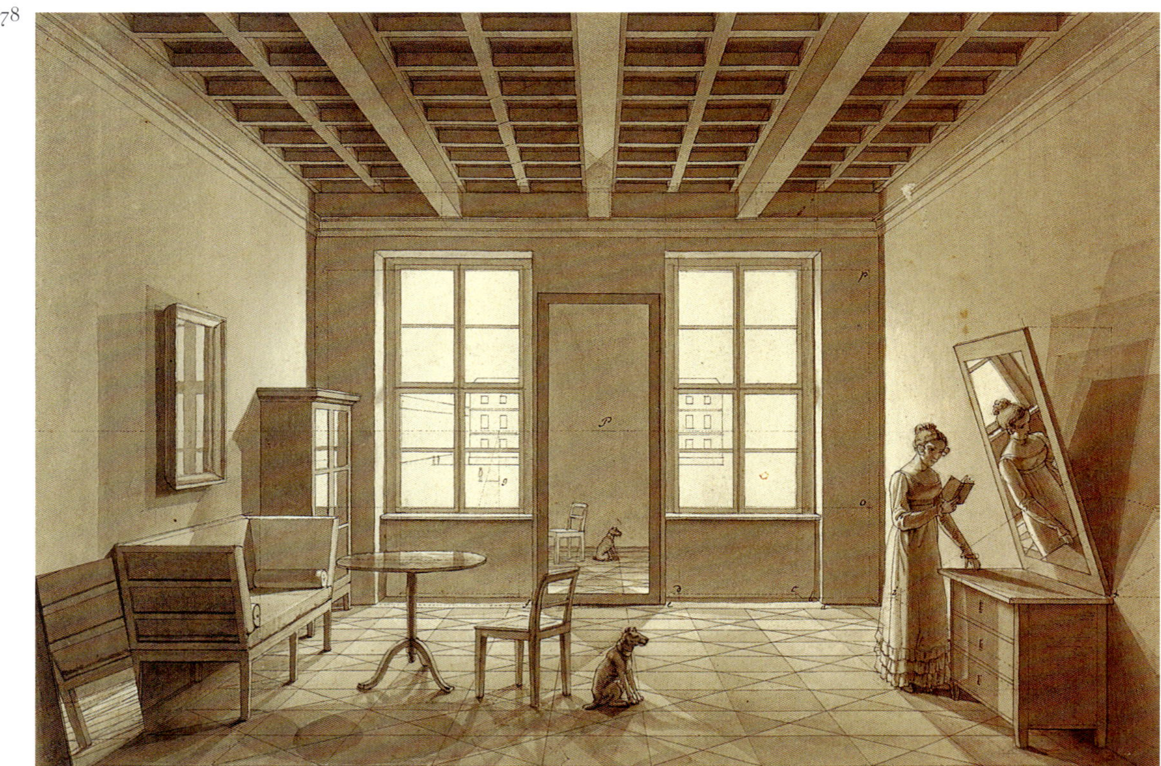

78

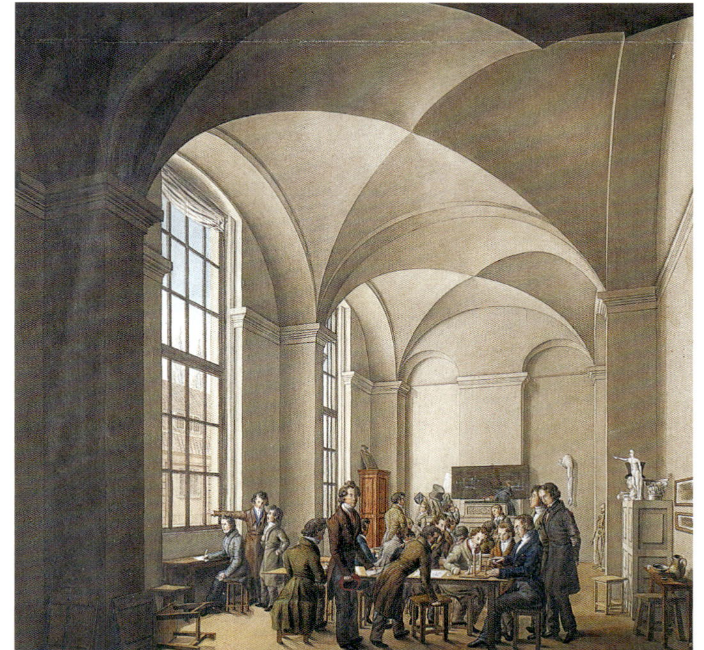

79

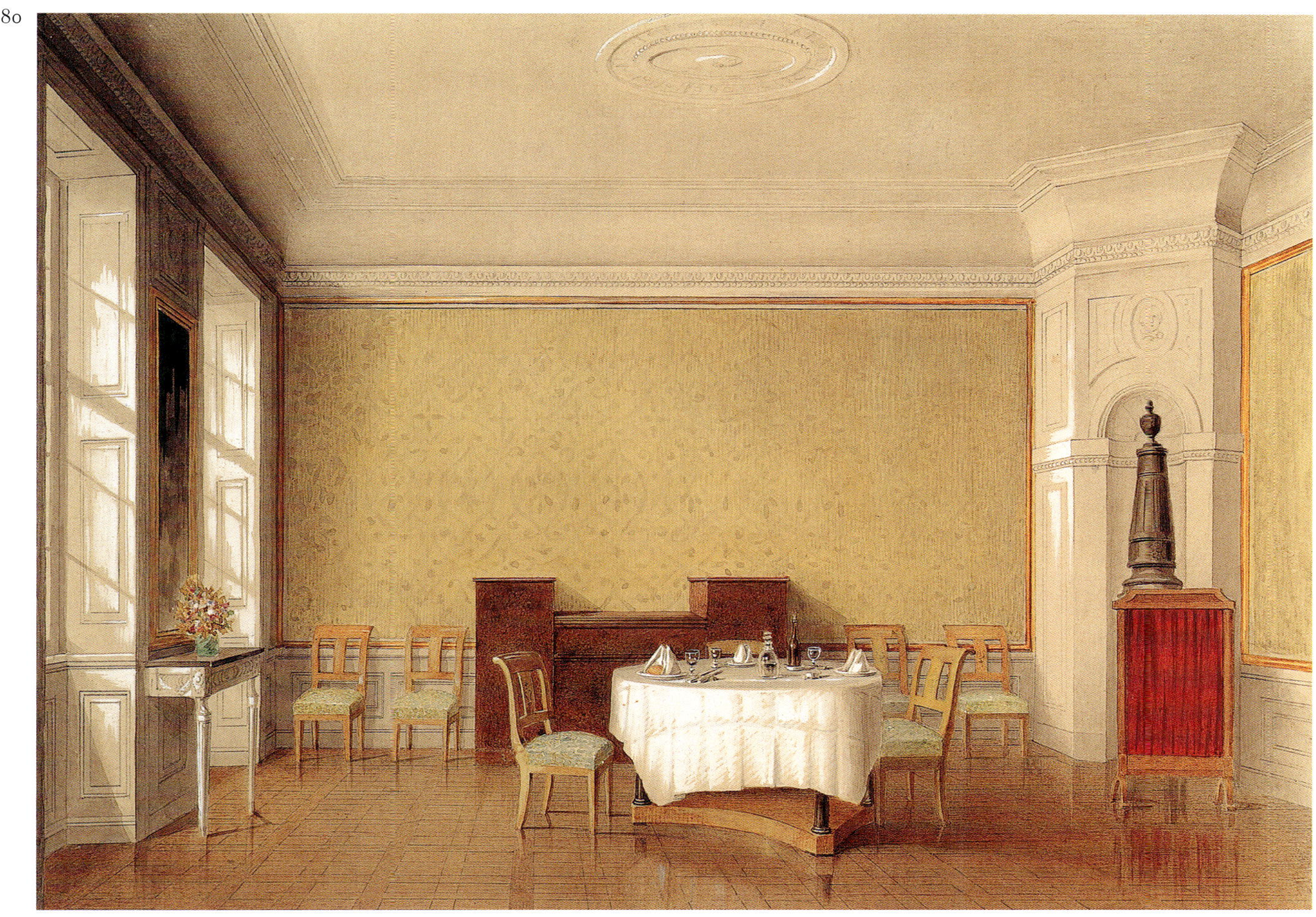

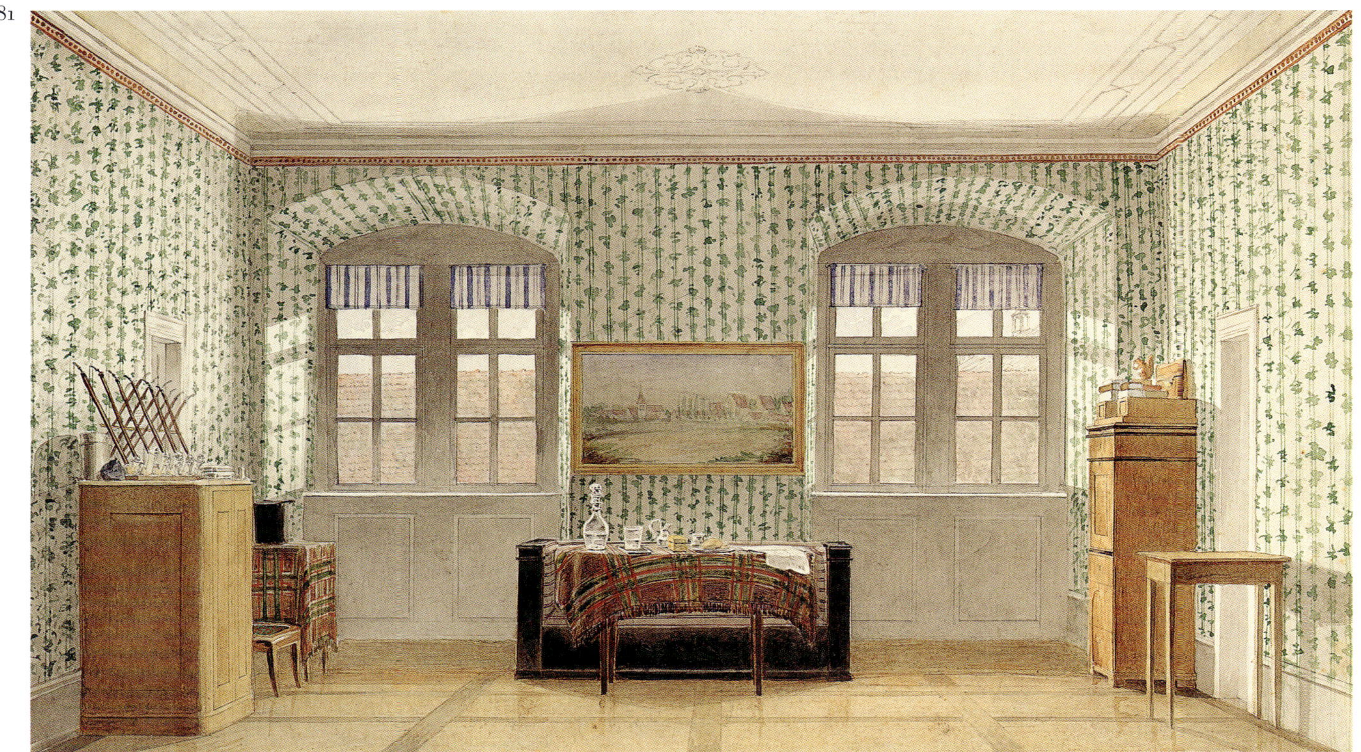

82
Monogrammist EW
*The Study of Prince
Andreas Rasumofsky
in his Vienna Palace,*
Vienna, ca. 1820
Cat. IV-7

83
Leopold Zielcke
*The Artist's Studio
in His Apartment at
Friedrichstrasse 228*
Berlin, ca. 1825
Cat. IV-9

84
Stephanie von
Fahnenberg
*Living Room of
Alexander von
Fahnenberg at
Wilhelmstrasse 69*
Berlin, 1837/38
Cat. IV-8

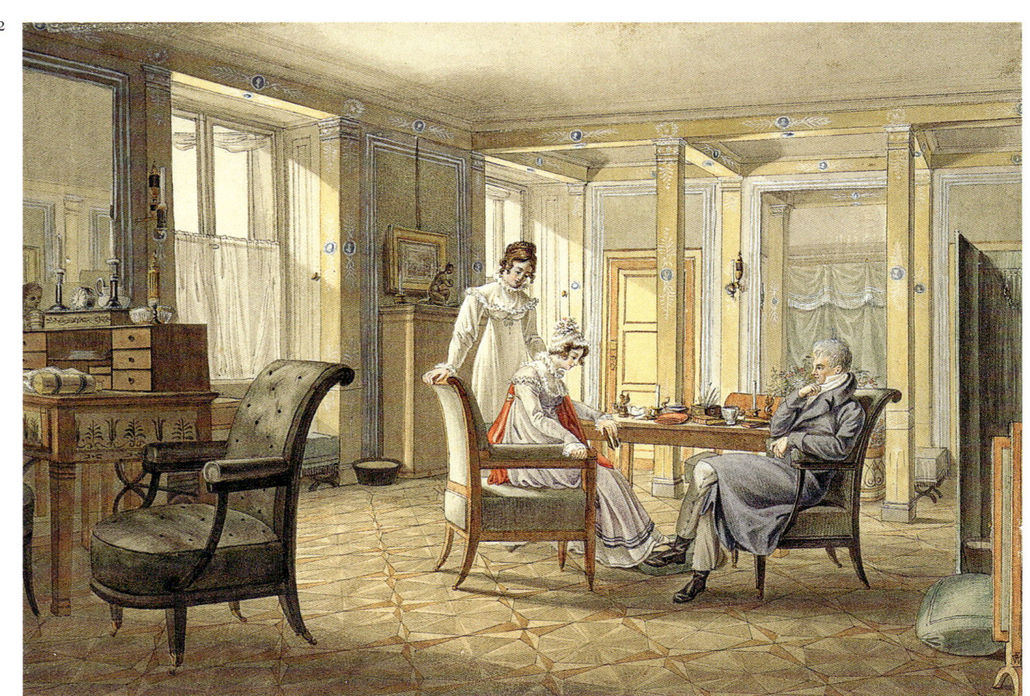

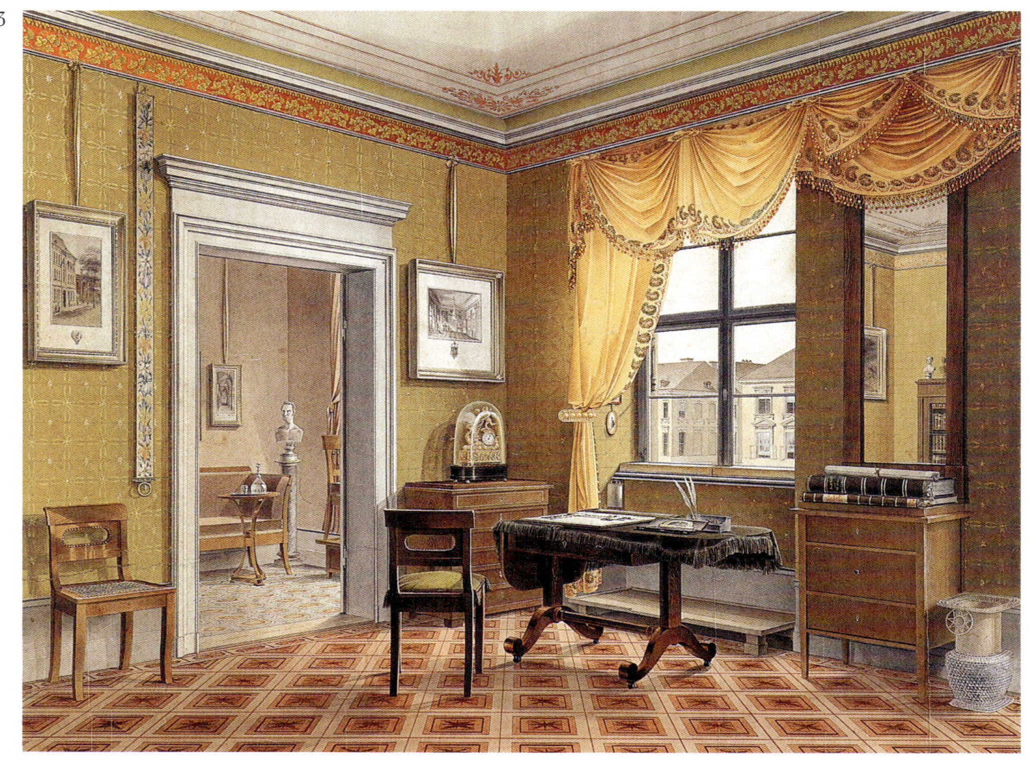

84

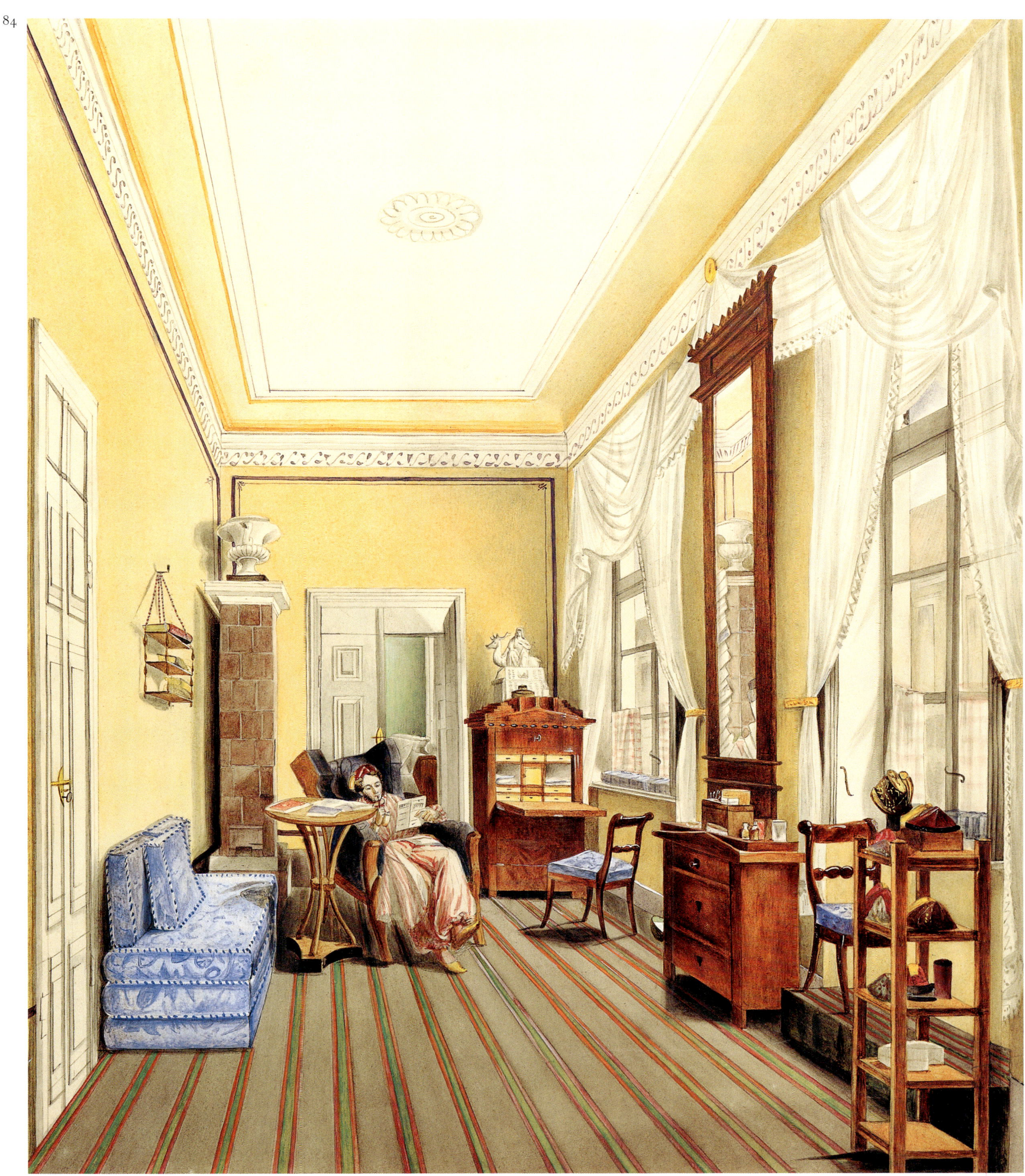

85
Heinrich Krüppel, Jr.
*Blue Room in
the Bürglass Palace
in Coburg*
Coburg, 1832
Cat. IV-10

86
Heinrich Krüppel, Jr.
*Yellow Room in
the Bürglass Palace
in Coburg*
Coburg, 1832
Cat. IV-11

87
Heinrich Krüppel, Jr.
*Carpet Room in
the Bürglass Palace
in Coburg*
Coburg, 1832
Cat. IV-12

88
Johann Baptist Hoechle
*A Room in
Schönbrunn Palace*
Vienna, ca. 1818
Cat. IV-13

89
Artist Unknown
My Room in Vienna
Vienna, 1837/42
Cat. IV-14

90
Franz von Maleck
*A Living Room
in Vienna*
Vienna, 1836
Cat. IV-15

91
Artist Unknown
*Room of the Gyulai
Family in Vienna*
Vienna, ca. 1829/31
Cat. IV-16

85

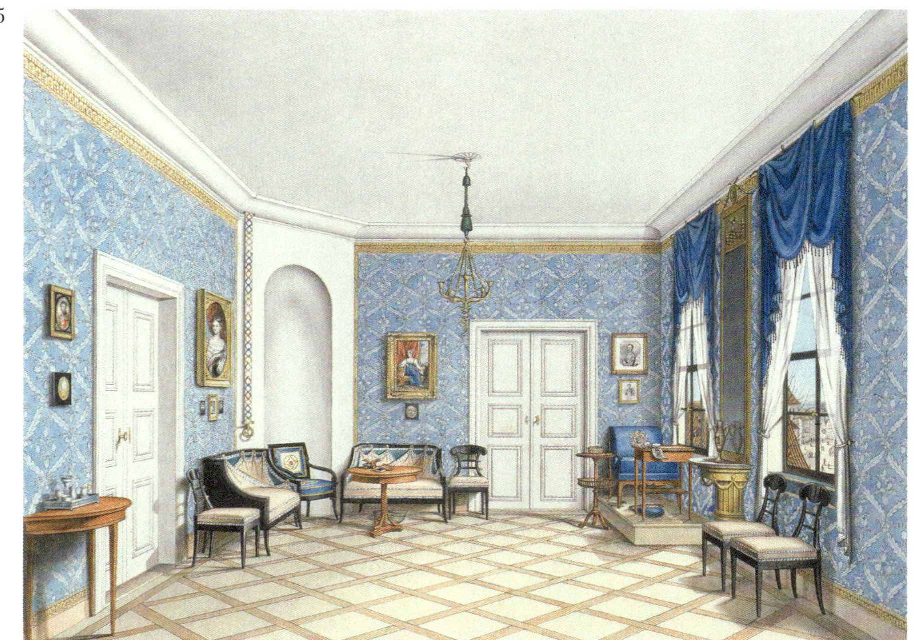

86

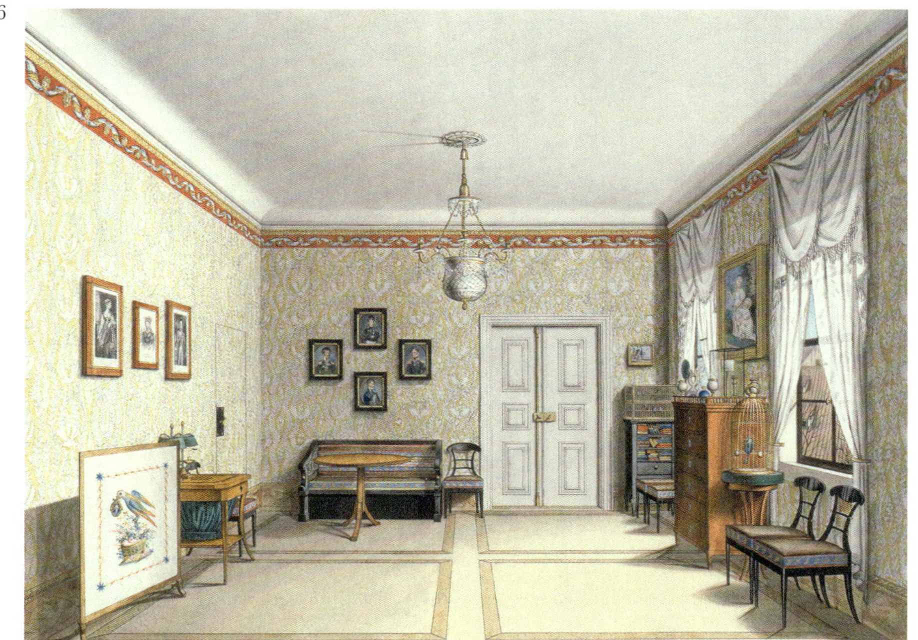

87

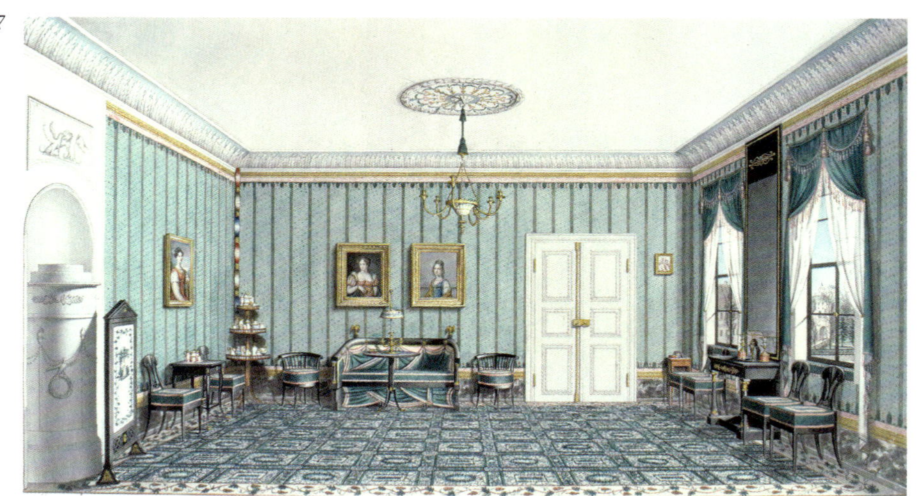

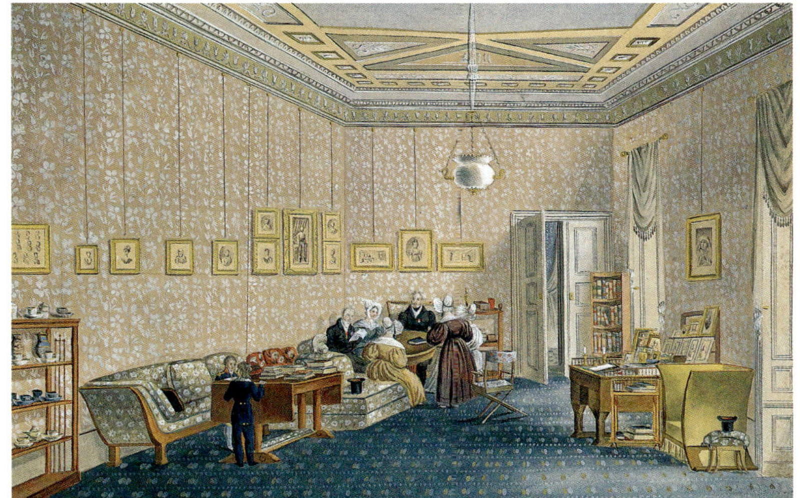

88

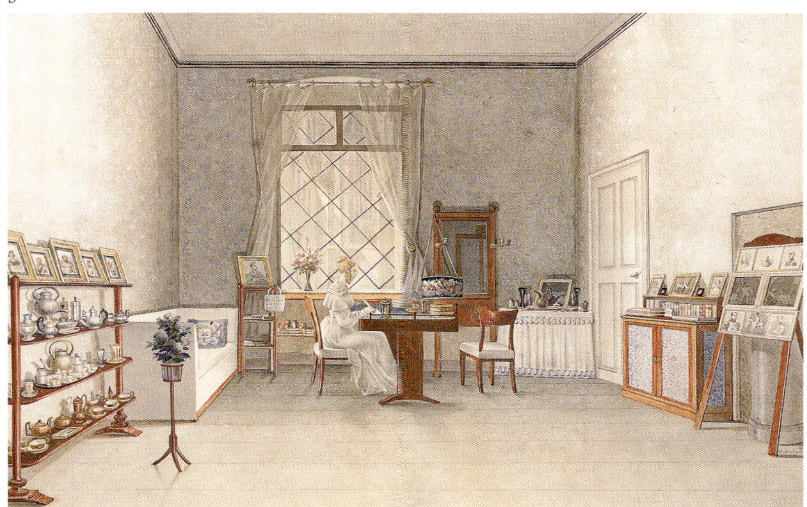

90

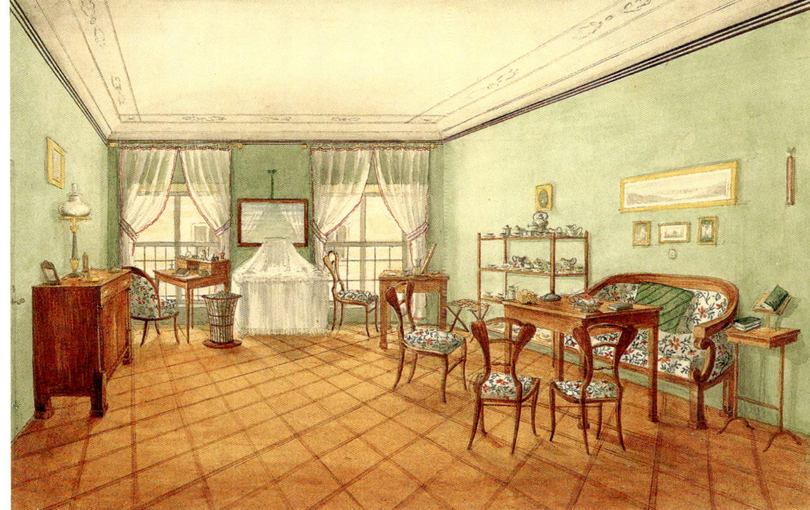

89

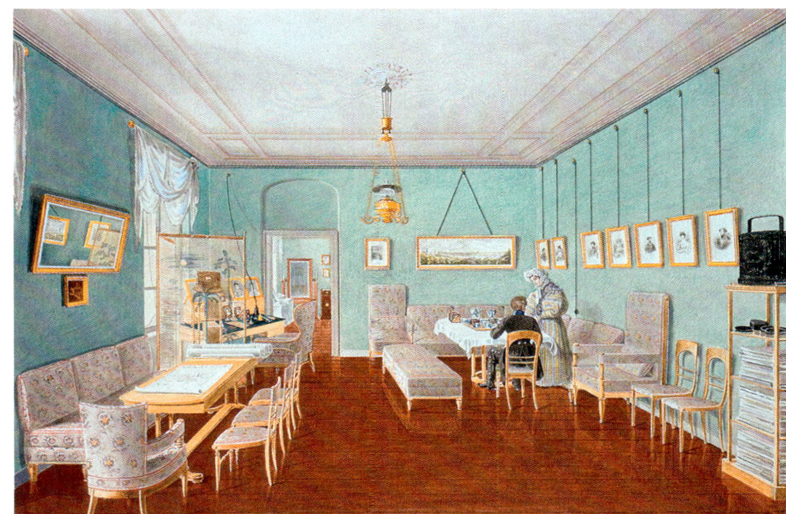

91

92
Artist Unknown
Room in Vinor Castle
Prague, 1836
Cat. IV-17

93
Artist Unknown
*Czernin Family
Interior at the Lazen
House at Chudenice*
Prague, ca. 1836
Cat. IV-18

94
Artist Unknown
*Room in the Apartment
of Princess Elisabeth*
Berlin, ca. 1840
Cat. IV-21

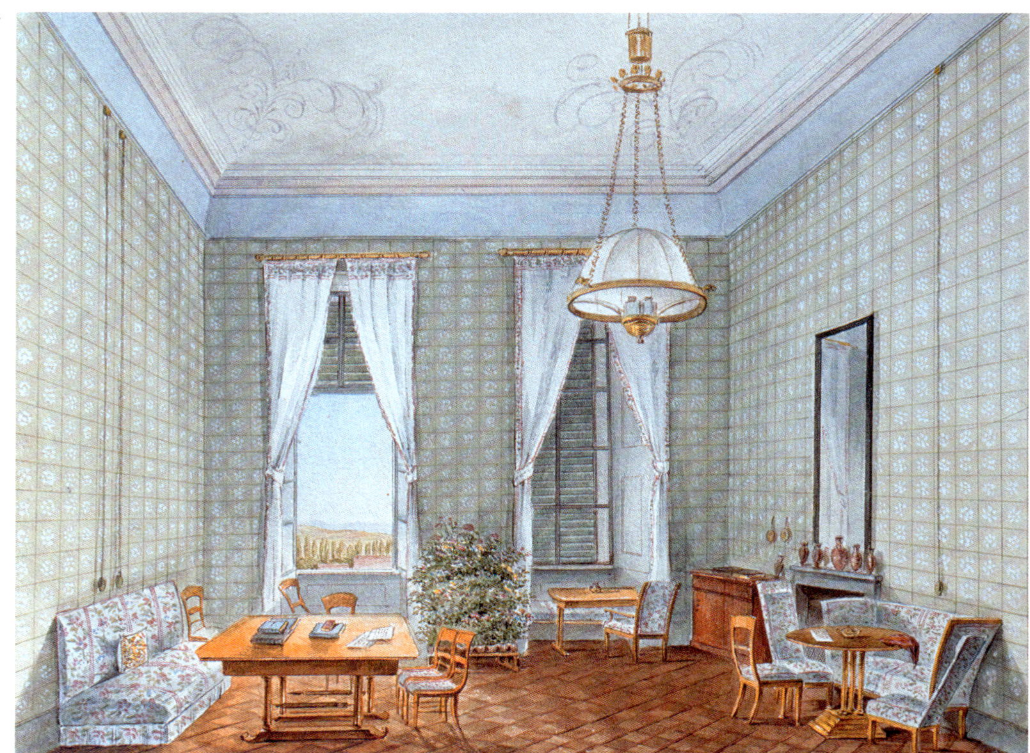

92

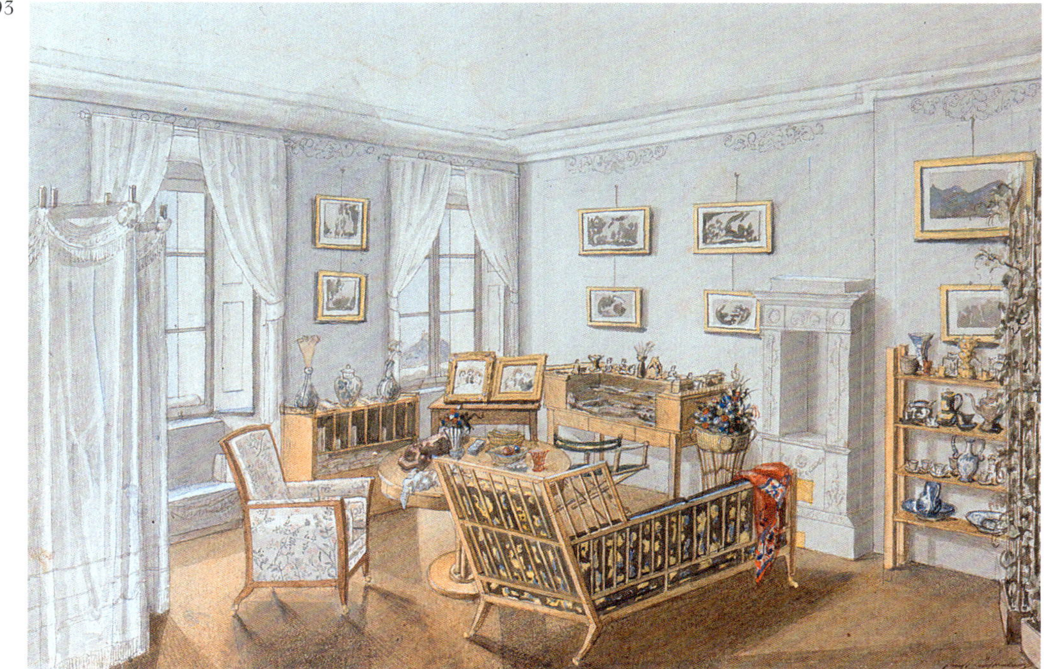

93

94

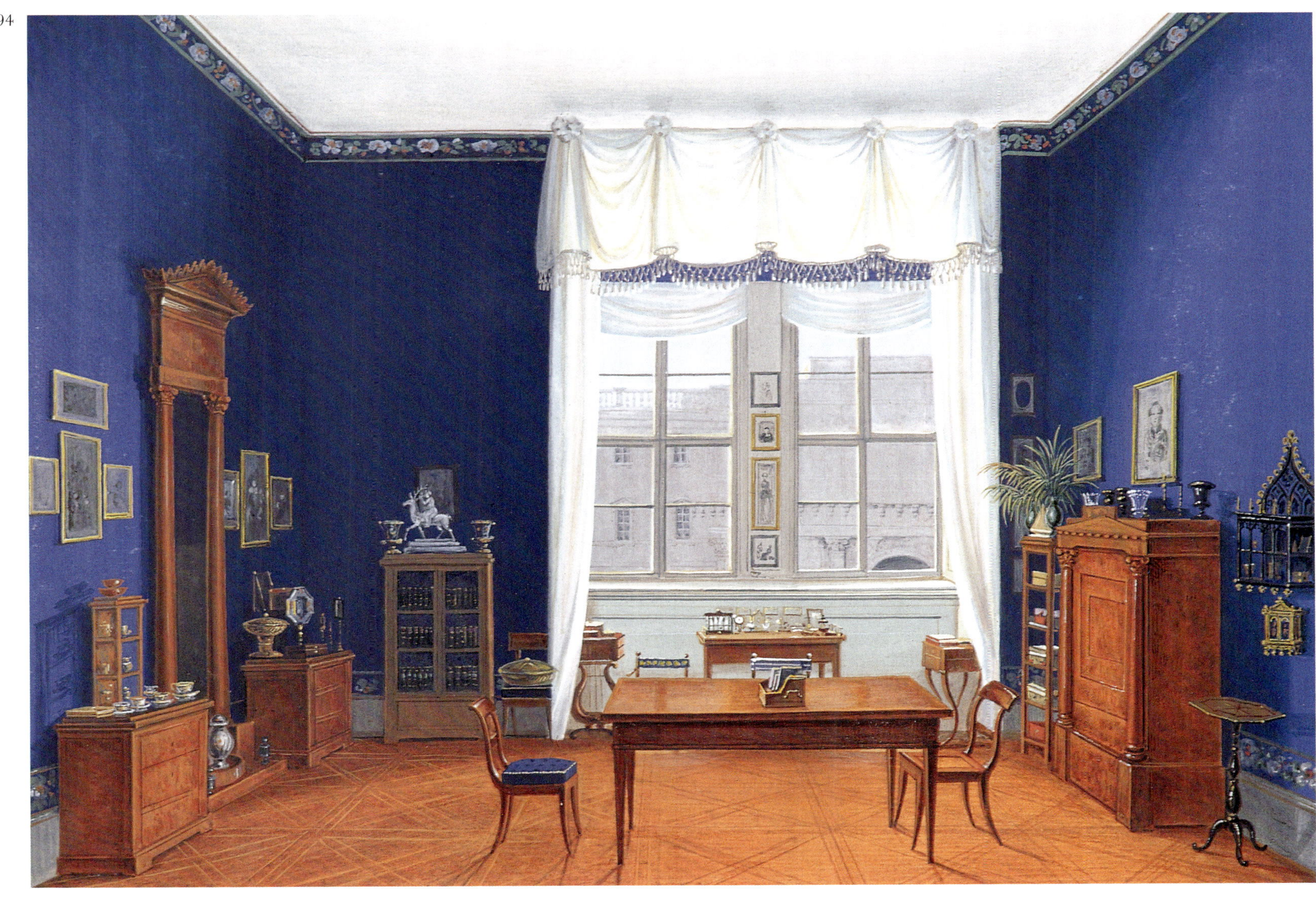

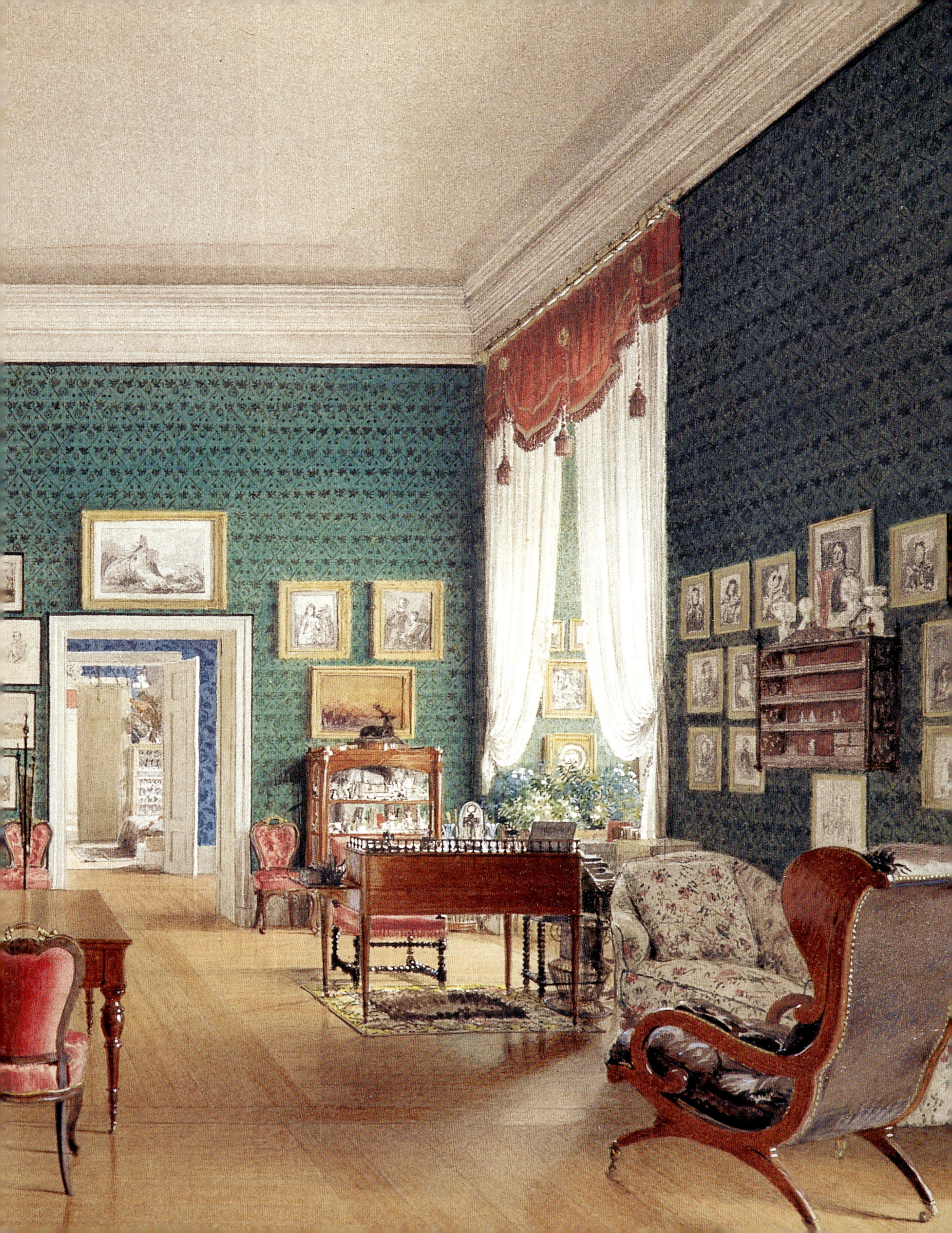

96
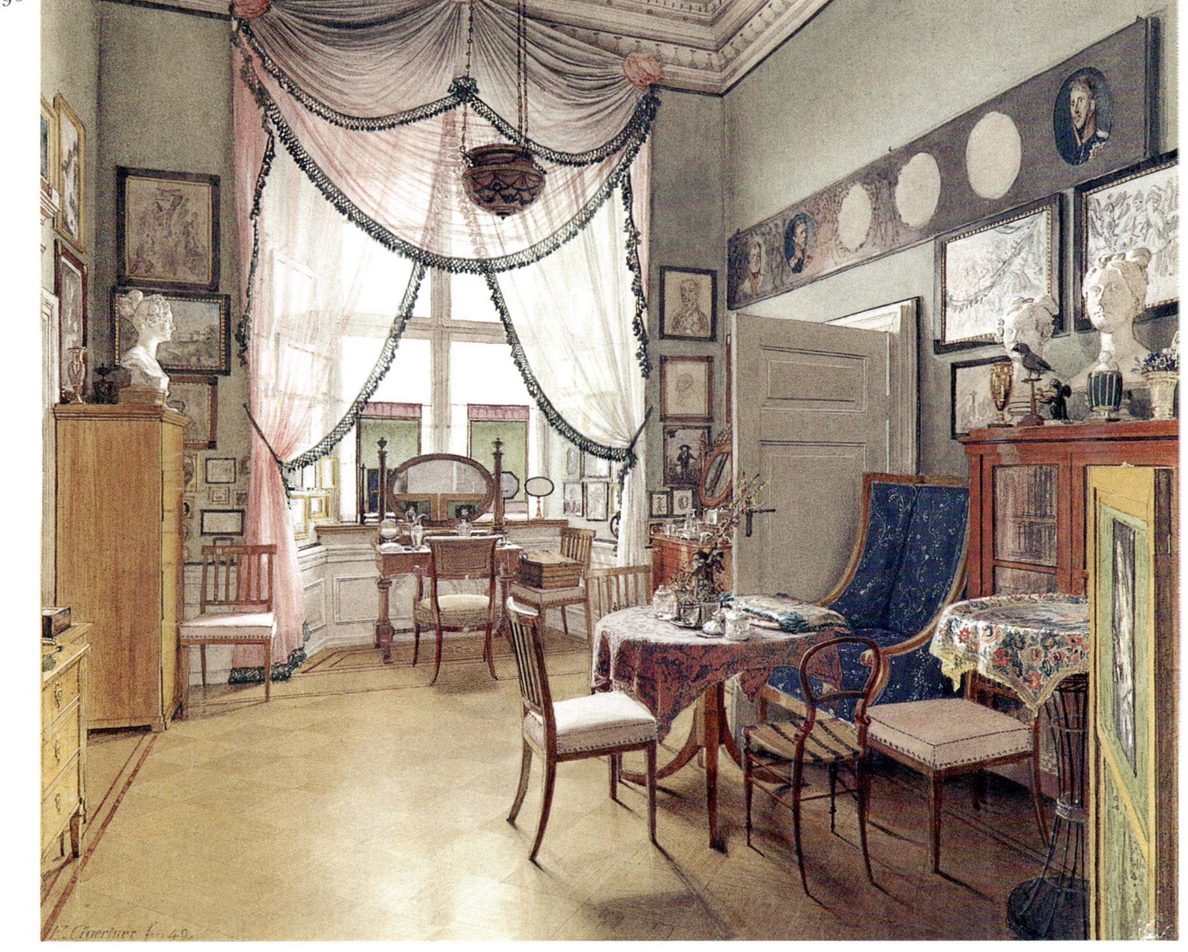

95
(Opposite)
Eduard Gaertner
*Prince Waldemar's
Living Room in
the Royal Palace*
Berlin, 1847
Cat. IV-22 (detail)

96
Eduard Gaertner
*Toilette Room in the
Apartment of Prince
Wilhelm and Princess
Marianne in the Royal
Palace*
Berlin, 1849
Cat. IV-24

97
J. Ferdinand Rothbart
Prince Albert's Salon,
the Former Salon of
Duke Ernst in Rosenau
Palace, Coburg
Coburg, ca. 1848
Cat. IV-25

98
J. Ferdinand Rothbart
The Queen's Salon,
the Former Salon of
the Duchess Luise in
Rosenau Palace, Coburg
Coburg, ca. 1848
Cat. IV-26

99
J. Ferdinand Rothbart
The Bedroom of Duke
Ernest in Rosenau
Palace, Coburg
Coburg, ca. 1848
Cat. IV-27

100
Georg Konrad Rothbart
The Room of the
Princes in Rosenau
Palace, Coburg
Coburg, ca. 1845
Cat. IV-28

97

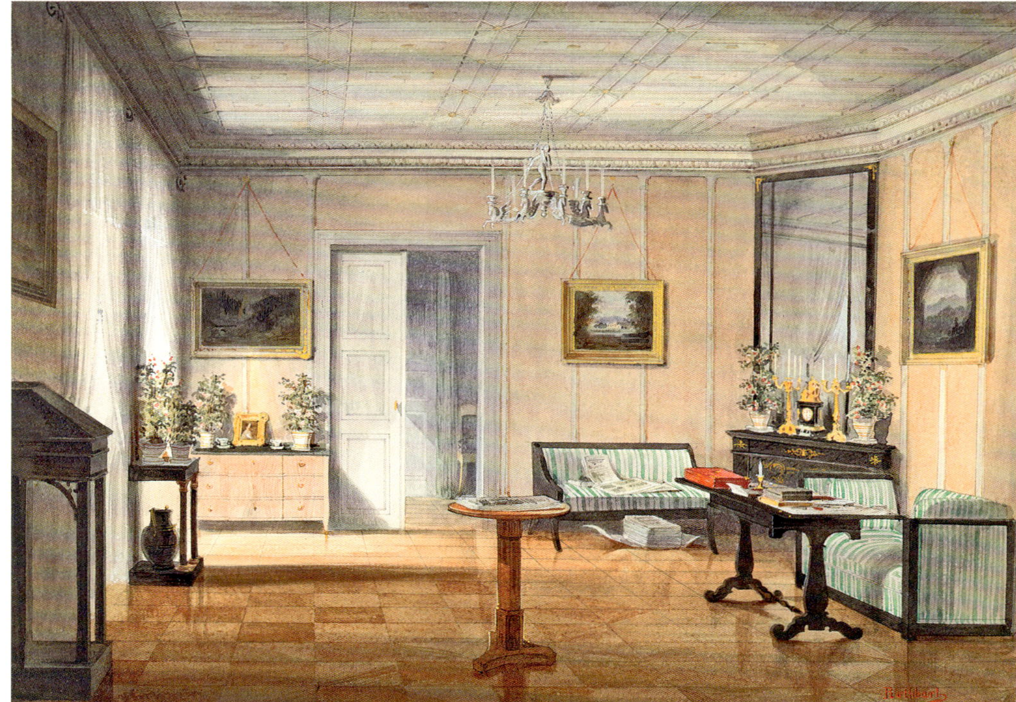

98

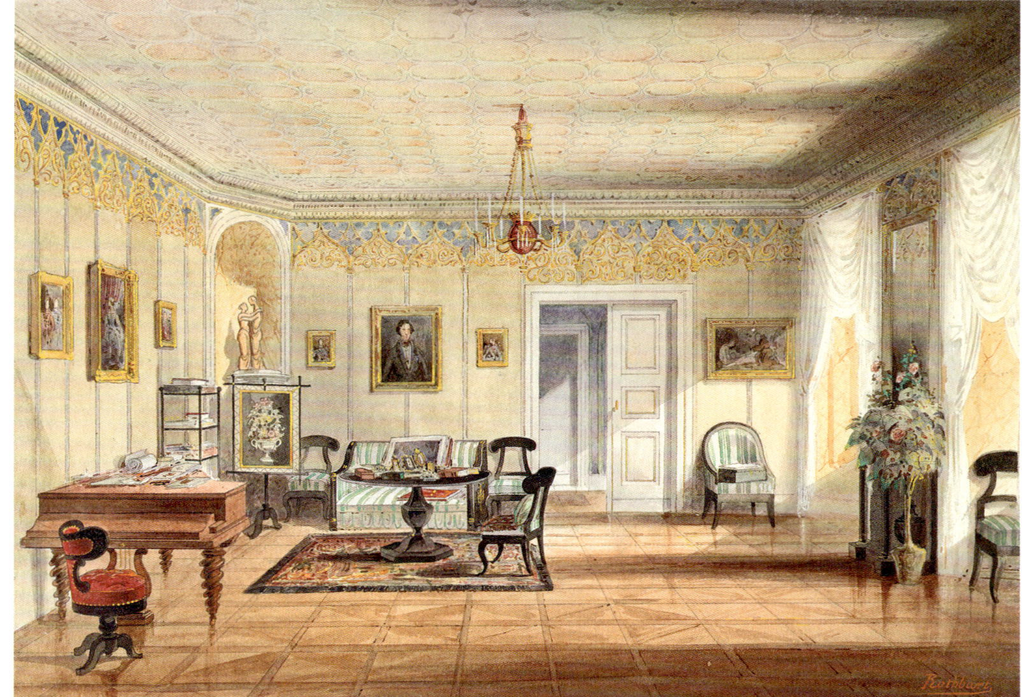

99

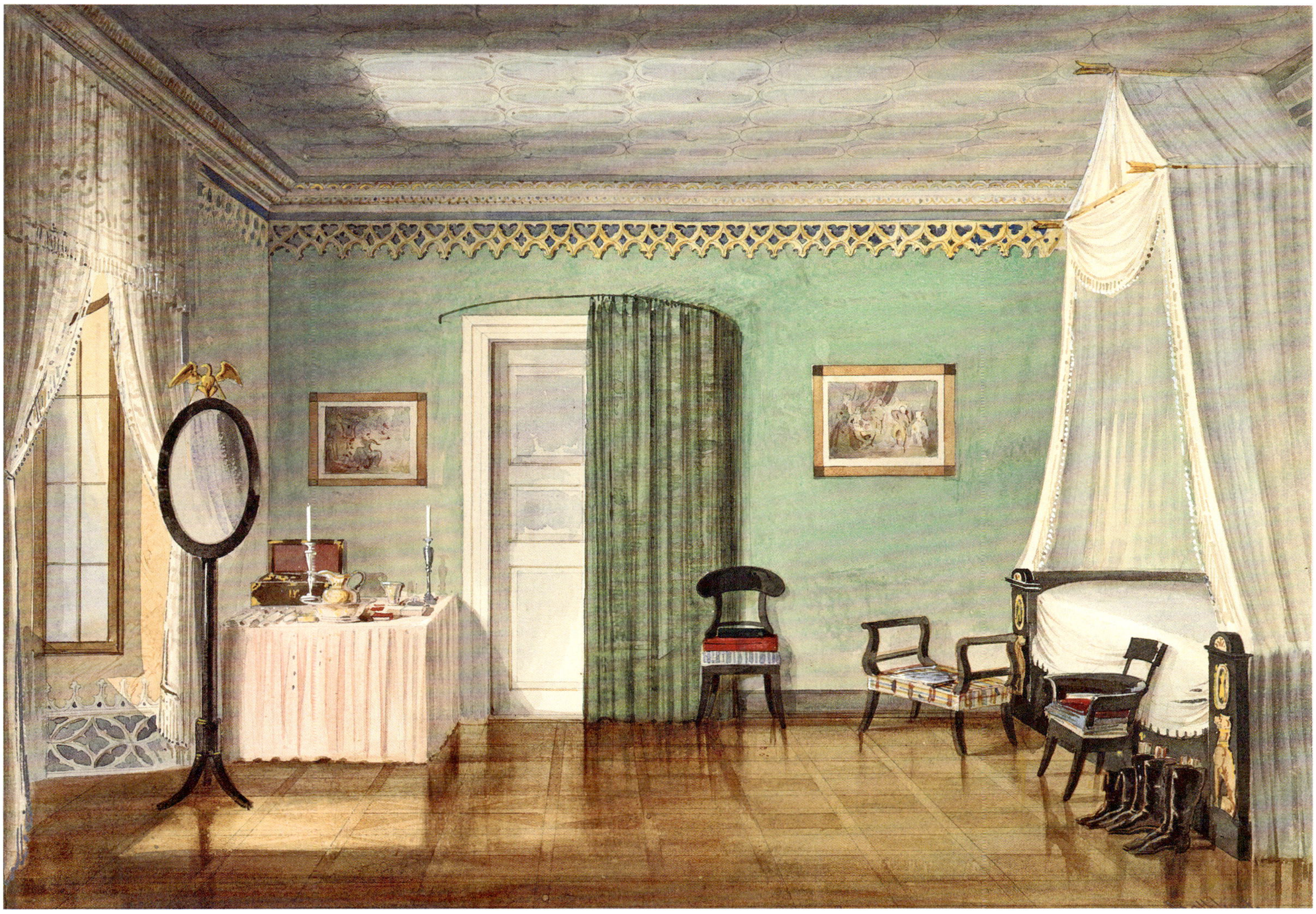

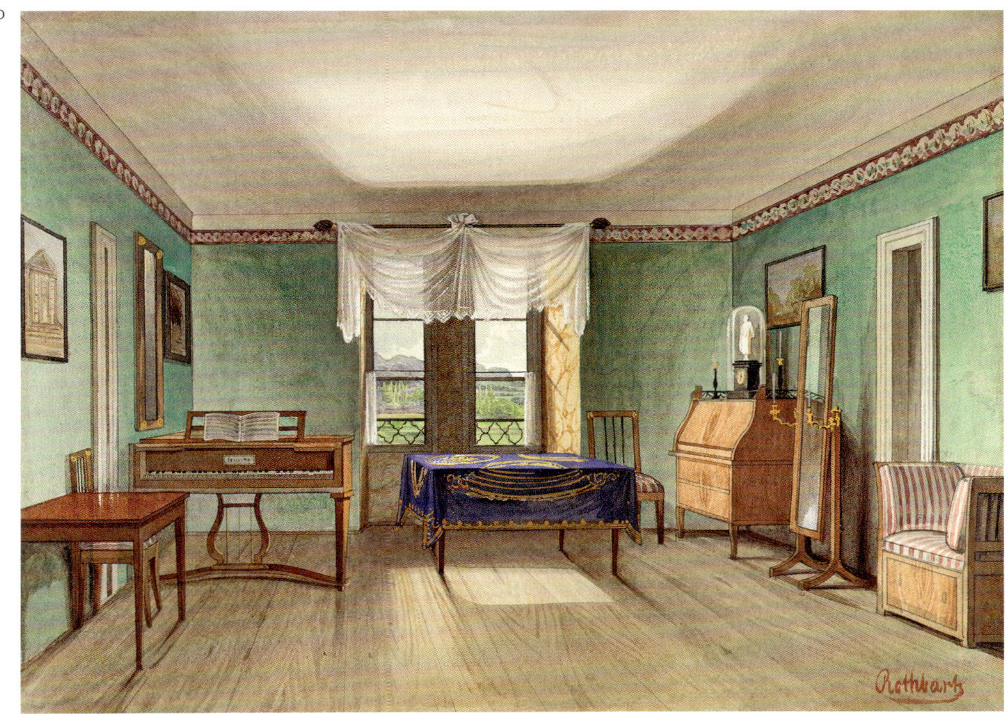

100

COLOR THEORY AND SCIENTIFIC INSTRUMENTS

SECTION V

Gisela Maul and Albrecht Pyritz

JOHANN WOLFGANG VON GOETHE

Gisela Maul

Johann Wolfgang von Goethe explored color theory for more than forty years. His book *Theory of Colors* (1810) was only his largest and most important single work in this area. Goethe's experimental apparatus, material samples, and drawings – his "chromatic equipment" – now in the Goethe-Nationalmuseum in Weimar, comprises some 1,100 items from his estate. The motivation for Goethe's investigation of color came from a desire to improve his own "mediocre" drawing and coloring skills by acquiring a firm grasp of the underlying theoretical principles. His first, rather cursory, glance through a prism dates from 1790. Observation of the edge spectra on the borders between the light and dark areas led him to postulate that Sir Isaac Newton's hypothesis that white light was made up of colored light was wrong. Spurred on by the prospect of refuting established theory, Goethe embarked on a detailed study of edge spectra, publishing his first findings in 1791 in a didactic treatise called *Contributions to Optics*. He remained fascinated by the subject throughout his life. The treatise was concerned exclusively with the physical-optical aspects of color theory; *Theory of Colors* published some twenty years later embraces every conceivable aspect of the subject.

Whereas Goethe first derived his color circle from the edge spectra observable through a prism, he later declared the phenomenon of complementary colored afterimages to be the physiological underpinning of chromatic harmony. The emergence of these afterimages, he argued, was evidence of the eye's craving for totality and harmony. In his color wheel, therefore, the complementary colors are always opposite each other. Whereas organic matter turns yellow upon exposure to light, the color of metals and the changes these undergo upon oxidation are evident from the color wheel. Of particular importance here are the sections on real and pseudo mixtures. In a real mixture, the primary colors yellow, blue, and red are paired together to produce purple, orange, and green; gray is the result if all are mixed together. The lighter the colors, the lighter the gray, approximating white; the darker the colors, the closer to black. This is where Goethe believed he could

refute Newton as the author of the "absurdity" that all the colors mixed together produce white. By bringing together the colors of the prismatic spectrum with a lens, Newton had obtained white light. Goethe commits a sleight of hand by equating Newton's spectral colors with his own pigment colors and assuming that combinations of the same must be subject to the same laws. He was unaware of the difference between additive and subtractive mixing. Goethe's pseudo mixtures are such as are created by a spinning top or disk or when colored dots or stripes are viewed from a distance.

The final chapter of *Theory of Colors* on the "sensuously moral effect of color" reflects on how colors and color combinations affect the human psyche, mood, and aesthetic sensitivity. Yellow, for example, as the color closest to light, is credited with an uplifting, mildly stimulating effect. Whereas the yellow and red phases belong firmly to the plus side, "the colors of the minus side," in Goethe's view, "are blue, reddish-blue and bluish-red," as the colors closest to darkness. He finds blue both soothing and stimulating; areas of blue tend to be retiring and can even evoke emptiness and a feeling of coldness. The red – also called pure red or purple red – obtained by mixing yellow intensified to yellowish-red with bluish-red is a color with a truly unique impact, claims Goethe, for "it gives an impression of both gravity and dignity and of grace and beauty." Green, meanwhile, as a mixture of the polar opposites blue and yellow, is genuinely pleasing to the eye and can be said to have a calming effect on both the eye and mind. Combinations of colors can produce harmonious, characteristic, or characterless compositions, depending on the extent to which the eye's desire for totality and harmony is gratified. Goethe's recommendations on the practical application of color, including the color of clothes to be worn on particular occasions and the color that various different rooms should have, are all based on his hypotheses regarding the psychological impact of color. Finally, applying the theories outlined above, he offers pointers on the use of color in painting, which in effect brings him full circle, his own artistic shortcomings having been the starting point of his inquiry.

Ever since its publication, Goethe's *Theory of Colors* has provoked passionate debate. His critique of Newton was anachronistic even when first published, and therefore caused much of his discussion about the physiology of perception to be overlooked, including his investigation of the complementary afterimages created in the eye, the way in which the dazzle effect gradually subsides, and the fact that shadows are colored. Goethe himself, however, was unmoved by the controversy, and in 1829 declared his color theory his most important achievement (Eckermann 1987, p. 283).

THE INFLUENCE OF SCIENCE AND
TECHNOLOGY ON THE DEVELOPMENT
OF NEW PERCEPTUAL STRUCTURES
Albrecht Pyritz

Goethe's *Theory of Colors* has attracted attention only in scholarly circles, although it is one of the most important sources for later theories of color aesthetics. In this work, Goethe gives precedence to human perceptual experience over objective scientific investigation. His in-depth examination of physiological principles and the aesthetic effects of color perception impacted nearly all modes of reception in the visual arts and applied arts through the practical application of his principles of simplicity in interior design, furnishing, and decoration.

During this period, science and art pursued essentially the same goal – namely that of exploring our natural habitat and unveiling its secrets. The scientific study of minerals and crystals is an outgrowth of early efforts to mine natural resources, of geological research devoted to establishing their origins, and ultimately of the development of principles of classification. Minerals were collected and displayed in courtly residences and studied systematically at newly established scientific institutes. The French mineralogist René-Just Haüy (1743-1822) discovered the law of symmetry in crystallography by chance in 1781. He built enlarged scale models of various crystalline forms to illustrate the principle and sent them to the most important European research institutes. The Berlin mineralogist Christian Samuel Weiss (1780-1856), who translated the writings of Haüy and others into German, boldly incorporating the results of his own research in the process, articulated the laws of crystal geometry in a simple classification of crystal surfaces. The most noteworthy early contribution to the field by a German was that of Abraham Gottlob Werner (1749-1817), a professor at the Freiberger Bergakademie (Mining Academy), who trained several generations of geologists and wrote a treatise presenting the first definitive system of classification for minerals. Werner was a leading exponent of the "Neptunist" theory that most rock layers in the earth's upper crust are the products of sedimentation in water. The "Vulcanists," however, contended that the

earth was formed in an evolutionary process generated by a "central fire" in its interior. Werner's most famous student, Alexander von Humboldt (1769-1859), confirmed this hypothesis during his expedition to South America in early 1802, by proving that granite, porphyry, and basalt are volcanic in origin and therefore volcanic rock.

The natural world came to be regarded as an object whose image offered scientific benefit and thus assumed new relevance. Landscape painters strove for precise depiction of geological structures, mountain formations, and different types of rock. Geognosis, the theory of the earth's origin, is expressed in the mountain scenes of Caspar David Friedrich and the landscapes of Carl Gustav Carus. Carus, in particular, regarded scientific knowledge as the foundation of his art. Precise scientific observation of nature became a guiding principle in art.

Intensive study of the structural systems of nature promoted the development of optical instruments. The royal courts of Berlin, Munich, and Vienna supported the construction of instruments for topographic surveying, in which theodolites were used to measure distances and elevations, and the manufacture of microscopes, goniometers, and telescopes. The primary goal was to enhance the optical quality of lenses, prisms, and mirrors while developing instruments with simple handling features and clearly defined functions to satisfy the growing number of new users. Munich became a center of instrument manufacturing.

Insights into the structural principles of order in nature inevitably led artists to focus on these phenomena as well and to develop suitable forms with which to depict them in art. The traditional associative, subjective, idealized representations of nature in painting gave way to precise mirror images. The intricately detailed, botanically authentic plant studies that appeared during this period exhibit the same degree of realism as the classifiable cloud formations in the paintings. The minerals themselves were used for jewelry and mineralogical ring cabinets. Painted imitations of agate, lapis lazuli, amethyst, and malachite adorn the surfaces of porcelain and enameled objects. Agates were copied in glass art; chemical pigments and prismatic primary colors in glass painting produced astonishing results.

101
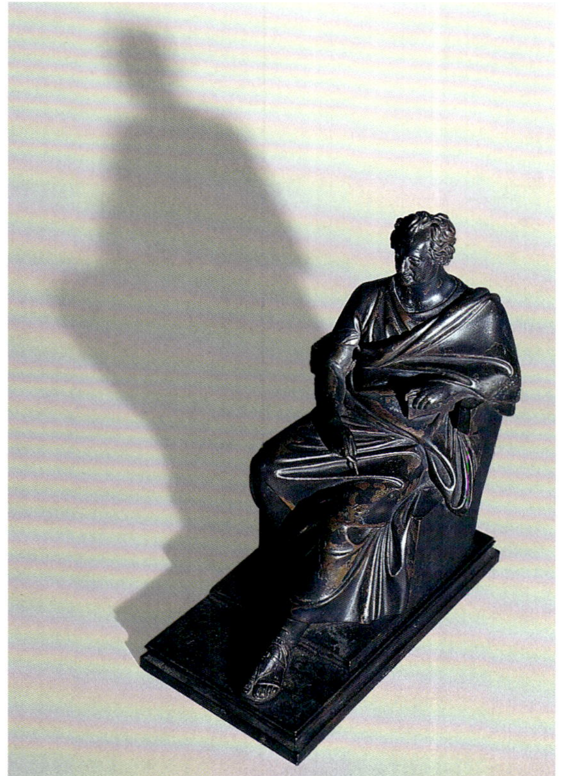

102
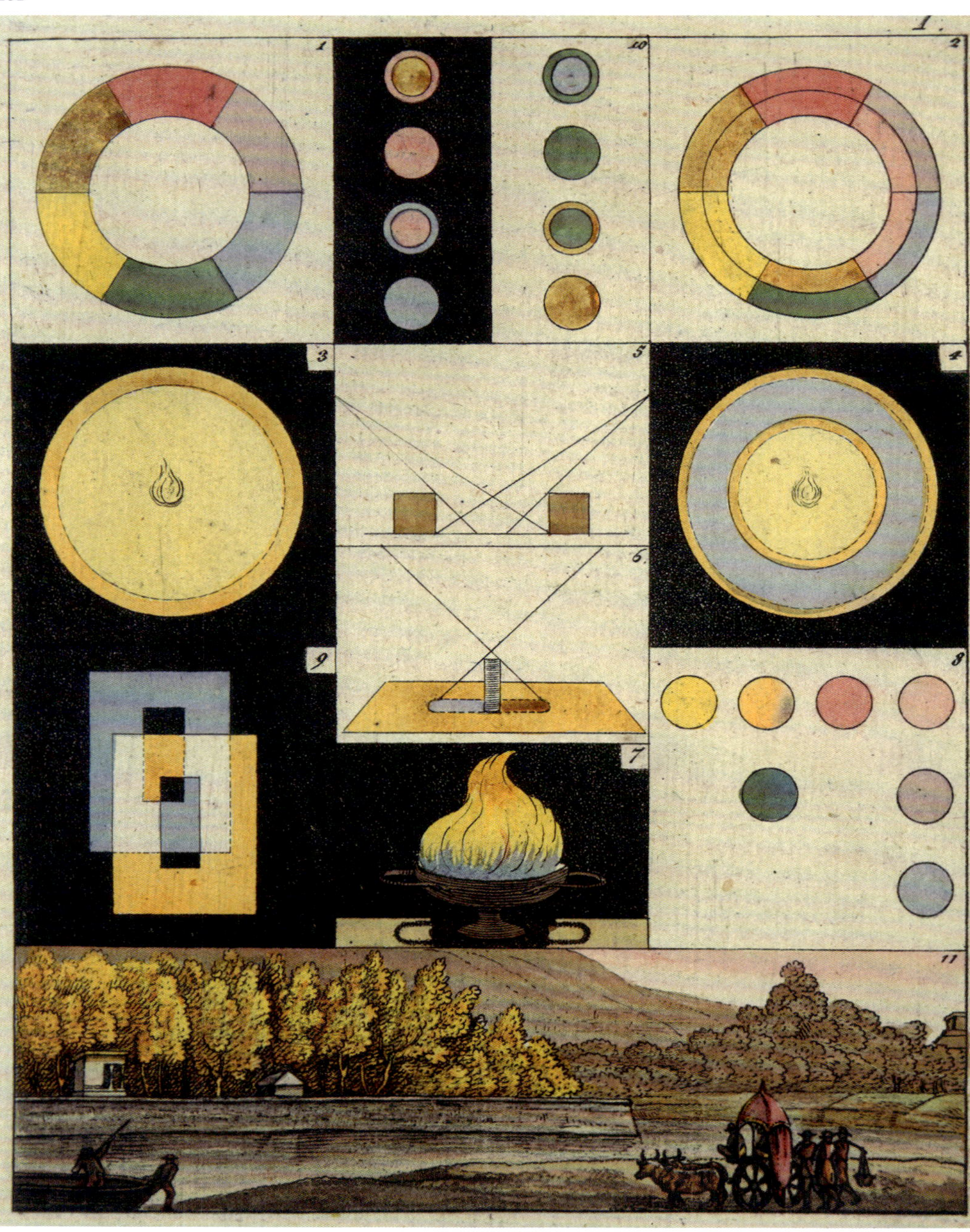

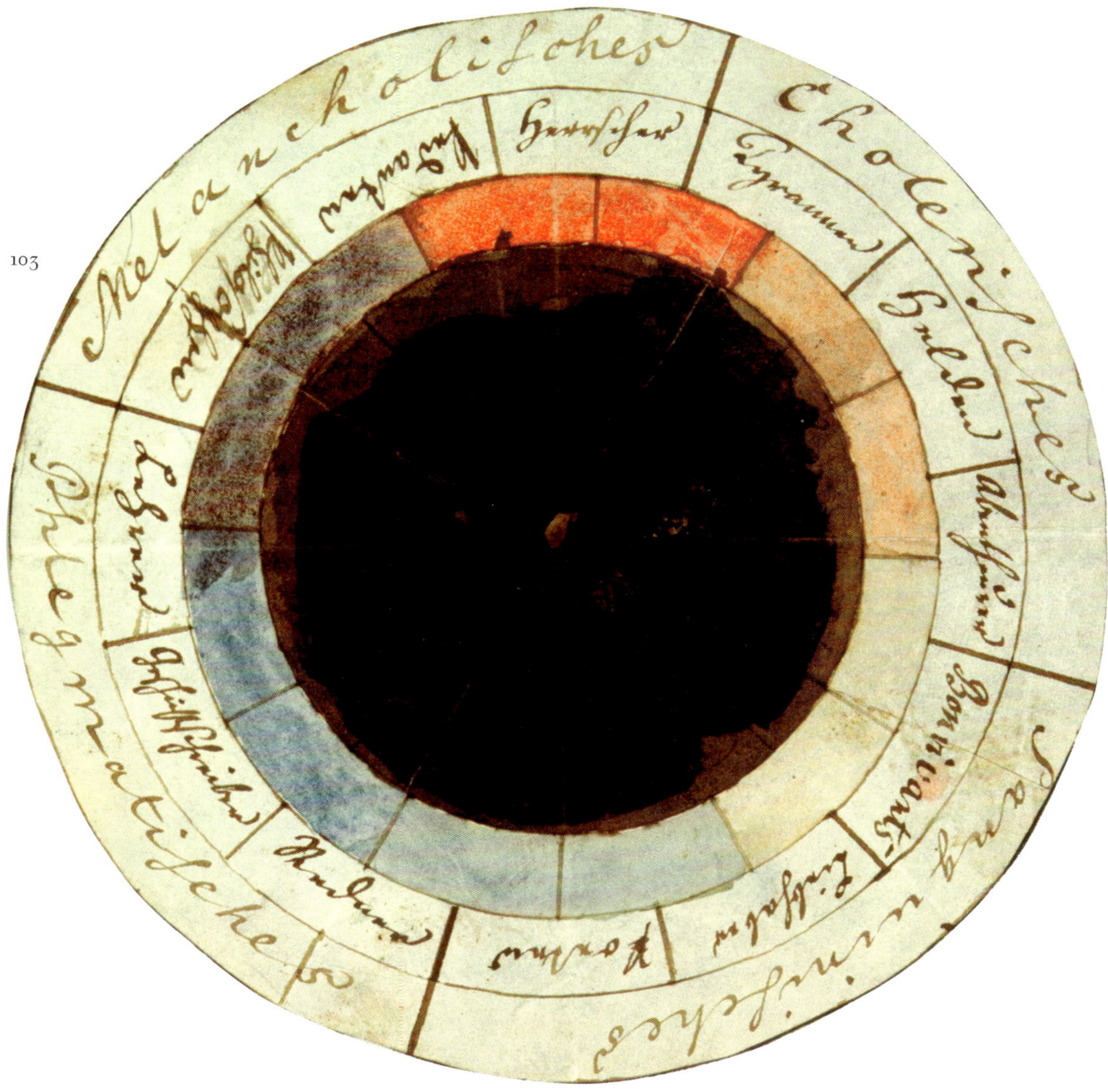

103

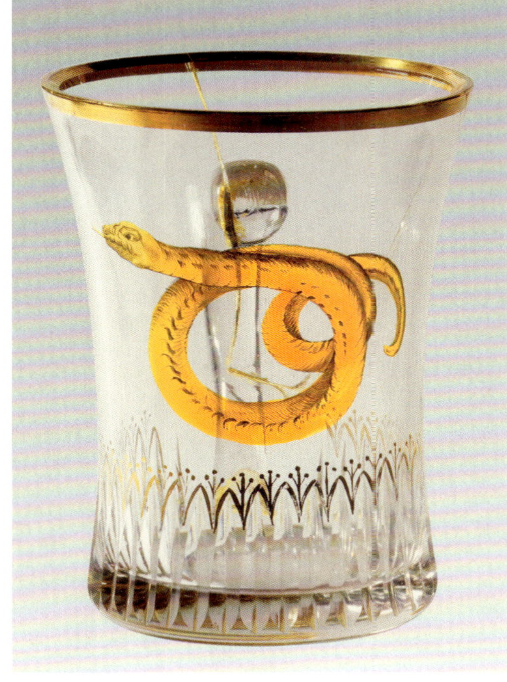

104

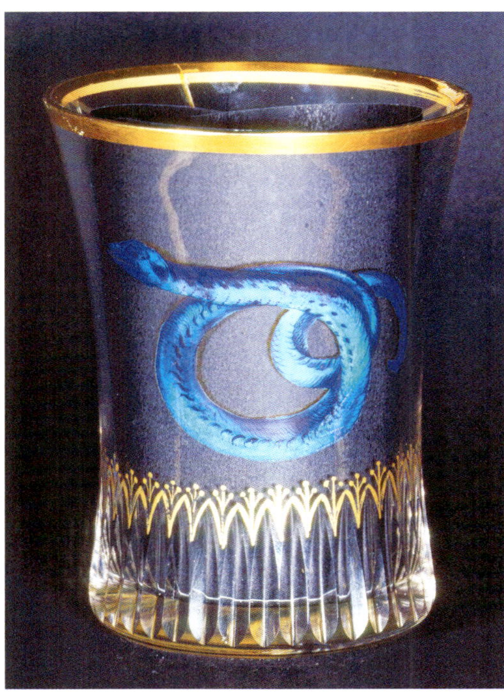

101
Christian Daniel Rauch
*Johann Wolfgang von
Goethe, Statuette after
a Draft for a Monument
in Frankfurt am Main*
(not realized)
Berlin, ca. 1825
Cat. v-1

102
Johann Wolfgang
von Goethe
Plate I of the Theory
of Colors, 1810
Cat. v-3

103
Johann Wolfgang
von Goethe and
Friedrich von Schiller
Rose of Temperaments
1798/99
Cat. v-5

104
Goethe's Handle Cup
Karlsbad, ca. 1810
Cat. v-11

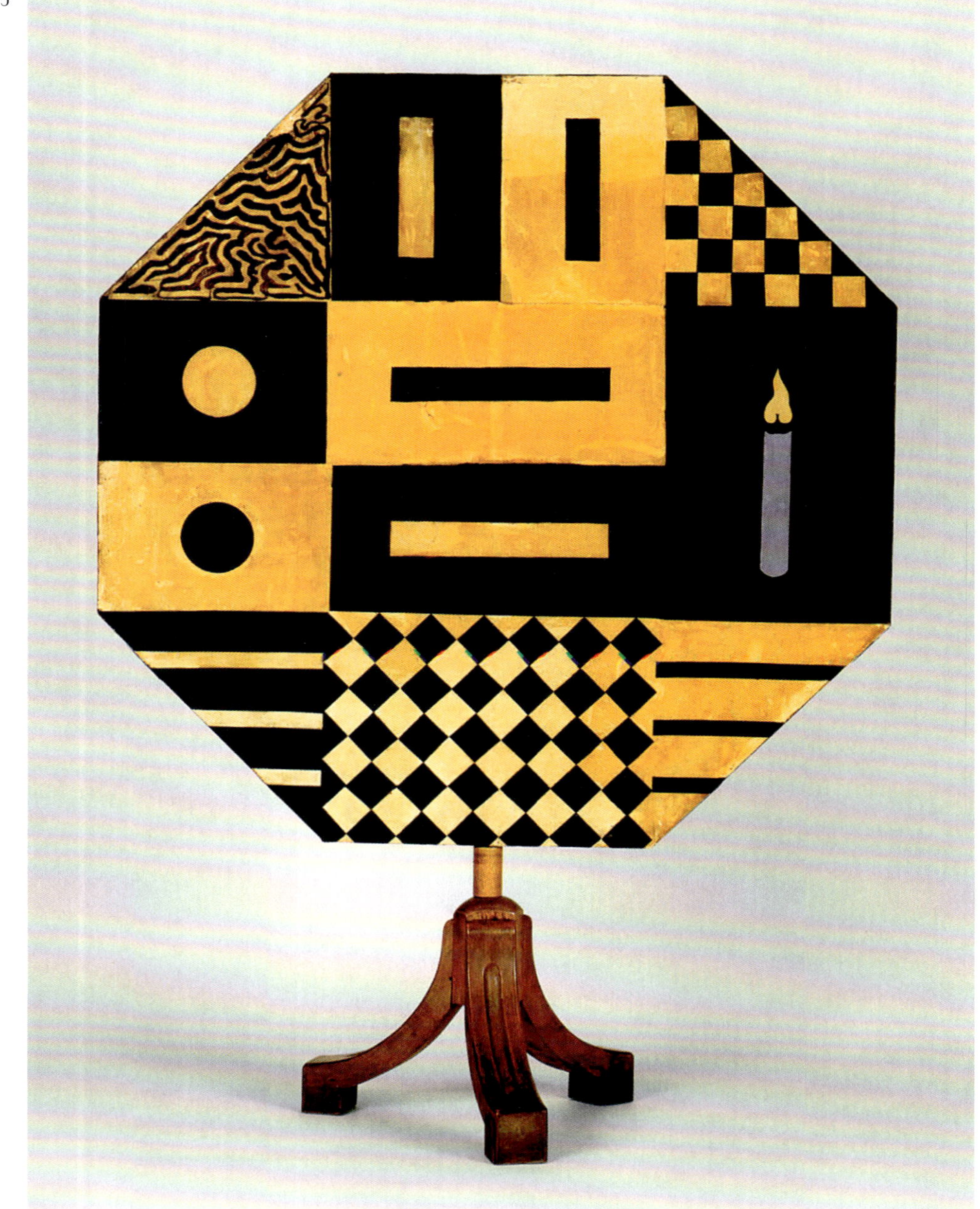

105

105
Screen for the Theory
of Colors *(Table)*
Weimar, 1791
Cat. v-6

106
Johann Wolfgang
von Goethe
Plate IIa of the Theory
of Colors, 1810
Cat. v-7

107
Johann Wolfgang
von Goethe
Plate III of the Theory
of Colors, 1810
Cat. v-8

108
*104 Samples of
German and French
Textiles from Goethe's
Sample Collection*
Weimar, ca. 1800
Cat. v-10

109
*Frame with
Prisms of Flint
and Crown Glass*
Jena, 1800
Cat. v-12

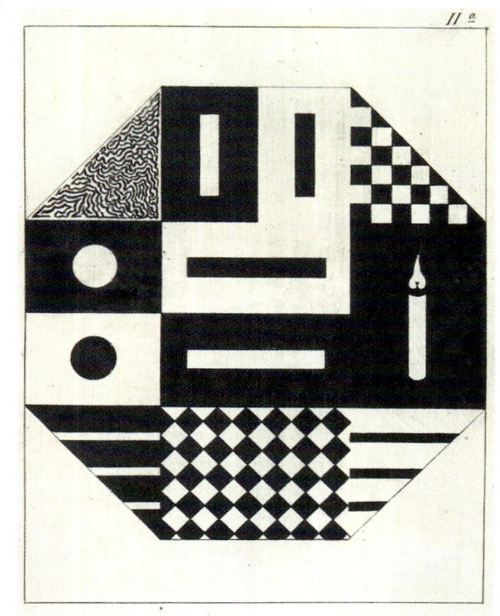

106

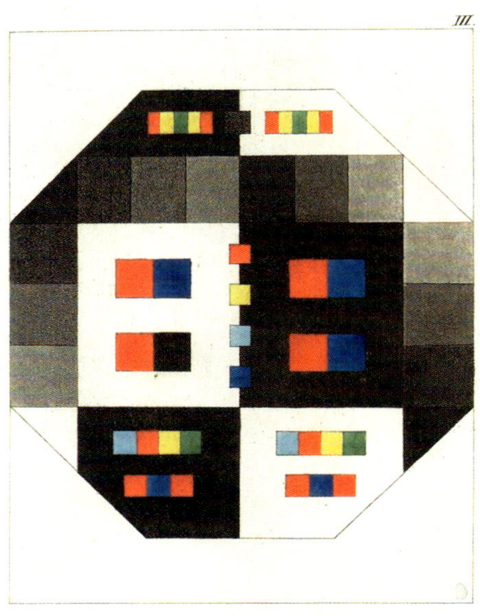

107

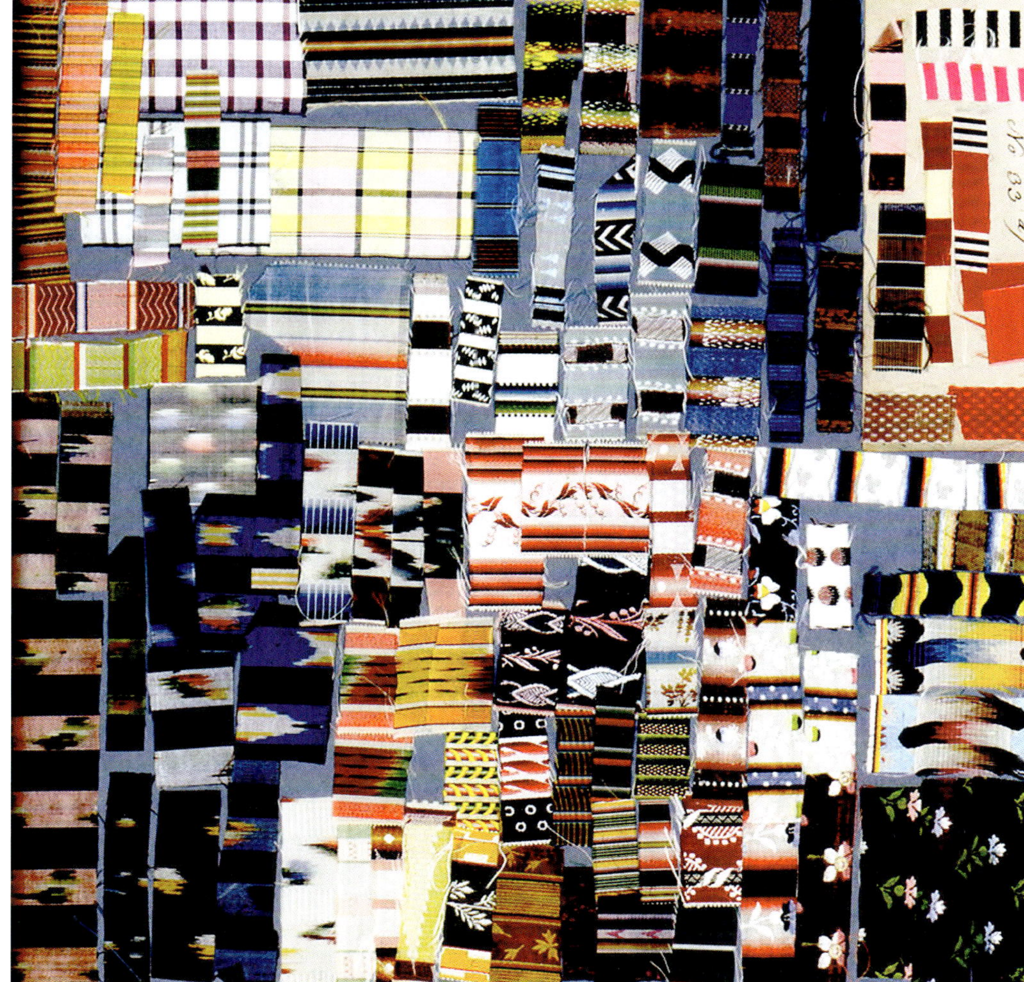

108

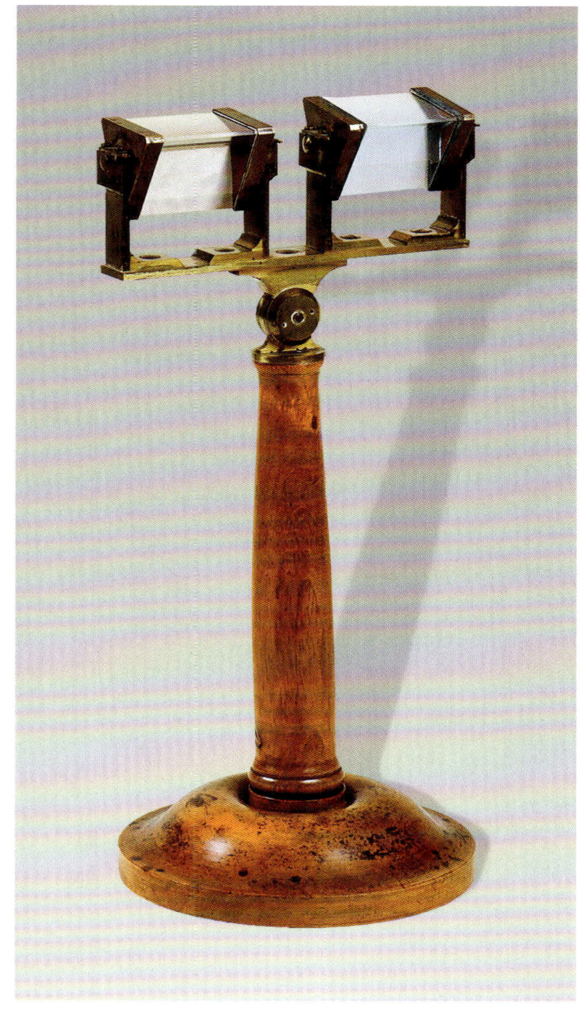

109

110
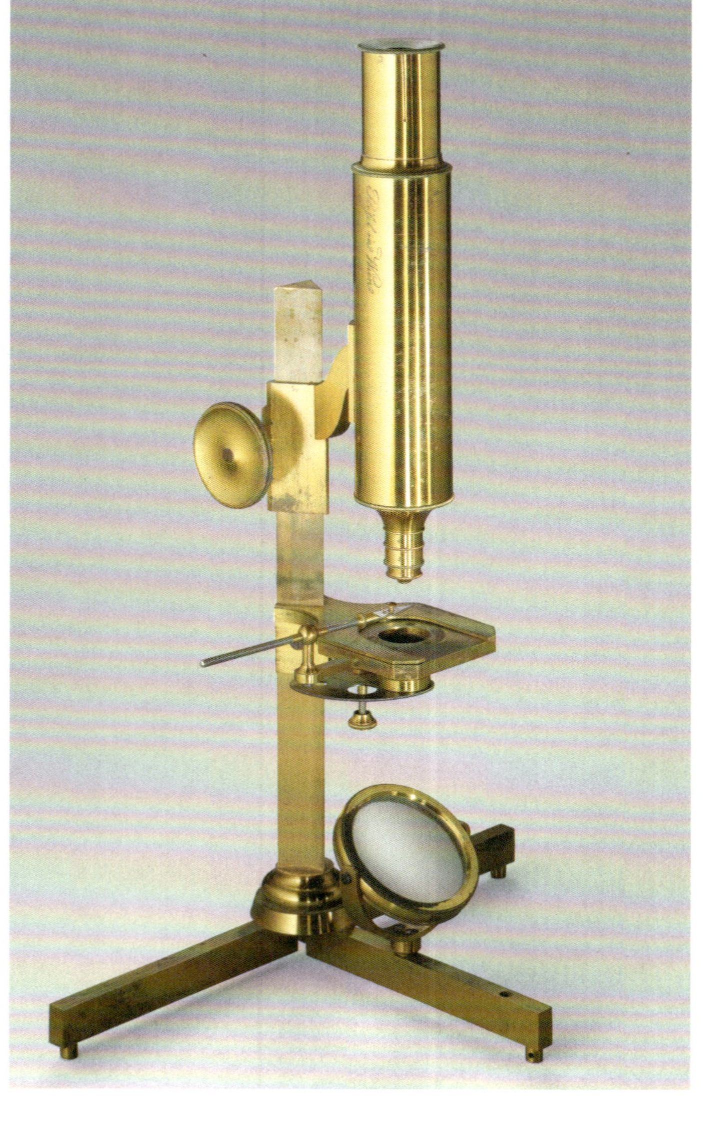

111
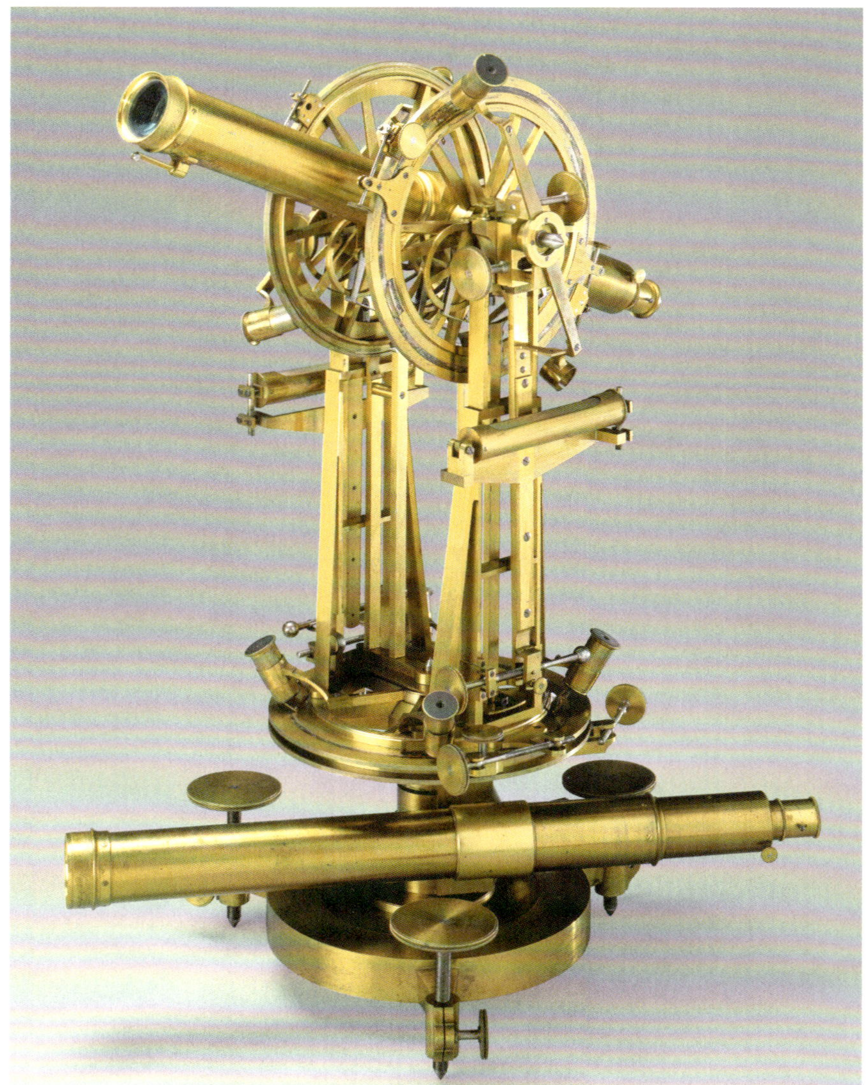

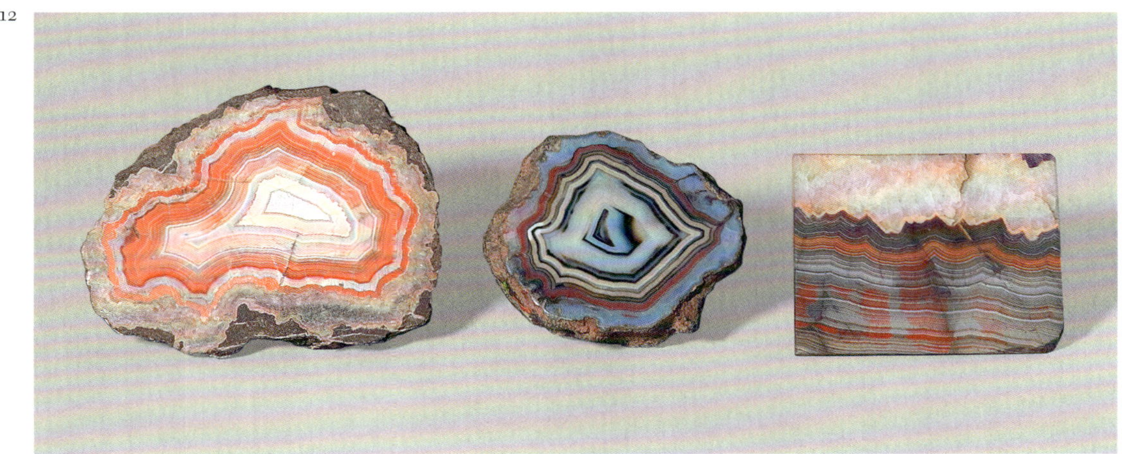

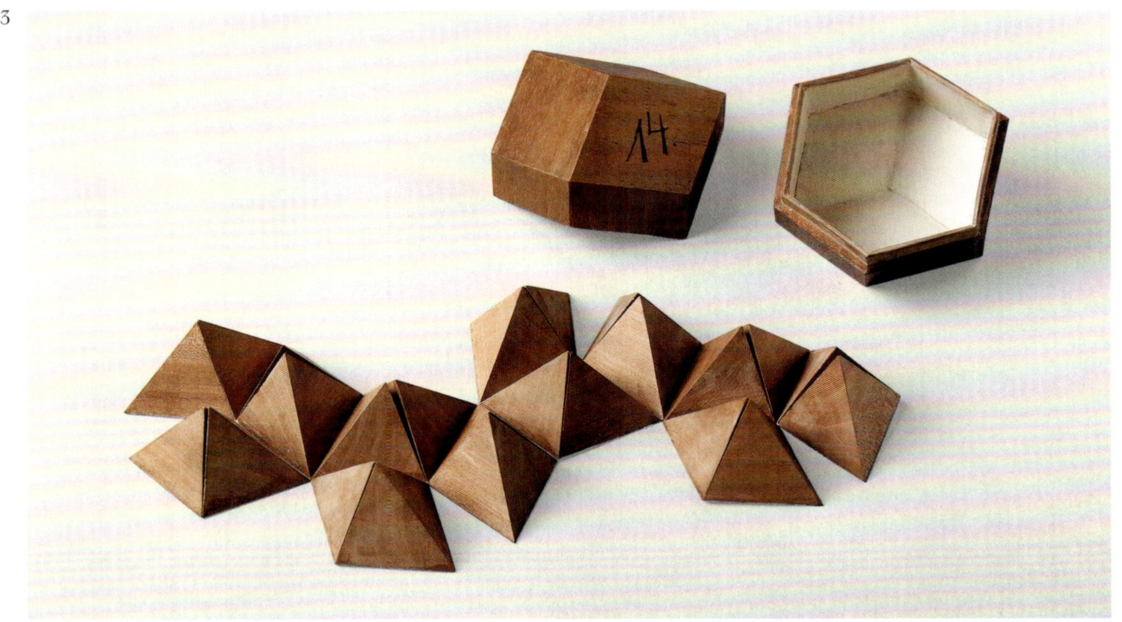

110
Microscope
Vienna, ca. 1835
Cat. v-14

111
*Theodolite, Eight-inch
Universal Instrument*
Germany, ca. 1830
Cat. v-15

112
Chalcedony (Agate)
Idar-Oberstein/
Rheinland-Pfalz,
ca. 1820

Chalcedony (Agate)
Idar-Oberstein/
Rheinland-Pfalz,
ca. 1820

*Chalcedony (Agate)
and Quartz*
Cunersdorf/Saxonia,
ca. 1820
Cat. v-20

113
*Crystal Model
with Removable
Structure Model*
1810
Cat. v-19

114
Mineralogical Ring Cabinet
probably Dresden,
ca. 1790
Cat. v-21

115
Alexander von Humboldt's Pocket Chronometer No. 224
Paris?, ca. 1809
Cat. v-23

116
Directoire Clock
Paris, ca. 1795
Cat. v-22

114

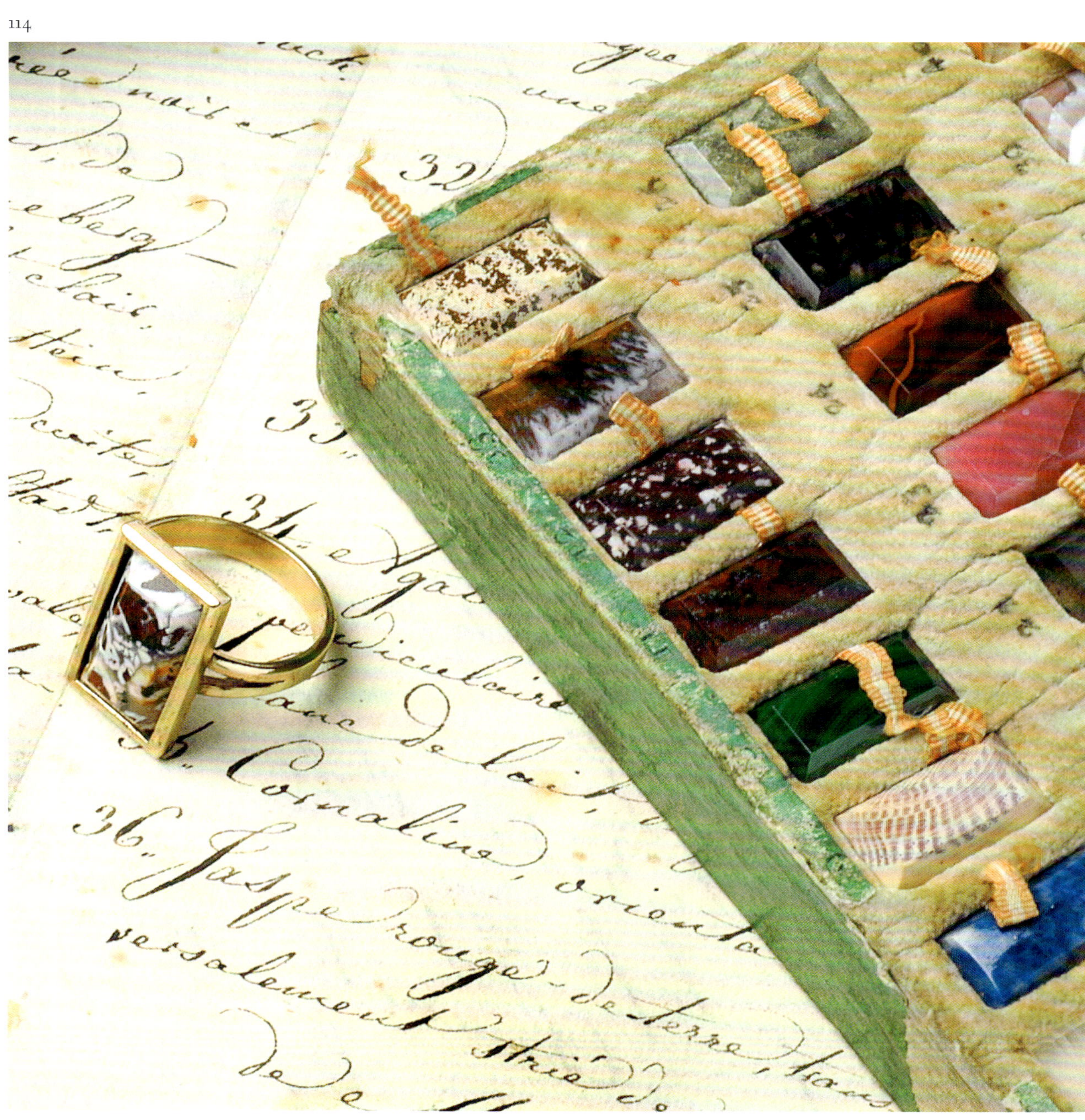

115

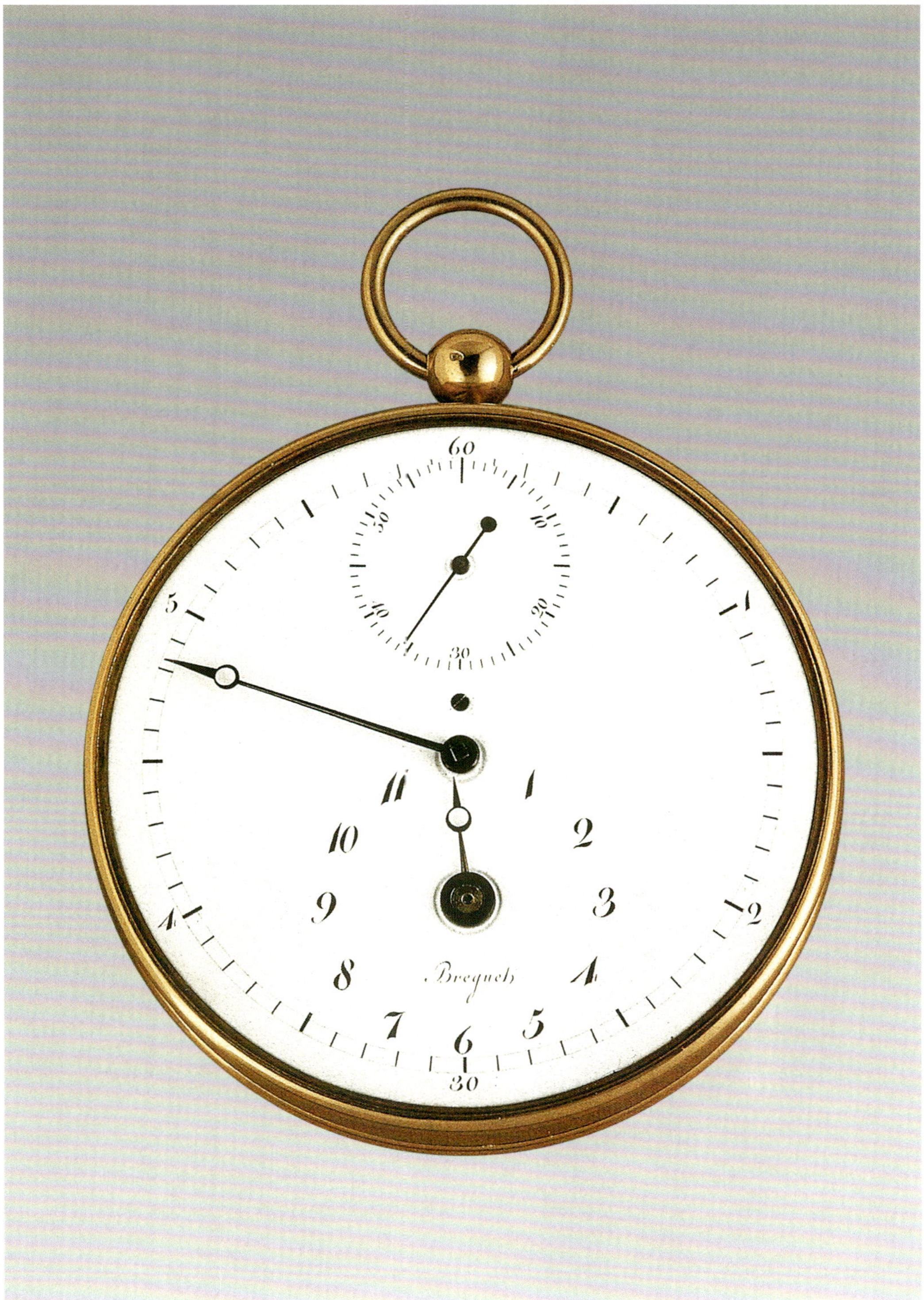

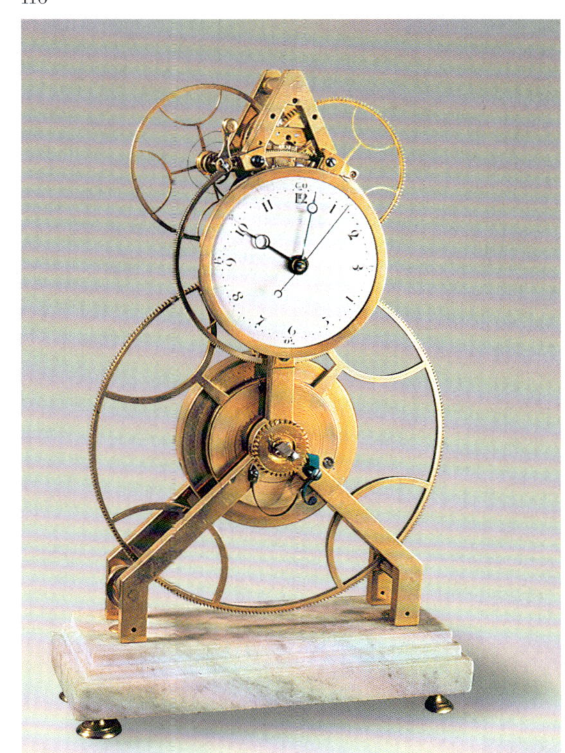

116

WALLPAPER

SECTION VI

Sabine Thümmler

THE AGE OF PAPER

"May I bother you with a small inquiry? I would like sixty-three yards of wallpaper in a pretty green and sixty-three yards of border, which I leave entirely up to your taste and theory of color." The person placing the order in 1796 was Friedrich Schiller; the individual being addressed, who carried out the assignment, was none other than Johann Wolfgang von Goethe, who responded: "I hope that the borders will appeal to you."

Paper wallpaper came into fashion at the end of the eighteenth century. During the Biedermeier period, it was already a standard component of interior furnishing because it offered a simple means of giving each room its own special atmosphere. Numerous fashion and interior decoration magazines published the latest wallpaper patterns. Building treatises and periodicals during the 1790s contained intense debates about the use of paper wallpaper, which was gradually replacing silk, chintz, or linen textiles, in part because it was cheaper. Additionally, in response to emerging thoughts about hygiene, paper was being universally praised for being cleaner and more resistant to insects than fabric. Nonetheless, increasingly foremost was its fashionability. Nobility and upper bourgeois circles paid considerable attention to current thinking. Consequently, numerous palaces and apartments were refurbished with modern paper wallpaper in the first quarter of the nineteenth century.

The new wallpapers first came through dealers from England, but France soon assumed the lead, with the work of manufacturers such as Réveillon. Elaborate wallpaper printed with fifteen colors was not uncommon. Shortly after 1800, wallpaper manufacturers emerged in the other European countries, such as Johann Christian Arnold in Kassel and Spörlin & Rahn in Vienna. Their wallpapers were of handmade paper, adhered together into rolls about fifty centimeters wide and ten meters long. In 1830, machine-made rolls of paper became available for printing. A unified ground color was applied, then carved wooden blocks and water-based distemper paint were used to create overlapping and layered colors.

THE SIMPLE WALL

Decorating with paper was an expression of a simple, unpretentious lifestyle in Jean-Jacques Rousseau's sense of a "return to nature." A virtue was seen in simplicity, in "distinguished moderation," which should be carried over to the home interior and elevated to an aesthetic principle. Thus, Biedermeier renounced luxurious materials and expansive ornament, for example, costly decorative textiles and wall-coverings. The wallpaper itself should emphasize color as a unifying element. Initial designs featured a rich interplay of hues and stylized geometric ornament; simplicity was achieved by avoiding any division of the fields and treating the wall as a decorative unity. Moldings installed as a base and a border under the ceiling enclosed the wall, as room designs by Antonin Friebel in Prague illustrate.

The color scheme provided for two complementary basic hues, accompanied by white, which facilitated color perception. Goethe had set forth this scheme in 1810 in his *Theory of Colors*, which was widely circulated in the form of popular excerpts. With wallpapering, it was also acceptable to play off two complementary base colors in the wall and its borders, with a ceiling of white or light gray. The two hues on the wall were echoed by the rest of the furnishings: upholstery, curtains, and rugs, right up through tablecloths and other accessories. Breezy white curtains or gathered partial drapes hung in the windows.

Biedermeier wallpaper was at first still pasted onto canvas and stretched on frames to be hung on the wall, like the textile coverings. Beginning in the 1830s, it became customary to affix this wallpaper with flour paste directly onto the plastered wall on a paper-pulp base. Edging along the margins imitated the woven borders used to conceal the ends of the textile coverings. In small, simple rooms, these ornamental bands were pasted horizontally over the baseboard and underneath the upper moldings; in more complex schemes, they framed the windows and doors and ran along the corners.

THE PATTERNS

These strikingly modest wallpapers display few colors and have simple geometric or floral patterns. They create the impression of a tranquil color accented by contrasting borders whose labor-intensive flowers, architectural elements, and drapery motifs sometimes echoed the basic pattern of the wallpaper. This restrained style was international; it is difficult to determine the origins of patterns discovered in France, Switzerland, Germany, or Sweden. The *Album Billot*, with patterns from Réveillon and its successor firm Jacquemart & Bénard, introduced many more than a hundred wallpapers with all-over patterns and stripes involving small plain motifs during the period 1800–20. They are strikingly similar to wallpapers distributed across Europe by the Kassel manufacturer Arnold. Designs discovered in Sweden or Switzerland are very similar, yet their drawing style differentiates them from those of the better-known fabrication centers.

Common to all these designs is their textile character, which suggests that these patterns were originally developed for fabrics. Cotton cloth, increasingly popular since the eighteenth century, experienced a boom at the beginning of the nineteenth, in conjunction with ground-breaking inventions in England. In 1785, machine weaving and rotational printing with engraved copper cylinders made possible the easy and rapid production of greater lengths of lightweight printed cottons. The pattern repeat now depended on the width of the cylinders (maximum fifty-five centimeters), so the technology favored small-detail patterns for fabrics produced using this process. Thus, it is also not surprising that the first typical Biedermeier swatches, bearing small, closely spaced geometric forms or highly stylized plant motifs, appeared on cotton fabrics made in England between 1800 and 1808. A wide spectrum of similar patterns is found around 1810 in the inventory of the Arnold firm. The longevity of such styles is demonstrated by Prague wall sketches drawn after 1825.

Popular patterns were unabashedly copied; manufacturers repeated the competition's innovations without hesitation. Nevertheless, from 1800 onward, pattern designers became increasingly important to the industry. The French academies of design set the standard for their training, primarily in drawing flowers and ornament. France also was the leader in technology and taste in wallpaper manufacture. It is not surprising that Johann Christian Arnold sent his son Carl Heinrich to Paris in 1811–12 to be trained by Jacquemart & Bénard and Joseph Dufour, the most renowned firms in the business, and that modified French patterns, even to the point of literal quotations, are found in his production. The pattern from the residence of the brothers Grimm constitutes one such direct adoption: the stepped squares set on their corners are repeated in offset rows, with small, white leaf-shapes softening the strictly geometric composition. Jacquemart & Bénard's design from 1801 differs only in the central classical rosette, which Arnold replaced with a starlike motif. Arnold also shamelessly copied as well as marketed wallpapers created by the famous Zuber company of Rixheim in Alsace.

Vienna also became an important center for Biedermeier wallpaper. In 1809, with Heinrich Rahn, Michael Spörlin, who had trained in the firm of his brother-in-law Jean Zuber in Rixheim, began production in Vienna. In 1816, Spörlin succeeded in developing wallpapers with the so-called "iris effect" – which was to make him world famous. In imitation of the shimmering effect of silk damask, colors gradually faded at their edges to transition to another hue. This new technique was first used in the sky portions of figural wallpapers. Three years later, working with Jean Zuber's son in Rixheim, Spörlin was able to refine the technique, and in 1822 he presented the first collection of iridescent wallpaper. Although first limited to the background color, iridescent printing subsequently also became possible for the motifs. In 1822 and 1823, Spörlin received two licenses for the process, which was used internationally for producing wallpaper but especially for printing calico fabrics – a link between these two domains. Stylized floral designs in contrasting colors appeared astonishingly novel and modern. Graphic surface interplay eschewed spatial illusionism in favor of flat optical effects, similar to the grained veneers favored in furniture. Scottish plaids represented another revolutionary type of ornamentation at this time. At first used only for lining men's coats, plaids came to play a role in women's outerwear and influenced wall-coverings as well. Appealing because of their Romantic connection to the unspoiled landscape and people of Scotland, they were used for whole walls as well as borders.

In addition to the cotton designs, iridescent silk effects, and Scottish plaids was the so-called drapery wallpaper. It reproduced a luxurious French Empire fashion, but radically simplified and given a linear character to accord with Biedermeier taste. It could be restricted to laboriously composed friezes, such as in the Arnold firm's scheme in which the double-leveled drapery motif runs around the top of the wall (evidently in regular alternation with drapery rods or threaded through rings of blossoms).

In summary, Biedermeier wallpapers were characterized by a formal language that spread very rapidly through Europe and determined the fashions of wall-covering for almost three decades. Following a beginning characterized by little change, the 1830s saw the development of richer internal patterns and lively floral decoration.

117
Five Wallpapers
from a Wallpaper
Pattern Book
Vienna, 1827
Cat. VI-1

117

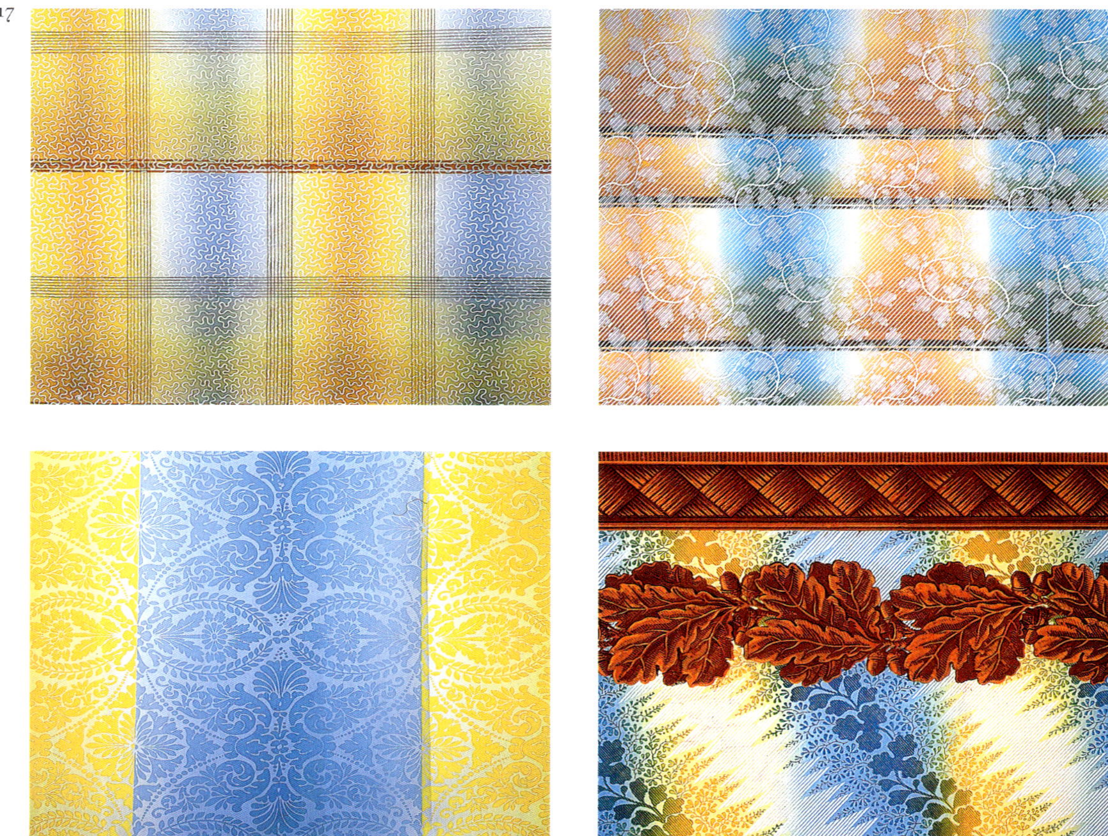

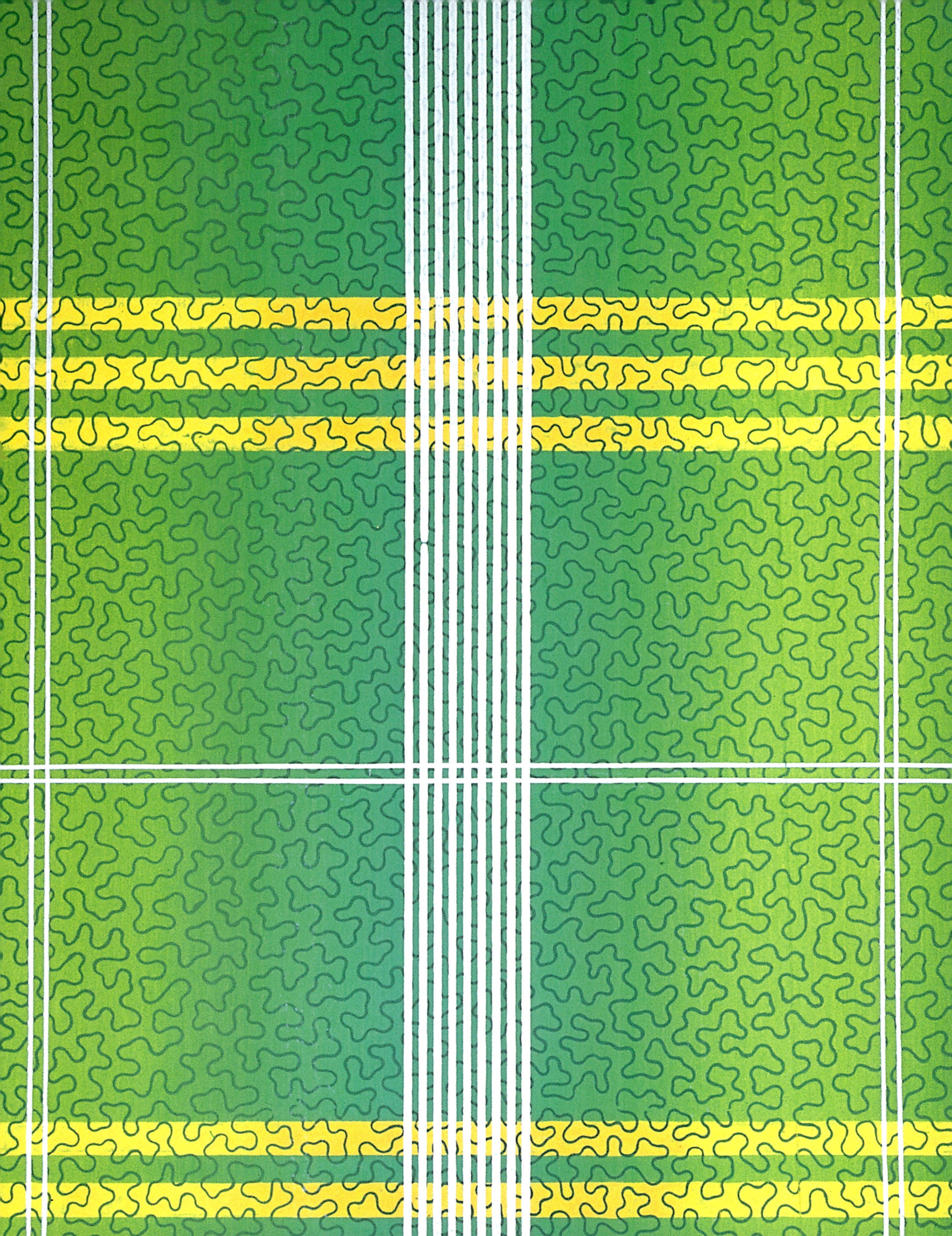

118
*Wallpaper from
a Wallpaper
Pattern Book*
Vienna, 1824
Cat. VI-2

119
*Two Wallpapers
from a Wallpaper
Pattern Book*
Vienna, 1828
Cat. VI-4

120
*Wallpaper from
a Wallpaper
Pattern Book*
Vienna, 1829
Cat. VI-5

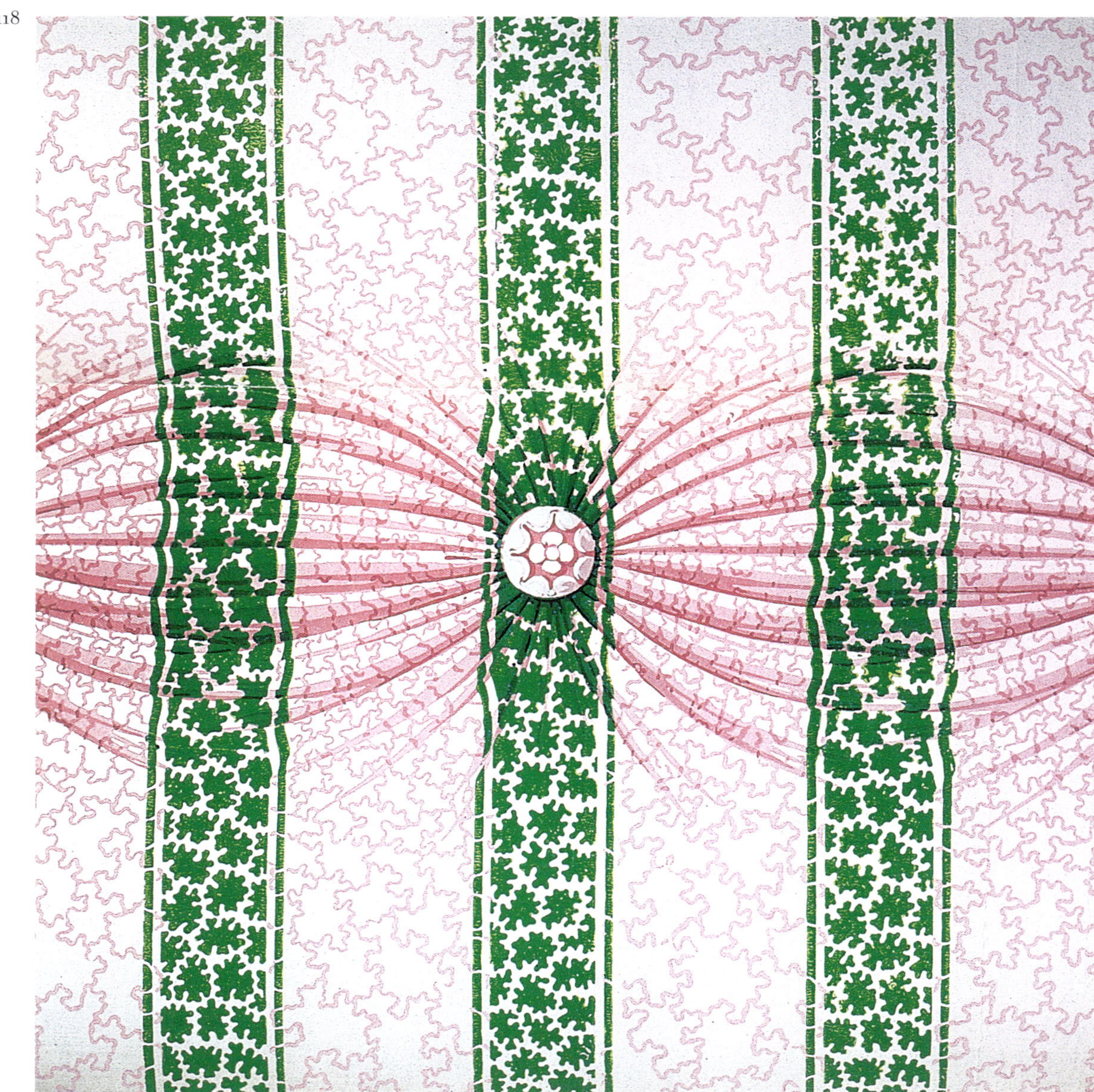

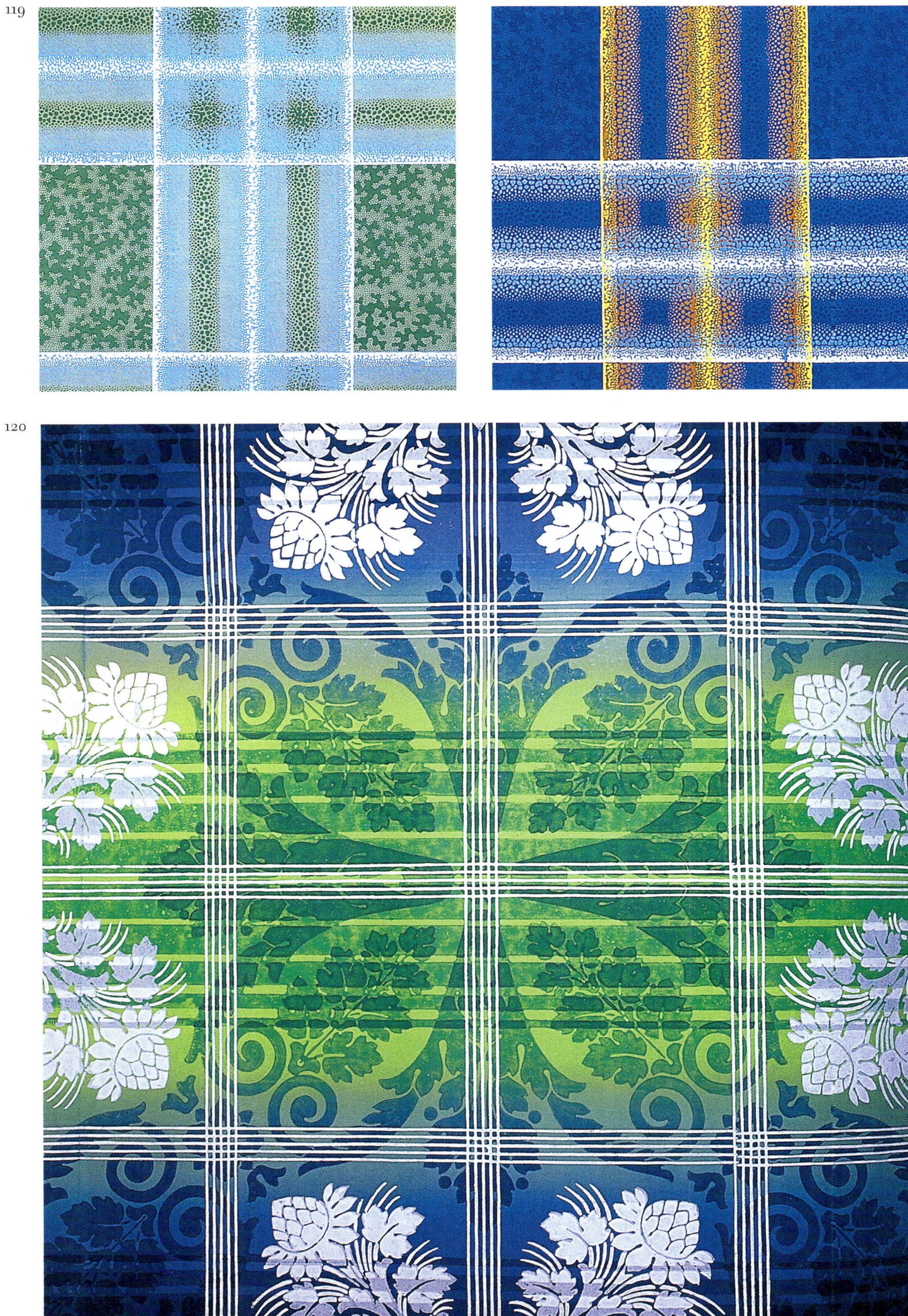

121
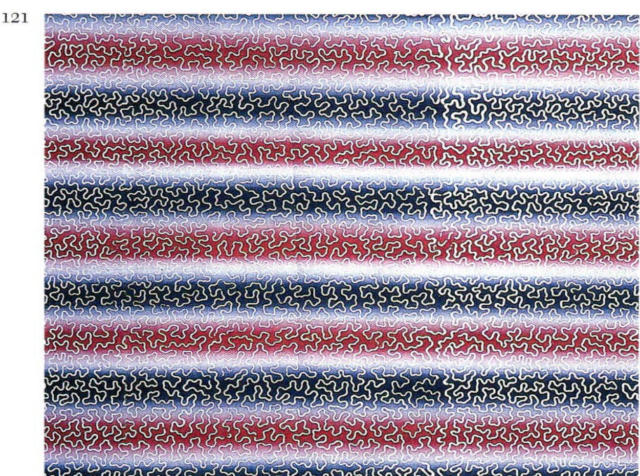
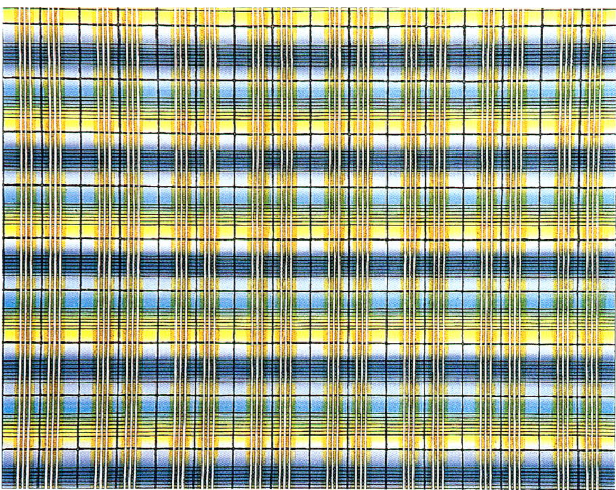

122
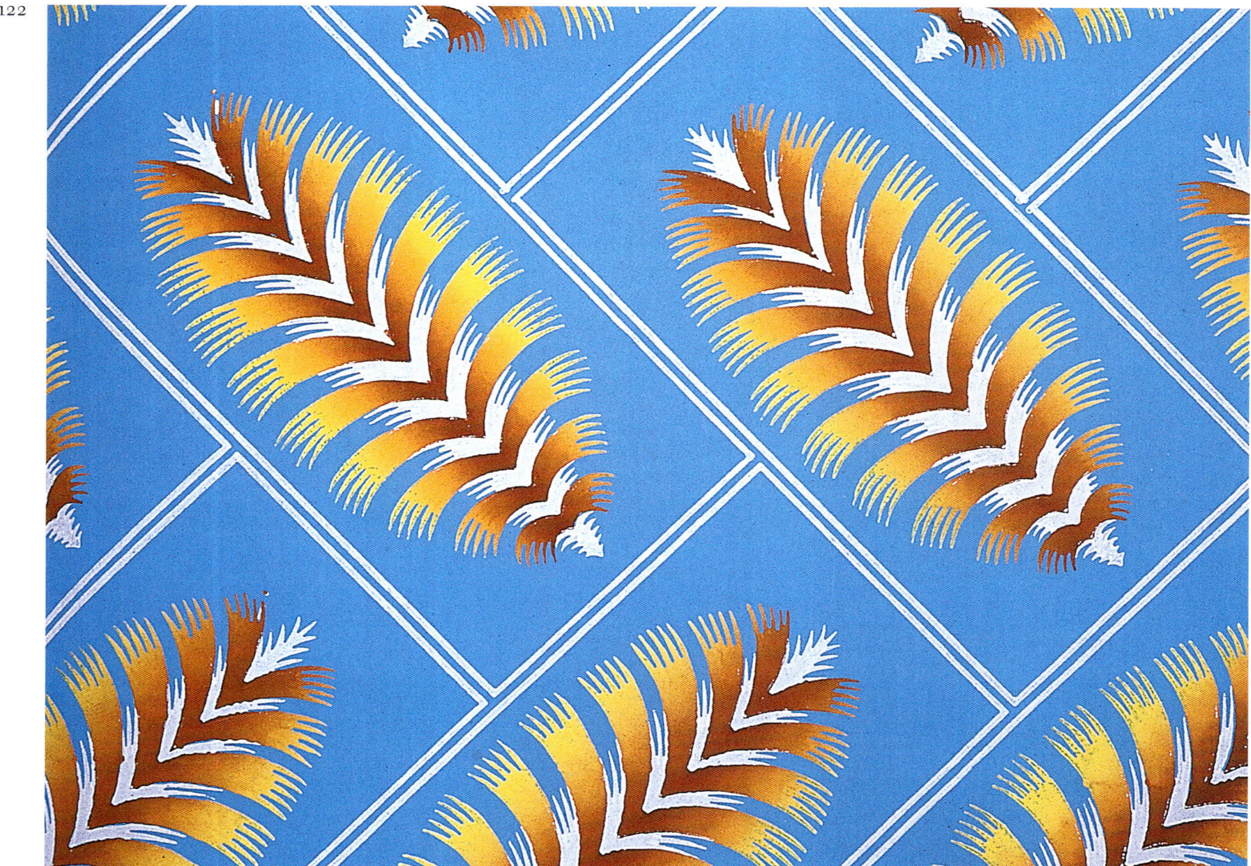

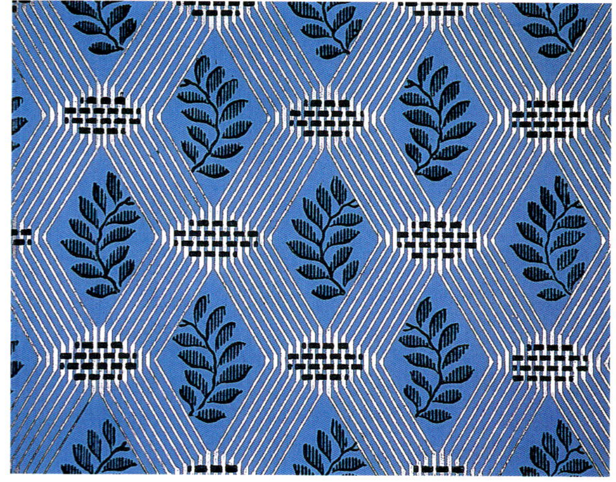
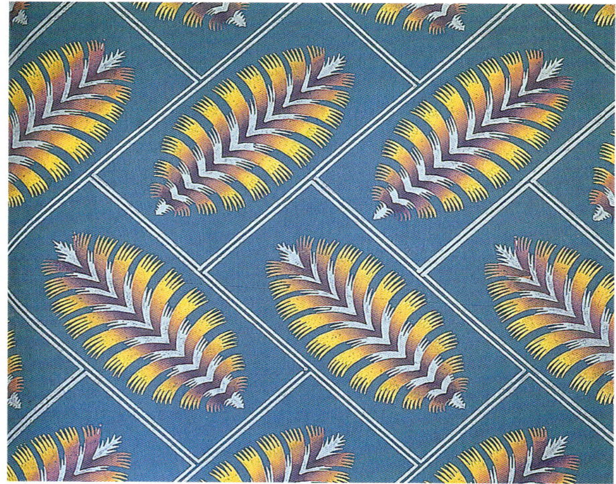

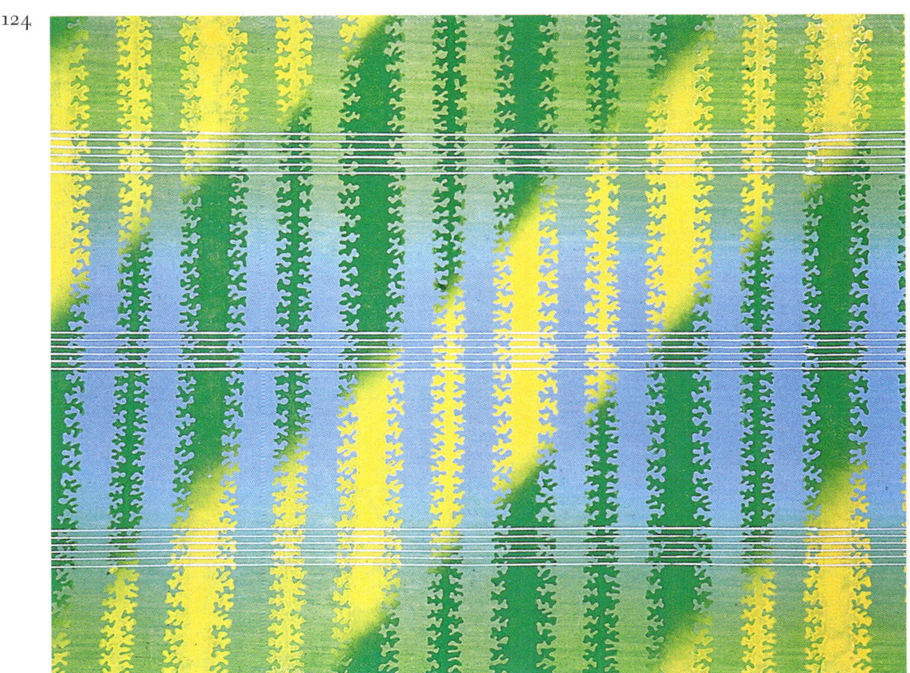

123

124

121
*Wallpaper and
Decorative Paper
from a Pattern Book*
Vienna, 1828
Cat. vi-6

122
*Decorative Paper
and Two Wallpapers
from a Pattern Book*
Vienna, 1827
Cat. vi-7

123
*Wallpaper from
a Wallpaper
Pattern Book*
Vienna, 1825
Cat. vi-8

124
*Wallpaper from
a Wallpaper
Pattern Book*
Vienna, 1823
Cat. vi-9

125
*Six Studies for
the Decoration of
Interior Walls*
Bohemia, 1837/50
Cat. VI-10 (selection)

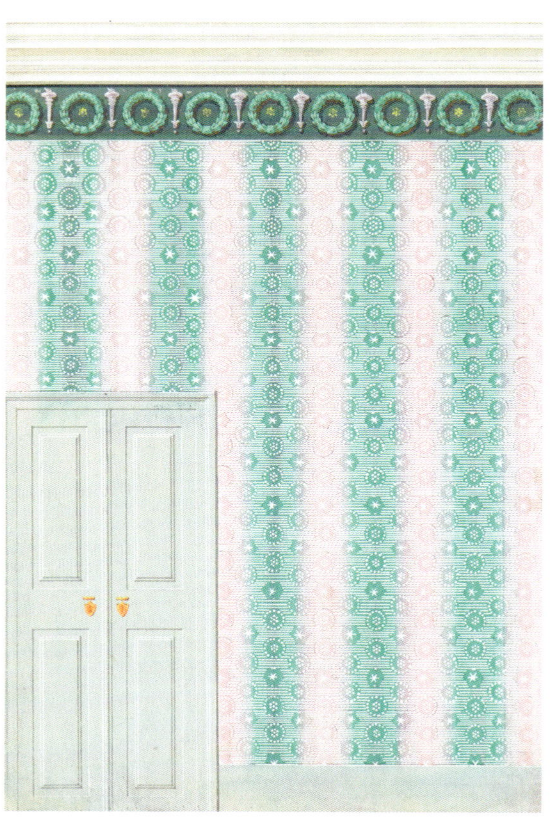

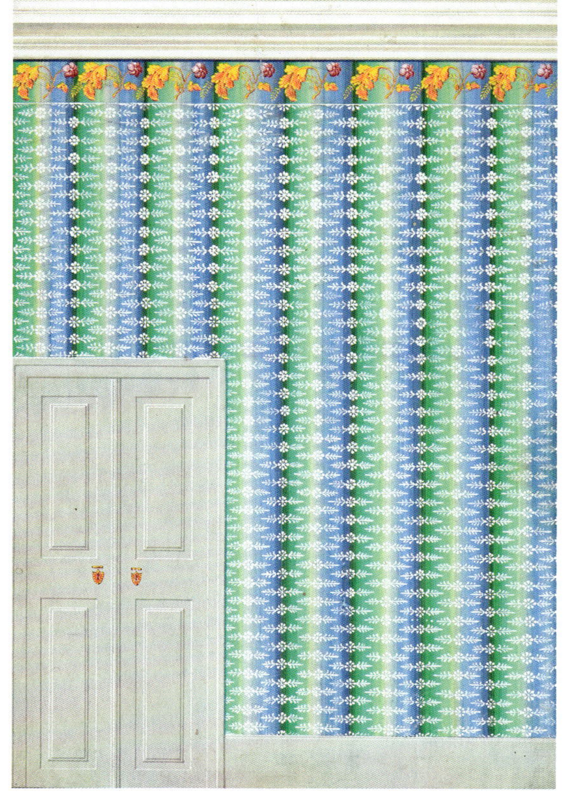

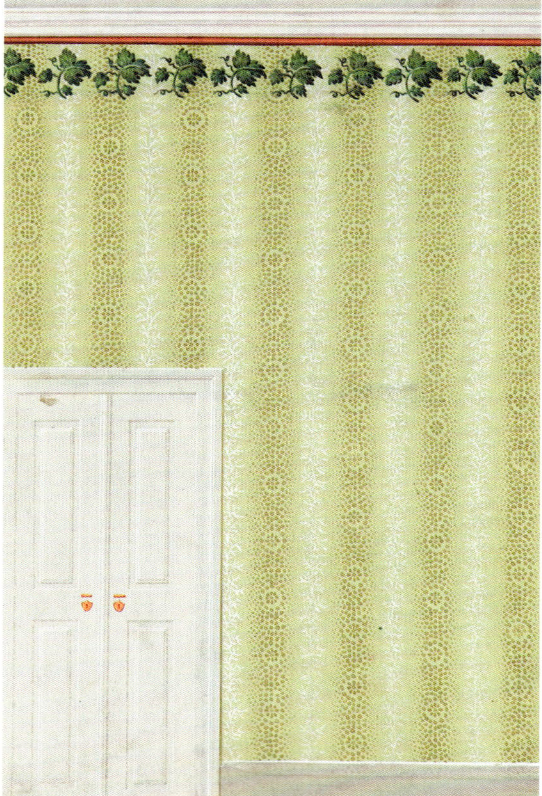

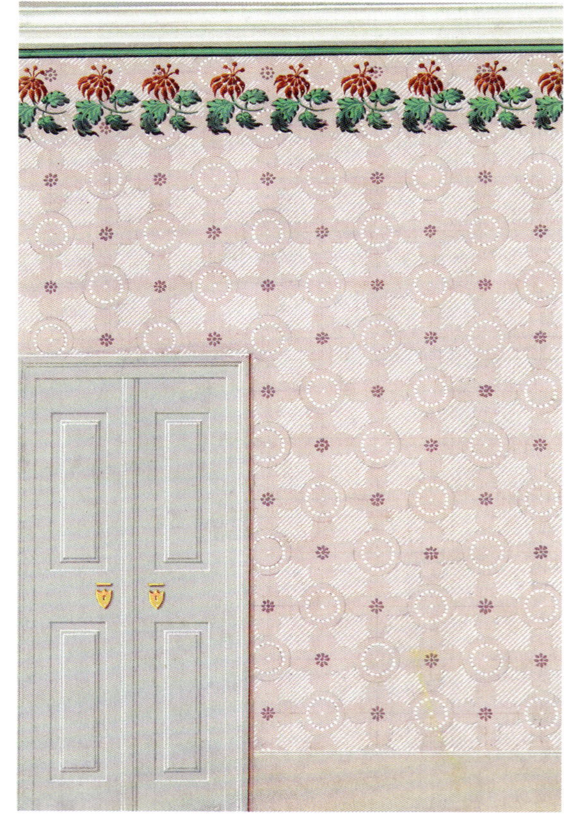

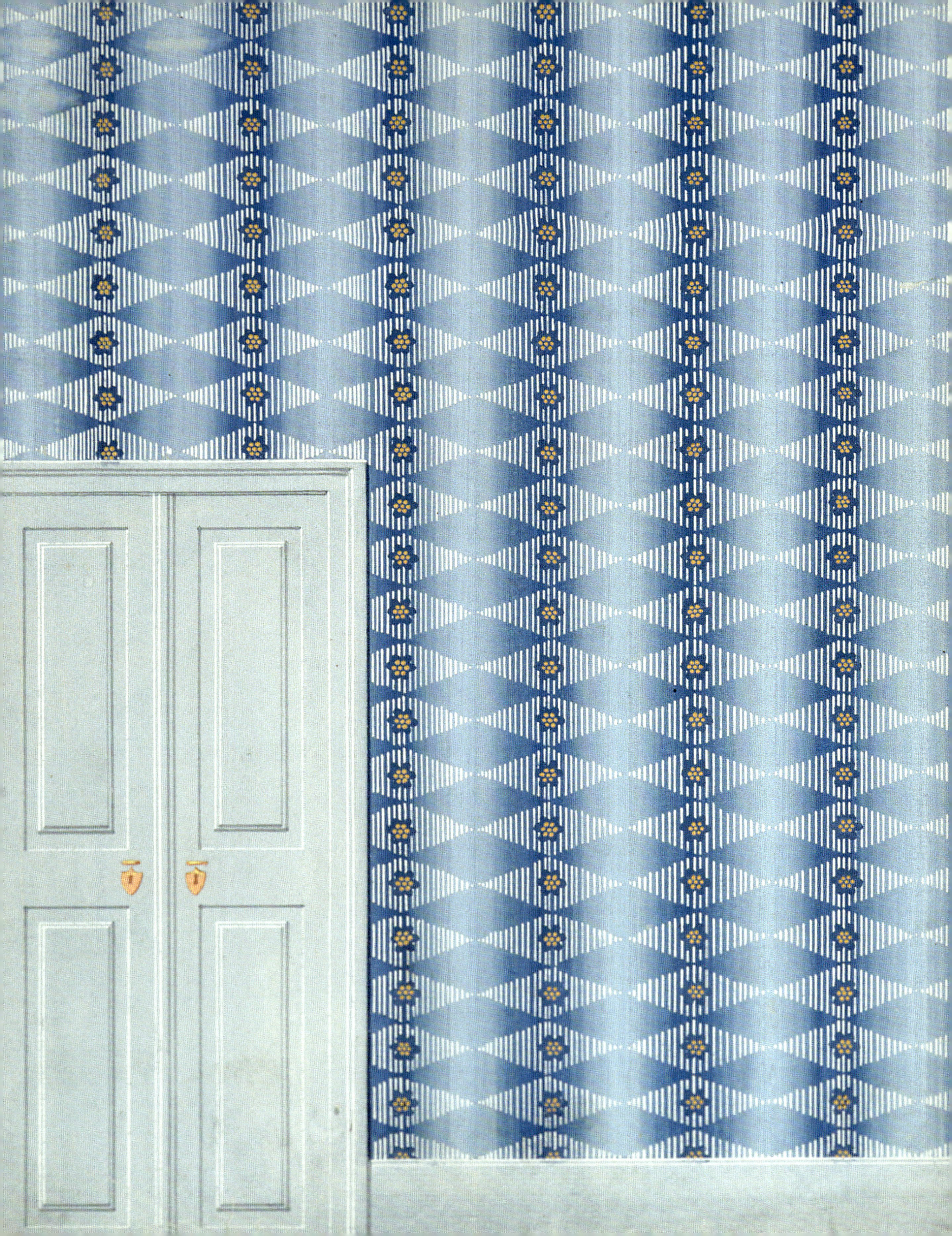

126

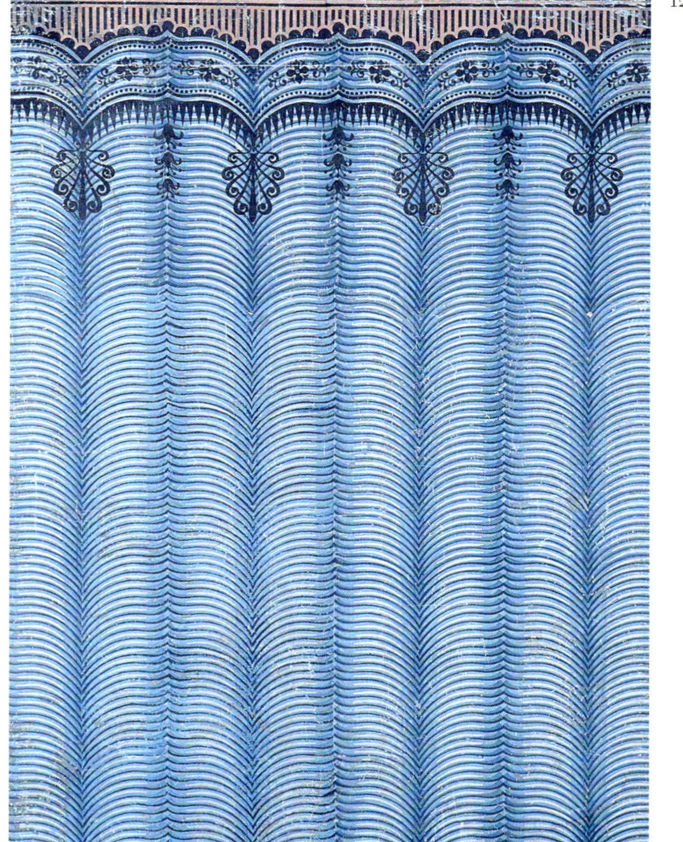

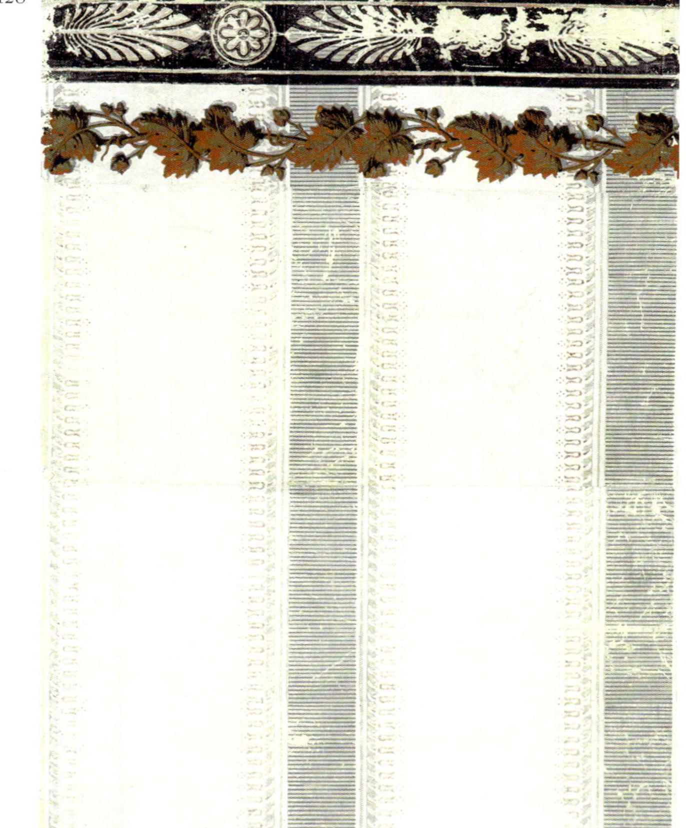

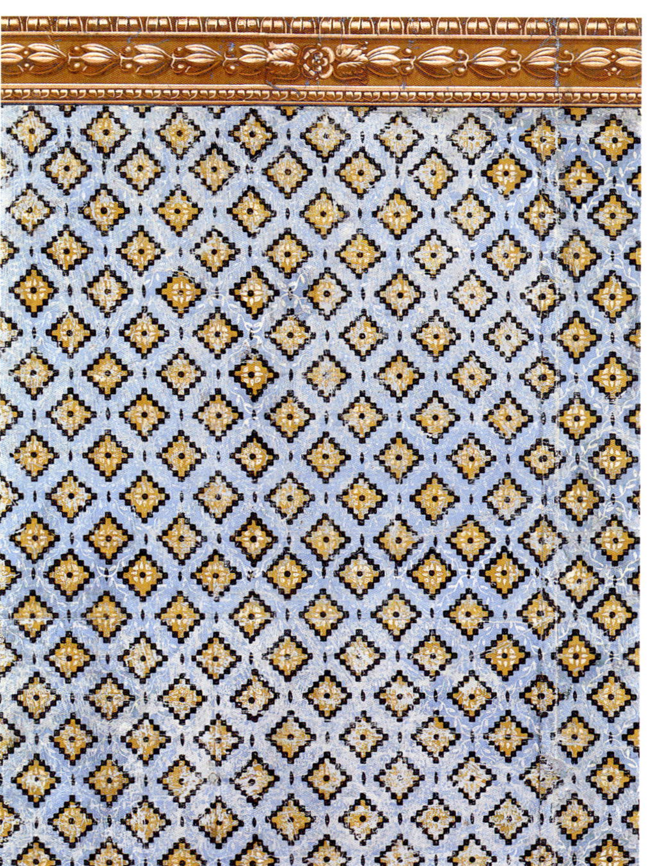

130

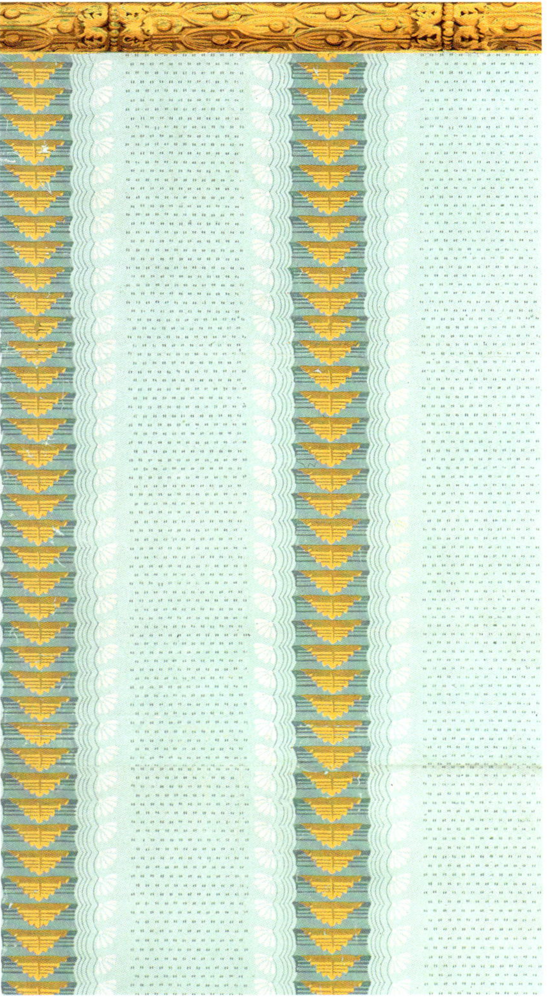

131

126
*Repeat Pattern
Wallpaper with
Upper and Lower
(French?) Borders*
Germany, ca. 1825
Cat. vi-11

127
*Repeat Pattern
Wallpaper with
Matching Upper
and Lower Borders*
Germany, 1800/10
Cat. vi-14

128
*Repeat Pattern
Wallpaper with
Matching Upper
and Lower Borders
in Two Parts*
Germany, 1815/20
Cat. vi-13

129
*Repeat Pattern
Wallpaper with
Upper and Lower
(French?) Borders*
Germany, 1808
Cat. vi-12

130
*Repeat Pattern
Wallpaper with
Matching Upper
and Lower Borders*
Germany, ca. 1820
Cat. vi-15

131
*Repeat Pattern
Wallpaper with
Lower Border*
Germany, 1820/30
Cat. vi-16

PORCELAIN

SECTION VII

Albrecht Pyritz

The development of Biedermeier porcelain began around 1790 when modelers began simplifying their shapes and designs in line with the models and archetypes of classical antiquity as the source of all Western art. The Attic Greek amphora served as the model for many of the straight-walled cylindrical or conical vessels created during this period. Their handles, too, while bent off at right angles to enhance the linearity of the "neo-Greek style," nevertheless resemble those of Attic Greek kylikes and kraters. The plates and saucers are either "antique smooth" or "conical" with a sloping inside rim characteristic of the porcelain produced throughout the Biedermeier period.

Alongside this smooth, straight-walled porcelain, the Empire style that became popular from 1805 onward and that bore the stamp of the French porcelain factories led to an increase in both round-bellied "Campanian style" and almost egg-shaped "Etrurian style" vases. Most of these objects are designed with an indented foot and furnished with either elongated ribbon handles or swan handles. Decoration ranges from simple white to extravagant floral and foliate ornamentation.

In 1790, when Duke Peter of Kurland commissioned a 450-piece dinner service from the Königliche Porzellanmanufaktur Berlin, it marked in Prussia the advent of this new style of tableware. Completed in 1794, the Kurland Service shows its indebtedness to antique models in its simplicity and the smoothness of its surfaces; the plain white conical walls are decorated only with a frieze around the rim and angular handles. Tablewares with such neoclassical designs appealed to both the aristocracy and bourgeoisie alike. Many of the models were soon copied by rival factories (Berlin 2003, p. 14). It was also at this time that most porcelain factories in the German-speaking world began systematically expanding their repertory of patterns with the intention to ensure that their designs would retain their marketability well into the future. Among the services produced prior to 1800 were several with floral patterns, plates that artfully alternated matte and glazed surfaces, and vessels with a black or colored ground, narrow strip friezes, and contrasting wave band patterns. These design elements were taken a step further in the first decade of the nineteenth century and by 1820 had a firm place in Biedermeier porcelain's expressive canon.

An important precondition for the economic development of the porcelain manufactories was the comprehensive modernization of factories that began in Berlin and Vienna around 1790. By the early nineteenth century, most plants had state-of-the-art equipment. Improved kilns permitted more sophisticated firing techniques; steam engines could be used to produce large quantities of very fine and homogeneous porcelain pastes and glazes. Technical innovations around 1800 led to changes in the quality and the application of porcelain paints. While the porcelain painters of the late eighteenth century had only high-glaze colors and limited enamel paints to choose for underglazing, years of experimentation with metal oxides produced significant improvements and meant also that no fewer than thirty-five different hues were now available for overglaze painting as well (Faÿ-Hallé and Mundt 1983, p. 60). These colors could then be combined with gold, silver, and platinum trim, also improved enormously as a result of new polishing and etching methods.

The production of such exquisitely decorated porcelain required painters trained in the art of historical and landscape painting or in floral and foliate, purely ornamental, or so-called "pattern painting." The modelers and formers had to be skillful designers. In order to secure a sufficiently skilled workforce, the porcelain factories began to cooperate with the art academies of the royal palaces. Starting in 1785 in Vienna and in 1788 in Berlin, these schools began offering classes to the porcelain painters and modelers. The porcelain factories also opened schools of their own that in the early nineteenth century developed into full-fledged colleges of applied art. In 1815, for example, the painting department of the Nymphenburger Porzellanmanufaktur was elevated to the status of an institute of applied art. In that same year, the Königliche Porzellanmanufaktur Berlin opened its own drawing and painting school and attached great importance to perspectival drawing, hiring Leopold Zielcke, professor at the Kunstakademie, to teach the subject. His pupils Eduard Gaertner and Johann Heinrich Hintze were to profit enormously from their lessons with him.

The end of the Napoleonic Wars in 1815 triggered a boom in the porcelain business, with many of Europe's ruling families ordering huge services in honor of their victory. Vases, cups, and whole series of individually decorated but otherwise identical models in a dazzling array of colors were also produced as commemorative or memorial pieces. Some items were sold unpainted so that customers could order individualized decorative schemes. The new look in domestic interiors of the Biedermeier era with their glass showcases and cabinets transformed porcelain from an exquisite, but primarily functional, object into something that formed an integral part of the décor and whose sole purpose was to give aesthetic pleasure.

Under its artistic director Johann Peter Melchior (1742–1825), the Nymphenburger Porzellanmanufaktur near Munich became one of Europe's leading producers. Its "antik" series of tableware, for example, evinces a formal language of universal validity throughout Europe (Munich 1997, ill. p. 276). Responding to the prevailing taste, Melchior oversaw the production of a plethora of cylindrical tableware and countless busts, figurines, and medallions containing portraits of members of the ruling Wittelsbach dynasty. Large series of plates and platters bearing copies of paintings in the royal art collections were also popular. When the architect Friedrich von Gärtner (1792–1847) took over from Melchior in 1822, the Nymphenburg factory intensified its engagement with the language of classical antiquity. In his new version of the exquisite 1810 "antik C" service, Gärtner sought to build upon the design feats of his predecessor. The service displays a strikingly elegant simplicity in the combination of its plain, matte blue finish and extravagant gold trim.

An important influence on the porcelain of this period was the interest in the natural world. Voyages of discovery and overland expeditions undertaken with the aim of proving the most disparate theories regarding the origins of life and the laws of nature had been the principal line of scientific inquiry since the end of the eighteenth century. They found their way into art as well, denoting a clear shift away from idealized depictions of nature toward a more scientific representation. Like the scientists, the artists of this era began to take a keen interest in both their native environment and in more exotic countries. The opening to the public of the natural history collections of the courts of Vienna, Paris, and Berlin had consequences for the applied arts, too. Even before 1800, the porcelain factories in Paris and Vienna followed by Berlin began producing vases, cups, and plates based on models in these collections. They were painted to look like agate, lapis lazuli, amethyst, and malachite, with bases and plinths that resembled blocks of porphyry or marble. Vienna and Berlin even produced decorative plates, cups, and vases consisting entirely of reproduction agates

and carnelians. This wide range of collectors' items continued to find enthusiastic buyers right up to the 1840s.

Out of concern for accuracy, the porcelain factories usually took their floral and foliate motifs from scientific works, depicting each plant as a typical example of a particular species or variety (Berlin 1999, p. 202), a textbook effect that is further enhanced by noting the botanical name on the underside of the porcelain. The 1,800-piece "Flora Danica" dinner and dessert service (1790–1802) created by the Königliche Porzellanmanufaktur Kopenhagen is not only one of the most magnificent examples of royal tableware ever produced. but is also the largest known collection of botanical porcelain (Berlin 1999, pp. 205f.). In 1806, during the French occupation of Prussia, the Porzellanmanufaktur Berlin received an order for a dessert service for the Empress Joséphine of France, bearing motifs taken from the *Jardin de la Malmaison* collection of colored engravings by Pierre-Joseph Redouté (1759–1840) that the empress had commissioned. The few surviving dessert dishes show meticulously drawn flowers, painstakingly painted onto a colored or black ground and framed by a gilded inner rim; on the outer rim is an exquisitely etched garland. The Wiener Porzellanmanufaktur in 1818 began work on a series of "dessert plates with all kinds of flowers" for the royal household that was originally to have comprised thirty-six, but in the end ran to ninety-six, items. The decorative scheme was based on scientific watercolor studies of various native and some exotic plants in the imperial gardens. Painted onto a brown-black ground, these plants demonstrate an extraordinary vitality that is enhanced by their frame of gold borders and beige-colored rims. In the late 1820s, these dark-ground plates were followed by a series of white flower plates with a gold border that marked the last expression of the era of exquisite botanical porcelain.

132
Coffee Service
Nymphenburg, ca. 1825
Cat. VII-1

133
(Opposite)
Coffee Bowls
Vienna, ca. 1835
Cat. VII-4

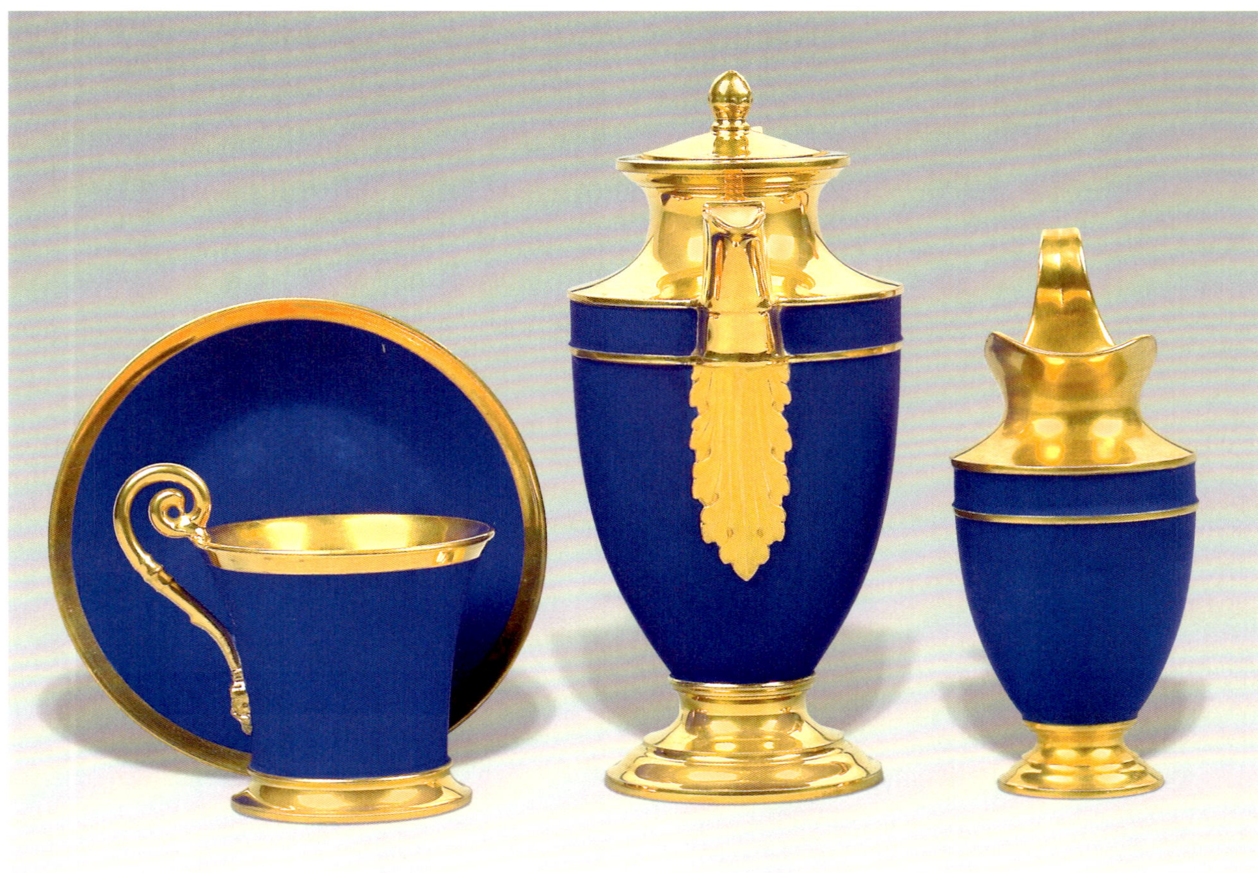

132

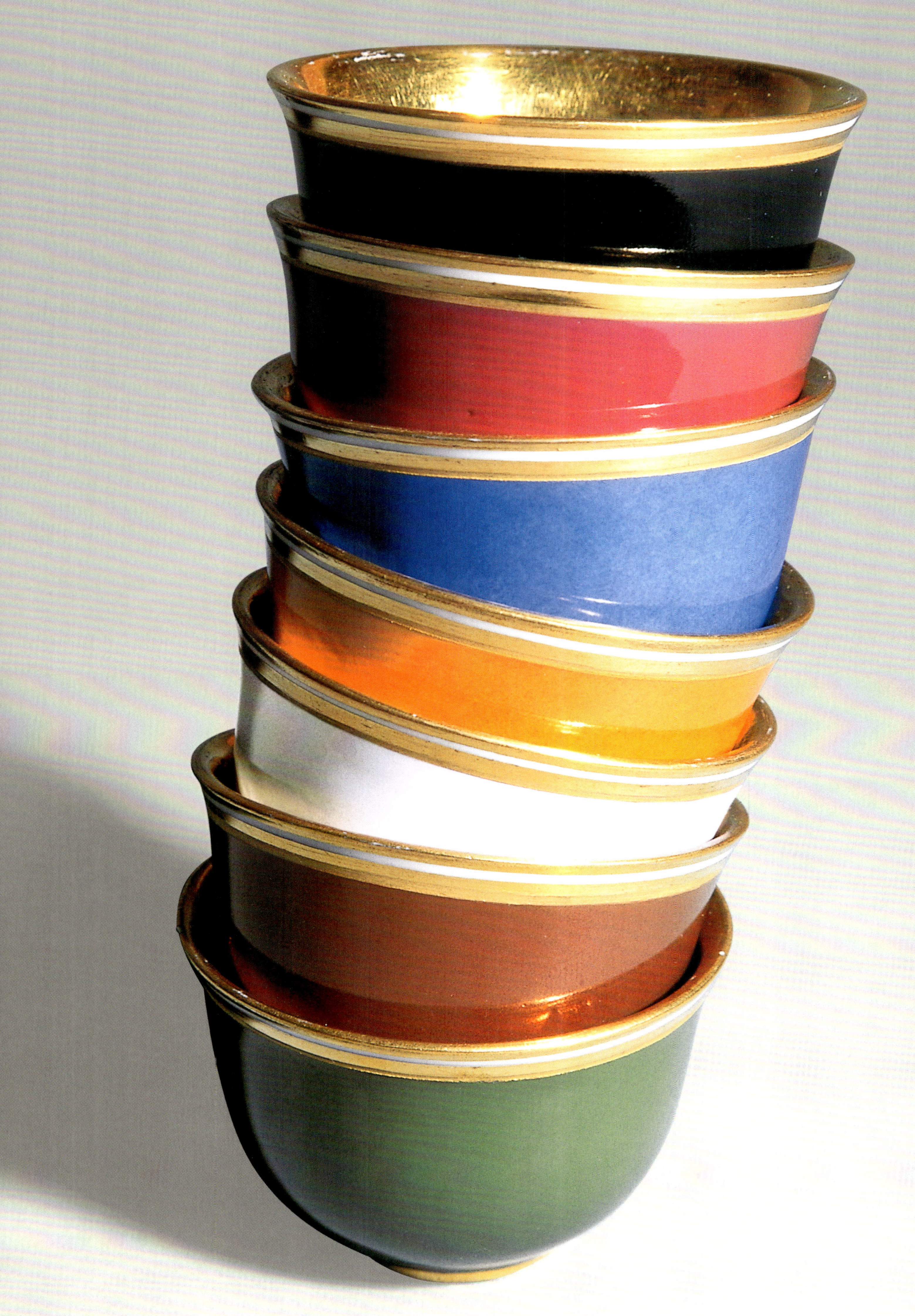

134

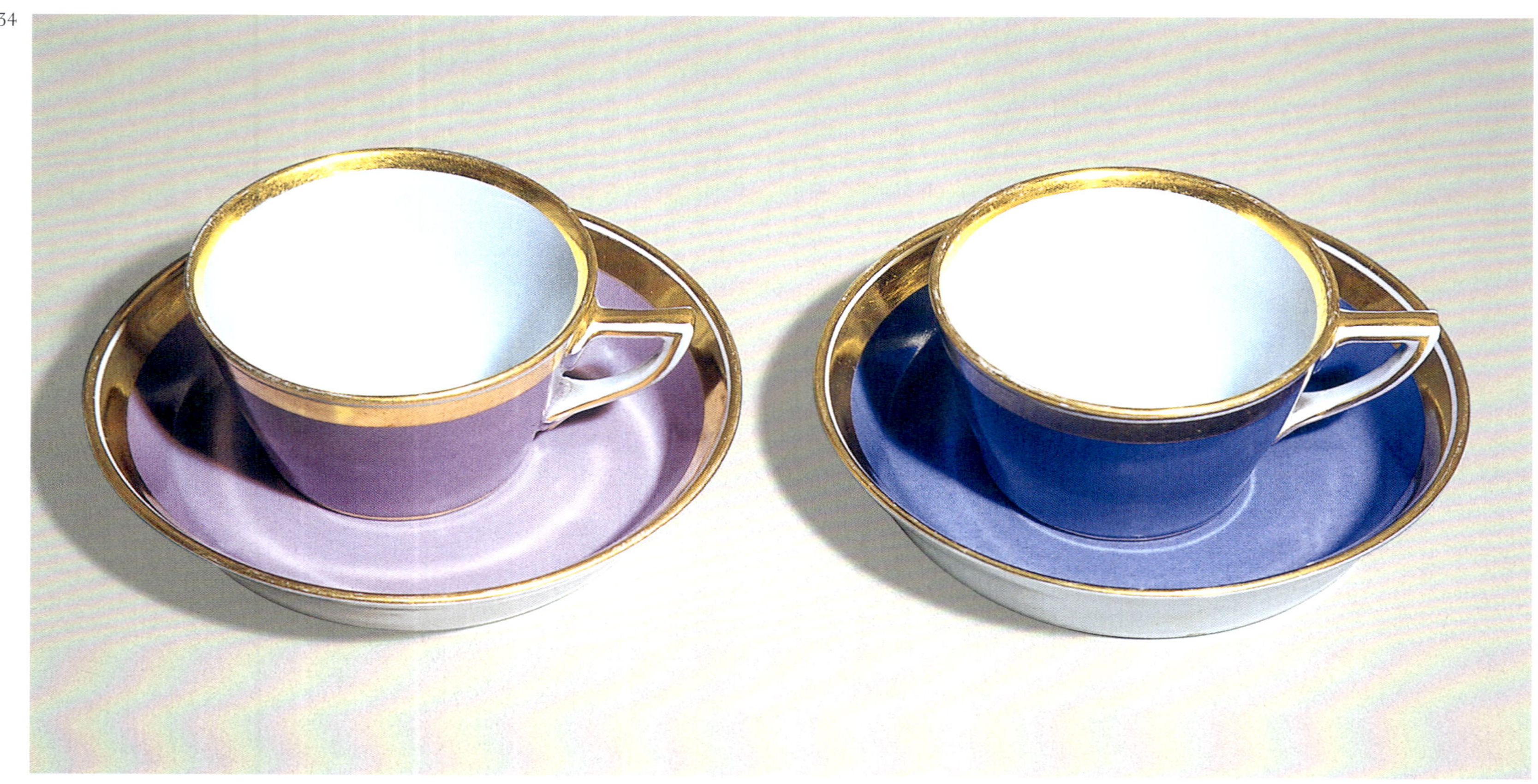

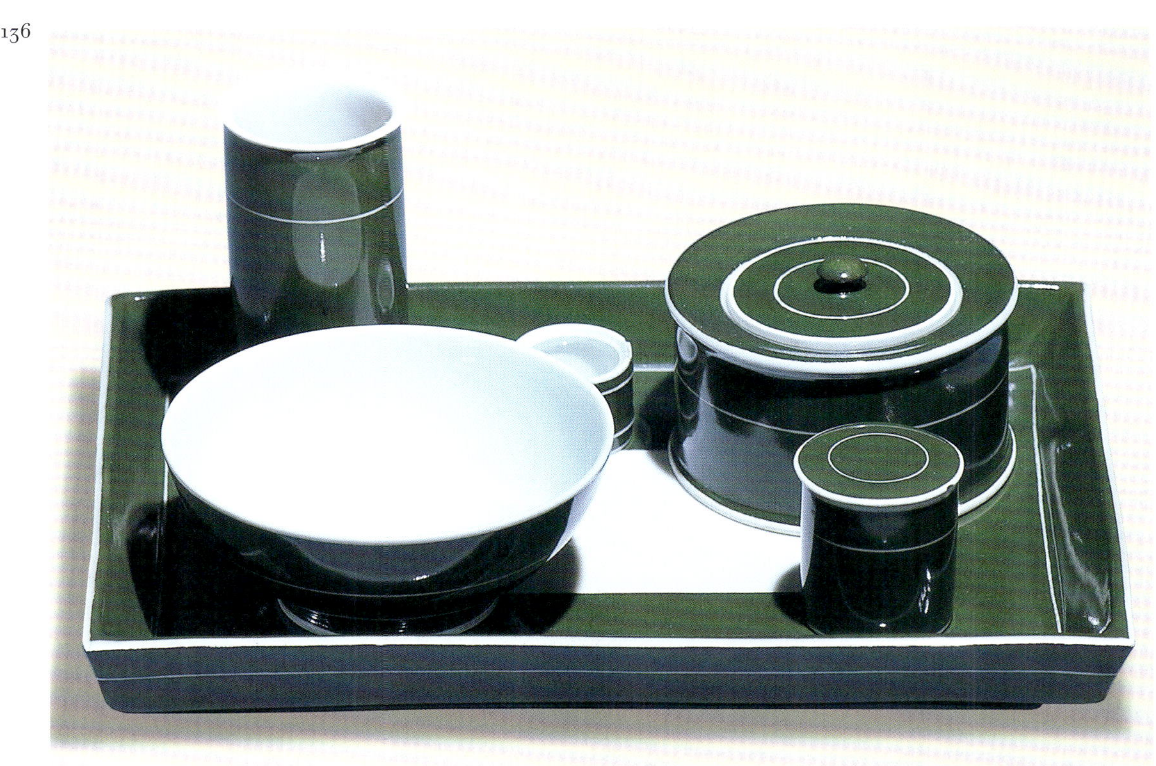

135

136

134
Two Cups and Saucers
Vienna, 1814/17
Cat. VII-2

135
Tea Service
Vienna, 1811
Cat. VII-5

136
Writing Set
Vienna, 1823/24
Cat. VII-6

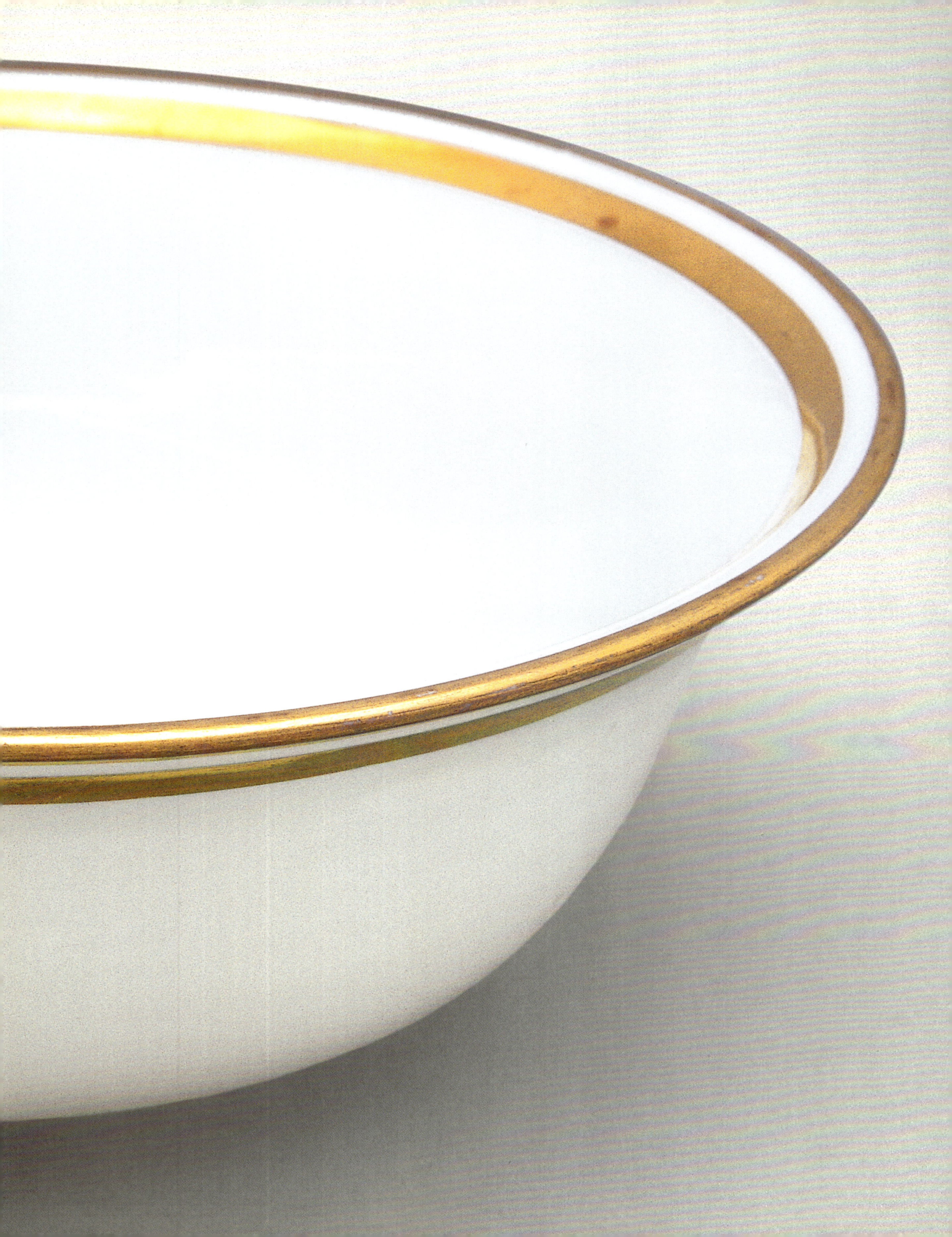

138

137
(Opposite)
*Family Dinner Service of
Emperor Franz II (I)*
Vienna, 1814/40
Cat. VII-7 (detail)

138
*Tea Service with Coffee
Pot*
Berlin, 1820/40
Cat. VII-8 (selection)

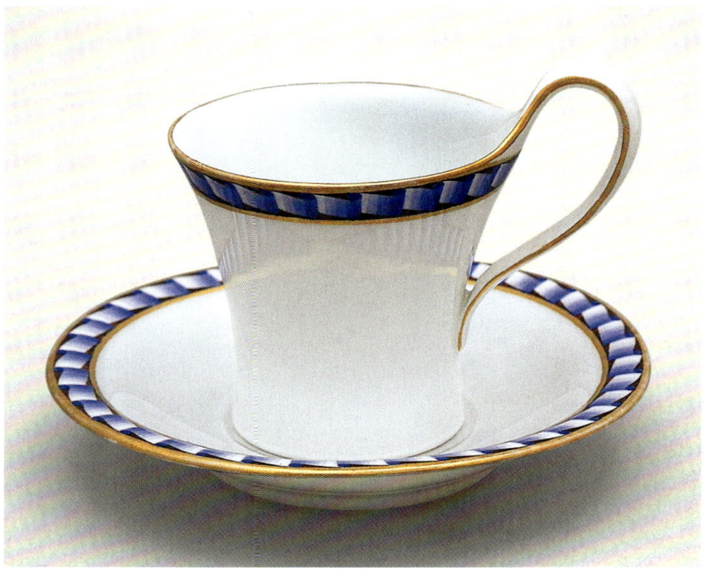

139

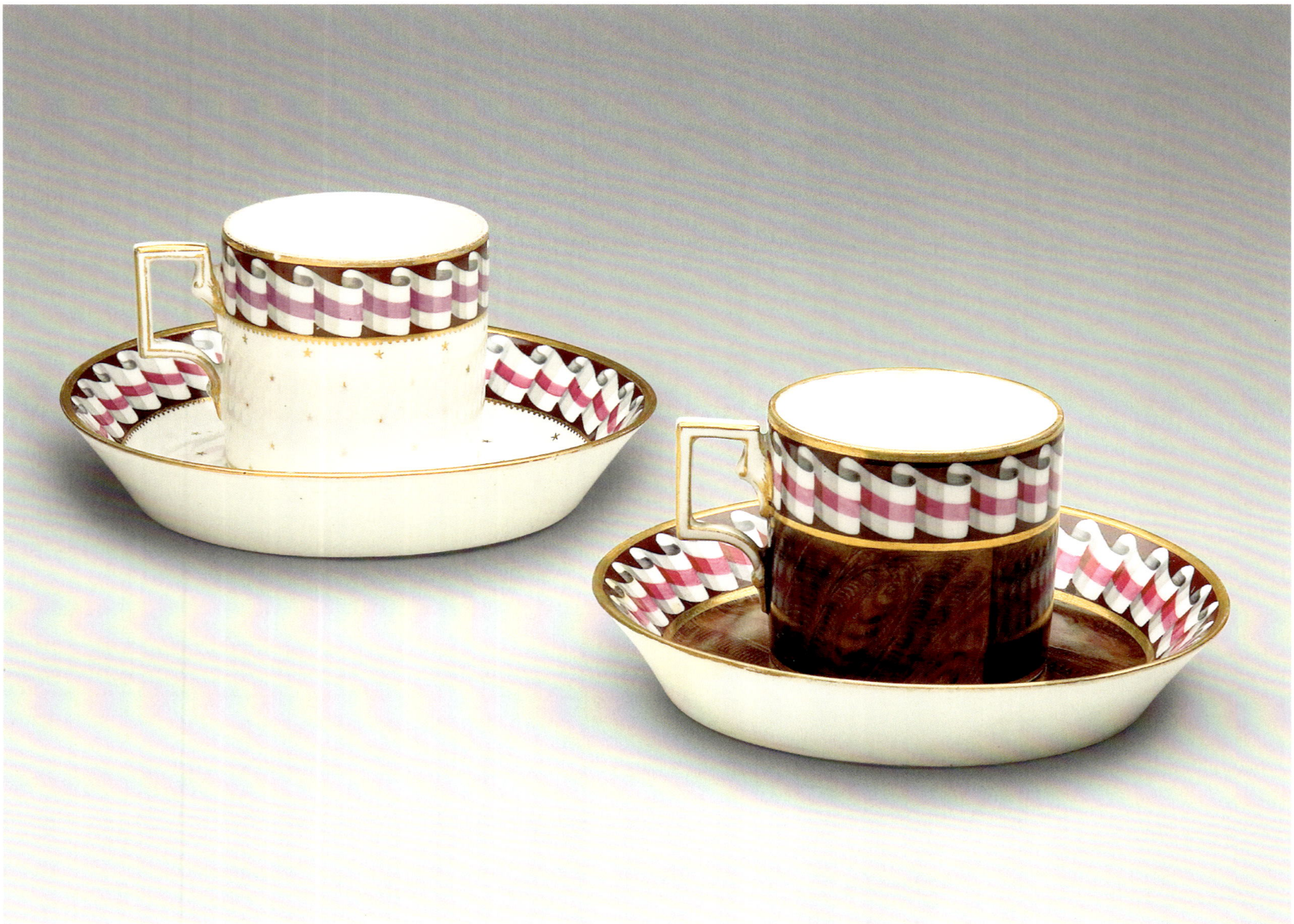

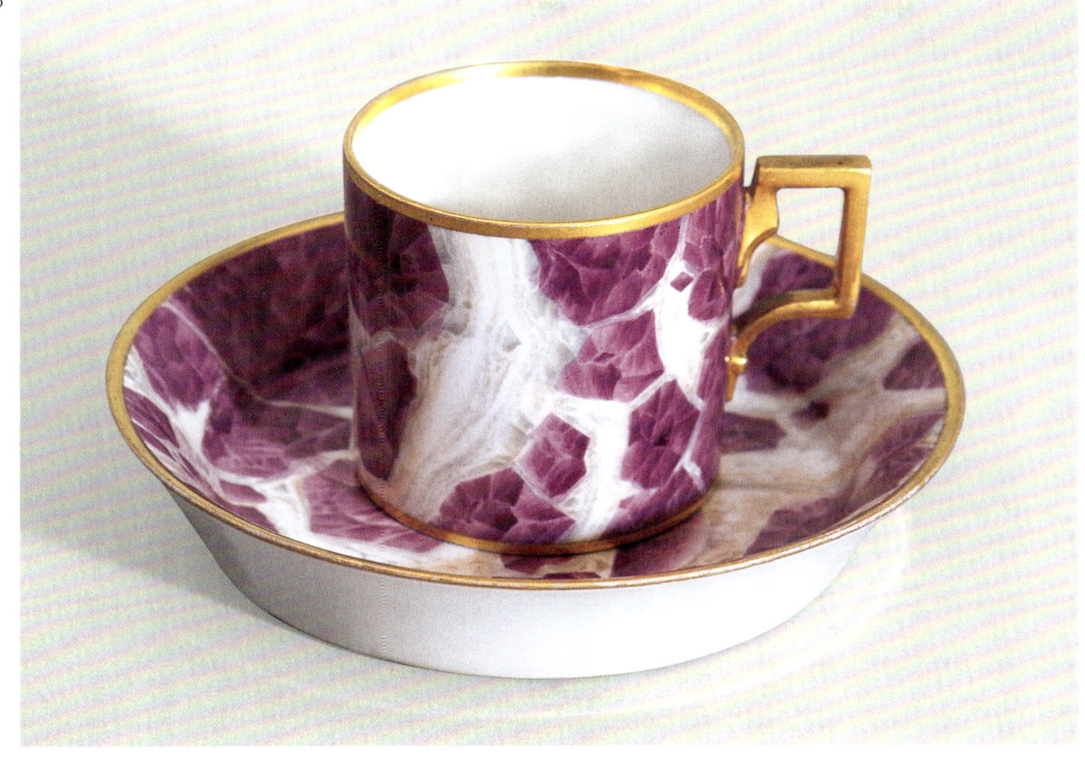

140

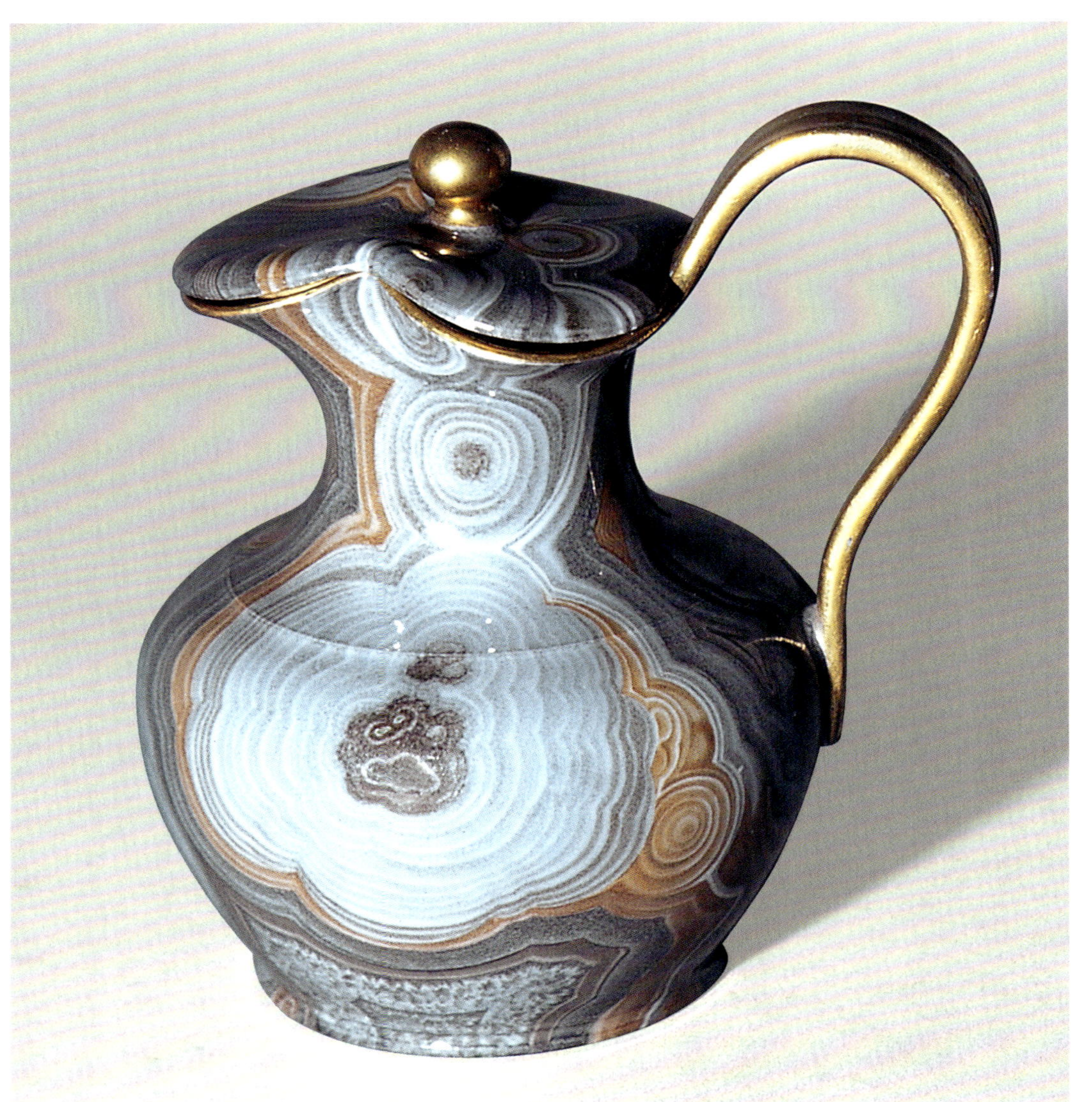

141

139
Two Cups and Saucers
Vienna, ca. 1800
Cat. VII-10

140
Cup and Saucer with
Amethyst Pattern
Vienna, ca. 1804
Cat. VII-11

141
Pitcher with
Agate Pattern
Vienna, 1810
Cat. VII-12

142
Flower Plates
Vienna, 1818/27
Cat. VII-13 (selection)

143
Flower Plates
Vienna, 1833
Cat. VII-14

142

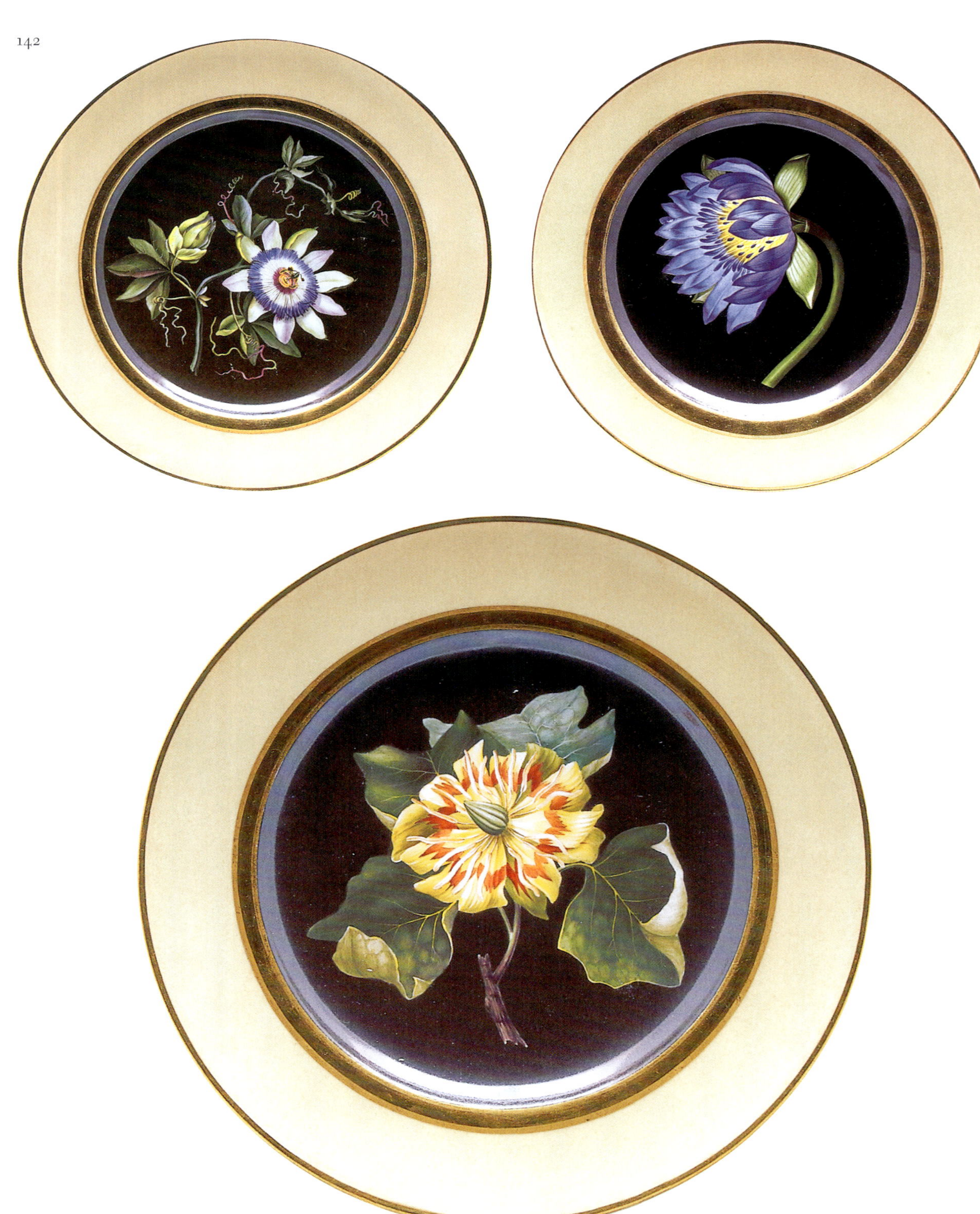

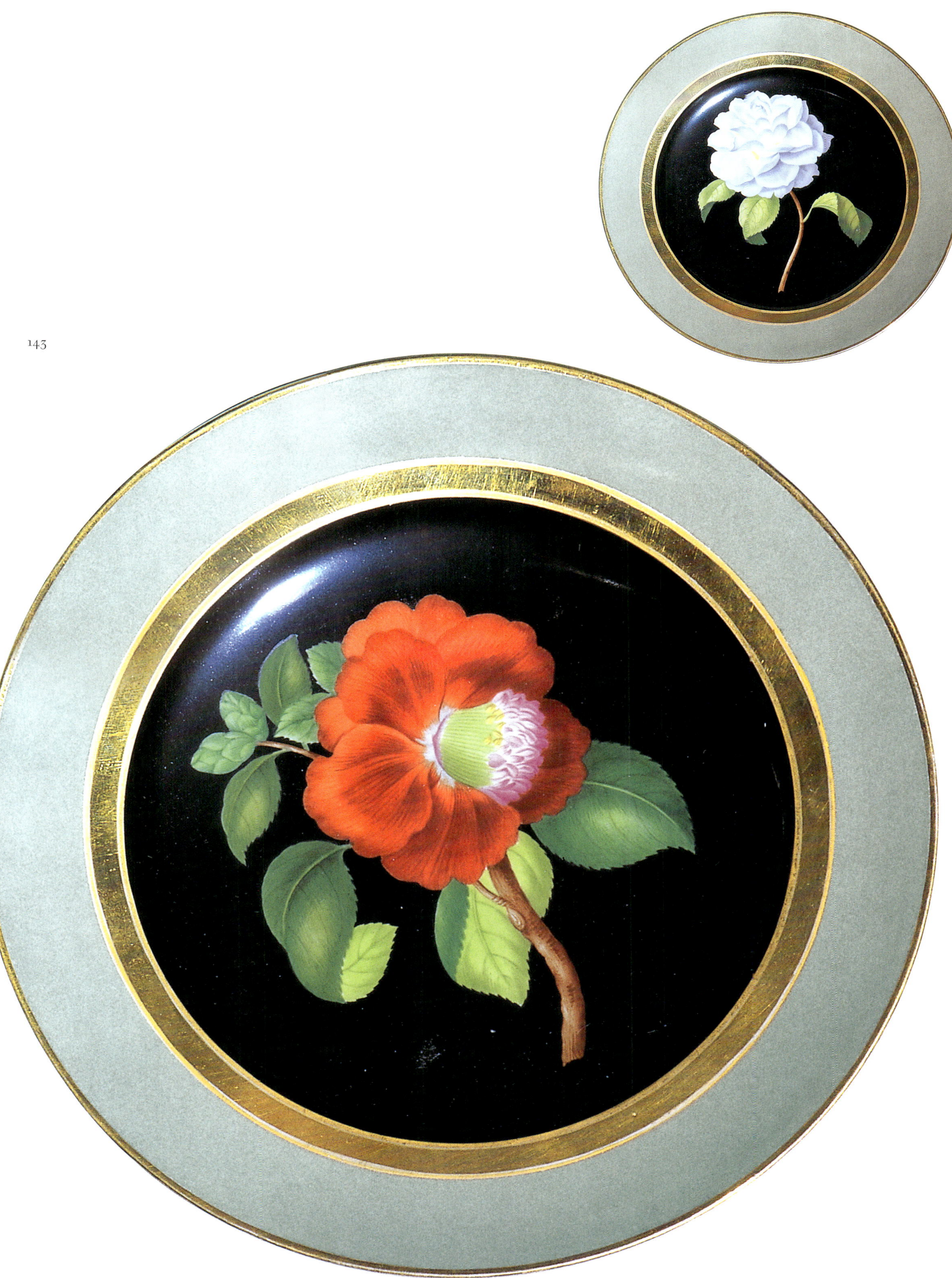

143

144
Botanical Plates
Berlin, 1803/13
Cat. VII-17

145
Plates from the
Exotic Plants Dessert
Service for Empress
Joséphine of France
Berlin, 1806–1807
Cat. VII-16

146
Botanical Plate with
Bromelia Pinguin
Berlin, 1803/13
Cat. VII-15

144

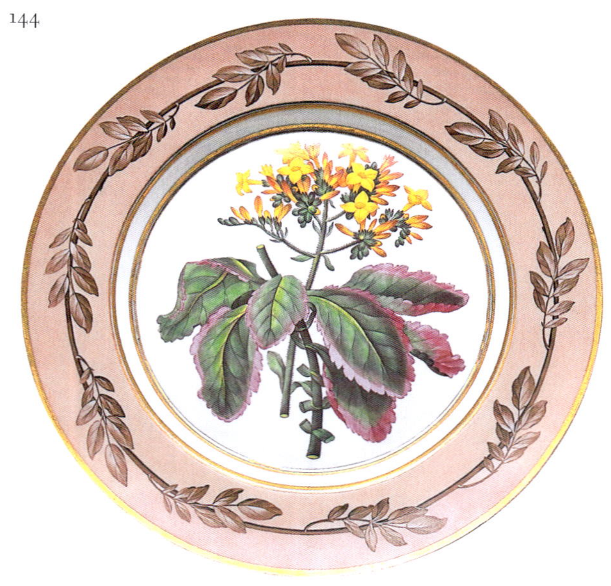
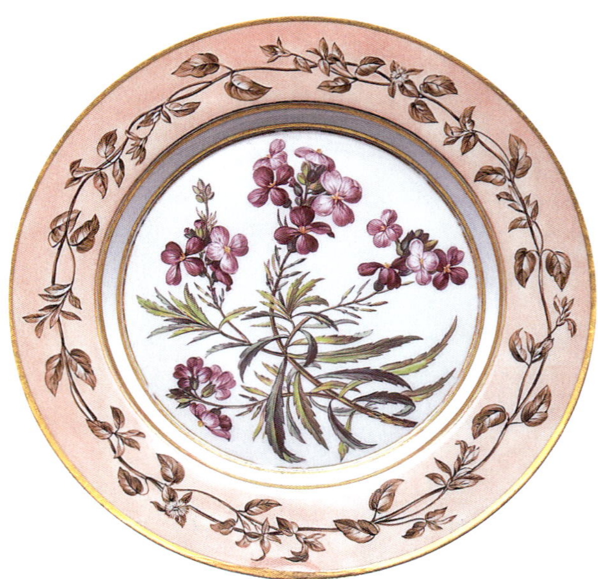

145

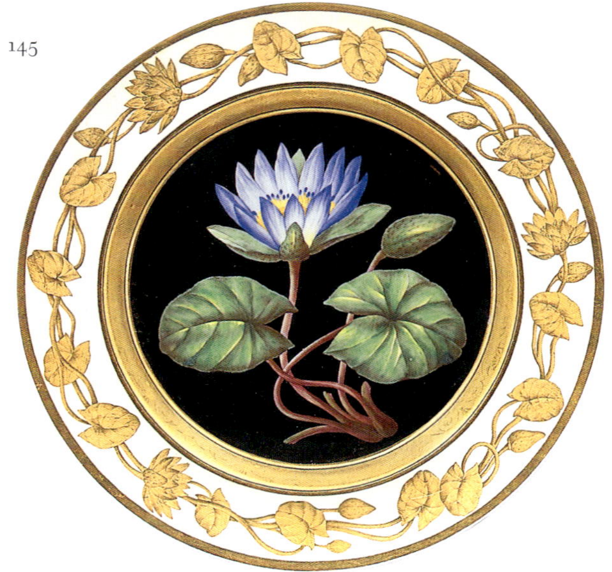
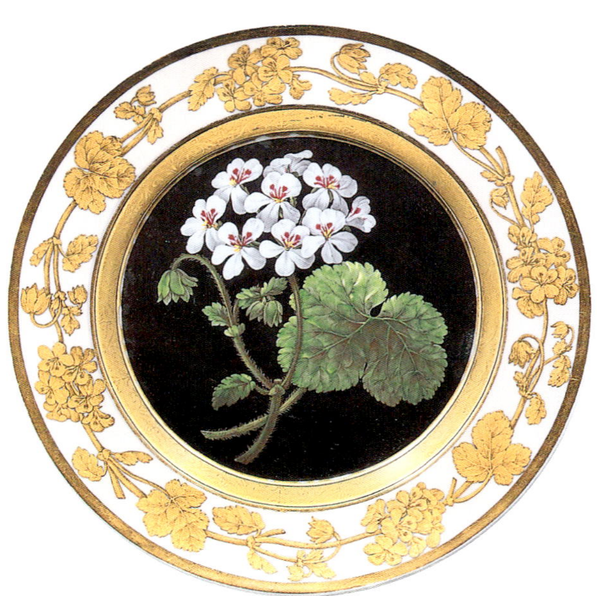

146

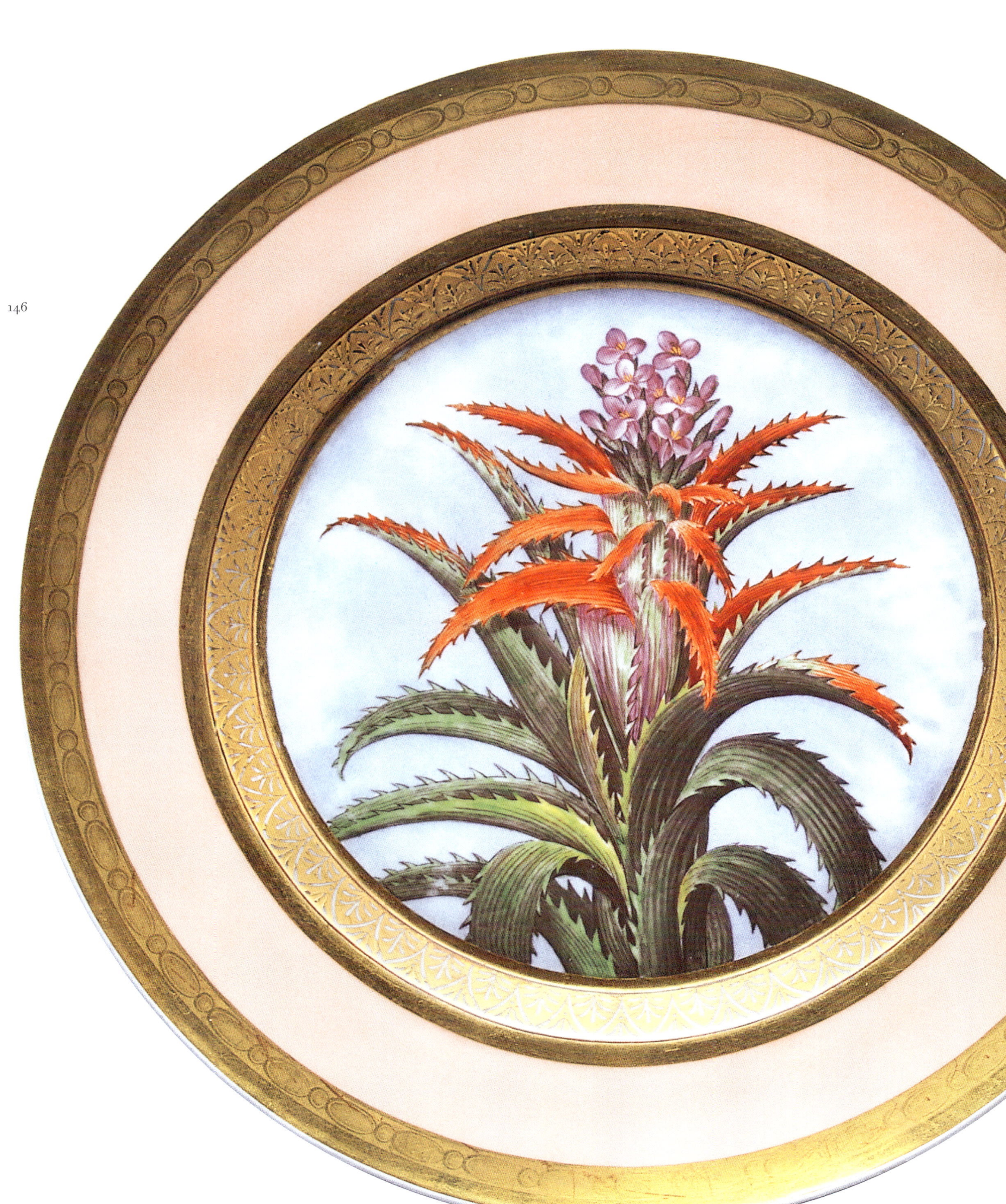

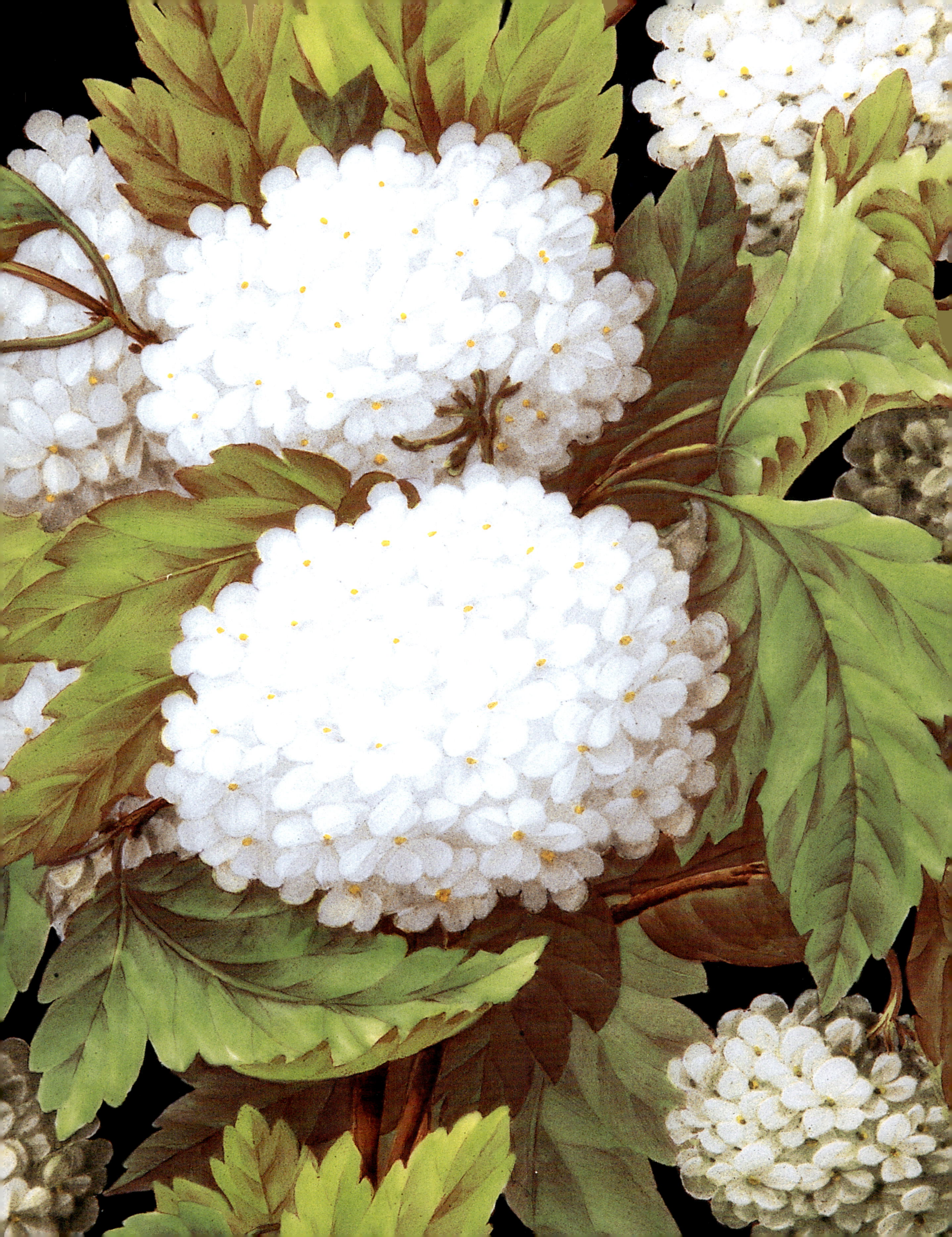

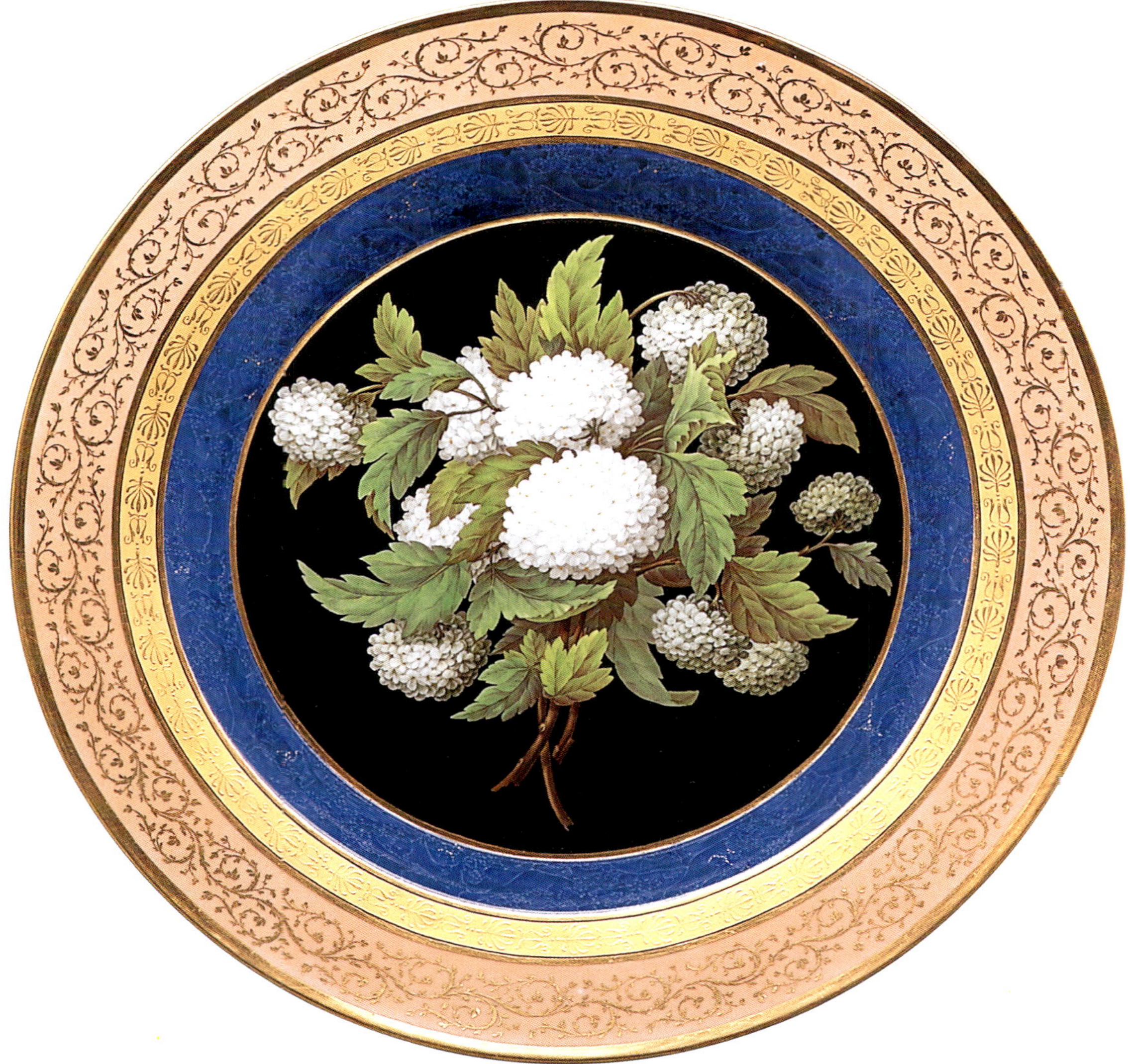

147
Snowball Flowers Platter
Berlin, 1803/13
Cat. VII-18

GLASS

SECTION VIII
Jutta Annette Page

Ornamental and table glass made in Continental Europe in the early nineteenth century reflects the prevailing aesthetic and philosophical ideals of the Biedermeier period. The classicism favored at the Court of Napoleon Bonaparte – adopted by francophile (and French-occupied) Europe – lingered well into the 1830s, and gradually evolved into a taste for more simplified shapes and new color schemes. A fondness for color in all artistic areas fostered rapid advances in glass technology, resulting in polychrome ware with sophisticated forms and surface decorations that reflect an interest in Christian subjects and an unbridled taste for naturalism. During the Biedermeier period, the foundation was laid for the stylistic pluralism that unfolded later in the century.

By the beginning of the nineteenth century, English lead glass had completely influenced international taste in favor of highly refractive cut glass; it continued its triumphal market success among the Continental European elite. Diamonds, with their remarkable refractive qualities and cutting, provided the model for this glassware. The primary tastemaker of the period, the French court, with its well-known penchant for diamonds, led this development. The execution of such glass, done largely by Bohemian immigrant craftsmen, was time-consuming and required great skill acquired through extensive, specialized training.

The Napoleonic Wars' devastating effect on European economies left the Bohemian glass industry, which had dominated Continental glass production in the eighteenth century, in a dismal state. The price of potash, an essential raw material of Bohemian glass, increased considerably and with it the price of the glassware. Export trade nearly collapsed and many of the once flourishing glasshouses closed permanently. Fashionable vessel styles produced for the remaining Continental clientele were based predominantly on cylindrical forms, sometimes flaring at the rim. King Frederick II of Prussia introduced import embargos of glassware to his territories (including occupied Silesia) as a protectionist measure for the Prussian glass industry. The venerable glasshouse at Zechlin near Berlin initiated new designs to appeal to the tastes of its privileged customers. It adapted the Venetian renaissance technology of "calcedonio," producing polychrome vessels imitating the appearance of agate and other hard stones.

Bohemian trade regained strength around 1820, when its former Eastern markets (especially Hungary and Turkey) were restored. The rebounding glass industry had improved its traditional potash formula to make a more refined colorless glass which, although inferior in quality to the Anglo-Irish lead-based glass, was cheaper because of the lower wages paid to the craftsmen; it created considerable competition. Export wares with a slightly pink tinge were bound for England and North America; wares with a silvery-blue hue were intended to suit French tastes.

Northern Bohemian cutters played a vital role in the production of an ever-changing repertory of forms. The most gifted Bohemian glass engraver was Dominik Biemann (1800–1857) from Neuwelt, whose creations on exclusively colorless glass remain unsurpassed. Biemann's residence of choice was the fashionable spa of Franzensbad (Františkovy Lázne), which provided him with an affluent clientele for his rather costly souvenirs. The high point of glass engraving has always been the portrait. Like other engravers, Biemann used prints as models for his images, but he was also the sole engraver able to work directly from life – a rare skill and one that only his wealthiest sitters could afford. His popularity waned when the daguerreotype became the preferred (and less expensive) option for spa portraits.

The Biedermeier period also witnessed an increasing preference for color. Growing interest in watercolor paintings fueled the popularity of transparent enameling on glass. At the beginning of the nineteenth century, the decoration of glass with colored enamels was the domain of the Northern Bohemian glass refineries. Their decorations owed much to the exquisite products of the German painter Samuel Mohn (1762–1815) and his son Gottlob Samuel Mohn (1789–1825), independent decorators ("Hausmaler") in Dresden. Samuel Mohn had invented a transparent enamel paint for glass that could be fired for permanency and was noted for its brilliance. His production included beakers with popular city views executed after prints by well-known artists. A floral border near the rim increased their price considerably. His son Gottlob, who had moved to Vienna by 1811, continued to paint glasses with the familiar repertory of motifs, as well as porcelain for the Wiener Porzellanmanufaktur. However, his colleague Anton Kothgasser (1769–1851), an equally talented gold and "dessin" (scene) painter employed at the manufactory from 1805 until 1816, became the most prolific independent painter of the period. Few Bohemian painters could compete with his skill. His works included a wide range of ornamental glassware depicting naturalistic motifs, idealized landscapes, "vedute" (scenes), and portraits, reflecting the current interest in drawing, graphic arts, and watercolor painting. His workshop stocked beakers and drinking sets decorated with naturalistic butterflies; customers could also place special orders. The specific meaning of these scenes remained elusive unless accompanied by an inscription. Motifs with tender mottos of friendship and love are prolific and executed with sensitivity and care, employing the language of flowers to transmit sentimental messages. The four-leaf clover is still a well-known symbol of luck, and the pansy (derived from French "pensée" or thought) subtly alludes to fond memories. One of the most romantic beakers executed in Kothgasser's workshop is decorated with a continuous view of a night sky – an image able to be fully appreciated only when the cup is handled.

Silver-staining, a technique involving using a brush to produce transparent, golden-yellow surface treatments, had been used in stained glass since the fourteenth century. The younger Mohn used the technique, albeit sparingly. However, it may have been the technological experiments of Friedrich Egermann (1777–1864) of Blottendorf (Polevsko) near Haida in Northern Bohemia, one of the most important glass refiners in the nineteenth century, who inspired Kothgasser's unusual wood-grained beaker. The decoration emulates the blond hardwoods favored by furniture makers of the Biedermeier period.

The quest for complex colored glass formulas resulted in one of the most striking inventions of the period. In 1816, Count Georg of Buquoy developed in his glasshouse Georgenthal near Gratzen a black, obsidianlike glass he named "hyalith" (glass stone), emphasizing his desire to develop not only a new glass but one that imitated black stone. Hyalith was marked by complete opacity, great hardness, and a very shiny surface to which initially only cut ornamentation was applied. By 1819, Georgenthal was producing exclusively hyalith glass, but because of the dearth of painters expert in gilded decoration, the glass blanks were sent to the refineries in Schaiba near Haida. By this time, the factory also made red hyalith. It was very similar to the red ("rot-welsche") glass that had been made by the Count Harrach glasshouse in Neuwelt since 1764, a glass production that had been dormant for two generations. Red hyalith was even more expensive to produce than the black variety.

Four types of decorations existed: facet cutting, veining (creating swirling veins on the surface by making a twisted motion while blowing), gilding, and silver-staining. The glass bore a startling resemblance to oriental lacquer and forms inspired by Japanese and Chinese ceramics and porcelain, and by 1824, gilded "chinoiserie" motifs appeared. Despite Buquoy's exclusive privilege, Harrach also produced vessels with relief cutting in many shades resembling hard and semiprecious stone.

The quest for color intensified during the 1820s to undermine the dominance of English lead glass, resulting in new formulas and technological advances in colored decoration. Egermann's "lithyalin" glass, resembling marble and a broad range of semiprecious stones, joined the spectrum of Bohemian glasses. However, this period of artistic creativity and technological innovation was soon followed again by economic decline. Higher duties to German states, such as Bavaria and Prussia, led to a stagnation of exports. French and Belgian glassware producers became the greatest economic threat: they designed and accepted orders only for large series, whereas the Bohemians had always accommodated special orders and requests from private patrons, thereby incurring a less efficient and relatively expensive production. To stay economically viable, Northern Bohemian merchants responded by selling undecorated, cheap glass, as well as offering polychrome designs achieved by thin overlays of transparent and opaque glass in two and later three colors developed in the chemical factories in Prague. By the 1830s and 1840s, the second Rococo with its exuberant forms and decorations began to dominate glassware for the fashionable table.

148
*Water Carafe, Water
Glass, Champagne Glass*
Southern Germany,
ca. 1800
Cat. VIII-1

149
Agate Vase
Zechlin, ca. 1800
Cat. VIII-12

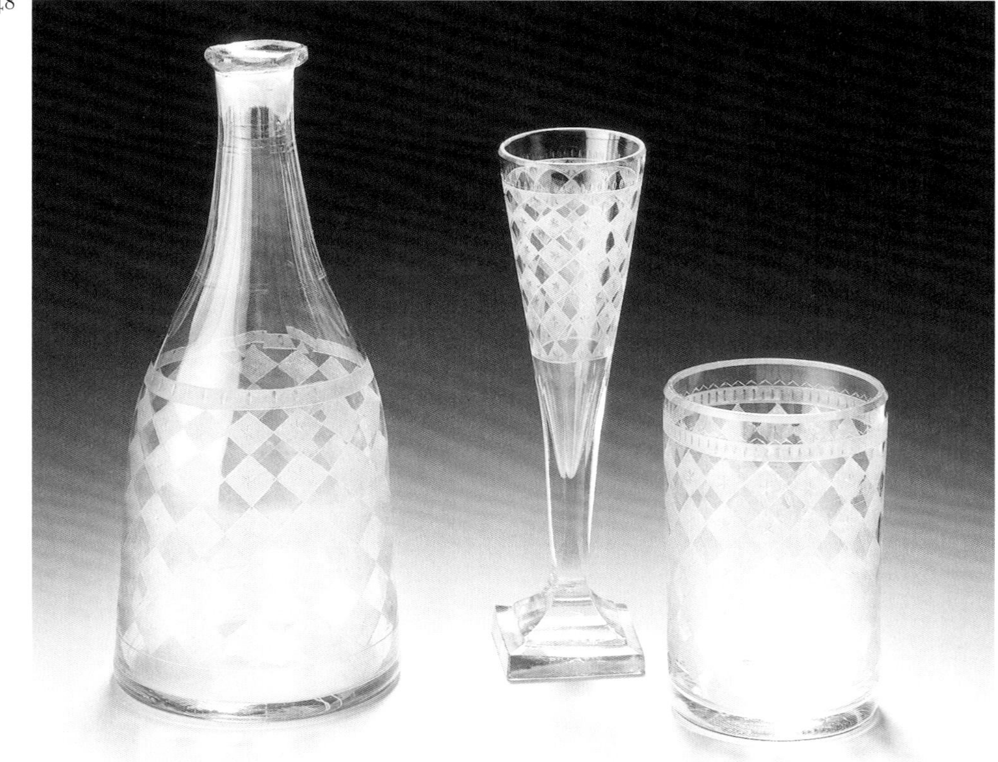

148

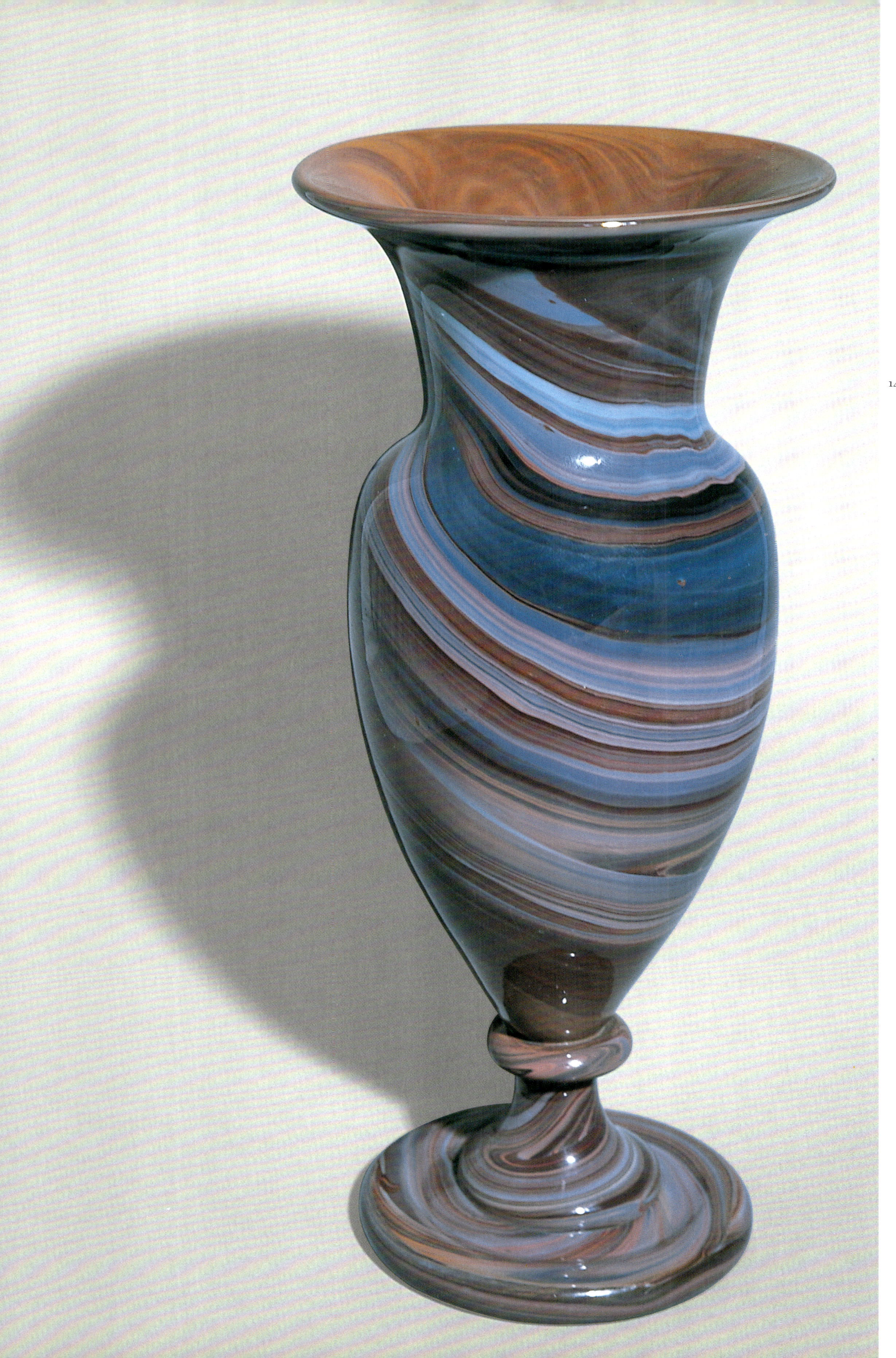

150

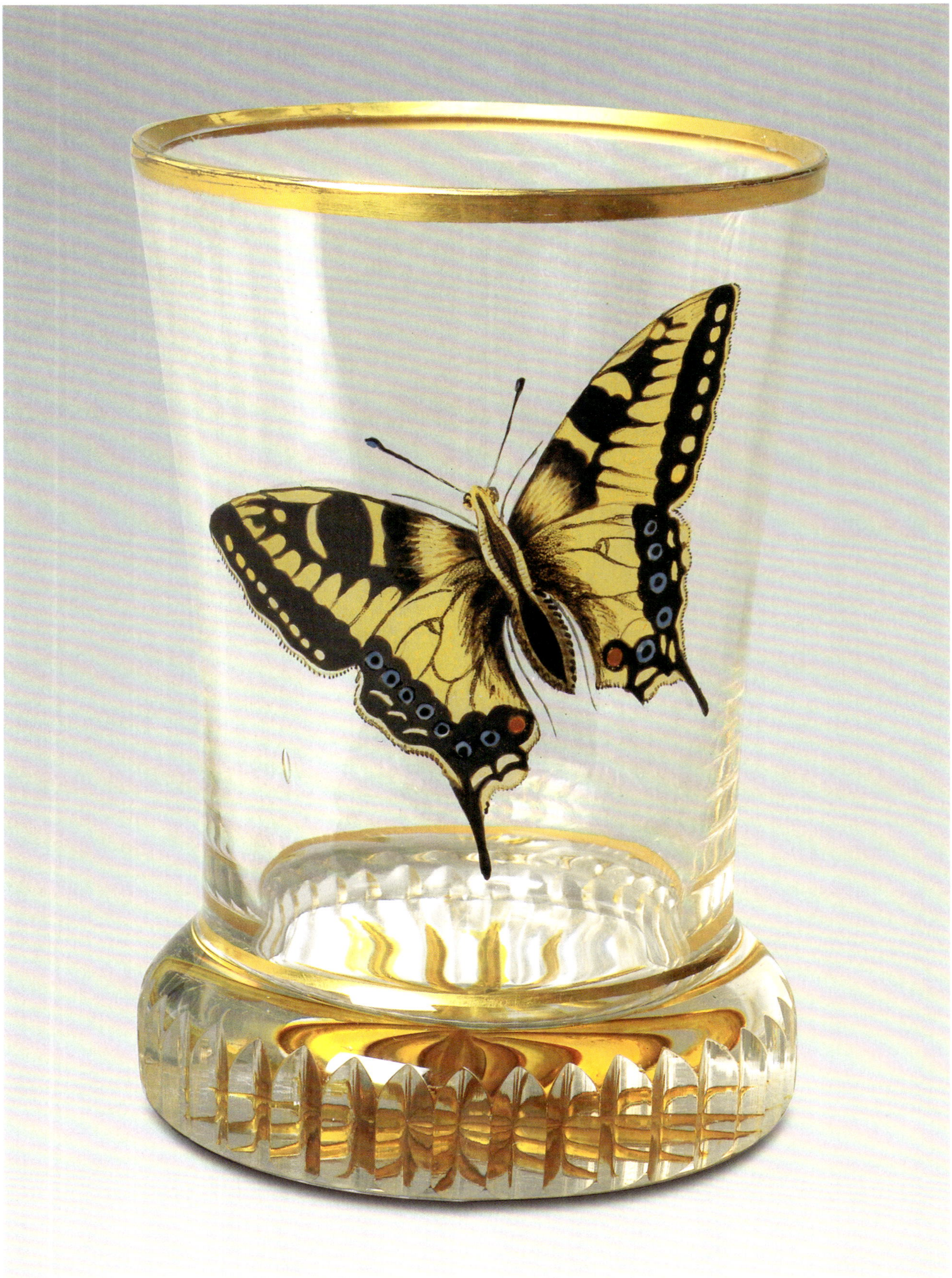

151

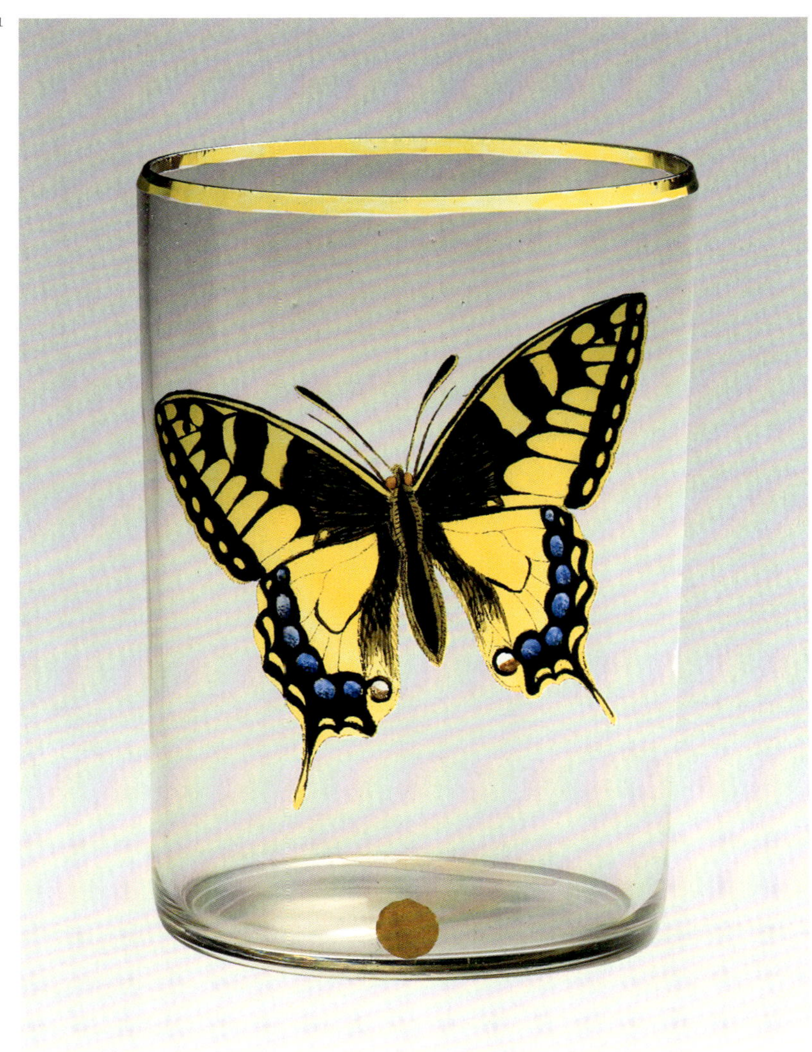

150
Beaker (Ranftbecher)
with a Butterfly
Vienna, ca. 1815
Cat. VIII-7

151
Beaker with a Butterfly
Vienna, ca. 1815
Cat. VIII-6

152
Travel Beaker Set
(graduated set of seven)
Northern Bohemia or
Russia, 1820/30
Cat. VIII-8

152

153

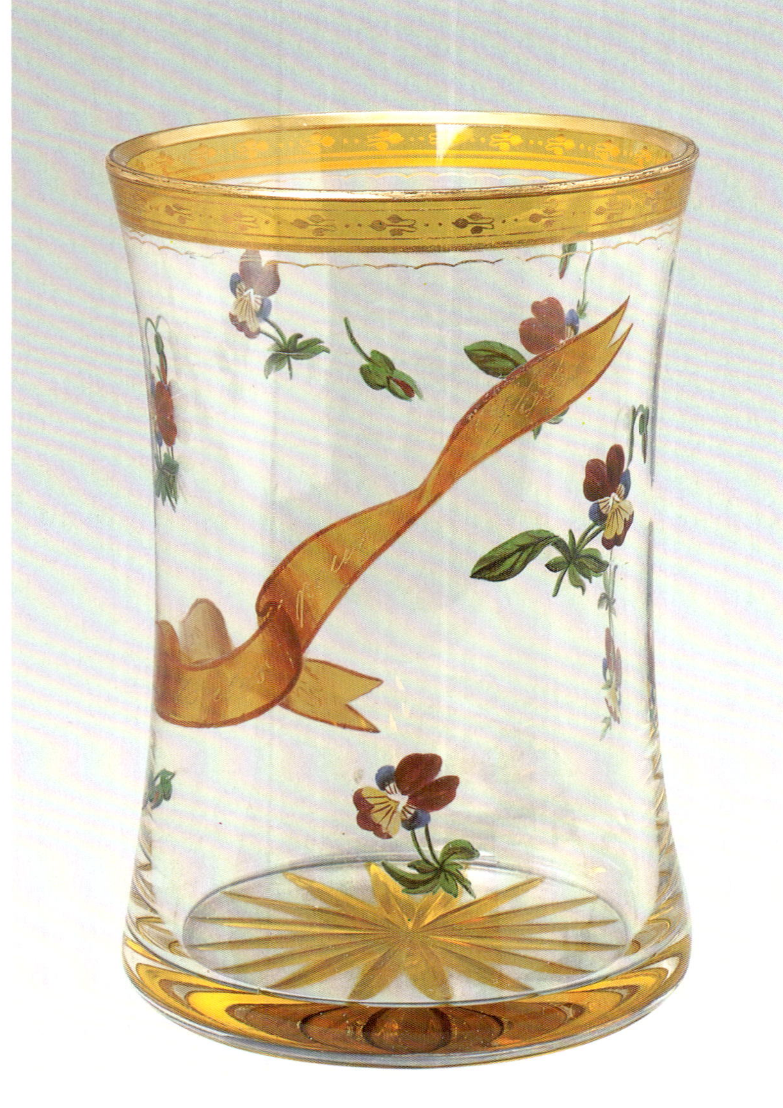

154

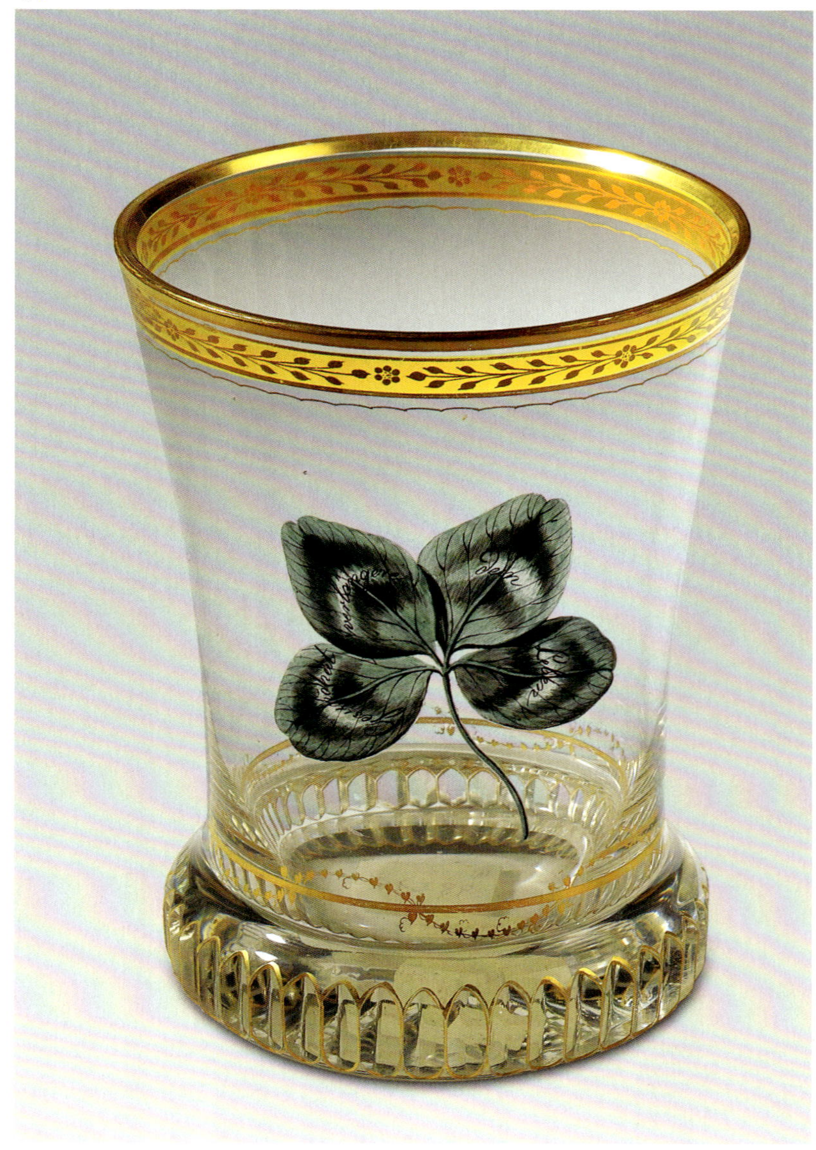

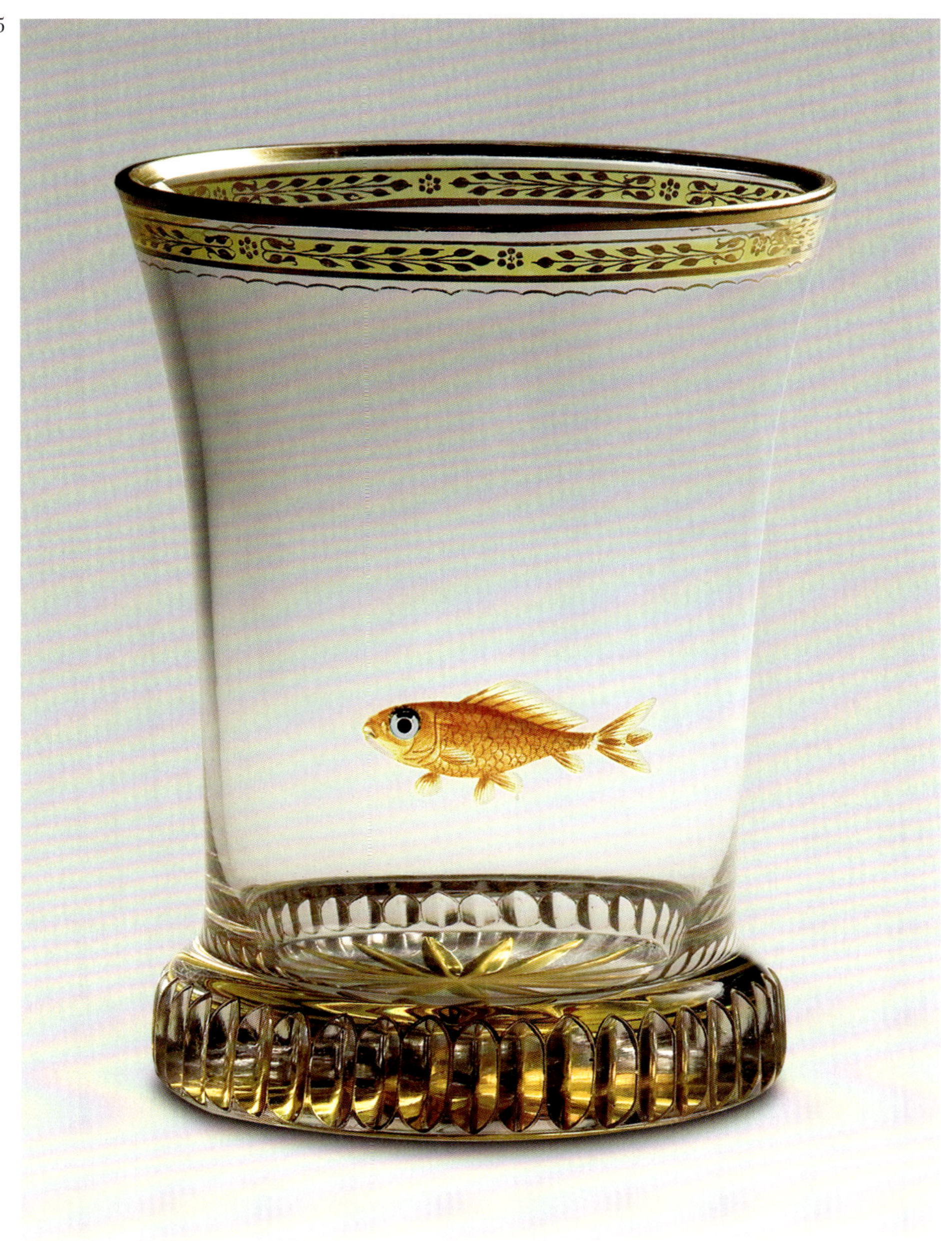

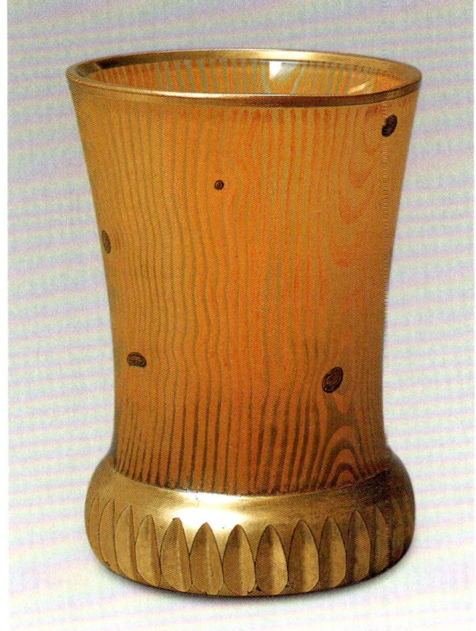

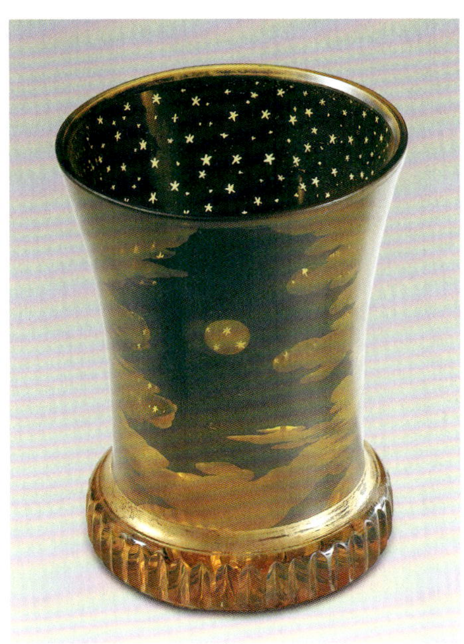

153
Beaker with Pansies
Vienna, 1815/20
Cat. VIII-3

154
Beaker (Ranftbecher)
with a Four-Leaf Clover
Vienna, ca. 1820
Cat. VIII-4

155
Beaker (Ranftbecher)
with Goldfish
Vienna, 1820/30
Cat. VIII-9

156
Beaker (Ranftbecher)
with Wood Grain
Vienna, ca. 1825
Cat. VIII-11

157
Beaker (Ranftbecher)
"Moon Glass"
Vienna, ca. 1825
Cat. VIII-10

158
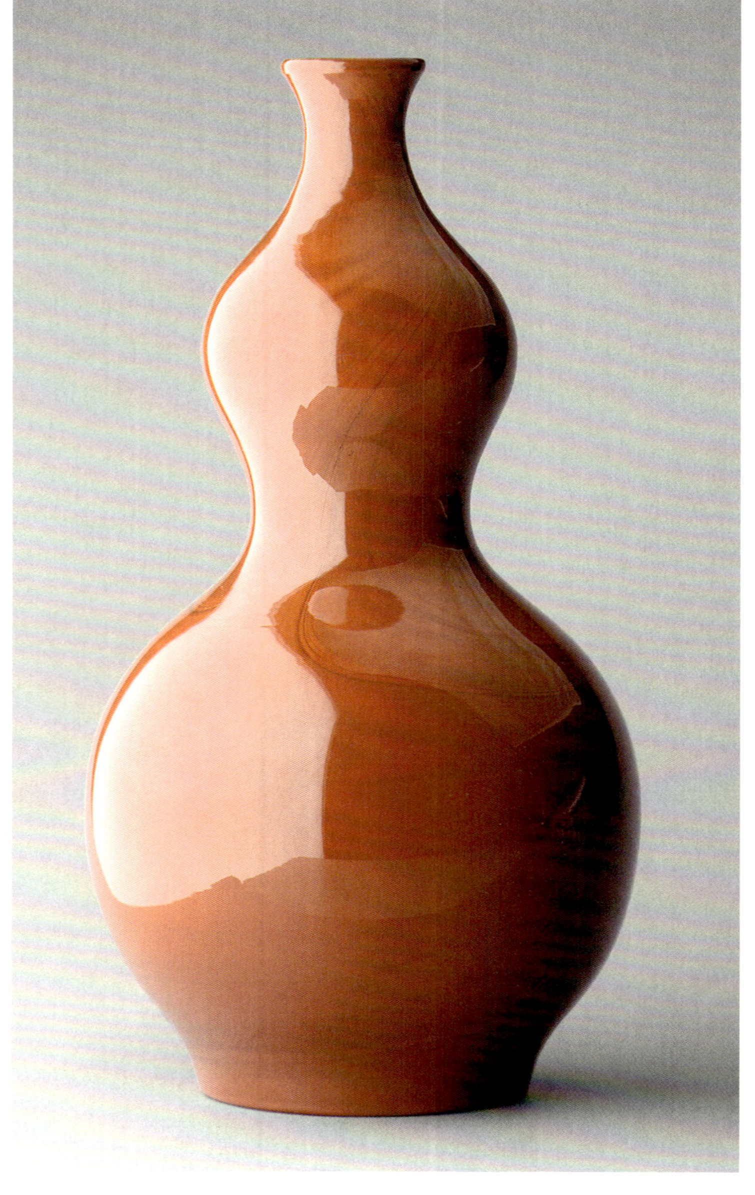

159
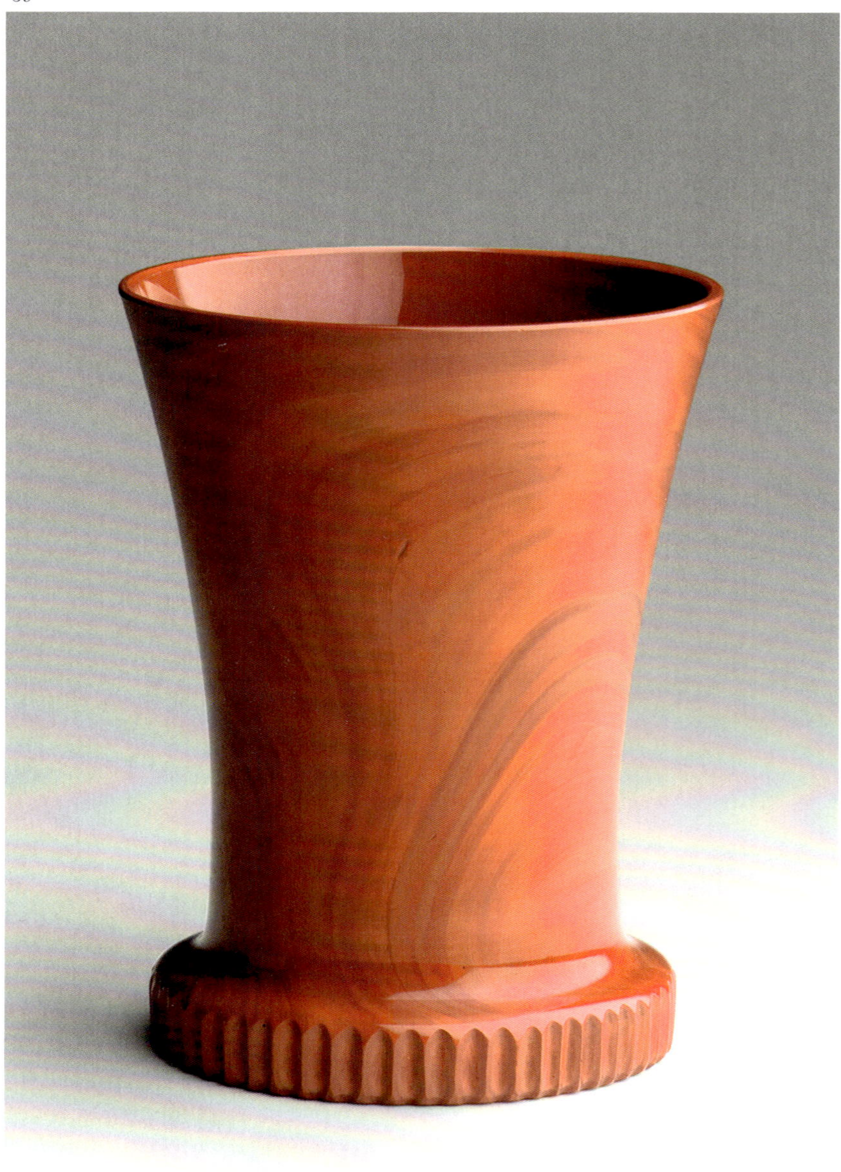

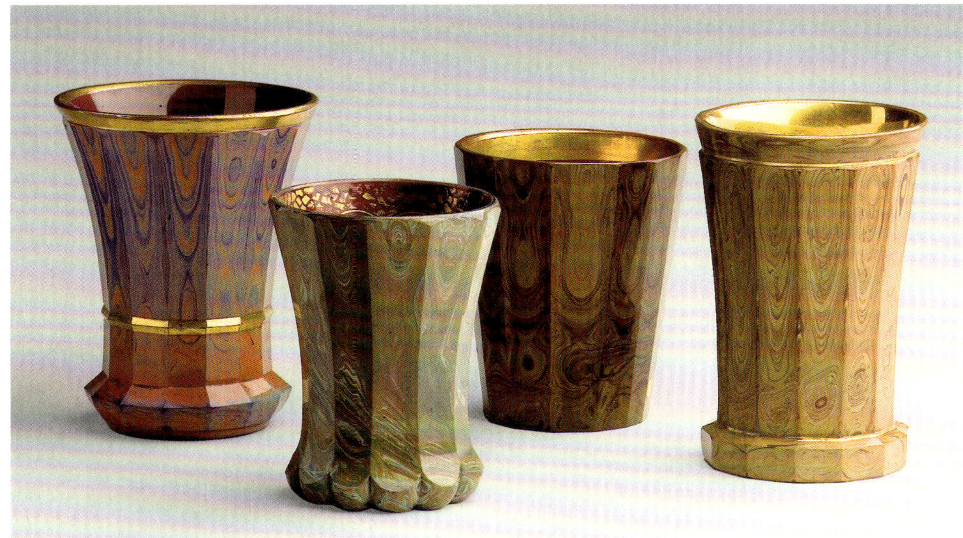

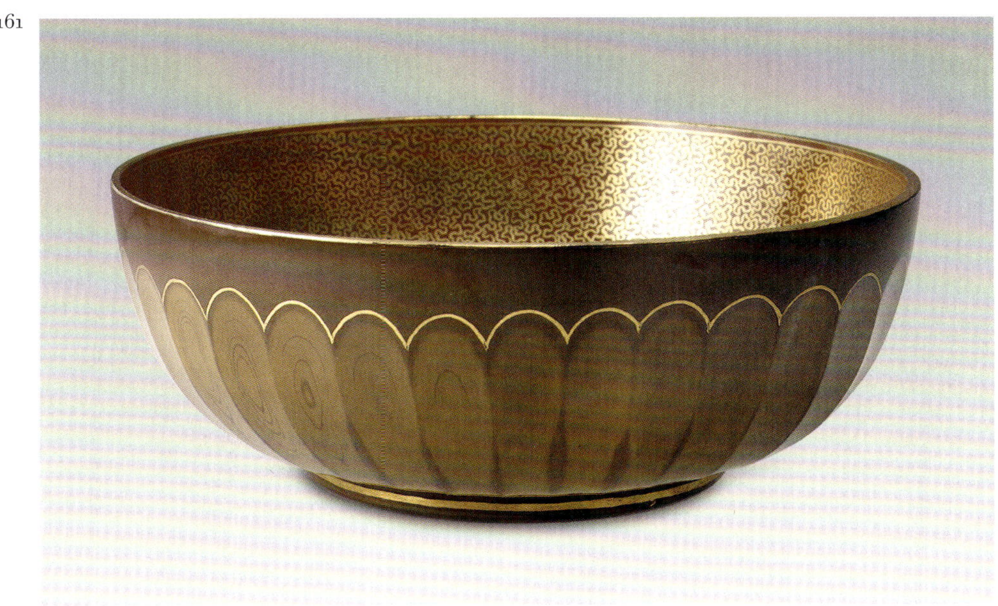

158
Gourd-Shaped Vase
Bohemia, 1820
Cat. VIII-13

159
Beaker (Ranftbecher)
Bohemia, ca. 1825
Cat. VIII-15

160
Beaker (Ranftbecher)
Bohemia, ca. 1830
Cat. VIII-17

Beaker (Ranftbecher)
Bohemia, ca. 1830
Cat. VIII-18

Beaker
Bohemia, ca. 1830
Cat. VIII-19

Beaker (Ranftbecher)
Bohemia, ca. 1830
Cat. VIII-20

161
*Small Bowl with
the Motif of the
Endless Road*
Bohemia, ca. 1830
Cat. VIII-21

SILVER

SECTION IX

Paul Asenbaum and Albrecht Pyritz

VIENNESE SILVER
Paul Asenbaum

Vienna can look back on a long tradition of artistry in silver- and goldsmithing, with the first known regulation of the craft dating back to 1566. Despite the quality of its craftsmanship, Vienna nevertheless was stylistically dependent on the most important goldsmith centers of the German-speaking realm, Nuremberg and Augsburg.

Until the middle of the eighteenth century, no new ideas emerged from the silver workshops of Vienna, despite the city's being an imperial capital and residence and the third largest city in Europe. The few surviving gold and silver objects from the court of Maria Theresa still adhere to the formal canon of the Baroque, unlike their contemporary Rococo creations coming out of other European centers. By the end of the 1770s, all of Europe, including Vienna, fell under the stylistic influence of classicism as defined by the shapes and decorations produced by French workshops during the reign of Louis XVI. The middle of the 1780s saw a rise in the authority of England and a simpler classical style influenced by the architect Robert Adam. If France was the land of tasteful and refined luxury items, then England, according to a 1788 issue of the *Journal des Luxus und der Moden*, was the producer of goods that bore "the mark of practicality and public benefit."

Both qualities corresponded to an enlightened, rational mindset that became widespread in Vienna during the reign of Joseph II, who himself came to exemplify the new ideals. A reformer and an enlightened despot, he broke with the existing monarchical styles of representation and renounced flamboyance in favor of a distinct simplicity and modesty. A clear example of this is a chocolate pot made for him around 1780 by silversmith Ignaz Sebastian Würth. The tapering, vaguely conical, cylinder with a flat lid bears no ornamentation other than an engraved crown and the royal monogram. The style, named for the emperor, was the local response to French classicism and can be seen as heralding the general trend toward simplification that became more apparent after 1800.

At the beginning of the nineteenth century, Vienna's silversmiths offered up work characterized by coexisting, but distinct, stylistic influences and tendencies – a spectrum ranging from objects rich with decoration to those entirely lacking in ornament. From today's point of view, the unadorned Viennese objects, widely produced in 1800-30, were a sign of innovative designs to come. These objects have been emancipated, leaving their models behind them. By reducing the object to its fundamental structure, while allowing for a playful interaction with archetypal forms, new shapes were derived that express two particular ideals of classicism: antiquity and geometry. Amphoral and columnar forms as well as rectangles, balls, cylinders, and cones formed the starting point for new interpretations.

The feeling of balance inherent in these silver objects has its origins in the training of the Viennese silversmiths. Like all Viennese craftsmen after 1785, they had to become certified as masters in the art of drawing. One aspect of their training was the analysis of the classical formal canon, especially columnar order and its proportions.

Starting in 1800, the appearance of silver objects is marked by a graphically precise, legible outline, a consequence of the concentration on form. Around 1820-25, the sharp contours start to have more rounded edges, emphasizing the object's voluminous shape and serving as a transition to the softer, more imaginative forms of the Biedermeier style. At about the same time, the influence of classicism begins to slacken. Another aspect that distinguishes these objects is the deliberately functional design, which places less value on the representational image. To elevate material simplicity and practicality to an aesthetic norm is a demand that has its roots in the previous century and is associated with the ideal of antiquity.

The restrained use or total discarding of decoration in Viennese silver strengthens the attention to form as well as purpose. Decoration in this silver serves to ornament the surface without disturbing the silhouette of the form. Ornament serves as an organizing principle of a vertically oriented object's horizontal pattern, denoting areas or the entire surface; for the most part, the ornamentation bows to the laws of geometry. Ornament is also used functionally, as evidence, as it were, of an intended purpose, such as the groove of a node as a handle for candlesticks. Most of the examples from 1800 to 1830 are distinguished by a complete renunciation of ornament. The relinquishment of all forms of embellishment is a radical break with a millennium-old tradition and one of the forward-looking characteristics of a modernist tendency in design.

GERMAN AND DANISH SILVER
Albrecht Pyritz

Whereas the simple elegance of the silver being produced in Vienna around 1800 soon made it more popular than the extravagant designs of the period, the early nineteenth century saw the advent of a rigorously proportional classicistic style in all the great European silversmithing centers. The deliberate incorporation of contrasting elements is very much in evidence in the tableware, flatware, and items of everyday use from this period. Far from being highly ornate luxury goods, these table decorations, candlesticks, cups, dishes, and boxes, to say nothing of the samovars then in vogue, exemplify the new ideals of simplicity. Their standardized bodies are sparingly adorned and only with antique embellishments and figures. While their shape was determined largely by function, their ornamentation often amounted to nothing more spectacular than somewhat arbitrarily applied appliqués that underscored one particular feature or part. From around 1805 onward, these principles of simplicity and functionality came to dominate the new style of silverware that was becoming widespread in the leading courts of Europe.

The master silversmiths pioneering this trend, for the most part descendents of Huguenot immigrants who settled in Europe's large urban centers, had been schooled or learned their trade in France. Their creations from the mid-eighteenth century onward display an elegant artlessness that reflects the enlightened, yet puritanical, spirit of their Protestant makers. Late eighteenth-century English silver was extremely influential, its patterns disseminated throughout the Habsburg monarchy in German periodicals such as the *Journal des Luxus und der Moden.* In addition, beginning in 1800, large numbers of English plans and patterns for plain tableware and flatware began circulating on the Continental market.

One of the most important causes behind this new plain style is assumed to have been the shortage of funds and resources suffered by most of the big European courts, especially in the war years 1792–1806 and 1813–15. Yet, the desire for a less profligate style, and the financial difficulties presumed to have necessitated it, can both be dated back to the mid-eighteenth century. In 1754, for example, there were complaints at the Court of Kassel about the austerity and plainness of the silverware being made by the Huguenot craftsmen who worked there. Some critics even insinuated

that these silversmiths were simply not skilled enough in the art of embellishment. Nevertheless, the objects created for the Court of Kassel remained primarily functional and deliberately unostentatious right up to the end of the century – stylistic features that earned appreciation only after 1800. The silversmiths of the early nineteenth century, meanwhile, profited from the introduction of new metalworking methods. For example, rolled sheet metal freed them from having to beat each individual vessel into shape; they were instead able to switch to small-scale mass production, except for the more extravagant designs. The highly traditional, but now remarkably simple travel and toilette sets produced around this time provide a good example of this development. Comprising some twenty or more matching items, these sets derive much of their charm from the quality of their surfaces, which could be polished or even fire-gilt and monogrammed. Elegant traveling cases veneered with tropical wood also reflect this newfound fascination with surface.

The quality of the items is especially apparent in large tea services, whose plain teapots and coffee pots vary only in the shape of the spout or handle. As in the porcelain pots produced during this period, the handles are most often attached either at a right angle to the pot ("Greek style") or pointing upward beyond the upper rim of the pot ("Campanian style" referring to the Italian "campagna" or countryside).

The emphasis on surfaces is particularly noticeable in small items of tableware such as beakers, goblets, and candlesticks. These often have a square or round base and indented foot and are decorated, if at all, by narrow, horizontal chasing, fluting, or friezes. Silver caskets and boxes, meanwhile, are invariably reduced to their geometrical fundamentals. What all Biedermeier silver has in common, however, is the way in which it derives its stylistic value from the importance attached to functionality and surface finish.

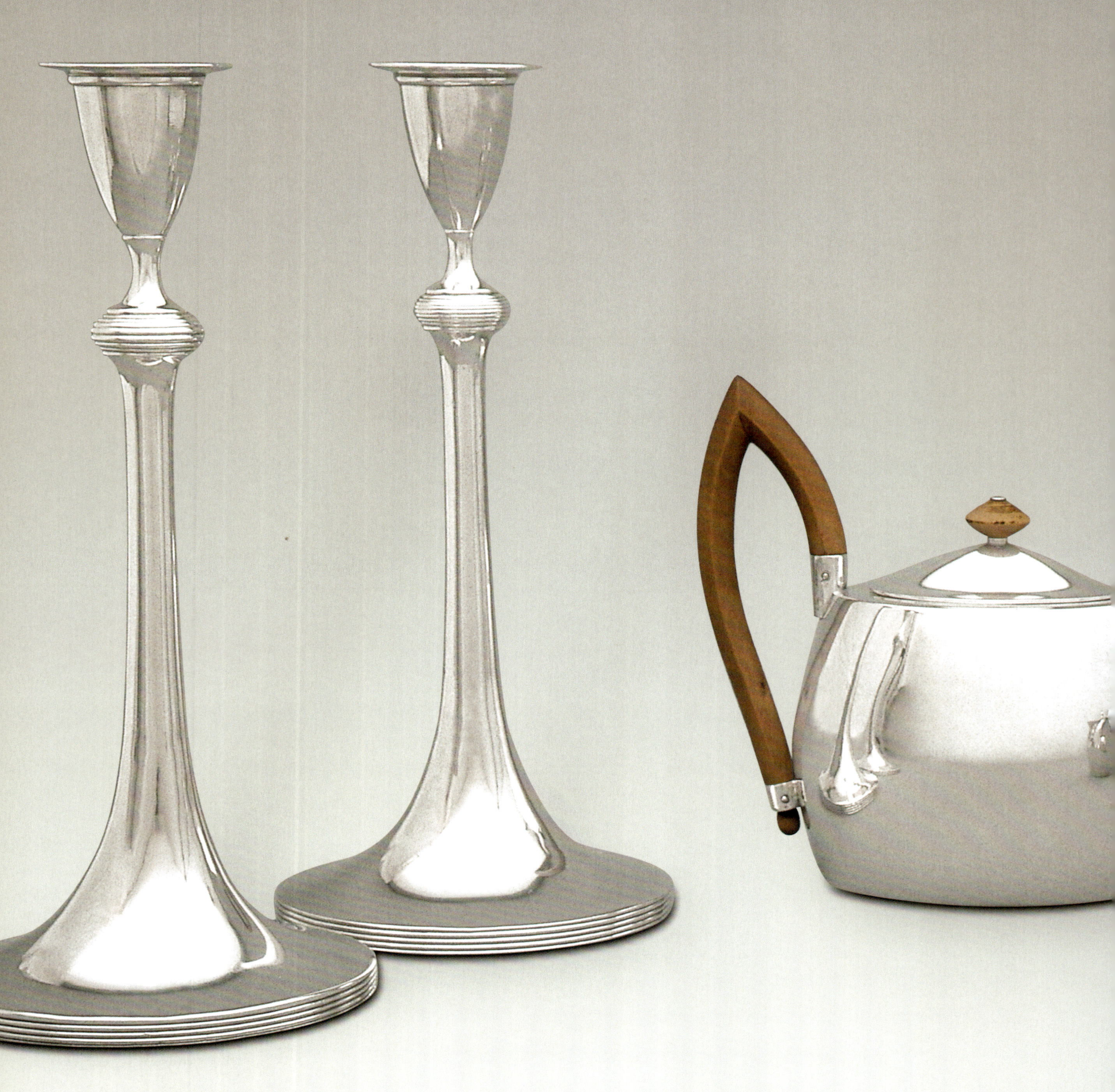

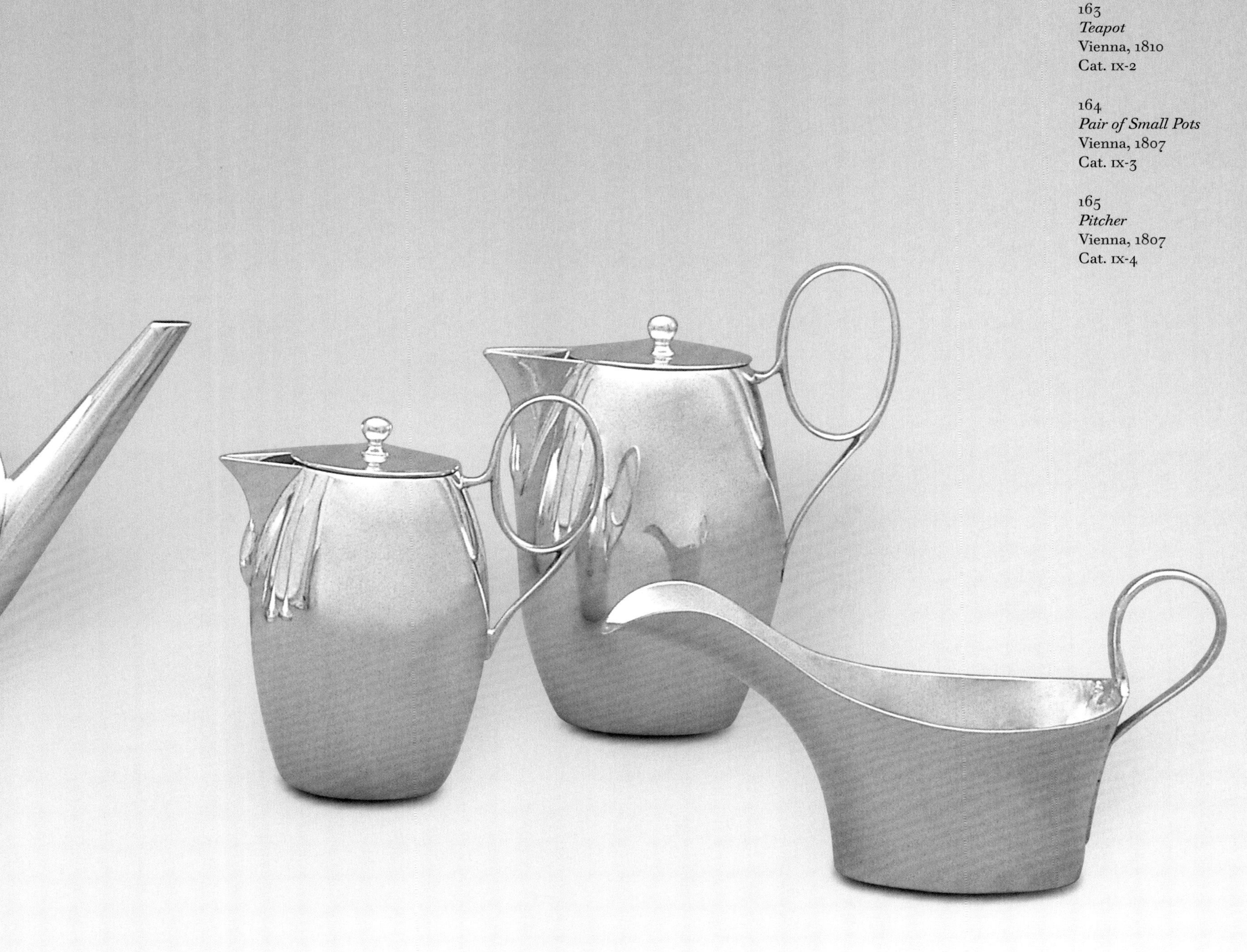

162
Pair of Candlesticks
Vienna, 1800
Cat. IX-1

163
Teapot
Vienna, 1810
Cat. IX-2

164
Pair of Small Pots
Vienna, 1807
Cat. IX-3

165
Pitcher
Vienna, 1807
Cat. IX-4

166
Cream Pitcher
Germany, ca. 1816
Cat. ix-58

167
Goblet
Germany, 1804
Cat. ix-53

168
Pair of Cups
Munich, 1817
Cat. ix-61

169
Water Pitcher
Vienna, 1817
Cat. ix-6

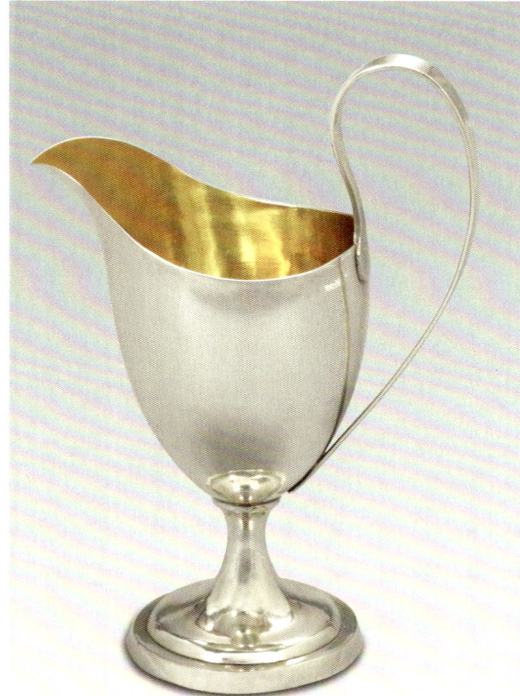

166

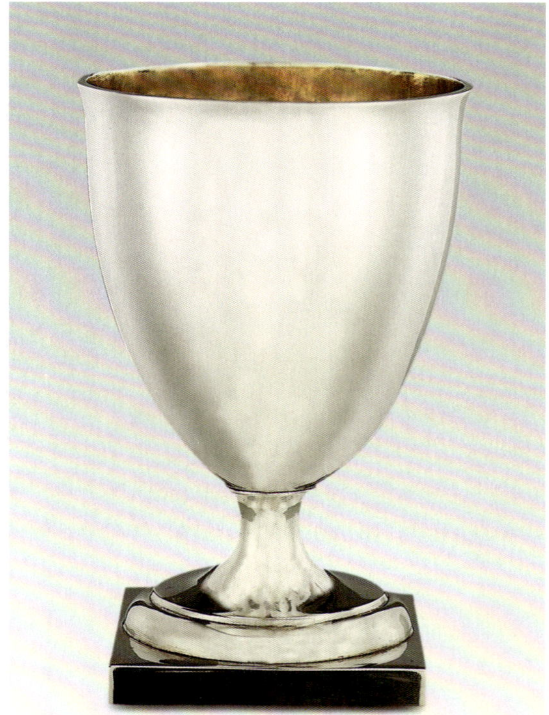

167

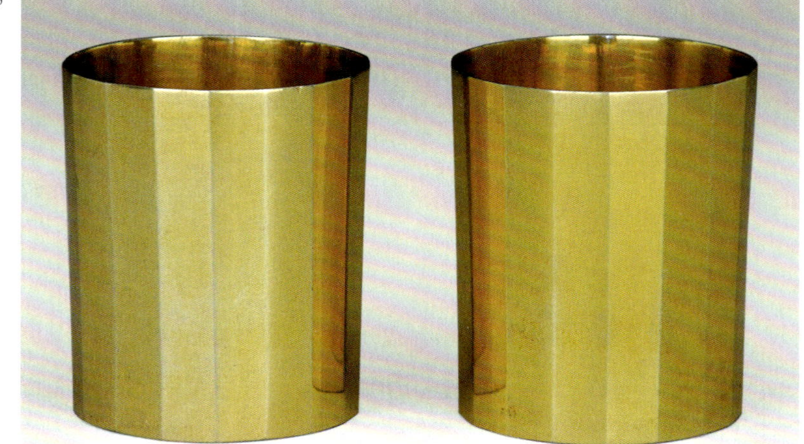

168

169

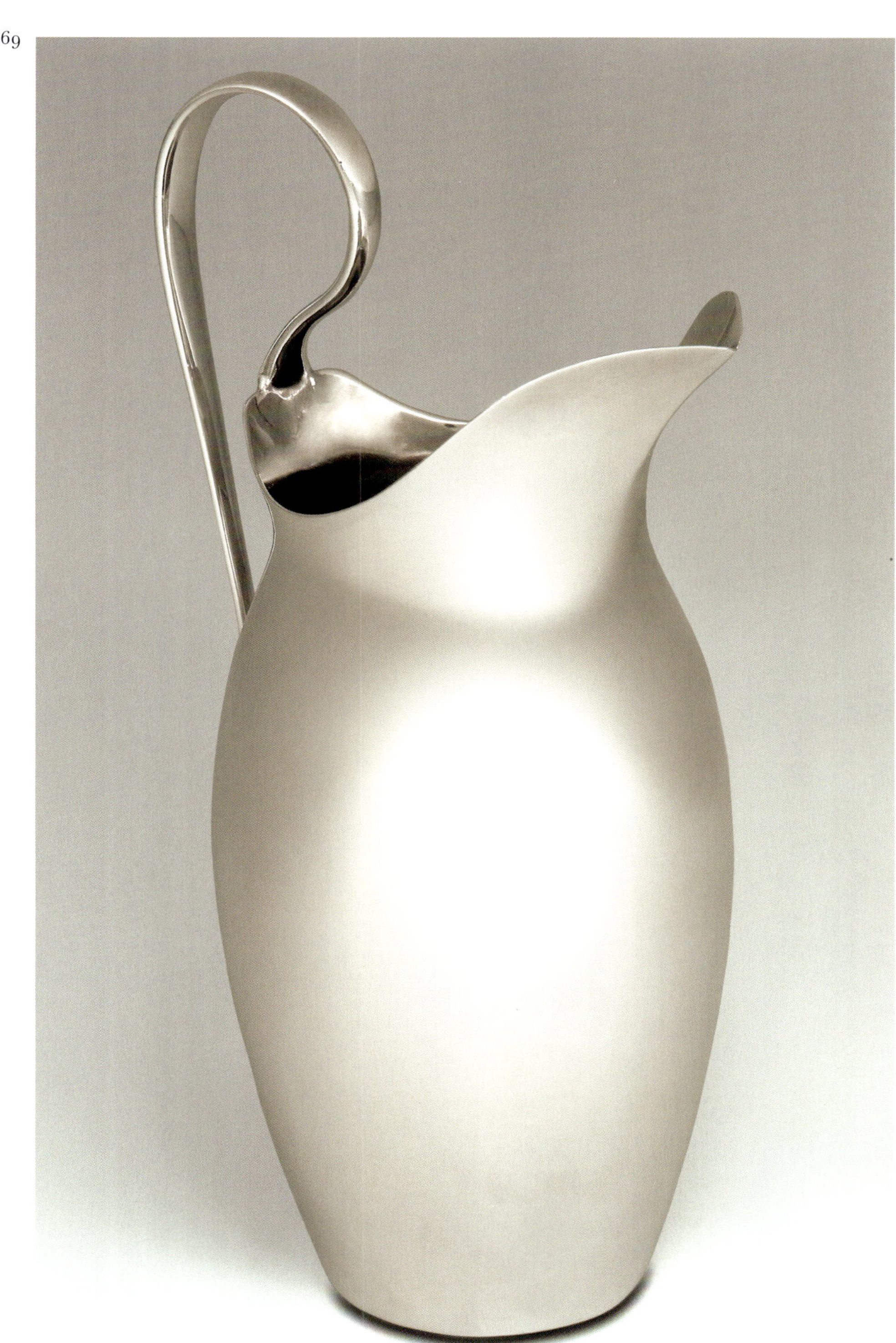

170

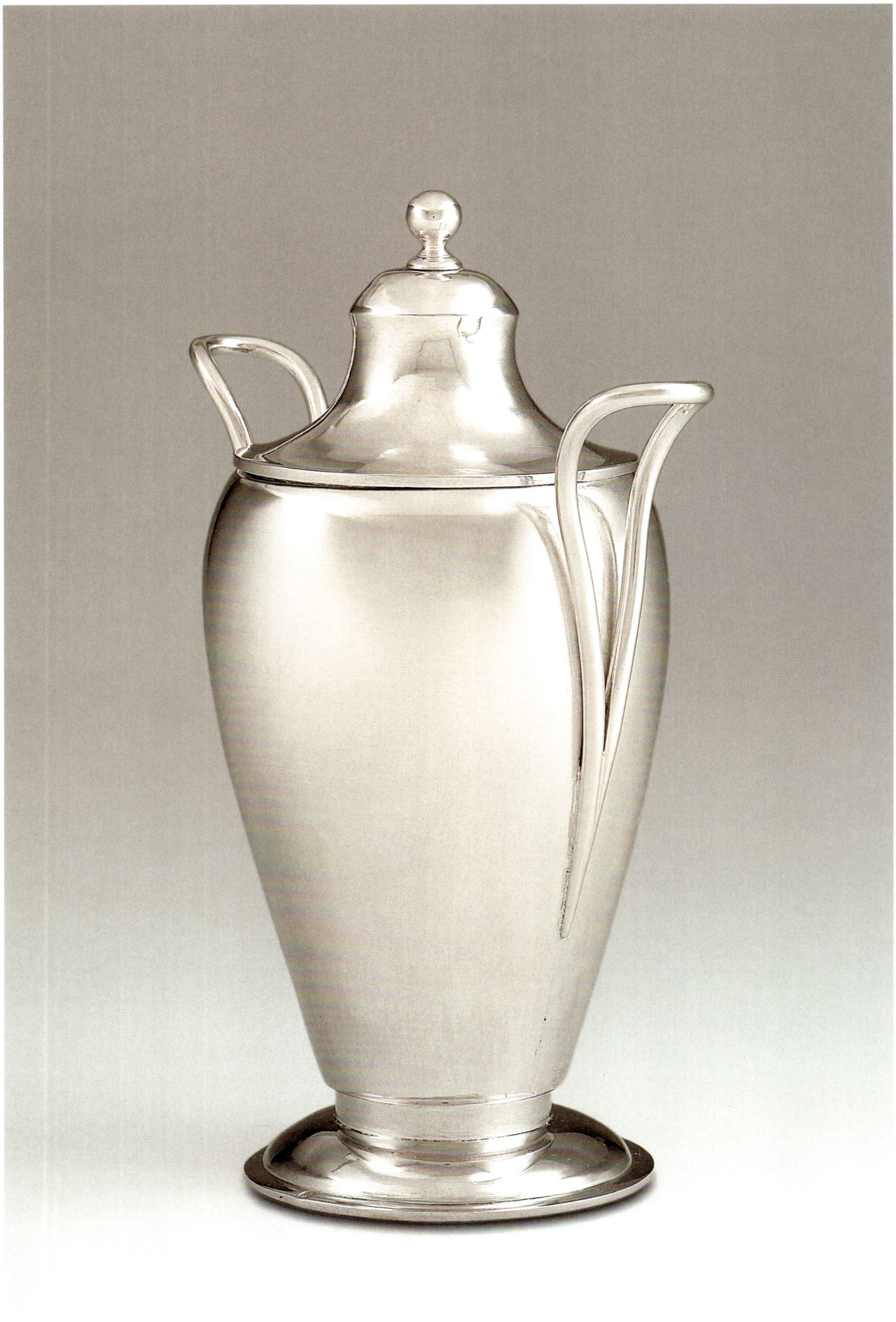

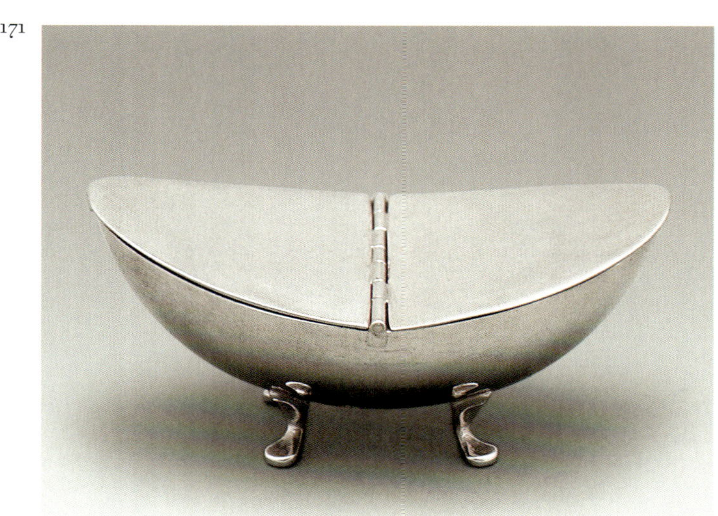

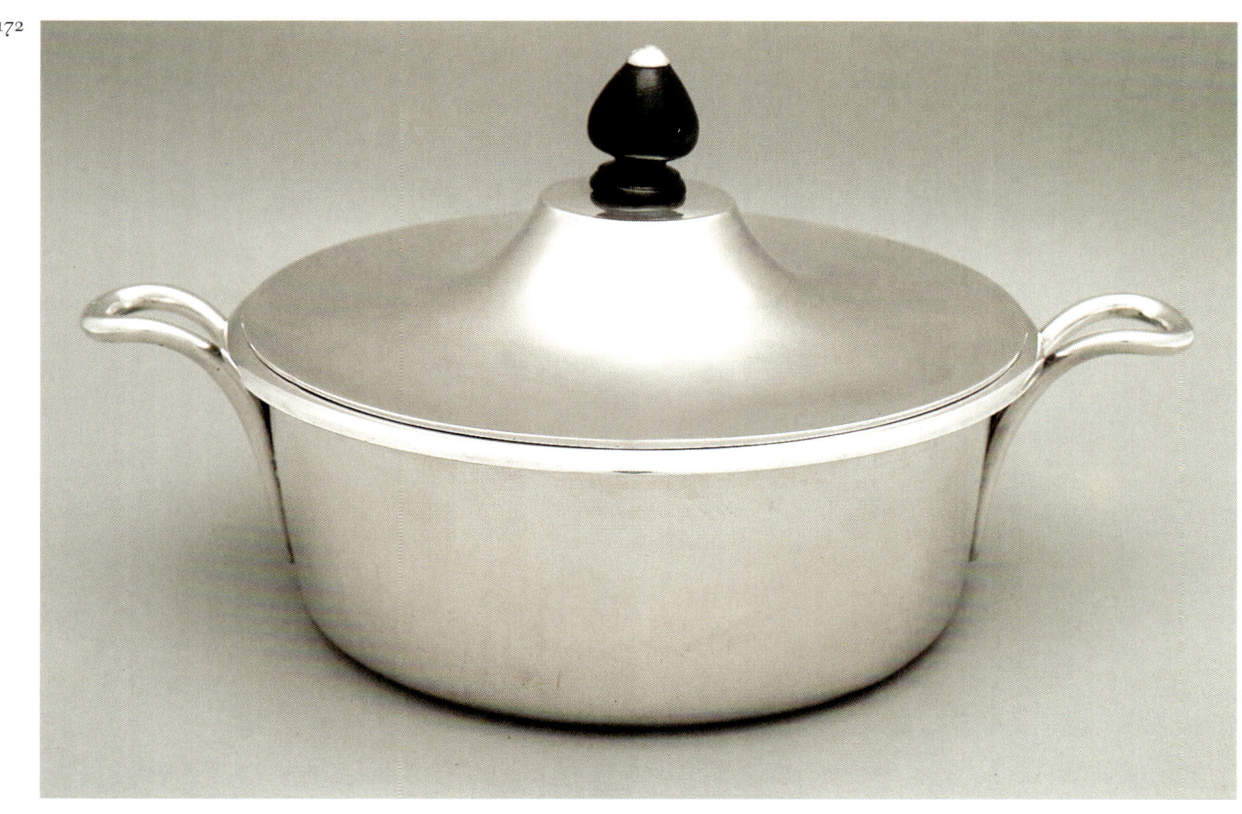

170
Sugar Urn
Vienna, 1814
Cat. IX-8

171
Spicebox
Vienna, 1821
Cat. IX-7

172
Tureen
Vienna, 1814
Cat. IX-10

173
Caster
Vienna, 1810
Cat. IX-25

Caster
Vienna, 1807
Cat. IX-26

Caster
Vienna, 1813
Cat. IX-27

174
Table Bell
Vienna, 1818
Cat. IX-9

175
(Opposite)
Caster
Vienna, 1827
Cat. IX-42 (detail)

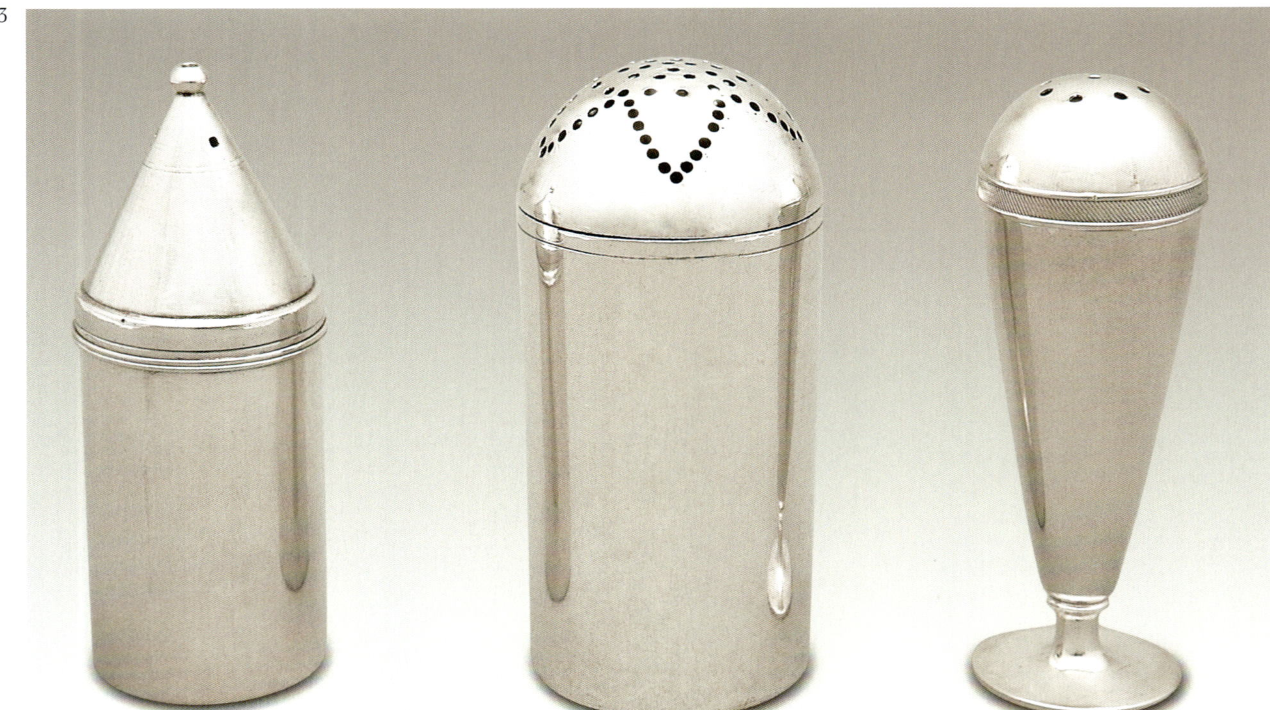

173

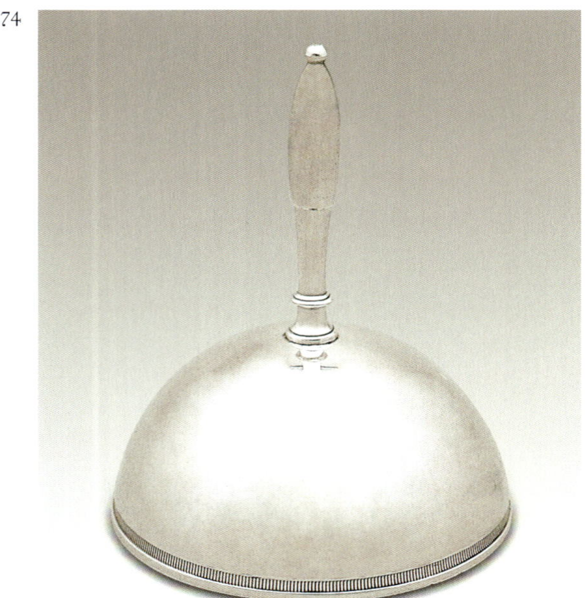

174

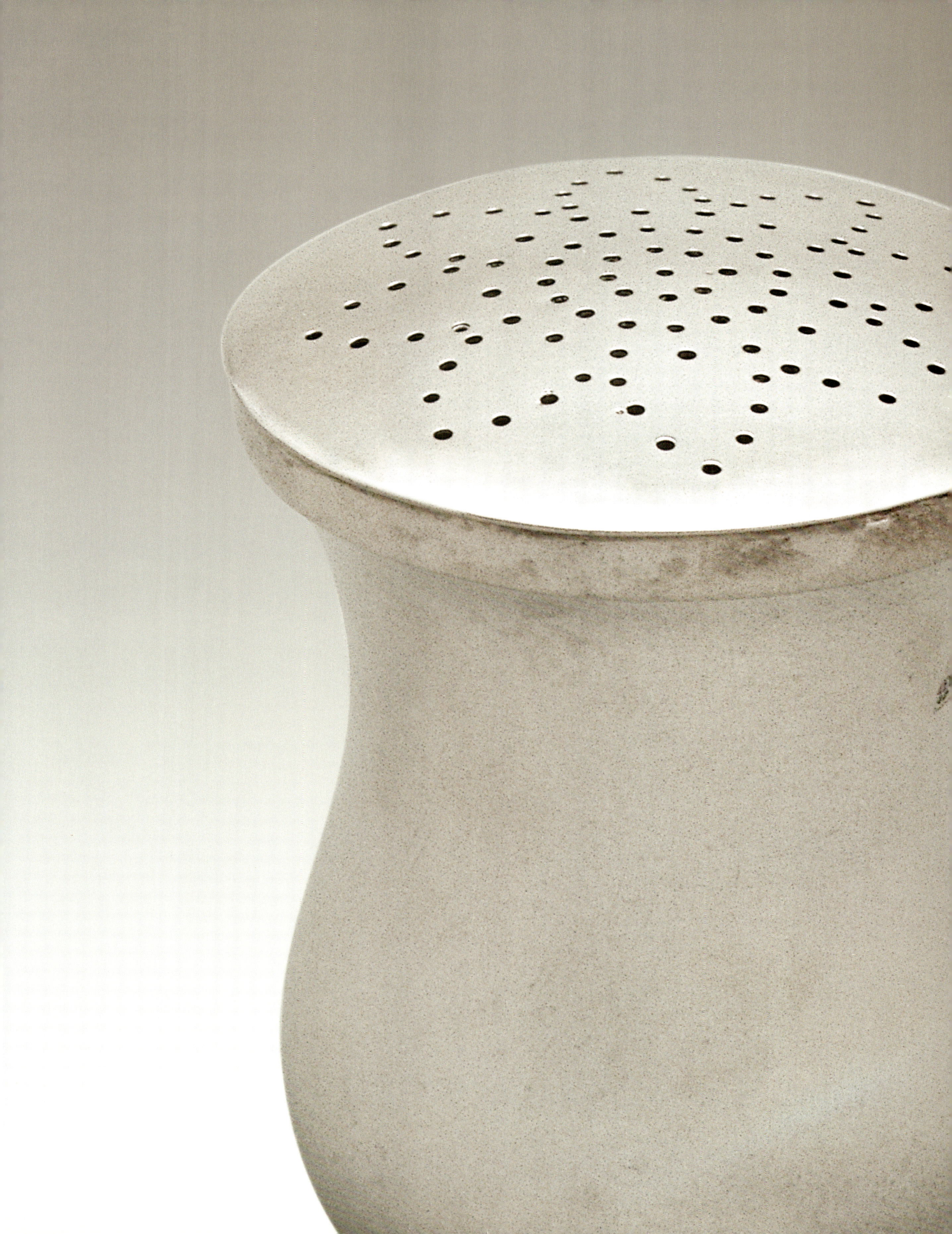

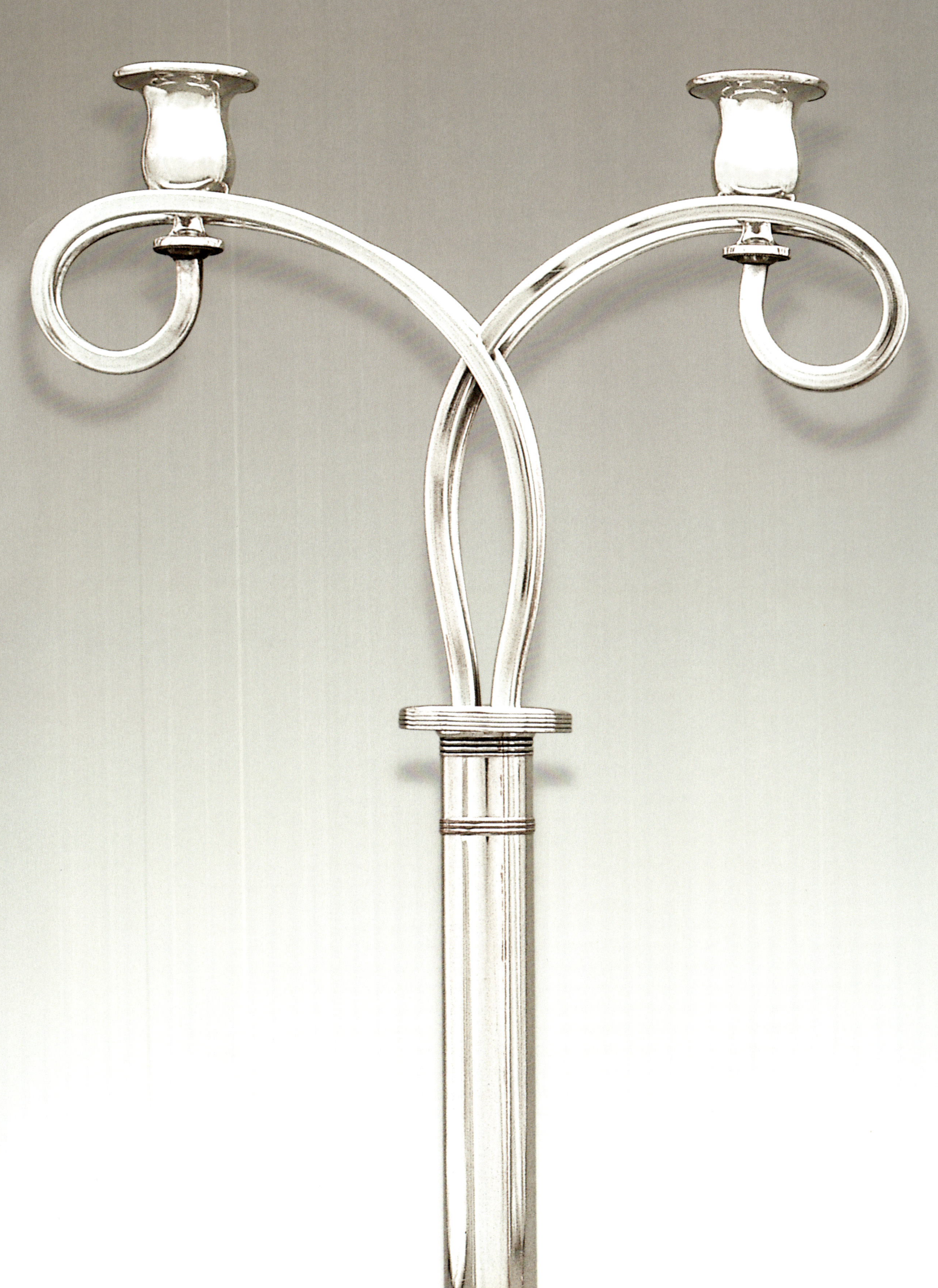

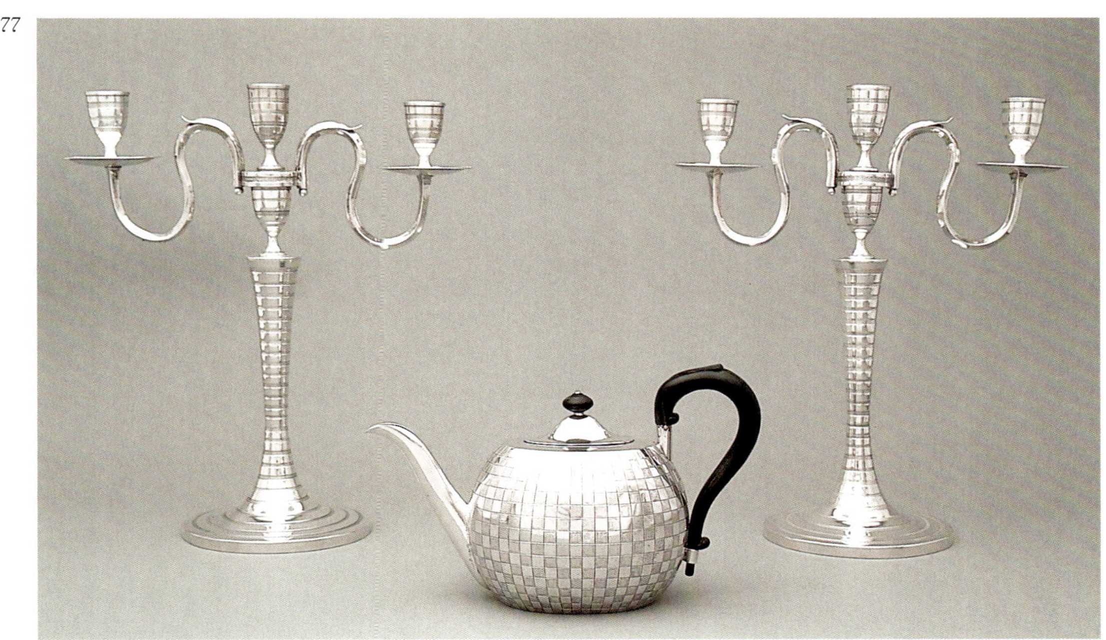

177

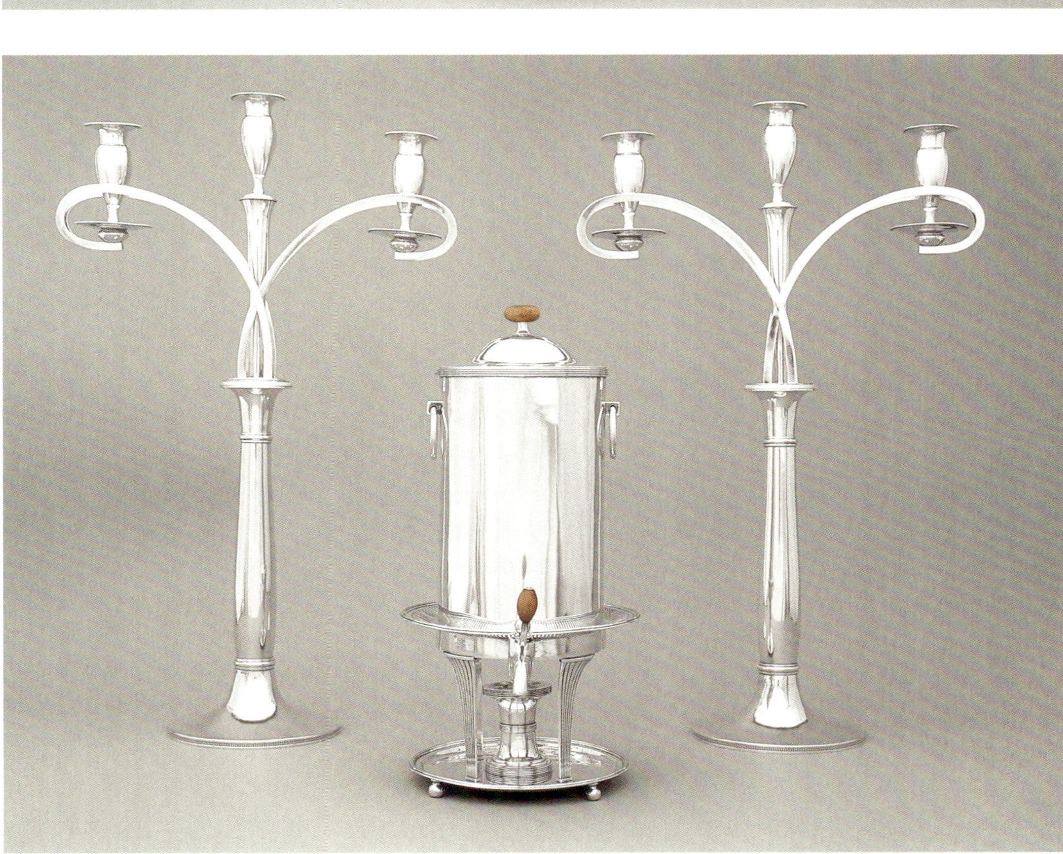

178

176
(Opposite)
Pair of Candelabra
Vienna, ca. 1820
Cat. IX-47 (detail)

177
Pair of Candelabra
Vienna, 1804
Cat. IX-16

Teapot
Vienna, 1802
Cat. IX-17

178
Pair of Candelabra
Vienna, 1825
Cat. IX-50

Samovar
Vienna, 1820
Cat. IX-51

179
Tea Kettle and Stand
Vienna, 1816
Cat. IX-32

180
Teapot
Vienna, 1803
Cat. IX-28

181
Teapot
Berlin, ca. 1805
Cat. IX-54

182
Coffee Pot
Berlin, ca. 1805
Cat. IX-55

183
Teapot
Copenhagen, ca. 1800
Cat. IX-63

179

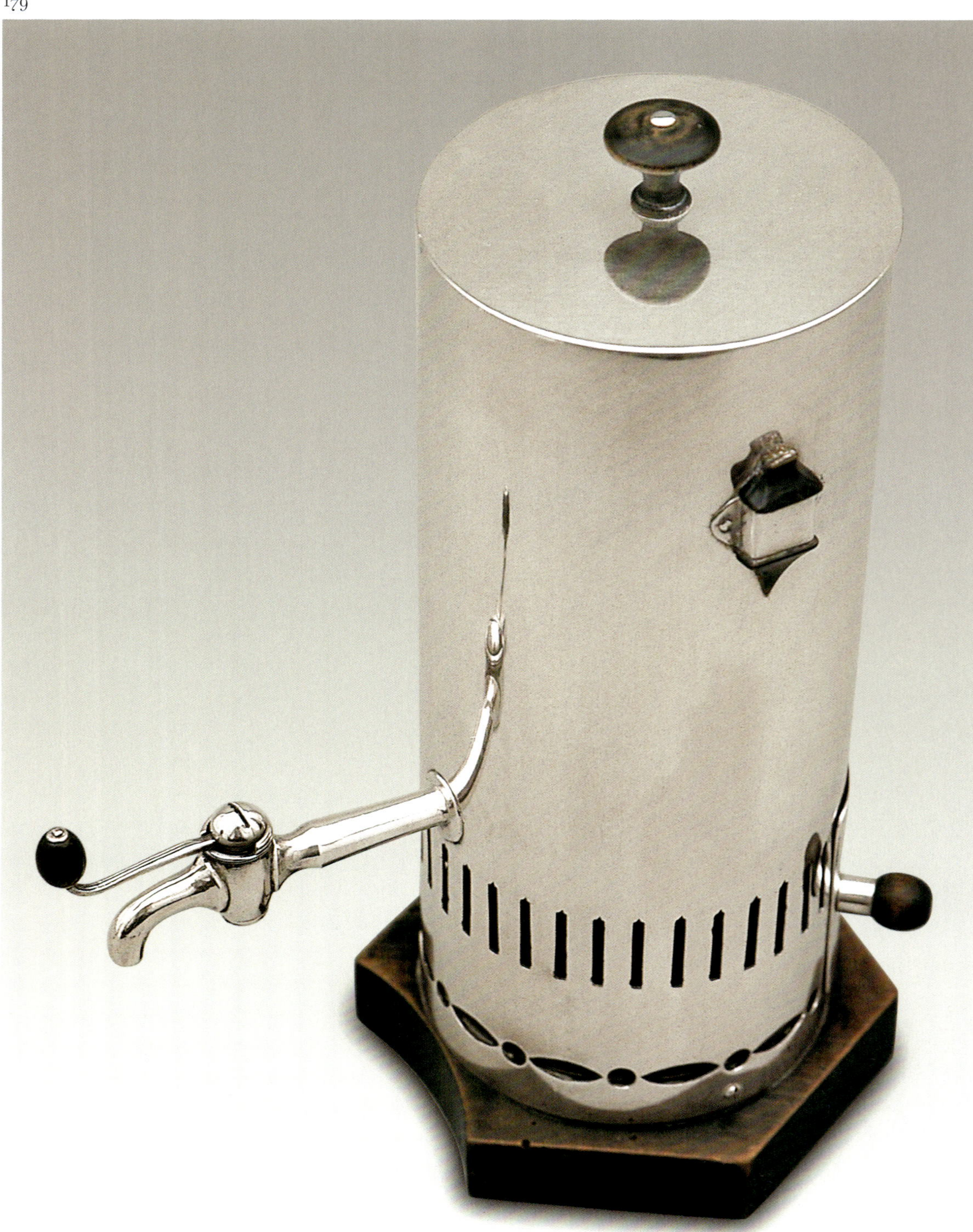

180

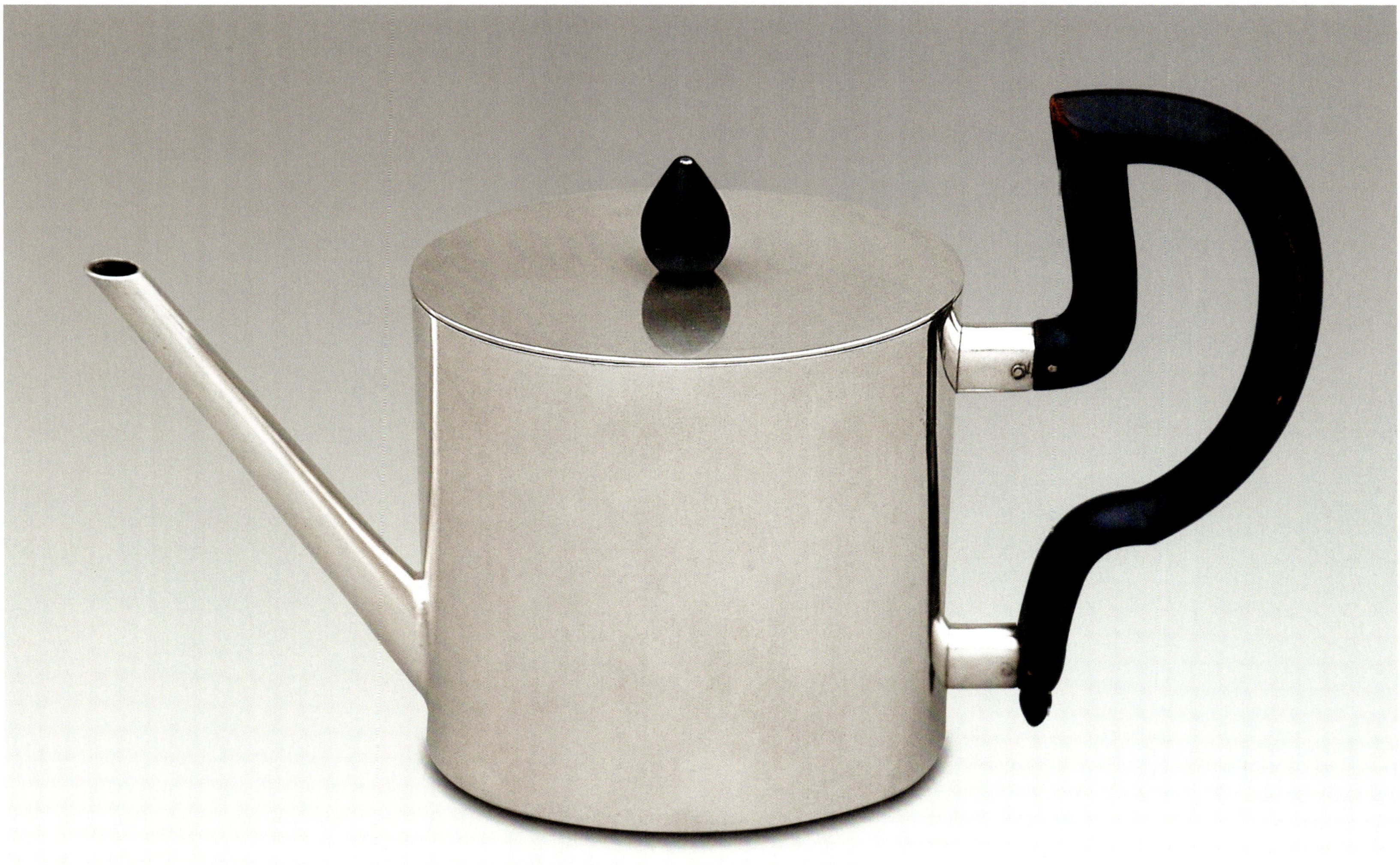

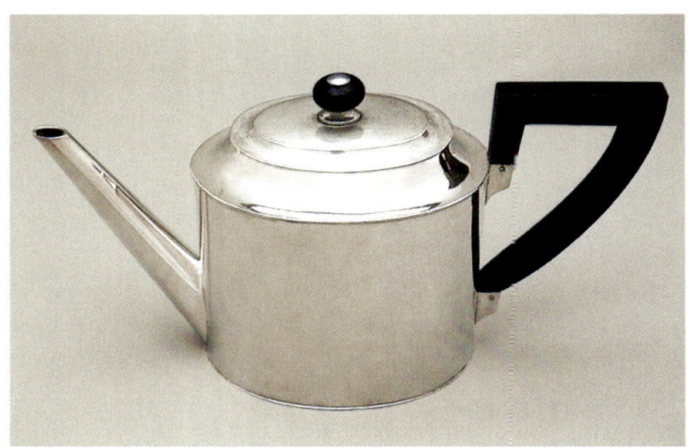

181

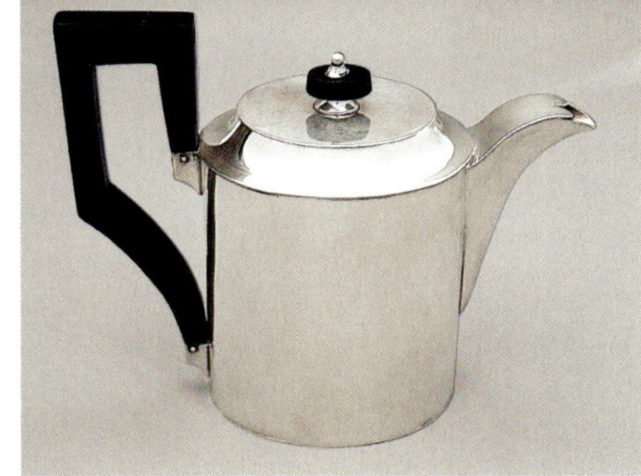

182

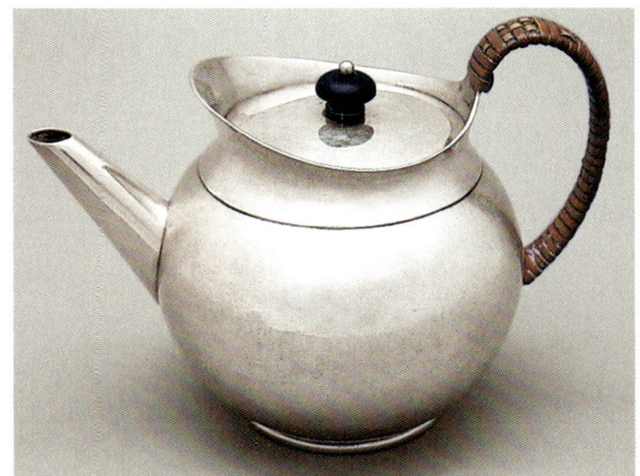

184
*Coffee Pot and
Percolator*
Vienna, 1818
Cat. IX-35

185
Coffee Set
Vienna, 1821
Cat. IX-48

184

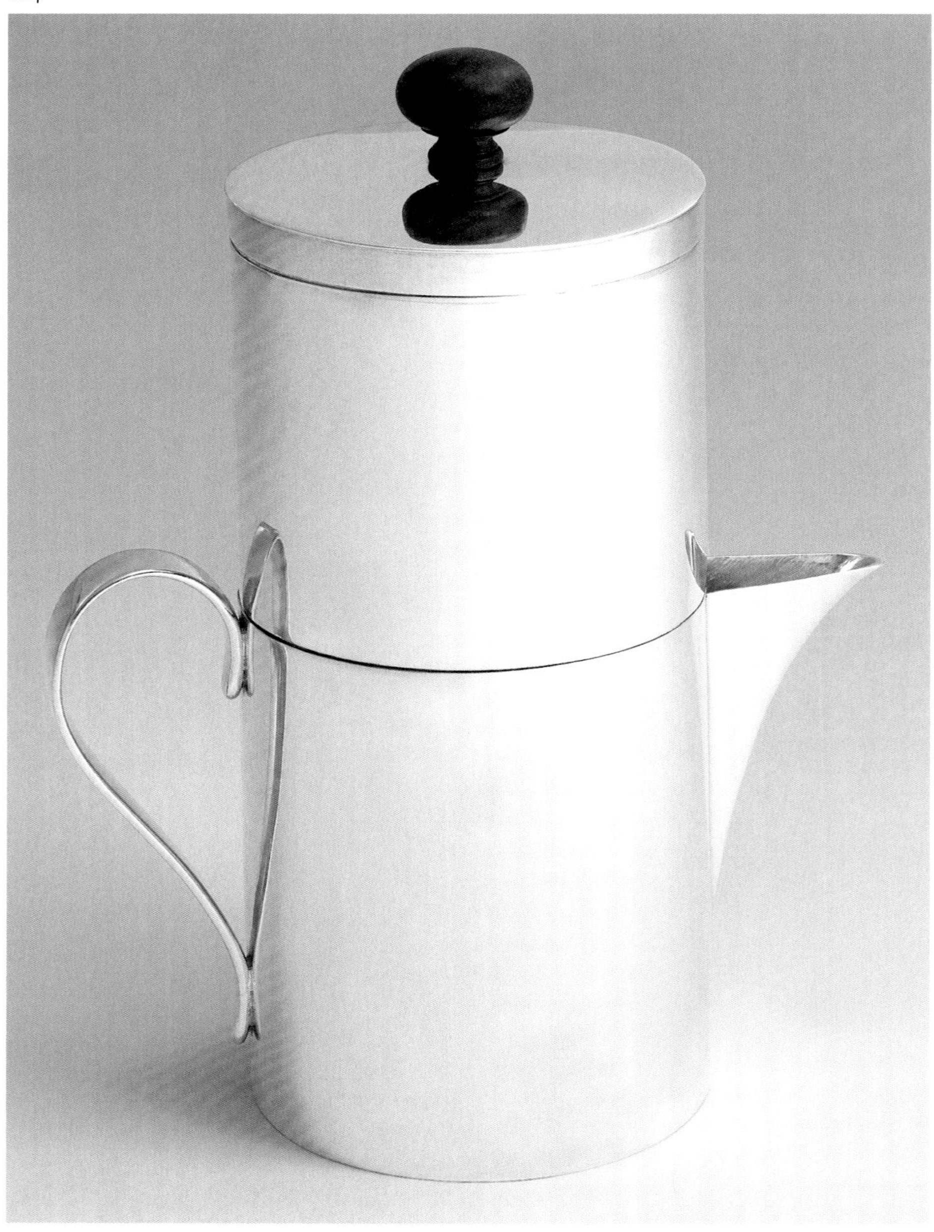

185

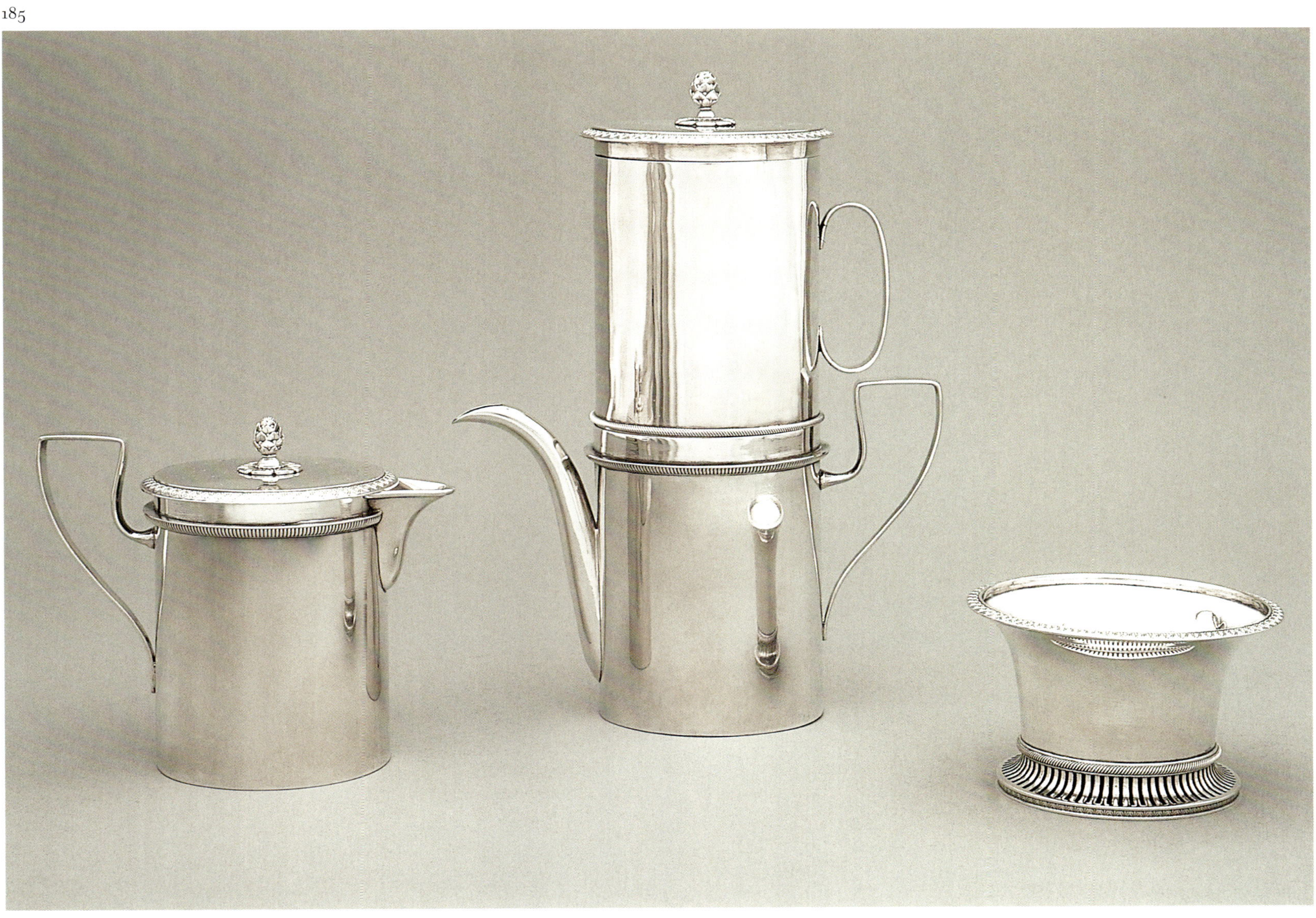

186
*One of a Pair of
Candlesticks*
Vienna, 1815
Cat. ix-38

Pair of Candlesticks
Vienna, 1816
Cat. ix-37

Casserole
Vienna, 1815
Cat. ix-36

187
Casserole
Vienna, 1807
Cat. ix-29

188
Pair of Candlesticks
Vienna, 1806
Cat. ix-31

189
*Casserole with Lid
from a Traveling Service*
Berlin, ca. 1805
Cat. ix-56

186

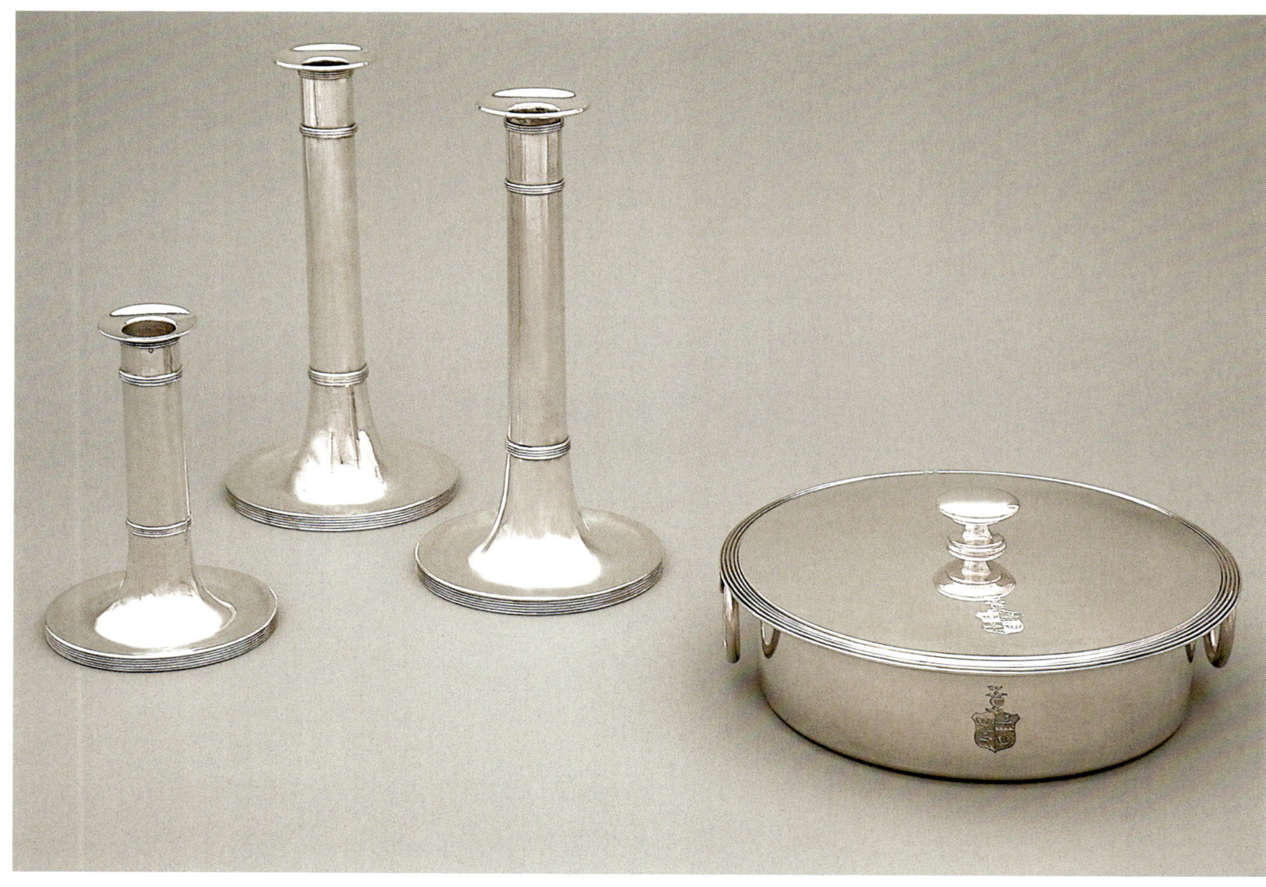

187
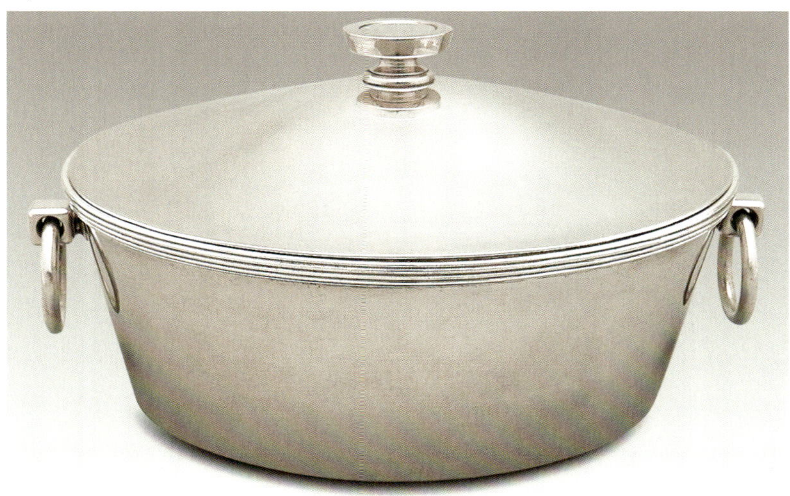

188
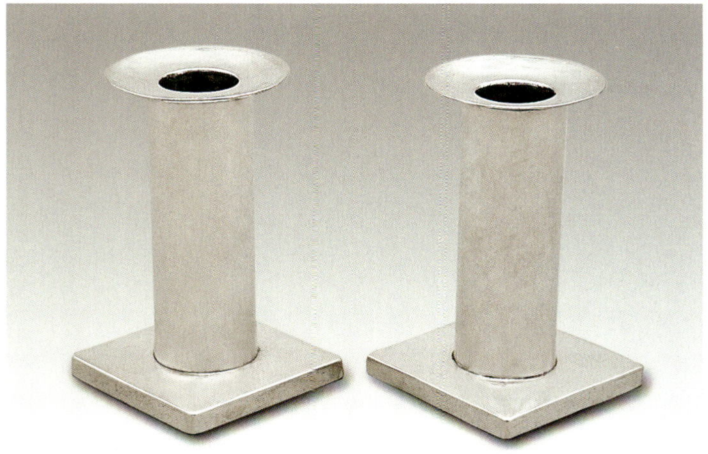

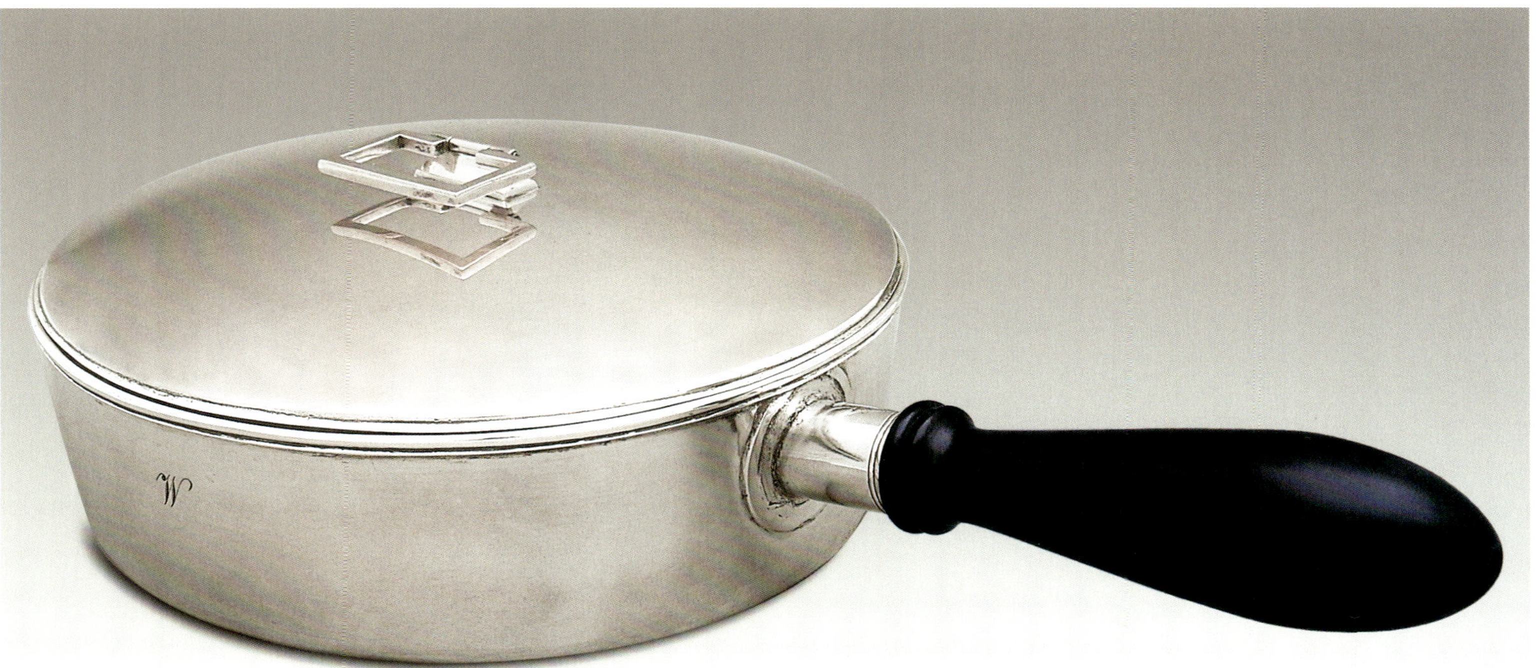
189

190
Box
Vienna, 1807
Cat. IX-30

191
Box with Handle
Vienna, 1813
Cat. IX-34

192
*Box from a Toilette
Service*
Vienna, 1807
Cat. IX-33

193
*Box from a Toilette
Service*
Vienna, 1834
Cat. IX-45

194
Sugar Box
Vienna, 1819
Cat. IX-39

195
*Box from a Toilette
Service*
Vienna, 1828
Cat. IX-40

190 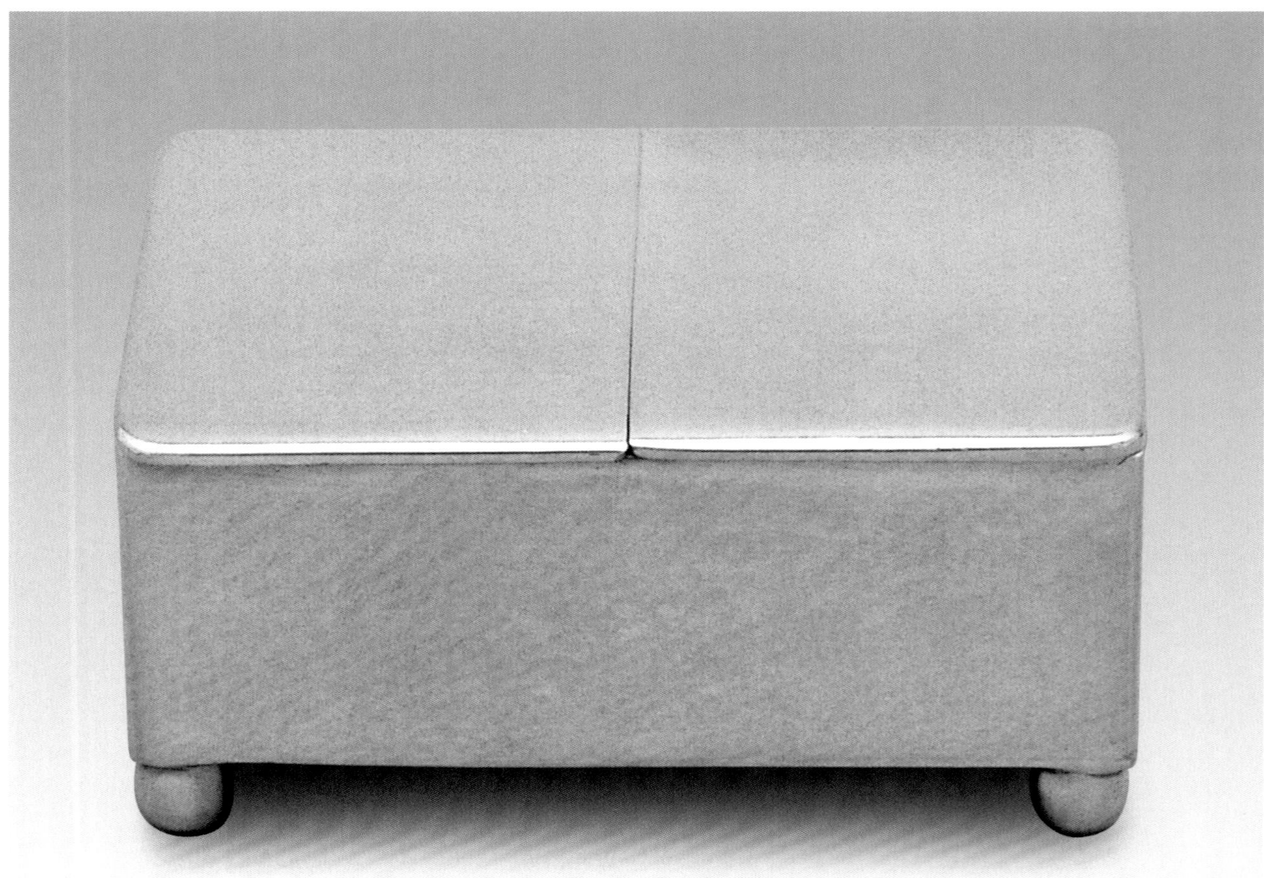

191 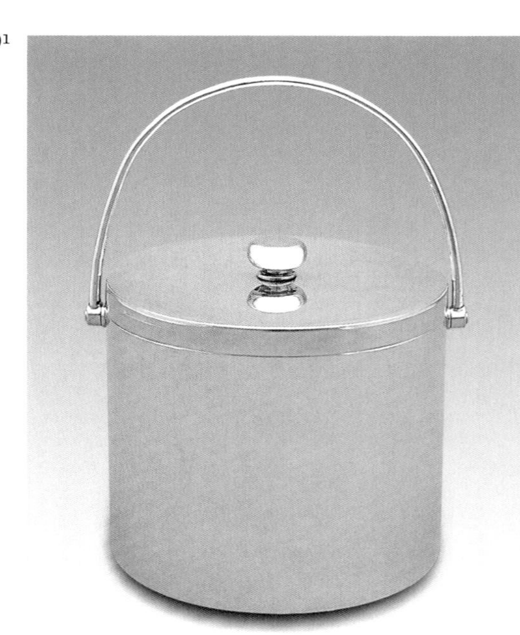

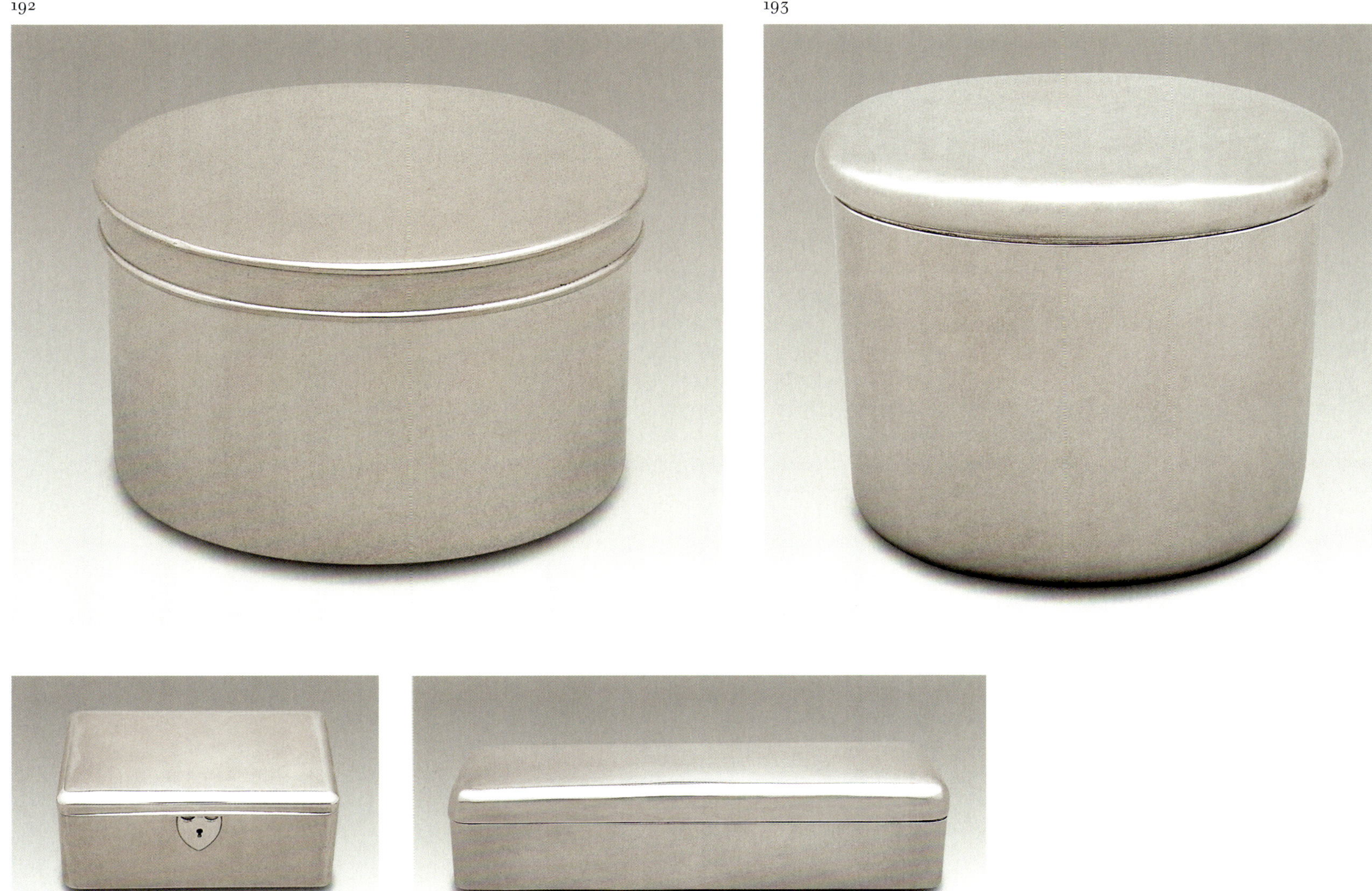

192   193

194   195

196
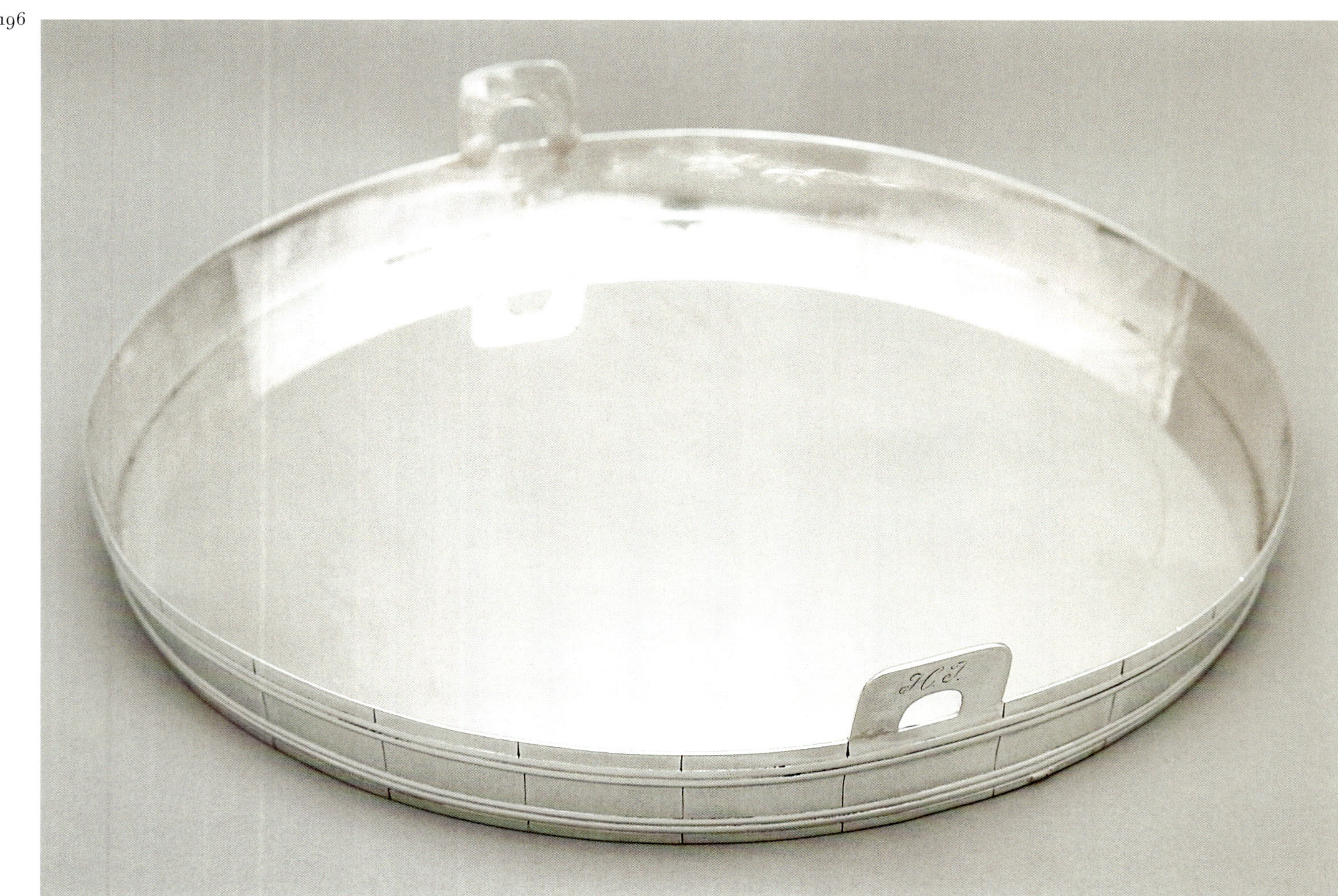

197
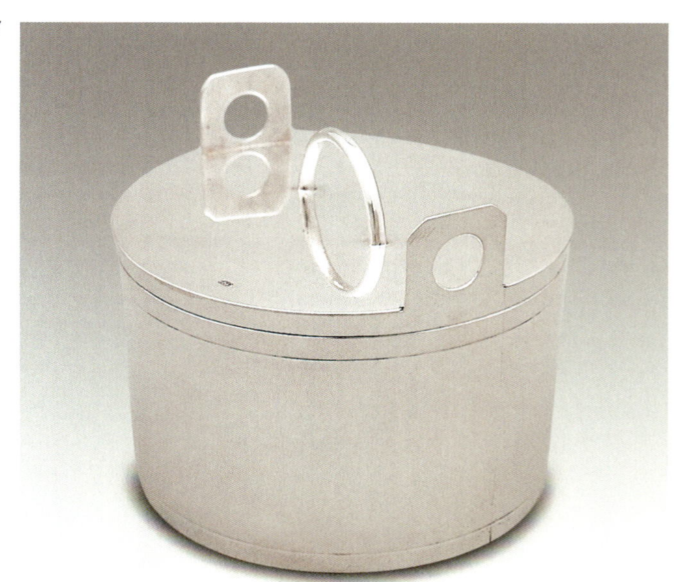

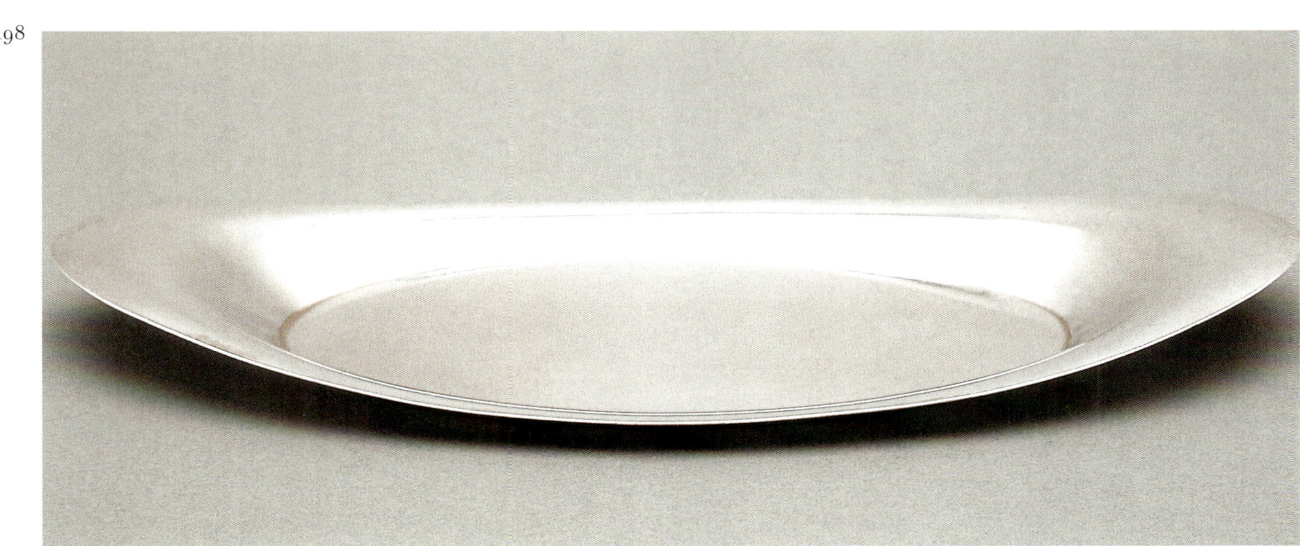

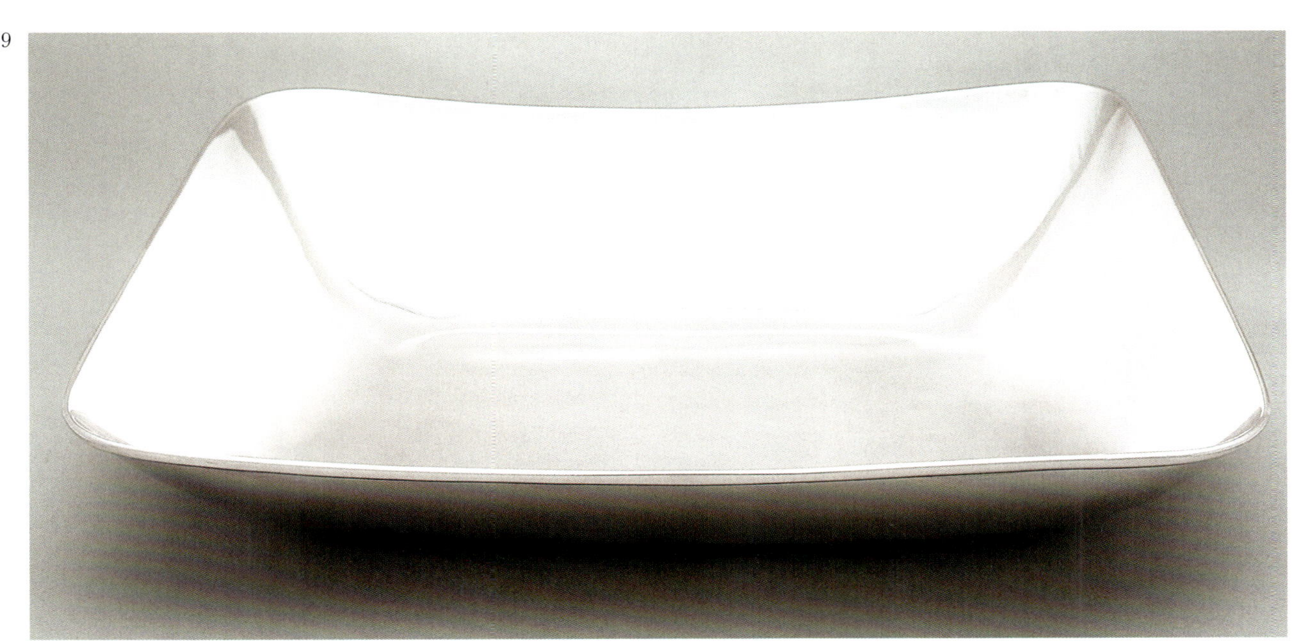

196
Tray
Vienna, 180?
Cat. IX-24

197
Butter Tub
Vienna, 1802
Cat. IX-23

198
Small Tray
Vienna, 1819
Cat. IX-46

199
Bowl
Vienna, 1826
Cat. IX-43

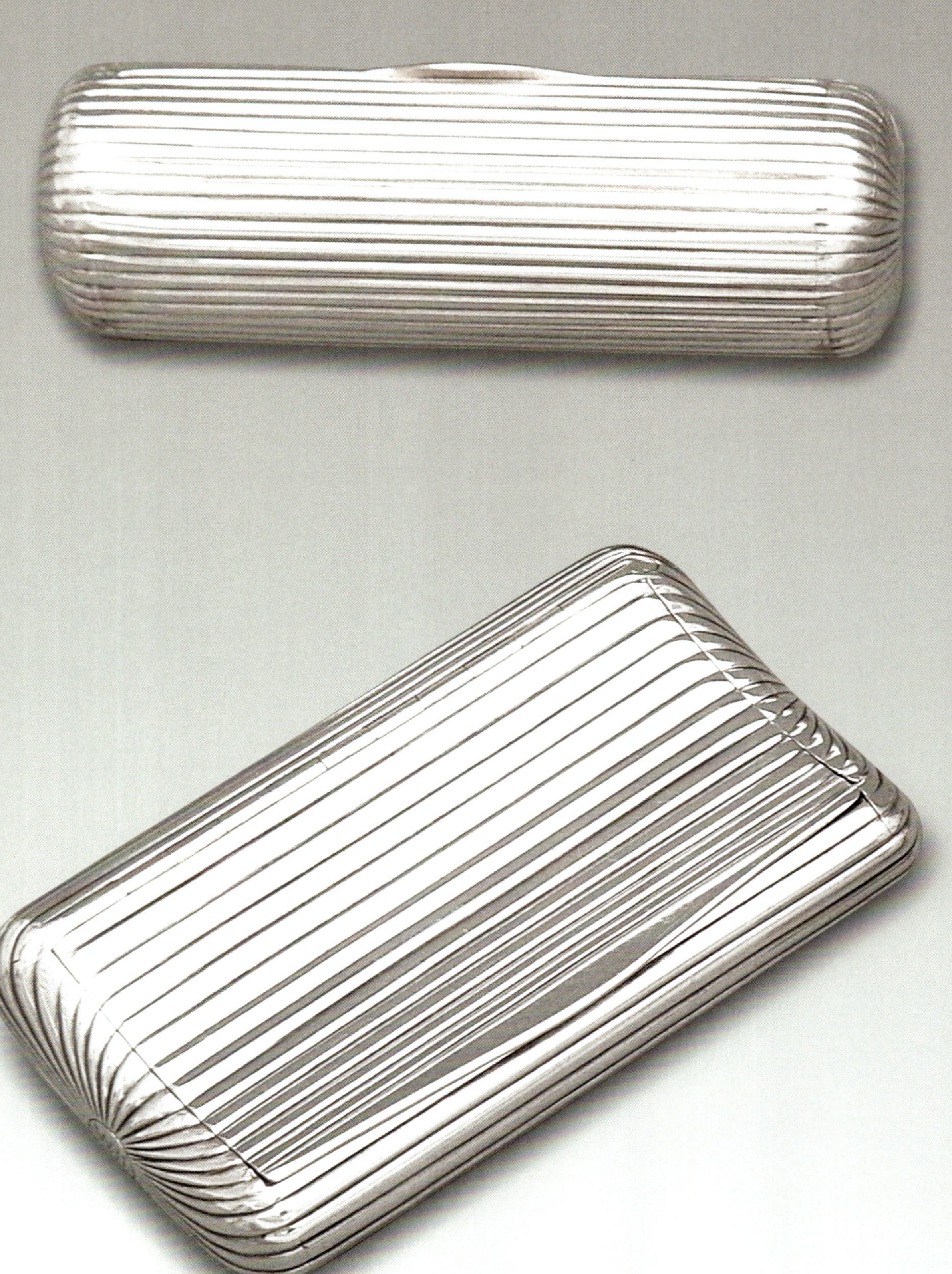

200
(Top left)
Box
Vienna, 1818
Cat. IX-19

(Top middle)
Box
Vienna, 1807
Cat. IX-21

(Top right)
Box
Vienna, 1813
Cat. IX-22

(Bottom left)
Box
Vienna, 1822
Cat. IX-18

(Bottom right)
Box
Vienna, 1803
Cat. IX-20

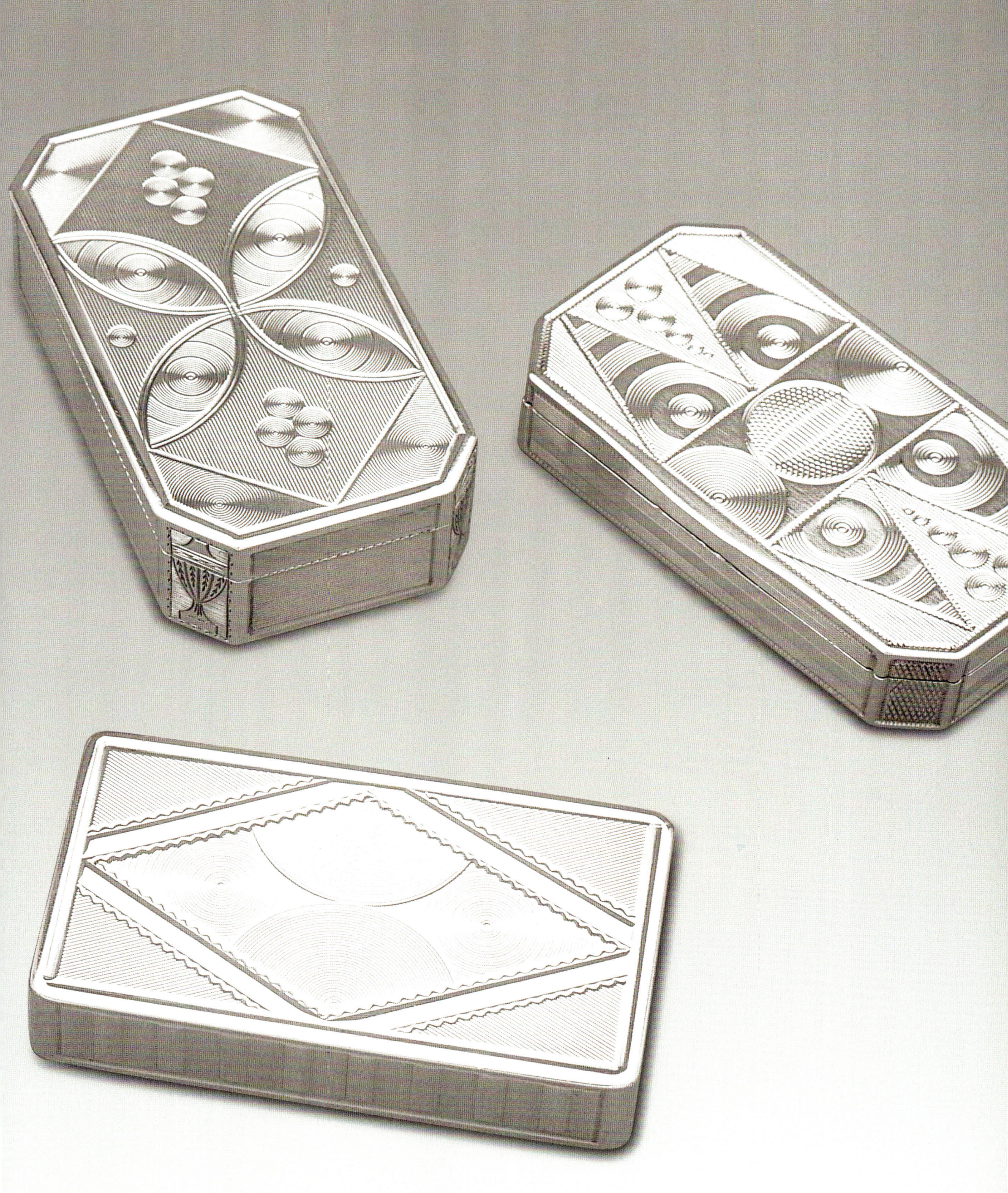

201
Brushes from a
Toilette Service
Vienna, 1821
Cat. IX-44

202
Travel Set
Vienna, 1816
Cat. IX-15

203
Travel Toilette Set
Kassel, 1802
Cat. IX-52

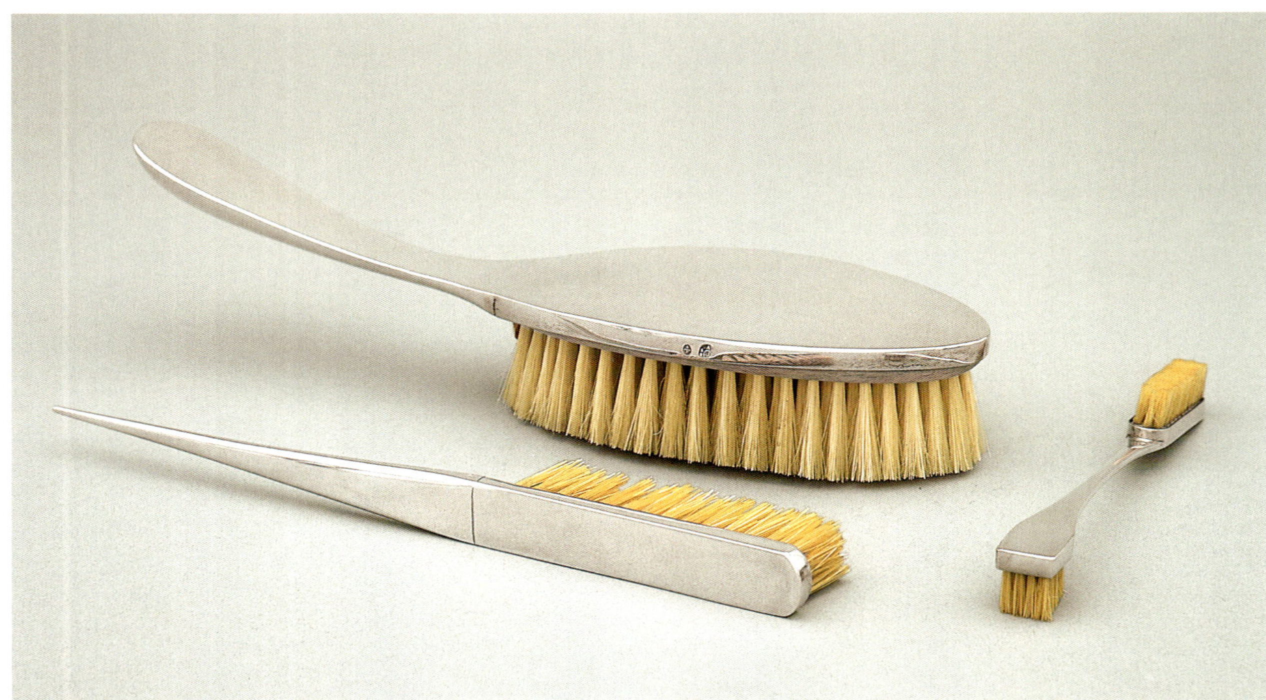

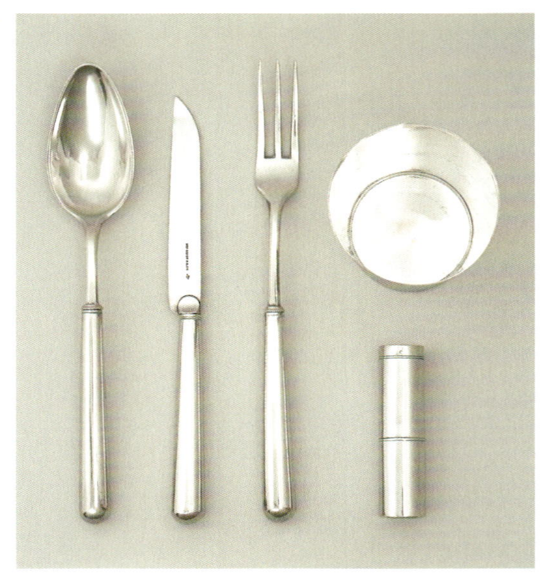

203

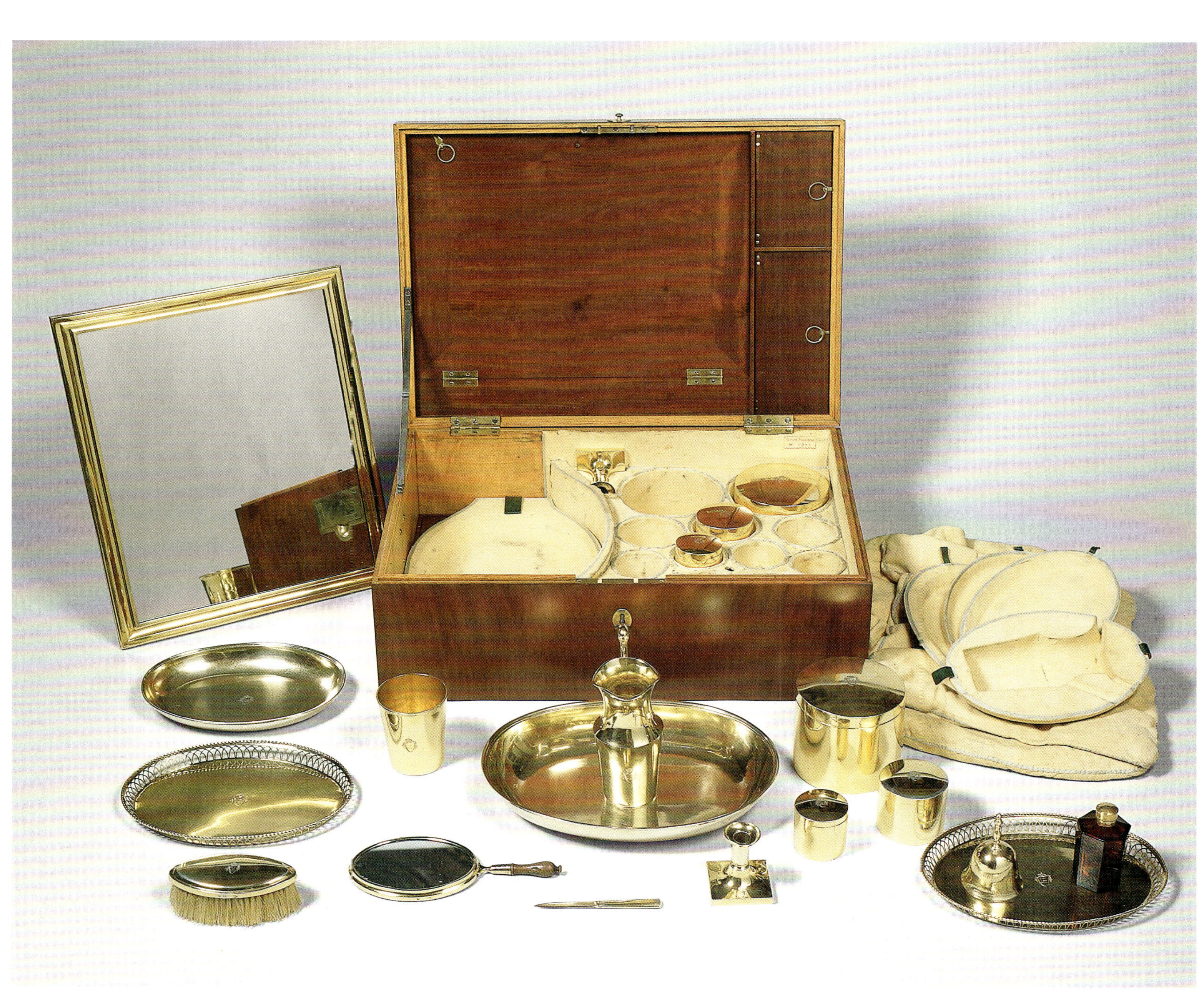

METALWORK

SECTION X

Albrecht Pyritz

THE ART OF METALWORK

With the production of handicrafts still in the hands of small-scale manufacturers, early Biedermeier metalwork exhibited a pronounced preindustrial character. This began to change around 1800 with the establishment of state-owned factories that began producing goods of outstanding technical quality and specialized in the serial production of art objects. This development took place primarily in foundries and metalworking shops, in which improved production methods and new casting and forming techniques were developed. This mirrored changes in the highly traditional state-owned porcelain and glass manufactories, where extensive technical modernization programs were undertaken to meet the declared economic objective of competing successfully in the national and international markets and achieving independence from imports of raw materials and utilitarian goods that were subject to customs duties.

CAST IRON

With its characteristic flat black appearance, cast iron represented a form of expression in Biedermeier art defined primarily by the plain look of the material. Works designed by artists themselves or commissioned for casting in iron represented a style that relied upon material simplicity as opposed to the material luxury of the waning eighteenth century. This opposition between the extravagant ornamentation of the Empire style and reductive iron art oriented toward clear contours assumed programmatic significance within the context of the anti-Napoleonic climate in Prussia. The "material of our fatherland, ennobled by the highest art" became an expression of patriotism and an embodiment of the functional and objective qualities of Biedermeier art.

The development of cast iron can be traced back to the seventeenth century. With the revival of the metalworking industry and the establishment of numerous foundries after 1750, the Prussian state built the first consolidated network of production facilities. New sources of raw materials and manufacturing processes led to new transportation routes and systems. The upgraded foundries were based on the English model and the systematic training of molding and casting specialists benefited primar-

ily the newly established Königliche Preussische Eisengiessereien (Royal Prussian Iron Foundries) in Gleiwitz (1798–1945) and Berlin (1804–1873), but also the ironworks in Mariazell (1742–1898) and Horowitz (1785–ca. 1850) in the Austrian Empire.

The basic prerequisites for ironworking included both technical training and artistic training of casting and forming specialists at art academies, which set up drawing classes for craftsmen and factory workers in order to promote "general education in taste." Free afternoon and Sunday courses in drawing, architecture, and geometry were offered at the Berlin Academy beginning around 1790; public lectures were given on the arts and architecture of ancient Greece and Rome. This aesthetic and artistic training had a significant impact on the quality of commercial handicrafts produced in Prussia.

Equally important impulses for the design of cast-iron objects were pattern books and imported models. In 1790, Friedrich Wilhelm Count von Reden (1752–1815), Director of the Upper Mining Office for the Silesian provinces, acquired pewter models and glass plates with ancient motifs from the same series used by Josiah Wedgwood (1730–1795) in Staffordshire. Cast medallions bearing relief portraits from Greek and Roman coins were prepared from these examples in Gleiwitz and became very popular. The Berlin works specialized initially in the production of small, rectangular plaques bearing images of innovations in casting technology and large cast-iron objects. The Gleiwitz and Berlin items reflected the deliberate expression of a primarily technical and increasingly artistic development that appealed to a large group of collectors and other buyers.

In 1806, the Berlin foundry began specializing in cast art objects, including the first portrait medallions and articles of jewelry. These activities were interrupted by the French occupation of the city in 1807–12. In 1808, the French requisitioned numerous cast art objects and models for the purpose of establishing iron-casting operations in Paris, but these efforts came to nothing. Only with the outbreak of the Wars of Liberation in 1813 did artistic iron casting resume on a large scale in Berlin. Launching the campaign "I gave gold for iron," the state borrowed from the people to fund the war. Citizens turned in their gold, and iron jewelry became a fashionable expression of patriotism. The "Eisernes Kreuz" (Iron Cross) established by the Prussian King Friedrich Wilhelm III (1770–1840), which was produced from a design by Karl Friedrich Schinkel (1781–1841) in 1813, underscored the symbolic power of iron embodied in a military badge of honor.

Cast-iron figures were among the most aesthetically appealing creations that emerged from the Prussian and Austrian iron foundries. In 1810, noble families began commissioning leading sculptors to execute portrait busts, initially in marble or stone and later in cast iron. The Berlin sculptor Christian Daniel Rauch (1777–1857) and the Vienna artist Johann Nepomuk Schaller (1777–1842) belonged to a generation that had educated themselves by copying ancient models during periods of study in Rome and developed a classicist style of art characterized by clearly defined forms and contours. Rauch, who had already created the gravestone for Queen Luise of Prussia (1776–1810) following her untimely death, was commissioned by Friedrich Wilhelm III to execute a marble bust of the queen in 1816 and a companion bust of the king himself in 1818. The bust of Luise was based on an antique model of Demeter Valata in Rome, guardian of the ordered state and marriage, yet characterized at the same time by striking realism. Rauch's portraits of the Prussian king and queen were cast in iron at the Berlin foundry in 1818 and exhibited that same year at the Akademie der Künste, where they earned the highest acclaim.

The Königliche Eisengiesserei Berlin also engaged leading artists to design its art objects. With inventiveness and love of experimentation, Schinkel, who had already achieved great success with interior decorations and furniture for the royal palace, was eminently qualified to meet the challenges of designing iron furniture. His diverse, broadly varied designs in basic cast-iron forms and details, created in collaboration with the foundry, began to appear in outdoor furniture for the newly furnished royal residences. They exhibit the same characteristics as his designs for wood furniture for the Prussian royal family: an emphasis on contours and a homogeneous surface design composed of interconnected structures and applied ornaments. Schinkel's furniture built for the public areas of Prussian residences exemplifies the Empire style; pieces for the private quarters of the royal families of Prussia exhibit the clearer, simpler lines of Biedermeier.

In 1808, for the Chamois Room in the palace of the crown prince, Schinkel designed a seating group with crossed legs that calls to mind the ancient Roman "sella curulis," a scissor-legged chair based on an English adaptation of the original form. In a parallel development, the *Klismos Chair* derived from Greek illustrations became increasingly popular after about 1800. This chair, with its typical flared, sword-shaped legs and concave back, was produced by court cabinetmakers for the Danish royal family, then moved to England and from there to Germany, where it could be found in nearly all royal residences of Central Europe after 1815. Schinkel designed several different versions of this type as a dining chair. For the Weisser Saal of the Neues Palais and in Paretz Palace, the chair was made of birch. Schinkel used both types of chair, the *Klismos Chair* and the "sella curulis," as models for iron furniture. Initially, he designed a sofa, the centerpiece of room furnishings, and later an armchair and dining chair. Schinkel achieved complete mastery of the basic forms, to which he added a variety of decorative elements. Yet the open backs and sides of the sofas and chairs posed new challenges for the artist.

In addition to the Königliche Eisengiesserei, private foundries in Berlin also played a significant role in the production of cast-iron art, most notably in the manufacture of delicate jewelry. Of particular note in this context are the foundries of Johann Conrad Geiss (1772–1846) and Simeon Pierre Devaranne (1789–1859), whose rivalry produced a number of extraordinary artistic achievements. Especially beautiful are the delicate, precisely fashioned bracelets and necklaces composed of separate elements arranged in alternating patterns representing motifs from nature. They also created parures that offered a wide range of variations for women's fashions. This jewelry was worn in combination with accessories made of matching materials – pocketbooks and bracelets of woven iron wire, clasps and pins with cast-iron appliqués.

ENAMEL ART BY STOBWASSER

The enameled pieces made of white sheet iron or cast tin and placed in monochrome settings by the Manufaktur Stobwasser, which operated production facilities in Braunschweig and Berlin, were conceived as articles for everyday use. They exhibit a simple design reduced to the elementary forms of the object. In contrast to the numerous versions with painted decorative motifs, these simple pieces vary only with regard to settings and appliqués. The use of monochromatic, pure primary colors of red, blue, and yellow exactly follows the theory of colors proposed by Johann Wolfgang von Goethe, who is known to have possessed many such pieces.

204
Christian Daniel Rauch
*Bust of Queen
Luise of Prussia*
ca. 1818
Cat. x-1

205
Christian Daniel Rauch
*Bust of Friedrich
Wilhelm III of Prussia*
1816
Cat. x-2

206
(Opposite)
Chair
Gleiwitz, ca. 1830
Cat. x-6

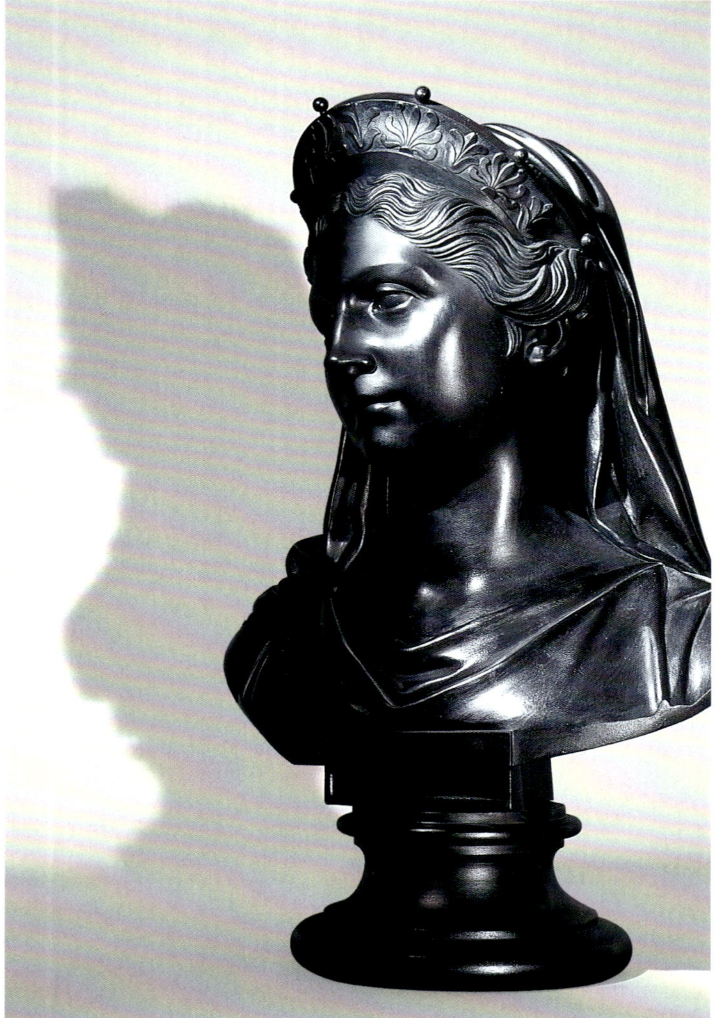

204

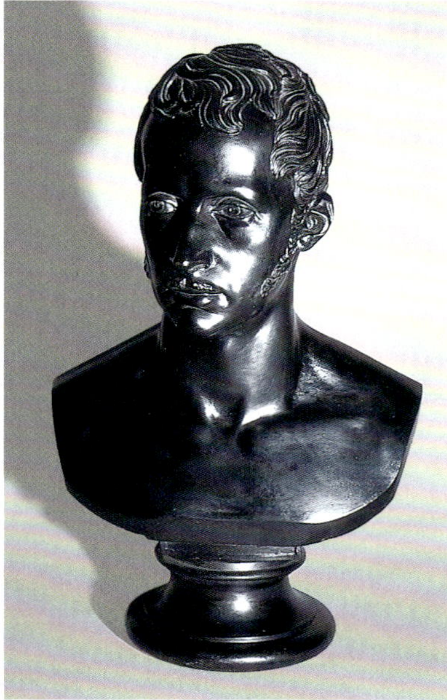

205

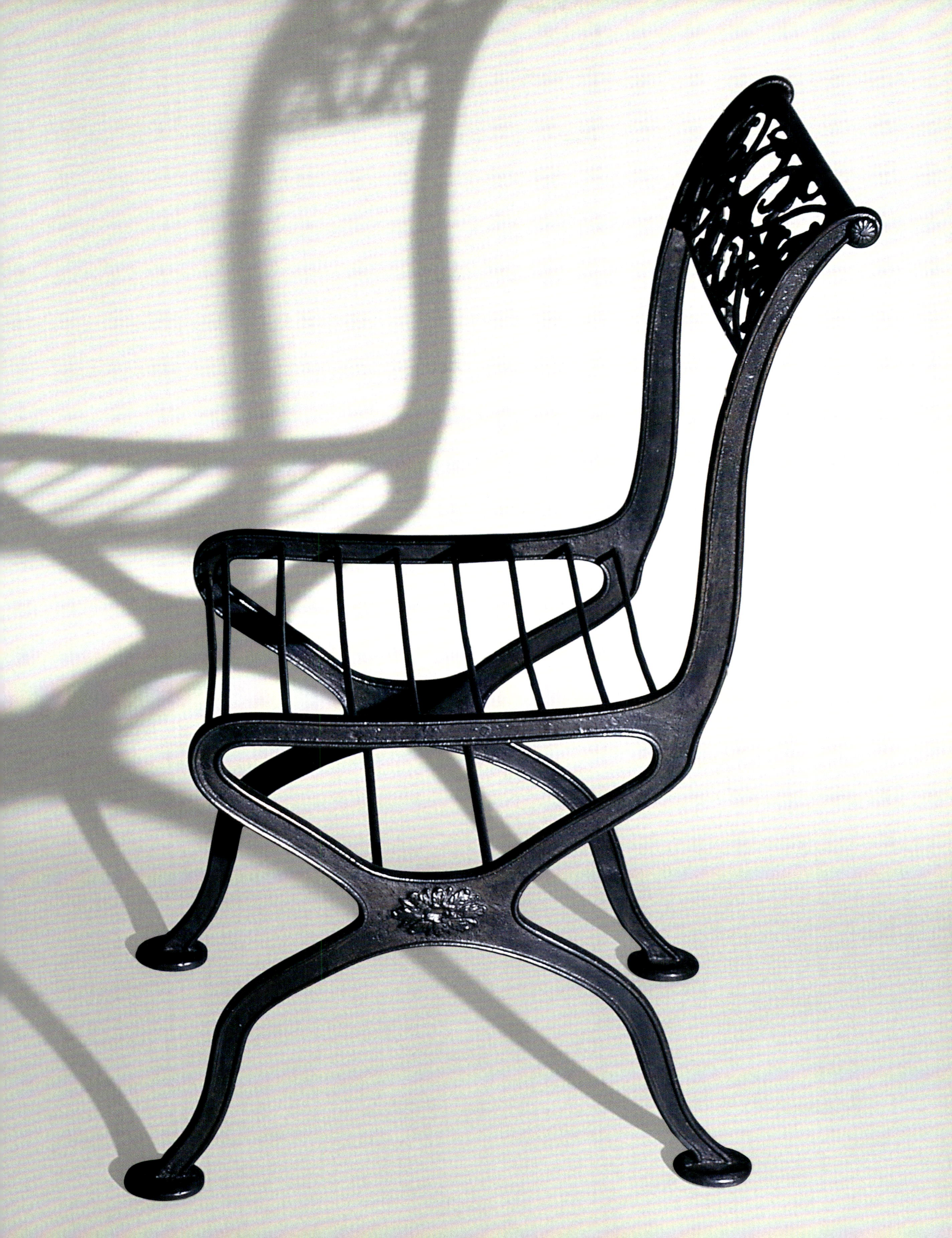

207 

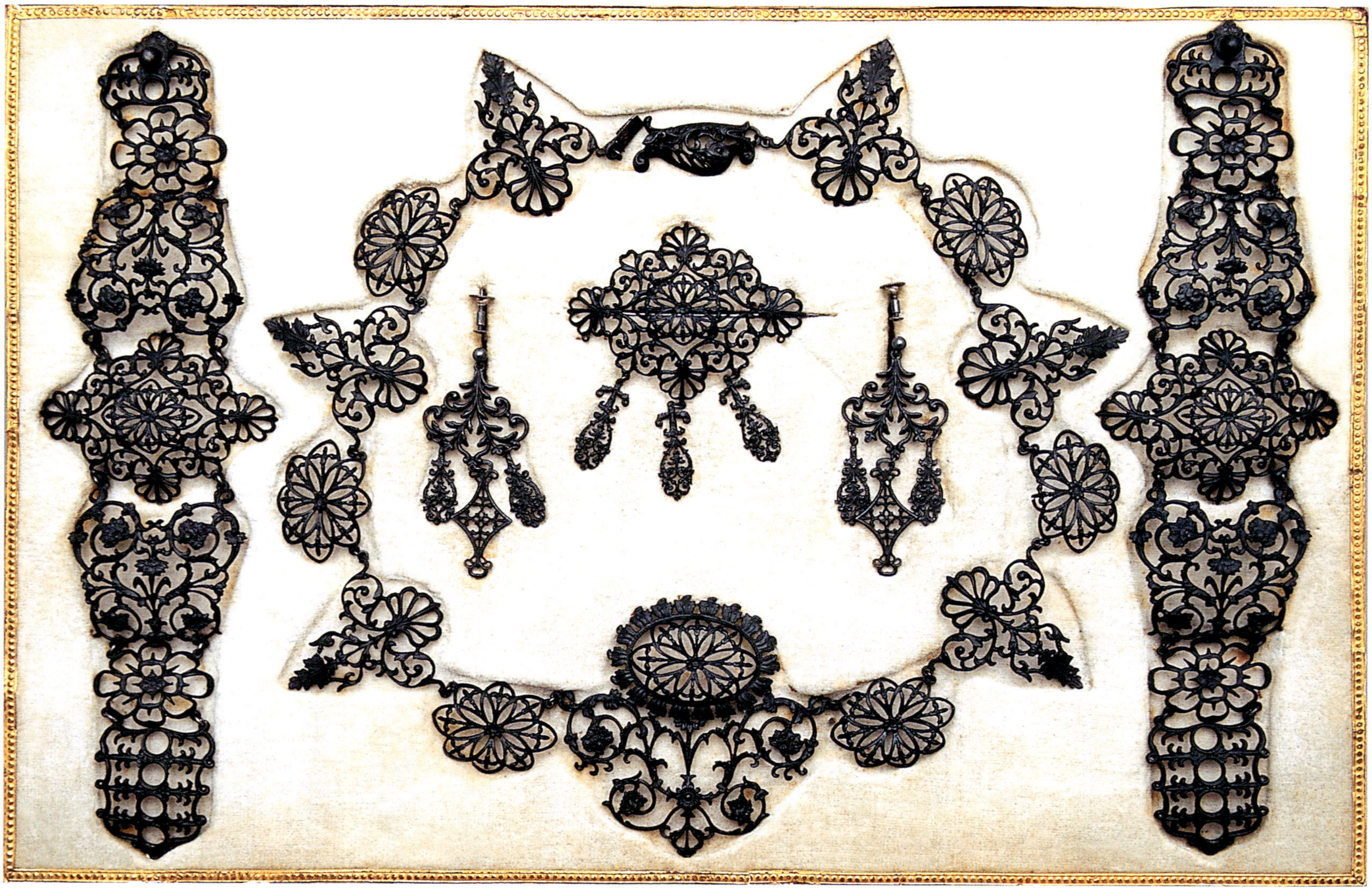

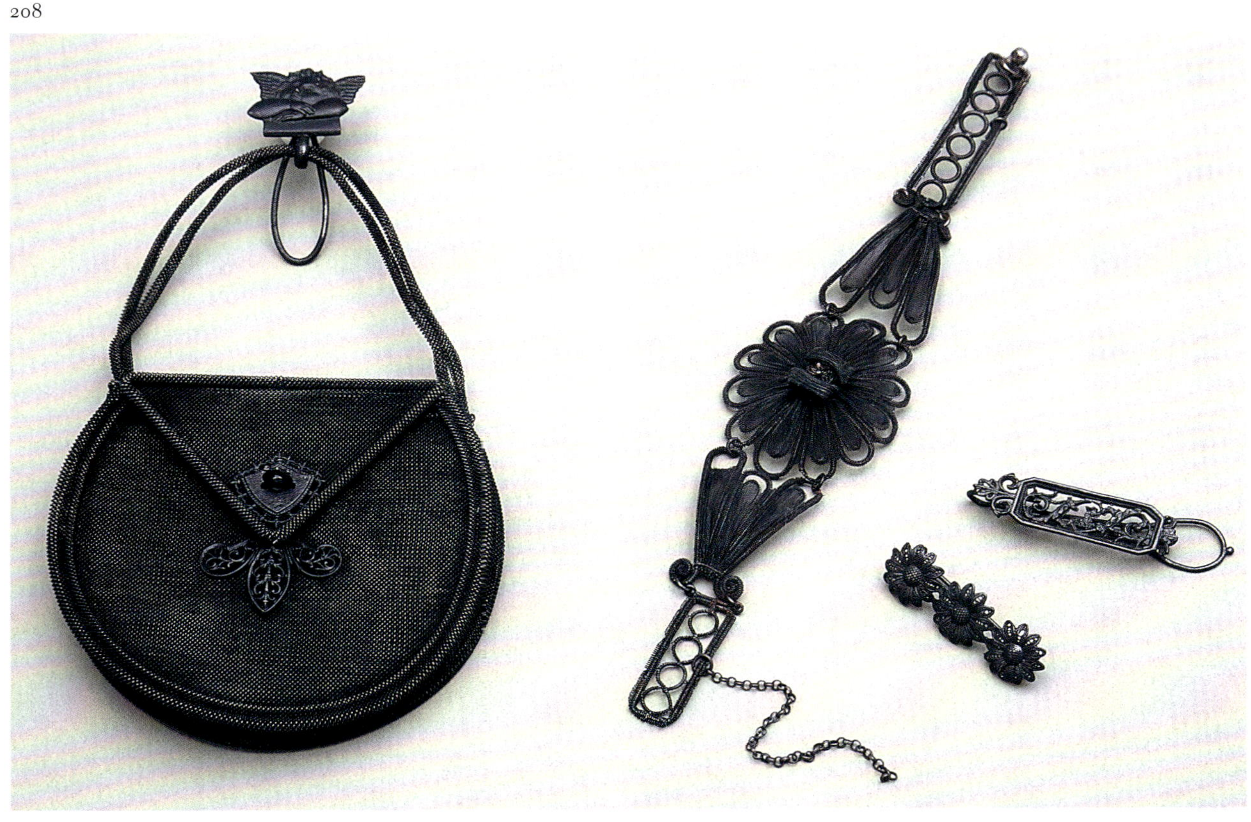

208

207
Jewelry Set (Parure)
Berlin, 1830/40
Cat. x-3

208
*Purse with Belt
Hook, Bracelet, Pin,
and Brooch*
Berlin, ca. 1830
Cat. x-5

209
*Necklace with
Butterflies*
Berlin, ca. 1840
Cat. x-4

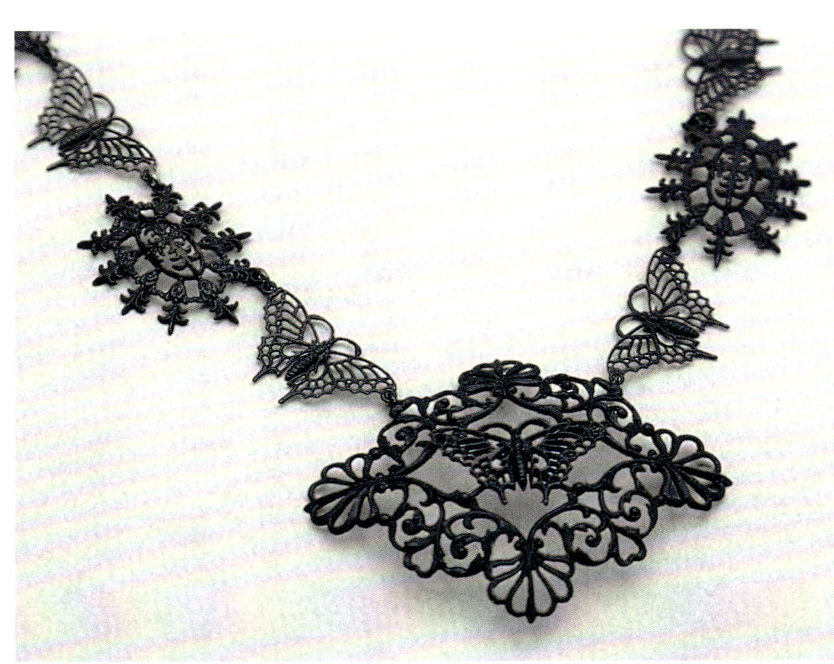

209

210

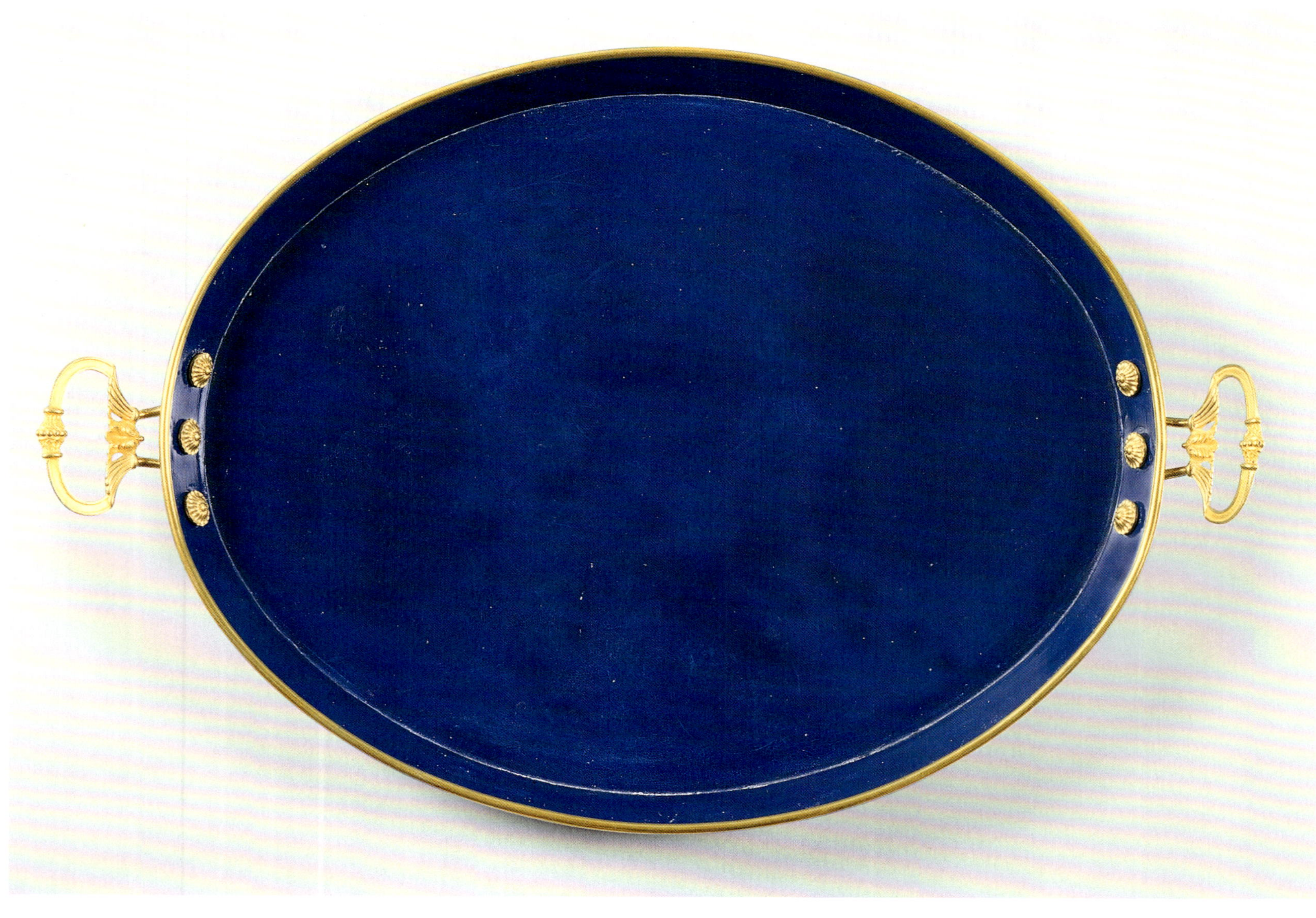

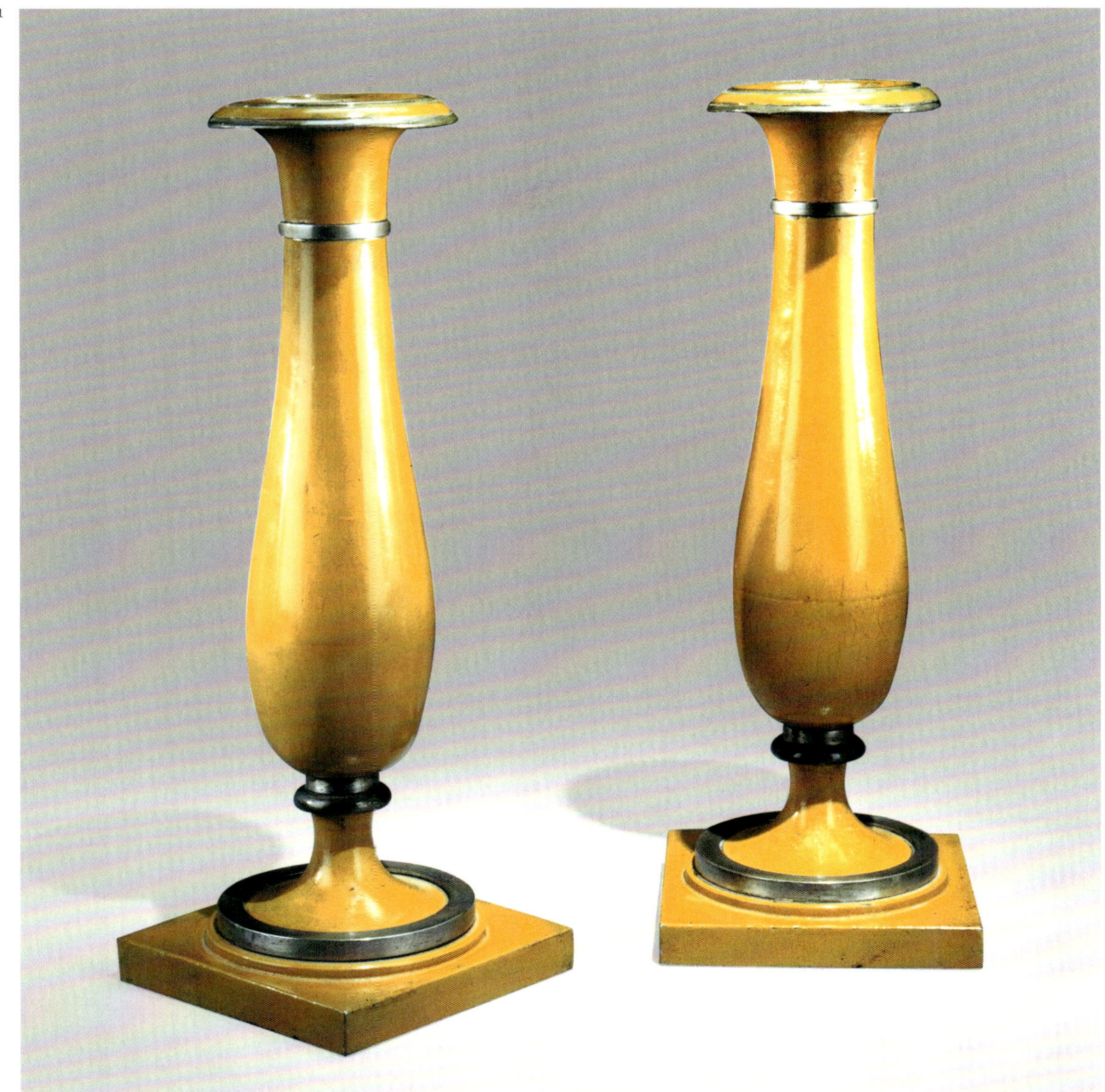

210
Oval Tray
Braunschweig, ca. 1825
Cat. x-10

211
Pair of Candlesticks
Braunschweig, ca. 1820
Cat. x-11

212
Tea Caddy
Braunschweig/Berlin,
ca. 1800
Cat. x-9

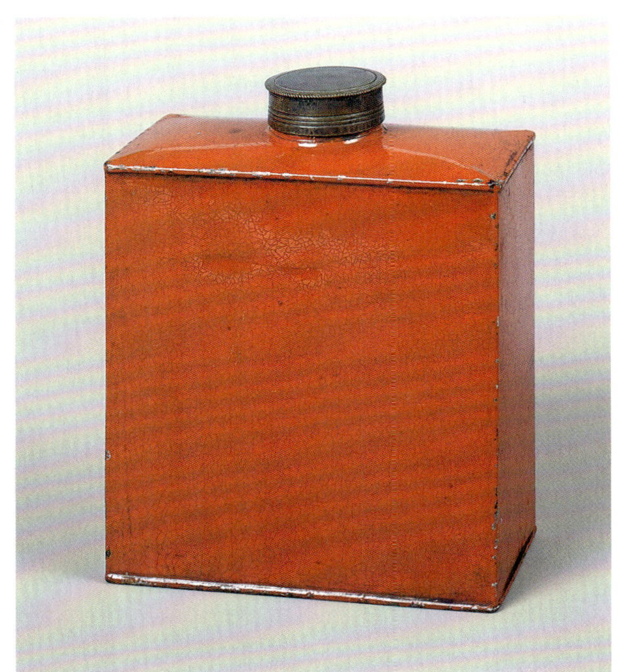

CLOTHING

SECTION XI
Regina Karner

Women's clothing of the Biedermeier period began as girlish and playful, became substantially more feminine, and by the end of the era, much more erotic. In contrast to earlier courtly styles, this clothing appealed to both the aristocracy and the bourgeoisie. Its development is often divided into Early Biedermeier (1814/15–24), High Biedermeier (1825–35/36), and Late Biedermeier (1836–48). Throughout the entire period, couturiers used a variety of cottons and silks and offered style options. Strong colors and patterns, such as Scottish plaids, floral stripes, and large checks with a bouquet of flowers in the middle enjoyed great popularity.

Early Biedermeier dress silhouettes capitalized on the simplicity of the Empire period: straightforward, high-waisted, with a deep décolleté and long narrow sleeves slightly puffed at the shoulder. The gently flaring skirt had a tie or ribbon-pull closure at the back. Lace that was bleached or steamed, embroidery, openwork, and relief decoration often embellished the necklines, ends of sleeves, and the hem of the skirt. For daytime, women wore at the neck filmy frills of batiste or "vapeur," and fichus (white batiste cloths folded into a triangle and placed in the décolleté). The dominant fashion color was white, along with sweet pastels such as lemon yellow, pink, or bright blue. During the High Biedermeier period, waists moved lower, reaching their anatomically correct place around 1836. The fashionable hourglass silhouette was characterized by leg-of-mutton sleeves, wasp waists, and ankle-length skirts; a corset was essential. Flounced skirts and relief ornamentation on the bodice, as well as on the skirt between knee and hem, were very popular. The volumetric sleeves formed over an armature of horsehair or fishbone reached their apex in 1836, then immediately receded to allow for slim-fitting, lightly puffed, or flounce-ornamented alternatives.

During the late 1830s and 1840s, Rococo fashion was an influence, emphasizing grace, sweetness, and elegance. Women wore a narrow, tight-fitting bodice that ended in a lip, making the waist seem thinner; and a wide, round skirt, revealing only the tips of the shoes. Horsehair petticoats maintained the shape. Daytime dresses had a deep décolleté, covered with a fichu, or were high-necked. Sleeves were usually long, narrow to the elbow, puffed on the forearm, and banded at the wrist. Evening dresses displayed a deep, seductive décolleté, embellished with a wide lace trimming ("berthé") or fitted into a collar held on the shoulders with clasps. During the 1840s, attention shifted from the upper body to the skirt, often decorated with alternating stripes further emphasized by bows, rosettes, or stitching; another option was an overskirt open at the front to reveal a contrasting skirt. Daytime wear blended pastel silks and cottons with checked or floral or striped patterns; for evening, fabrics were velvet, moiré silk, damask, brocade, and tulle.

For outerwear, women could choose the "spencer" (a short fitted jacket); the "pelerine" or velvet cape; or the "redingote" (a long coat following the cut of the dress). The capelike "wickler" was all the rage around 1822. The luxurious cashmere shawl, monochrome with colored borders often bearing orientalized palm-leaf motifs, became a fashion "must"; these were also known as "Turkish shawls." As early as 1800, they provided an important color accent for the quiet dresses. Initially long and narrow, they became full-scale wraps. Eventually, wraps and fur capes dominated outerwear, along with mantillas and fitted coats. Winter versions were of heavy silk, velvet, or wool, often trimmed or lined with fur.

The typical women's headgear of the Biedermeier period was the fabric or straw bonnet with a high crown and wide brim richly garnished with bows, ribbons, and artificial flowers. At home, a lady wore a starched caplet of white batiste or tulle, decorated with white embroidery, pleats, and braiding or piping. Social occasions called for an artfully wound turban adorned with a brooch and heron feathers. In the Late Biedermeier period, toques, birettas, and small-brimmed bonnets sparingly ornamented with feathers, ribbons, lace, bows, or artificial flowers came into fashion.

Shoes were cross-banded in black, cream, or pastel satin, or made of soft kidskin, embellished with small bows and rosettes. Bootlets, initially flat and later with small heels, offered an alternative.

Other accessories provided essential fashion statements. During the Early Biedermeier period, gloves reached as high as halfway up the upper arm, yet in the later periods, just to the wrist, terminating in a band. This short form, interestingly called "half-long," was appropriate for daytime and evening. The gloves were of doeskin, patent leather, deerskin, or chamois, in white, beige, or natural hues. In winter, women additionally carried muffs of ermine, marten, or fox. Fans were obligatory, not only for function and ornamentation, but also for coquetterie. They were made of gauze embellished with gold- and silver-foil, of embroidered silk, or of painted or printed paper ornamented with gold and silver, held together by fragile rods of ivory or wood. Biedermeier handbags began with little spangled, embroidered, or glass-pearl-trimmed reticules, which hung from the wrist on thin cords. In addition, there were cylinder-shaped bags with narrow leather handles, and small square bags of silver mesh. These were followed by handbags shaped like small baskets. The parasol was another fashion element, offering protection from the sun and a serving as a device for daytime flirting corresponding to the fan in the evening. These were usually silk, with a wood or fishbone pole and a carved ivory or turned-wood handle.

MEN'S FASHIONS

Men's fashions during the Early Biedermeier period underwent a dramatic change: "pantalons," or long pants, became acceptable to wear in public during the day. The daytime suit consisted of a darker frock-coat worn over long light-colored pants that were secured over the bootlets by means of stays; a vest in a contrasting color; a white shirt (with a high collar until around 1820); and an artfully arranged necktie. Until the late 1840s, evening dress still demanded knee breeches.

The slender silhouette of the Early Biedermeider period expanded during the High Biedermeier years. The sleeves of the coat and frock coat were gathered in folds on the shoulders and increased in bulk, making the waistline appear narrower; the frock coat received broad coat-tails. In Late Biedermeier men's clothing, sleeves became somewhat narrower. Checked pants combined with a frock coat of another color; brilliant vests and checked vests with checked long pants were both very popular. Brown, blue, and green dominated the frock coat for daytime wear; the evening tail coat was blue and, at the end of the 1840s, black. Outerwear options included coats cut like the frock coat, often embellished with braid, or capelike cloaks. Coat, frock coat, and pants were most often wool. Daytime footwear was bootlets fastened at the sides; formal evenings called for "escarpins," or flat black slippers. At home, under the influence of orientalist styles, the gentleman donned a bathrobe of cashmere or a shawl with palmette motifs or of velvet; comfortable light wool pants; a shirt with a large collar, around which he loosely wound a scarf; a fezlike head-covering; and slippers.

The most important piece of gentleman's clothing during the Biedermeier era was the vest, which provided a colorful accent to the suit. Cream-colored and embroidered with a floral pattern, colored stripes, checks, or dots, it allowed for the personal expression of one's fashion sophistication. Owning fifty vests was in no way to be viewed as luxury. The vest of silk, velvet, piqué, or cashmere had to be of the latest cut and have the newest number and style of buttons. Neckwear likewise expressed its wearer's individual taste. Daytime ties were colorful and patterned, those for evening gleamed in black or white. Modes of fastening, twisting, and knotting them occasioned a flood of literature. Honoré de Balzac wrote: "The art of fastening his tie is for the man of the world what the art of giving a dinner is for the statesman."

The elegant gentleman wore a top hat of felt or straw. The shape of its brim and the height of its crown changed often, but it remained the desirable head-covering and was viewed as the hat of the patriotic, conservative citizen. During the 1830s, the "Calabresian" cap came into fashion. The beret worn by artists, liberals, and intellectuals ten years later was a visible declaration of a free-thinking orientation. Short gloves, a pocket watch with a chain, a lorgnette, and a walking stick were fashionable accessories during this era. This was the golden age of the walking stick, which was chosen to suit the occasion and mood. It was made of Spanish cane, bamboo, various woods, painted, and tipped with metal; handles displayed ball- and egg-shaped pommels and various animal heads of ivory, silver, bronze, horn, and tortoise shell.

Following the Biedermeier period, at the time of the 1848 Revolution, male fashion continued to move toward monochromatic and simpler, more functional clothing. The trend confirmed Beau Brummel's statement: "The elegance of a man's suit does not consist in being noticed, but rather expresses itself only via excellent cut and perfect fit."

213

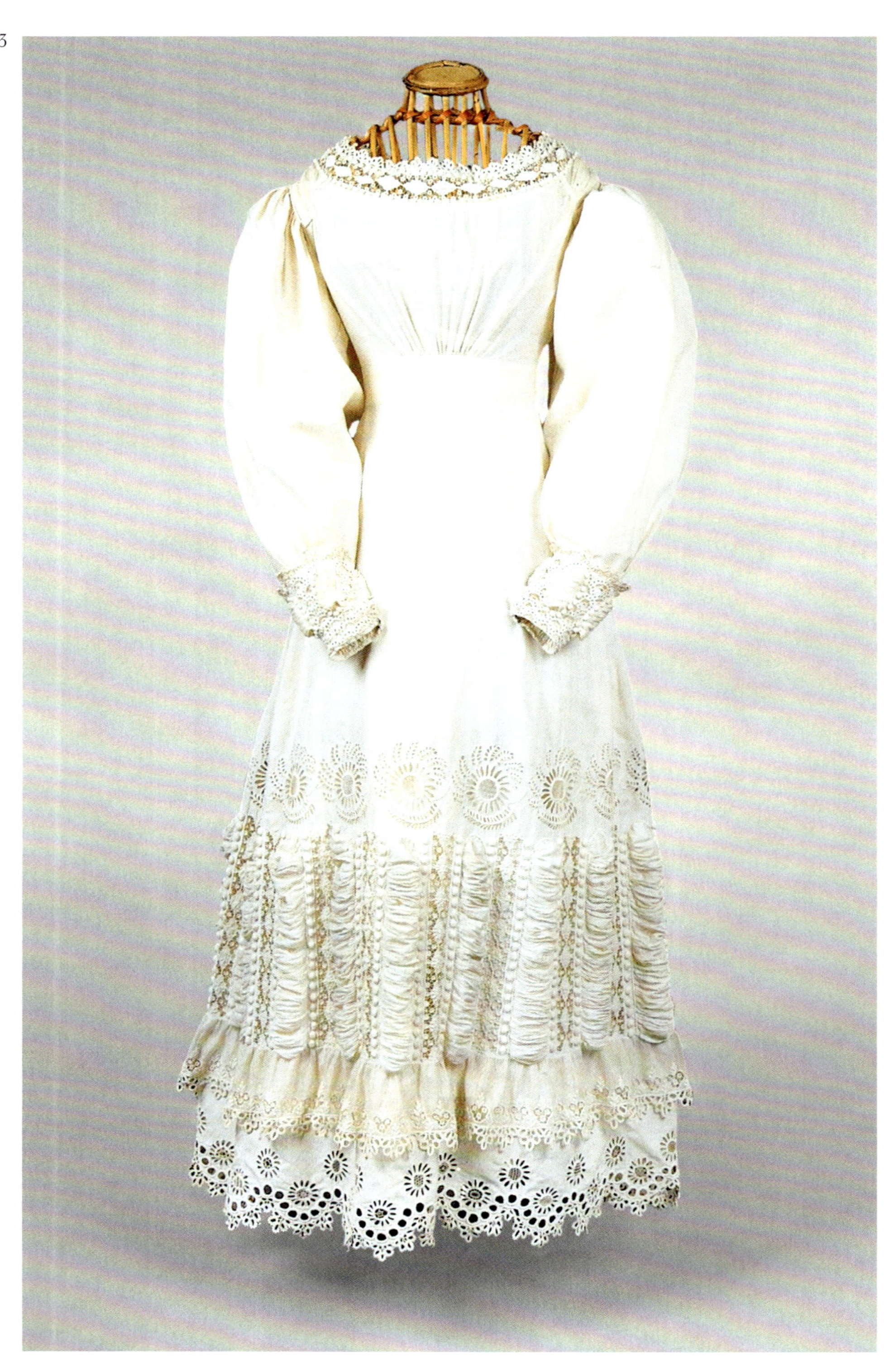

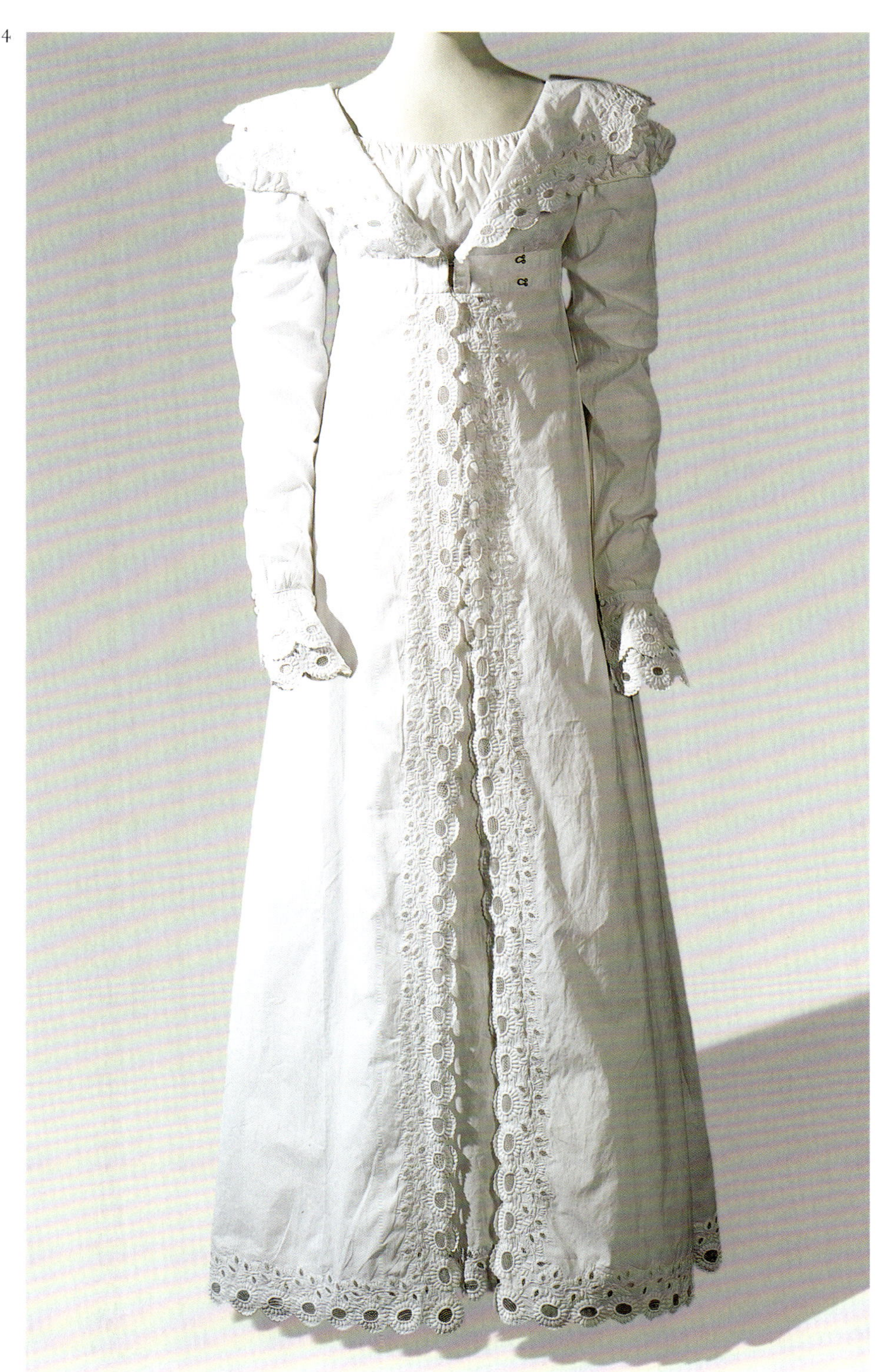

213
Summer Dress
Bohemia, ca. 1830
Cat. XI-1

214
Dress and Coat Set
Germany, ca. 1810
Cat. XI-2

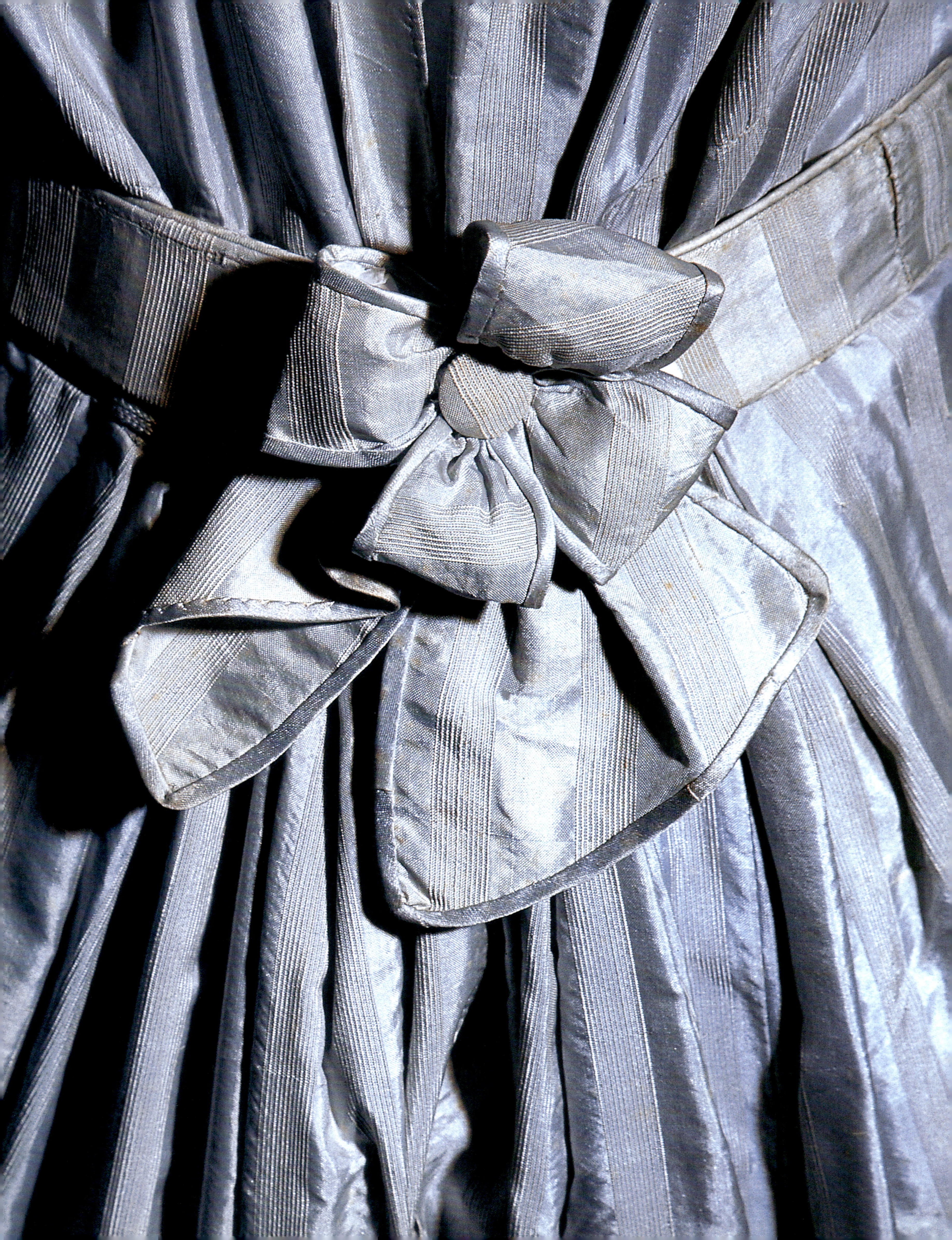

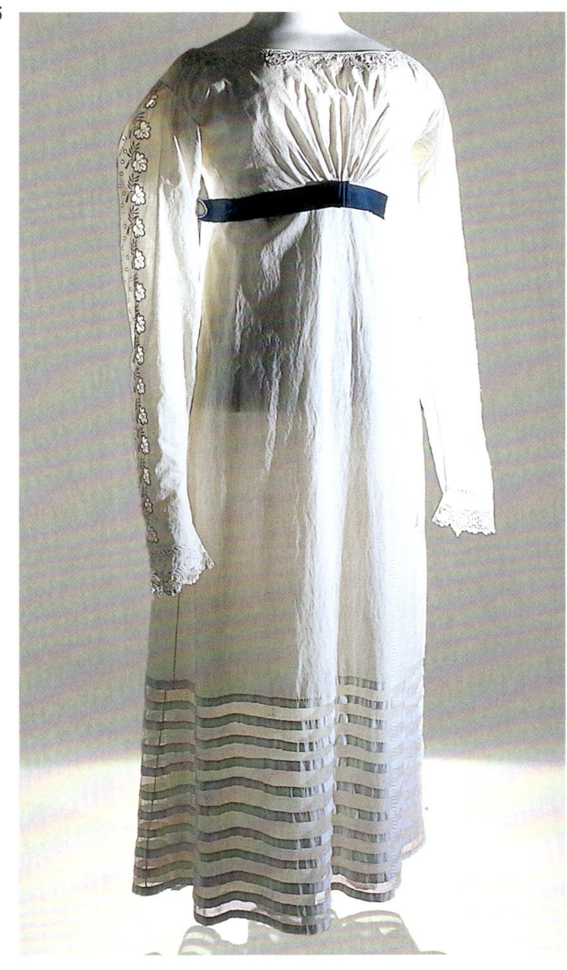

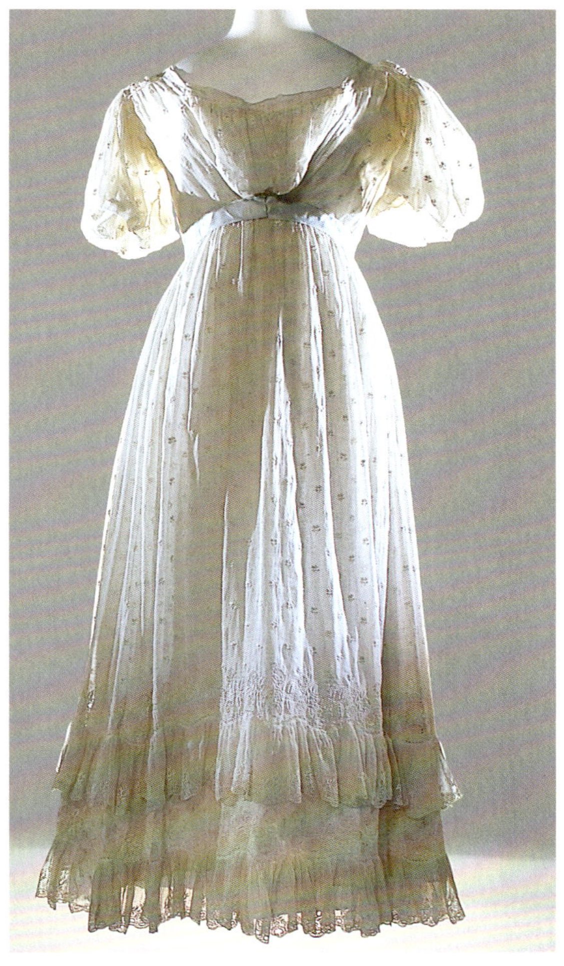

215
(Opposite)
Party Dress
Austria, ca. 1824
Cat. XI-7 (detail)

216
Daytime Dress
Austria, ca. 1815/16
Cat. XI-3

217
Woman's Dress
Vienna, ca. 1825
Cat. XI-4

218

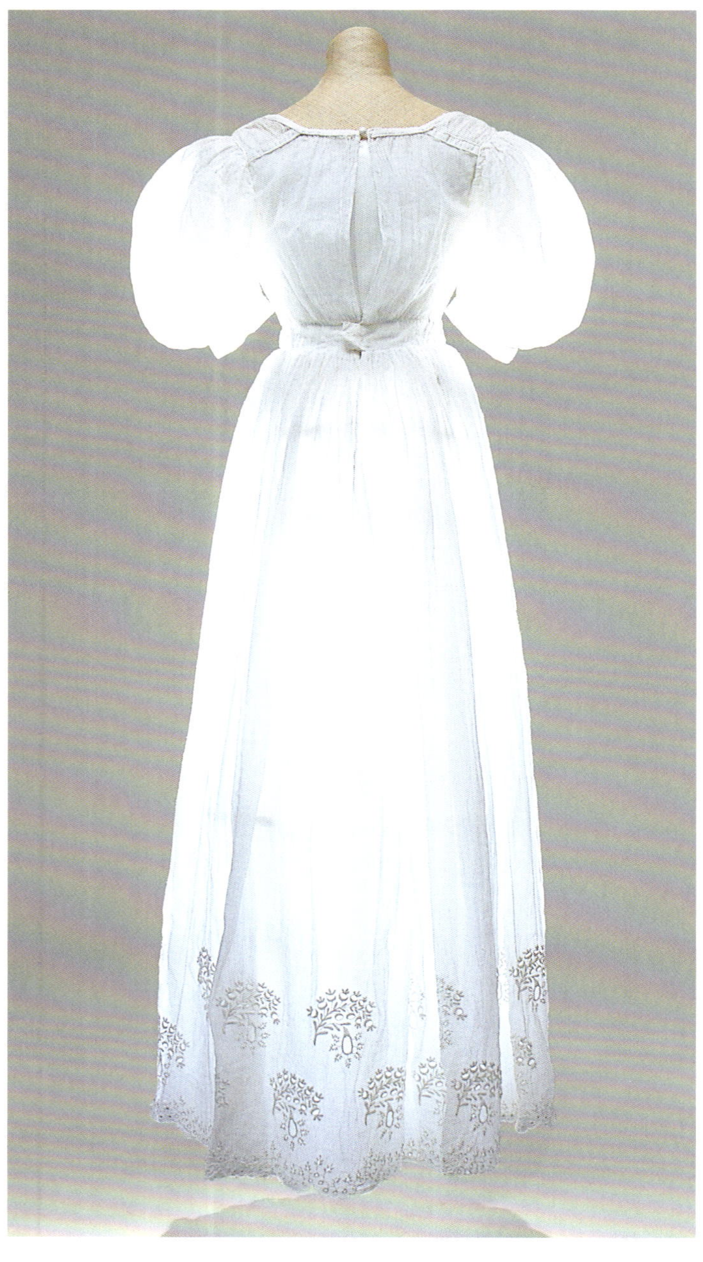

219

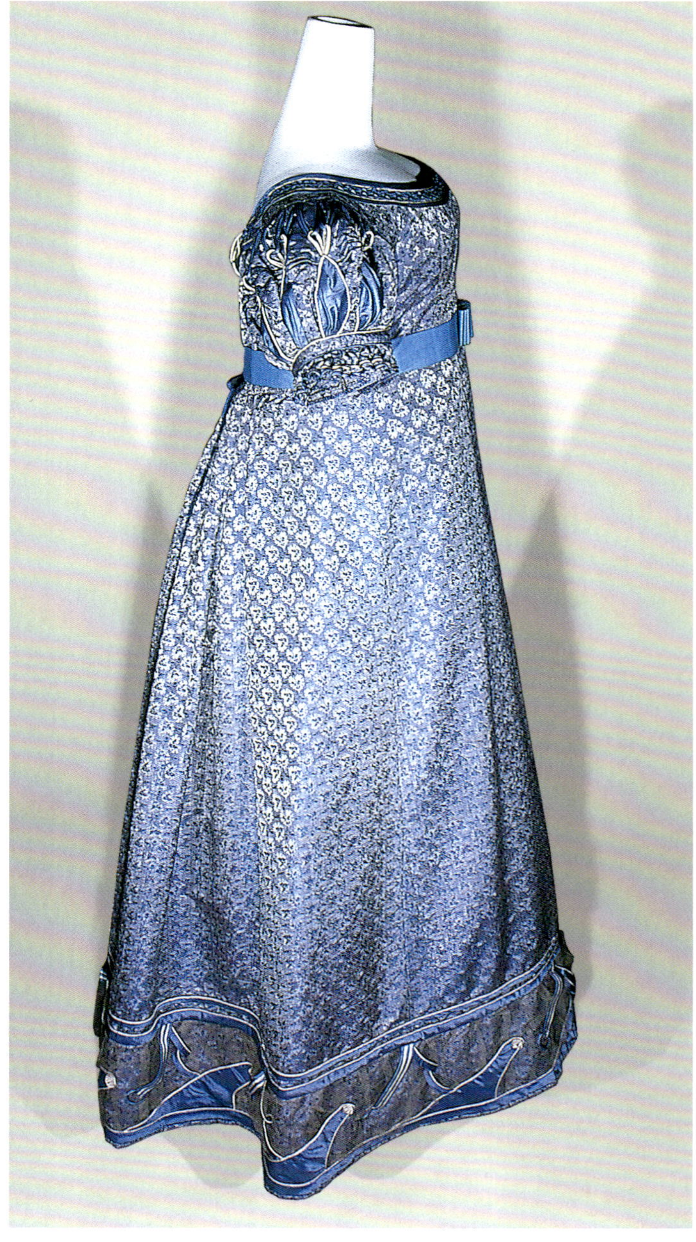

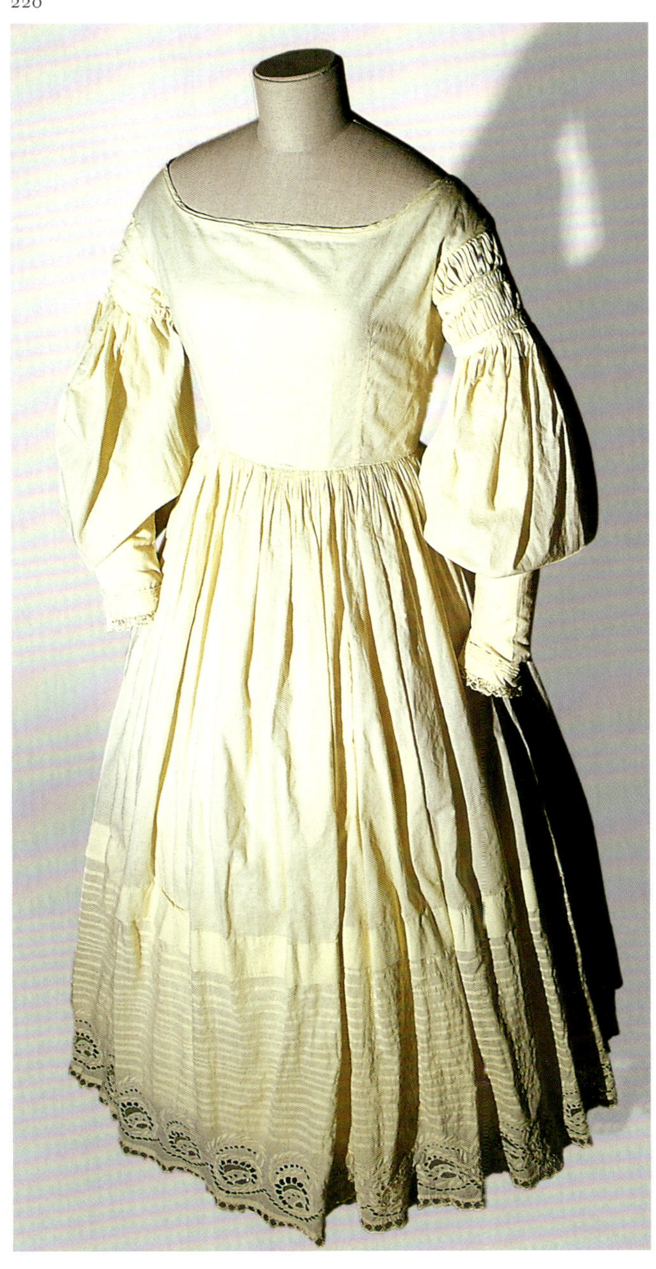

220

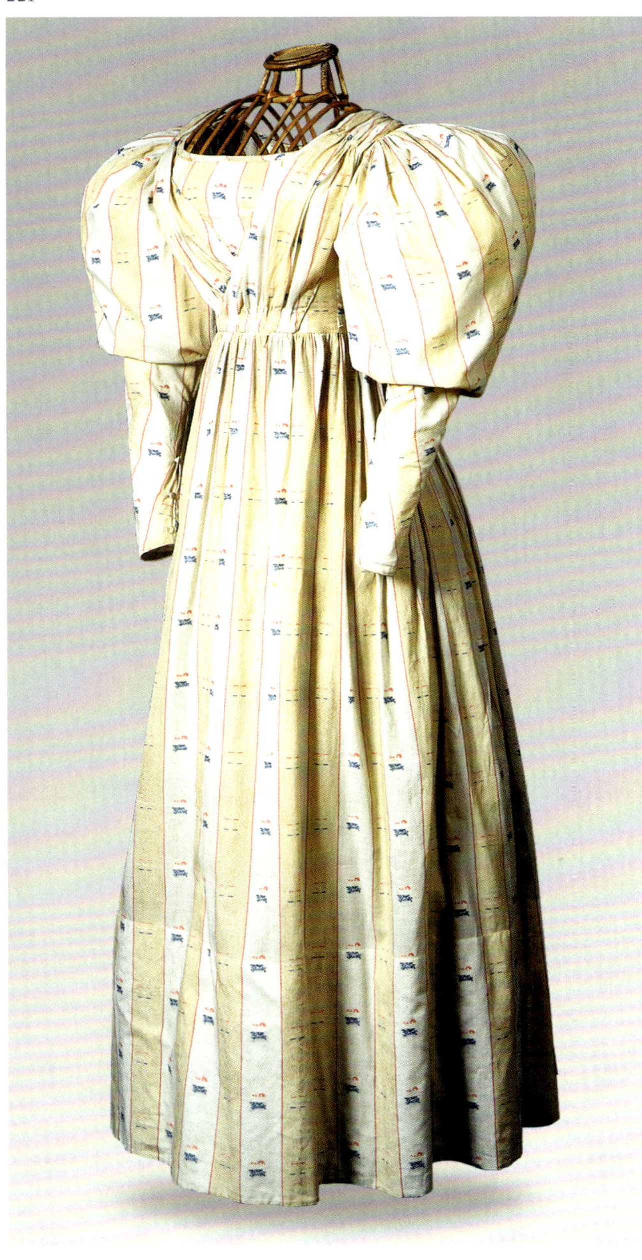

221

218
*Young Girl's
Summer Dress*
Germany, ca. 1825
Cat. XI-5

219
Party Dress
Austria, ca. 1820
Cat. XI-6

220
Woman's Dress
Berlin, ca. 1837
Cat. XI-9

221
Woman's Dress
Bohemia, Písek,
ca. 1830
Cat. XI-8

222
Bonnet
Austria, ca. 1845
Cat. XI-11

223
Bonnet
Austria, ca. 1841/48
Cat. XI-10

224
(Opposite)
Bonnet
Austria, ca. 1841/48
Cat. XI-12

222 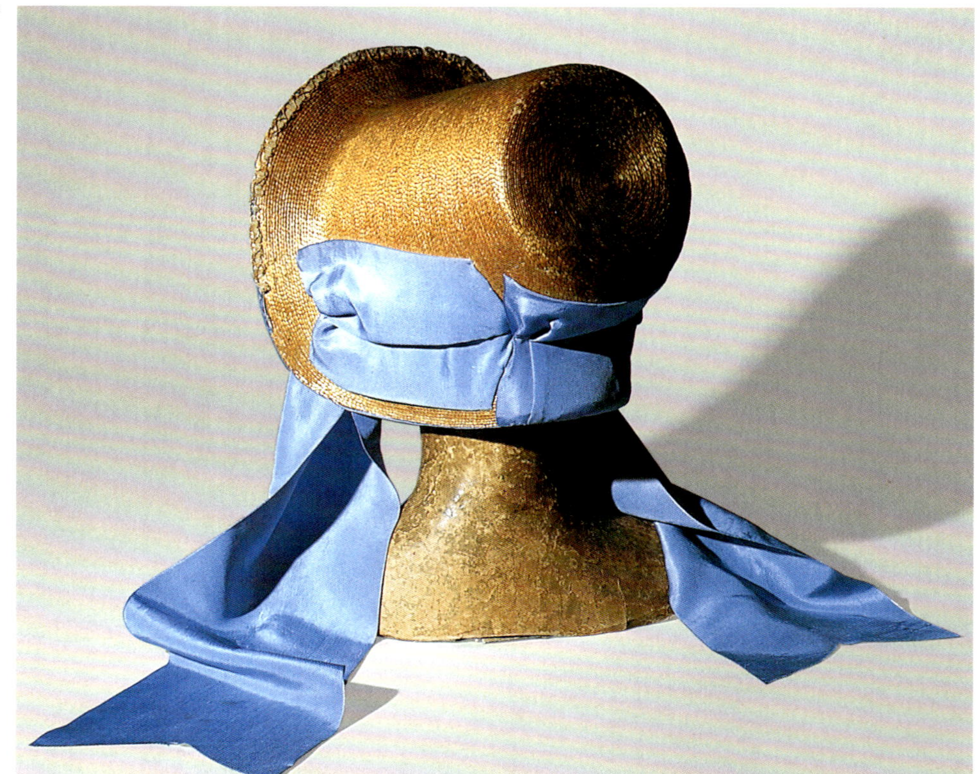

223 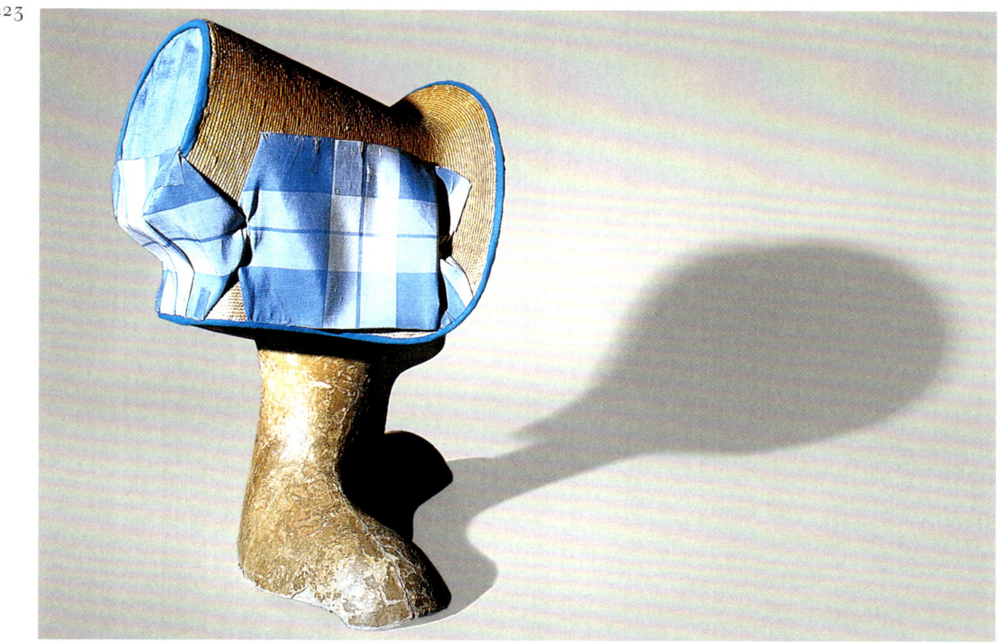

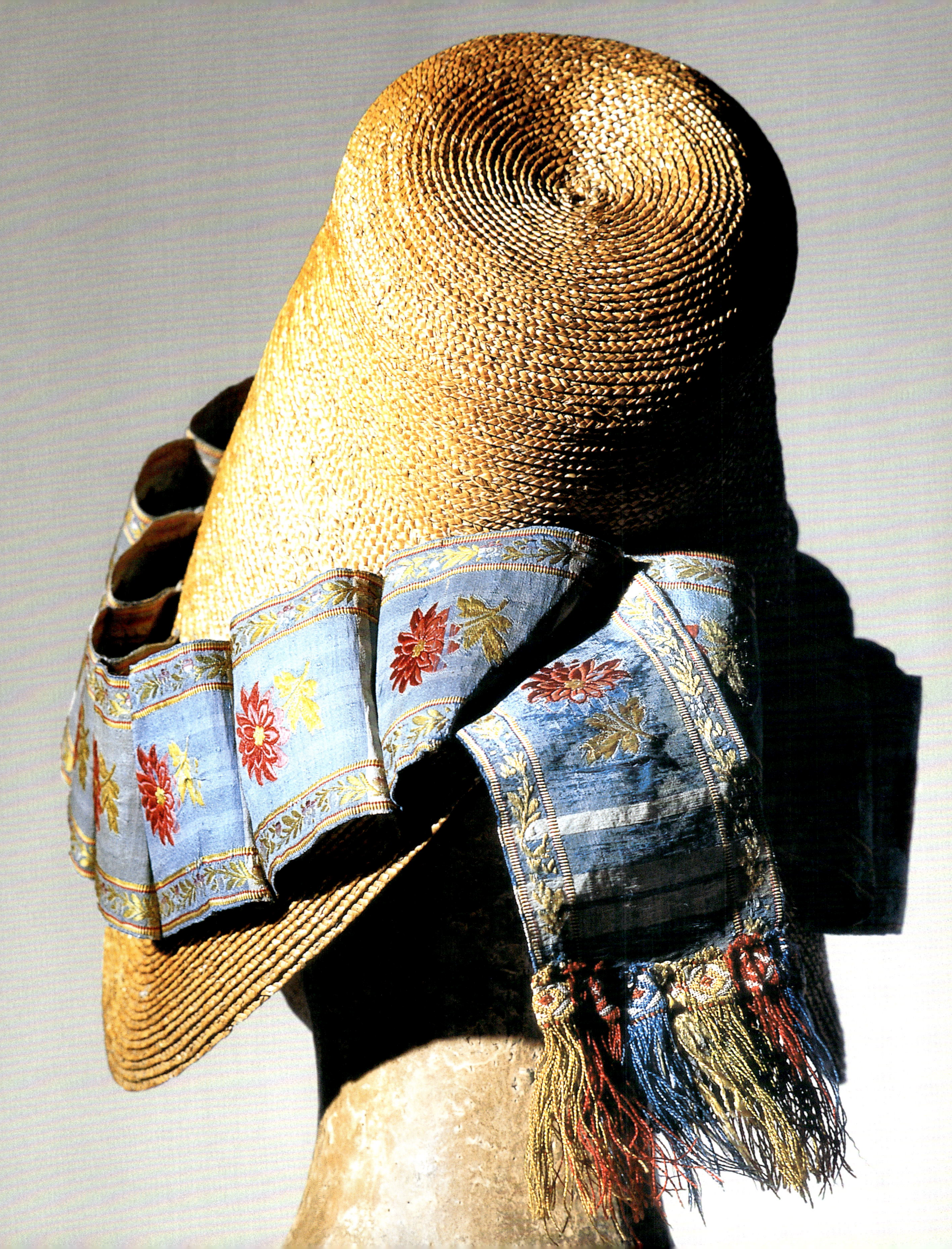

225

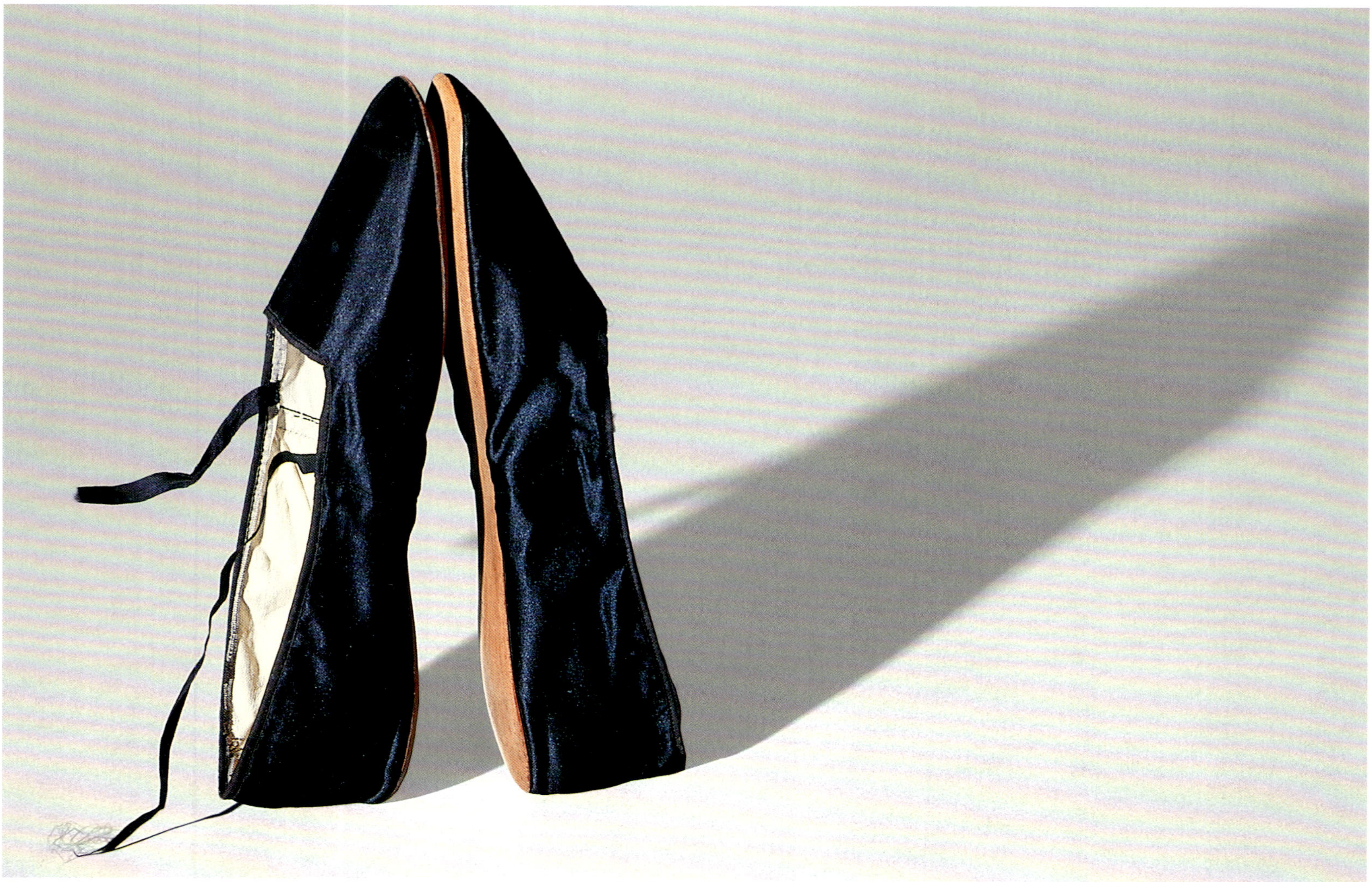

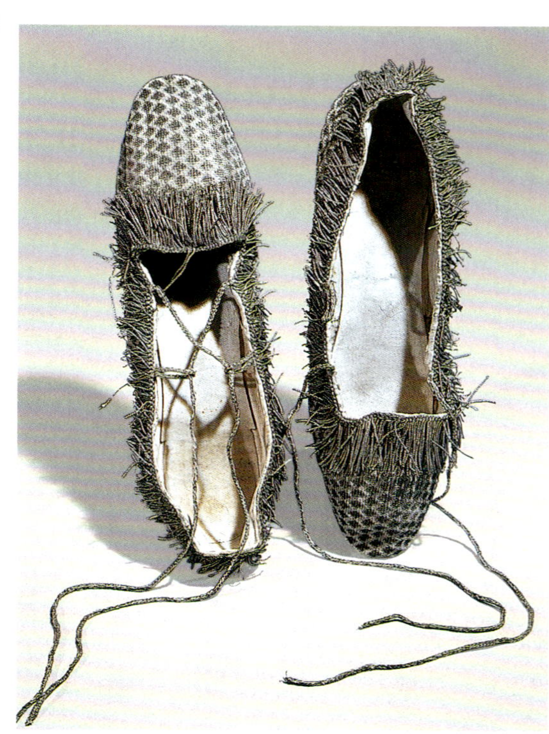

226

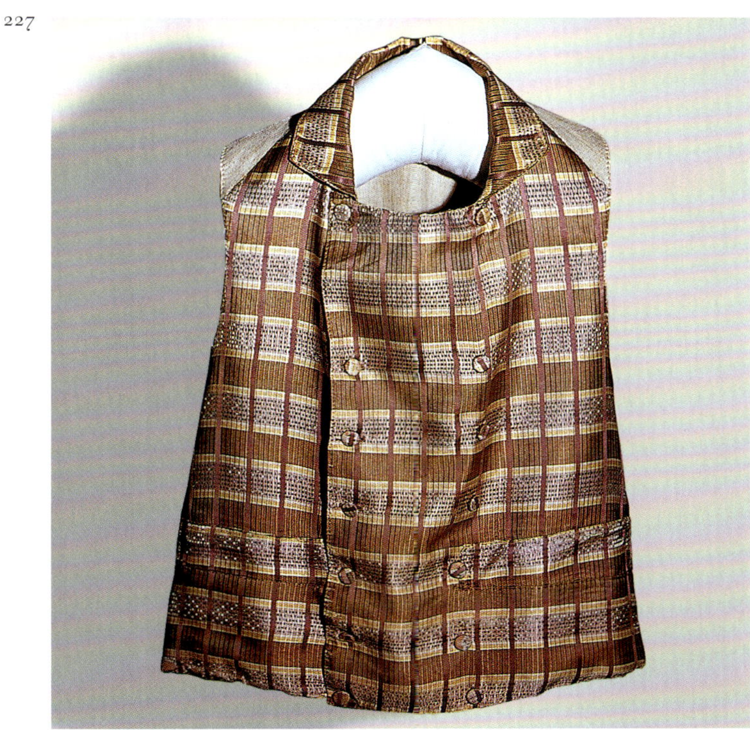

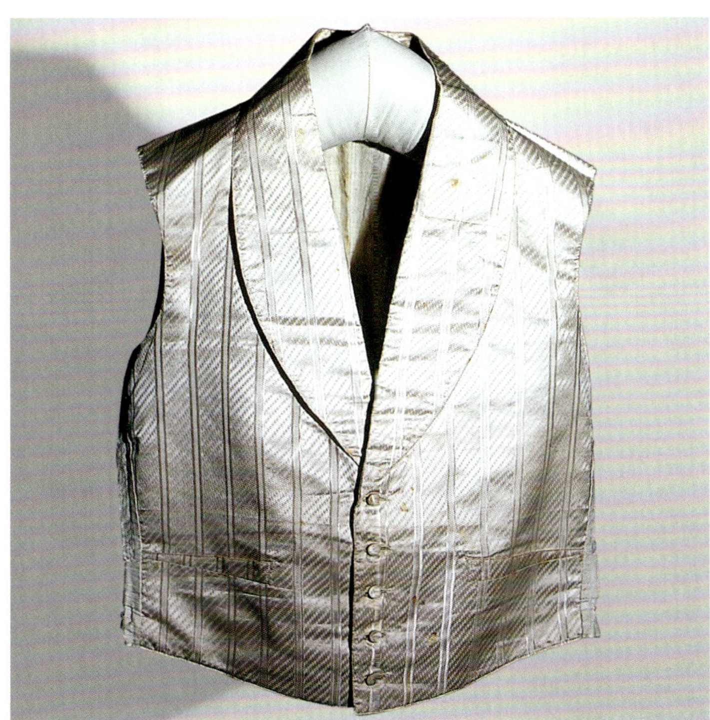

225
Shoes with
Ribbon Ties
Austria, ca. 1820
Cat. XI-14

226
Shoes
Berlin, ca. 1830
Cat. XI-16

227
Man's Vest
Austria, ca. 1830
Cat. XI-18

228
Man's Vest
Austria, ca. 1831
Cat. XI-19

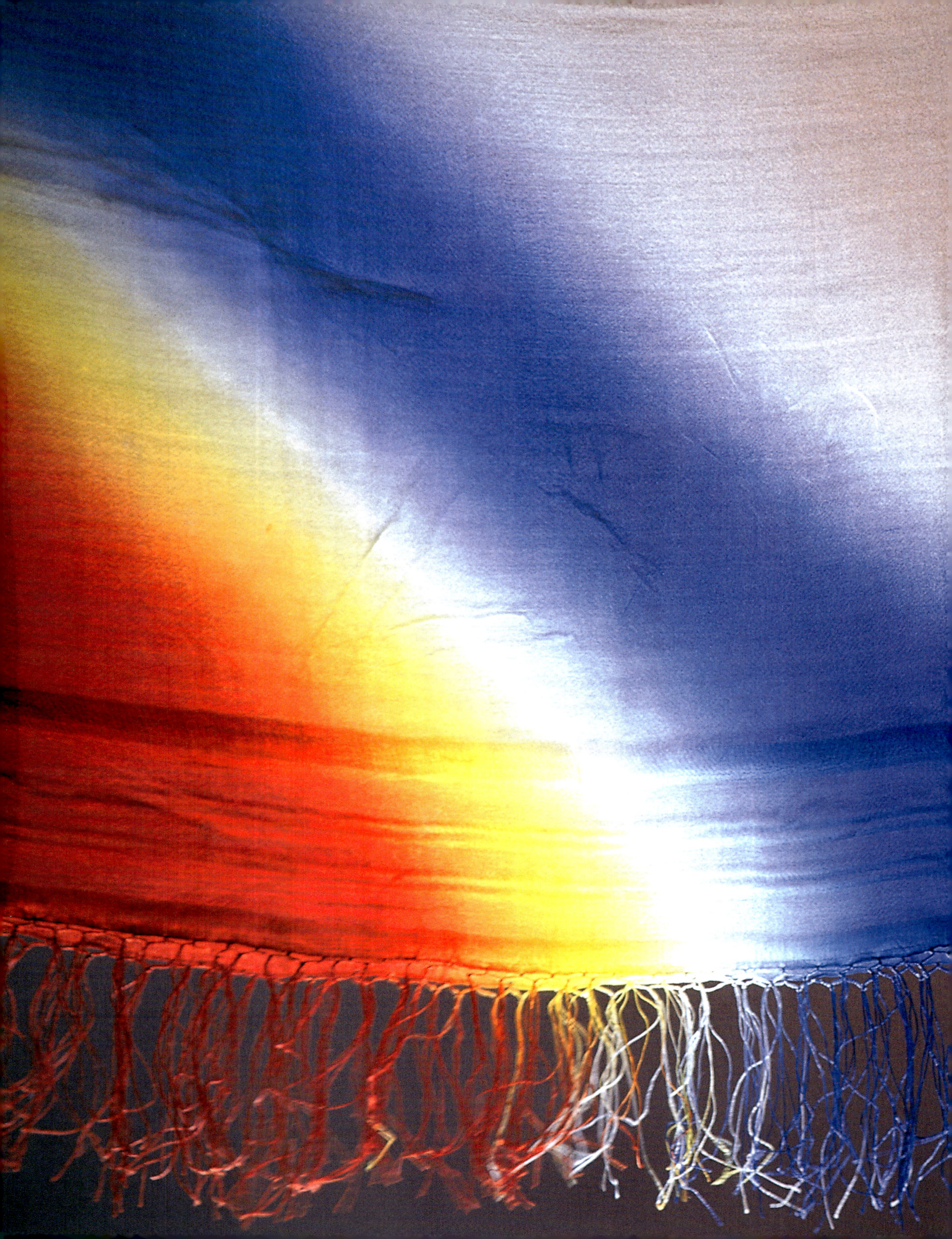

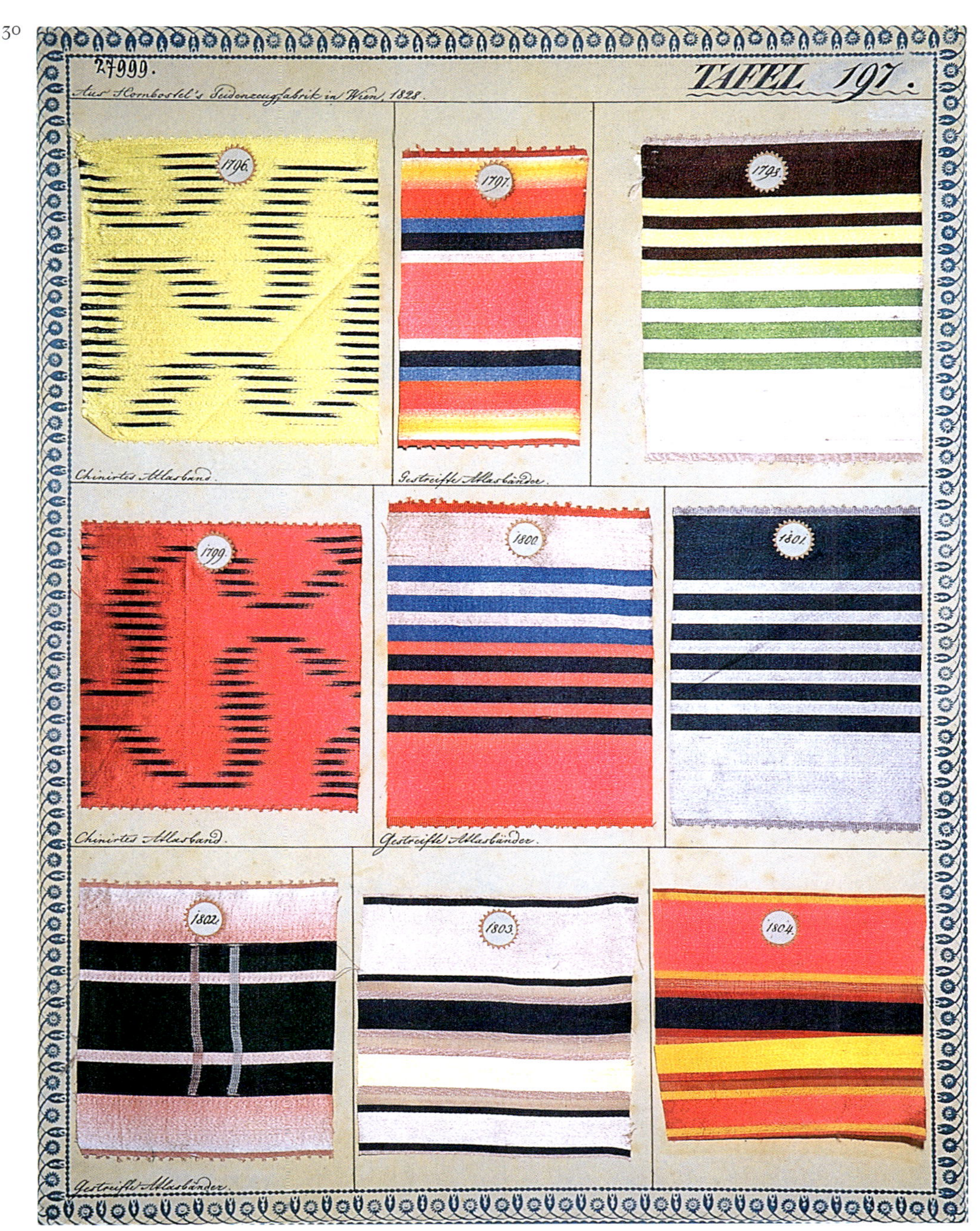

229
(Opposite)
Shawl
Vienna, 1827
Cat. XI-13 (detail)

230
*Nine Satin Ribbon
Pattern Samples*
Vienna, 1828
Cat. XI-21

NORTHERN EUROPEAN PAINTING AND DRAWING

SECTION XII

Laurie Winters

The Biedermeier period followed in the wake of German Romanticism and was profoundly influenced by this intellectual movement. Romanticism flourished with particular vitality in Northern Europe and German writers working between 1770 and 1800, such as Johann Wolfgang von Goethe and Johann Gottfried von Herder, extolled Jean-Jacques Rousseau's cult of nature – with dramatic effects for philosophy, literature, and the visual arts. The turn of the century saw Germany's romantic energy channeled into religious revivals, supported by philosophers who looked back to artists of the Middle Ages and the Renaissance for the clearest expression of God's design. The Protestant counterpart to Catholicism found its expression in mysticism. Friedrich Wilhelm Joseph von Schelling's *Naturphilosophie* united nature with mind in a co-dominion constituting God, a tenet that was to become one of the guiding principles of the Romantic Movement (Norman 1987, p. 17).

Schelling's philosophy profoundly influenced landscape painters such as Caspar David Friedrich and Carl Gustav Carus, who, in painting nature, felt they were painting the manifestations of God. Friedrich developed a landscape style filled with personal religious symbolism. He freed landscape from traditional categories – the "veduta" and the topographical view – seeking instead to convey the meditative experience of devotion to nature. Using motifs such as ships at sea, craggy oak trees, Gothic ruins, isolated figures, and majestic mountain peaks, he encoded spiritual content in a vocabulary of "divine symbols." His method encouraged painstaking attention to reality, and therein provided the seed of Biedermeier realism.

After Friedrich, Carus was the leading landscape painter of the German Romantic Movement. The two men formed a close friendship, traveling the countryside of Saxony together in search of suitable motifs. Carus, however, eschewed the symbolic and religious overtones in Friedrich's landscapes and in the 1820s increasingly embraced emerging realist tendencies. In *Neun Briefe über Landschaftsmalerei* (*Nine Letters about Landscape Painting*), Carus developed the concept of the "earth-life image" (Erdlebenbild), which defines nature not as a divinely laden place but as a living organism characterized by dynamic processes and subject to scientific examination. Goethe, whom

he had met in Weimar in 1821, also encouraged this inclination toward pictorial realism, characteristic of the transition from Romanticism to Biedermeier's more objective translation of the world. Carus's majestic mountains and private interiors with open windows became recurrent themes of the Biedermeier period.

A very different catalyst for Biedermeier painting was the work of the neoclassical landscape painter Joseph Anton Koch. Trained in the classical heroic landscape tradition of Nicolas Poussin and Claude Lorrain, Koch was also keenly interested in the natural sciences, especially geology, and he made frequent trips into the Swiss Alps and the Roman Campagna to draw from nature. Although his art represents the high point of German neoclassical landscape painting, not Romanticism, he became a pivotal figure in the Romantic Movement through his role as a teacher in Rome when the Nazarenes arrived. Nazarene founders Franz Pforr and Johann Friedrich Overbeck came under his tutelage and an entire generation of young artists in their Roman circle in the 1820s was instilled with the importance of sketching from nature to ensure "truth" in the paintings they later composed in the studio. Echoes of Koch's intellectual rigor can be found in the work of Friedrich and Ferdinand Olivier, Julius Schnorr von Carolsfeld, and generally in the precise drawing and fidelity to nature of the Biedermeier period.

DANISH ARTISTS

In a politically fragmented Northern Europe following the Congress of Vienna, no single art center took the lead. Munich, Dresden, and Berlin were important art centers in Germany and Copenhagen was prominent in Denmark; proximity made it a simple matter for German artists to study at the Copenhagen Academy, where no tuition was charged. In the early nineteenth century, many German artists, including Friedrich, studied there and continued to exhibit there after returning home.

One of the most influential Danish artists of the time was Christoffer Wilhelm Eckersberg. He trained at the academy and in Paris under Jacques-Louis David, before becoming a professor at the Copenhagen academy and establishing what was to become the Danish school of Biedermeier painting.

He developed a fresh, unostentatious realism that he applied equally to diverse subjects. His portraits and nudes demonstrate a close study of nature combined with a high finish that is characteristic of the French school. Eckersberg's fascination with navigation combined with his interest in mechanics and perspective naturally led him to Copenhagen's harbors and shipyards. His advice to students to draw from nature without any particular overarching compositional hierarchy is evident in his own landscapes and marine subjects. His ordinary, everyday subjects, rendered in a clear, light palette, epitomize Danish Biedermeier and inspired the generation of painters who followed, such as Christen Købke and Martinus Rørbye.

The Biedermeier era in Denmark, referred to as "The Golden Age," is also called "The Age of Købke" in honor of the man now considered the greatest Danish artist of his time. As a pupil of Eckersberg in Copenhagen, Købke absorbed Eckersberg's realism, but gradually adopted a freer, more naturalistic rendering of atmospheric effects. His calm, monumental landscapes capture Copenhagen and the more rural environment of his family home near Blegdammen and Lake Sortedam. Unusual viewpoints and perspectives established in the buildings of his later views suggest a similar approach to Berlin's architectural painters of the Biedermeier period.

GERMAN ARTISTS

One of the dominant artistic spirits in the German Confederation was the artist and architect Karl Friedrich Schinkel, who spearheaded a building campaign to transform Berlin following the Napoleonic Wars. The furious pace of Schinkel's building program heightened awareness of the city's architecture and influenced the next generation of artists. His transformation of Berlin is evident throughout Eduard Gaertner's famous panorama of the city painted from the roof of Schinkel's newly completed Friedrichwerder Church in Berlin. Gaertner was Berlin's most distinguished architectural artist. Although the Prussian King Friedrich Wilhelm III commissioned the work, Gaertner did not show Berlin as a royal residence but rather as a town of citizens whose activities he narrated with pride and even humor. He took more than two years to complete the multipanel panorama and consistent with the Biedermeier era's emphasis on family, he included himself, his wife, and their children on the rooftop in the finished picture.

A professor of perspective and optics at the Akademie der Künste in Berlin, Johann Erdmann Hummel ("Perspektivhummel") reflected in his art the period's characteristic interest in architecture and science in his pictures showing the manufacture and installation of the massive bowl in front of Schinkel's new museum. Reflections of the surrounding garden and onlookers are mirrored on the underside of the bowl. Hummel's bowl records not only the period's interest in science but the rapt attention of the bourgeois class as they venture into Berlin's newly created public spaces and gardens. In contrast to the characteristic Biedermeier culture of private life, here Hummel captured a rare moment of public participation and self-identification with the emerging grandeur of Berlin.

Outside the bustling city, Wilhelm von Kobell captured in his paintings the quiet resonance of the civilized countryside. He worked as court painter to Elector Karl Theodor of Bavaria and for Crown Prince Ludwig of Bavaria, moving from commissioned scenes commemorating victories during the Napoleonic Wars to small-scale rural and anecdotal views of seemingly accidental "encounters" in the countryside. These chance encounters are distant reflections of the Romantics' dramatic encounters with a majestic nature. In the Biedermeier period, nature was reduced to something knowable, familiar, even cozy.

Cultural life during this period was centered almost entirely in the home, and the women of the family were particularly important in determining its character. Cities like Berlin, Copenhagen, and Munich doubled in size during this period, and new neoclassically designed apartment buildings sprang up to accommodate expanding populations. Houses were built with pairs of windows, creating brightly lit interiors that often looked onto busy streets or well-kept gardens. Families delighted in their elegant, well-ordered lives and a restrained neoclassically inspired Biedermeier style of furniture, interior design, and costume emerged to complement their domestic bliss. In genre painting and portraiture, the subjects are almost always shown in real interiors, usually their own homes or gardens, and the furnishings are affectionately depicted, often reflecting and reinforcing their characters.

This concept of the interior is clearly represented in Georg Friedrich Kersting's small, private, almost intimate pictures that include portraits of his friends or family. Kersting relied on the concept of the "window picture" that had become popular in German Romantic painting and had been used by his Dresden colleague and friend Caspar David Friedrich. For Friedrich, the window functioned as a highly charged symbol conveying a sense of yearning for nature and the external world. His pictures posit an uneasy juxtaposition between internal and external. For Kersting, the open window reinforced the primacy and comfort of the interior world and the identification of the sitters with their surroundings.

231

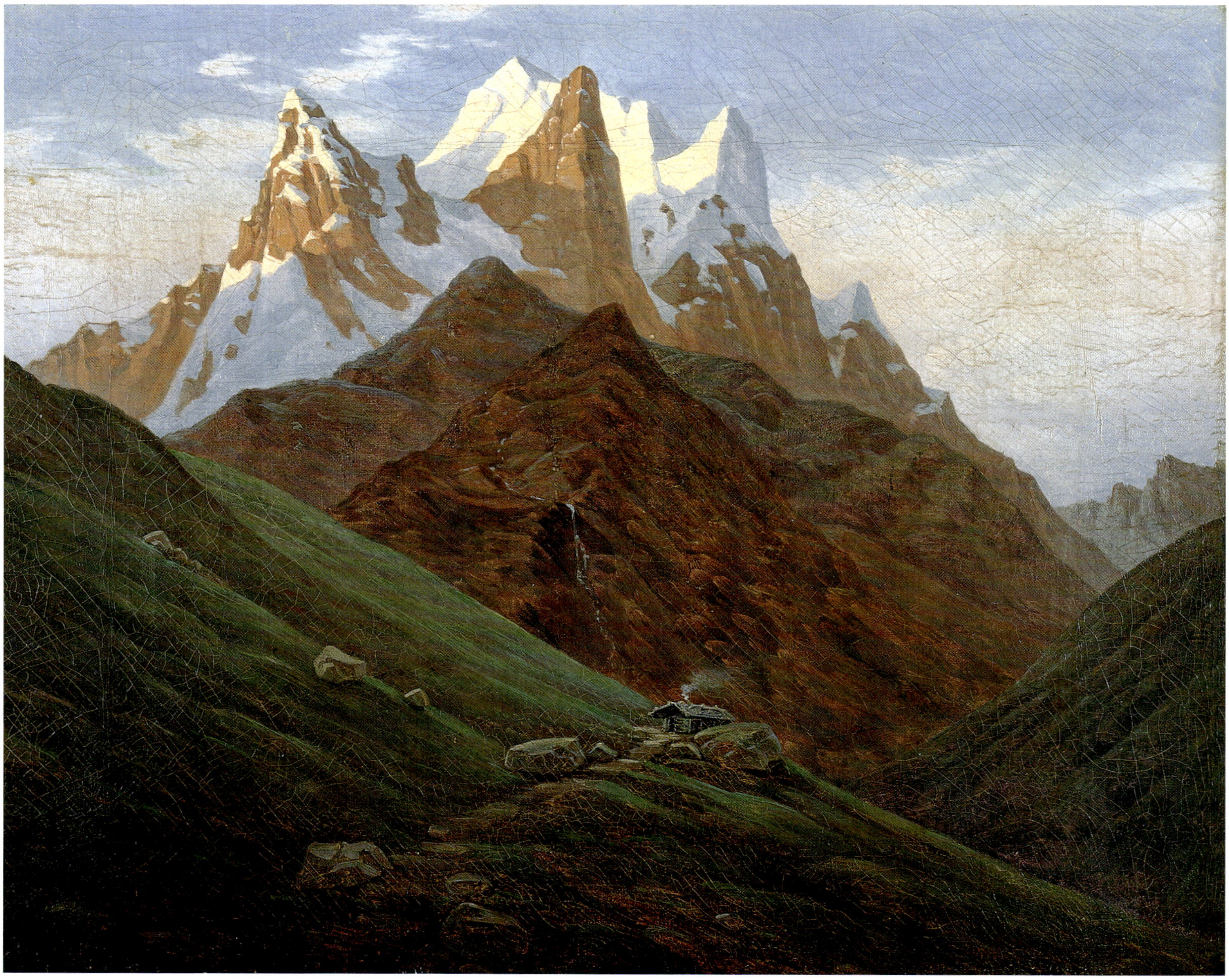

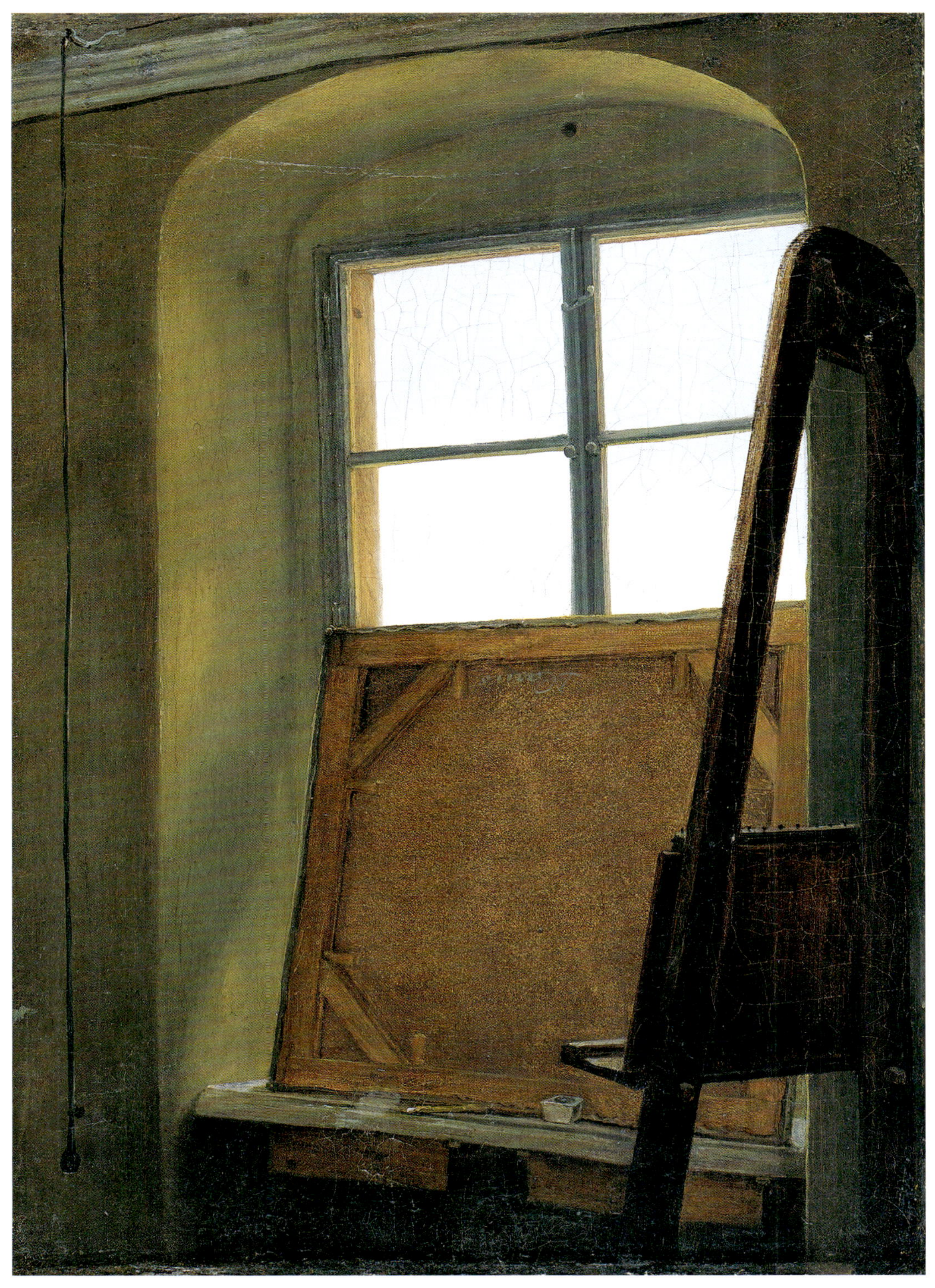

232

231
Carl Gustav Carus
Swiss Landscape
ca. 1822
Cat. XII-1

232
Carl Gustav Carus
The Artist's Studio
1823/24
Cat. XII-2

233 

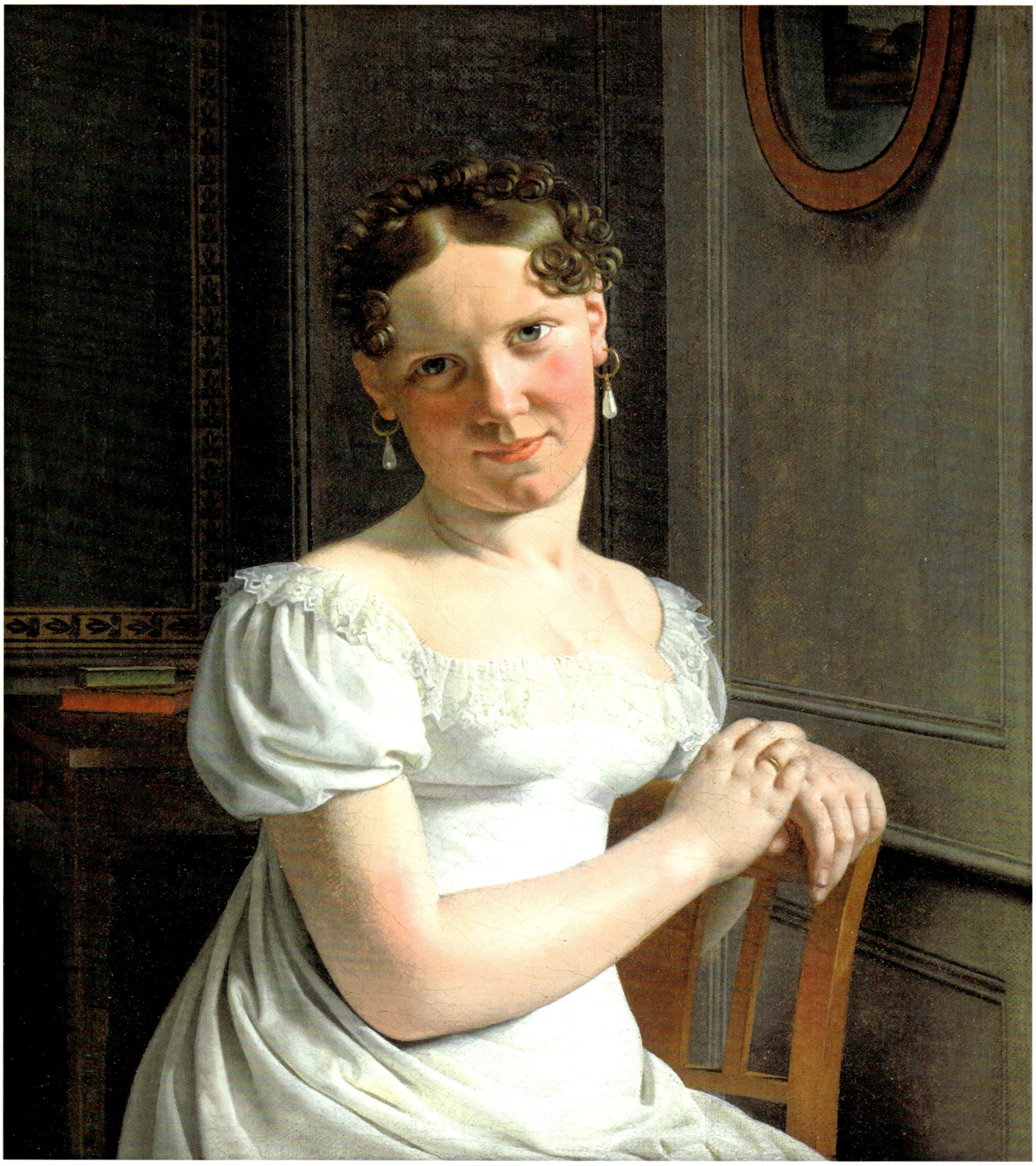

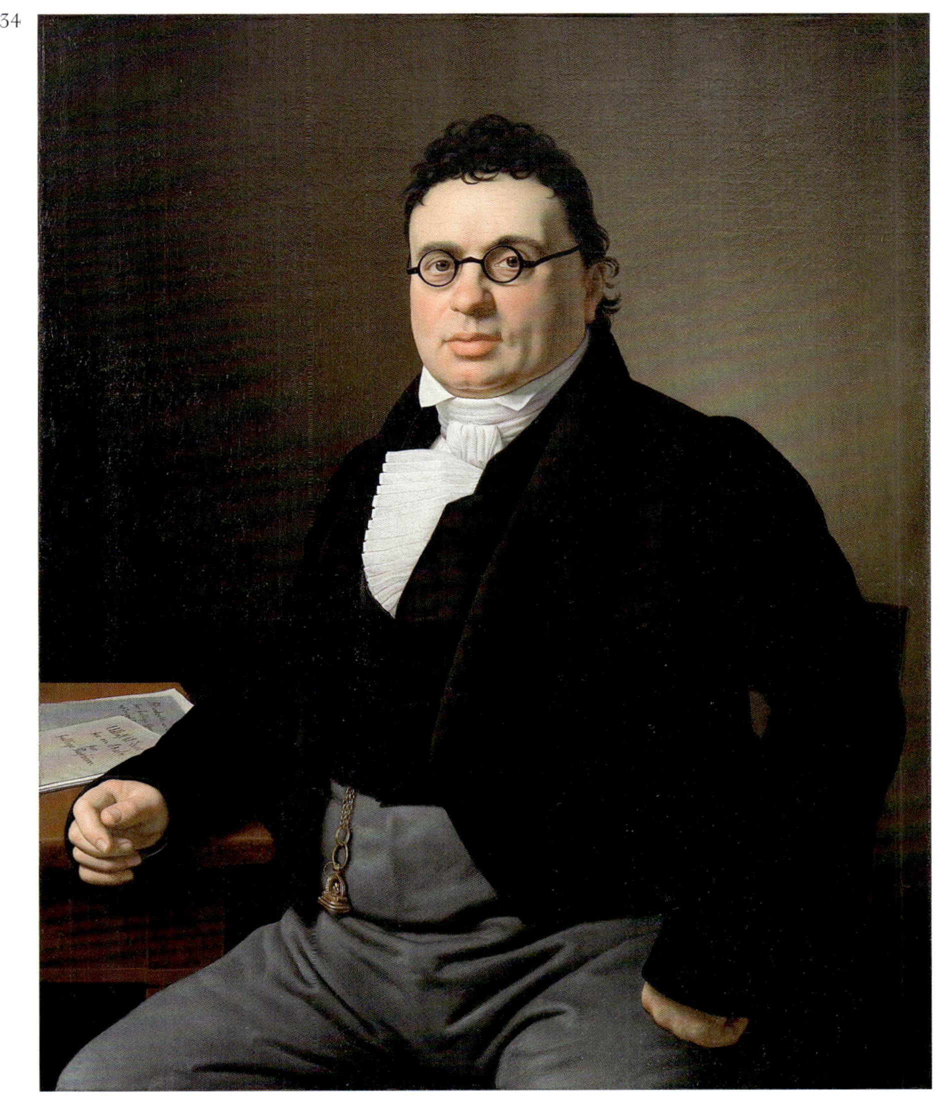

234

233
Christoffer Wilhelm
Eckersberg
*Julie Eckersberg,
née Juel, the Artist's
Second Wife*
1817
Cat. XII-3

234
Christoffer Wilhelm
Eckersberg
*Portrait of the
Merchant
Joseph Raphael*
1824
Cat. XII-5

235
Christoffer Wilhelm
Eckersberg
*Mendel Levin
Nathanson's Eldest
Daughters, Bella
and Hanna*
1820
Cat. XII-4

236
Christoffer Wilhelm
Eckersberg
*Nude Putting on
Her Slippers*
1843
Cat. XII-10

235

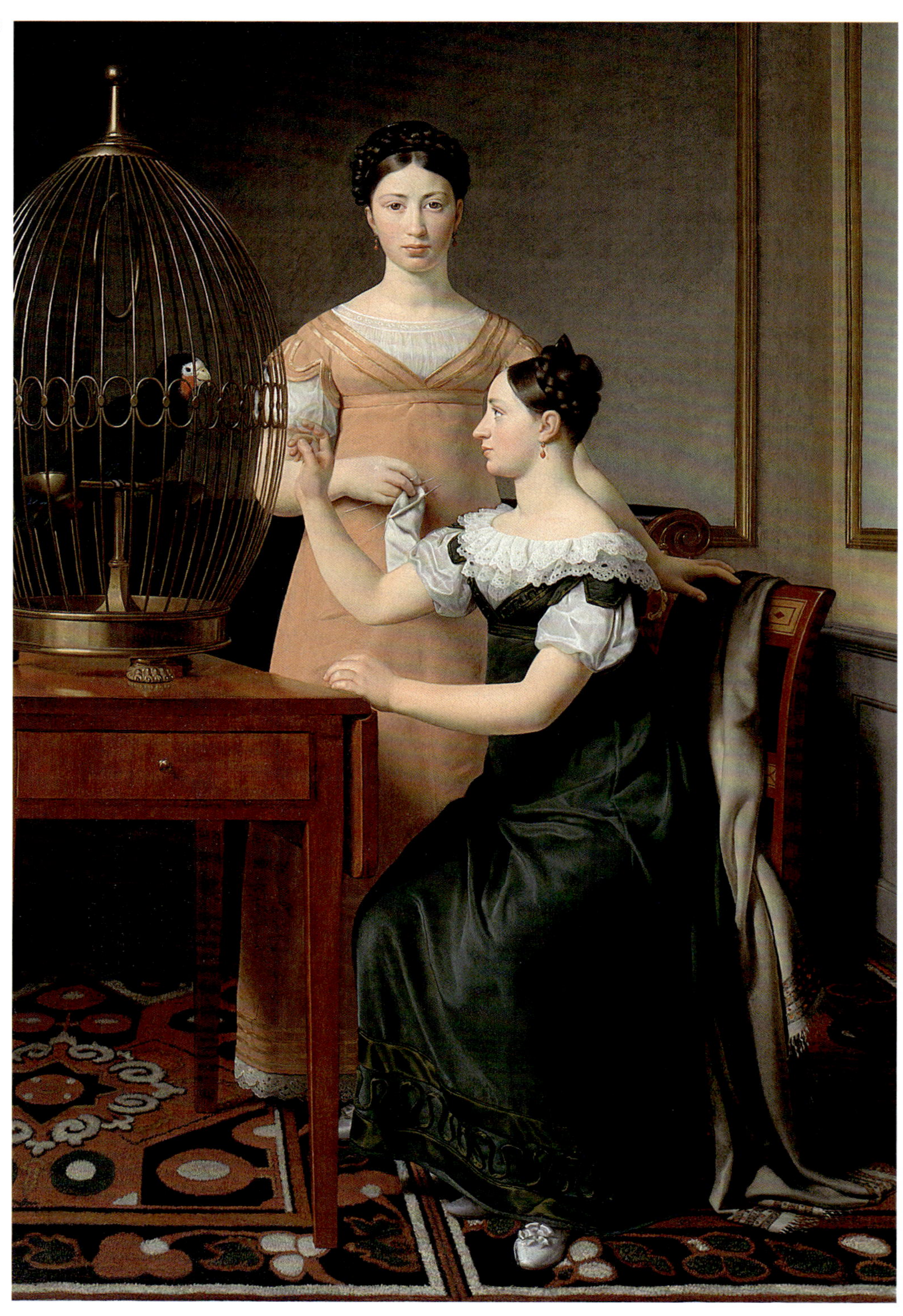

236

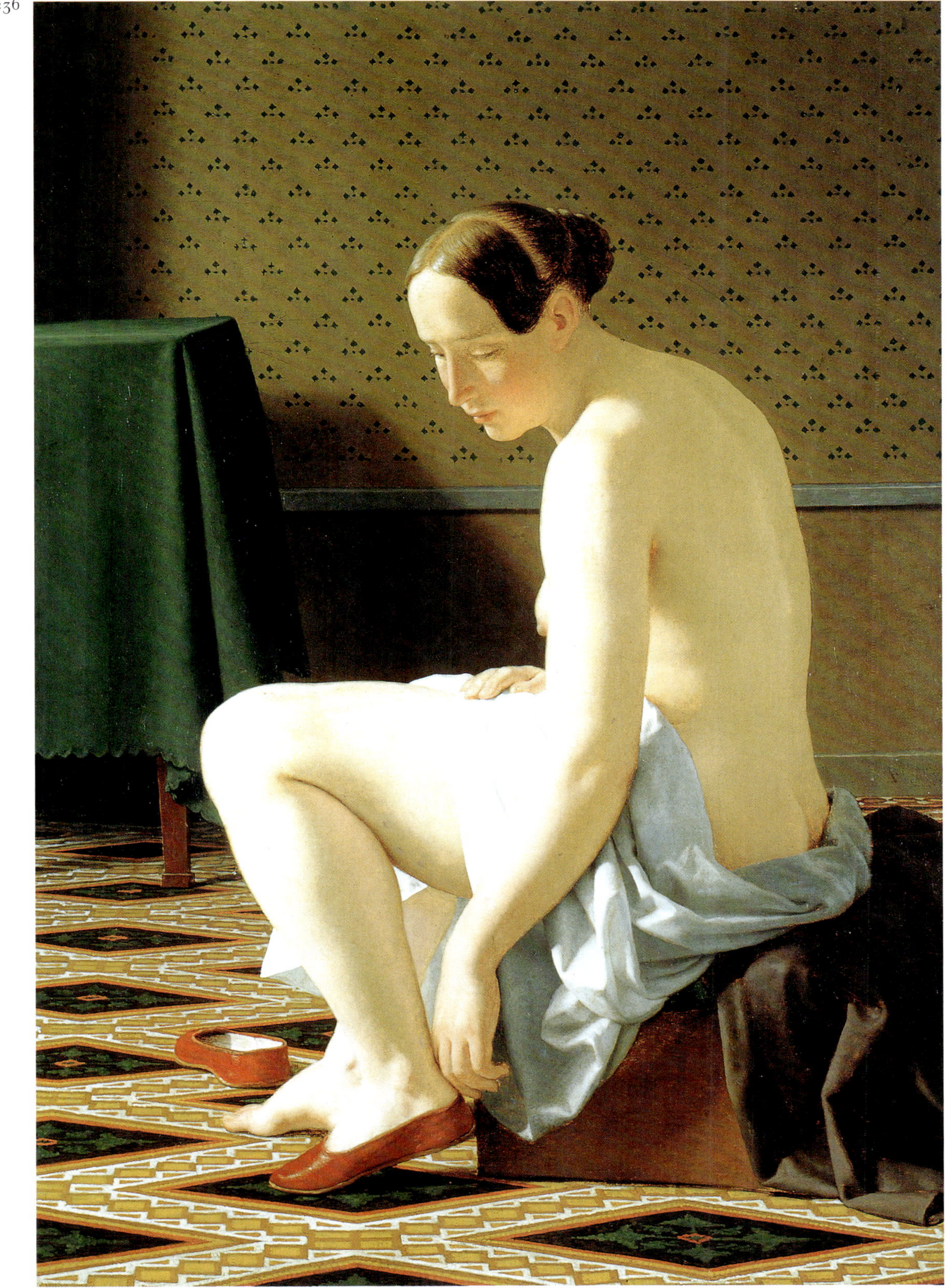

237

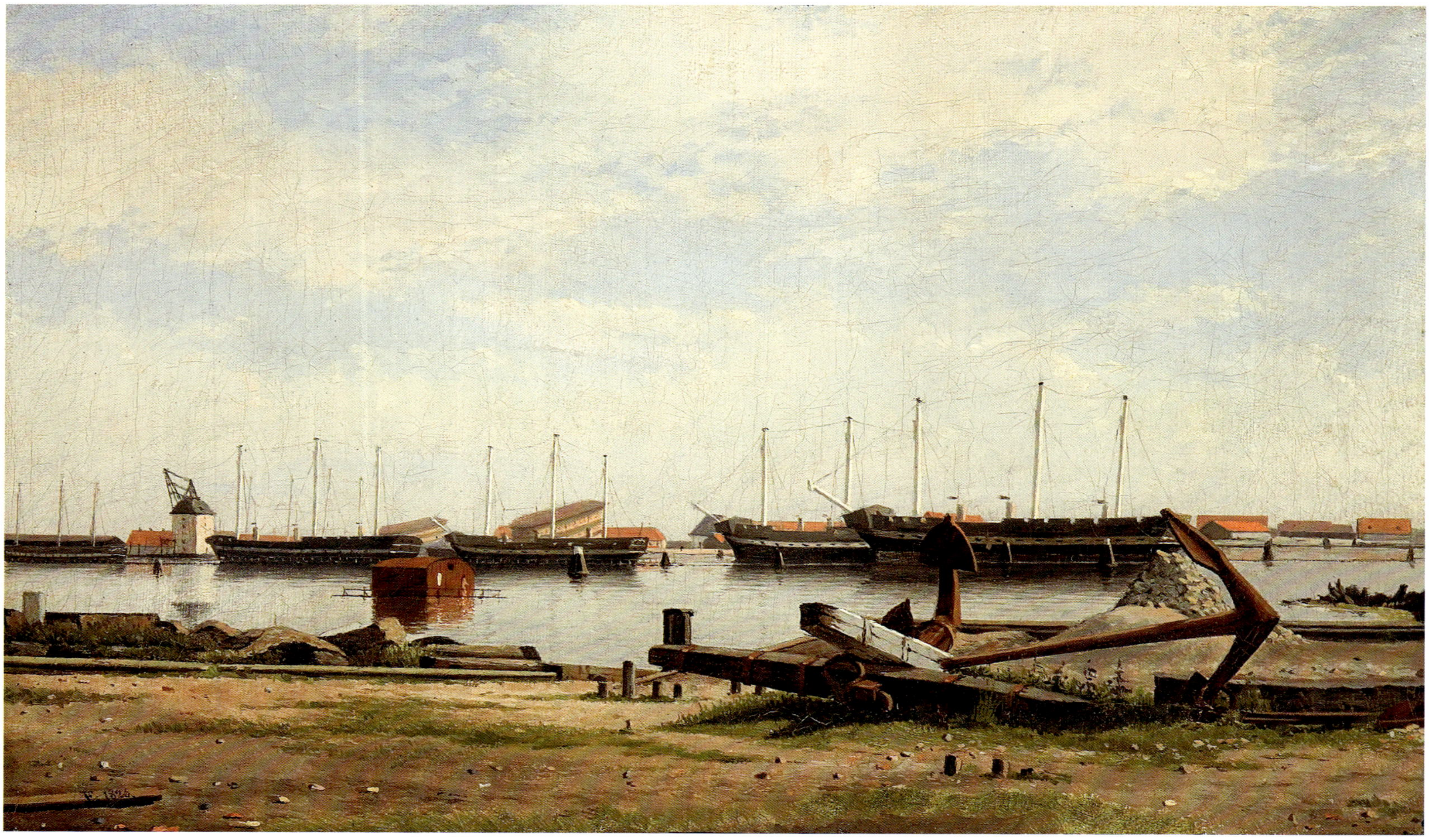

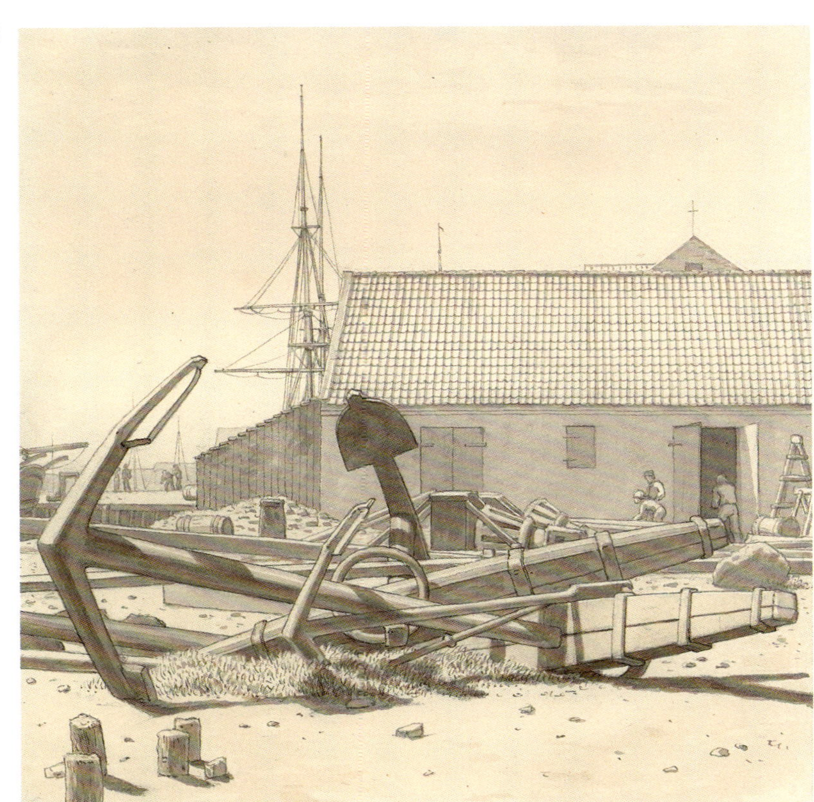

237
Christoffer Wilhelm
Eckersberg
*A View toward the
Wharf at Nyholm with
Crane and Warships*
1826
Cat. XII-6

238
Christoffer Wilhelm
Eckersberg
The Timbers of a Ship
1827
Cat. XII-7

239
Christoffer Wilhelm
Eckersberg
*Anchors at Larsen's
Wharf, Copenhagen*
1838
Cat. XII-8

240

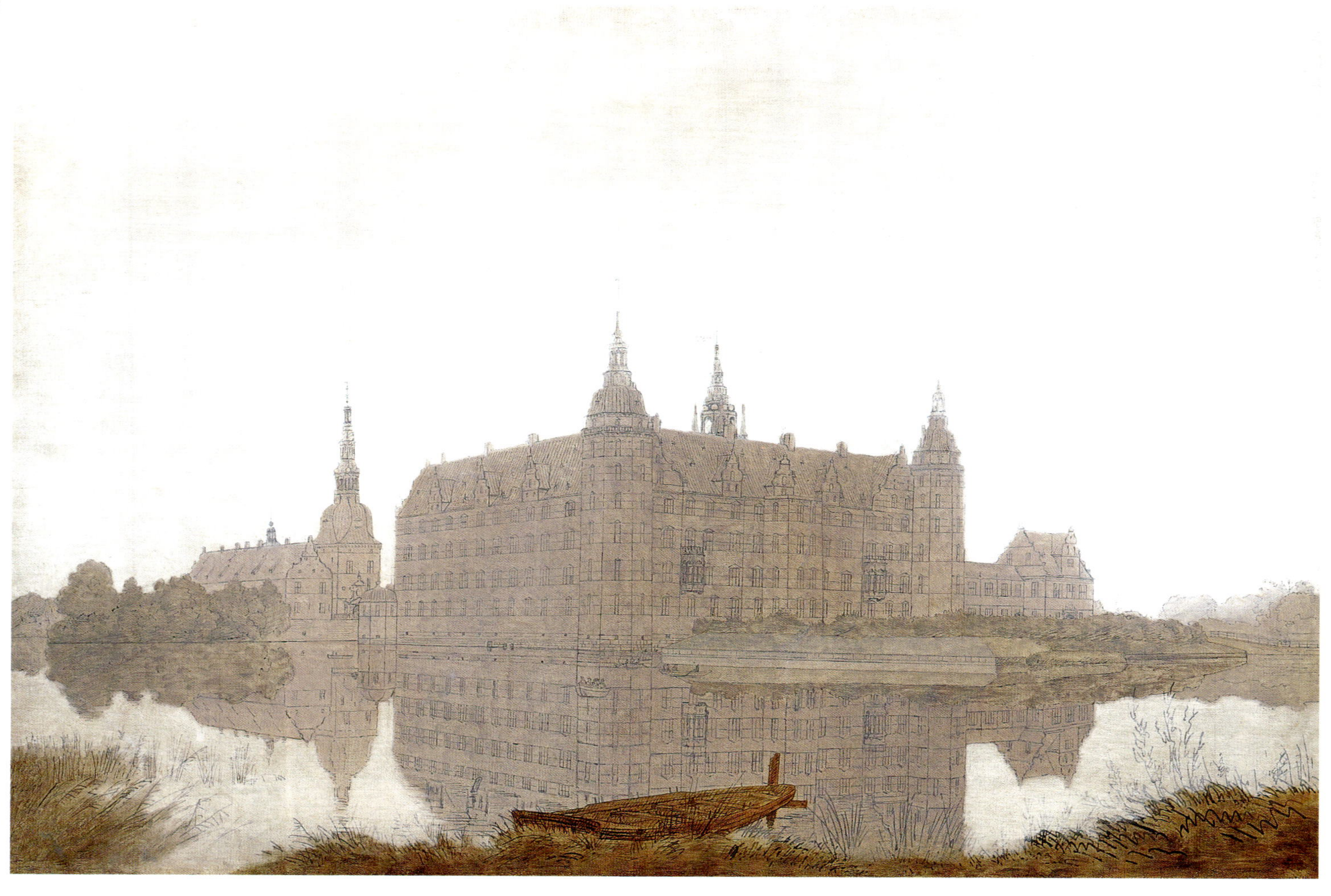

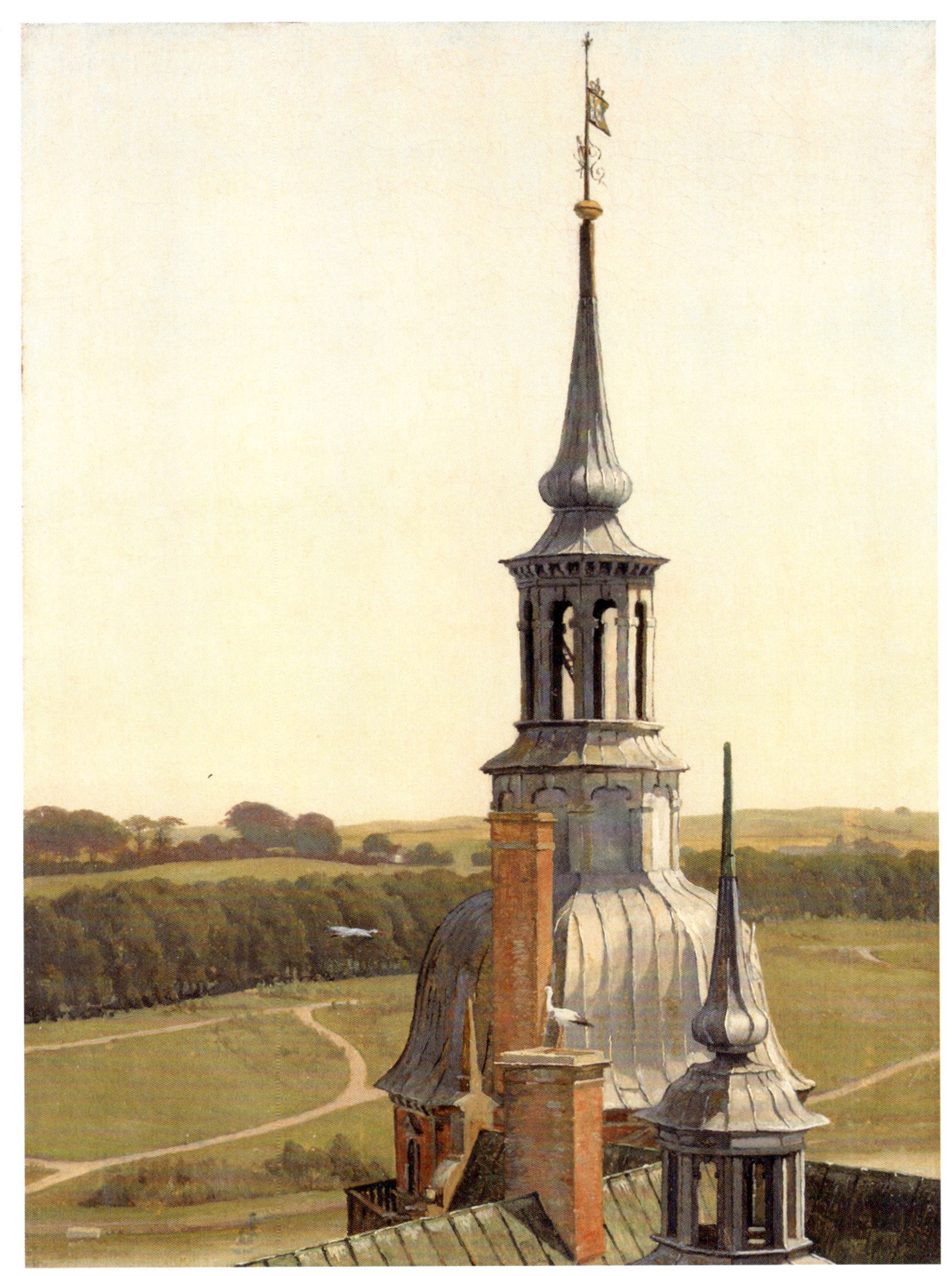

241

240
Christen Købke
*Frederiksborg Castle
Seen from Jaegerbakken*
ca. 1835
Cat. XII-38

241
Christen Købke
*One of the Small
Towers from Castle
Frederiksborg*
ca. 1834
Cat. XII-36

242
Christen Købke
*View from
the Grain Loft*
1831
Cat. XII-35

243
Martinus Rørbye
*Vester Edege Church
with Gisselfeld Convent
in the Background*
1832
Cat. XII-39

242

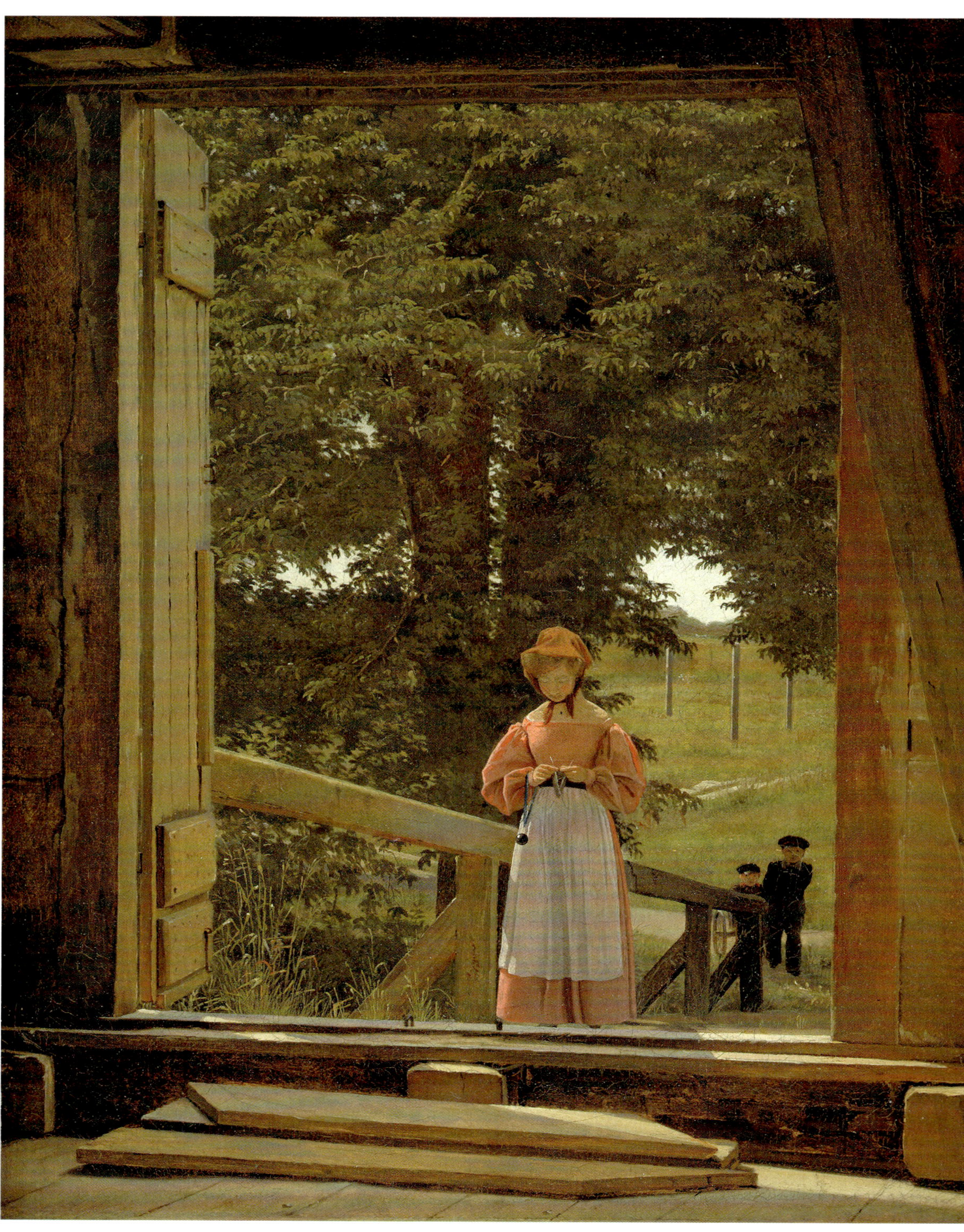

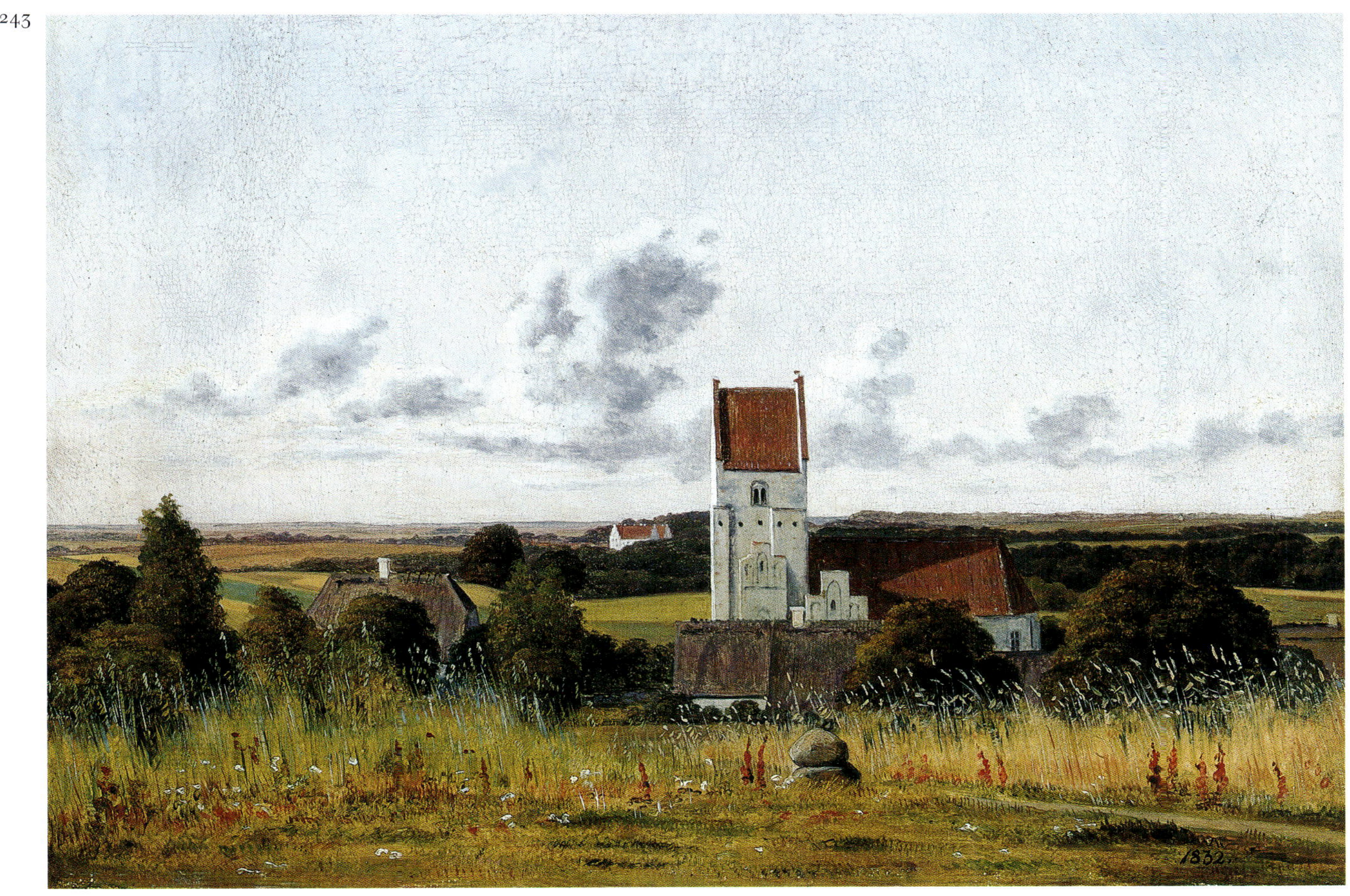

244

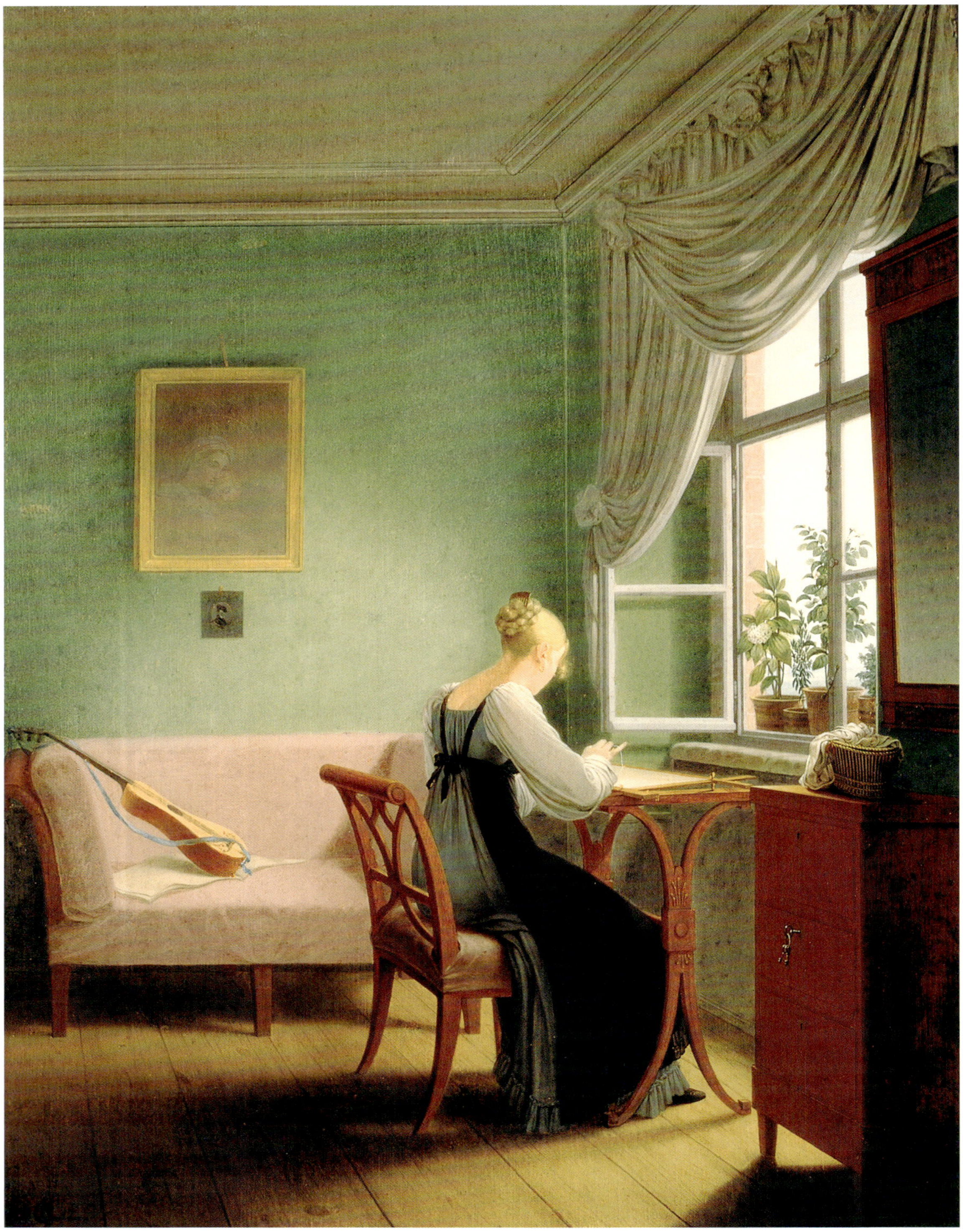

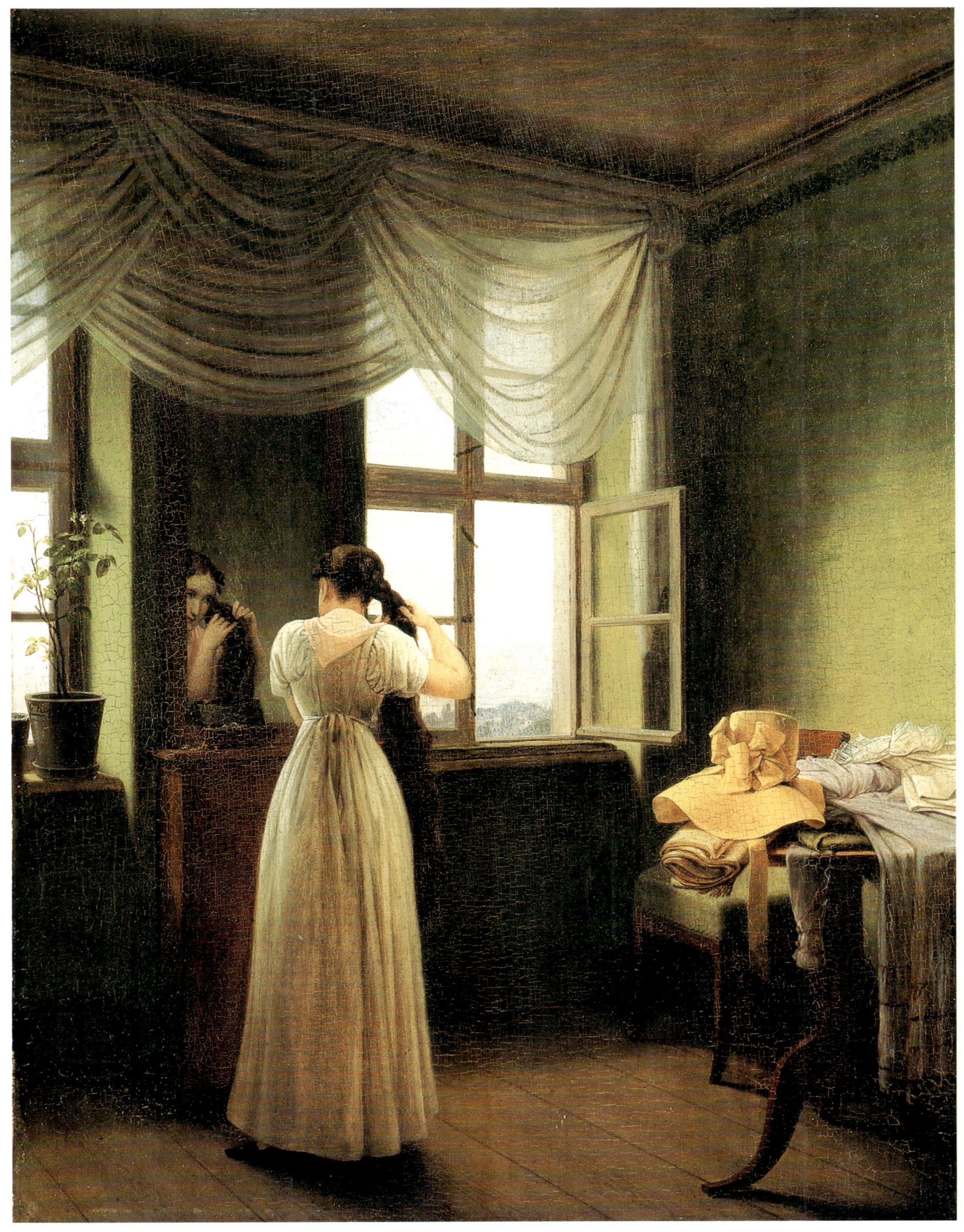

244
Georg Friedrich
Kersting
Woman Embroidering
1817
Cat. XII-17

245
Georg Friedrich
Kersting
Before the Mirror
1827
Cat. XII-18

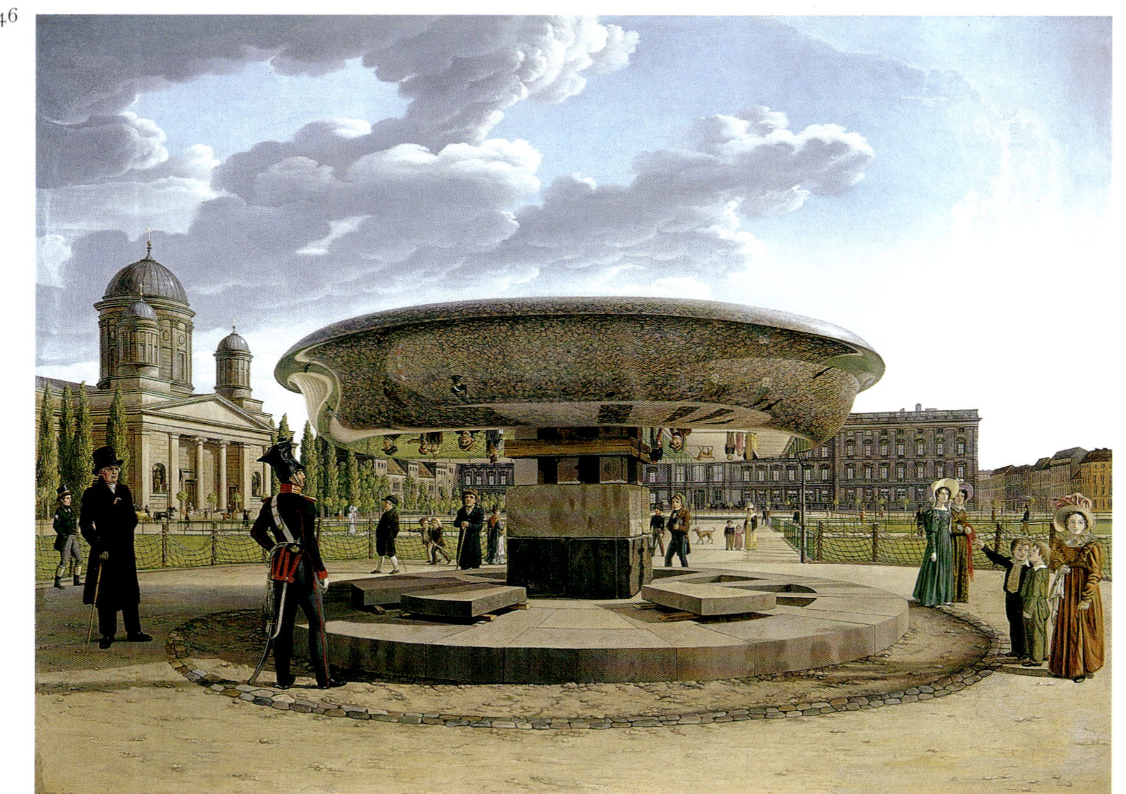

246

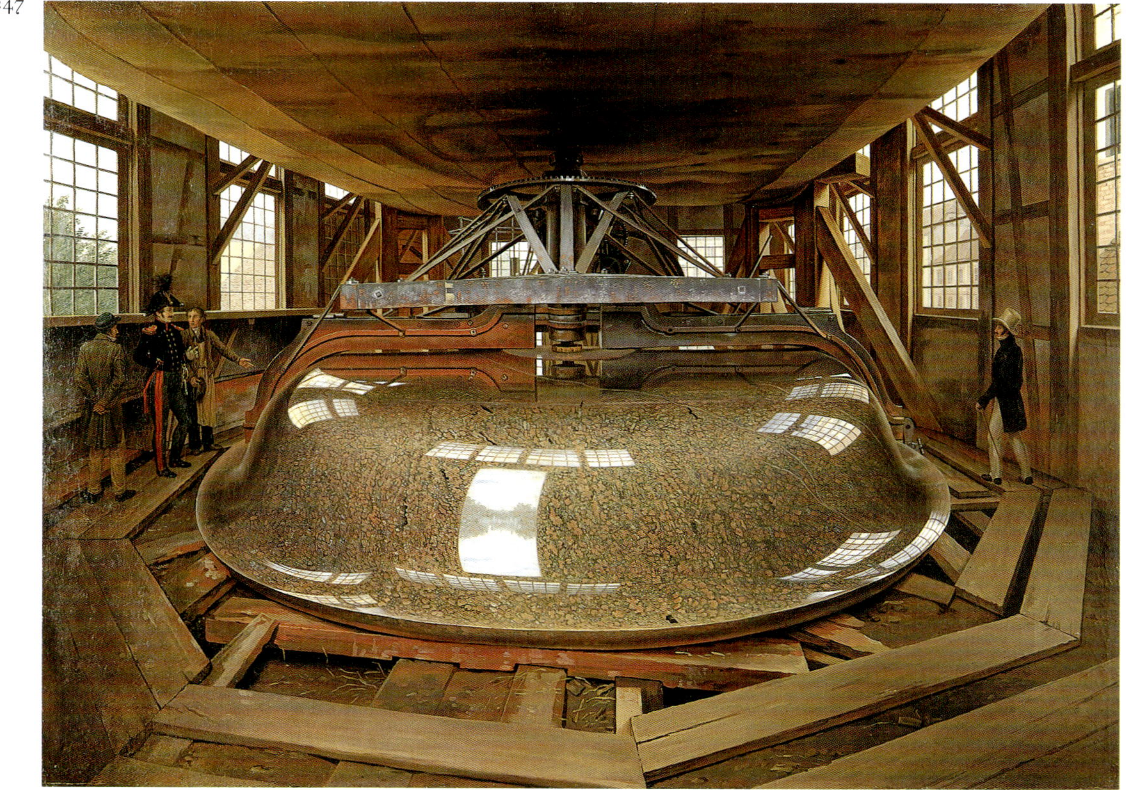

247

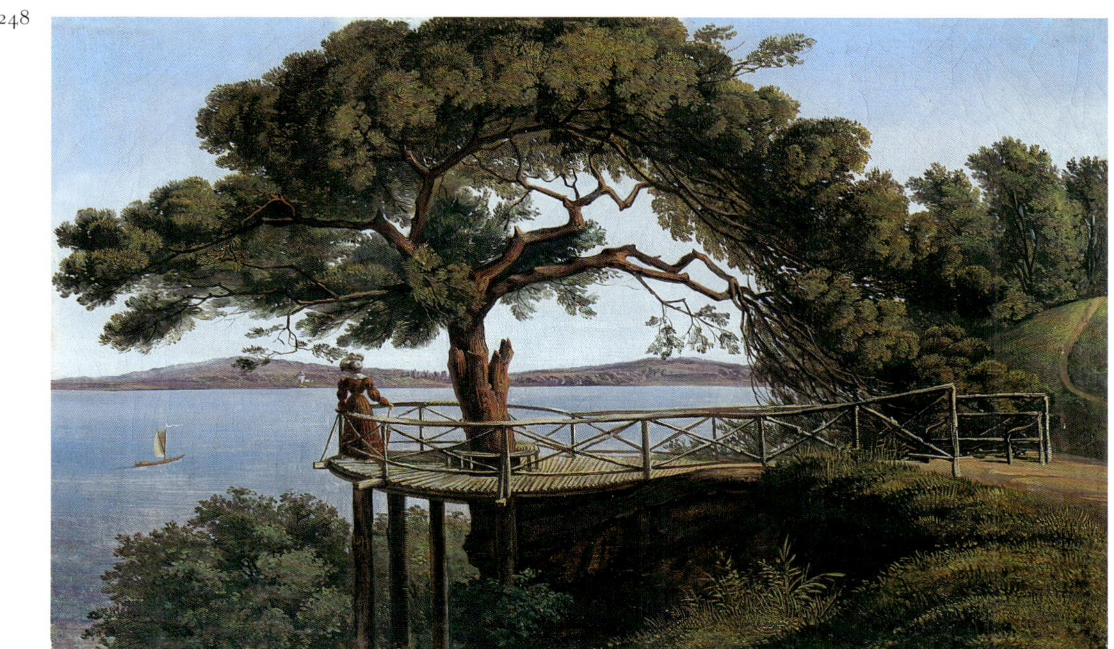

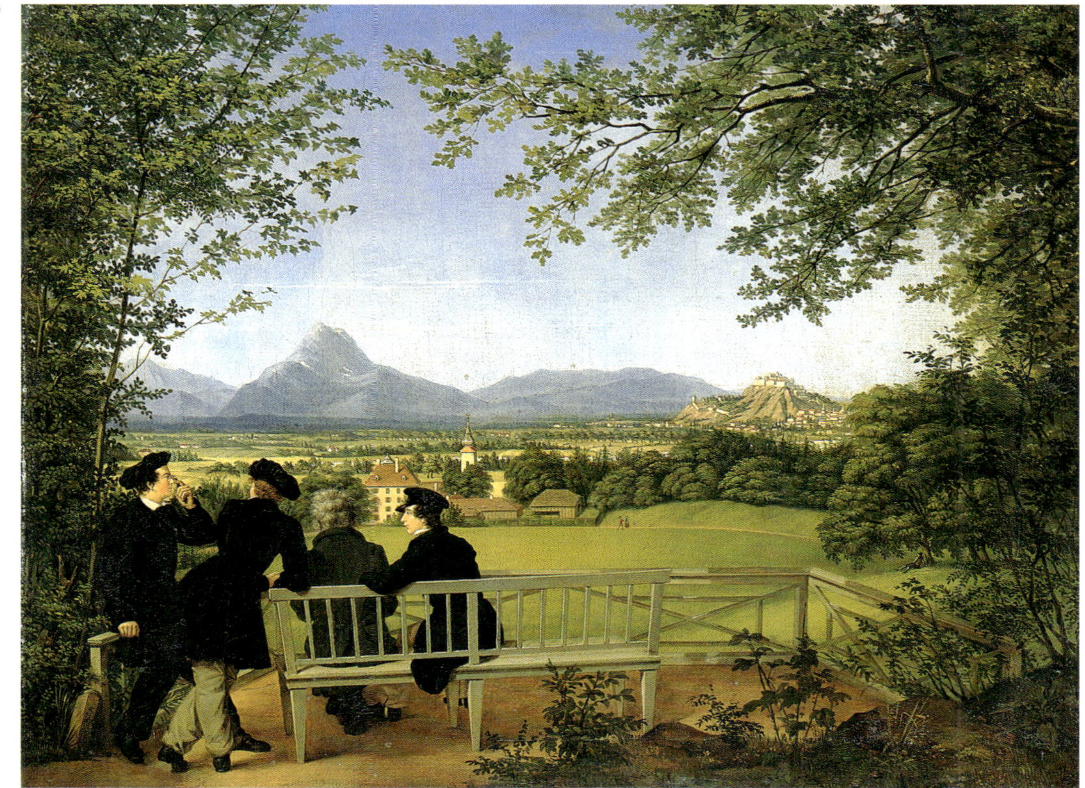

246
Johann Erdmann
Hummel
*The Granite Basin in
the Berlin Lustgarten*
1831
Cat. XII-15

247
Johann Erdmann
Hummel
*Polishing the Granite
Basin for the Lustgarten*
1831/32
Cat. XII-16

248
Julius Schoppe
*The "Emperor's
Pine" in the Park of
Kleinglienicke*
1827
Cat. XII-41

249
Julius Schoppe
View of Salzburg
1817
Cat. XII-40

250
Eduard Gaertner
*Studio of the Gropius
Brothers*
after 1832
Cat. XII-12

251
Eduard Gaertner
*View from the Roof
of the Church of
Friedrichswerder over
the Friedrichsforum,
Berlin*
1835
Cat. XII-13

250

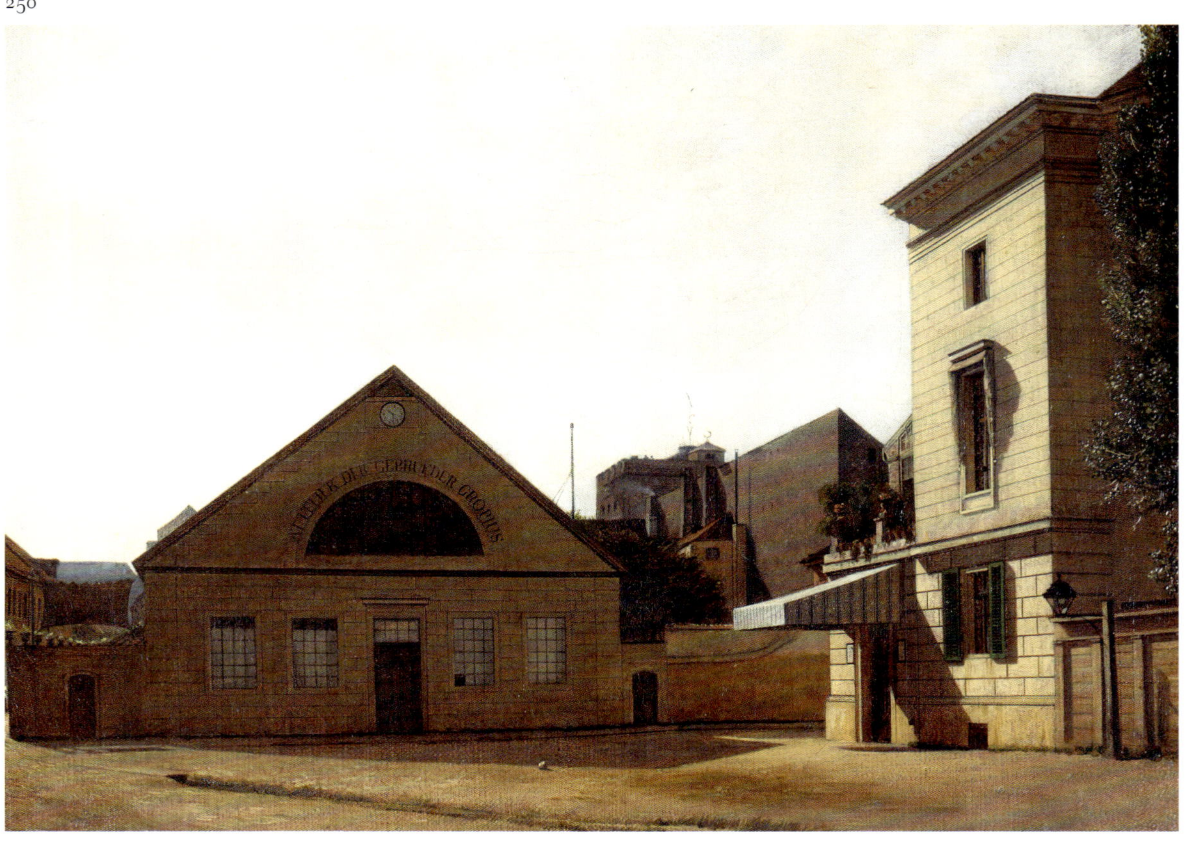

251

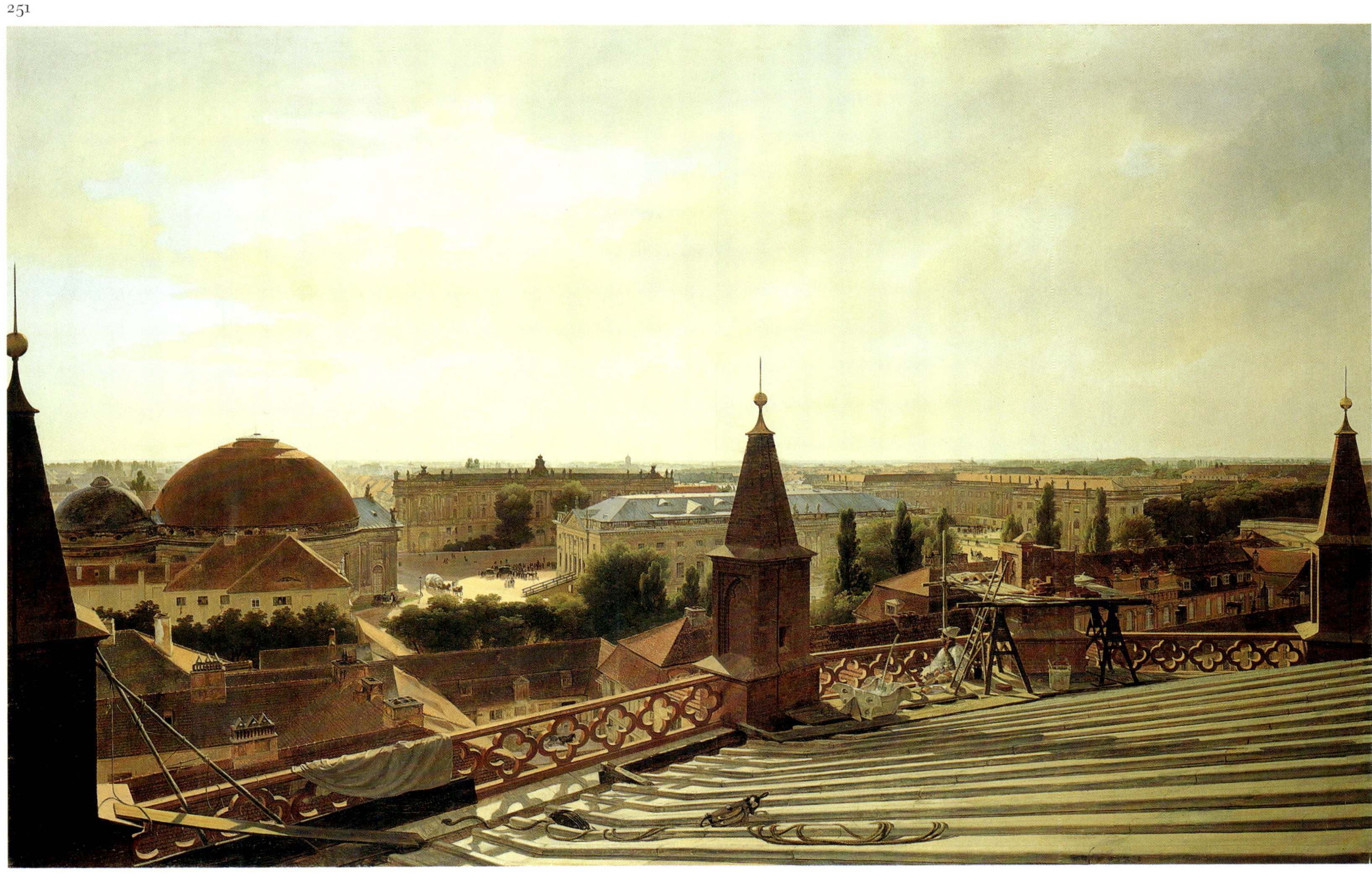

252

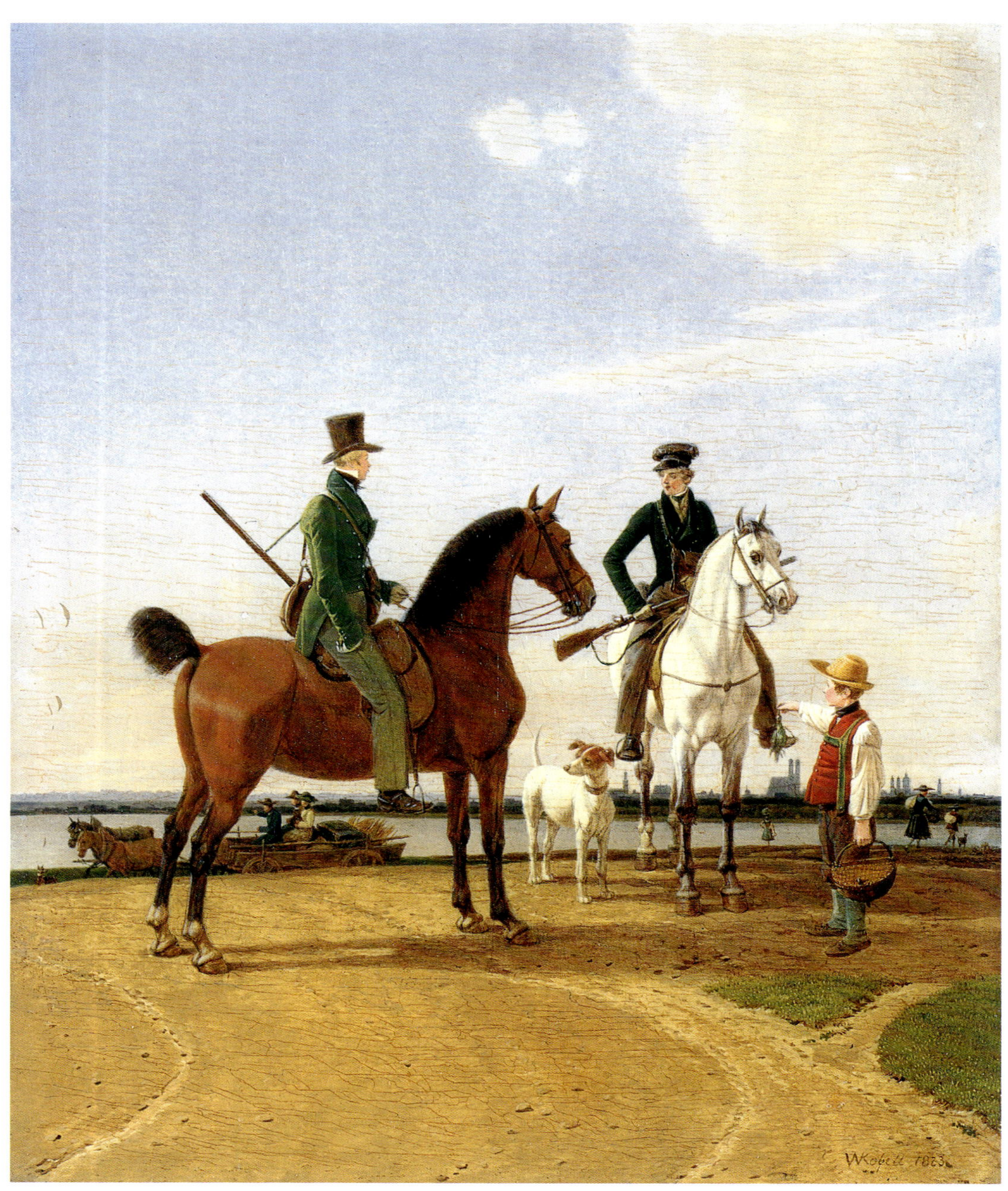

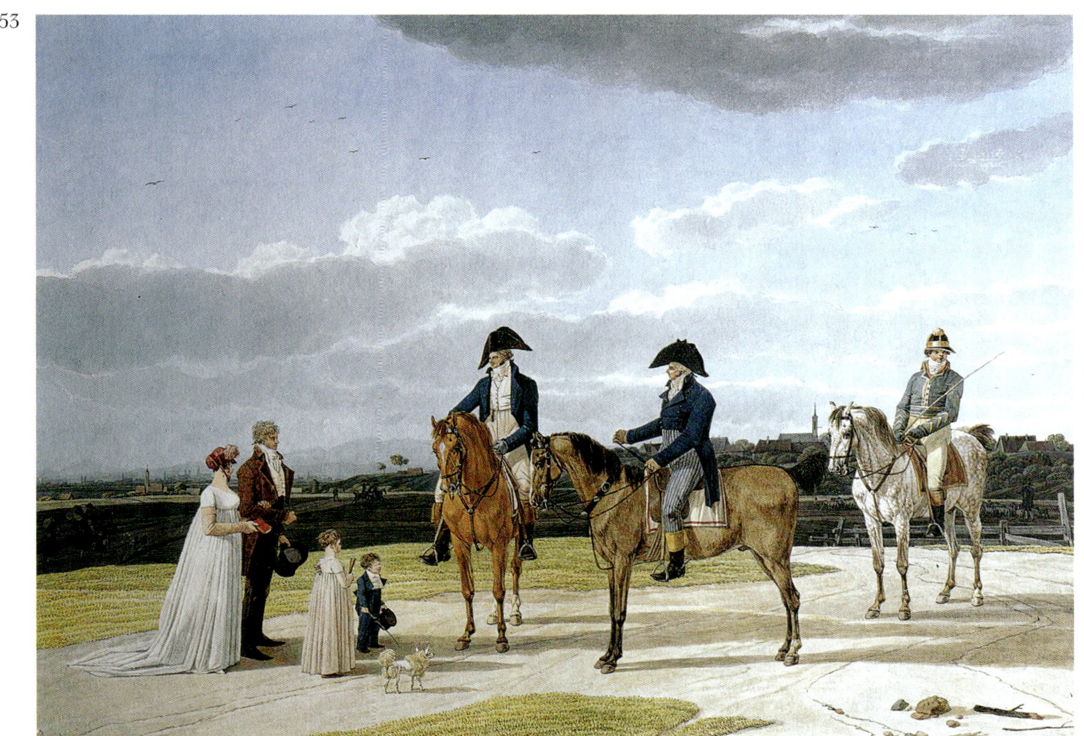

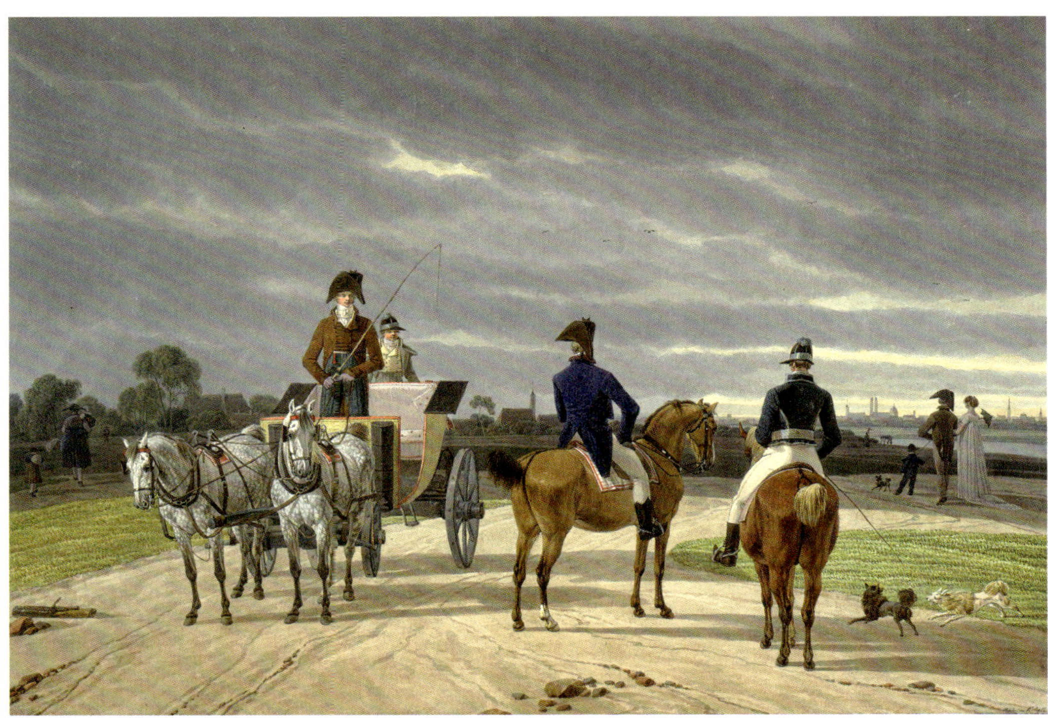

252
Wilhelm von Kobell
*Hunter and Lord
at the River Isar with
View of Munich*
1823
Cat. XII-34

253
Wilhelm von Kobell
*Encounter between
Elegant Horsemen
and a Family*
1803
Cat. XII-22

254
Wilhelm von Kobell
*Encounter of Riders
and a Hunting Chaise
Drawn by Two Horses
outside Munich*
1803
Cat. XII-24

255
Wilhelm von Kobell
*Village Landscape
with Goats, Shepherd,
and a Horse at a
Watering Place*
1798
Cat. XII-21

256
Wilhelm von Kobell
*Austrian Infantrymen
and Hussars*
ca. 1806
Cat. XII-28

257
Wilhelm von Kobell
*Cattle Market outside
the Town of Constance
(?) on Lake Constance*
1820
Cat. XII-33

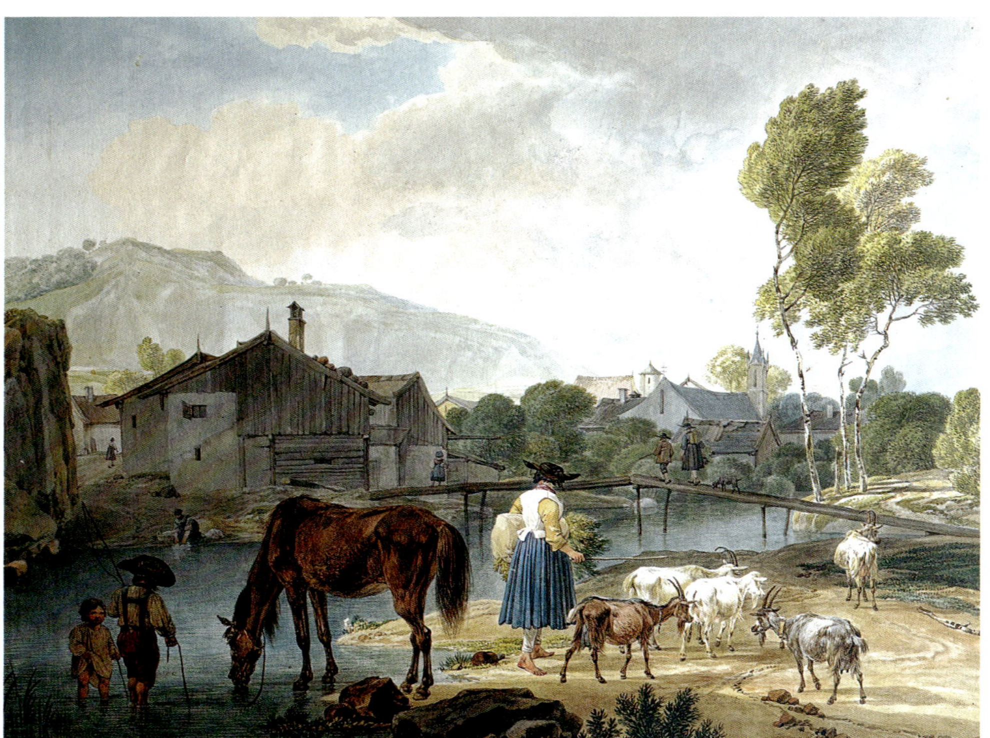

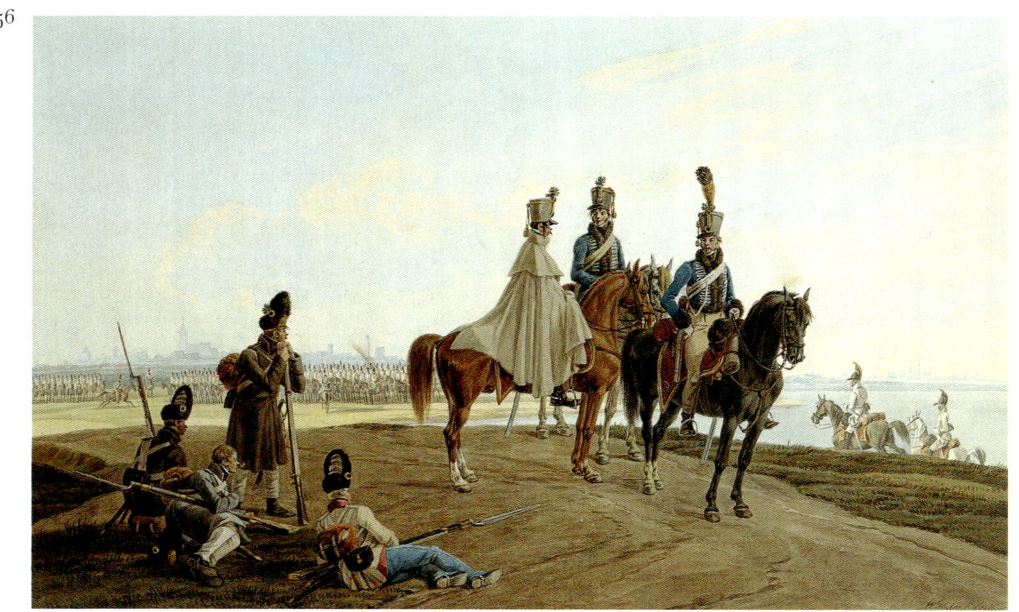

257

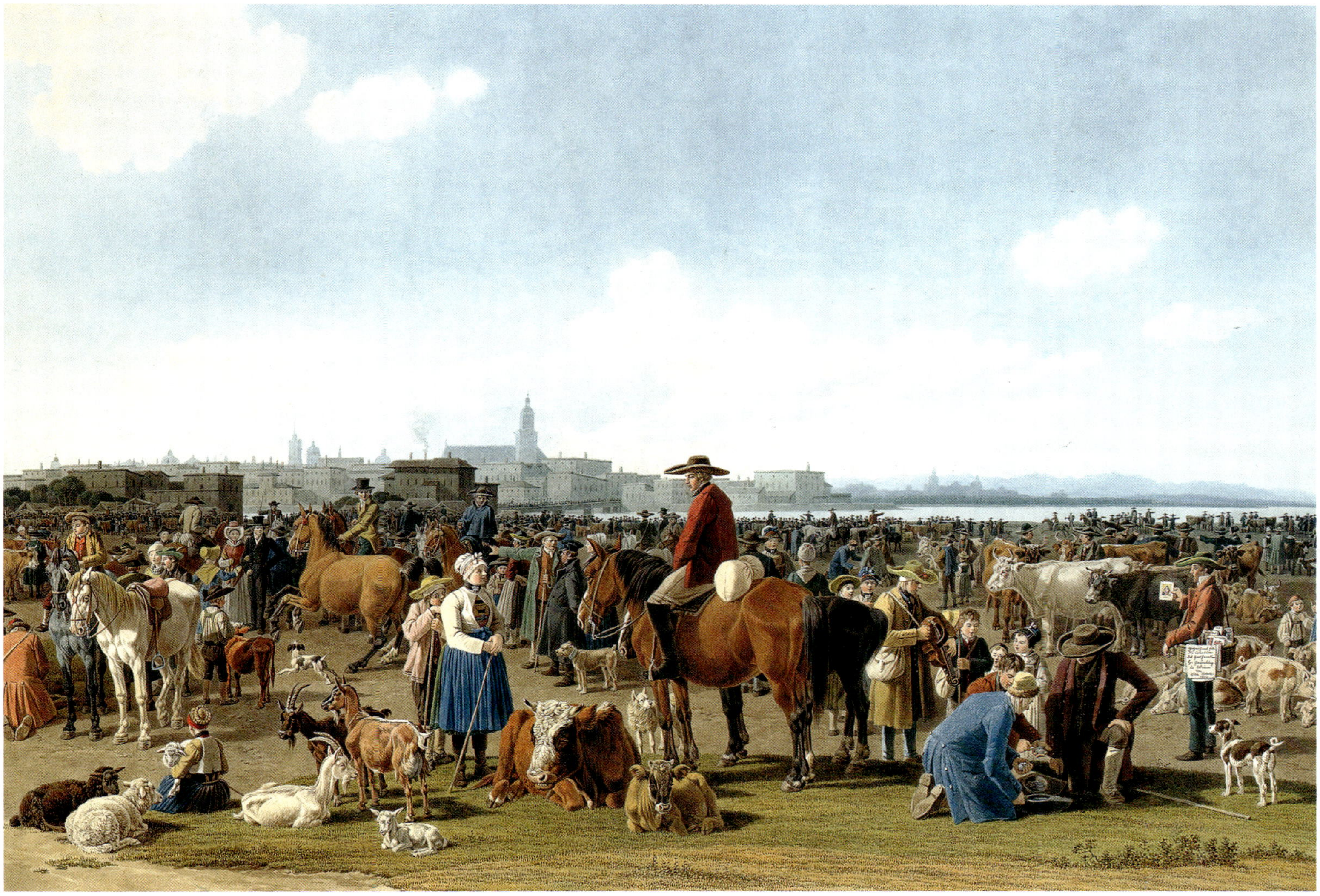

CENTRAL EUROPEAN PAINTING AND DRAWING

SECTION XIII

Cornelia Reiter

THE POETRY OF REALITY

The Biedermeier years fall within The Golden Age of Austrian painting and drawing. Biedermeier's emphasis on reality, on what is empirically graspable, without romantic, symbolic, or ennobling overstatement, was revolutionary in its time. The immediate "visual experience" – in the newly discovered local landscape or in the reality of the human image devoid of all idealization – became an autonomous, valid pictorial subject in its own right.

Landscapes and city scenes were core subjects of paintings, watercolors, and drawings. One important factor contributing to the development of landscape painting in the waning eighteenth century was an increased demand for pictures among the upper strata of the bourgeoisie, manifested above all in numerous, popular series of "voyages pittoresques." Jakob Alt occupies an important position within this context. A visionary synthesis of "free" landscape and cityscape, *View of Vienna from "Spinnerin am Kreuz"* is one of his early masterpieces. From this popular prospect south of the city, the artist developed a panoramic, true-to-life view of the silhouette of Vienna.

The discovery of the Salzkammergut, a region of Austria depicted in numerous watercolors and oil paintings of the Biedermeier period, is attributed primarily to Ferdinand Olivier. While Olivier viewed the landscape primarily as a symbol of complex, predominantly religious, allegories, Biedermeier artists concentrated on visible phenomena. Alt himself – often accompanied by his son Rudolf – took hikes to the lakes of the Salzkammergut, which he painted in intricately executed gouaches in which realism is blended with a subtle, occasionally Romantic, atmosphere of light.

Franz Steinfeld's painting *The Hallstättersee in Upper Austria* is regarded as the work that "gave birth" to Viennese painting of the Biedermeier period. Here, perspective is expanded far beyond the scope of the sensitive nature studies of earlier years and realism with its obsession with detail for the first time controls the entire composition. Ferdinand Georg Waldmüller chose a similar point of view in his *View of Hallstatt*, in which the almost palpable forms of light-drenched buildings surpass even Steinfeld in terms of realism. Waldmüller's Salzkammergut landscapes from the mid-1820s are considered highlights of Biedermeier

painting by virtue of their unpretentious subjects and the often almost surreal depiction of light.

A key figure in the development of new regions and themes as worthy subjects for painting was Archduke Johann Baptist of Austria, a leading intellectual of his time. He was passionate about documenting not only the local landscape but also the customs and indigenous culture of the region. Devoid of all external symbols of class and noble background, Leopold Kupelwieser's austere, objective portrait vividly conveys the strong-willed man who broke with many of the prevailing conventions of his age. The court painters he appointed and instructed to document the alpine landscape of the Steiermark were among the leading landscapists of the time. For example, Matthäus Loder, appointed court painter in 1816, painted *View of Brandhof* around 1824. The Brandhof was the archduke's estate, which later was furnished and decorated by various artists. Loder painted a series of outstanding watercolors of Austrian alpine landscapes in the service of the archduke. Loder's successor was Thomas Ender, one of the period's most prominent landscape painters and watercolorists, whose powers of observation were honed during an expedition to Brazil in 1817/18. In addition to his nearly 800 Brazil works are the fascinating, geologically detailed documentary images of the high alpine landscape, many executed in series from different perspectives. Especially notable are his views of the Grossglockner and the Pasterze glacier, executed following an ascent of the Glockner massif in the company of Archduke Johann. Jakob Gauermann, father of the more famous landscape painter Friedrich Gauermann, also was associated with Archduke Johann. His paintings of a cushion dance at Lake Grundl and a wedding procession to the Church of Scheuchenstein are outstanding documentations of folk life and customs.

Another project, this one spearheaded by the emperor, significantly increased commissions for artists and promoted the art of watercolor painting: "Des Kaisers Guckkasten" (The Emperor's Peepshow) – a series of large-scale views of beautiful spots in the Austrian Empire and neighboring countries commissioned in 1833 for Archduke Ferdinand, the crown prince who became Emperor Ferdinand I in 1835. Reportage attention to detail in watercolors of impressive stylistic refinement was implicit in the commission specifications. This series, originally comprising more than 300 works, could be viewed in three-dimensional projection through a box equipped with a concave mirror. The best watercolorists of the period, among them the court painter Eduard Gurk, were engaged to create the illustrations. The works selected included Gurk's views of Prague, Pilsen, and Baden near Vienna, where he painted the Kaiserhaus (emperor's residence) with the Ferdinandsbrunnen (Ferdinand's Fountain) as well as several views of the countryside around Mariazell. The Guckkasten featured not only images of major cities, architectural structures, and landscapes but also seemingly ordinary subjects such as the studio of Jakob Alt with a view of the suburb of Alser. In this loving description of his easel and drawing table in front of a window open to a sunlit suburban setting, a casually pushed aside armchair serves as a substitute for the physical presence of the artist. Here, in contrast to the transcendental quality of the Romantic topos of the view from a window, the incidental has come to triumph over all forms of idealized exaggeration.

In portraiture, one of the most admired pictorial genres of the Biedermeier period, increasingly sought after among the upper bourgeoisie, Ferdinand Georg Waldmüller was certainly one of the most uncompromising advocates of a new "truth to nature." His portraits from the 1820s are rightly regarded as an incunabulum of realistic portrait painting. Such examples as *Catharina Baroness von Koudelka* from 1821/22 and *The Burgtheather Actor Maximilian Korn (1792–1854) in a Landscape* from 1828 assert a direct and unrhetorical approach to representation, while celebrating the refinement and material elegance valued by the Vienna aristocracy. Waldmuller's bright color schemes, precision of detail, neutral backgrounds, and near frontal poses convey a sense of comfortable self-assurance and integrity. In other later and more personal portraits, Waldmüller – evidently inspired by English artists – placed his models in expansive landscape settings, as in *Portrait of Baron von Moser in front of a Salzkammergut Landscape with Loser and Sandling*. By depicting action, Waldmüller often transformed the portrait into a genre painting.

Along with Waldmüller, Friedrich von Amerling, who trained his eye primarily on the English paintings of such artists as Thomas Lawrence, was a preferred portraitist among the nobility and the affluent bourgeoisie in Vienna, especially during the 1830s and 1840s. The appeal of his portraits lies in his refined painting style, as reflected, for example, in the depiction of porcelain skin or his effective color harmonies, primarily warm, vibrant browns. The description of reality is often combined with heightened sentimentality, especially in his greatly admired children's portraits. The mere posture of a young girl gazing dreamily into the distance with her head resting on her arm in an emphatic gesture of melancholy clearly implies the sentimental concentration of expression in a moody image of adolescence.

The world of simple craftsmen – often viewed under aspects of social criticism – now became worthy of depiction for the first time. The "industrial painting" as an invention of the Biedermeier is embodied in an early gouache by Carl Agricola showing a blacksmith's shop. Before then, such a motif would have been conceivable only in a mythological context, such as a depiction of the furnace of Vulcan (Hephaestus). Johann Baptist Reiter and Franz Eybl would continue the evolution of similar themes into the 1830s and even the 1840s.

Flower paintings occupied a privileged position in Austrian Biedermeier art. While an interest in exotic plants was confined primarily to a small circle of aristocrats until the eighteenth century, the lovingly tended house garden now became an important place of retreat in bourgeois households. Erasmus von Engert, who has been unjustly ignored by most scholars, depicted the idyllic setting of such a house garden in Vienna. Moritz Michael Daffinger's fine flower paintings exhibit close affinities to botanical illustrations. A highly successful portraitist during the Biedermeier period, he devoted his attention during the last two decades of his life to the theme that had always been closest to his heart – the illustration of local flora. Extraordinarily well versed in botany, the painter labeled the intricately depicted plants, among them such plain and ordinary varieties as daisies, primroses, and thistles, with Latin designations and the locations at which they were found, most of which were in lower Austria. Daffinger captured not only the often vividly colored blossoms of the plants but also their complex root systems as important aspects of characterization. The subtitle of the present exhibition, "The Invention of Simplicity," is probably most clearly reflected in the unpretentious depiction of the nearby real world in Daffinger's impressive illustrations.

258

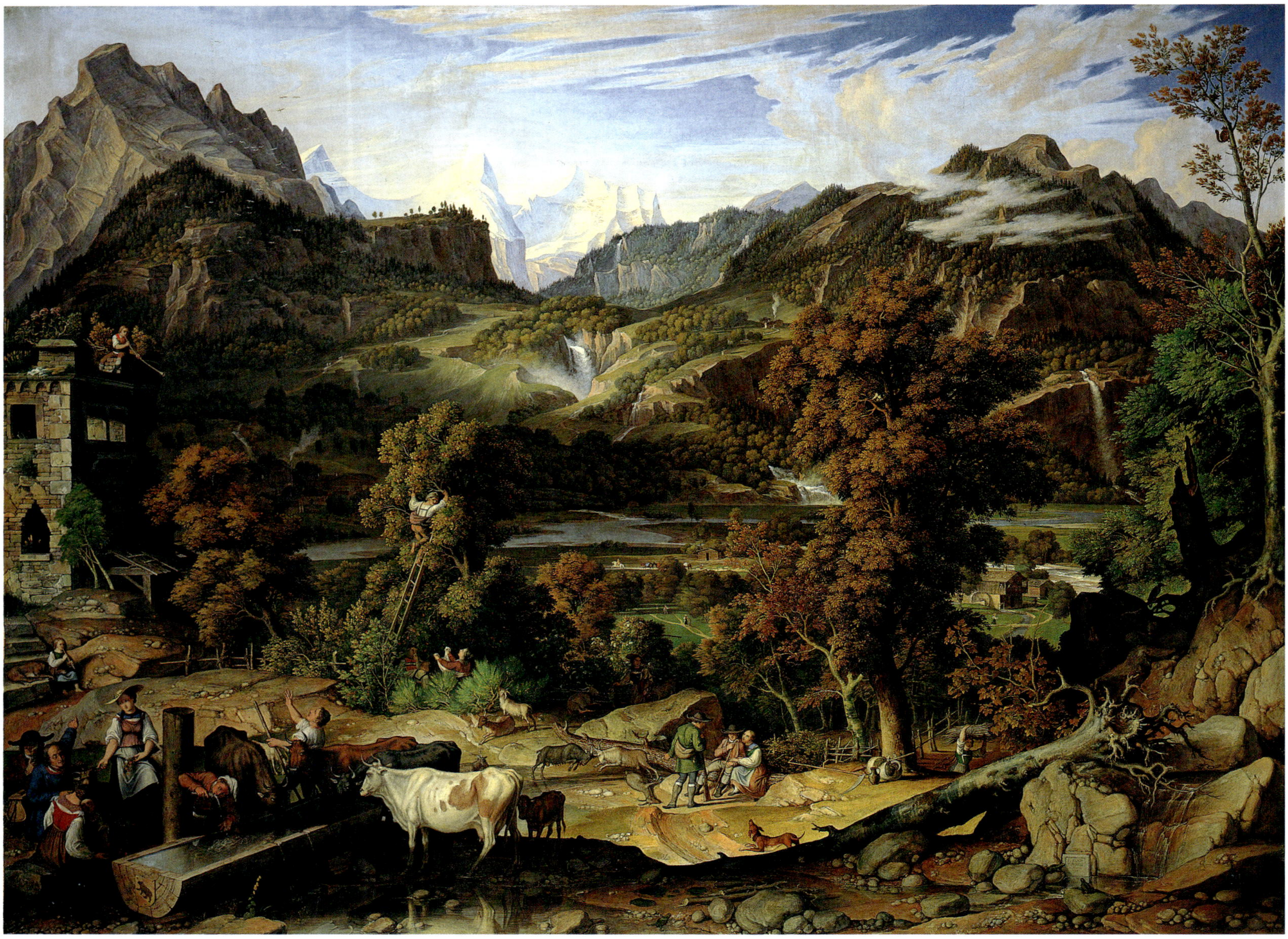

259

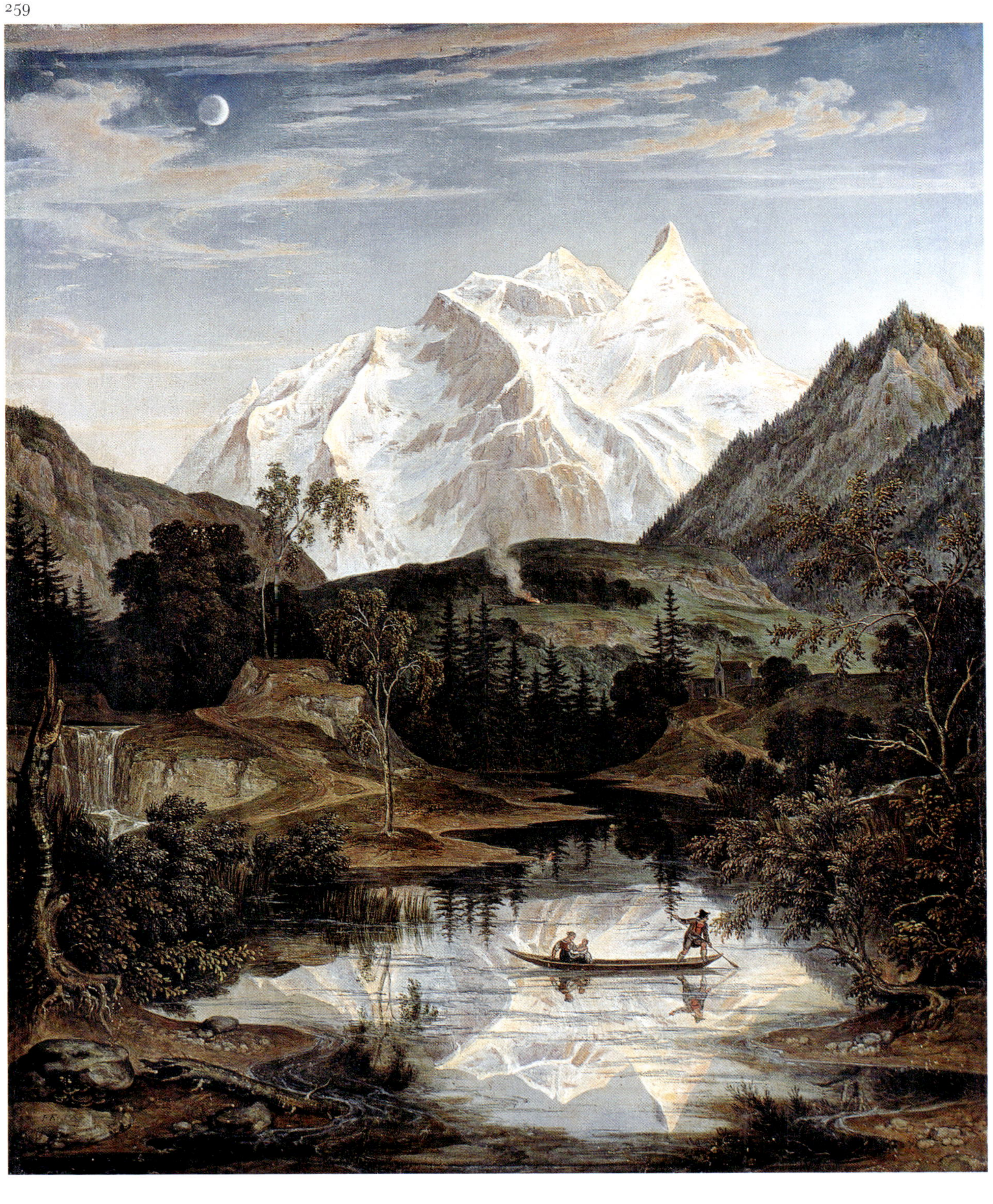

258
Joseph Anton Koch
*The Hasli Valley
near Meiringen*
1817
Cat. XIII-49

259
Joseph Anton Koch
*Mountain Landscape
with Lake*
after 1830
Cat. XIII-50

260
Franz Pforr
Self-Portrait
1810
Cat. XIII-66

261
Julius Schnorr von
Carolsfeld
*Portrait of Henriette
Schnorr von Carolsfeld*
1817
Cat. XIII-70

262
Johann Evangelist
Scheffer von
Leonhardshoff
Self-Portrait
ca. 1809
Cat. XIII-68

260

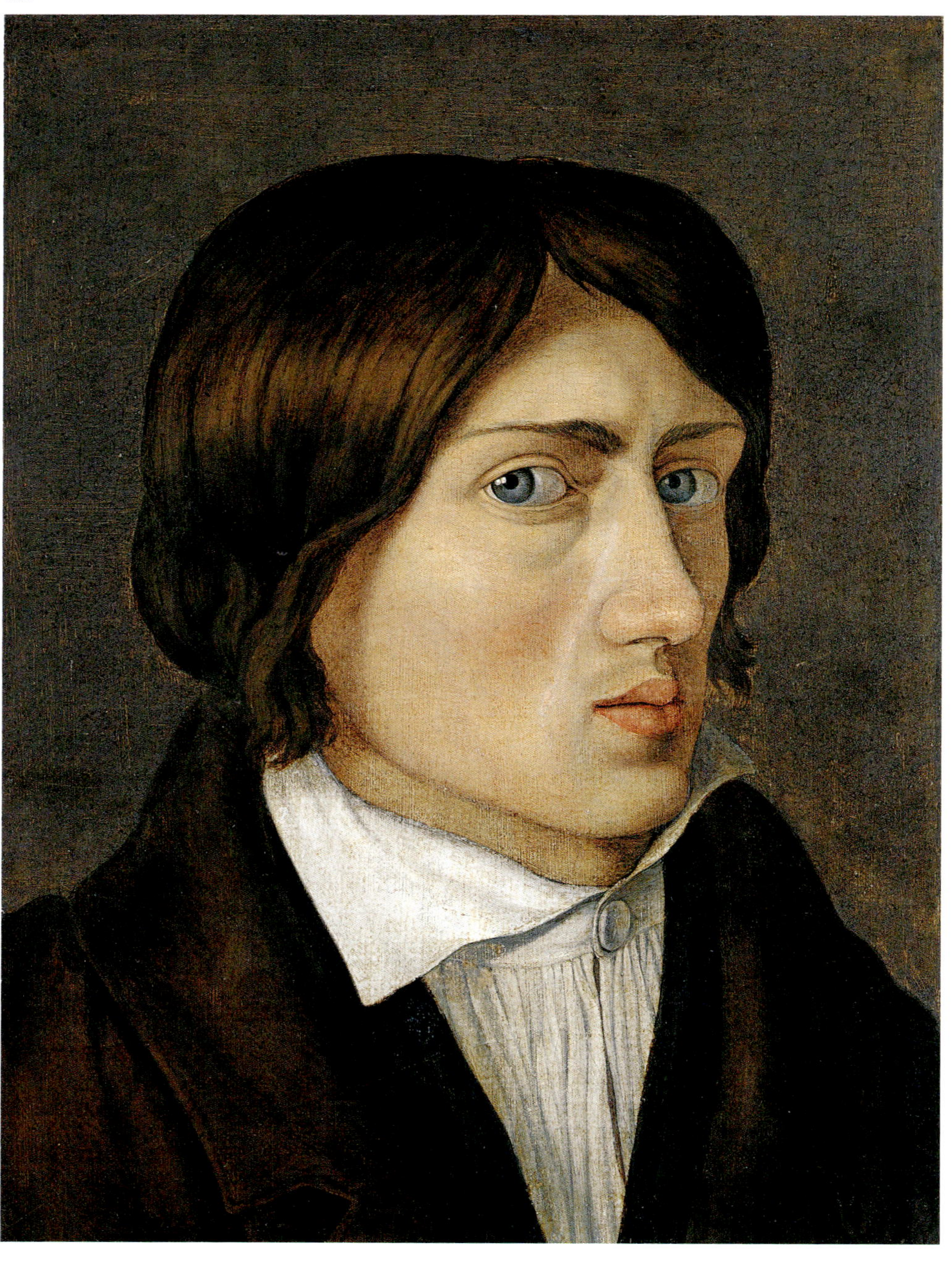

261

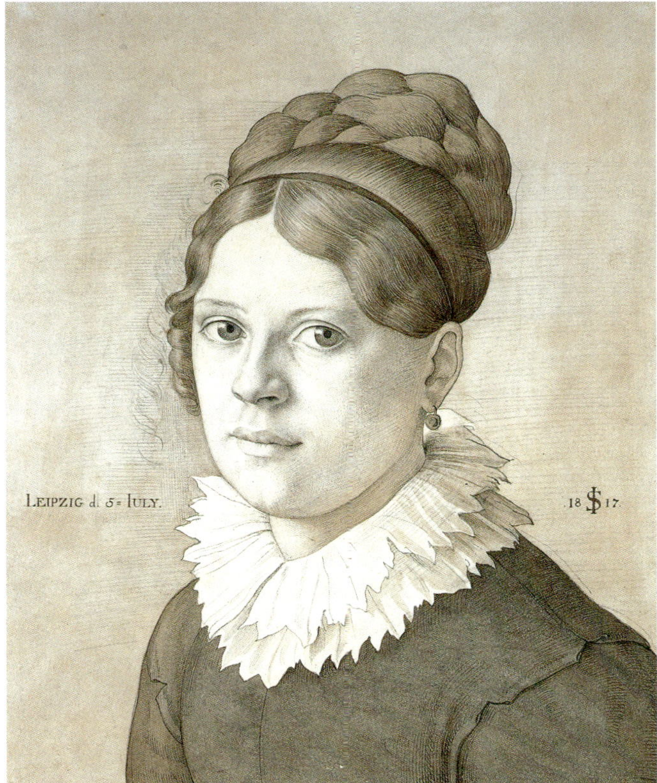

262

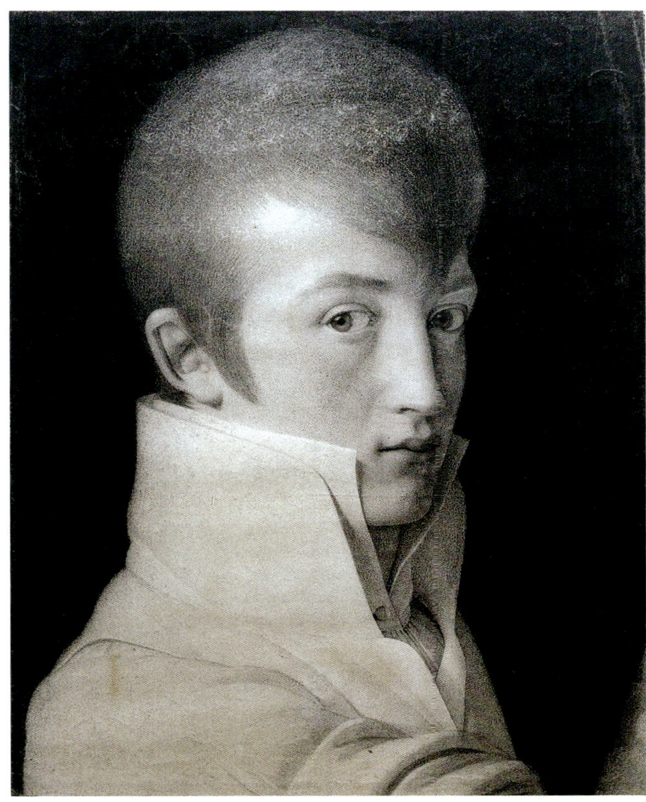

263 and 264
Ferdinand Olivier
*Seven Regions
from Salzburg and
Berchtesgaden:
Wednesday. Footpath
on the Mönchsberg
near Salzburg*, and
*Monday. Roseneck
Garden outside
Salzburg*
1823
Cat. XIII-63

265
Johann Friedrich
Overbeck
Head of a Boy
1811/18
Cat. XIII-65

263

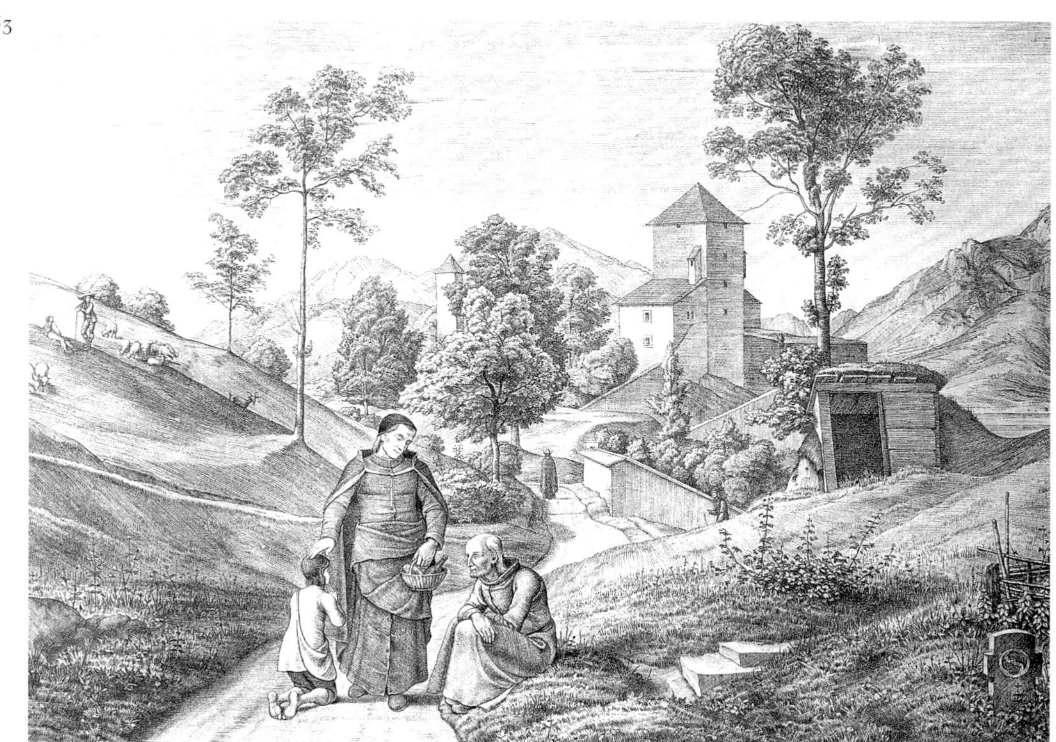

264

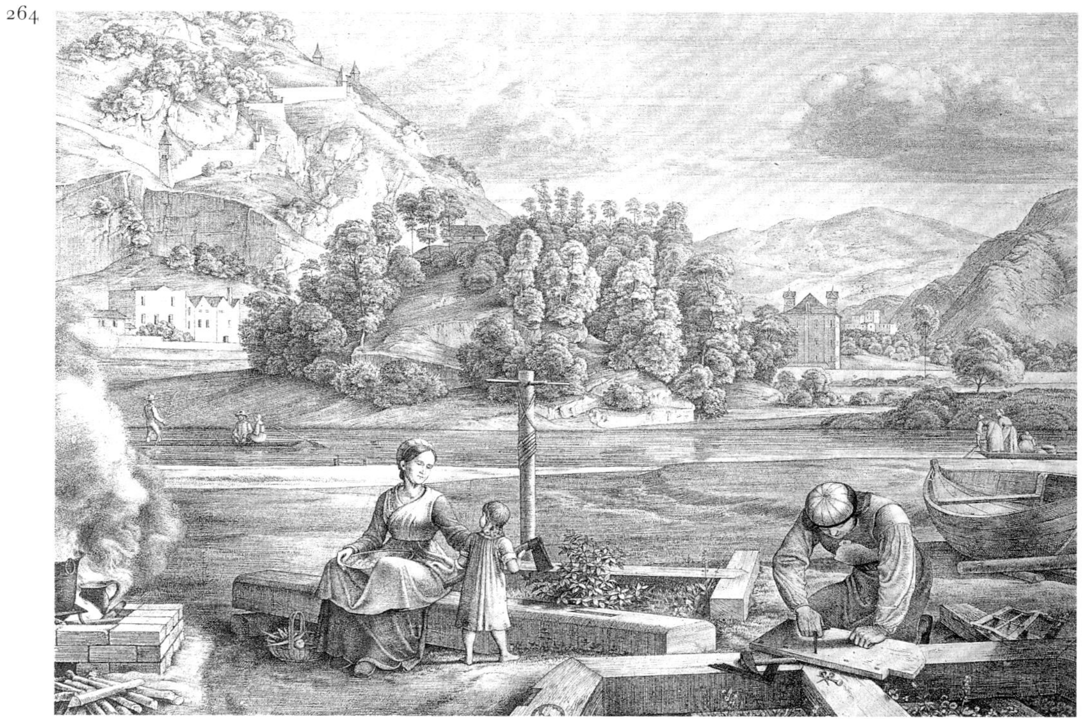

265

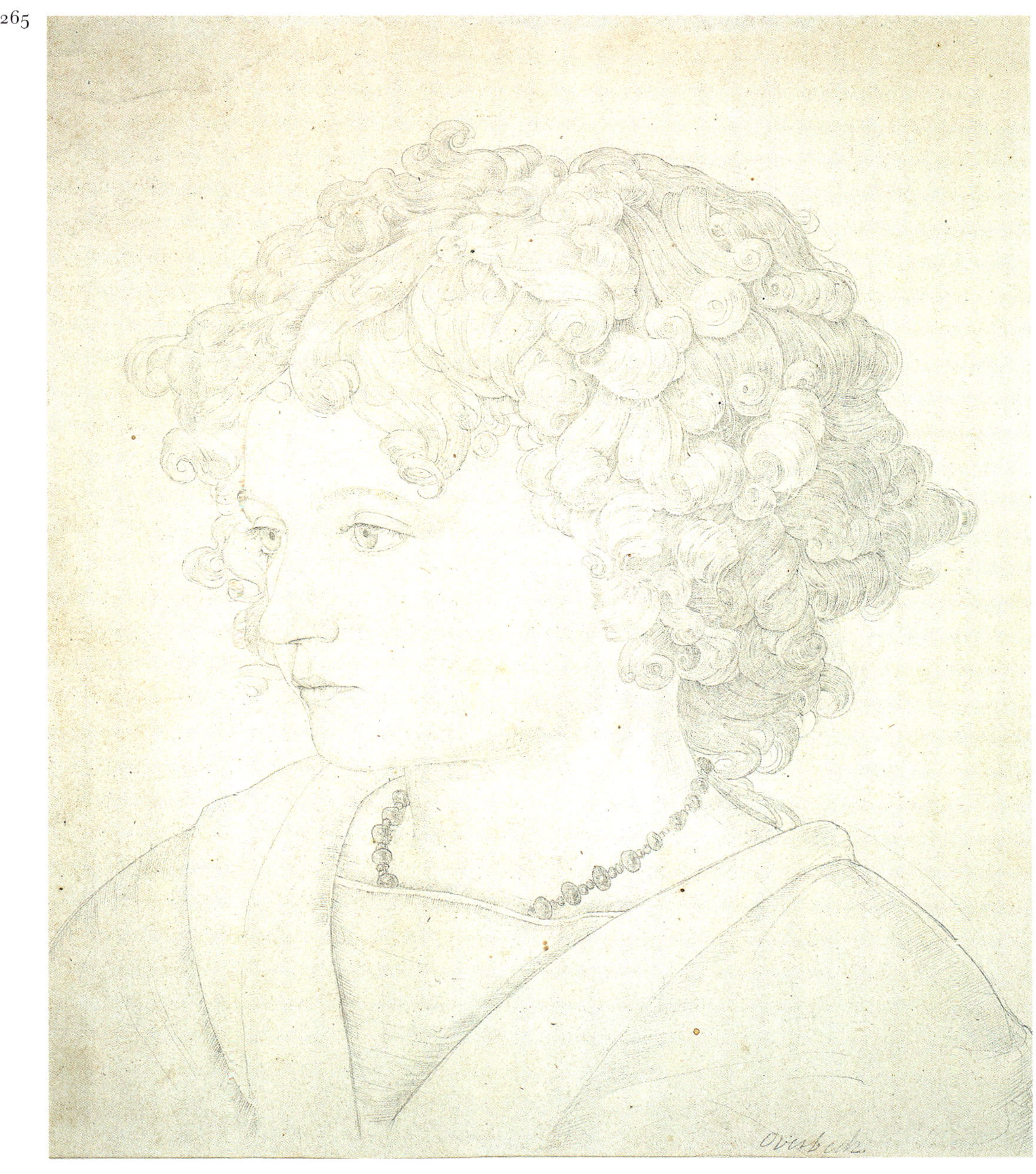

266

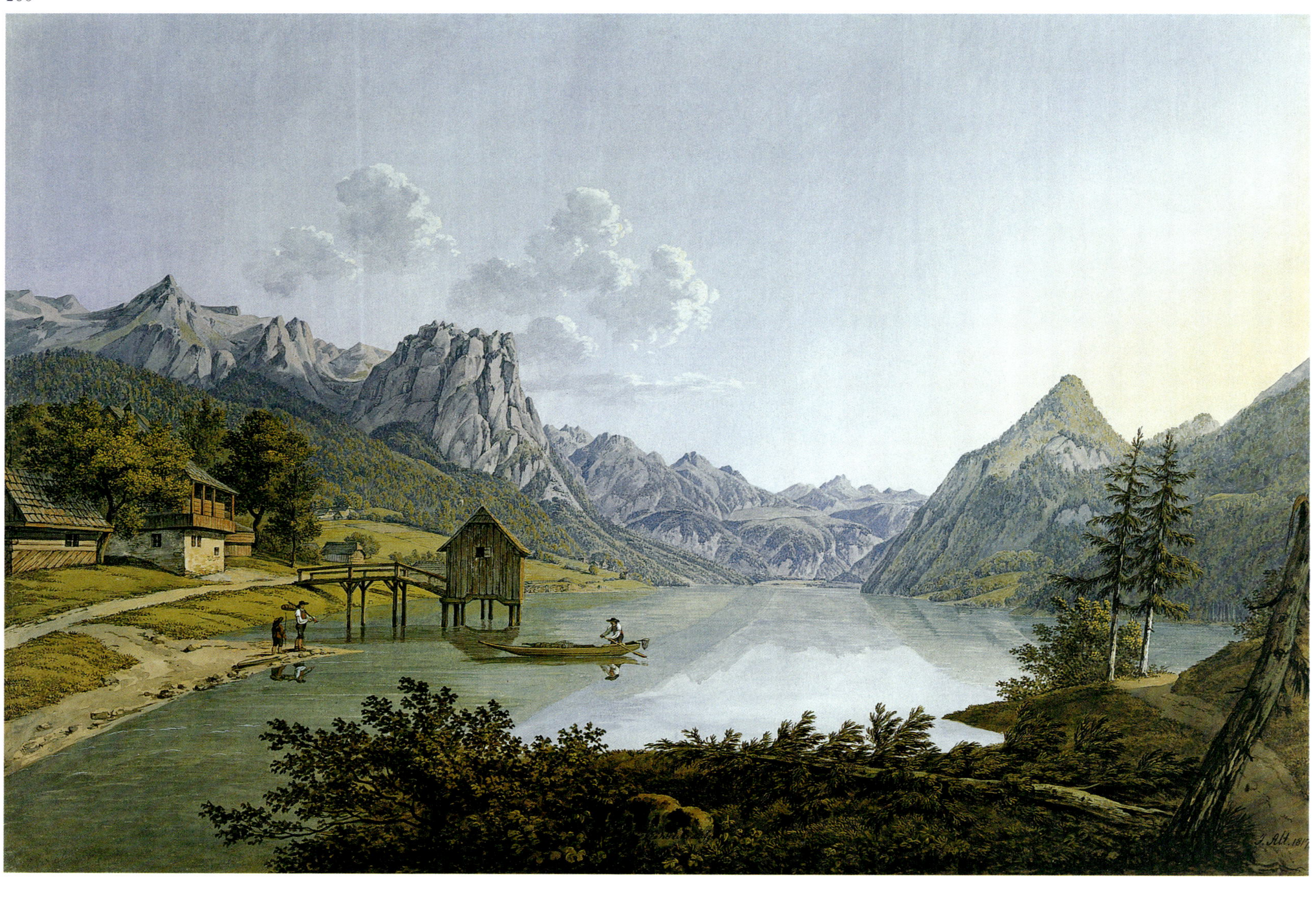

267

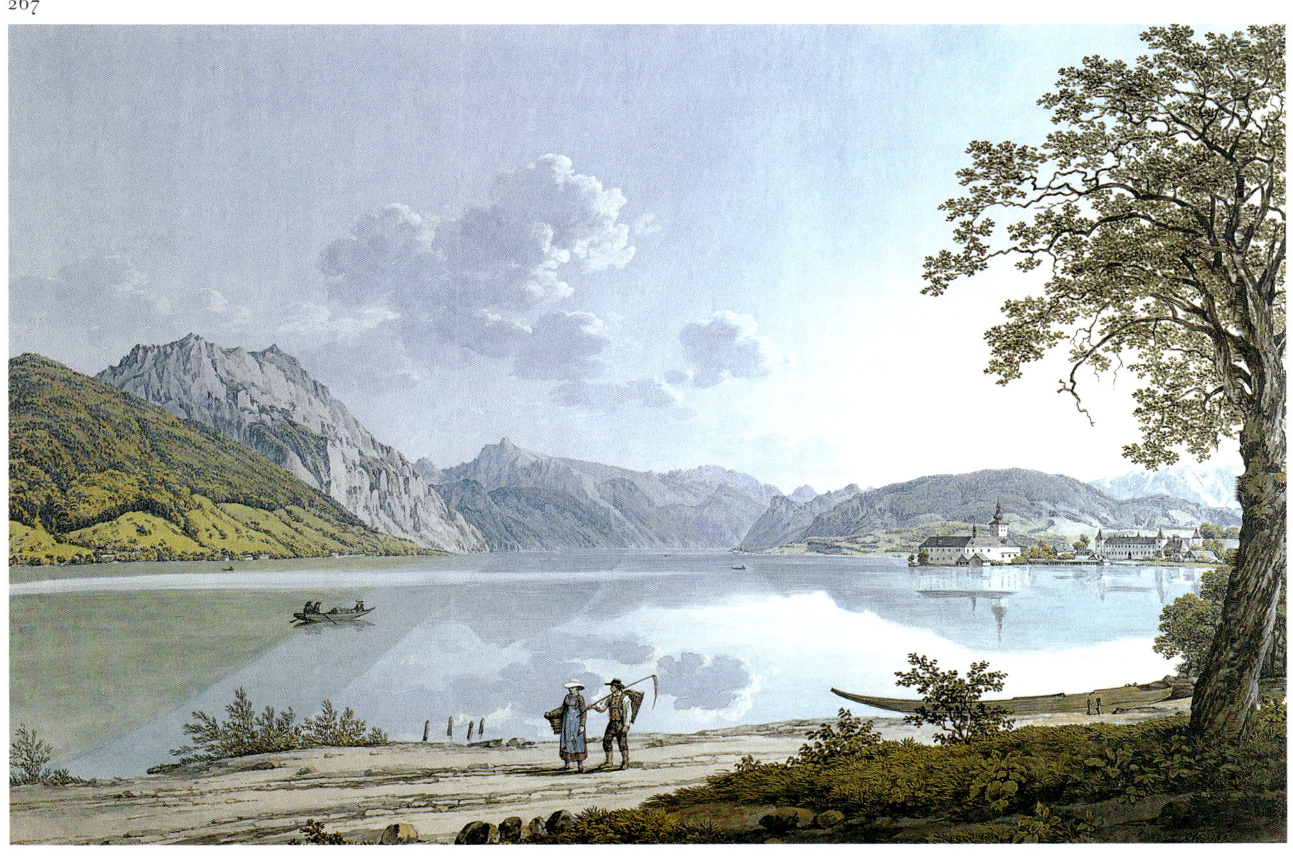

266
Jakob Alt
The Grundlsee
1817
Cat. XIII-3

267
Jakob Alt
*The Traunsee
with Ort Castle*
1817
Cat. XIII-4

268
Jakob Gauermann
*Wedding Procession
to the Church of
Scheuchenstein*
1821
Cat. XIII-37

269
Jakob Gauermann
*Polsterltanz
[Cushion Dance]
at the Grundlsee*
1821
Cat. XIII-36

270
Leopold Kupelwieser
*Archduke Johann
Baptist of Austria*
1828
Cat. XIII-51

268

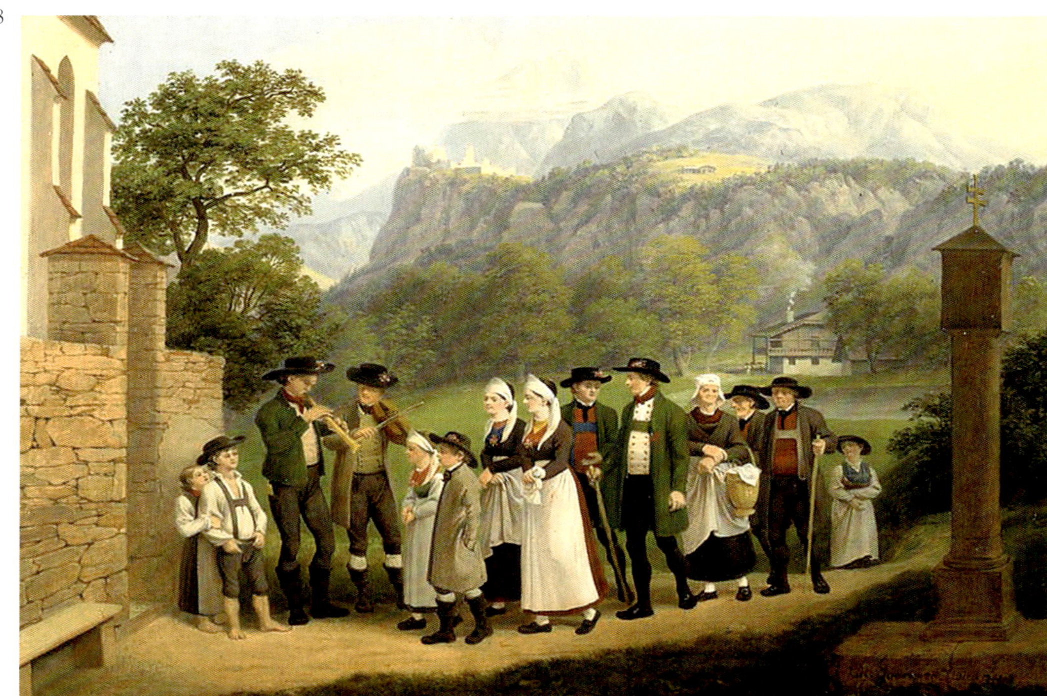

269

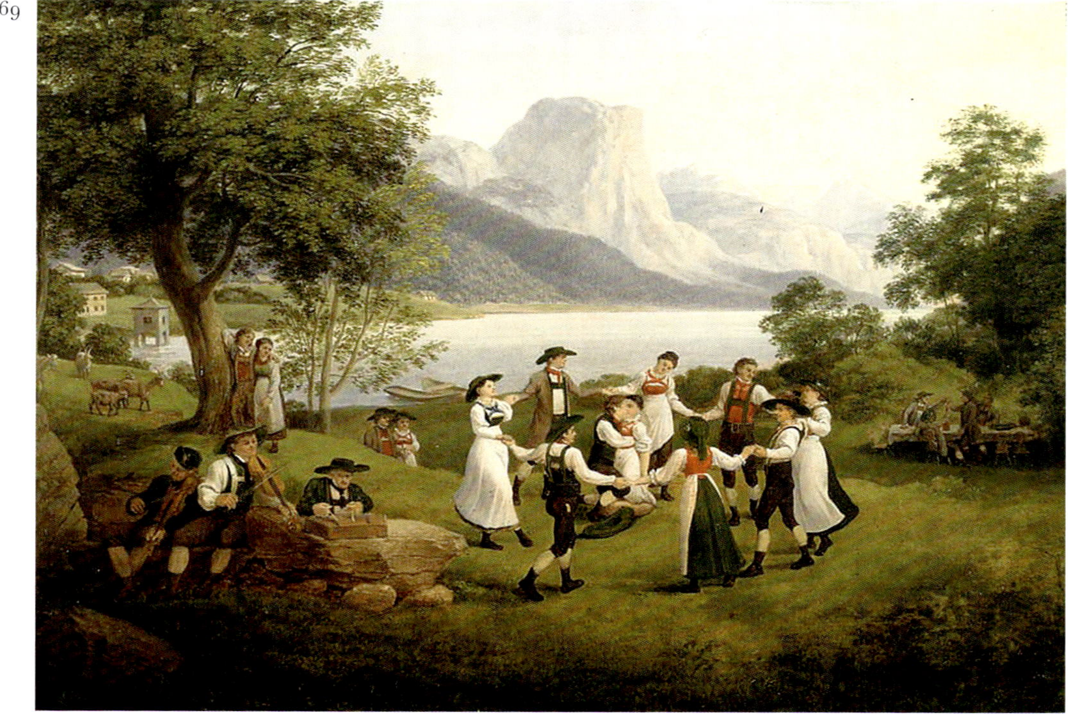

270

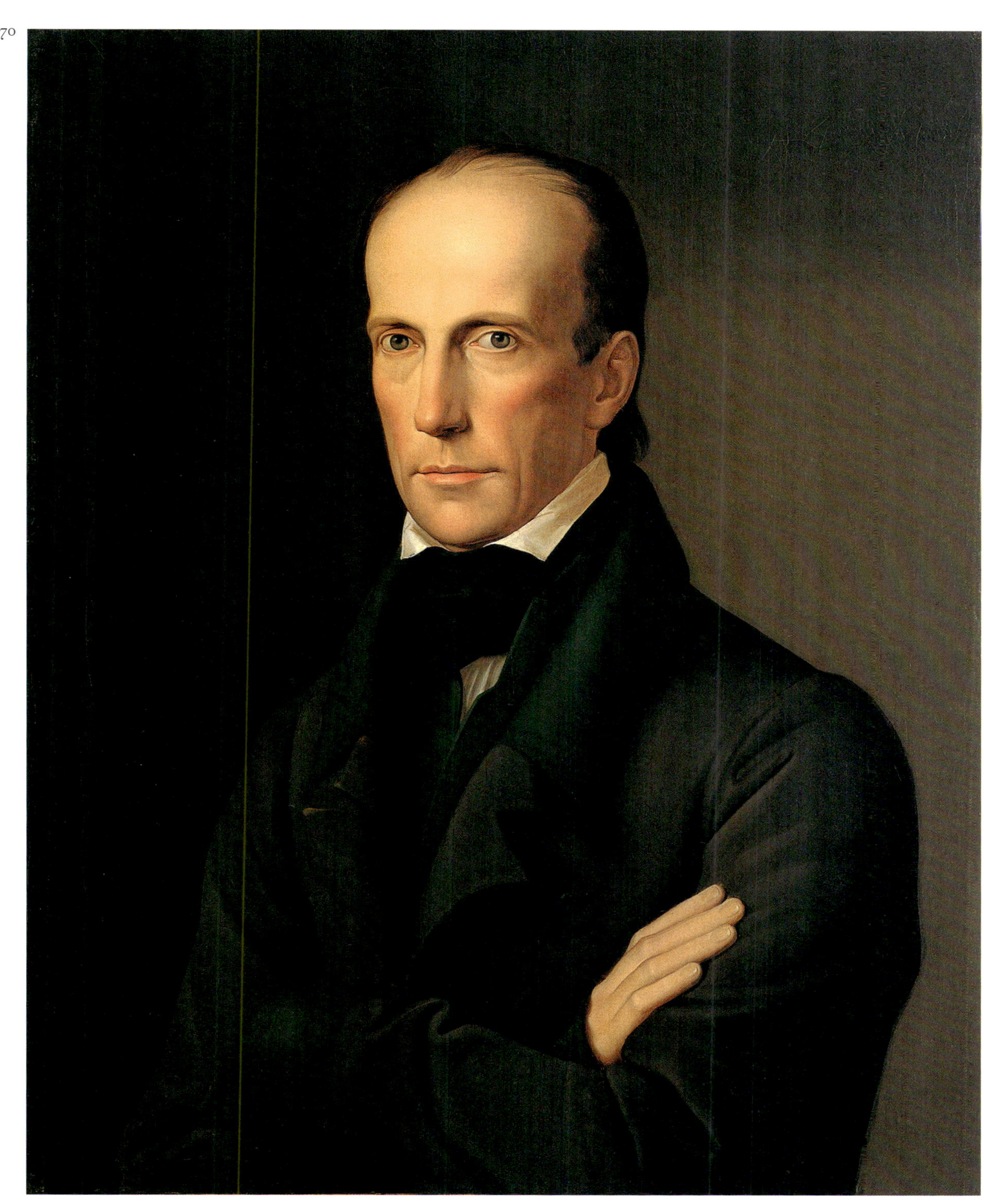

271 

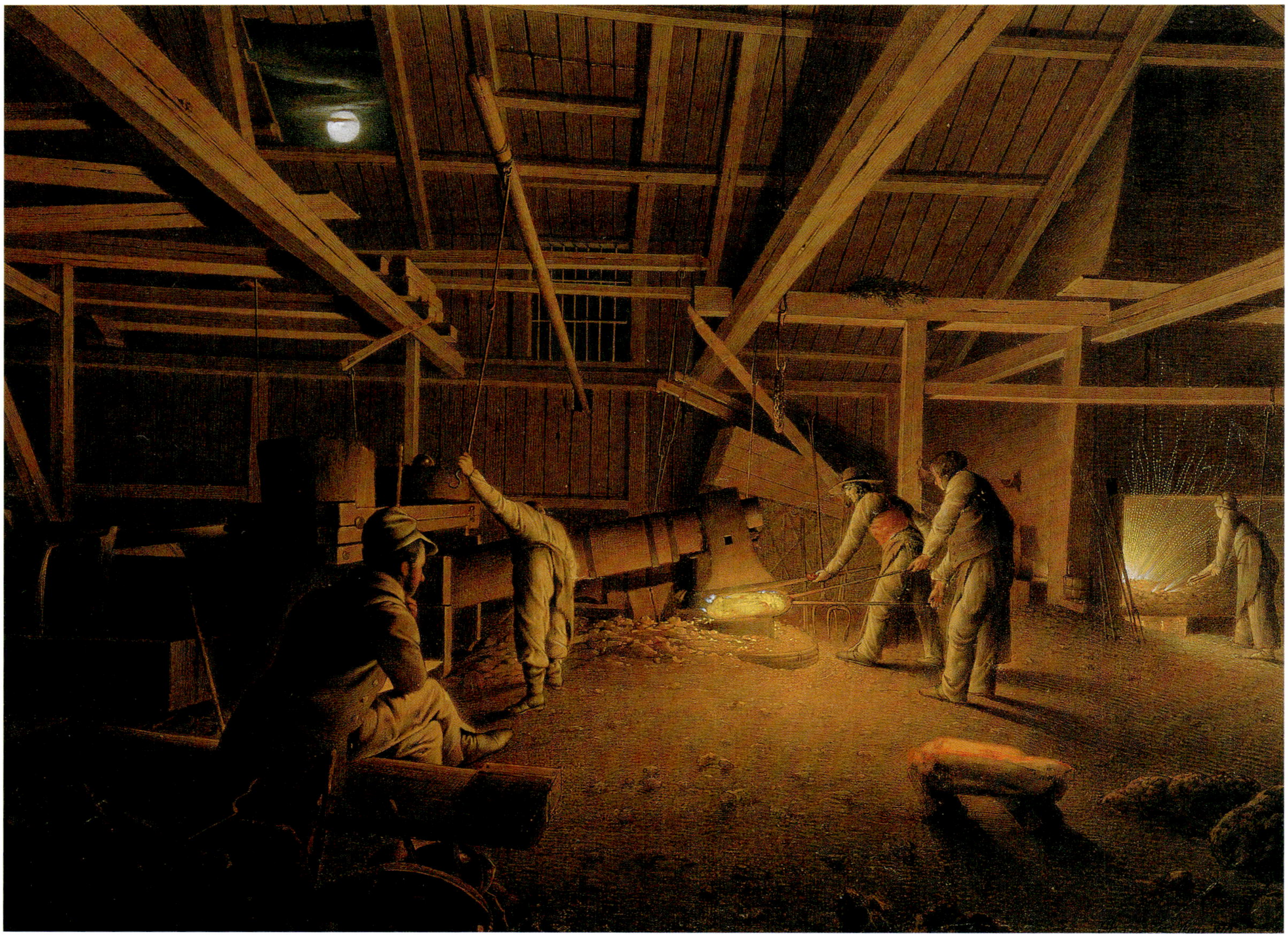

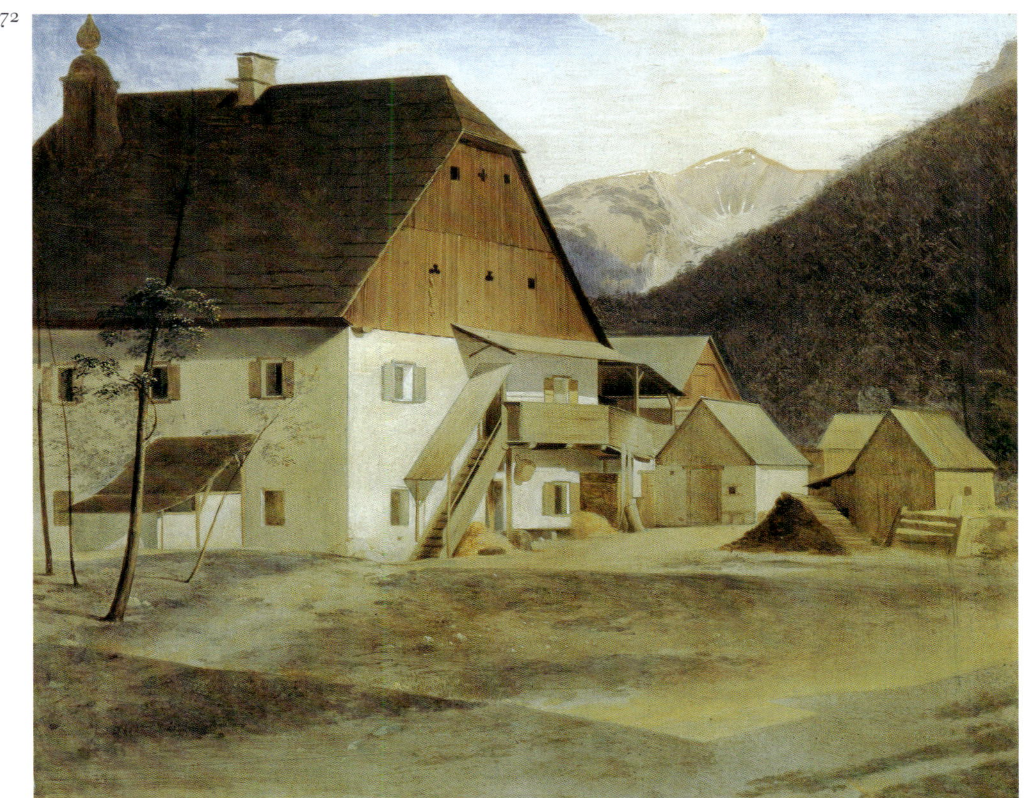

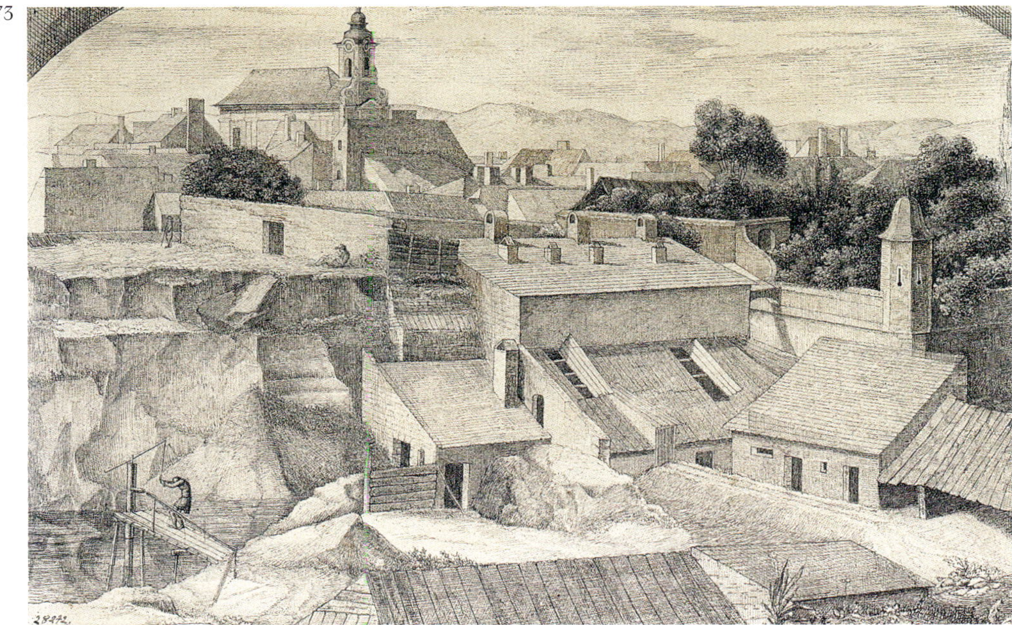

271
Carl Agricola
*Interior of a
Blacksmith's Shop*
1810
Cat. XIII-1

272
Erasmus von Engert
*The Big
Hammerhaus
in Hirschwang
an der Rax*
1825
Cat. XIII-28

273
Ferdinand Olivier
*View of the Clay Pits
in Matzleinsdorf
and the Parish Church
St. Florian*
1814/15
Cat. XIII-62

274

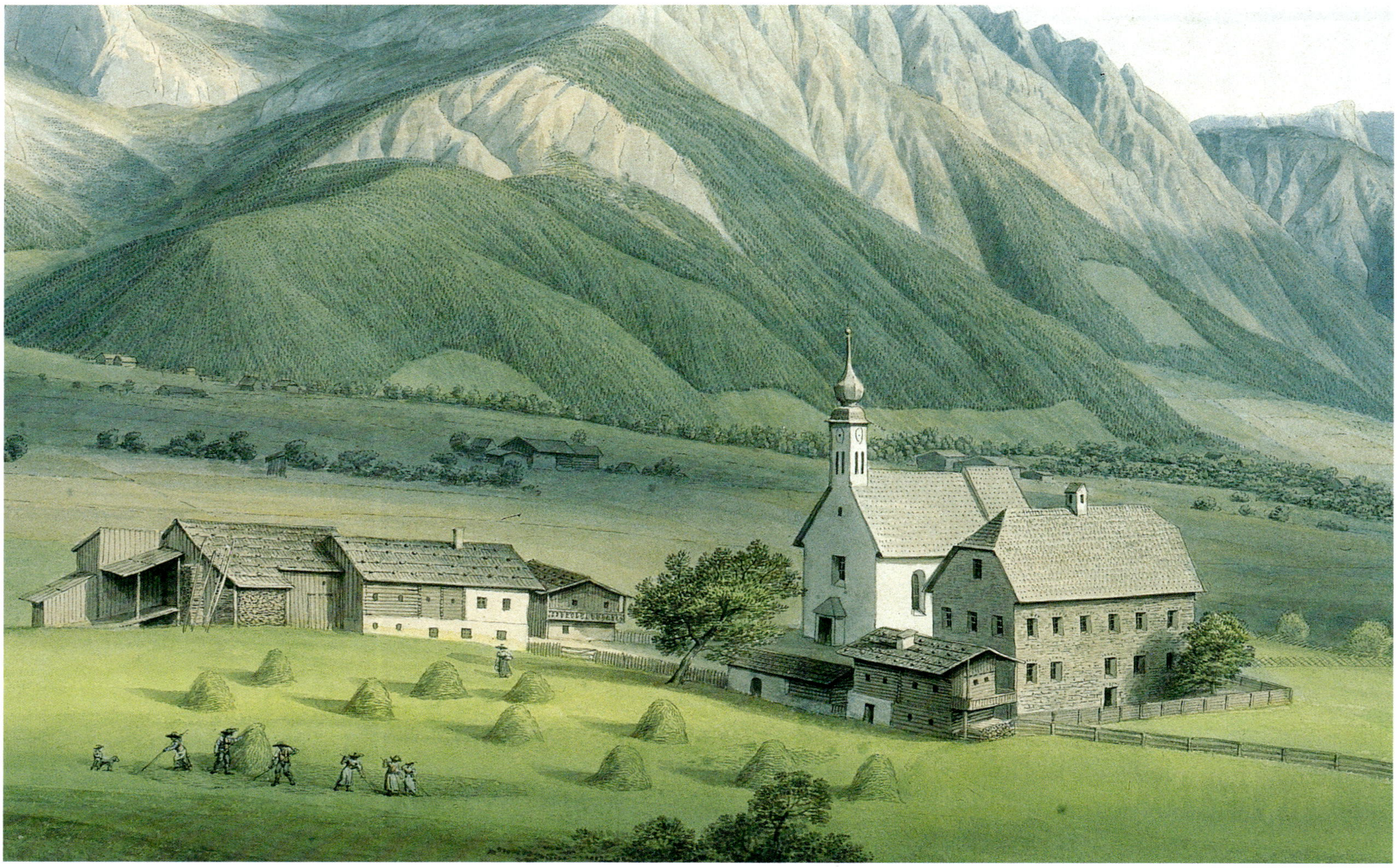

275

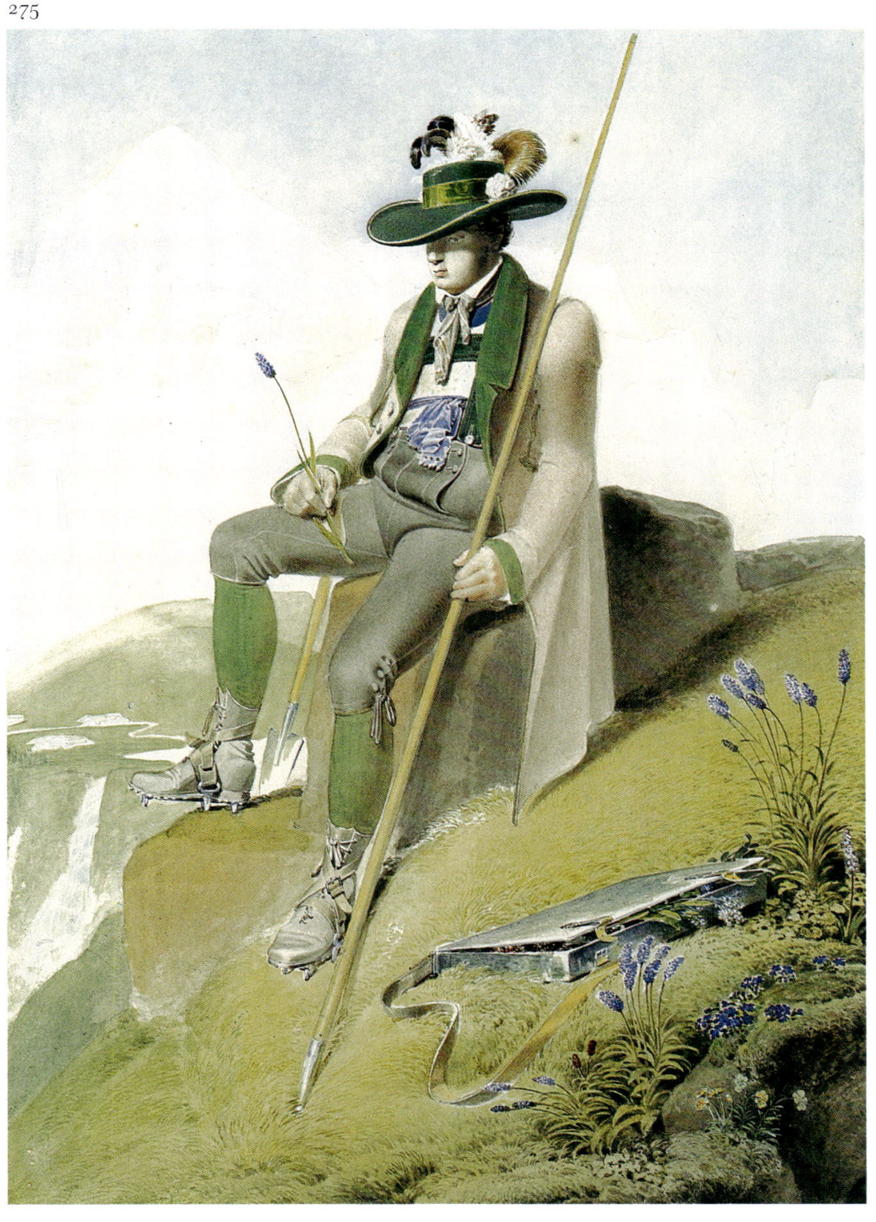

274
Jakob Gauermann
In the Ramsau
ca. 1820
Cat. XIII-38
(detail)

275
Matthäus Loder
Johann Zahlbruckner,
Botanist and Private
Secretary of Archduke
Johann of Austria
ca. 1820
Cat. XIII-53

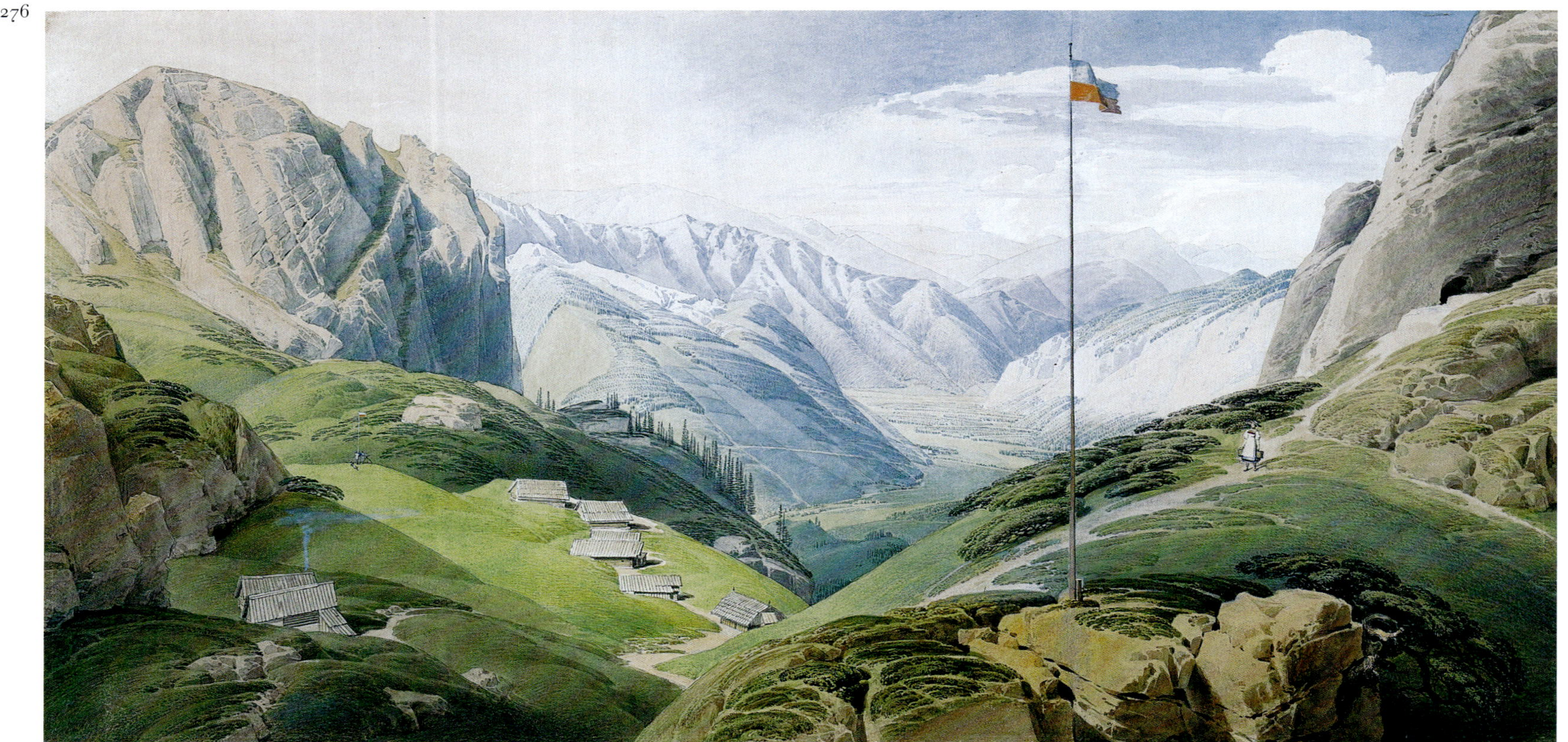

276

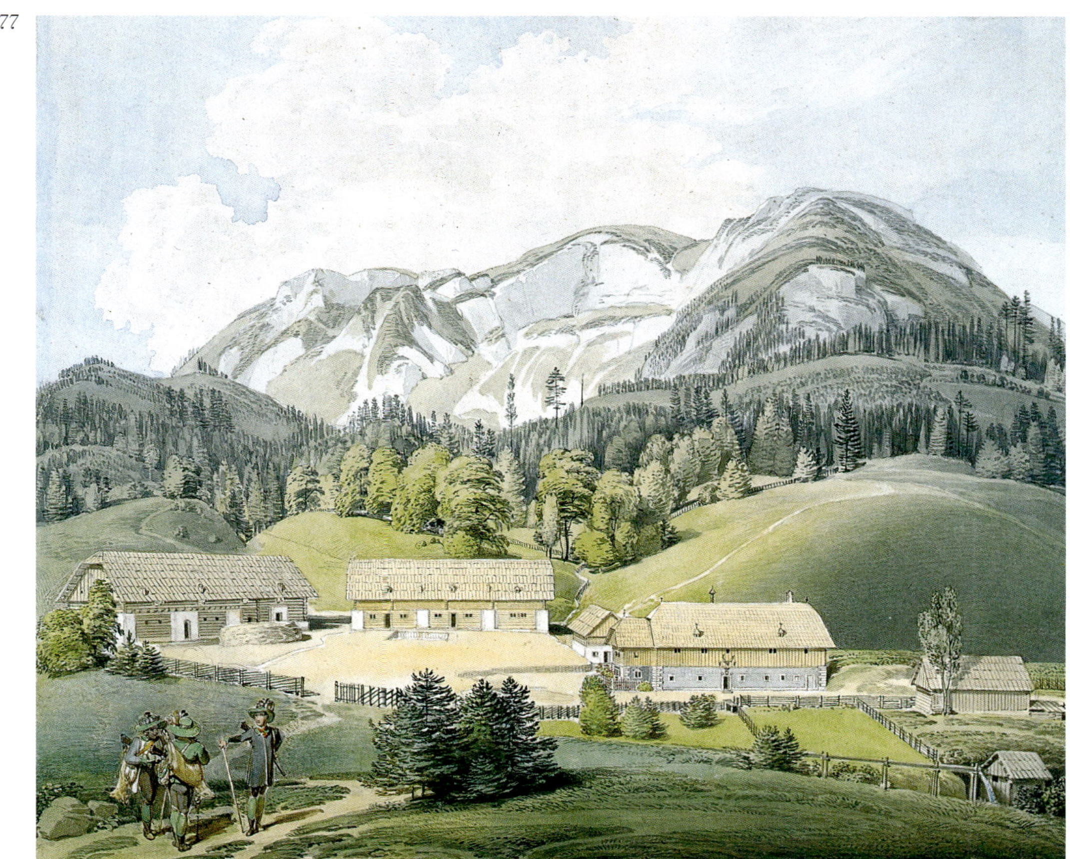

277

278

276
Matthäus Loder
*Survey on the
Sonnschienalm*
1820/21
Cat. XIII-55

277
Matthäus Loder
View of Brandhof
ca. 1824
Cat. XIII-56

278
Matthäus Loder
*Böckstein near
Wildbad Gastein*
1828
Cat. XIII-57

279 

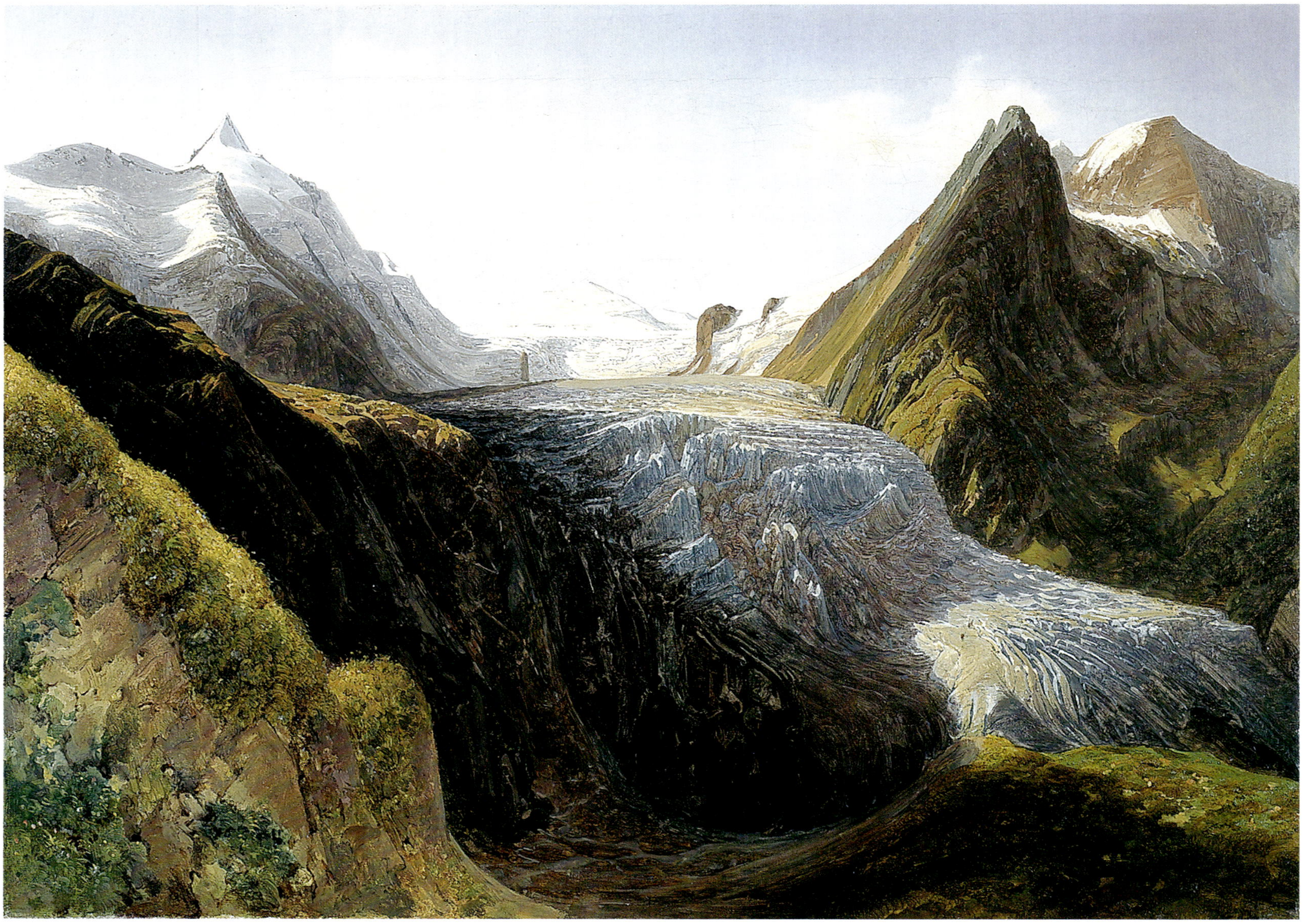

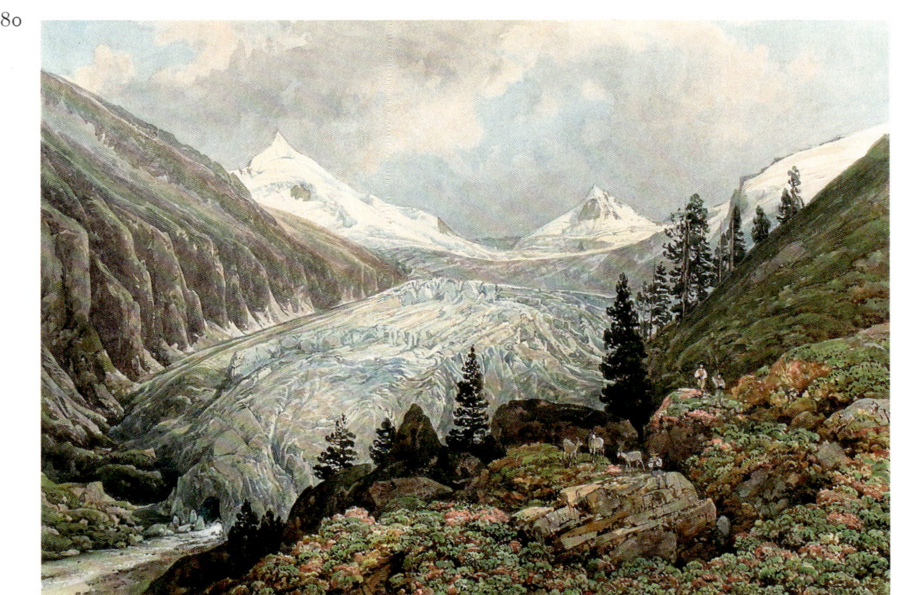

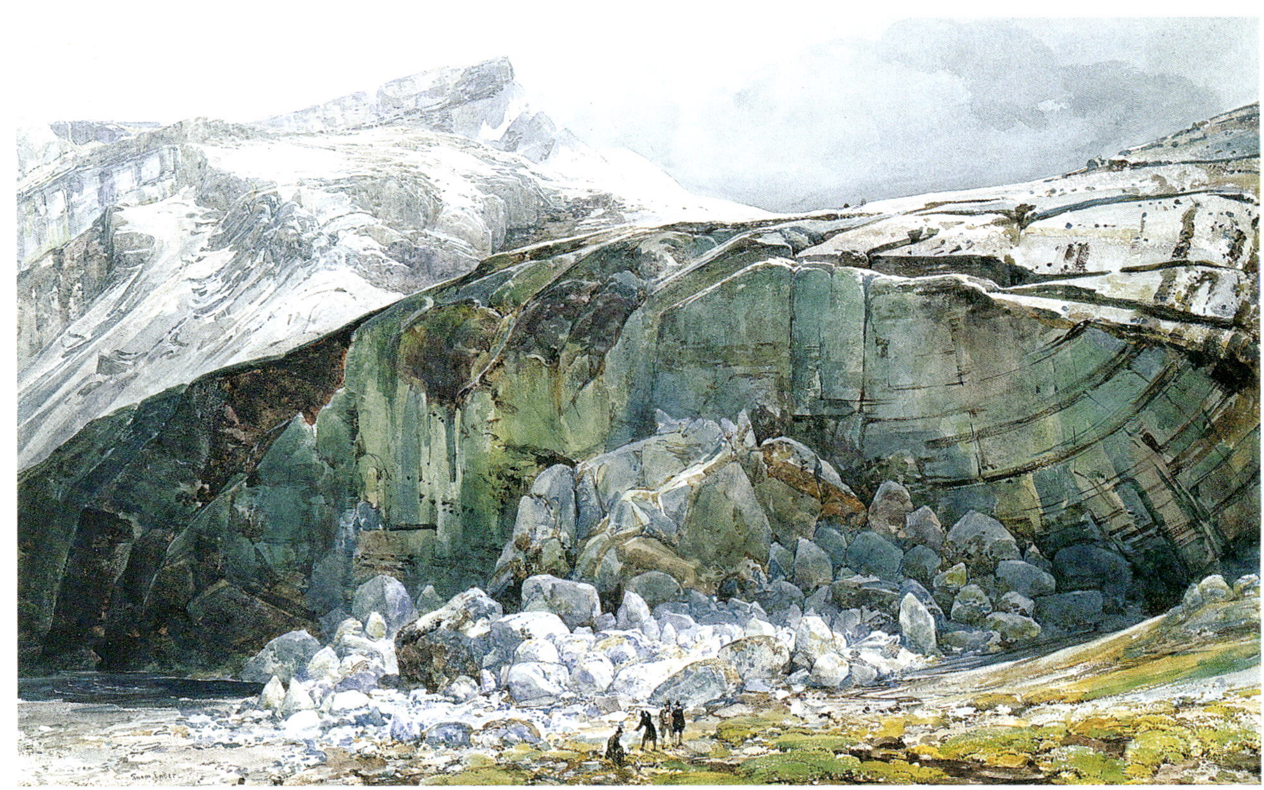

279
Thomas Ender
The Upper and Lower Pasterze with the Grossglockner and the Johannisberg near Heiligenblut
1834
Cat. XIII-24

280
Thomas Ender
Upper Sulzbachkees with Grossvenediger
ca. 1834
Cat. XIII-25

281
Thomas Ender
View of the "Ausgussgletschers" in Kaprun
1830
Cat. XIII-23

282
Jakob Alt
*The Palace of
Duke Albert von
Sachsen-Teschen*
1816
Cat. XIII-2

283
Jakob Alt
*View of Vienna
from "Spinnerin
am Kreuz"*
1817
Cat. XIII-5

282

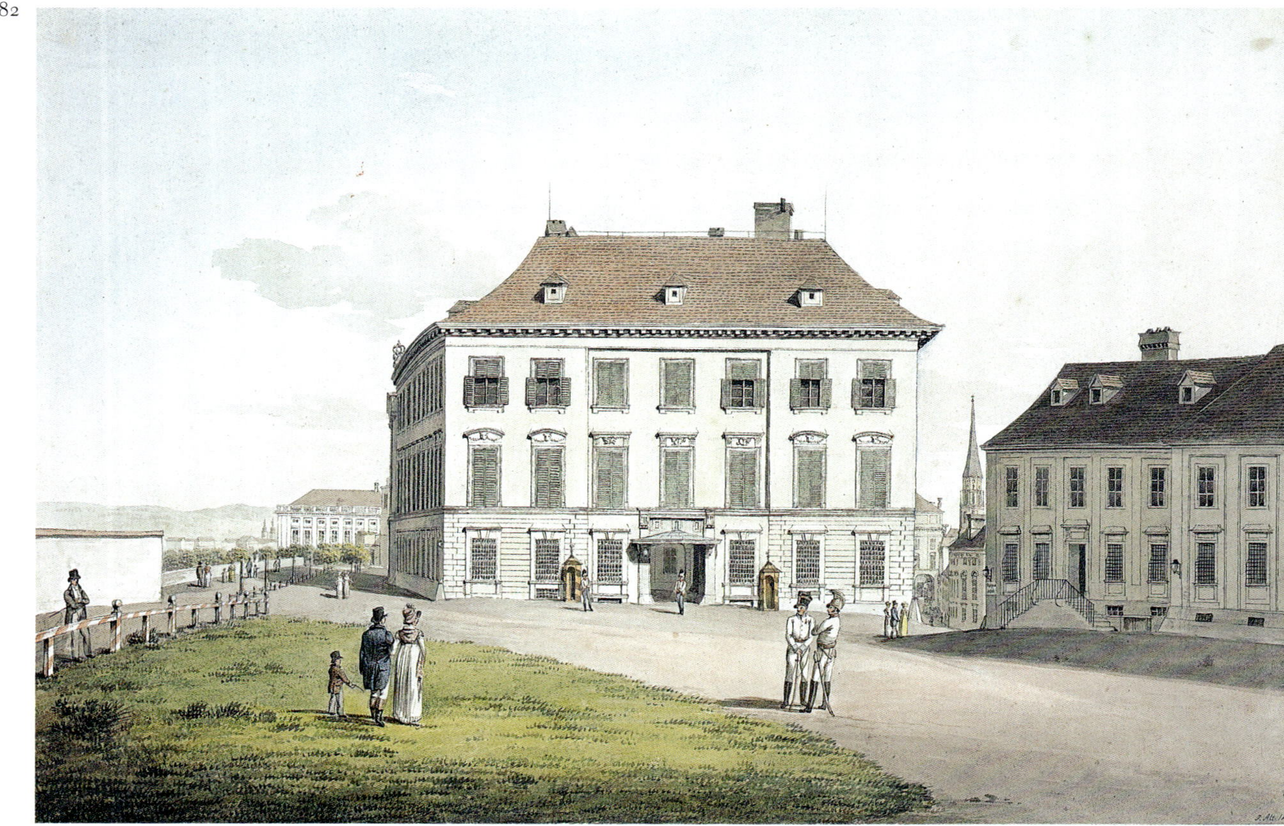

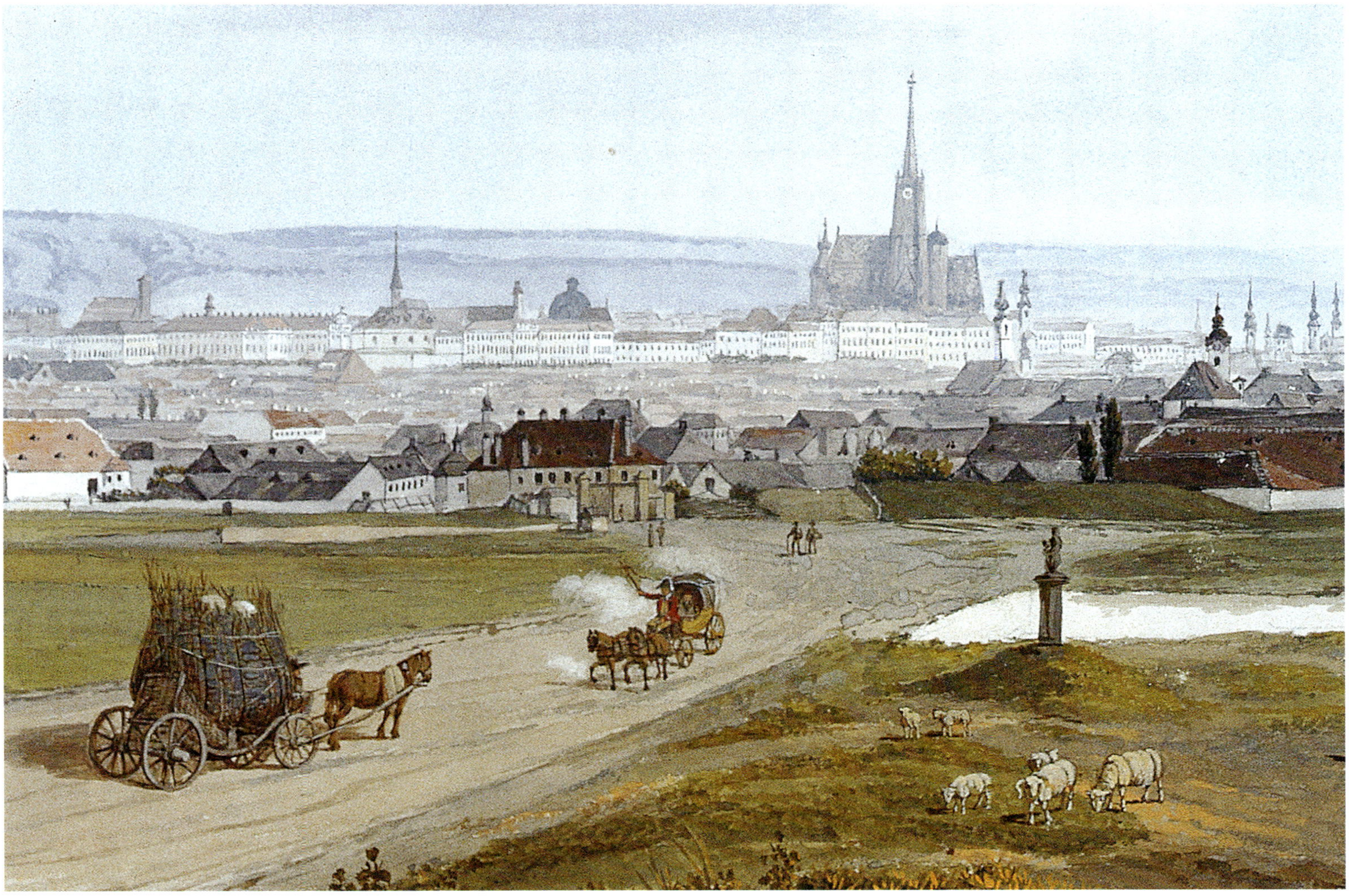

283

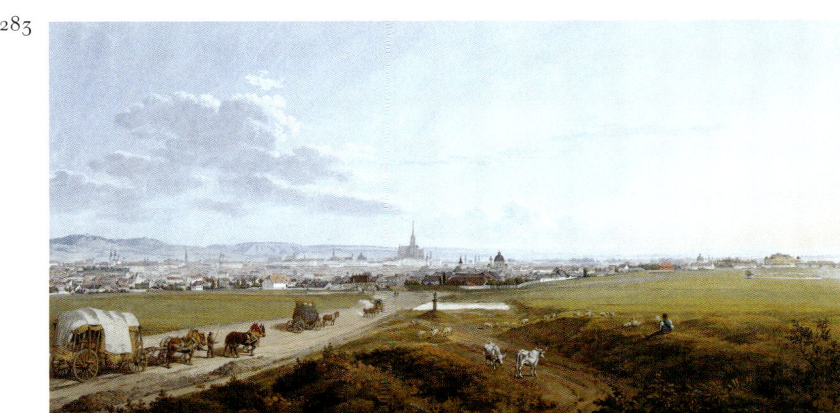

284
Nikolaus Moreau
*View from a Window
of the Diana Bath*
1830
Cat. XIII-61

285
Johann Stephan Decker
*Emperor Franz I in
His Study*
after 1821
Cat. XIII-21

286
Jakob Alt
*View from the Artist's
Studio in Alservorstadt
toward Dornbach*
1836
Cat. XIII-7

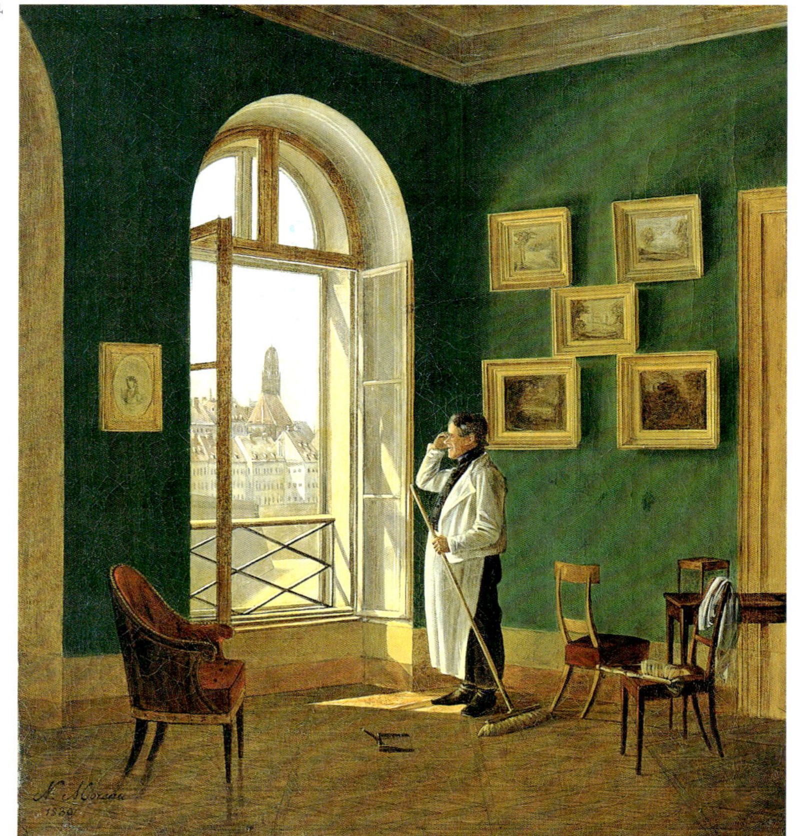

284

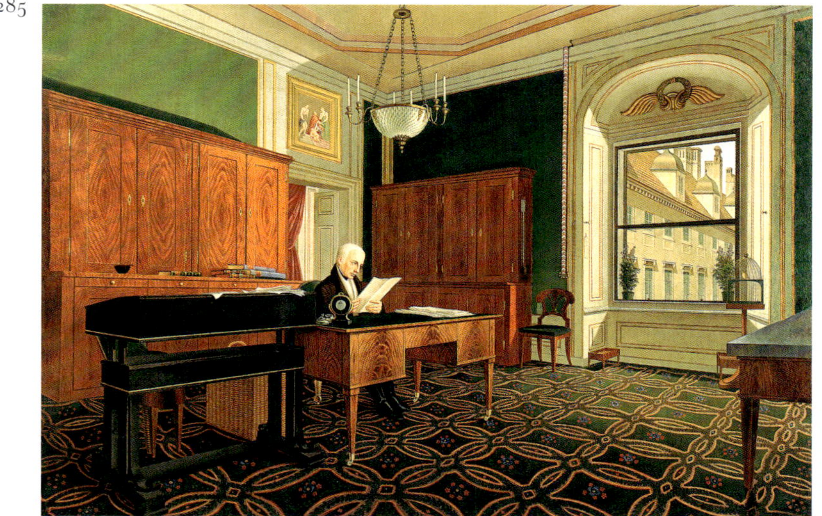

285

286

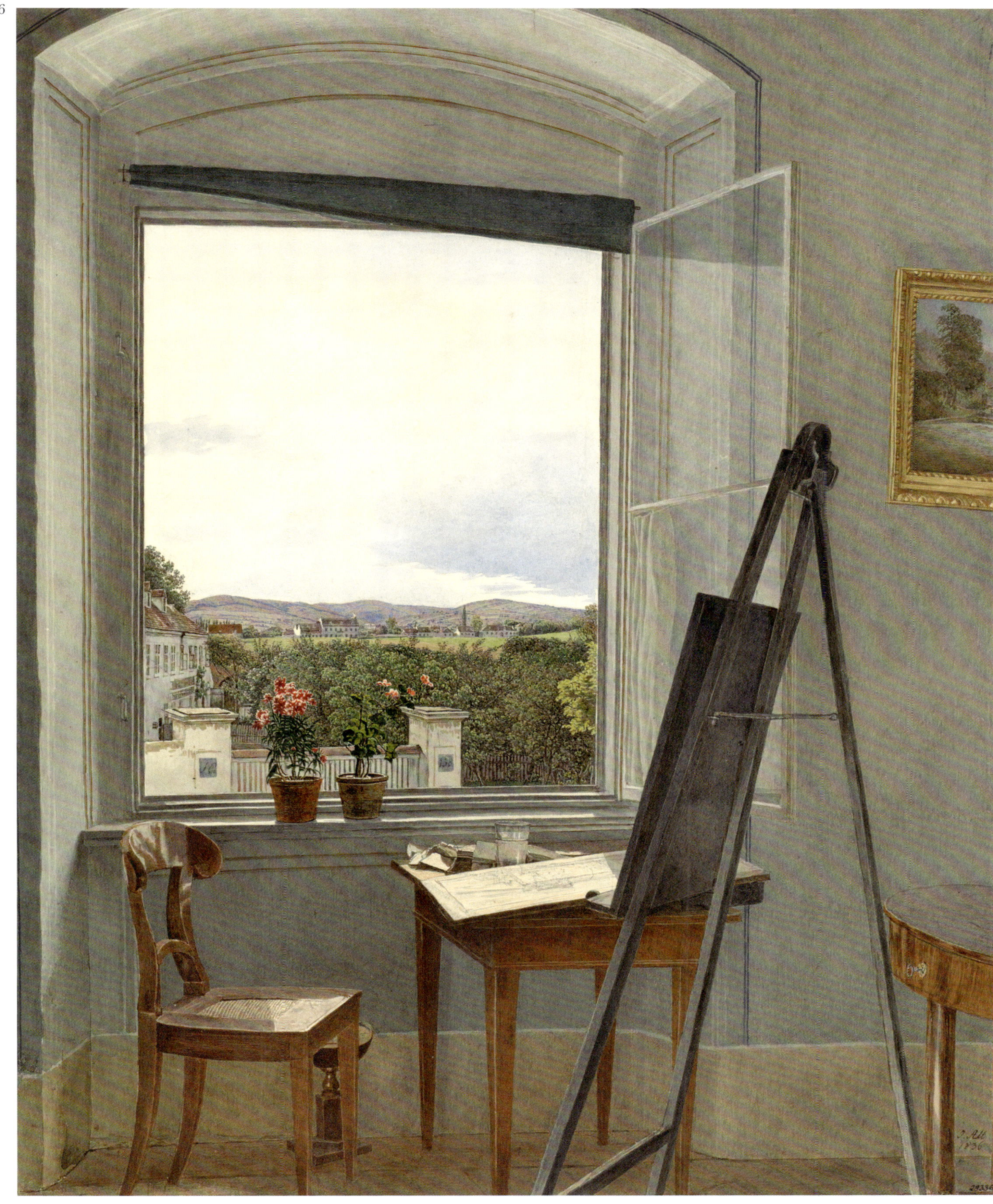

287
Thomas Ender
Gate to the Graveyard
ca. 1820
Cat. XIII-22

288
Friedrich Loos
*Motif from
Oberschützen*
1838
Cat. XIII-60

289
Erasmus von Engert
Girl in an Arbor
ca. 1828
Cat. XIII-29

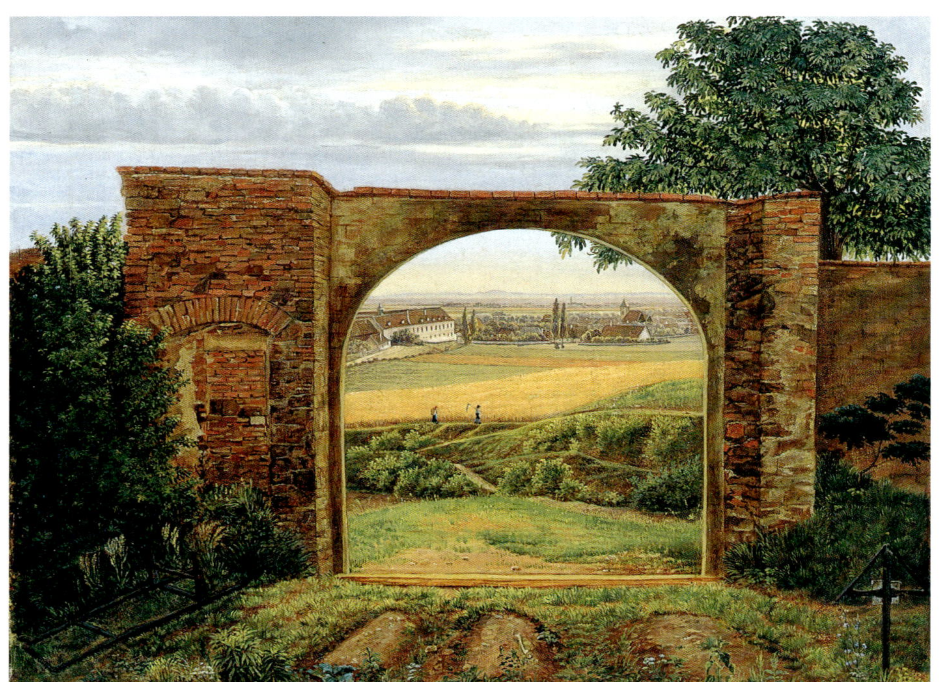

287

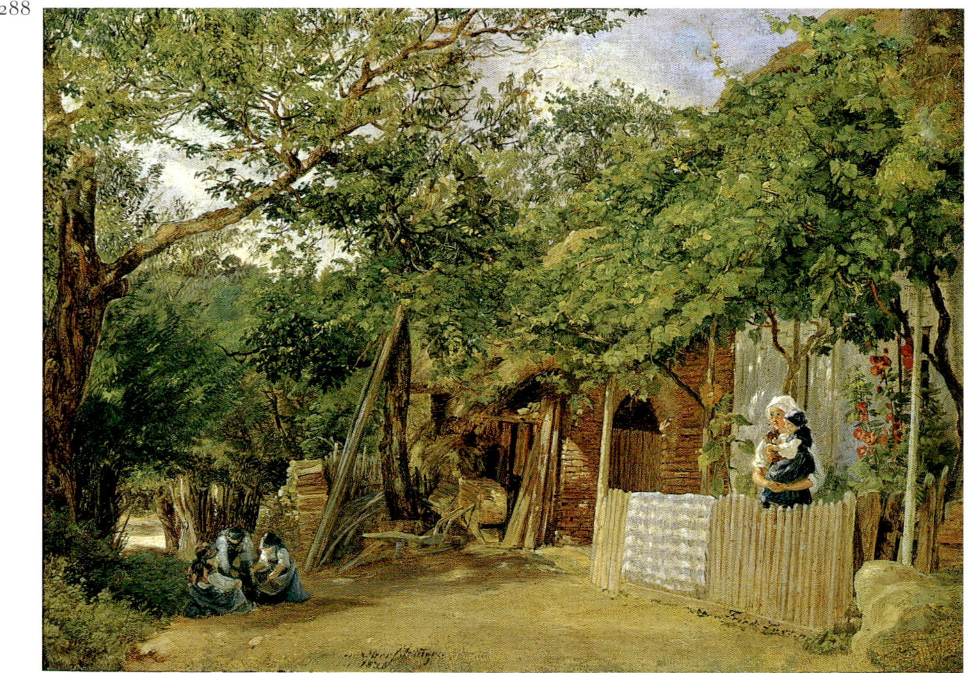

288

289

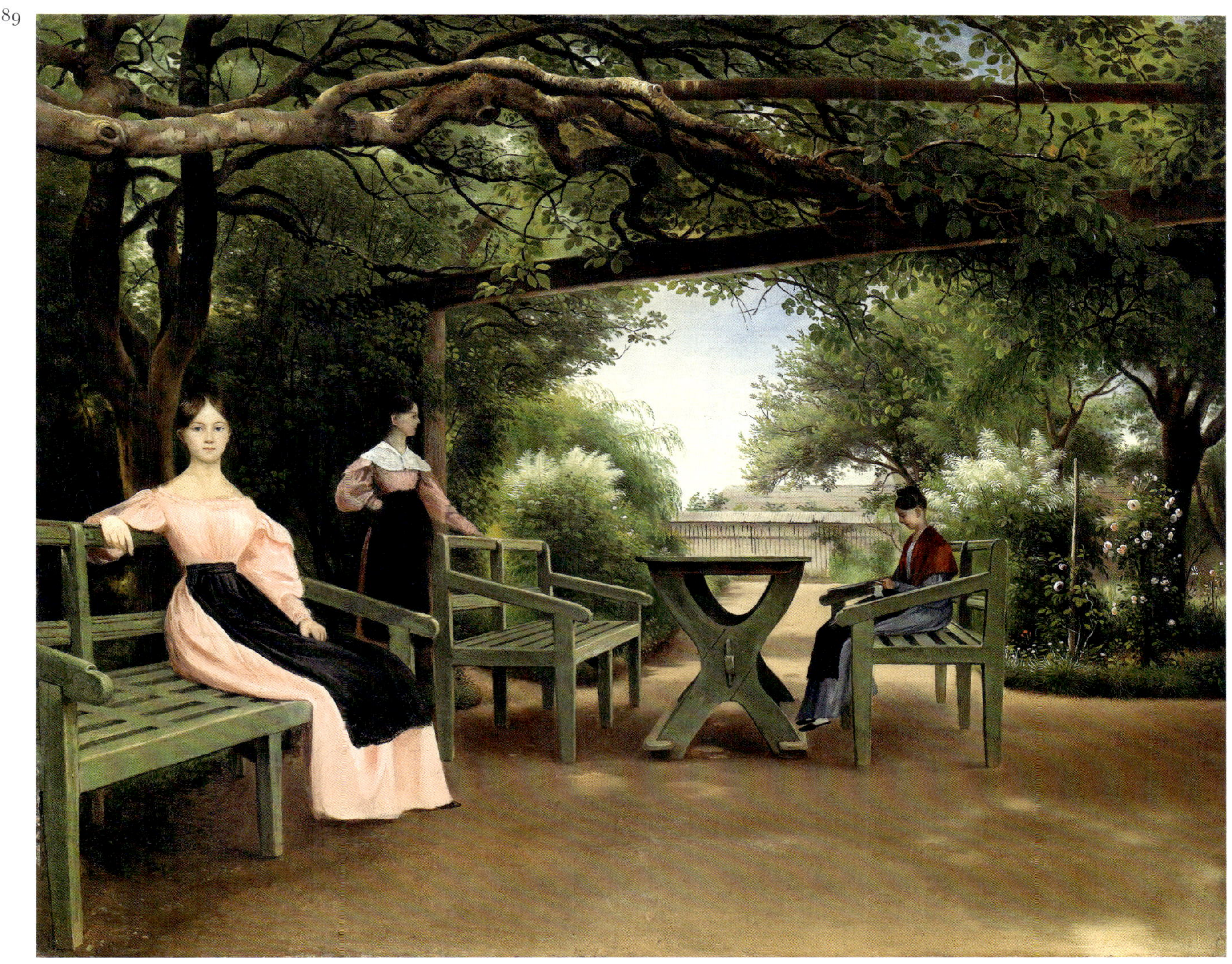

290
Eduard Gurk
*The Imperial Palace
with the Ferdinand
Fountain in Baden
near Vienna*
1833
Cat. XIII-42

291
Eduard Gurk
*On the Hradschin
in Prague*
1838
Cat. XIII-48

292
Eduard Gurk
*The Basilica of
Mariazell Seen from
the Churchyard*
1833
Cat. XIII-41

290

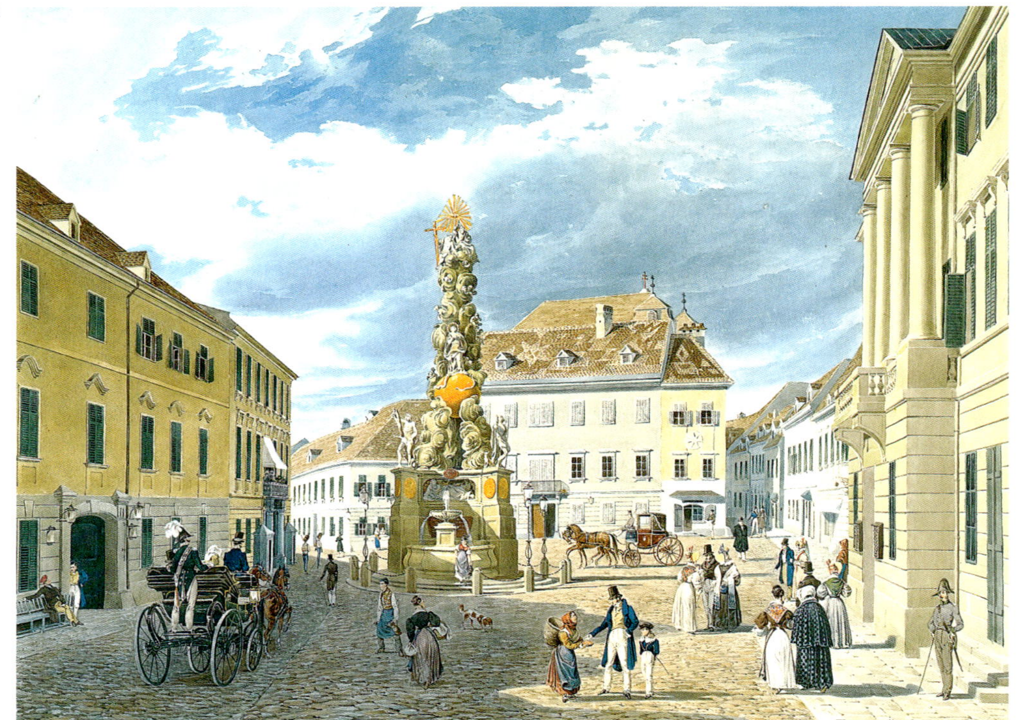

291

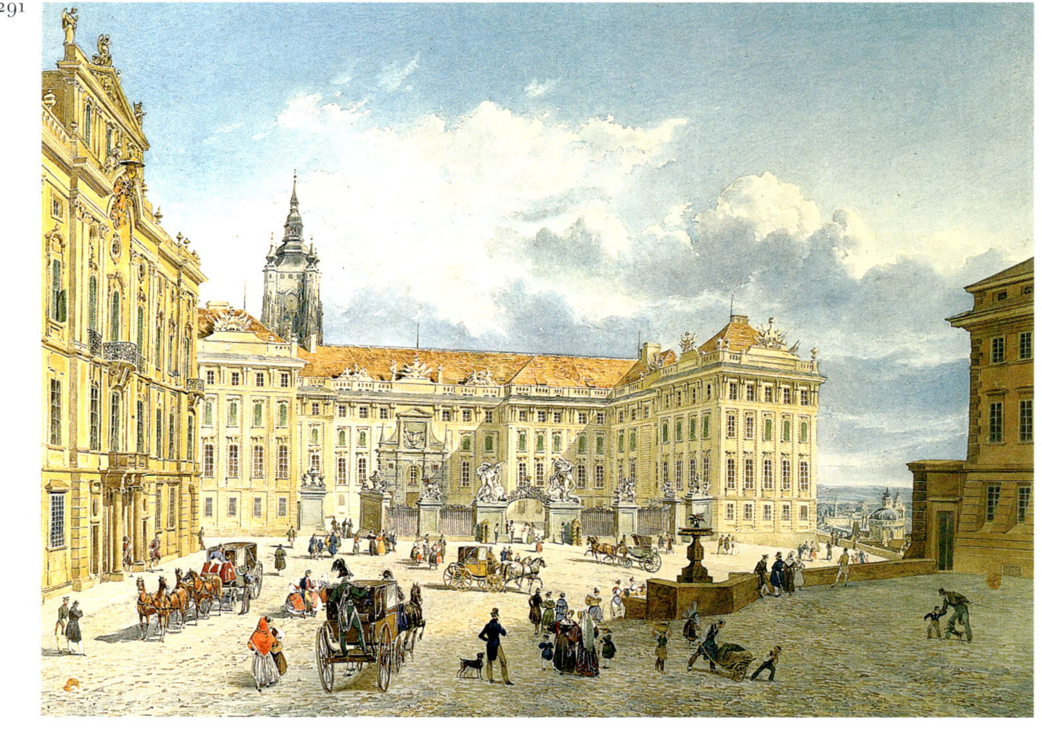

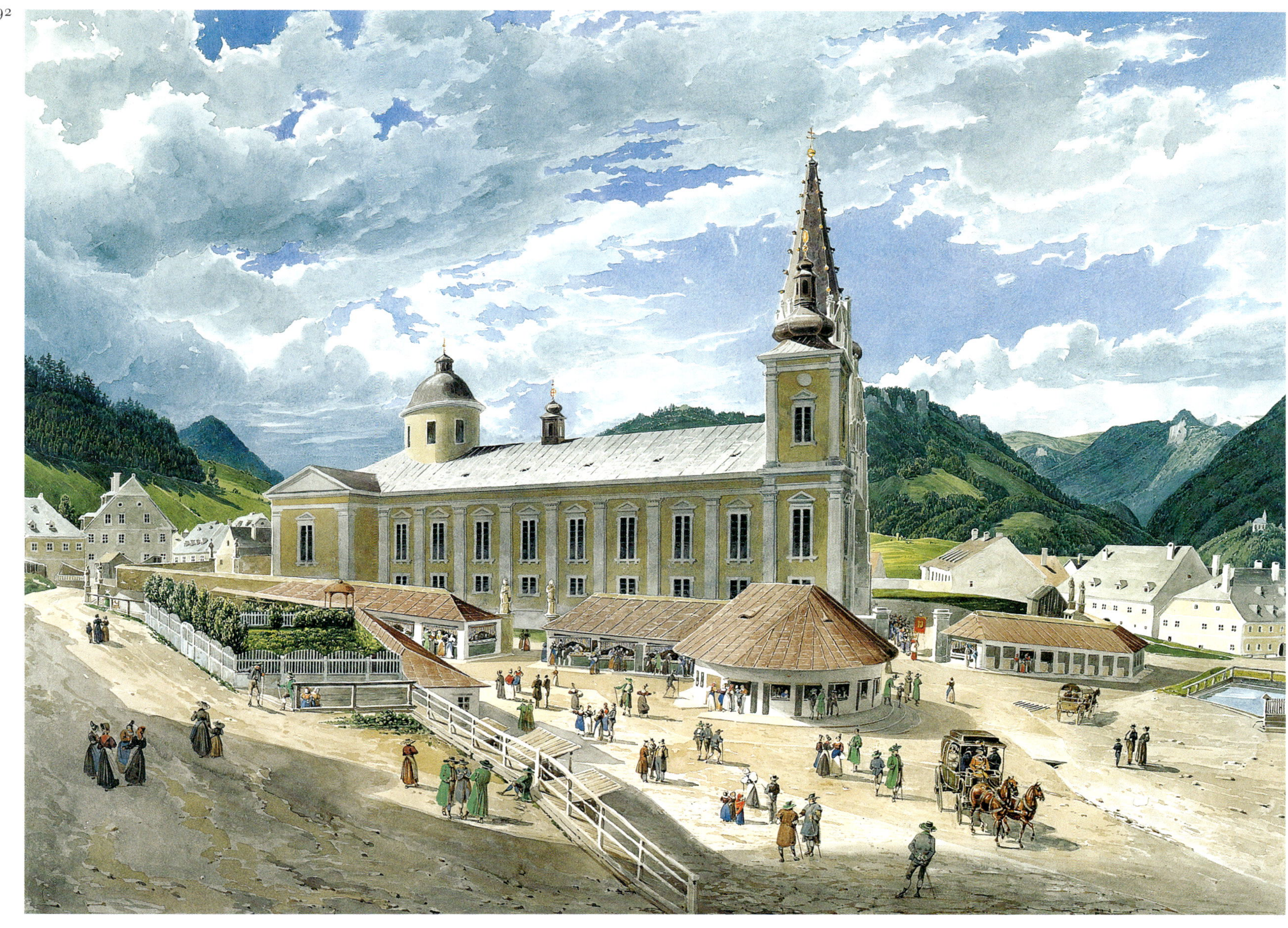

292

293 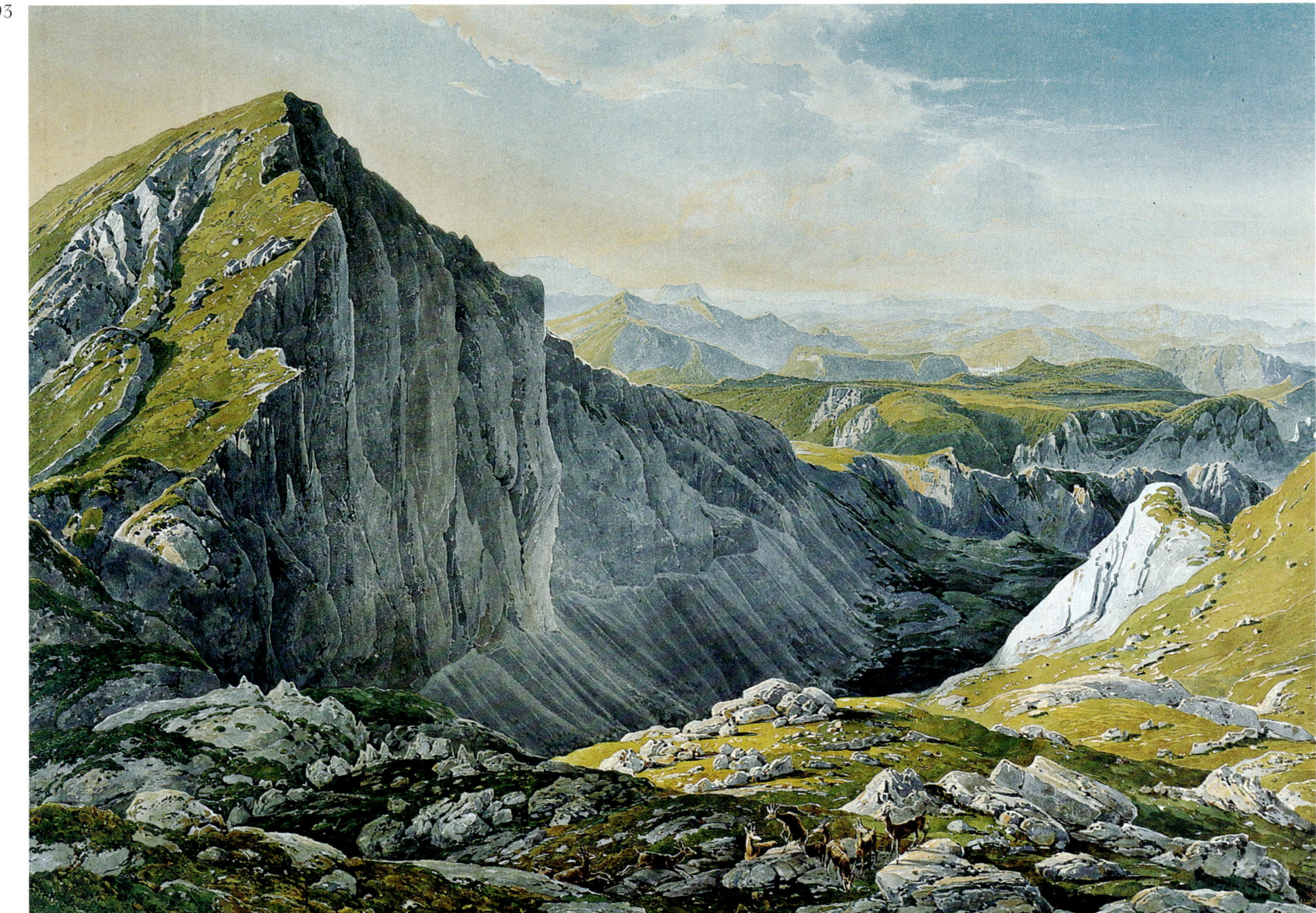

294 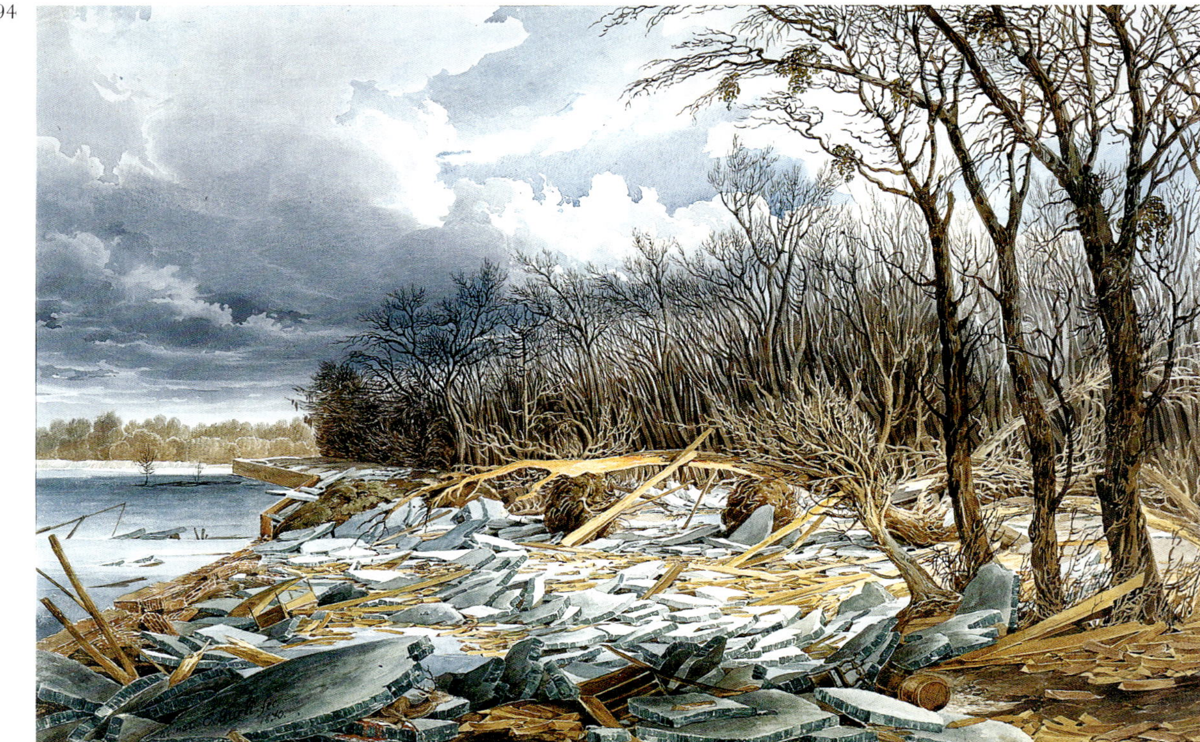

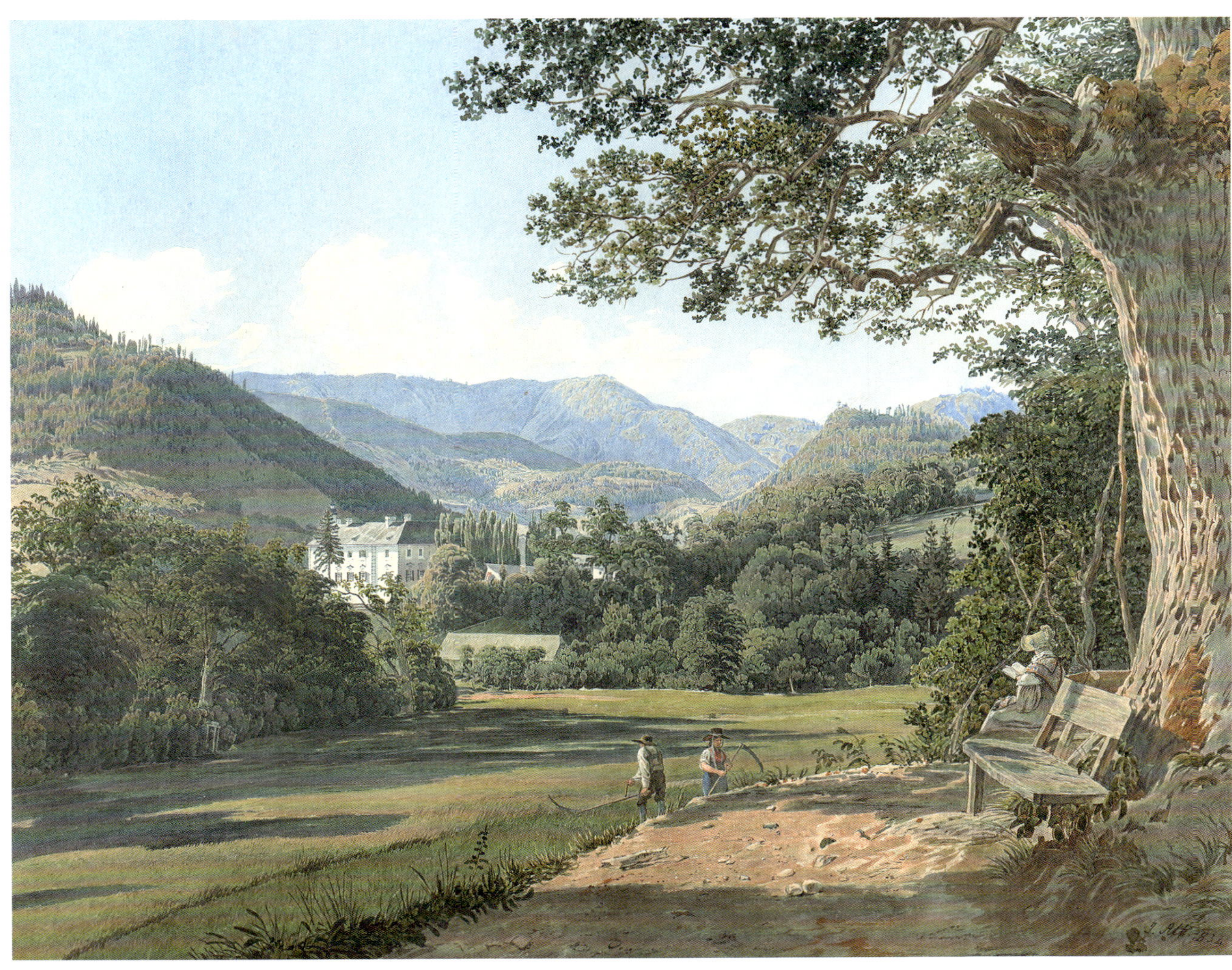

295

293
Eduard Gurk
*Distant View from
Grosser Höllstein
toward Mariazell*
1835
Cat. XIII-44

294
Eduard Gurk
*On the Embankment
next to the Augarten
on March 3, 1830*
1830
Cat. XIII-39

295
Jakob Alt
*View to Stiebar
Castle near Gresten
in Lower Austria*
1834
Cat. XIII-6

296
Friedrich Gauermann
*The Dachstein from
Plassen near Hallstatt*
ca. 1827
Cat. XIII-33

297
Friedrich Gauermann
*View from
Scheuchenstein
toward Gauermannhof
with Schneeberg
in the Background*
ca. 1835
Cat. XIII-35

298
Friedrich Loos
*The Ramsau near
Berchtesgaden*
1836
Cat. XIII-59

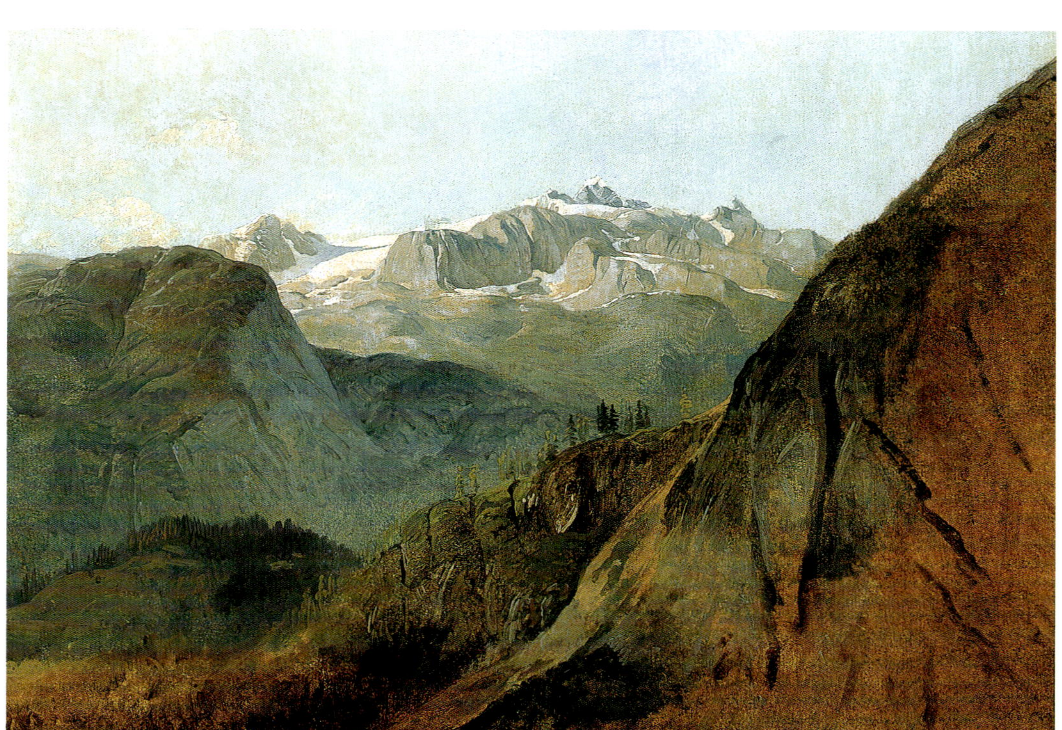

296

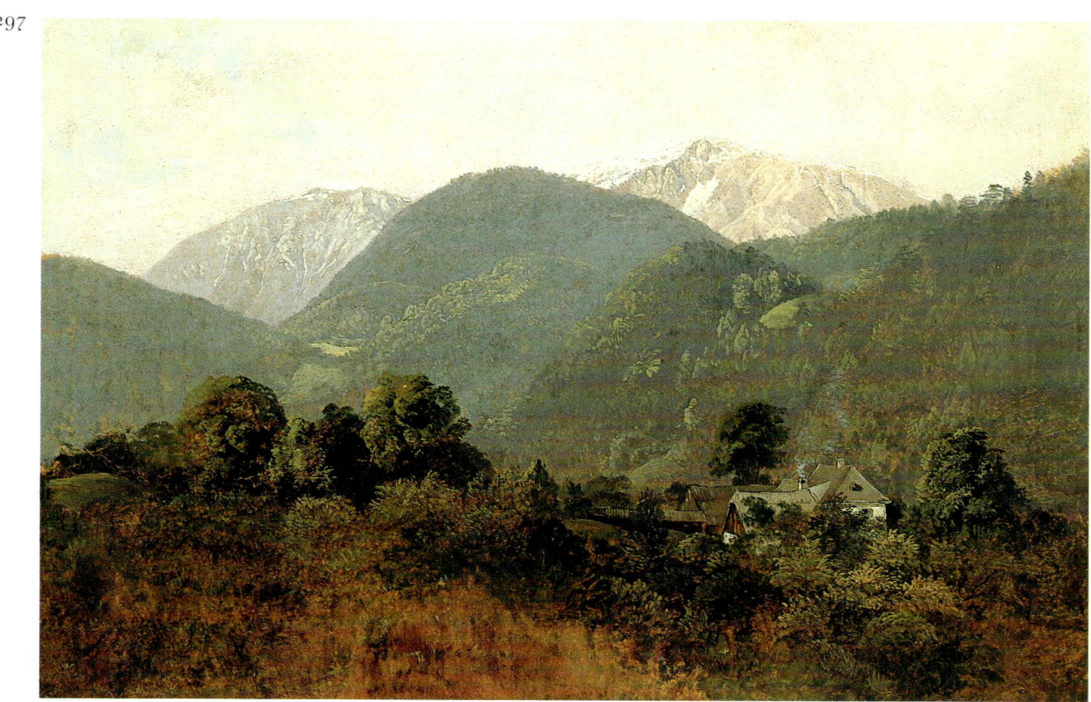

297

298

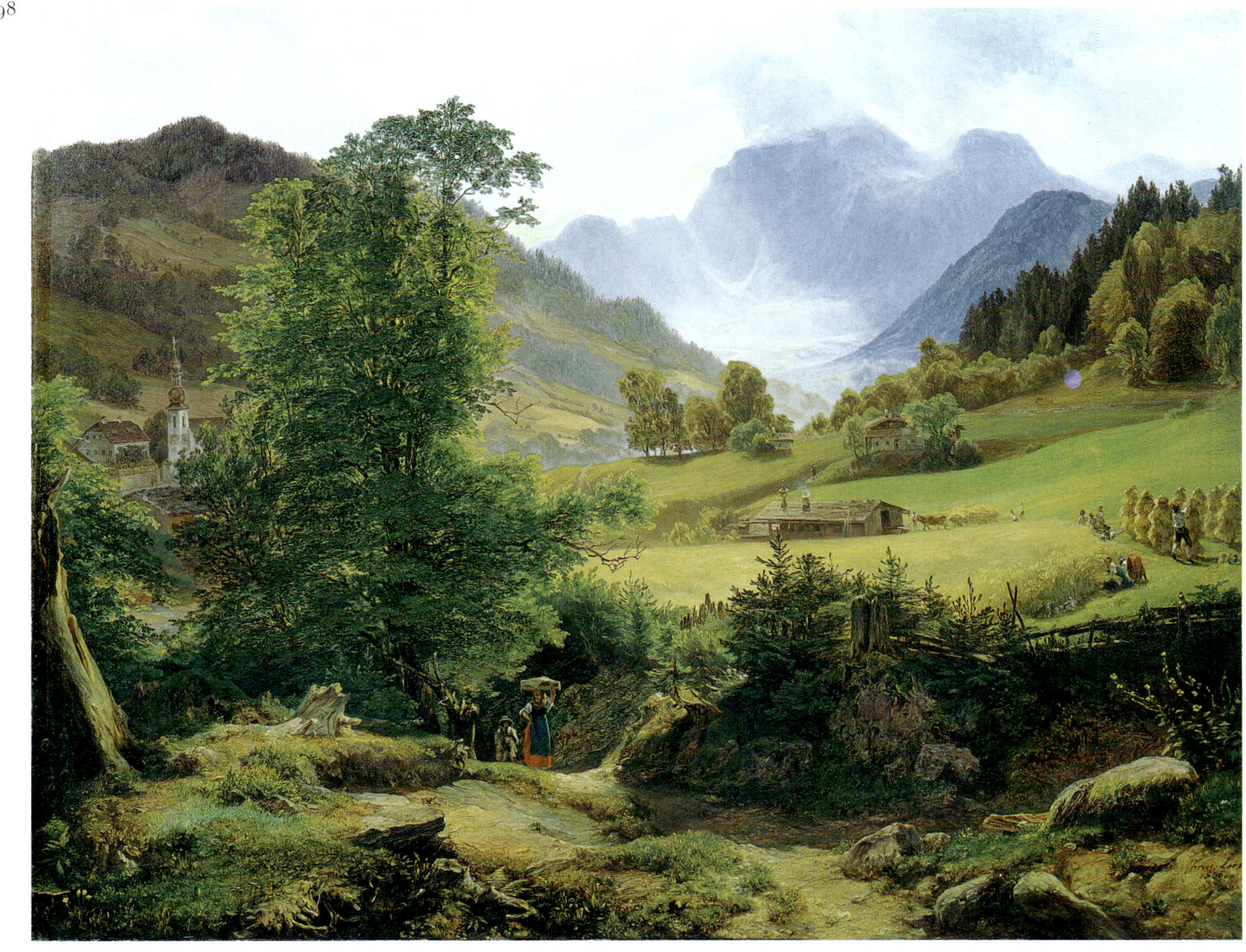

299
Franz Steinfeld
*The Hallstättersee
in Upper Austria*
1824
Cat. XIII-71

300
Ferdinand Georg
Waldmüller
View of Hallstatt
1839
Cat. XIII-94

301
Franz Steinfeld
The Hallstättersee
before 1834
Cat. XIII-74

299

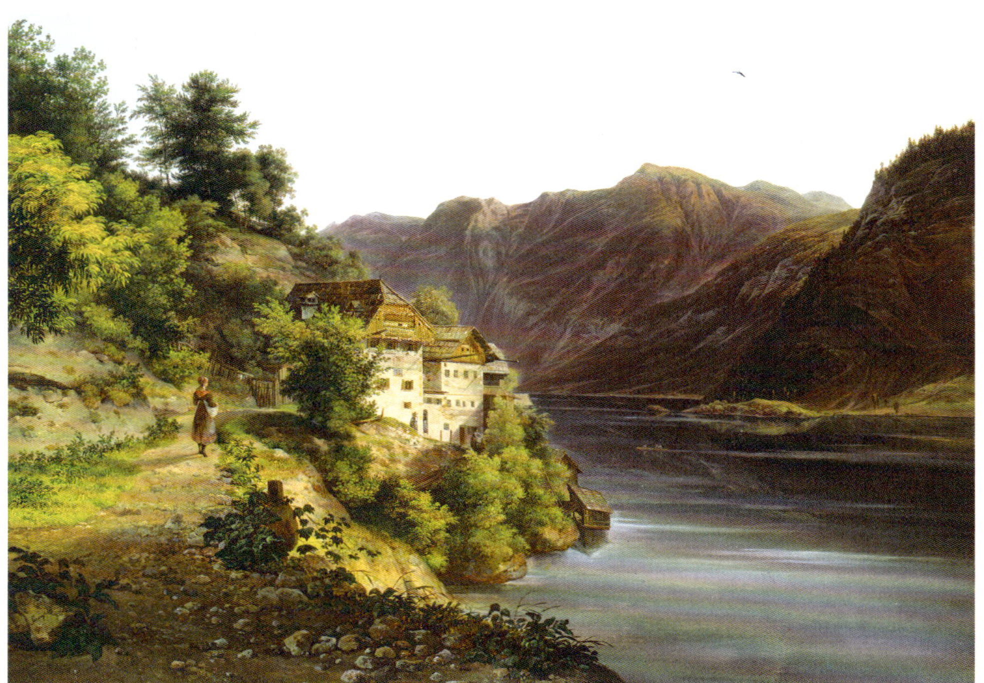

300

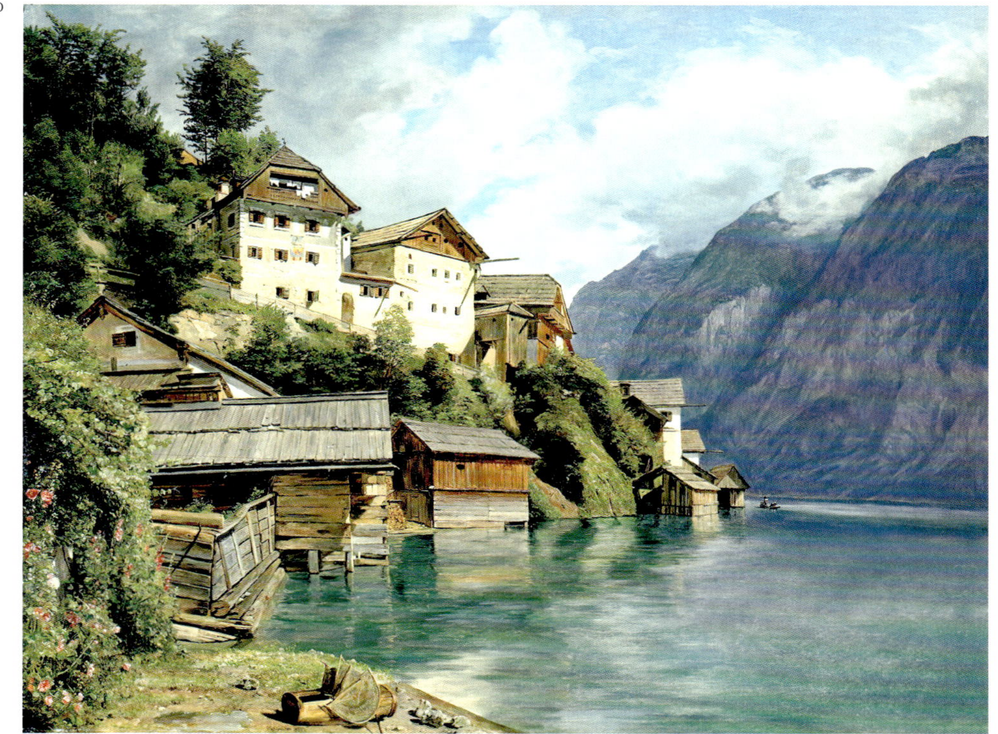

301

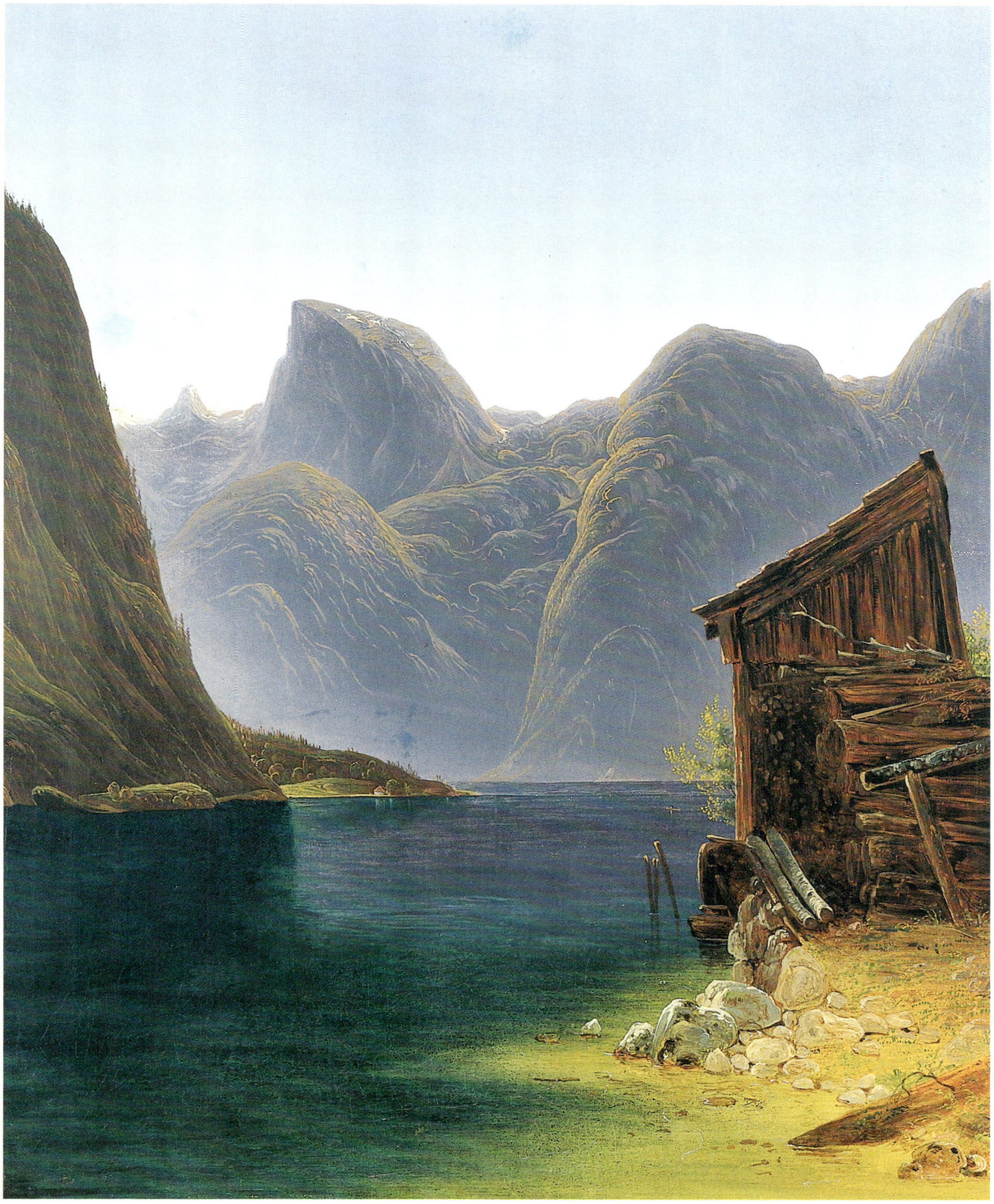

302
Ferdinand Georg
Waldmüller
*The Dachstein
with the Gosausee*
1834
Cat. XIII-88

303
Ferdinand Georg
Waldmüller
*The Dachstein from
Sophien-Doppelblick
near Ischl*
1835
Cat. XIII-90

302

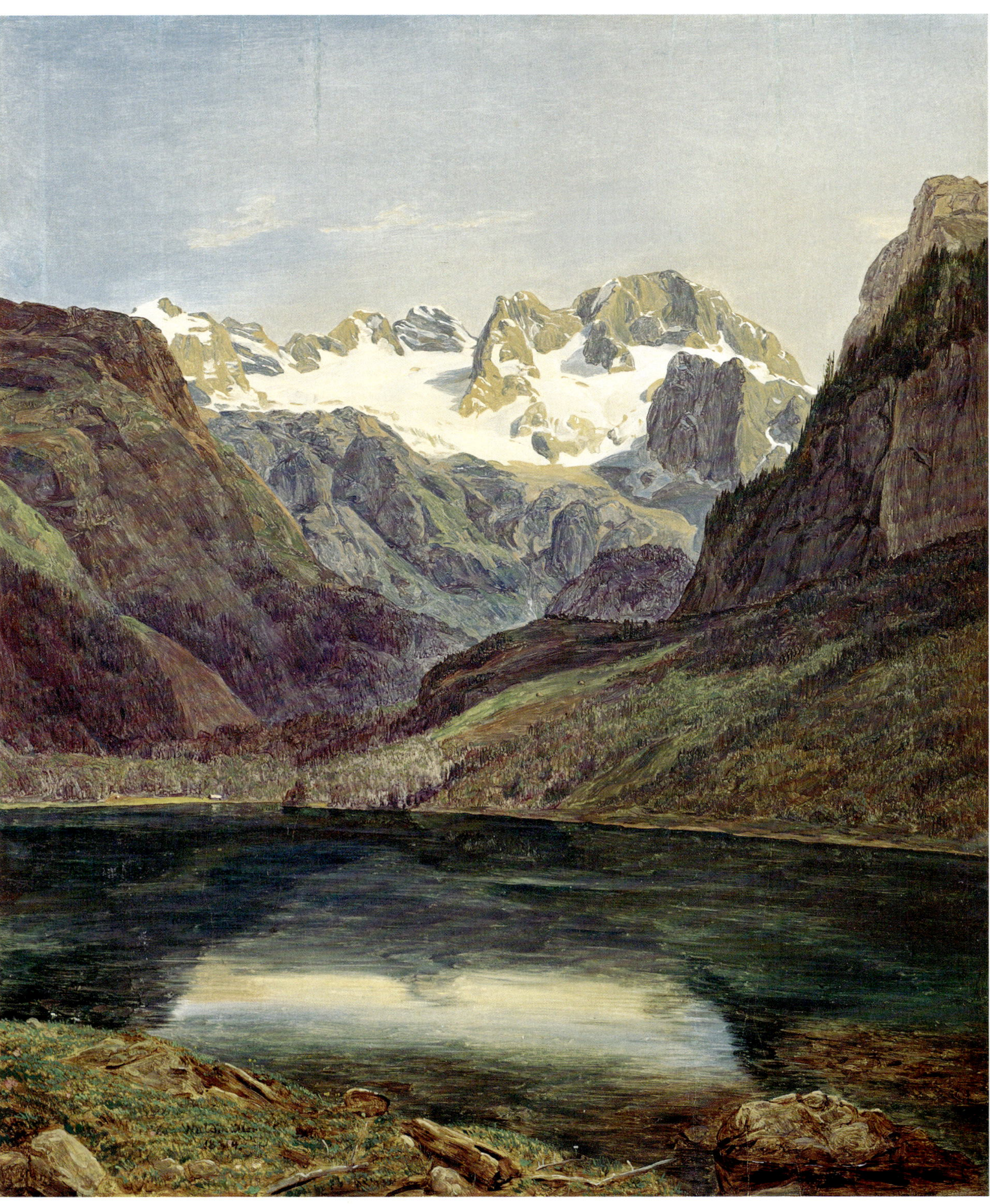

303

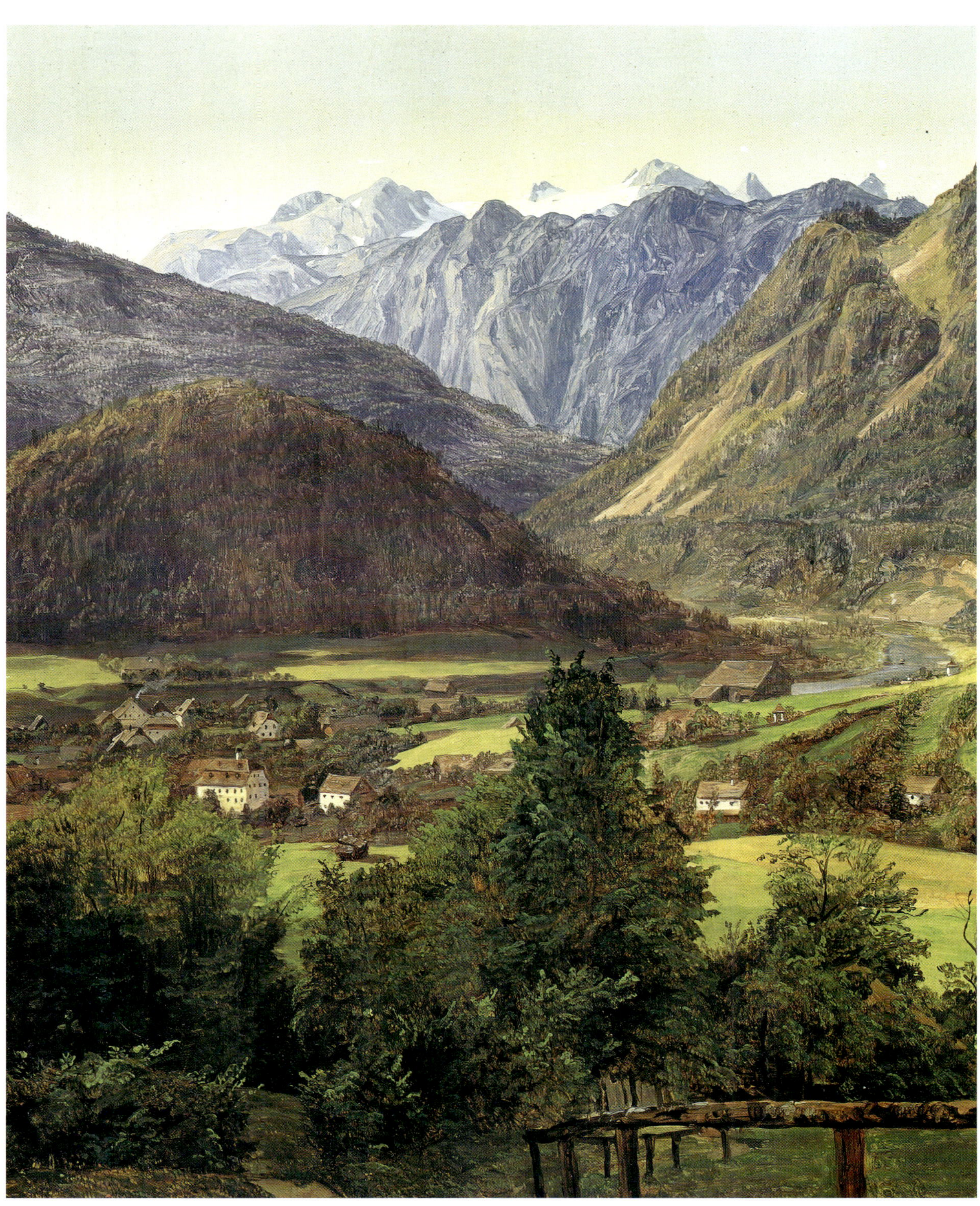

304
Ferdinand Georg
Waldmüller
The Traunsee
with Ort Castle
ca. 1834/35
Cat. XIII-89

305
Ferdinand Georg
Waldmüller
View from the Höllental
to the Schneeberg
(Nature Study)
ca. 1840
Cat. XIII-95

306
Ferdinand Georg
Waldmüller
The Ziemitzberg Seen
from the Village Ahorn
1831
Cat. XIII-86

304

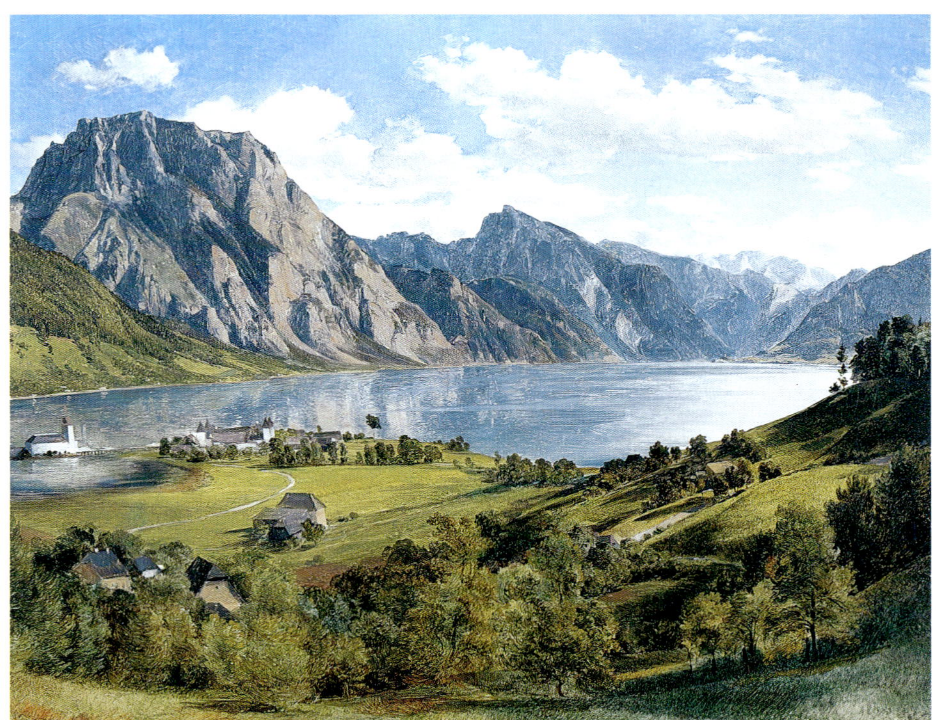

305

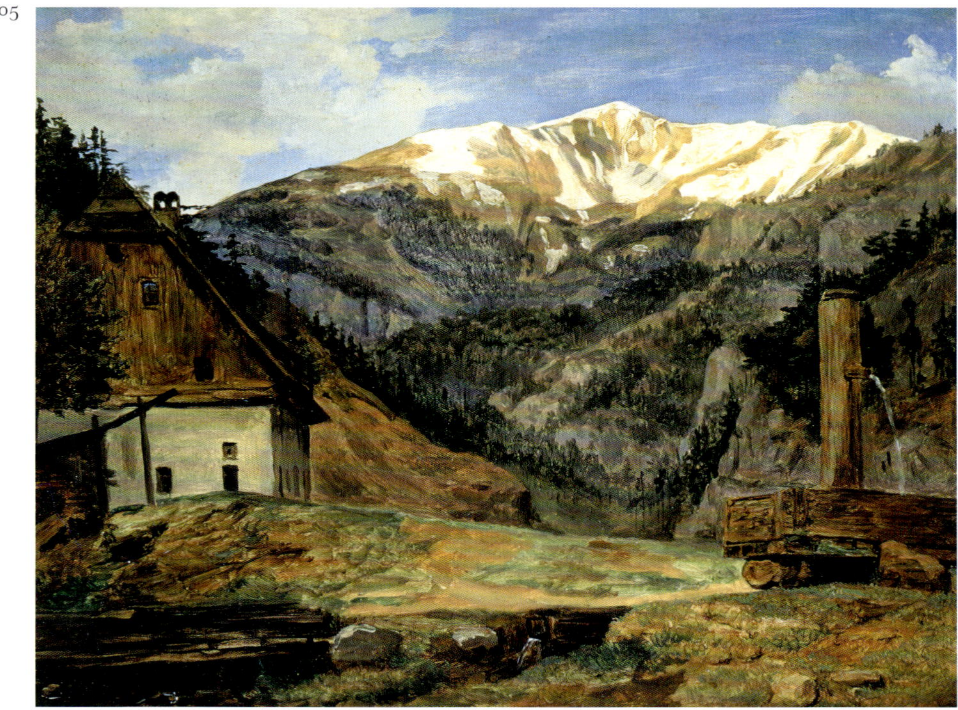

306

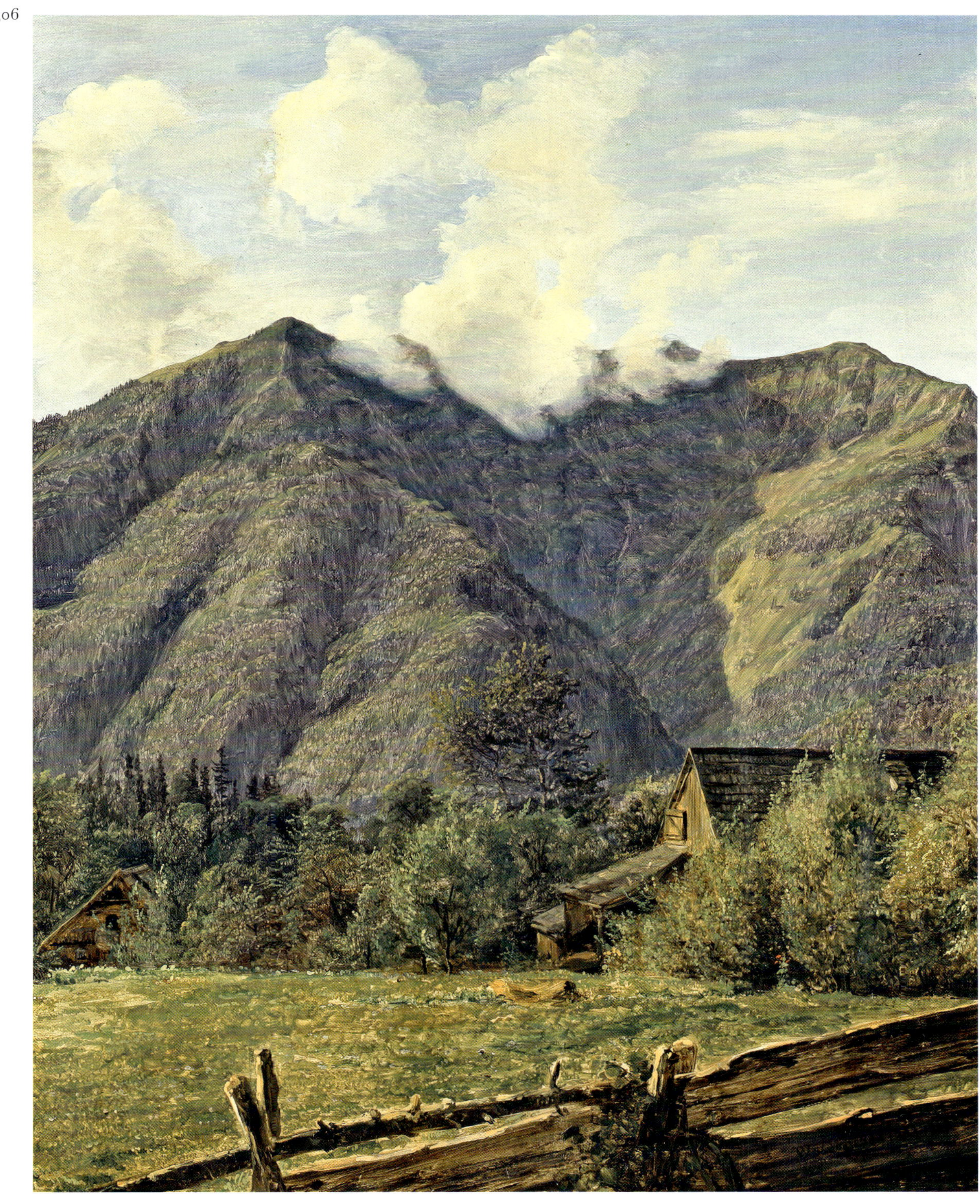

307
Moritz Michael
Daffinger
Rosa gallica L,
Gallic Rose
1830s/40s
Cat. XIII-19

308
Moritz Michael
Daffinger
Convallaria majalis L,
Common Lily of the
Valley
1830s/40s
Cat. XIII-15

309
Moritz Michael
Daffinger
Var. Hepatica triloba
D.C., Liverwort, variants
in different colors
1830s/40s
Cat. XIII-20

310
Moritz Michael
Daffinger
Arnica Montana L,
Mountain Arnica
1830s/40s
Cat. XIII-12

311
Moritz Michael
Daffinger
Primula veris acaulis L,
Common Primrose
1830s/40s
Cat. XIII-18

307

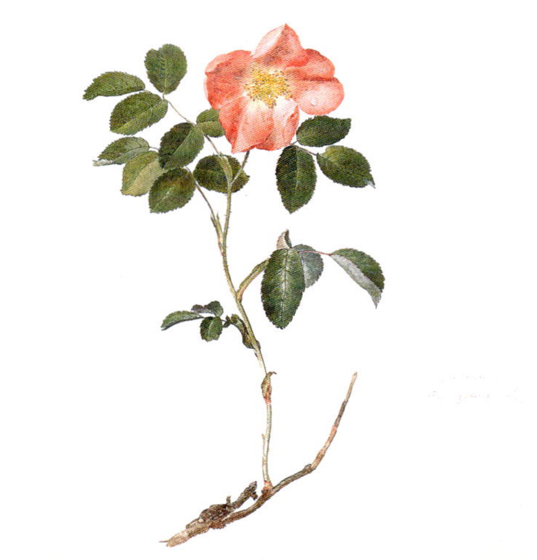

308

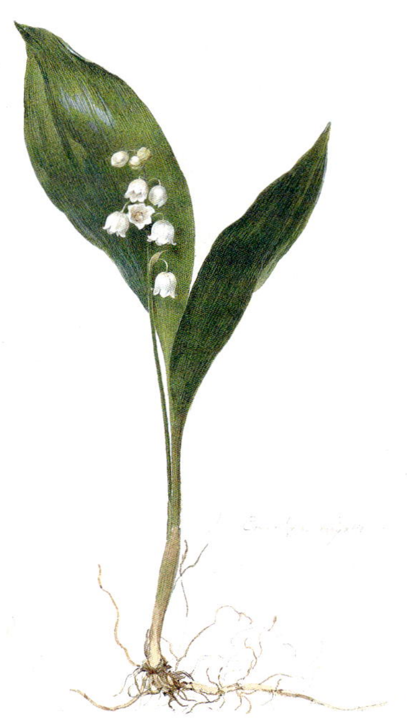

309

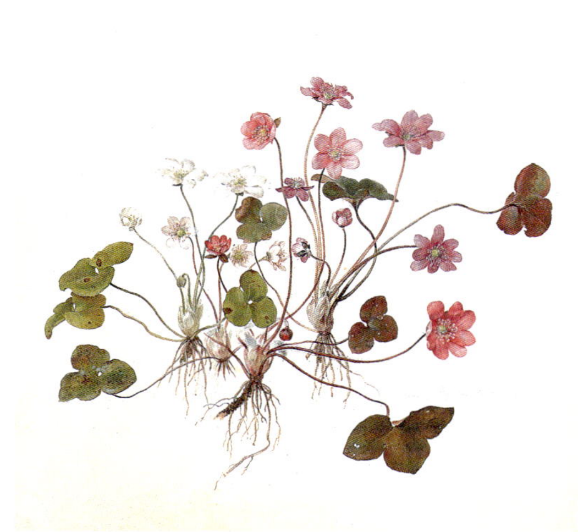

310

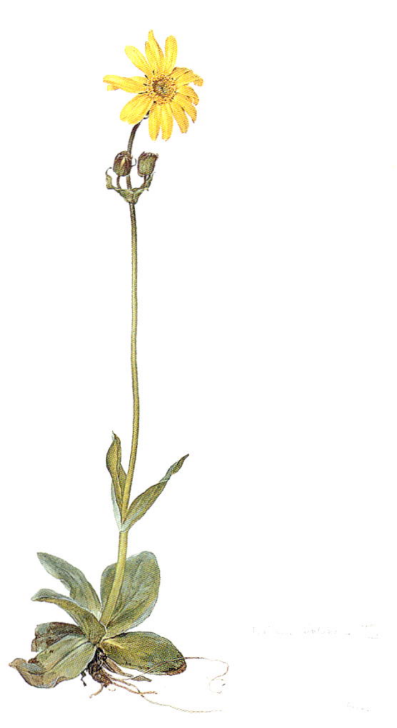

311

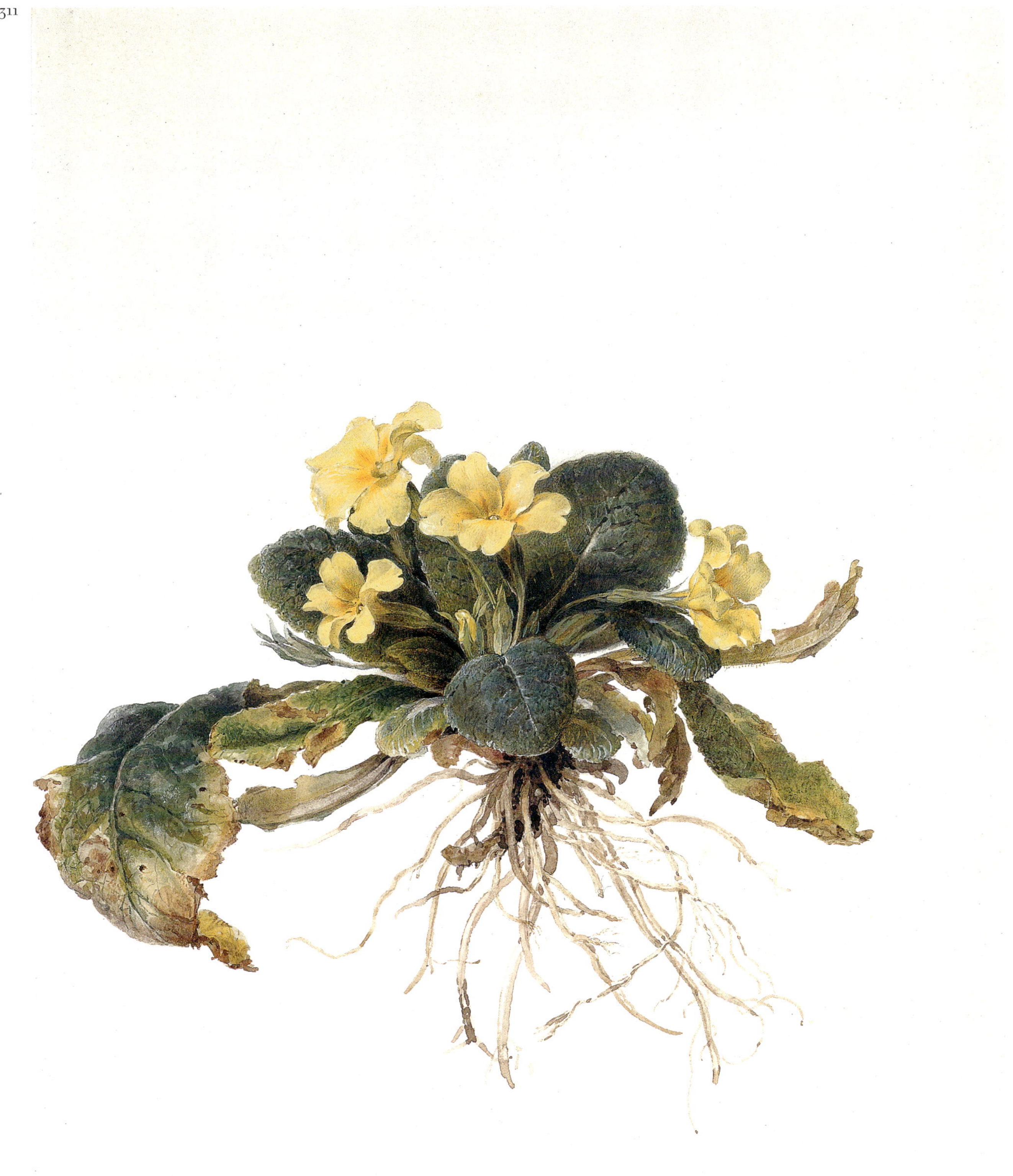

312
Ferdinand Georg
Waldmüller
*Catharina Baroness
von Koudelka*
1821/22
Cat. XIII-78

313
Ferdinand Georg
Waldmüller
*The Burgtheater
Actor Maximilian
Korn (1792–1854)
in a Landscape*
1828
Cat. XIII-83

314
Ferdinand Georg
Waldmüller
*Portrait of a Gentleman
in a Travel Coat*
1829
Cat. XIII-84

315
Ferdinand Georg
Waldmüller
*Portrait of Baron
von Moser in front
of a Salzkammergut
Landscape with
Loser and Sandling*
1833/35
Cat. XIII-87

316
Ferdinand Georg
Waldmüller
Girl with a Straw Hat
ca. 1824
Cat. XIII-80

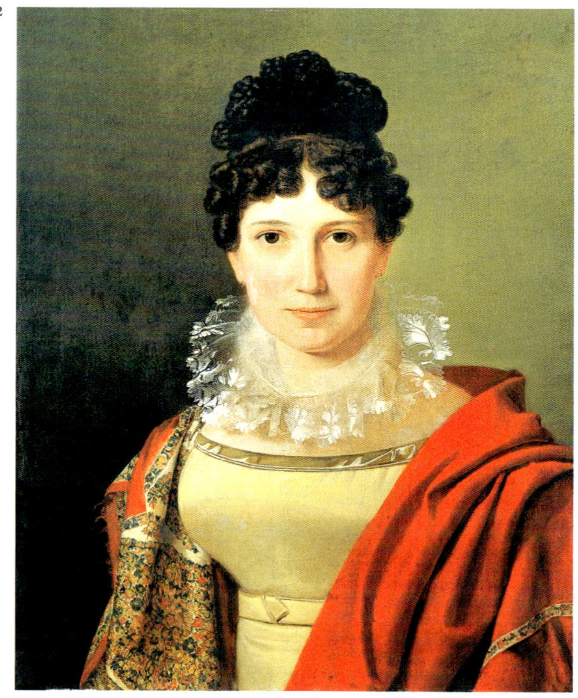

312

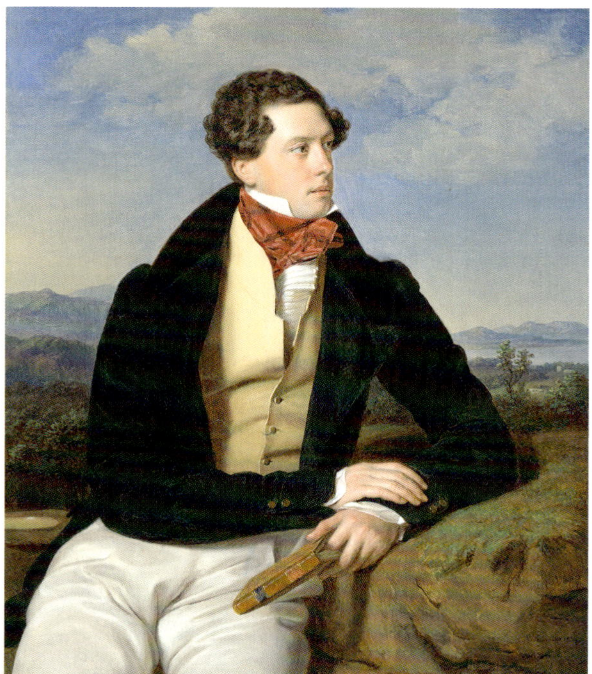

313

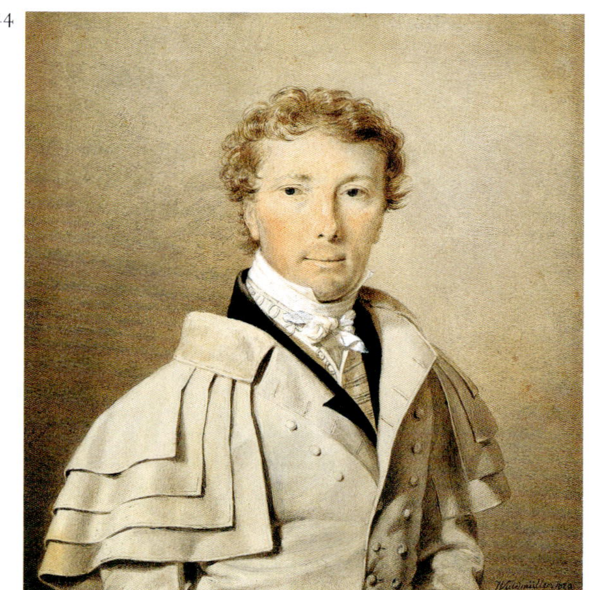

314

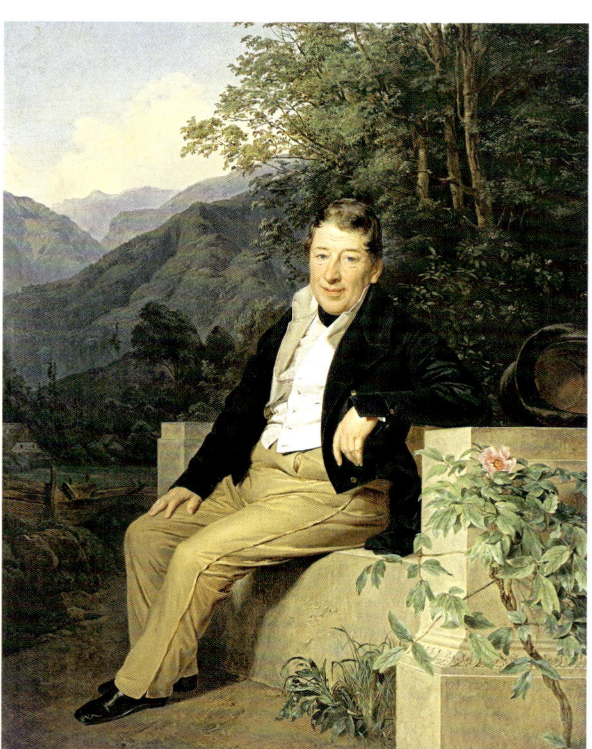

315

316

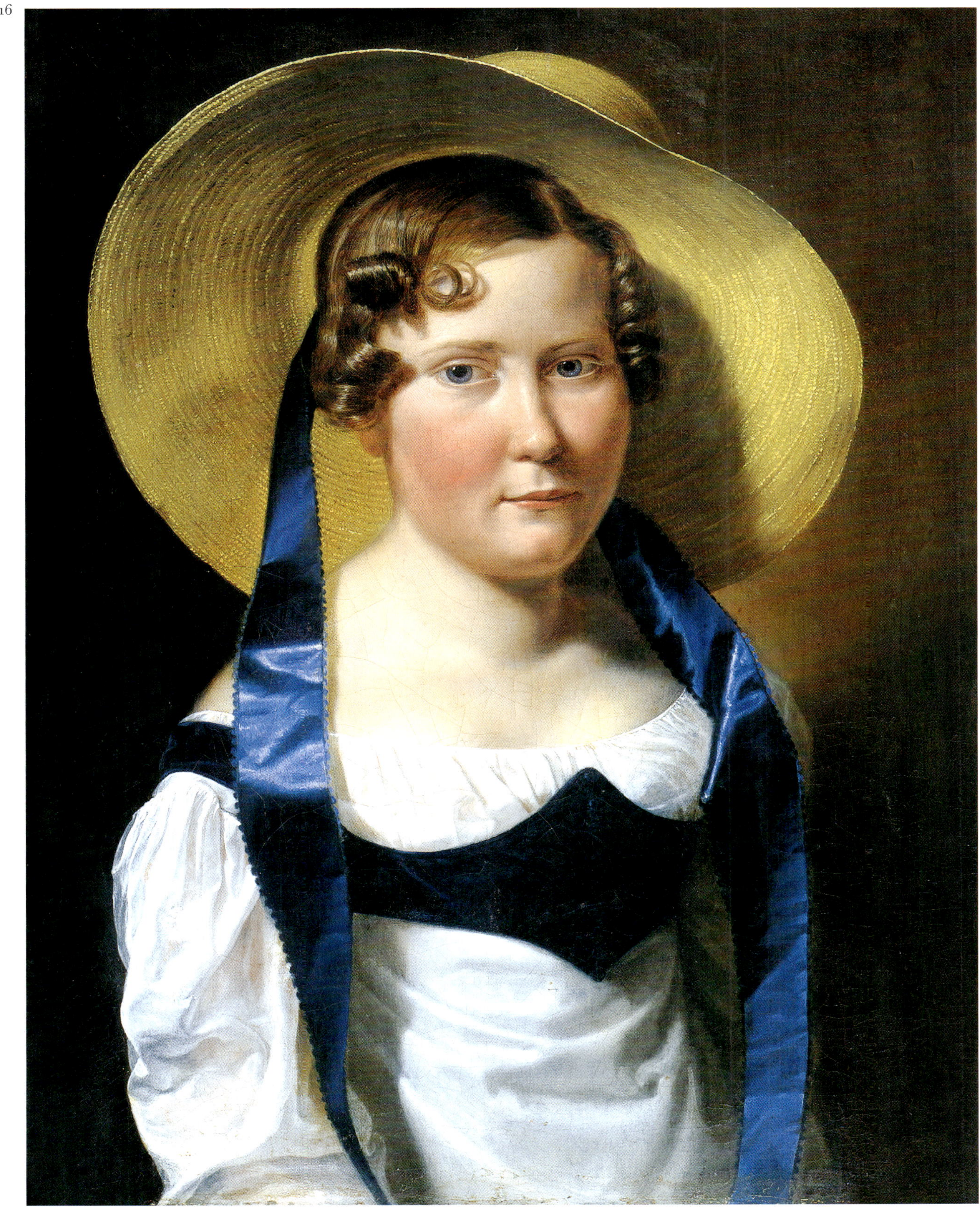

317 

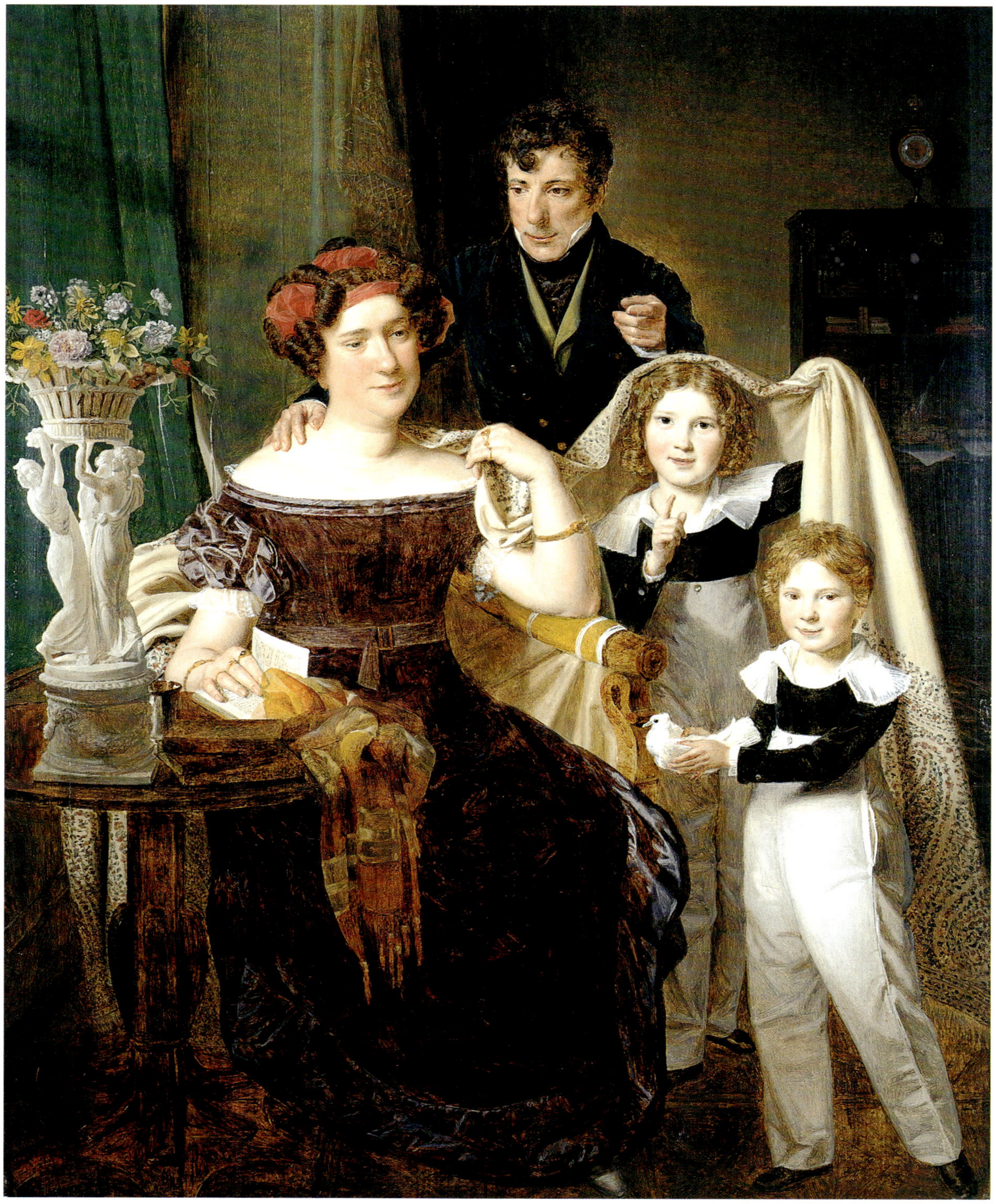

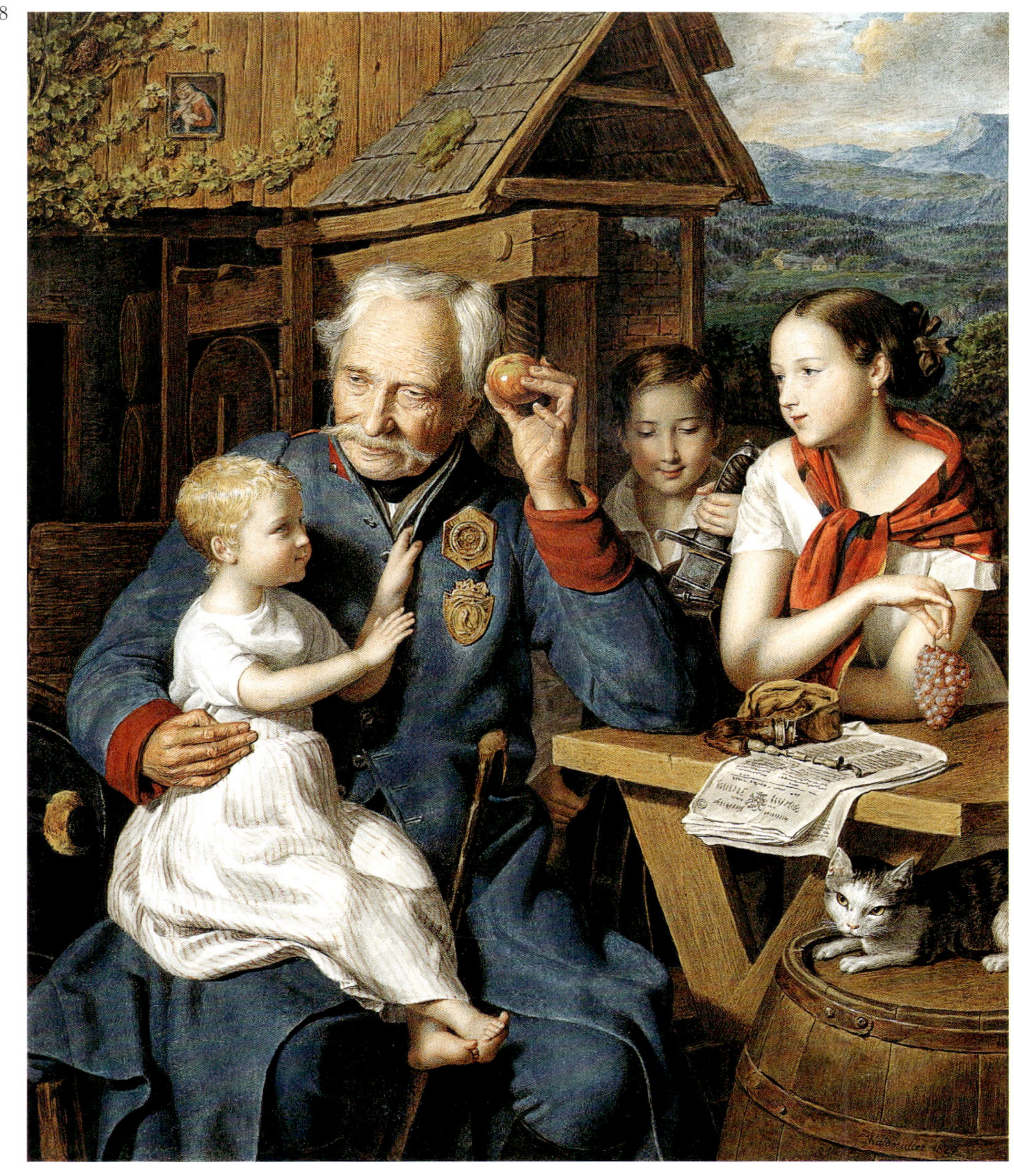

317
Ferdinand Georg
Waldmüller
Baron von Odkolek
with His Wife and
Their Two Sons
1826
Cat. XIII-81

318
Ferdinand Georg
Waldmüller
Old Soldier with
Three Children
1827
Cat. XIII-82

319
Ferdinand Georg
Waldmüller
*Portrait of the Son of
Mr. and Mrs. Werner*
1835
Cat. XIII-93

320
Ferdinand Georg
Waldmüller
*Portrait of the Daughter
of Mr. and Mrs. Werner*
1835
Cat. XIII-92

321
Ferdinand Georg
Waldmüller
*Portrait of Comtesse
Julia Apraxin*
1835
Cat. XIII-91

322
Friedrich von Amerling
*Alexander Baron
von Vesque-Püttlingen
as a Child*
1836
Cat. XIII-10

323
Friedrich von Amerling
*Prince Viktor
Odescalchi in a Fancy-
Dress Costume*
1838
Cat. XIII-11

319

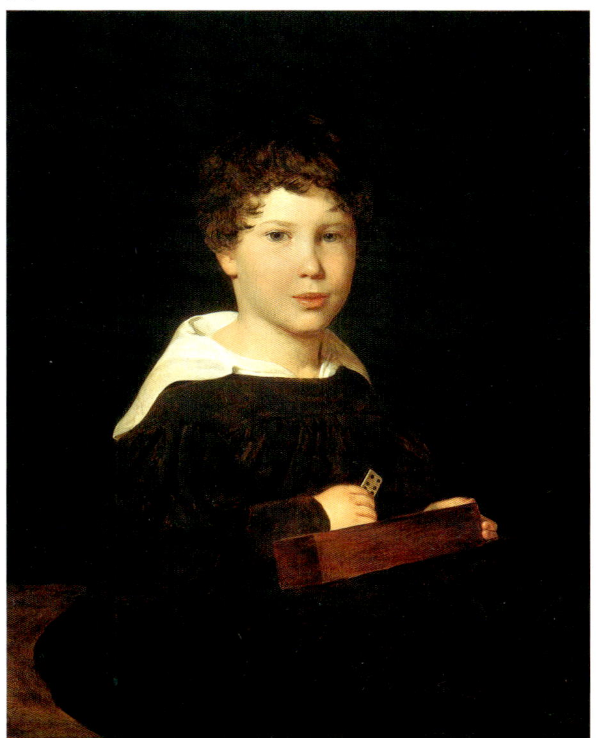

320

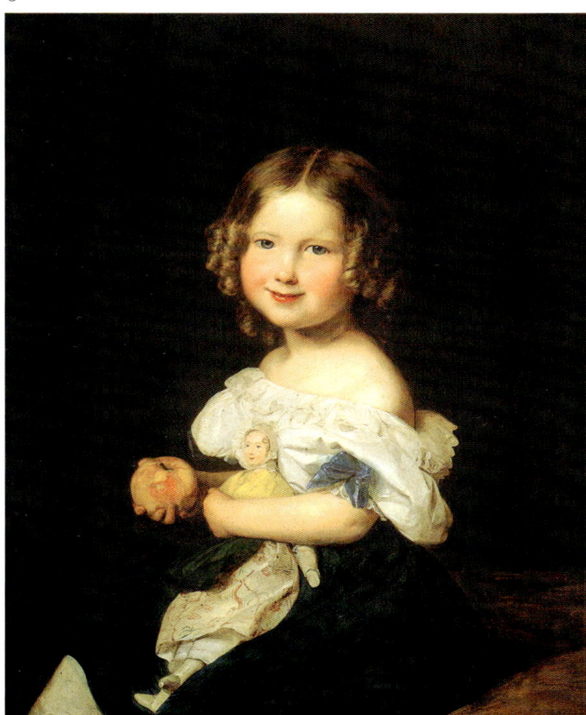

321

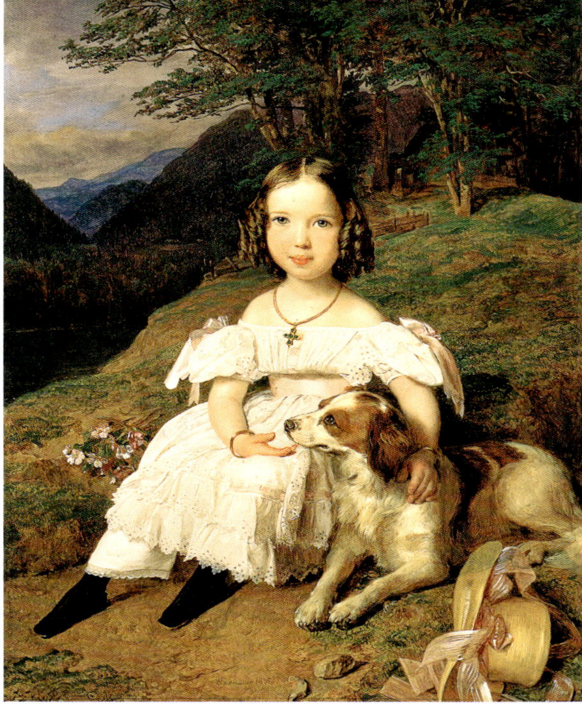

322

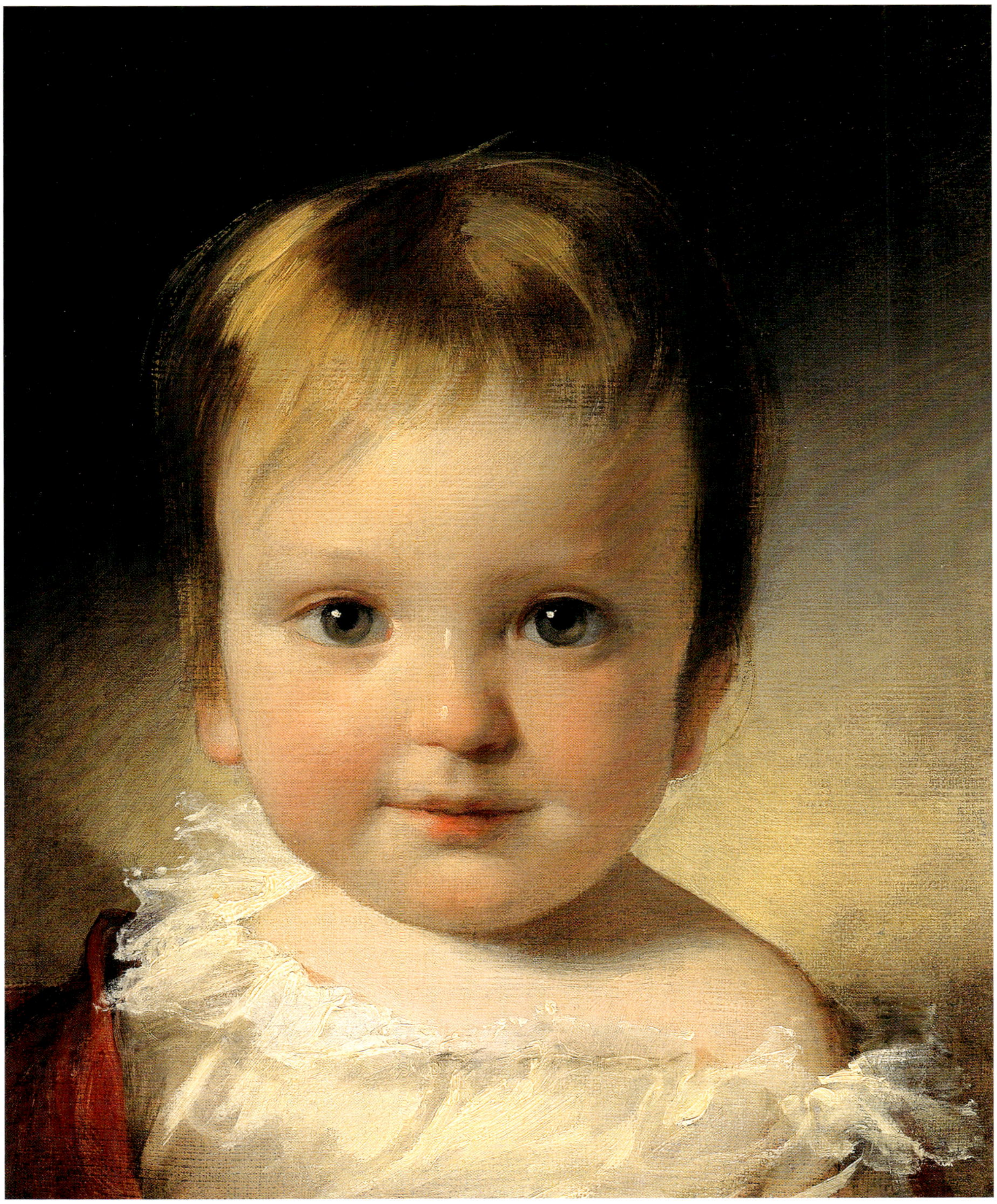

323

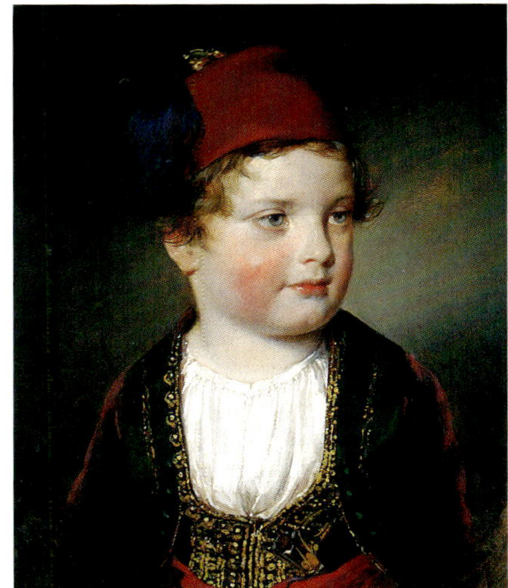

324

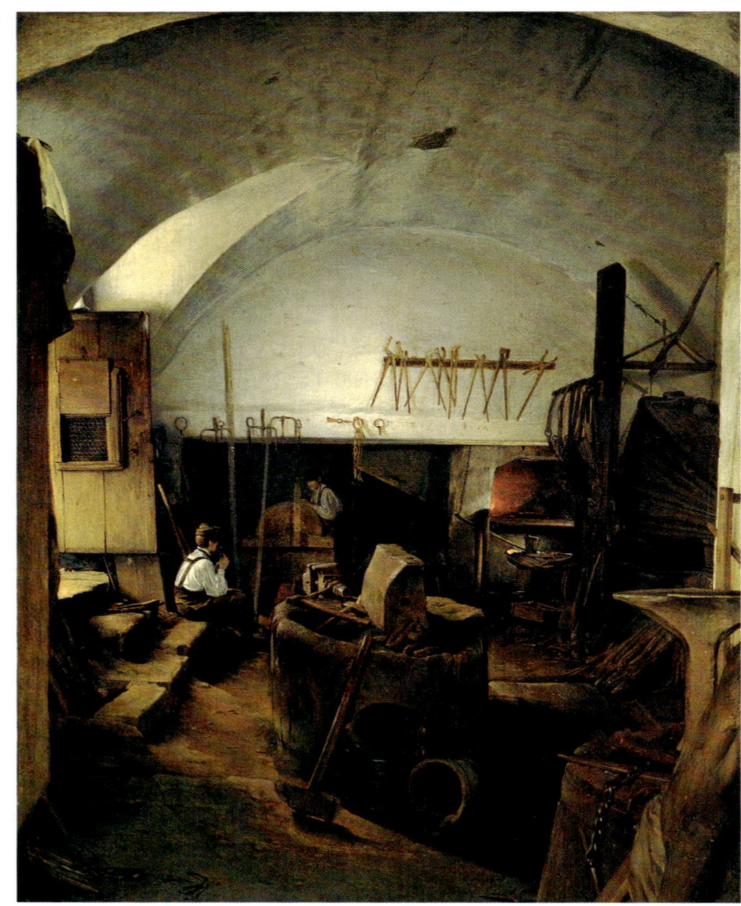

325

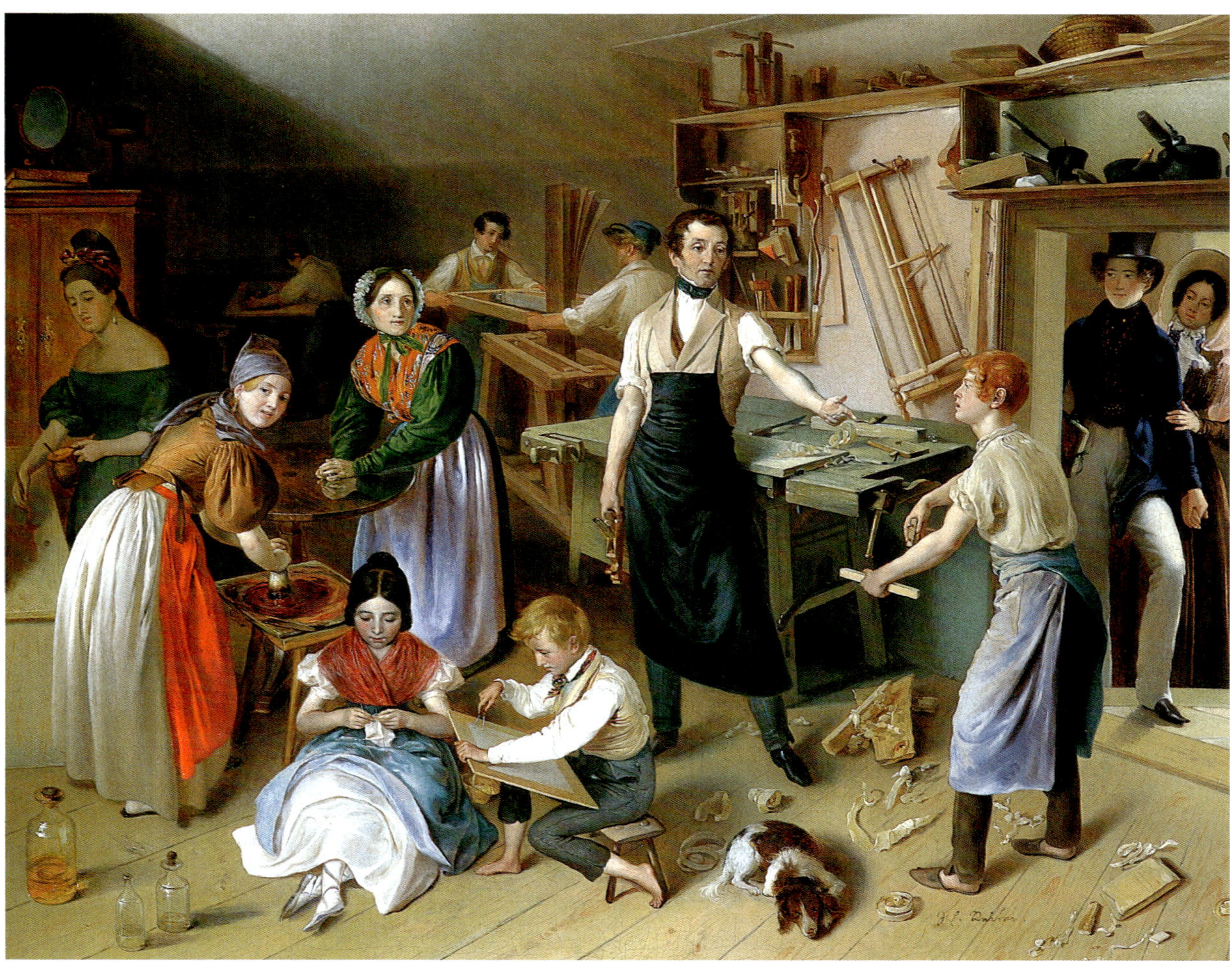

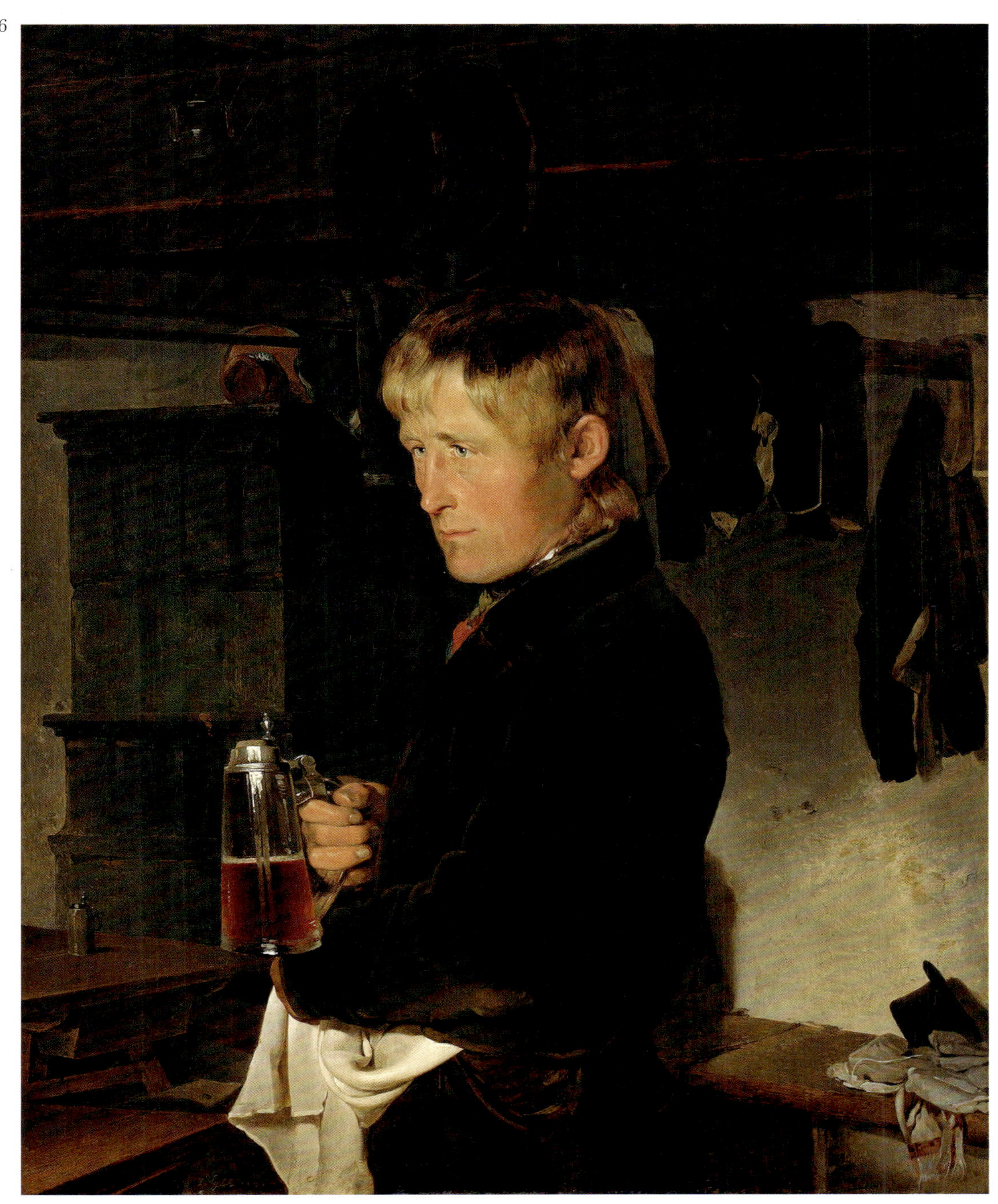

326

324
Franz Eybl
*Inside of a
Blacksmith's Shop*
1847
Cat. XIII-31

325
Johann Baptist Reiter
*The Hard-Working
Joiner Family*
before 1838
Cat. XIII-67

326
Franz Eybl
*The Landlord
at the Krottensee*
1835
Cat. XIII-30

CATALOGUE

OF THE EXHIBITION

CABINET FURNITURE

SECTION I

I-1   *Writing Cabinet*, Munich, ca. 1810, Hofkistlerei Daniel, attributed to, cherry, cherry veneer, 176 x 105 x 47 cm, Berlin, Deutsches Historisches Museum (35/2224), Prov. Munich, Galerie am Herzogpark, Lit. Ottomeyer 1994, cat. 7, ill. p. 83, PLATE 3

This writing cabinet, built in Munich and attributed to the firm of Daniel, court cabinetmakers, is reduced to the clear contours of its surface. Streaked cherry veneer covers the entire body of the piece in a symmetrical pattern. To enhance the homogenous effect of the veneer surfaces, the craftsmen dispensed with furniture fittings and framed the keyhole with a diamond-shaped intarsia. The dual function of the cabinet is evident when the doors are opened; the cabinet transforms into a standing desk, and a board can also be pulled out as a writing surface for a seated user.

I-2   *Writing Cabinet*, Vienna, 1810/15, mahogany, maple veneer, ebonized pear, mother of pearl, paint, gilding, 155 x 92 x 46 cm, Milwaukee Art Museum, Gift of René von Schleinitz Memorial Fund, by exchange (M2001.60), Prov. Vienna, Strubecker-und-Hollhuber Haus, from ca. 1850; Munich, Möbel und Kunst des Biedermeier, Lit. Vienna 1996, fig. 6, p. 56; Winters 2004, pl. 4; Milwaukee 2004, cat. 23, p. 19, PLATE 2

Two Vienna writing cabinets (cats. I-2, I-3) from the same period exemplify the new spectrum of options available on the furniture market. Both are luxury pieces covered with precious wood veneers. While the one cabinet relies on the traditional representational effect of sculptural décor, the other draws its quality from the natural persuasive power of the wood grain.

I-3   *Writing Cabinet*, Vienna, ca. 1810, ash, maple, yew, ebonized and gilded wood, brass and copper marquetry, gilt-brass bronze, 147.3 x 83.2 x 38.1 cm, Paris, Private Collection, Courtesy Didier Aaron & Cie, Prov. Paris, Didier Aaron & Cie, Lit. Vienna 1987B, ill. p. 372; Witt-Dörring 1989, p. 60, fig. 8a-b, PLATE 1

I-4   *Pair of Cabinets*, Vienna, 1825/30, walnut, walnut veneer on pine, each 169 x 110 x 52.5 cm,

Asenbaum Collection, Prov. Asenbaum Family, by descent since 1960s, PLATE 6

Although reduced to the bare formal necessities, this pair of cabinets succeeds in setting a strikingly individual accent, enhanced by the carefully selected veneer pattern and the restrained architectural configuration. A secret drawer activated by a spring mechanism is concealed beneath the tops of the cabinets.

I-5   *Cabinet*, Copenhagen, late 1830s, Christen Købke (Copenhagen 1810-1848 Copenhagen), attributed to, mahogany, boxwood inlay, 162 x 73.5 x 48.5 cm, Copenhagen, The Danish Museum of Decorative Art, Bequest of Juliane Købke 1926 (B 67/1926), Lit. Copenhagen 2004, pp. 174ff.

The Danish painter Christen Købke also designed interiors with Pompeian landscape paintings and furniture. Based on Attic Greek stele, this cabinet is divided into a pedestal section with two drawers, a lean upright body, and a plinth-shaped top segment with an additional drawer. The mahogany-veneered spandrels and the middle panels of the doors, which are slightly rounded toward the sides, are inlaid with boxwood laurel branches and fruit.

I-6   *Chiffonier*, Munich, ca. 1810, Hoftischlerei Daniel, attributed to, cherry veneer, dark stained inlay, spruce on the interior, 151 x 87 x 43 cm, Munich, Münchner Stadtmuseum (35/2132), Prov. Munich, Residenz, Lit. Munich 1991, cat. 37, p. 125, PLATE 4

In this chiffonier attributed to the court cabinetmakers Daniel, visual means are employed to create a contrast between the uniform design of the surface and the functional structure of the piece. The drawers are aligned with the frame, which, like the drawer frames, are offset with a strip of intarsia. The keyhole plates are dark, umbrella-shaped wood inlays. The intensely streaked grain displays the typical pattern of cherry veneer.

I-7   *Chiffonier*, Vienna, ca. 1820, Danhauser'sche Möbelfabrik (1814-42) (Chiffonier Model No.17), mahogany, mahogany veneer on oak, gilded fittings, 145.5 x 95 x 47 cm, Munich, Bayerisches Nationalmuseum (93/288), Prov. Regensburg,

1-5

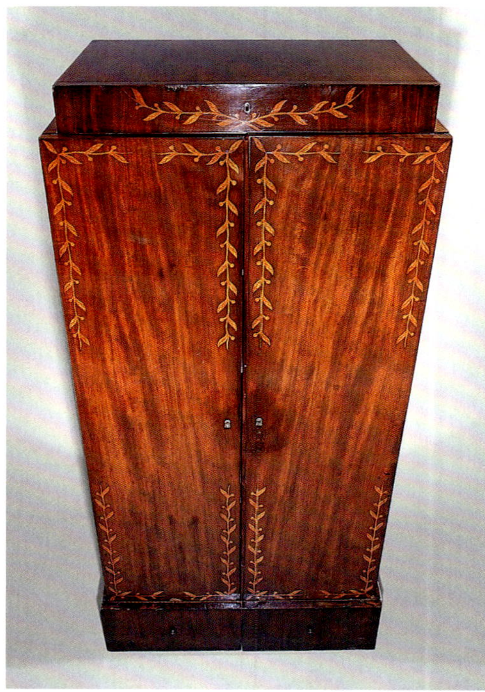

1-20

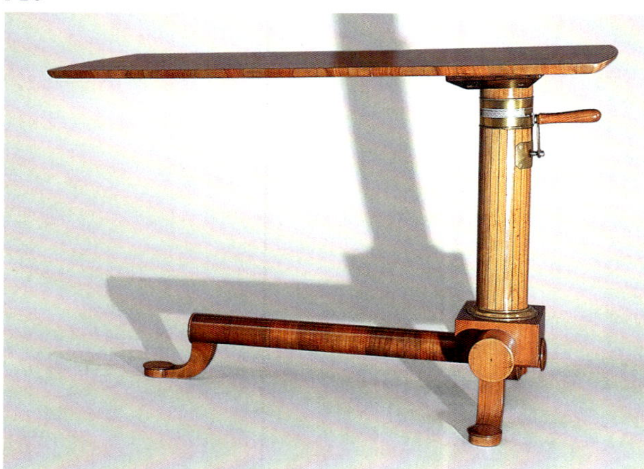

1-25

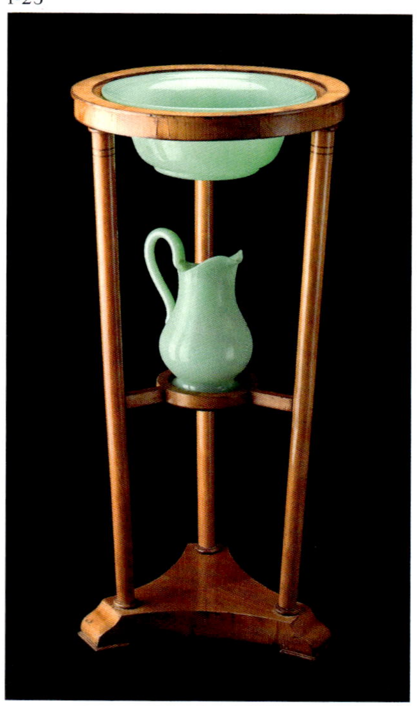

St. Emmeran Palace, Princes Thurn und Taxis;
Vienna, Palais Archduke Karl of Austria
(Albertina), Lit. Himmelheber 1973, cats. 3, 4;
Kreisel and Himmelheber 1968–73, cat. 360;
Sangl 1994, pp. 3199ff., PLATE 7

This eight-drawer console achieves its striking effect by virtue of its expansive form in which
all intricate detail is eliminated. A base, two curved
side panels, which appear on the front as edge
molding, a ledge top, and the carefully worked,
consistent veneer pattern are the sole elements of
design. The elongated S-shaped side panels and the
vertical veneer pattern provide a dynamic counter-
weight to the piece's volume.

1-8   *Cabinet with Drawers*, Vienna, 1815/20,
Danhauser'sche Möbelfabrik (1814–42)
(Chiffonier Model No. 19), cherry veneer, maho-
gany inlays, old brasses, 152 x 100 x 36 cm, Vienna,
Private Collection, Prov. Vienna, Agathe Galvagni,
by descent to Carl and Maria Auböck, 1961, Lit.
Vienna 1981, cat. 159, p. 221, PLATE 5

This entirely frontally constructed piece
presents an aura of solidity. It exhibits an interplay
of closed and open volumes and of sharply angular and softly curving contours. The shelves that
extend from each side link the solid body of drawers with the room, while the concave spandrels
join the base in a sweeping curve and enhance the
impression of stability.

1-9   *Writing Desk*, Vienna, 1820/30, walnut, walnut veneer on pine, maple on the interior, 77 x
124 x 73 cm, Asenbaum Collection, Prov. United
States, Private Collection, PLATE 8

1-10   *Column Desk*, Vienna, ca. 1825, ebonized
pear veneer on softwood, 101.5 x 152 x 71 cm,
Prague, Galerie Zlatá Husa, Prov. Prague, Iliad
Antik, PLATE 9

This oval, free-standing desk supported by
two columnar legs is a model produced by several
different firms, including the Danhauser'sche
Möbelfabrik in several versions in Vienna between
1825 and 1930. Integral components of the design
are the two hollows in the tops of the legs, which
serve as flower vases, and the footrest positioned
between the legs.

1-11   *Patent Writing Cabinet*, Vienna, ca. 1820,
maple, maple veneer, ebonized wood, 131.5 x 70 x
41.5 cm, Vienna, Private Collection, Prov. Vienna,
Private Collection, Courtesy Galerie Martin Suppan,
Lit. Suppan 1987, p. 42, pl. 6; Vienna 1996, p. 60,
ill. 13, PLATE 10

1-12   *Standing Desk*, Vienna, 1825/30, walnut,
walnut veneer on oak and softwood, felt covering,
102 x 85 x 53.5 cm, Vienna, Bundesmobilienverwaltung, Hofmobiliendepot. Möbel Museum Wien
(MD 35052), Prov. Vienna, Laxenburg Palace, PLATE 11

I-13   *Table*, Vienna, ca. 1825, walnut, walnut veneer on beech and softwood, H 78.5 x Dia 121 cm, Vienna, Bundesmobilienverwaltung, Hofmobiliendepot. Möbel Museum Wien (MD 50499), Prov. Vienna, The Viennese Court, PLATE 12

I-14   *Table*, Vienna, 1826, Danhauser'sche Möbelfabrik (1814–42), mahogany, mahogany and pear veneer, pine core, brass casters, 76.8 x 158 x 80.5 cm, Milwaukee, Milwaukee Art Museum, Purchase, with funds from Collectors' Corner, Avis and James K. Heller, and René von Schleinitz Memorial Fund, by exchange (pending acquisition 2006), Prov. Vienna, Private Collection since 1950s; Vienna, Asenbaum Collection, Lit. Ottillinger and Hanzl 1997, pl. 37; Hanzl-Wachter 2002, p. 274, PLATE 13

The same model of table now in the collection of the former Wiener Hofmobiliendepot is part of a seating group originally built for the music room of Archduchess Sophie at Laxenburg Palace (cat. II-20). A leg composed of four columnar sections mediates between the quatrefoil base and the oval table top.

I-15   *Console Table*, Vienna, 1826, Danhauser'sche Möbelfabrik (1814–42), mahogany, mahogany veneer, maple veneer, beech and pine core, 89.5 x 89 x 26 cm, Vienna, Bundesmobilienverwaltung, Hofmobiliendepot. Möbel Museum Wien (MD 50255), Prov. Vienna, Laxenburg Palace, Blue Court, Salon or Music Room of Archduchess Sophie (L1945), Lit. Hanzl-Wachter 2002, ill. p. 274; Vienna 1987B, cat. 8/53, p. 398

I-16   *Tea Table*, Vienna, ca. 1825, Danhauser'sche Möbelfabrik (1814–42) (Model No. 34), maple, maple veneer on beech and softwood, mahogany inlays, H 82 x Dia 116 cm, Sitzenberg-Reidling, Private Collection, Prov. Sitzenberg-Reidling, Private Collection, by descent since mid-nineteenth century, Lit. Baden 1988, cat. 321, ill. p. 21; Witt-Dörring 1989, unpag., PLATE 14

In contrast to the oval models, this round tea table was usually equipped with a fold-up top that suggested mobility. This variable feature also enabled the user to exhibit the top, which was often decorated with an elaborate veneer pattern, in a vertical position. In the case of this particular table, the tilted top and the carved foot together present an image resembling a flower on a stem.

I-17   *Center Table*, Austria, 1825/30, walnut veneer, H 76.8 x Dia 99 cm, New York, Collection of Christopher Forbes, Prov. New York, Angus Wilkie, Lit. Wilkie 1987, p. 89, ill. 66, PLATE 15

I-18   *Table*, Vienna, ca. 1820, Walnut veneer, maple and bone inlay, 78.5 x 125 x 62 cm, New York, Collection of Ellen and Bill Taubman, Prov. Vienna, Asenbaum Collection, PLATE 17

I-19   *Tea Table*, Vienna, ca. 1825/30, Danhauser'sche Möbelfabrik (1814–42) (Model No. 2), cherry, cherry veneer on softwood, 75 x 126 x 71.7 cm, Chicago, The Art Institute of Chicago, gift of Tiffany Blake, Mr. and Mrs. Ernest Brummer, Walter Brewster, Mrs. Richard Crane, R. E. Danielson, Frank Harding, Howard van Doren Shaw, and Mary P. Withers, restricted gift of Edna Olive Johnson; the Richard T. Crane Jr. Memorial, and Florene May Schoenborn and Samuel Marx funds, by exchange (1986.179), Prov. London, Sotheby's, 1985; New York, Frederick P. Victoria and Son, Lit. Witt-Dörring 1989, ill., unpag., PLATE 16

I-20   *Bedside Table*, Vienna, ca. 1825, cherry, cherry veneer on softwood, mahogany inlay, brass, 77.5 x 118 x 55 cm, Asenbaum Collection, Prov. Austrian Art Market, 1970s

I-21   *Pair of Night Stands (Column Cabinets)*, Vienna, ca. 1820, Danhauser'sche Möbelfabrik (1814–42) (Model No. 16), walnut veneer with Kehlheim sandstone top, each H 89 x Dia 42 cm, Chicago, Rita Bucheit, Prov. Vienna, Private Collection, PLATE 18

I-22   *Dumb Waiter*, Vienna, 1815/20, walnut, walnut veneer on oak and softwood, 114 x 44.5 x 44.5 cm, Vienna, Private Collection, Prov. Austrian Art Market, 1990s, PLATE 19

I-23   *Etagère (Music Stand)*, Vienna, ca. 1820, pear, pear veneer on softwood, ebonized, 147.5 x 51.5 x 43.5 cm, Vienna, Private Collection, Prov. Austrian Art Market, 1990s, PLATE 20

I-24   *Pair of Dumb Waiters*, Vienna, ca. 1822/23, Danhauser'sche Möbelfabrik (1814–42) ("Servantes" Model No. 33), mahogany veneer on beech and softwood, gilt bronze fittings, each H 157 x Dia 51 cm, Vienna, Albertina, Prov. Vienna, Palais Archduke Karl of Austria (Albertina), Vienna, C. Bednarczyk, Lit. London 1972, cat. 1591a, p. 739; London 1979, cats. 30, 86, PLATE 21

Designed and built by the Danhauser'sche Möbelfabrik for the Palais Archduke Karl of Austria (now the Albertina), these two dumb waiters are among the most innovative designs of the period. With shelves that decrease in size from bottom to top, supported at the side rather than by a central post, this model offers completely unobstructed surfaces for presentation.

I-25   *Washstand with Wash Bowl and Pitcher*, Bohemia or Moravia, ca. 1840, walnut, cast green opaline glass, table H 85.5 cm; bowl Dia 35 cm; pitcher H 23.3 cm, Prague, Museum of Decorative Arts, Acquisition, 1951 (31.479, 31.480a, b), Prov. J. Cuřinová, Lit. Padua 2000, cat. 433, ill.

I-26   *Tilt Mirror*, Vienna, 1825, maple veneer on softwood, mahogany inlay, metal mounts, 171 x 121 x 48.5 cm, Vienna, Bundesmobilienverwaltung, Hofmobiliendepot. Möbel Museum Wien (MD 34965), Prov. Vienna, The Viennese Court, PLATE 24

I-27   *Coat Rack*, Vienna, ca. 1825, walnut, walnut veneer on softwood, 183.5 x 45 x 45 cm, Vienna, Private Collection, Prov. Vienna, Vienna Art Market, 1970s, PLATE 23

I-28   *Wastepaper Basket*, Vienna, 1828, walnut and maple veneer on softwood, ebonized inlays, 68 x 64 x 40 cm, Vienna, Bundesmobilienverwaltung, Hofmobiliendepot. Möbel Museum Wien (MD 771), Prov. Vienna, Laxenburg Palace, Archduke Franz Karl and Archduchess Sophie (L 10880), Lit. Vienna 1987B, ill. p. 399, cat. 8/54

I-29   *Spittoon*, Vienna, 1825/30, walnut veneer on softwood, H 33 x Dia 25.3 cm, Vienna, Bundesmobilienverwaltung, Hofmobiliendepot. Möbel Museum Wien (MD 60656), Prov. Innsbruck, Hofburg Innsbruck (I 650), PLATE 22

Spittoons were standard interior furnishings beginning in the late eighteenth century. An outgrowth of the traditional metal or ceramic spittoons of earlier eras, they were not hidden discreetly in a corner. Rather, they were often deliberately and elaborately designed to match the other furniture in a room and positioned symmetrically on each side of a fireplace. They were equipped with a removable metal container and usually filled with lavender, sand, or crushed shells.

I-30   *Spittoon*, Vienna, 1825/30, cherry veneer on pine, H 32 x Dia 28 cm, Vienna, Bundesmobilienverwaltung, Hofmobiliendepot. Möbel Museum Wien (MD 59252), Prov. Vienna, Laxenburg Palace, Blue Court, Salon of the Archduchess Sophie, Lit. Schallaburg 1997, ill. p. 64, pl. 21, PLATE 22

I-31   *Spittoon*, Vienna, 1825/30, cherry, turned, cherry veneer on softwood, 29 x 20. 5 x 20.5 cm, Vienna, Bundesmobilienverwaltung, Hofmobiliendepot. Möbel Museum Wien (MD 59237), Prov. Vienna, The Viennese Court, Lit. Vienna 1987B, ill. p. 400, cat. 8/61, PLATE 22

I-32   *Spittoon*, Vienna, 1825/30, Danhauser'sche Möbelfabrik (1814–42) (Spuckkastel Model No. 46), cherry, turned, cherry veneer on softwood, H 52 x Dia 28 cm, Vienna, Bundesmobilienverwaltung, Hofmobiliendepot. Möbel Museum Wien (MD 41239), Prov. Vienna, The Viennese Court, Lit. Vienna 1987B, ill. p. 400, cat. 8/63, PLATE 22

I-33   *Spittoon*, Vienna, 1825/30, Danhauser'sche Möbelfabrik (1814–42) (Spuckkastel Model No. 25), walnut, turned, walnut veneer on softwood, 39.5 x 18.5 x 18.5 cm, Vienna, Bundesmobilienverwaltung, Hofmobiliendepot. Möbel Museum Wien (MD 46335), Prov. Vienna, Schönbrunn Palace (S 2275), PLATE 22

I-34   *Spittoon*, Vienna, 1825/30, walnut veneer on softwood, H 31 x Dia 23 cm, Vienna, Bundesmobilienverwaltung, Hofmobiliendepot. Möbel Museum Wien (MD 408), Prov. Vienna, Schönbrunn Palace (S 15624), PLATE 22

I-35   *Spittoon*, Vienna, ca. 1825/30, cherry, turned, cherry veneer on softwood, H 42 x Dia 29 cm, Vienna, Bundesmobilienverwaltung, Hofmobiliendepot. Möbel Museum Wien (MD 43938), Prov. Baden near Vienna, Flora Villa, Bedroom of Archduke Franz Karl and Archduchess Sophie (BA 1973), Lit. Vienna 1987B, ill. p. 400, cat. 8/59; Hanzl-Wachter 2002, ill. p. 272, PLATE 22

I-36   *Spittoon*, Vienna, 1825/30, cherry veneer on softwood, H 24 x Dia 26 cm, Vienna, Bundesmobilienverwaltung, Hofmobiliendepot. Möbel Museum Wien (MD 4135), Prov. Vienna, Schönbrunn Palace (S 2292), PLATE 22

I-37   *Spittoon*, Vienna, ca. 1828, cherry, cherry veneer, mahogany inlay, H 38 x Dia 30 cm, Vienna, Bundesmobilienverwaltung, Hofmobiliendepot. Möbel Museum Wien (MD 59231), Prov. Baden near Vienna, Flora Villa, Archduke Franz Karl and Archduchess Sophie (BA 4469), Lit. Hanzl-Wachter 2002, p. 272, PLATE 22

I-38   *Long Case Clock*, Germany, ca. 1790, David Roentgen (Herrnhaag 1743–1807 Wiesbaden)/Roentgen Workshop, mahogany, spruce, brass, 189.5 x 57 x 22 cm, Berlin, Deutsches Historisches Museum, Purchase, 1997 (KG 97/36), Prov. Wuppertaler Uhrenmuseum Abeler, Purchase, 1997; Vienna Art Market, Lit. Greber 1980, vol. 1, p. 252; Fabian 1984, cat. 107, pp. 133f., 354, PLATE 26

The furniture factory operated by David Roentgen in Neuwied was one of the leading producers in Europe near the end of the eighteenth century. In collaboration with the Kinzing watchmaker family, Roentgen specialized in the manufacture of tall-case clocks that embodied the highest technical and aesthetic standards. Designed in the shape of a shortened obelisk, the body of this example rests on a two-step pedestal and has a door decorated with a fluted band and, above that, a square brass plate with a round opening for the clock face. The unusual clockwork displays the time with a self-extending hand that makes three revolutions around the twelve hours arranged in three concentric rings of four hours each.

I-39   *Long Case Clock*, Berlin, ca. 1820, poplar burr veneer, ebonized pear, 208.3 x 59.7 x 21.6 cm, Milwaukee Art Museum, Gift of René von Schleinitz Memorial Fund, by exchange (M2003.137), Prov. Munich, Parisius family, by descent from nineteenth century; Munich, Christa von Preussen, 1986–90; Munich, Klaus Spindler, 1990–92; New York, Karl Kemp, 1992–96; Chicago, William B. Demas, 1996–2002; New York, Karl Kemp, 2002–2003, Lit. Wilkie 1987, p. 180, ill.; Greenberg 1996, ill. p. 75; Chase and Kemp 2001, p. 393, ill. 392; Winters 2004, p. 178, pl. 1, PLATE 27

I-40   *Picture Clock, Emperor Franz I in His Study*, Vienna, 1829, L.C. Hofmeister, oil on copper, ox eye border, gilding, 64 x 80 cm, Vienna, D & S Antiques, PLATE 25

The picture clock, usually equipped with chimes, was a popular interior furnishing in the first half of the nineteenth century. Their pictures allude to social themes or landscape scenes. In this example, Emperor Franz I of Austria is depicted as the "highest civil servant" of the state. He is portrayed sitting in his office in the Vienna Hofburg, his thoughts focused on the welfare of his subjects.

SEATING FURNITURE
SECTION II

II-1 *Chair*, Weimar, ca. 1795, fruitwood, modern upholstery, 98 x 48.5 x 53 cm, Berlin, Deutsches Historisches Museum (KG 92/25.1-8), Prov. Weimar, Estate of Ottilie Goethe, Acquired 1992, Lit. Bertuch 1796, vol. 11, pl. 33, PLATE 28

The Weimar *Journal des Luxus und der Moden* published illustrations of numerous examples of "English chairs in a new form" beginning in 1786. These chairs were initially produced for the Weimar court and later in large series. A smoothly finished plinth runs between the square legs, which are tapered and flared toward the bottom. The only decorative elements in these table chairs are the open, ornamented backs, which were replaced by plain rungs and back panels in the early years of the nineteenth century.

II-2 *Chair*, Weimar, 1810/20, mahogany, modern upholstery, 92.2 x 46 x 50 cm, Berlin, Deutsches Historisches Museum (KG 2004/16), Prov. Weimar, Goethe House, Lit. Maul 1996, p. 69, PLATE 29

II-3 *Chair*, South German, ca. 1804/1805, maple, maple veneer, 87 x 46 x 43 cm, Berlin, Deutsches Historisches Museum, Purchase, 2005 (KG 2005/79), Prov. Hohenaltheim Schloss, Princes of Oettingen-Wallerstein, PLATE 30

II-4 *Klismos Chair*, Copenhagen, early 1790s, Nicolai Abraham Abildgaard (Copenhagen 1743-1809 Copenhagen), gilded beech, cane seat, 76.5 x 58 x 70 cm, Copenhagen, The Danish Museum of Decorative Art, Gift of V. Holten 1938 (B 42/1938), Lit. Boidi Sassone 2000, p. 514; Copenhagen 2004, pp. 52f., PLATE 32 (right)

The Klismos Chairs, modeled after the original ancient Greek type, were very popular in Denmark. The history painter Nicolai Abraham Abildgaard built these chairs as part of the furnishing for an "antiquity room" for which he executed a large wall painting based on Roman subjects. The widely flared legs and the broad, expansive back panel decorated with a palmetto frieze reflect motifs from Greek vase painting. The gold-painted surface of the early chairs is based on the assumption that the ancient models were made of metal; only later examples directly reference their wood construction.

II-5 *Klismos Chair*, Copenhagen, ca. 1840, Hermann Ernst Freund (Copenhagen 1786–1840 Copenhagen), beech, cane seat, horsehair cushion, 79 x 55 x 71.5 cm, Copenhagen, The Danish Museum of Decorative Art, permanent loan from the Staatens Museum for Kunst since 2000 (D 1753 m), Lit. Boidi Sassone 2000, p. 514; Copenhagen 2004, p. 80f., PLATE 32 (left)

II-6 *Klismos Chair*, Copenhagen, ca. 1840, mahogany, beech, modern upholstery, 79.3 x 53.5 x 55.7 cm, Copenhagen, The Hirsrchsprung Collection, Prov. Copenhagen, Painter Julius Exner, mid-nineteenth century; purchased by The Hirschsprung Collection, 1911, Lit. Gelfer-Jørgensen 1988, p. 394, ill.

II-7 *Chair*, Berlin, 1805/10, David Gilly (Schwedt 1748-1808 Berlin), attributed to, black polished beech, modern upholstery, 89 x 45 x 55 cm, First version: Milwaukee, Milwaukee Art Museum, Gift of René von Schleinitz Memorial Fund, by exchange (M2004.593), Prov. Berlin, Private Collection, Second version: Berlin, Deutsches Historisches Museum, Purchase, 2005 (KG 2005/84), PLATE 31

The Berlin dining chair is derived from the characteristic neoclassical style of the Klismos Chair, which is based on Greek models and appeared in numerous popular variations throughout the Biedermeier period. The front and rear legs are flared in opposite directions, and the backward-curving backrest is topped by a rail that protrudes beyond the edges of the chair. The more elegant variations of the chair are equipped with cushions, while the mass-produced versions have wicker or flat wood seats.

II-8 *Chair*, Berlin, ca. 1825, Design by Karl Friedrich Schinkel (Neuruppin 1781-1841 Berlin), polished beech, cane seat, 85 x 45 x 39.5 cm, Potsdam, Stiftung Preussische Schlösser und Gärten Berlin-Brandenburg (SPSG, unnumbered.), Prov. Berlin, New Pavillion King Friedrich Wilhelm III of Prussia, Lit. Sievers 1950, p. 23, ill. 122; Berlin 1981B, p. 225, ill. p. 226; Hamburg 2002, pp. 126-28, ill. p. 127, PLATE 33

II-9   *Kitchen Chair*, Berlin, ca. 1820, Design Karl
Friedrich Schinkel (Neuruppin 1781-1841 Berlin),
birch, white lacquer, 81 x 45 x 40 cm, Berlin,
Schloss Tegel Verwaltungs GmbH, Prov. Berlin,
Schloss Tegel, PLATE 34

II-10   *Chair*, Berlin, ca. 1820, mahogany,
mahogany veneer on oak, cane seat, 84.5 x 46 x
41 cm, Potsdam, Stiftung Preussische Schlösser
und Gärten Berlin-Brandenburg (SPSG, IV 203),
Prov. Potsdam, Schloss Charlottenhof, Rotes
Eckkabinett, PLATE 35

II-11   *Garden or Terrace Chair*, Vienna, ca. 1825,
Danhauser'sche Möbelfabrik (1814-42) (Model
No. 37), walnut veneer on beech and softwood,
walnut grain glaze, original webbing, 87 x 45.5 x
50 cm, Vienna, Bundesmobilienverwaltung, Hofmobiliendepot. Möbel Museum Wien (MD 54974),
Prov. Baden near Vienna, Flora Villa, Bedroom of
Archduke Franz Karl and Archduchess Sophie
(B. 3072), Lit. Vienna 1987A; Vienna 1987B, cat.
8/8, ill. p. 393, PLATE 36
    This simple chair was used as summer furni-
ture on patios or in winter gardens; its upholstery
is equally simple and functional. It is comparable to
the webbing used by the Shakers in seat upholstery.
The result is a chair with front legs exposed at the
top and a curved front frame element.

II-12   *Garden or Terrace Chair*, Vienna, ca. 1825,
Danhauser'sche Möbelfabrik (1814-42) (Model
No. 53), walnut veneer on beech and softwood,
reconstructed webbing, 92 x 46.5 x 41.5 cm,
Vienna, Bundesmobilienverwaltung, Hofmobilien-
depot. Möbel Museum Wien (MD 55047), Prov.
Vienna, Schönbrunn Palace and Laxenburg Palace
(L 625), Lit. Vienna 1987A, PLATE 36

II-13   *Chair*, Lavagna, ca. 1830, Giovanni
Battista Ravenna (? 1827-ca. after 1870?), cherry,
wicker seat, 85 x 42 x 38 cm, Paper label: DELLA
FABBRICA / DI / GIO. BATTISTA RAVENNA / Ai Cavi die
Lavagna presso CHIAVARI, Vienna, Collection of
Christian Witt-Dörring, Lit. Chiavari 1985, p. 18,
PLATE 37
    This lightweight chair, which as a type had
served as a movable complement to large seating
groups since the early nineteenth century, came to
be called the "Chiavari chair" in reference to its
place of origin. Located outside Genoa in Liguria,
Chiavari was the production center for this simple,
reasonably priced seating furniture, which was
available in a wide variety of design variations. It
spread throughout Europe and ultimately served
as a source of inspiration for Gio Ponti's 1957
"Superleggera chair."

II-14   *Bentwood Chair*, Boppard am Rhein,
1835/40, Michael Thonet (Boppard am Rhein

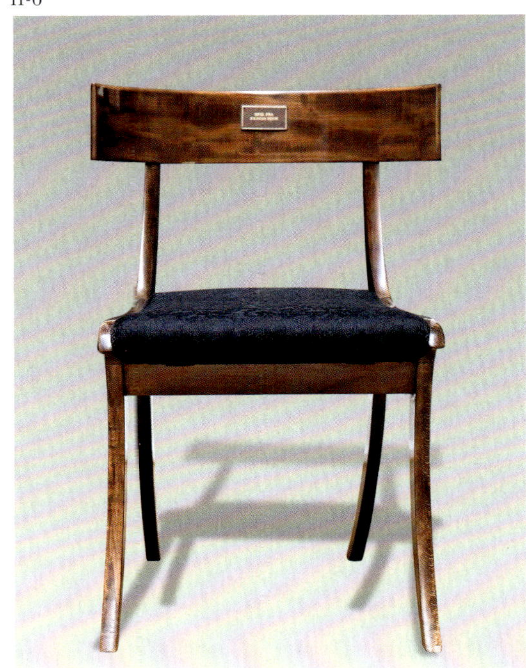

II-6

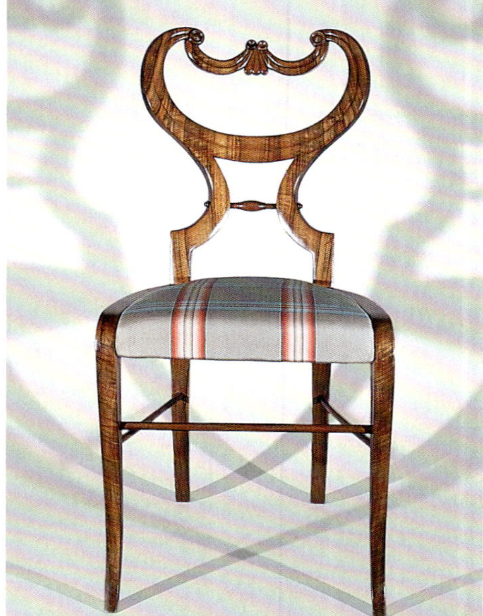

11-22

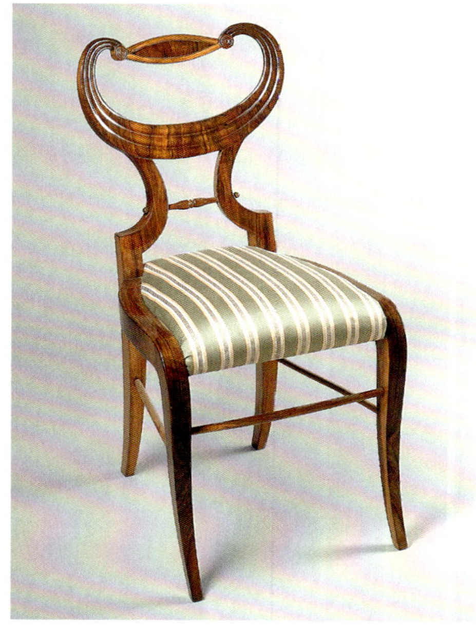

11-23

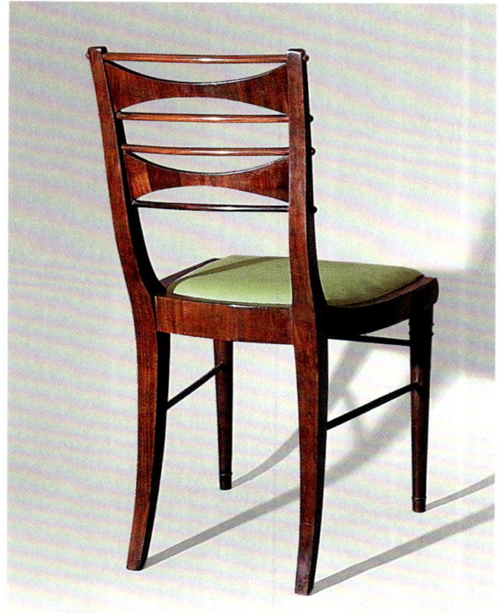

11-30

1796–1871 Vienna), walnut veneer on bent lami-nated wood, cane seat, 92 x 44 x 50 cm, First version: Chicago, Private Collection, Second version: Munich, Bayerisches Nationalmuseum (L86/225), Lit. Ottillinger 2003, cat. 3, ill., PLATE 38

This armchair is one of the first bentwood seating furniture models made by Michael Thonet while he was still working in Boppard am Rhine. Instead of building the currently popular curved furniture from solid wood covered with veneer—a time-consuming process—Thonet chose a cheaper method involving bent two-dimensional elements. To accomplish this, he glued individual strips of veneer previously bent to the desired shape by steaming them in iron molds.

11-15   *Chair*, Vienna, 1810, Design by Count Franz Anton Harrach (dates unknown), ebon-ized wood on beech, brown stained maple inlays, gilded bronze fittings, modern upholstery, 95 x 53 x 45 cm, Vienna, Bundesmobilienverwaltung, Hofmobiliendepot. Möbel Museum Wien (MD 2755), Prov. Hofburg, Vienna, Empress Maria Ludovika, Schönbrunn Palace (S 16061), Lit. Ottillinger and Hanzl 1997, p. 87, fig. 43; Schallaburg 1997, p. 60, pls. 12, 13, cats. 3.06, 3.07

Designed in 1810 by Count Franz Anton Harrach for the apartment of Empress Maria Ludovica on the third floor of the Vienna Hofburg, this transparent-looking chair is typical of the era yet exhibits extreme formal autonomy. The symmetrical contours of the chair are counteracted by the asymmetrical diagonal elements of the chair-back.

11-16   *Chair*, Vienna, ca. 1826, Danhauser'sche Möbelfabrik (1814–42) (Model No. 18), mahogany, mahogany veneer on beech, modern upholstery, 93.5 x 47.5 x 42.5 cm, Vienna, Bundesmobilien-verwaltung, Hofmobiliendepot. Möbel Museum Wien (MD 057108), Prov. Vienna, Laxenburg Palace, Blue Court of Archduchess Sophie, Lit. Vienna 1987B, ill. p. 393, cat. 8/4, PLATE 39

The curved chair-backs that were typical of the time are composed of individual sections and call to mind a bentwood chair. With this chair, Danhauser created a precursor to Thonet's bent-wood chair, Model No. 8, of 1856. Danhauser cut his curved sections from solid wood, whereas Thonet shaped them by bending.

11-17   *Chair*, Vienna, ca. 1825, mahogany, mahogany veneer on beech and softwood, modern upholstery, 95 x 47.5 x 47 cm, Paris, Musée du Louvre (OA 12193), Prov. Vienna Art Market, 1970s, Asenbaum Collection, PLATE 40

11-18   *Chair*, Vienna, ca. 1825, ebonized wood veneer on beech and softwood, modern upholstery, 91.5 x 47.8 x 42 cm, Vienna, Bun-desmobilienverwaltung, Hofmobiliendepot.

Möbel Museum Wien (MD 66231), Prov. Vienna, Schönbrunn Palace (S 5830), PLATE 41

II-19   *Chair*, Vienna, 1826, Danhauser'sche Möbelfabrik (1814–42) (Model No. 92), mahogany veneer on beech and softwood, turned maple, reconstructed upholstery, 93 x 47 x 53 cm, Vienna, Bundesmobilienverwaltung, Hofmobiliendepot. Möbel Museum Wien (MD 45872), Prov. Vienna, Laxenburg Palace, Blue Court, Salon or Music Room of Archduchess Sophie (L 10937), Lit. Hanzl-Wachter 2002, p. 274, figs. 318, 319; Schallaburg 1997, pp. 30–32, pl. 16, cat. 4.02, pl. 17, cat. 4.03, PLATE 42

This chair was originally part of the furnishings of the music room of Archduchess Sophie in Laxenburg Palace near Vienna. It is an excellent example of simplicity in frame and upholstery design. Despite the upholstered seat, Danhauser succeeded in preserving the transparent look of the chair-back by pleating the fabric in his design and stretching it lightly between the elements of the wood construction.

II-20   *Chair*, Vienna, ca. 1820, walnut veneer on beech, original leather, 91 x 47.5 x 44.3 cm, Vienna, Bundesmobilienverwaltung, Hofmobiliendepot. Möbel Museum Wien (MD 29412), Prov. Vienna, The Viennese Court, PLATE 44

II-21   *Chair*, Vienna, 1815/20, Danhauser'sche Möbelfabrik (1814–42), beech and pine, cherry veneer, ebonized mahogany, 94.3 x 47 x 55.3 cm, New York, The Metropolitan Museum of Art, Purchase, Friends of European Sculpture and Decorative Arts, 1996 (1996.417.1), Prov. Private Collection, South Germany, PLATE 48

II-22   *Chair*, Vienna, 1830/35, walnut, walnut veneer, modern upholstery, 91.2 x 43.4 x 50.8 cm, Milwaukee, Milwaukee Art Museum, Purchased with funds from Kenneth Treis (M2005.135), Prov. New York, Barry Friedman Gallery; Asenbaum Collection, Lit. Vienna 1987B, cat. 8/14, ill. p. 394, PLATE 43

The 1830s witnessed the development in Vienna of the so-called side-frame chair, which exhibited considerably greater lightness and transparency than the more solid furniture forms of the 1820s. The upholstery is flatter and extended over the front frame element. All visible structural elements are thinner and evoke a more vibrant effect.

II-23   *Chair*, Vienna, ca. 1820, Danhauser'sche Möbelfabrik (?) (1814–42), walnut veneer, maple inlays, modern upholstery, 95 x 45.7 x 48.3 cm, New York, Private Collection, Courtesy Iliad Antik, New York, Prov. New York, Iliad Antik

II-24   *Chair*, Vienna, ca. 1825, Danhauser'sche Möbelfabrik, walnut and birch veneer on beech and softwood, modern upholstery, 90 x 47.5 x 45 cm, Milwaukee, Milwaukee Art Museum, Gift of Helen Oberndorfer in Memory of Her Sister Jeanette Oberndorfer (M2004.565), Prov. Rita Bucheit, Ltd., Chicago, PLATE 45

II-25   *Chair*, Vienna, ca. 1825, Danhauser'sche Möbelfabrik (?), mahogany veneer, maple inlays, 92 x 50 x 53 cm, New York, Iliad Antik, PLATE 47

II-26   *Chair*, Vienna, ca. 1825, walnut and pear veneer on beech, penwork on maple, modern upholstery, 94 x 44.5 x 40 cm, Paris, Musée du Louvre (OA 12194), Prov. Vienna Art Market, 1970s; Vienna, Private Collection, Lit. Vienna 1987B, cat. 8/5, p. 391, PLATE 46

II-27   *Chair*, Vienna, 1815/20, Danhauser'sche Möbelfabrik (?) (1814–42), mahogany and Pyramid mahogany, veneer, upholstery, H 91.4 cm, New York, Collection of Ellen and Bill Taubman, Prov. Vienna, Asenbaum Collection, 1998, PLATE 49

II-28   *Chair*, Bohemia, 1815/20, walnut veneer on beech and softwood, 88 x 44 x 42 cm, Prague, Museum of Decorative Arts, Acquisition, 1971 (74.912/1971), Prov. Prague, L. Veselá, Lit. Padua 2000, cat. 160, fig. 74, PLATE 51

II-29   *Chair*, Austria, ca. 1820, walnut, 92 x 43 x 46 cm, New York, Collection of Ellen and Bill Taubman, Purchase, 1990, Prov. New York, Sotheby's; Vienna, Inge Zerunian and Susan Pisarcewicz, PLATE 50

II-30   *Chair*, Vienna, ca. 1830, mahogany, mahogany veneer on beech and softwood, modern upholstery, 89 x 47 x 48 cm, Asenbaum Collection, Prov. Vienna Art Market, 1980s

II-31   *Chair*, Vienna, 1815/20, walnut, walnut veneer, maple, ebonized wood on pine, 94 x 47 x 43.5 cm, Paris, Musée du Louvre (OA 12191), Prov. Vienna Art Market, 1970s; Asenbaum Collection, PLATE 52

II-32   *Armchair*, Vienna, ca. 1825, Danhauser'sche Möbelfabrik (1814–42) (Model No. 86), mahogany, mahogany veneer, pine core, modern upholstery, 116 x 76 x 76 cm, Vienna, Bundesmobilienverwaltung, Hofmobiliendepot. Möbel Museum Wien (MD 5227), Prov. Vienna, The Viennese Court, Lit. Vienna 1981, cat. 44, ill. p. 146, cat. 177, ill. p. 224; Vienna 1987B, cat. 8/21, ill. p. 369; Schallaburg 1997, p. 33, fig. 18, p. 79, pl. 54, PLATE 53

The innovative quality of this armchair is attributable not only to its simple shape but above all to the fact that it is upholstered with individual, removable elements. By placing the rigid structural components on the outside, providing tectonic support for the soft upholstery, Danhauser created an armchair that may be regarded as a precursor to Corbusier's "fauteuil grand comfort" of 1928.

II-33   *Pair of Armchairs*, Austria (?), 1825/30, ash veneer, maple, turned ebonized wood, ebonized inlays, modern upholstery, each 82.6 x 64.8 x 61 cm, New York, Daniel Romualdez Collection, Prov. New York, Juan Portela Antiques, 1980s, Lit. Wilkie 1987, p. 144, fig. 134, PLATE 55

II-34   *Pair of Armchairs*, Austria, ca. 1830, walnut veneer, modern upholstery, each 90.2 x 66 x 50.8 cm, New York, Collection of Christopher Forbes, Prov. New York, Christie's, 1987, Lit. Wilkie 1987, pp. 90–91, fig. 67, PLATE 54

II-35   *Settee*, Vienna, ca. 1815, Danhauser'sche Möbelfabrik (1814–42), mahogany veneer, gilding, reconstructed upholstery, 113 x 214 x 66 cm, Milwaukee Art Museum, Gift of René von Schleinitz Memorial Fund, by exchange (M2001.61), Prov. Munich, Art Fundus Biedermeiermöbel, Lit. Witt-Dörring 1993, figs. 1, 19, 20; Winters 2004, pls. 2, 2a; Milwaukee 2004, p. 19, cat. 22, PLATE 57

II-36   *Settee*, Austria, ca. 1820, maple veneer, mahogany veneer, upholstery, 100 x 194 x 70 cm, Munich, Schlapka KG, Axel Schlapka, Lit. Ottomeyer and Schlapka 2000, ill. p. 204; Pressler, Döbner, and Eller 2002, cat. 471, ill. p. 7, PLATE 56

II-37   *Settee*, Vienna, 1825/30, cherry, 99 x 192 x 82 cm, Vienna, Bundesmobilienverwaltung, Hofmobiliendepot. Möbel Museum Wien (MD 48394), Prov. Vienna, Laxenburg Palace (L 10885), Lit. Vienna 1987B, cat. 33, ill. p. 395, PLATE 58

This creation consisting of separate upholstered cushions is a variation on a Turkish divan. Danhauser gave it a curving wood base that provides tectonic support for the seating unit without detracting from the supposedly flexible character of the upholstered elements, which is achieved by the complete elimination of wood structural elements. The result is a tense balancing act between hardness and softness.

II-38   *Settee*, Vienna, 1825/30, ash, ash veneer, ebonized pear, modern upholstery, 94 x 180 x 68 cm, Asenbaum Collection, Prov. Munich Art Market, 1980s, PLATE 59

Reconstructed on the basis of original drawings, the upholstery of this settee exemplifies the use of appliqués and drapery elements as tectonic components that was typical of the period. Borders and cords define the individual upholstered elements. The drapery hung between the legs of the

settee counteracts the ponderous character of the piece and allows it to appear suspended in the air.

II-39   *Settee*, Vienna, 1825/30, walnut veneer on softwood, modern upholstery, 92.5 x 132 x 69 cm, Milwaukee Art Museum, Gift of René von Schleinitz Memorial Fund (M2005.146), Prov. Asenbaum Collection, PLATE 60

Although this settee appears to be composed of separate upholstered elements, the two lower horizontal sections consist of a single wood box covered with fabric. In a purely visual sense, the upholstery assumes a weight-bearing, tectonic function.

II-40   *Settee*, Vienna, 1825/30, Danhauser'sche Möbelfabrik (?) (1814–42), walnut, walnut veneer, modern upholstery, 97.2 x 141.6 x 65.5 cm, Paris and New York, Didier Aaron, Inc., and Barry Friedman, Ltd., Prov. Asenbaum Family; New York, Barry Friedman, Ltd., October 1999, PLATE 61

II-41   *Settee*, Vienna, ca. 1830, cherry, cherry veneer, turned mahogany, mahogany inlay, ebonized wood, reconstructed upholstery, 98 x 182 x 67.5 cm, Paris, Musée du Louvre (OA 12190), Prov. Vienna, Private Collection since 1920s; Asenbaum Collection, PLATE 62

II-42   *Daybed*, Vienna, 1825/30, walnut veneer on beech and softwood, maple inlays, modern upholstery, 92 x 230 x 75 cm, Vienna, Bundesmobilienverwaltung, Hofmobiliendepot. Möbel Museum Wien (MD 53296), Prov. Vienna, Schönbrunn Palace (S 19968), PLATE 63

CABINETMAKERS' DRAWINGS

SECTION III

III-1 *Drawing for a Simple Table*, Vienna, ca. 1815, pen and black ink, watercolor, gray wash, 31.5 x 45.5 cm, Vienna, Michael Huey, Prov. Vienna Art Market, 1990s, Lit. New York 2003, ill. pp. 90–91, PLATE 65

III-2 Christian N. Knudsen (dates unknown), *Patterns for Chairs*, Copenhagen, 1826, pen and black ink, 48.1 x 34.3 cm, Copenhagen, The Danish Museum of Decorative Art, Prov. Copenhagen Guild of Cabinetmakers' Archives, Lit. Gelfer-Jørgensen 2004, cat. 321, pp. 325f., PLATE 66

III-3 Christian N. Knudsen (dates unknown), *Patterns for Small Tables*, Copenhagen, 1826, pen and black ink, watercolor, 54.6 x 43.3 cm, Copenhagen, The Danish Museum of Decorative Art, Prov. Copenhagen Guild of Cabinetmakers' Archives, Lit. Gelfer-Jørgensen 2004, cat 323, pp. 325f., PLATE 64

III-4 Artist Unknown, *Design for a Writing Cabinet: Elevation, Cross Section, Groundplan*, Copenhagen, 1810/25, pen and black ink, watercolor, 44.7 x 34 cm, Copenhagen, The Danish Museum of Decorative Art, Prov. Copenhagen Guild of Cabinetmakers' Archives, PLATE 68

III-5 Artist Unknown, *Design Drawing for Two Writing Cabinets: Elevation, Cross Section, Groundplan*, Copenhagen, ca. 1820, pen and black ink, watercolor, 31.5 x 46.5 cm, Copenhagen, The Danish Museum of Decorative Art, Prov. Copenhagen Guild of Cabinetmakers' Archives, PLATE 67

III-6 Carl August Reichelt (Master 1828), *Design Drawing for a Writing Cabinet: Cross Section, Oblique View (open), Groundplan*, Austria, 1825, pen and black ink, watercolor 45 x 34.5 cm, Vienna, Akademie der bildenden Künste, Kupferstichkabinett (15040), Lit. Vienna 1996, cat. 67, ill. p. 76, PLATE 69

III-7 Andreas Pfeffer (Master 1819), *Drawing for a Settee or Tea Table: Front View, Side View with Part of Cross Section, Top View of the Pedestal with Groundplan*, Vienna, 1819, master

drawing, pen and black ink, watercolor, 40.6 x 33 cm, Vienna, Akademie der bildenden Künste, Kupferstichkabinett (14982), Lit. Vienna 1996, cat. 23, ill. p. 66, PLATE 70

III-8 Artist Unknown, *Six Views of the Linear Light-Dark Gradation of a Ball with Shadowing*, Copenhagen, 1820, pen and black ink, gray wash, 31.6 x 49.2 cm, Copenhagen, The Danish Museum of Decorative Art, Prov. Copenhagen Guild of Cabinetmakers' Archives, PLATE 71

III-9 Artist Unknown, *Three Views of the Interface of Roll Molding and Octahedron: Elevation, Cross Section, Groundplan*, Copenhagen, ca. 1820, pen and black ink, gray wash, 42.8 x 54.2 cm, Copenhagen, The Danish Museum of Decorative Art, Prov. Copenhagen Guild of Cabinetmakers' Archives, PLATE 72

III-10 Artist Unknown, *Two Views of a Stepped Gradation of a Crowning Ornament*, Copenhagen, ca. 1820, pen and black ink, watercolor, gray wash, 31.2 x 49.1 cm, Copenhagen, The Danish Museum of Decorative Art, Prov. Copenhagen Guild of Cabinetmakers' Archives, PLATE 73

III-11 Artist Unknown, *Four Views of Moldings: Elevation, Groundplan*, Copenhagen, ca. 1820, pen and black ink, watercolor, gray wash, 49 x 31.8 cm, Copenhagen, The Danish Museum of Decorative Art, Prov. Copenhagen Guild of Cabinetmakers' Archives, PLATE 74

III-12 Artist Unknown, *Six Views of Pilaster Moldings with Plinths: Elevation, Groundplan*, Copenhagen, ca. 1820, pen and black ink, gray wash, 65 x 49.9 cm, Copenhagen, The Danish Museum of Decorative Art, Prov. Copenhagen Guild of Cabinetmakers' Archives, PLATE 75

INTERIOR VIEWS

SECTION IV

IV-1   Johann Stephan Decker (Colmar 1784-1844 Vienna), *Room in the Apartment of Duchess Sophie in Blauer Hof in Laxenburg*, Vienna, 1826, gouache, 25 x 25.5 cm, Potsdam, Stiftung Preussische Schlösser und Gärten Berlin-Brandenburg (482), Prov. Former property of Queen Elisabeth of Prussia, Lit. Schallaburg 1997, cat. 4.02, pp. 64, 159f, PLATE 76

IV-2   Artist Unknown, *Tent Room, Charlottenhof Palace*, Potsdam, after 1830, pen and black ink, watercolor, 15.4 x 20.5 cm, Potsdam, Stiftung Preussische Schlösser und Gärten Berlin-Brandenburg (SPSG 3866), Prov. Former property of Queen Elisabeth of Prussia, Lit. Hamburg 2002, cat. 35, p. 146, PLATE 77

IV-3   Johann Erdmann Hummel (Kassel 1769-1852 Berlin), *Interior with Three Mirrors*, Berlin, ca. 1820, pen and black ink, gray wash, 22.5 x 32.5 cm, Berlin, Stiftung Stadtmuseum Berlin (VII 61/1171 w), Second version: Vienna, Collection of Christian Witt-Dörring, Prov. Erfurt, Georg Hummel, Lit. Hummel 1824-25, unpag., § 2; Vienna 1981, cat. 122, p. 206; Söntgen 2004, pp. 315f., fig. 4, PLATE 78

IV-4   Leopold Zielcke (Danzig 1791-1861 Berlin), *Erdmann Hummel Teaching Perspective at the Königliche Akademie der Künste*, Berlin, ca. 1830, pen and black ink, watercolor, 42.4 x 43.2 cm, Berlin, Deutsches Historisches Museum, Purchase, 2004 (Gr 2004/197), PLATE 79
Born and educated in Kassel, the architect and painter Johann Erdmann Hummel began teaching drawing at the Akademie der Künste Berlin in 1802. In 1809, he conducted a course in "Kunst- und Gewerkschule" (School for Art and Crafts) in the Architectural Drafting, Perspective, and Optics class at the Akademie. Leopold Zielcke became Hummel's assistant in 1820 and was appointed professor at the Akademie in 1826. His accurately detailed depiction of a simply furnished historical classroom at the Akademie shows Hummel and his students engaged in practical experiments in projection.

IV-5   Artist Unknown, *Living Room with Laid Table*, Berlin, ca. 1830, pencil, watercolor, gouache on cardboard, 17.2 x 29.7 cm, Nuremberg, Germanisches Nationalmuseum, Acquisition, 1936 (Hz 4250, Kaps. 712a), Prov. Berlin, Ernst Heinicke, Lit. Nuremberg 1995, cat. 21, ill. p. 33, PLATE 80

IV-6   Artist Unknown, *Dining Room with Laid Table*, Berlin, ca. 1840, pencil, watercolor, gouache on cardboard, 18.4 x 25.4 cm, Nuremberg, Germanisches Nationalmuseum, Acquisition, 1936 (Hz 4251, Kaps. 712a), Prov. Berlin, Ernst Heinicke, Lit. Nuremberg 1995, cat. 21, ill. p. 33, PLATE 81

IV-7   Monogrammist EW (dates unknown), *The Study of Prince Andreas Rasumofsky in his Vienna Palace*, Vienna, ca. 1820, pencil, pen and black ink, watercolor, gouache on cardboard, 18.6 x 25.5 cm, Nuremberg, Germanisches Nationalmuseum, Acquisition, 1915 (Hz 4300, Kaps. 712a), Prov. Berlin, S. S. Botkina Collection, Purchased by Willy Matthies, 1935, Lit. Berlin 1970, cat. 73, fig. 10; Nuremberg 1995, cat. 1, ill. p. 29, PLATE 82

IV-8   Stephanie von Fahnenberg (Munich 1817-ca. 1910 Munich), *Living Room of Alexander von Fahnenberg at Wilhelmstrasse 69*, Berlin, 1837/38, pen and black ink, watercolor, gouache, 28.6 x 24.1 cm, Nuremberg, Germanisches Nationalmuseum, Acquisition, 1939 (Hz 6112, Kaps. 1551b), Prov. Linz, A. M. Pachinger Collection, Lit. Nuremberg 1995, cat. 14, ill. p. 32, PLATE 84

IV-9   Leopold Zielcke (Danzig 1791-1861 Berlin), *The Artist's Studio in His Apartment at Friedrichstrasse 228*, Berlin, ca. 1825, pen and black ink, watercolor, gouache, 46.7 x 58.7 cm, Nuremberg, Germanisches Nationalmuseum, Acquisition, 1912 (Hz 5157, Kaps. 1011c), Prov. Berlin, Amsler and Ruthardt, Lit. Nuremberg 1995, cat. 39, ill. p. 36, PLATE 83

IV-10   Heinrich Krüppel, Jr. (? ca. 1814-1832?),
Blue Room in the Bürglass Palace in Coburg,
Coburg, 1832, gouache, 40.9 x 57.1 cm, Coburg,
Kunstsammlungen der Veste Coburg (z 4080),
Prov. Coburg, Landesbibliothek 1963, Lit. Seelig
1981, pp. 3ff., ill. p. 3, PLATE 85

IV-11   Heinrich Krüppel, Jr. (? ca. 1814-1832?),
Yellow Room in the Bürglass Palace in Coburg,
Coburg, 1832, gouache, 41 x 56 7 cm, Coburg,
Kunstsammlungen der Veste Coburg (z 4078),
Prov. Coburg, Landesbibliothek 1963, Lit. Seelig
1981, pp. 9f., ill. p. 8, PLATE 86

IV-12   Heinrich Krüppel, Jr. (? ca. 1814-1832?),
Carpet Room in the Bürglass Palace in Coburg,
Coburg, 1832, gouache, 33.8 x 57.3 cm, Coburg,
Kunstsammlungen der Veste Coburg (z 4076),
Prov. Coburg, Landesbibliothek 1963, Lit. Seelig
1981, pp. 3ff., ill. p. 4, PLATE 87

IV-13   Johann Baptist Hoechle (Klingnau/
Aargau 1754-1832 Vienna), *A Room in Schönbrunn
Palace*, Vienna, ca. 1818, gouache, 23.3 x 35 cm,
Vienna, Wien Museum (61.087), Prov. Vienna, Dr.
A. Heyman Collection, Lit. Waissenberger 1986,
cat. 60, p. 69, PLATE 88

IV-14   Artist Unknown, *My Room in Vienna*,
Vienna, 1837/42, gouache, 20 x 35.4 cm, Vienna,
Wien Museum (96.745/2), Prov. Vienna,
Auktionshaus Kende, Lit. Waissenberger 1986,
cat. 106, p. 111, PLATE 89

IV-15   Franz von Maleck (Austria 1787-1849),
A Living Room in Vienna, Vienna, 1836, watercolor, 25.8 x 38.1 cm, Vienna, Wien Museum 1937
(58.774), Prov. Vienna, Antiquariat Gilhofer und
Ranschberg, Lit. Waissenberger 1986, cat. 57,
p. 68; Schallaburg 1997, p. 10, PLATE 90

IV-16   Artist Unknown, *Room of the Gyulai
Family in Vienna*, Vienna, ca. 1829/31,
watercolor, 27.5 x 39.2 cm, Prague, Fürst Karl
zu Schwarzenberg, Prov. Prague, Orlik Castle,
Lit. Schallaburg 1997, cat. 9.16, p. 210, PLATE 91

IV-17   Artist Unknown, *Room in Vinor Castle*,
Prague, 1836, watercolor, 21.5 x 27 cm, Prague,
National Gallery (DK 4844/6), Prov. Prague, Vinor
Castle, PLATE 92

IV-18   Artist Unknown, *Czernin Family
Interior at the Lazen House at Chudenice*, Prague,
ca. 1836, watercolor, 17 x 25 cm, Prague, National
Heritage Institute, on depot to Jindřichův Hradec
Castle, Prov. Prague, Formerly Petrohrad Castle
(64/3666/818), Lit. Schallaburg 1997, cat. 6.48,
p. 191, PLATE 93

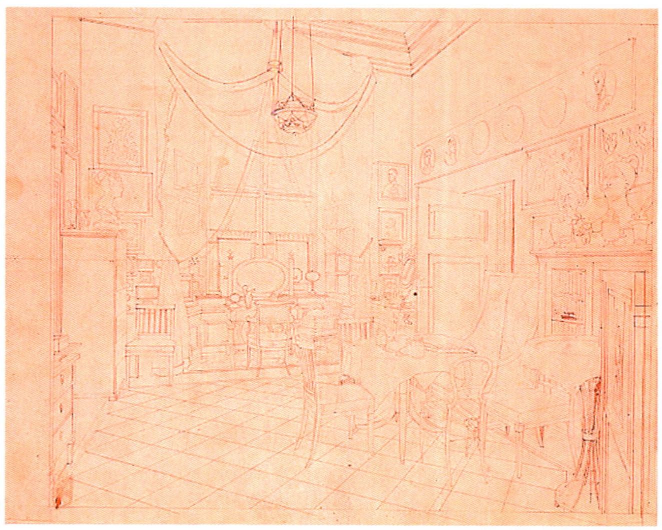

IV-19   M. Sekim (active 1840s), *A Room in the Governor's Residence*, Hermannstadt, 1841, watercolor, gouache, accents of gold paint, 36.9 x 53.3 cm, New York, Eugene V. Thaw Collection, Prov. New York, York House, Inc., Lit. Gere 1989, pl. 215; Gere 1992, cat. 16, ill., pp. 60-61

IV-20   Matthäus Kern (Riedhausen 1801–1852 Vienna), *Study Interior at St. Pölten*, 1837, watercolor, 24.1 x 31.8 cm, New York, Eugene V. Thaw Collection, Prov. London, Sotheby's, 1992

IV-21   Artist Unknown, *Room in the Apartment of Princess Elisabeth*, Berlin, ca. 1840, pencil, gouache, white highlights, 16.4 x 23.2 cm, Kronberg, Hessische Hausstiftung (StAD, D 23, Kasten 1/23), Prov. Fürstliche Schlösser im Besitz des Hauses Hessen, Lit. Eichenzell 2004, cat. no. 18, ill., pp. 72-73, PLATE 94

IV-22   Eduard Gaertner (Berlin 1801–1877 Zechlin, Brandenburg), *Prince Waldemar's Living Room in the Royal Palace*, Berlin, 1847, pencil, watercolor, gouache, highlights, 25.3 x 30 cm, Kronberg, Hessische Hausstiftung (StAD, D 23, Kasten 1/24), Prov. Fürstliche Schlösser im Besitz des Hauses Hessen, Lit. Eichenzell 2004, cat. no. 20, ill., pp. 76-77, PLATE 95

IV-23   Eduard Gaertner (Berlin 1801–1877 Zechlin, Brandenburg), *Toilette Room in the Apartment of Prince Wilhelm and Princess Marianne in the Royal Palace*, Berlin, 1849, pencil, 27.5 x 33 cm, Berlin, Stiftung Stadtmuseum Berlin (VII 59/53 w), Prov. Berlin, Estate of E. Gaertner, 1922, Lit. Eichenzell 2004, cat. no. 8, ill., pp. 46-47, see IV-24

IV-24   Eduard Gaertner (Berlin 1801–1877 Zechlin, Brandenburg), *Toilette Room in the Apartment of Prince Wilhelm and Princess Marianne in the Royal Palace*, Berlin, 1849, pencil, watercolor, gouache, highlights, 25.6 x 30.1 cm, Kronberg, Hessische Hausstiftung (StAD, D 23, Kasten 1/18), Prov. Fürstliche Schlösser im Besitz des Hauses Hessen, Lit. Eichenzell 2004, cat. no. 8, ill., pp. 46-47, PLATE 96

IV-25   J. Ferdinand Rothbart (Nuremberg 1823-1899 Rome), *Prince Albert's Salon, the Former Salon of Duke Ernst in Rosenau Palace, Coburg*, Coburg, ca. 1848, watercolor, 23.7 x 32.2 cm, Windsor, The Royal Library (RL 20470), Prov. SCG III 48a, Album with Interior Views of the Saxe-Coburg-Gotha Palace, former property of Queen Victoria of England, Lit. Seelig 1981, pp. 5ff., ill. p. 5; Millar 1995, cat. 4804, p. 769, PLATE 97

IV-26   J. Ferdinand Rothbart (Nuremberg 1823-1899 Rome), *The Queen's Salon, the Former Salon of the Duchess Luise in Rosenau Palace, Coburg*,

Coburg, ca. 1848, watercolor, 23.3 x 32 cm,
Windsor, The Royal Library (RL 20471), Prov.
SA III 17, Album with Interior Views of the Saxe-
Coburg-Gotha Palace, former property of Queen
Victoria of England, Lit. Seelig 1981, pp. 5ff.,
ill. p. 5; Millar 1995, cat. 4802, p. 768, PLATE 98

IV-27   J. Ferdinand Rothbart (Nuremberg
1823–1899 Rome), *The Bedroom of Duke Ernest in
Rosenau Palace, Coburg*, Coburg, ca. 1848, watercolor, 26.8 x 36.7 cm, Windsor, The Royal Library
(RL 20473), Prov. SCG III 48b, Album with Interior
Views of the Saxe-Coburg-Gotha Palace, former
property of Queen Victoria of England, Lit. Seelig
1981, pp. 5ff., ill. p. 4; Millar 1995, cat. 4803,
p. 769, PLATE 99

IV-28   Georg Konrad Rothbart (1817–1896),
*The Room of the Princes in Rosenau Palace,
Coburg*, Coburg, ca. 1845, watercolor, 22.6 x 31 cm,
Windsor, The Royal Library (RL 20468), Prov.
SCG III 49a, Album with Interior Views of the Saxe-
Coburg-Gotha Palace, former property of Queen
Victoria of England, Lit. Heym 1990, pp. 14ff.,
ill. p. 23; Millar 1995, cat. 4789, ill. p. 767,
PLATE 100

COLOR THEORY AND SCIENTIFIC INSTRUMENTS

SECTION V

V-1   Christian Daniel Rauch (Arolsen 1777-1857 Dresden), *Johann Wolfgang von Goethe, Statuette after a Draft for a Monument in Frankfurt am Main* (not realized), Berlin, ca. 1825, bronze, 29 x 13.5 x 24.5 cm, Berlin, Deutsches Historisches Museum, Acquisition 2004 (Pl 2004/10), Lit. Eggers 1889, pp. 81, 86, 102f.; Dresden 1993, pp. 58f.; Simson 1996, cat. 124.1-4, PLATE 101

The Frankfurt banker Simon Moritz von Bethmann commissioned Christian Daniel Rauch to design a Goethe monument. Rauch modeled three slightly different plaster statuettes depicting the poet seated in an armchair, dressed in an ancient toga and wearing Roman sandals. Students at Rauch's Berlin Foundry made a bronze cast of the third model. None of Rauch's models was ever realized as a monument. (Leonore Koschnick)

V-2   Johann Wolfgang von Goethe (Frankfurt am Main 1749-1832 Weimar), *Symbolic Approximation to Magnets*, after 1798, watercolor, 16.1 x 19.8 cm, Weimar, Stiftung Weimarer Klassik, Goethe-Nationalmuseum (GFZ 142), Prov. Estate of J. W. von Goethe, Lit. Matthaei 1963, cat. 142, pp. 51f., pl. 81; Matthaei 1971, p. 54, fig. 51; Paris 2003, p. 114, fig. 6

The two rectangles on the right in the colors of edge spectra provide the starting point for this diagram; the superimposition of these colors produces the variants shown in the center. The magnets illustrate the idea of polarity that is so central to the color wheel. Yellow and blue, as the colors derived from light and dark, are shown here as opposites that become orange and bluish-red respectively.

V-3   Johann Wolfgang von Goethe (Frankfurt am Main 1749-1832 Weimar), *Plate I of the* Theory of Colors, 1810, etching, aquatint, watercolor, 29.2 x 22.5 cm, Weimar, Stiftung Weimarer Klassik, Goethe-Nationalmuseum (GFZ 139), Prov. Estate of J. W. von Goethe, Lit. Matthaei 1963, cat. 139, p. 49, pl. 82, PLATE 102

This first plate brings together all the fundamental principles of Goethe's color theory from the complementarity of mutually evocative physiological colors and the polarity of physically and chemically produced colors to the "sensuously

moral effect of colors." Plates II-XI that follow are devoted to what Goethe called the physiological colors.

V-4   Johann Wolfgang von Goethe (Frankfurt am Main 1749-1832 Weimar), *First Draft for Plate I of the* Theory of Colors, 1810, pen and black ink, watercolor, 22 x 18.5 cm, Weimar, Stiftung Weimarer Klassik, Goethe-Nationalmuseum (GFZ 137), Prov. Estate of J. W. von Goethe, Lit. Matthaei 1963, cat. 137, p. 48, pl. 79

This sketch by Goethe is a draft for Plate I of the supplementary volume to his *Theory of Colors*. The coloration of the color wheel is especially well preserved.

V-5   Johann Wolfgang von Goethe (Frankfurt am Main 1749-1832 Weimar) and Friedrich von Schiller (Marbach am Neckar 1759-1805 Weimar), *Rose of Temperaments*, 1798/99, watercolor, Dia 15.3 cm, Weimar, Stiftung Weimarer Klassik, Goethe-Nationalmuseum (GFZ 144), Prov. Estate of J. W. von Goethe, Lit. Matthaei 1963, cat. 144, p. 53; Paris 2003, p. 115, fig. 10, PLATE 103

The color wheel that brings together the principles of polarity and enhancement, the activity of the plus side and passivity of the minus side, as well as the complementarity and totality of opposing colors is here symbolically transferred to the temperaments, as represented by specific groups of people. This results in some extraordinary pairings, such as hero/historiographer, adventurer/teacher, and ruler/poet.

V-6   *Screen for the* Theory of Colors *(Table)*, Weimar, 1791, wood, paper, Dia 184 cm, Weimar, Stiftung Weimarer Klassik, Goethe-Nationalmuseum (GNF 0128), Prov. Estate of J. W. von Goethe, Lit. Paris 2003, p. 118, fig. 16, PLATE 105

The chromatic equipment in Goethe's estate included demonstration screens in a variety of sizes. These were used for lectures and experiments in front of large audiences. The size chosen depended upon the scale of the room and distance of the audience.

V-7   Johann Wolfgang von Goethe (Frankfurt am Main 1749-1832 Weimar), *Plate IIa of the* Theory of Colors, 1810, etching, aquatint, 21 x 17.7 cm, Weimar, Stiftung Weimarer Klassik, Goethe-Nationalmuseum (GFZ 172), Prov. Estate of J. W. von Goethe, Lit. Matthaei 1963, cat. 172, p. 59; Paris 2003, p. 119, fig. 18, PLATE 106

Goethe himself described Plate II as an "insert" showing the most important subjective prismatic color experiments. These are performed by looking through a prism at the various figures on the plate. The colored peripheries or edge spectra and combinations of the same observed here show all six colors of the color wheel.

v-8   Johann Wolfgang von Goethe (Frankfurt am Main 1749–1832 Weimar), *Plate III of the* Theory of Colors, 1810, etching, aquatint, watercolor, 26.6 x 21.8 cm, Weimar, Stiftung Weimarer Klassik, Goethe-Nationalmuseum (GFZ 178), Prov. Estate of J. W. von Goethe, Lit. Matthaei 1963, cat. 178, p. 60, pl. 83, PLATE 107

Plates II and III were created for experiments with a prism, the purpose of which was to explore physical colors. The patterns are arranged in much the same way as in a plate in the second chapter of *Contributions to Optics* of 1792 that was intended for subjective prismatic experiments using both colored and gray areas.

v-9   *Eighteen Samples of German and French Wallpaper from Goethe's Sample Collection*, Weimar, ca. 1800, paper, various sizes, Weimar, Stiftung Weimarer Klassik, Goethe-Nationalmuseum (GNF 0396), Prov. Estate of J. W. von Goethe, Lit. Hölz 1999, pp. 126f., ill. p. 127

v-10   *104 Samples of German and French Textiles from Goethe's Sample Collection*, Weimar, ca. 1800, textiles, various sizes, Weimar, Stiftung Weimarer Klassik, Goethe-Nationalmuseum (GNF 0389), Prov. Estate of J. W. von Goethe, PLATE 108

These material samples were used to showcase the "sensuously moral effect of color" discussed in the "Didactic Section" of *Theory of Colors*. The focus here is on how certain colors and color combinations affect the eye and the human psyche, the underlying principles being those that informed the color wheel as well. While yellow, yellowish-red, and reddish-yellow belong firmly on the plus side, blue, reddish-blue and bluish-red are allocated to the minus side. Combinations of colors that are opposite each other on the color wheel are "harmonious," according to Goethe, in that they answer the eye's instinctive need for totality and harmony. Goethe describes the interaction of two colors separated by a third as "characteristic," while that of neighboring colors is "characterless."

v-11   *Goethe's Handle Cup*, Karlsbad, ca. 1810, Gottlob Samuel Mohn (Weissenfels 1789–1825 Laxenburg), colorless glass, fluorescent transpar-

ent and silver corroding paint, gilding, H 10 x Dia 8 cm, Weimar, Stiftung Weimarer Klassik, Goethe-Nationalmuseum (GNF 0085), Prov. Estate of J. W. von Goethe, Lit. Berlin 1981A, pp. 175., PLATE 104

Opaque materials such as the snake on this mug turn yellow, orange, and then red the dimmer the ambient light becomes or, starting from darkness, turn blue to bluish-purple the lighter it becomes. Goethe interprets this effect as an enhancement of the simple polarity between yellow, as the color closest to light, and blue, as the color closest to darkness. He used this cup around 1810 in Karlsbad to demonstrate the original phenomenon.

v-12   *Frame with Prisms of Flint and Crown Glass*, Jena, 1800, Johann Friedrich Körner (Weimar 1778–1847 Jena), wood, brass, bronze, glass, 35.4 x 17.5 cm, Weimar, Stiftung Weimarer Klassik, Goethe-Nationalmuseum (F 0151), Prov. Estate of J. W. von Goethe, PLATE 109

Flint glass is made of lead crystal with a high refractive index and high material dispersion. Because of its high phosphate content, crown glass has a much lower refractive index and material dispersion. The different refractive properties of these two types of prisms were of interest to Goethe in connection with achromasia and hyperchromasia, which he thought could be treated by using an appropriate combination of prisms to diminish or enhance the color effects of optical refraction.

v-13   *Kaleidoscope*, Vienna, ca. 1840, Gebrüder Voigtländer & Sohn (1756–1972), wood, glass, paper, L 21 x Dia 6.5 cm, Vienna, Technisches Museum Wien (15.743)

In view of the increasing scientific interest in the natural world, instruments designed to enhance the perception of nature were a logical development. At practically the same time (1816/17), the Augsburg watchmaker Christoph Kaspar Höschel (1744–1820) and the Scottish physicist David Brewster (1781–1868) registered patents for two variations of the kaleidoscope. Rather than considered as optical toys, they were viewed as scientifically sound constructions with practical benefits especially for those working in the arts and creating decorative patterns (Yelin 1818, p. 9).

v-14   *Microscope*, Vienna, ca. 1835, Georg Simon Plössl (Weiden 1794–1864 Wien), brass, optical glass, H 55 cm, Munich, Deutsches Museum, Purchase, 1983 (1983–292), Prov. Diozösesammlung des bischöflichen Seminars Eichstätt, Lit. Munich 1971, p. 87, fig. 9, PLATE 110

v-15   *Theodolite, Eight-inch Universal Instrument*, Hohenbaum company, Germany, ca. 1830, brass, optical glass, 60 x 50 x 48 cm, Munich, Deutsches Museum, Purchase, 1918 (46506),

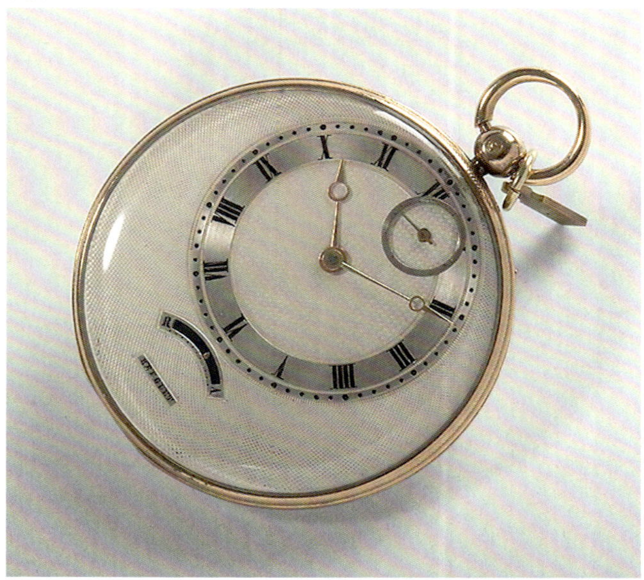

Prov. Sammlung der königlich preussischen Landesaufnahme Berlin, Lit. Munich 1971, p. 87, fig. 12, PLATE 111

v-16 *Travel Goniometer for Measuring Angles of Crystals*, Germany, ca. 1830, brass, steel, H 15 cm, Berlin, Humboldt-Universität zu Berlin, Museum für Naturkunde, Prov. Bought in early nineteenth century

v-17 *Goniometer (Contact Goniometer) for Measuring Angles of Crystals*, Germany, ca. 1820, brass, steel, Dia 12 cm, Berlin, Humboldt-Universität zu Berlin, Museum für Naturkunde

v-18 *Three Crystal Models*, Paris, 1810, René Just Haüy (Paris 1743–1822 Paris), porcelain, 7.5 x 3 cm; 4 x 4 cm; 5 x 4 cm, Berlin, Humboldt-Universität zu Berlin, Museum für Naturkunde, Prov. Donation of René Just Haüy

v-19 *Crystal Model with Removable Structure Model*, 1810, René Just Haüy (Paris 1743–1822 Paris), wood, leather, 7 x 7 cm; 14 x 6 cm, Berlin, Humboldt-Universität zu Berlin, Museum für Naturkunde, Prov. Donation of René Just Haüy, PLATE 113

v-20 *Chalcedony (Agate)*, Idar-Oberstein/ Rheinland-Pfalz, ca. 1820; Chalcedony (Agate), Idar-Oberstein/Rheinland-Pfalz, ca. 1820; Chalcedony (Agate) and Quartz, Cunersdorf/ Saxonia, ca. 1820, W 14 x L 11 cm; W 10 x L 8.5 cm; W 10 x L 8 cm, Berlin, Humboldt-Universität zu Berlin, Museum für Naturkunde (2000-4489/9363/9349), PLATE 112

v-21 *Mineralogical Ring Cabinet*, probably Dresden, ca. 1790, Johann Christian Neuber (dates unknown), attributed to, box with forty-one half jewel stone inserts, ring, and booklet with descriptions, wood, paper, fabric, gold, stones, box 20.3 x 11.5 cm; stones 1.7 x 0.9 cm, Munich, Kunstkammer Georg Laue München, Prov. France, Private Collection, Lit. Neuwied 2004, pp. 34f., PLATE 114

v-22 *Directoire Clock*, Paris, ca. 1795, marble, brass, enamel, steel, H 33 cm, Zurich, Uhrenmuseum Beyer Zürich, Purchase, 1992 (4060.06), Prov. Zurich, Collection of René and Theodore Beyer 1959, Lit. Kassel 1999, cat. 22.3.1, p. 533, PLATE 116

The technical precision of watches and clocks reached previously unimaginable heights near the end of the eighteenth century; design and construction followed suit. The functional features for the measurement of time were openly displayed as a sign of the artistry of their manufacturers. Producers of "skeleton clocks" dispensed with all decorative elements, as works themselves

were the ornament. The pocket watches made by
Abraham-Louis Breguet (cats. v-23, v-24) combined superior technical quality with simplicity
and clarity in design. They were equipped with a
self-winding mechanism, minute-by-minute repetition, a perpetual calendar, a thermometer, and an
independent second hand. The enameled and metal
faces are true works of art. Breguet had no qualms
about departing from symmetrical arrangements.
The plain, slim hands are fashioned with inimitable
elegance.

v-23   *Alexander von Humboldt's Pocket
Chronometer No. 224*, Paris?, ca. 1809, Abraham-
Louis Breguet (Neuchâtel 1747–1823 Paris), gold,
brass, enamel, steel, H 1.8 x Dia 6.1 cm, Zurich,
Uhrenmuseum Beyer Zürich, Purchase, 1967
(0555.61), Prov. Berlin, Estate of Alexander von
Humboldt (1769–1859); Basel, Collection of
Mr. E. Gschwind, Lit. Kassel 1999, cat. 22.3.4,
pp. 534f., PLATE 115

v-24   *Pocket Watch No. 4021*, Paris, ca. 1824,
Abraham-Louis Breguet (Neuchâtel 1747–1823
Paris), gold, brass, enamel, steel, Dia 4.2 cm,
Zurich, Uhrenmuseum Beyer Zürich (B2352.61),
Prov. London, Mannheimer Collection; Zurich,
Collection of Theodore Beyer 1976, Lit. Kassel
1999, cat. 22.3.6, p. 536

WALLPAPER

SECTION VI

VI-1   *Five Wallpapers from a Wallpaper Pattern Book*, Vienna, 1827, Fabrik Spörlin und Rahn Wien (1809–ca. 1847), woodblock print on paper, book 37 x 46.4 x 3 cm, unfolded sheets, each approx. 47/52-41/46 cm, Vienna, Technisches Museum Wien (36.877), Prov. Vienna, kaiserlich-königliches National-Fabriksprodukten-Kabinett Wien, PLATE 117

VI-2   *Wallpaper from a Wallpaper Pattern Book*, Vienna, 1824, Fabrik Spörlin und Rahn Wien (1809–ca. 1847), woodblock prints on paper, book 33 x 45.5 x 2 cm, unfolded sheet 51.5 x 45 cm, Vienna, Technisches Museum Wien (61.153), Prov. Vienna, kaiserlich-königliches National-Fabriksprodukten-Kabinett Wien, PLATE 118

VI-3   *Three Wallpapers from a Wallpaper Pattern Book*, Vienna, 1822–24, Fabrik Spörlin und Rahn Wien (1809–ca. 1847), woodblock prints on paper, book 33.5 x 43 x 2.5 cm, unfolded sheets, each approx. 30 x 43 cm, Vienna, Technisches Museum Wien (30.144), Prov. Vienna, kaiserlich-königliches National-Fabriksprodukten-Kabinett Wien

VI-4   *Two Wallpapers from a Wallpaper Pattern Book*, Vienna, 1828, Fabrik Spörlin und Rahn Wien (1809–ca. 1847), woodblock prints on paper, book 47 x 41 x 2 cm, unfolded sheets, each approx. 44.5 x 40.5 cm, Vienna, Technisches Museum Wien (61.112), Prov. Vienna, kaiserlich-königliches National-Fabriksprodukten-Kabinett Wien, PLATE 119

VI-5   *Wallpaper from a Wallpaper Pattern Book*, Vienna, 1829, Fabrik Spörlin und Rahn Wien (1809–ca. 1847), woodblock print on paper, book 46.5 x 41.5 x 2.5 cm, unfolded sheet 64.5 x 52 cm, Vienna, Technisches Museum Wien (61.124), Prov. Vienna, kaiserlich-königliches National-Fabriksprodukten-Kabinett Wien, PLATE 120

VI-6   *Wallpaper and Decorative Paper from a Pattern Book*, Vienna, 1828, Fabrik Spörlin und Rahn Wien (1809–ca. 1847), two woodblock prints on dyed, printed, pressed paper, book 51.5 x 39 x 2.5 cm, unfolded sheets each approx. 45 x 30/35 cm, Vienna, Technisches Museum Wien (61.104), Prov. Vienna, kaiserlich-königliches National-Fabriksprodukten-Kabinett Wien, PLATE 121

VI-7   *Decorative Paper and Two Wallpapers from a Pattern Book*, Vienna, 1827, Fabrik Spörlin und Rahn Wien (1809–ca. 1847), woodblock prints on paper, book 47 x 42 x 2 cm, unfolded sheets each approx. 45 x 42 cm, Vienna, Technisches Museum Wien (30.176), Prov. Vienna, kaiserlich-königliches National-Fabriksprodukten-Kabinett Wien, PLATE 122

VI-8   *Wallpaper from a Wallpaper Pattern Book*, Vienna, 1825, Fabrik Spörlin und Rahn Wien (1809–ca. 1847), woodblock print on paper, book 46 x 34 x 2 cm, Vienna, Technisches Museum Wien (24.652), Prov. Vienna, kaiserlich-königliches National-Fabriksprodukten-Kabinett Wien, PLATE 123

VI-9   *Wallpaper from a Wallpaper Pattern Book*, Vienna, 1823, Fabrik Spörlin und Rahn Wien (1809–ca. 1847), woodblock print on paper, book 44 x 34 x 2 cm, Vienna, Technisches Museum Wien (24.651), Prov. Vienna, kaiserlich-königliches National-Fabriksprodukten-Kabinett Wien, PLATE 124

VI-10   *Six Studies for the Decoration of Interior Walls*, Bohemia, 1837/50, Antonín Friebel the Elder (Choustníkovo Hradiště 1819–1905 Prague), gouache studies, each on three sheets of paper, each 39.5 x 26 cm, Prague, Museum of Decorative Arts (13.502/36, 71, 94), Lit. Padua 2000, p. 75, PLATE 125

VI-11   *Repeat Pattern Wallpaper with Upper and Lower (French?) Borders*, Germany, ca. 1825, Tapetenmanufaktur Johann Christian Arnold (1790–1883), woodblock print on primed paper, 201 x 68.5 cm, Kassel, Staatliche Museen, Tapetenmuseum (1138), Prov. Kassel, Nahl'sches House, Miss von Griesheim, 1931, Lit. Thümmler 1998, cat. 10, p. 78, PLATE 126

VI-12   *Repeat Pattern Wallpaper with Upper and Lower (French?) Borders*, Germany, 1808, Tapetenmanufaktur Johann Christian Arnold (1790–1883), woodblock print on primed paper, 170 x 61 cm, Kassel, Staatliche Museen, Tapetenmuseum (1137), Prov. Kassel, Brothers

Grimm House, 1936, Lit. Thümmler 1998, cat. 4, p. 72, PLATE 129

VI-13   *Repeat Pattern Wallpaper with Matching Upper and Lower Borders in Two Parts*, Germany, 1815/20, Tapetenmanufaktur Johann Christian Arnold (1790-1883), woodblock print on primed paper, 196 x 63 cm, Kassel, Staatliche Museen, Tapetenmuseum (1022), Prov. Kassel, Nahl'sches House, Gebr. Kölsch, Lit. Thümmler 1998, cat. 39, p. 110, PLATE 128

VI-14   *Repeat Pattern Wallpaper with Matching Upper and Lower Borders*, Germany, 1800/10, Tapetenmanufaktur Johann Christian Arnold (1790-1883), woodblock print on primed paper, 262 x 106 cm, Kassel, Staatliche Museen, Tapetenmuseum (1066), Prov. Weilberg, Weilburg Castle, 1938, Lit. Thümmler 1998, cat. 56, p. 130, PLATE 127

VI-15   *Repeat Pattern Wallpaper with Matching Upper and Lower Borders*, Germany, ca. 1820, Tapetenmanufaktur Johann Christian Arnold (1790-1883), woodblock print on primed paper, 197 x 69.5 cm, Kassel, Staatliche Museen, Tapetenmuseum (1084), Prov: Kassel, Nahl'sches Haus, Miss von Griesheim, 1931, Lit. Thümmler 1998, cat. 40, p. 112, PLATE 130

VI-16   *Repeat Pattern Wallpaper with Lower Border*, Germany, 1820/30, Tapetenmanufaktur Johann Christian Arnold (1790-1883), woodblock print on primed paper, 139 x 58 cm, Kassel, Staatliche Museen, Tapetenmuseum (1166), Prov. Kassel, Nahl'sches House, Miss von Griesheim, 1931, Lit. Thümmler 1998, cat. 48, p. 121, PLATE 131

PORCELAIN

SECTION VII

VII-1 *Coffee Service*, Nymphenburg, ca. 1825, design by Friedrich von Gärtner (Coblenz 1792–1847 Munich) and Johann Peter Melchior (Lintorf 1742–1825 Nymphenburg), Königliche Porzellanmanufaktur Nymphenburg (1757–present), porcelain, matte-blue glaze, gilding, Coffee pot H 19.5 cm; milk jug H 14.5 cm; coffee cup 8.2 cm; saucers each Dia 13.5 cm, Marks MM; RM: L, 1/5, Berlin, Deutsches Historisches Museum, acquired 2006 (KG 2006/9.1–4), Prov. Vienna, Dorotheum, Lit. Munich 1993, cat. 13.2.1, p. 237; Munich 1997, cat. 925, 929–934, 936, pp. 286–87, 937–38, PLATE 132

Designed in 1810, this coffee service is clearly influenced by French models, as is evident in its smooth, elegant forms. Although tea and coffee pots with bird's-head spouts, cylindrical necks, and band handles with leaf ornamentation were widespread in Europe, it is the contrast between the dull blue of the bodies and the polished gilding that make this elegant service so appealing.

VII-2 *Two Cups and Saucers*, Vienna, 1814/17, Wiener Porzellanmanufaktur (1718–1864), porcelain, colored underglaze, cups each H 5 cm; saucers each Dia 13.8 cm, Marks MM; JM: [1]814, [1]817; MN: 69,29,59,33, Vienna, Private Collection, Prov. Vienna Art Market, 1980s, PLATE 134

VII-3 *Two Cups and Saucers*, Vienna, 1825, Wiener Porzellanmanufaktur (1718–1864), porcelain, colored underglaze, green cup H 6.5 cm; saucer Dia 8.5 cm, red cup H 8.5 cm; saucer Dia 14.8 cm, Marks MM; WN: 27; MN: 33 and MM; WN: 2[7]; MN: 2, Vienna, Michael Huey, Prov. Vienna Art Market, 1990s

VII-4 *Coffee Bowls*, Vienna, ca. 1835, Wiener Porzellanmanufaktur (1718–1864), porcelain, colored overglaze, gilding, each H 4 cm, Dia 6.3 cm, Marks MM, Vienna, Technisches Museum Wien (19.254-55, 19.257, 19.323, 19.329, 36.822-23, 36.825-26), Prov. Vienna, kaiserlich-königliches National-Fabriksprodukten-Kabinett, Lit. Vienna 2004B, p. 94ff., PLATE 133

Designed after Turkish models, these small coffee bowls without handles illustrate the broad spectrum of colors used in Vienna, thanks to pigments ground from metal oxides. Executed with precious paints, the bodies of the bowls stand out appealingly against the gilding on the bottom ring and the rim accentuated by two rim lips.

VII-5 *Tea Service*, Vienna, 1811, porcelain, red-brown overglaze, white interior, teapot H 13.4 cm; cup H 7.5 cm; saucer Dia 15.2 cm, Prague, Museum of Decorative Arts (29.616/1,3), Prov. Prague, Auktionshaus Zdenek Jerábek, Lit. Aukce 1945, cat. 1277; Geismeier 1979, cat. 264, p. 361, PLATE 135

VII-6 *Writing Set (Large Box with Lid, Inkpot, Box with Lid, Beaker for Writing Tools, Bowl, and Tray)*, Vienna, 1823/24, Wiener Porzellanmanufaktur (1718–1864), porcelain, green underglaze, tray 3.8 x 29.6 x 21.6 cm, Marks MM; JM: [1]823/[1]824; WN: L; MN i2 [12], i3 [13], Vienna, Bundesmobilienverwaltung, Silberkammer Wien (MD 039251, 001-008), Prov. Vienna, Ehemalige Hofsilber- und Tafelkammer, PLATE 136

The geometric forms and contrasting colors of this writing set embody two essential aspects of the style of simplicity. The geometry determines not only the basic shape but also influences the form of details as an element of design. The chromium-oxide green surfaces are set off as contrasting elements against the white porcelain.

VII-7 *Family Dinner Service of Kaiser Franz II (I)*, Vienna, 1814/40, Wiener Porzellanmanufaktur (1718–1864), porcelain, gilding, round plate Dia 33.4 cm; oval plate 27.8 x 19.6 cm; salad bowl H 10.3 x Dia 27.2 cm; large platter 40.5 x 28.5 cm, Marks MM; JM; WN, Vienna, Bundesmobilienverwaltung, Silberkammer Wien (MD18.0058/023B, MD18.0058/028, MD18.0058/027, MD18.0058/031), Prov. Vienna, Ehemalige Hofsilber- und Tafelkammer, PLATE 137

VII-8 *Tea Service with Coffeepot*, Berlin, 1820/40, Königliche Porzellanmanufaktur Berlin (1763–present), porcelain, colored overglaze, teapot H 14.5 cm; coffee pot H 26 cm; cups each H 8/8.6, saucers each Dia 13.5/13.8 cm, Marks MM, Berlin, Stiftung Stadtmuseum Berlin (KH 2004/21 PB a-j), Prov. Berlin, Sammlung Albrecht Schütze, Bequest, 2002, Lit. Berlin 2003, p. 17, ill p. 10, PLATE 138

Originally produced as a tea service and later supplemented with a coffee pot in a corresponding design, this set reflects the tradition of the Königliche Porzellanmanufaktur Berlin as evidenced by the plain, white porcelain that underscores the quality of the forms and is accentuated only by an ornamental frieze and gilding on the contour lines. The remarkably three-dimensional painting of the wave frieze appears as a harmonizing design element in early pieces of Vienna porcelain.

VII-9   *Box with Faux Wood Decoration*, Vienna, 1796, Wiener Porzellanmanufaktur (1718–1864), porcelain, colored underglaze, H 6.6 cm, Dia 8.5 cm, Vienna, Collection of Christian Witt-Dörring, Prov. Vienna Art Market, 1990s

VII-10   *Two Cups and Saucers*, Vienna, ca. 1800, Wiener Porzellanmanufaktur (1718–1864), porcelain, colored overglaze, left cup H 5.6 cm; saucer Dia 13.7 cm, right cup H 5.5 cm; saucer Dia 13.5 cm, Bez. MM; JM: [18]00, Prague, Museum of Decorative Arts, Purchased 1954 (10.712ab and 39.253ab), Prov. Prague, Mici Bondy; Prague Art Market, PLATE 139

VII-11   *Cup and Saucer with Amethyst Pattern*, Vienna, ca. 1804, Wiener Porzellanmanufaktur (1718–1864), porcelain, colored overglaze, gilding, cup H 6.1; saucer Dia 13.4 cm, Marks MM; RM: 11; MM: 47' JM: [1]804, Vienna, Private Collection, Prov. Vienna Art Market, Lit. Berlin 1982, cat. 672, pl. 92, PLATE 140

VII-12   *Pitcher with Agate Pattern*, Vienna, 1810, Wiener Porzellanmanufaktur (1718–1864), porcelain, colored overglaze, gilding, H 13 cm, Marks MM; JM: [1]810, Vienna, Collection of Christian Witt-Dörring, Prov. Vienna Art Market, 1990s, PLATE 141

VII-13   *Flower Plates*, Vienna, 1818/27, Wiener Porzellanmanufaktur (1718–1864), porcelain, colored overglaze, gilding, Nymphea coerulea, 1827; Mesenbryanthemum, 1821; Capparis spinosa, 1821; Lirodendron tulipifera, 1821; Viola odorata, 1821; Dianthus caryophyllatuss, 1821; Dianthus caryophyllatuss, 1821; Primula auricula, 1821; Passiflora, 1821; Zinnea elegans, 1818; Bellis perennis, 1821, each H 3.5 x Dia 24.3/6 cm, Marks MM; JM: [1]818-[1]834; WN: 3, 13, 15, 18, 37, 46, 98; MN: 38, Vienna, Bundesmobilienverwaltung, Silberkammer Wien (MD 180076/105; 076; 130; 091; 125; 036; 071; 077; 111; 004; 039), Prov. Vienna, Ehemalige Hofsilber- und Tafelkammer, Lit. Faÿ-Hallé and Mundt 1983, p. 62; Berlin 1999, pp. 236–37, 270, 275, PLATE 142

The plant motifs painted on the brownish-black glazed centers of these plates exhibit extraordinary detail and liveliness. The flower painters at the Wiener Porzellanmanufaktur were masters in depicting even the finest nuances in the colors of leaves and blossoms. This series of more than ninety-six dessert plates with beige outer rings was supplemented by another series of green-rimmed plates in 1833 (VII-14), although the plant motifs in the later series have lost a great deal of plasticity.

VII-14   *Flower Plates*, Vienna, 1833, Wiener Porzellanmanufaktur (1718–1864), porcelain, colored overglaze, gilded, Camelia japonica alba, Camelia japonica, each Dia 24 cm; 24.5 cm, Vienna, Bundesmobilienverwaltung, Silberkammer Wien (MD 180076/163 and 167), Prov. Vienna, Ehemalige Hofsilber- und Tafelkammer, PLATE 143

VII-15   *Botanical Plate with Bromelia Pinguin*, Berlin, 1803/13, Königliche Porzellanmanufaktur Berlin (1763 – present), porcelain, colored overglaze, gilding, Dia. 23.8 cm, Marks MM; US, Berlin, Stiftung Preussische Schlösser und Gärten Berlin-Brandenburg, KPM-Porzellansammlung des Landes Berlin (B 77,68), Prov. Berlin, Private Collection, 1977, Lit. Berlin 1979, p. 79, PLATE 146

VII-16   *Plates from the Exotic Plants Dessert Service for Empress Joséphine of France*, Berlin, 1806–1807, Königliche Porzellanmanufaktur Berlin (1763 – present), porcelain, colored overglaze, gilding, Pelagonium echinatum, Nymphaea caerulea, each Dia 24.1 cm, Marks MM; US, Berlin, Stiftung Preussische Schlösser und Gärten Berlin-Brandenburg, KPM-Porzellansammlung des Landes Berlin (XII 8073; B 96/2), Prov. Wiesbaden Art Market, 1990; Private Collection, 1996, Lit. Berlin 1999, pp. 252, 255, figs. 46–48, PLATE 145

VII-17   *Botanical Plates*, Berlin, 1803/13, Königliche Porzellanmanufaktur Berlin (1763-present), porcelain, colored overglaze, gilding, Cheiranthus longefolius, Rafina triflora, Dia 23.8; Dia 24 cm, Marks MM; US, Berlin, Stiftung Preussische Schlösser und Gärten Berlin-Brandenburg, KPM-Porzellansammlung des Landes Berlin (B 81/3; B 77/2), Prov. Cologne Art Market, 1977, Lit. Berlin 1979, pp. 66–73; Berlin 1999, pp. 252, 255, figs. 46–48, PLATE 144

VII-18   *Snowball Flowers Platter*, Berlin, 1803/13, Königliche Porzellanmanufaktur Berlin (1763- present), porcelain, colored overglaze, gilding, Dia. 40 cm, Marks MM; US; MZ; PM: IIII 16, Berlin, Stiftung Preussische Schlösser und Gärten Berlin-Brandenburg, KPM-Porzellansammlung des Landes Berlin (83/10), Prov. Cologne Art Market, 1983, Lit. Berlin 1989, p. 53, PLATE 147

The flower plates produced by the Königliche
Porzellanmanufaktur Berlin differ from the later
examples from Vienna by virtue of the variable
coloration of the center and rim and the more
abundant use of leaf ornaments in which the depicted
plants are repeated as a silhouette. The liveliness
of the plants is particularly impressive in the large
showcase plates.

VII-19   *Fruit Basket from the Service of Princess
Luisa of Prussia and Prince Friedrich of the
Netherlands*, Berlin, 1825, design possibly by
Karl Friedrich Schinkel (Neuruppin 1781-1841
Berlin), Königliche Porzellan Manufaktur Berlin
(1763-present), glazed porcelain and biscuit
porcelain with open work, colored overglaze,
gilding, H 29 cm, Dia 28.8 cm, Potsdam, Stiftung
Preussische Schlösser und Gärten Berlin-
Brandenburg, Acquired 1962 (KS VIII 193.c.1),
Prov. Stockholm, Private Collection

GLASS

SECTION VIII

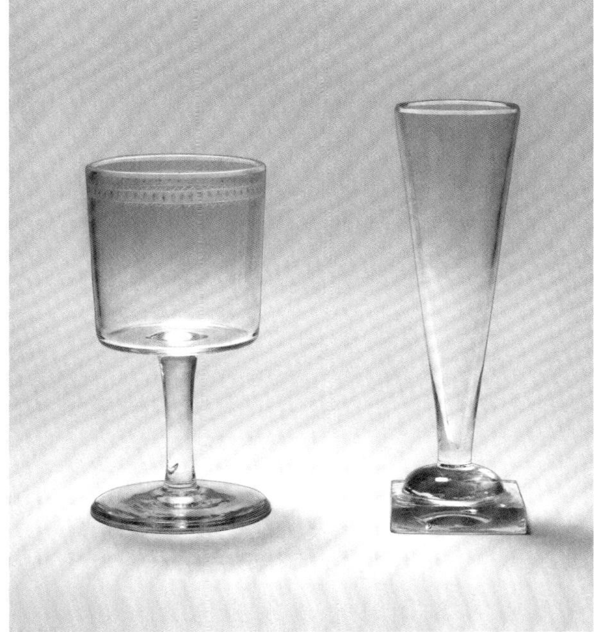

VIII-1 *Water Carafe, Water Glass, Champagne Glass*, Southern Germany, ca. 1800, colorless glass, matte engraved, cut, carafe H 21.2 cm, champagne glass H 17.2 cm; water glass H 10.7 cm, Munich, Münchner Stadtmuseum (48/249; L120; L92), Prov. Munich, Collection Ebenbuck, Lit. Munich 1993, cat. 12.2.5, fig. 228; Brožová 1995, vol. 2, fig. II.297, PLATE 148

VIII-2 *Wine Glass and Champagne Flute*, Vienna, ca. 1815, colorless glass, engraved, wine glass H 15.6 cm; champagne glass H 18.2 cm, Wernberg, Private Collection, Prov. By descent with same family, Lit. Vienna 1981, cats. 91, 92

VIII-3 *Beaker with Pansies*, Vienna, 1815/20, Anton Kothgasser (Vienna 1769–1851 Vienna), colorless glass, slightly convex side, on the underside a sixteen-pointed yellow-stained cut star, gilded edge, gilded inscription on yellow-stained banderole: "Elles sont toutes pour Vous," H 10.5 cm, Vienna, Kovacek Spiegelgasse Glas, Lit. Vienna 2003B, cat. 38, PLATE 153

VIII-4 *Beaker (Ranftbecher) with a Four-Leaf Clover*, Vienna, ca. 1820, Anton Kothgasser (Vienna 1769–1851 Vienna), colorless glass, transparent paint, Inscr.: "Gesundheit / verlängere / dein / Leben," H 11 cm, Vienna, Wien Museum, Purchase, 1927 (48.515), Prov. Vienna Art Market, Lit. Pazaurek and von Philippovich 1979, p. 208; Spiegl 1983, fig. 22; Vienna 1987B, cat. 6/1/25; Vienna 2000, cat. 18, pp. 36f., PLATE 154

VIII-5 *Beaker (Ranftbecher)*, Vienna, 1825/30, Anton Kothgasser (Vienna 1769–1851 Vienna), colorless glass, cut, yellow stained, transparent paint, gilded, H 11 cm, Prague, Museum of Decorative Arts, donated 1949 (30.532), Prov. Prague, Collection V. Butta

VIII-6 *Beaker with a Butterfly*, Vienna, ca. 1815, Anton Kothgasser (Vienna 1769–1851 Vienna), colorless glass, cut, yellow stained, transparent paint, gilded, H 10.2 cm, Prague, Museum of Decorative Arts, donated 1932 (17.712), Prov. Prague, Collection G.E. Pazaurek, PLATE 151

VIII-14

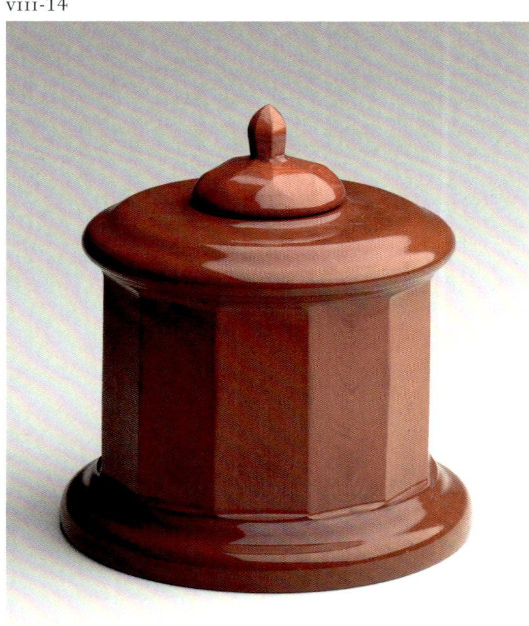

VIII-16

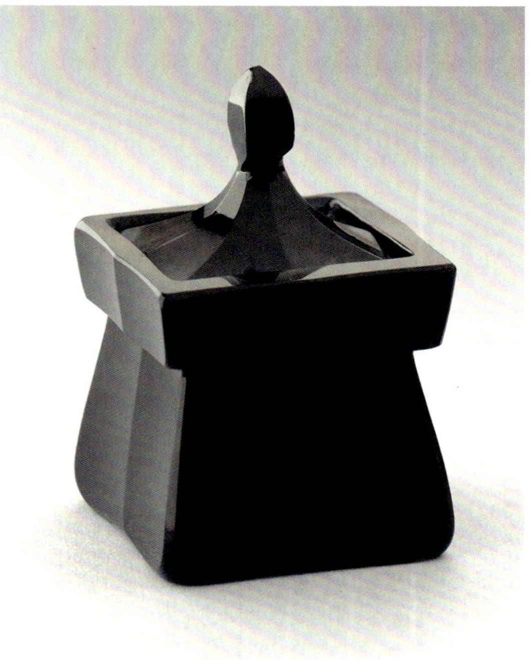

VIII-7 *Beaker (Ranftbecher) with a Butterfly*, Vienna, ca. 1815, Anton Kothgasser (Vienna 1769–1851 Vienna), colorless glass, mallet edge, on the underside a fifteen-pointed yellow-stained cut star, transparent enamel paint, gilded, H 10.2 cm, Vienna, Kovacek Spiegelgasse Glas, PLATE 150

VIII-8 *Travel Beaker Set (graduated set of seven)*, Northern Bohemia or Russia, 1820/30, colorless glass, enamel paint, gilded, cut, and polished, largest beaker H 10.7 cm x Dia. 9.8 cm, Toledo, Ohio, Toledo Museum of Art; Purchased with funds from the Libbey Endowment, gift of Edward Drummond Libbey (2004.1), Prov. Hokuriku, Japan, Hida Takayma Museum of Art, until 2002 (H105), PLATE 152

VIII-9 *Beaker (Ranftbecher) with Goldfish*, Vienna, 1820/30, Anton Kothgasser (Vienna 1769–1851 Vienna), colorless glass, cut, yellow stained, transparent paint, and gilded, H 11 cm, Prague, Museum of Decorative Arts, Purchase, 1961 (52.259), Prov. Prague, Antiquities Artia, PLATE 155

VIII-10 *Beaker (Ranftbecher)*, "Moon Glass," Vienna, ca. 1825, Anton Kothgasser (Vienna 1769–1851 Vienna), colorless glass, transparent paint, on the underside a sixteen-pointed star, H 10.8 cm, Vienna, Wien Museum, Purchase, 2000 (194.137), Prov. Vienna Art Market; Vienna, Collection Irmagard Müller-Mezin, Lit. Strasser [1977], p. 23, ill. 10, Pazaurek and von Philippovich 1979; PLATE 157

VIII-11 *Beaker (Ranftbecher) with Wood Grain*, Vienna, ca. 1825, Anton Kothgasser (Vienna 1769–1851 Vienna), colorless glass, mallet and gilded edge, gilded rim, rolled bottom, yellow stained, transparent enamel paint, H 10.5 cm, Vienna, Kovacek Spiegelgasse Glas, PLATE 156

VIII-12 *Agate Vase*, Zechlin, ca. 1800, Zechliner Glashütte (1741–1890), colored glass, H 29.2 x Dia 12.9 cm, Berlin, Stiftung Stadtmuseum Berlin (II 62/531 A), Prov. Berlin, Collection Stropp Ruppin, purchased Lepke Auction House, 1890, Lit. Berlin 1987, p. 23f., PLATE 149

VIII-13 *Gourd-Shaped Vase*, Bohemia, 1820, Jiříkovo Údolí (Georgenthal) Glassworks (eighteenth to early twentieth centuries), hot-shaped red hyalith, H 32 cm, Prague, Museum of Decorative Arts, Purchase, 1982 (91.377), Prov. Prague, Prague Antiquities, Lit. Zaragoza 2004, cat. 201, ill. p. 187, PLATE 158

VIII-14 *Covered Box*, Bohemia, ca. 1820, Jiříkovo Údolí (Georgenthal) Glassworks (eighteenth to early twentieth centuries), cut red hyalith, H 11.3 cm, Prague, Museum of Decorative Arts, donated by T. Bat'a, 1916 (14.260ab), Prov. Prague, Collection Joh. Novotný, Lit. Prague 2001, cat. 50, fig. 50; Zaragoza 2004, cat. 205, ill. p. 194

VIII-15   *Beaker*, Bohemia, ca. 1825, Jiříkovo Údoli (Georgenthal) Glassworks (eighteenth to early twentieth centuries), cut red hyalith, H 10.7 cm, Prague, Museum of Decorative Arts, Purchase, 1925 (94.437), Prov. Prague, Collection L. Bondy, Lit. Zaragoza 2004, cat. 203, ill. p. 188, PLATE 159

VIII-16   *Inkstand*, Bohemia, ca. 1830, Jiříkovo Údolí (Georgenthal) Glassworks (eighteenth to early twentieth centuries), cut black hyalith, H 10 cm, Prague, Museum of Decorative Arts, Purchase, 1978 (86.333), Prov. Prague, J. Zeman, Lit. Zaragoza 2004, cat. 177, ill. p. 180

VIII-17   *Beaker (Ranftbecher)*, Bohemia, ca. 1830, Friedrich Egermann (Sluknov 1777–1864 Nový Bor [Haida]), lithyalin, stained, cut and gilded, H 11.2 cm, Prague, Museum of Decorative Arts, transferred 1950 (83.260). Prov. State property, Lit. Winterthur 1993, cat. 64, ill. p. 56, PLATE 160

VIII-18   *Beaker (Ranftbecher)*, Bohemia, ca. 1830, Friedrich Egermann (Sluknov 1777–1864 Nový Bor [Haida]), lithyalin, stained, cut and gilded, H 9.6 cm, Prague, Museum of Decorative Arts, donated 1932 (18.139), Prov. Prague, Collection G. E. Pazaurek, PLATE 160

VIII-19   *Beaker*, Bohemia, ca. 1830, Friedrich Egermann (Sluknov 1777–1864 Nový Bor [Haida]), lithyalin, stained, cut and gilded. H 9.3 cm, Prague, Museum of Decorative Arts, donated 1932 (18.109), Prov. Prague, Collection G. E. Pazaurek, PLATE 160

VIII-20   *Beaker (Ranftbecher)*. Bohemia, ca. 1830, Friedrich Egermann (Sluknov 1777–1864 Nový Bor [Haida]), lithyalin, stained, cut and gilded, H 11.4 cm, Prague, Museum of Decorative Arts. donated 1932 (18.112), Prov. Prague, Collection G. E. Pazaurek, PLATE 160

VIII-21   *Small Bowl with the Motif of the Endless Road*, Bohemia, ca. 1830, Jiříkovo Údoli (Georgenthal) Glassworks (eighteenth to early twentieth centuries), cut red hyalith, stained and painted in gold, H 6.7 cm x Dia 13 cm, Prague, Museum of Decorative Arts, donated by T. Bat'a, 1916 (14.261), Prov: Prague, Collection Joh. Novotný, Lit. Prague 1976, cat. 84; Prague 2001, cat. 47, fig. 47; Zaragoza 2004, cat. 291, ill. p. 195, PLATE 161

SILVER

SECTION IX

MZ = Meisterzeichen/Masters mark
BZ = Beschauzeichen/Assayers mark
SM = Stadtmarke/Townmark
MM = Monatzeichen/Month mark
FG = Feingalt/Fineness of the silver amounts
G = Gravur/Engraving
MP = Manufakturpunze/Manufacturers privilege mark
BS = Befreiungsstempel/Liberation Mark

IX-1 *Pair of Candlesticks*, Vienna, 1800, Jakob Krautauer (Vienna ca. 1772-1845 Vienna), silver, each H 25.8 x Dia 11.6 cm, Marks SM: WIEN; MZ: K, Asenbaum Collection, Prov. Vienna Art Market, 1960s, Lit. New York 2003, cat. 18, ill. p. 51, PLATE 162

IX-2 *Teapot*, Vienna, 1810, Joseph Heinisch (Vienna 1765/70-1834?), silver, fruitwood, 16 x 20.3 x 8.5 cm, Marks SM: WIEN; MZ: IH; VP; T, Asenbaum Collection, Prov. Vienna Art Market, 1980s, Lit. New York 2003, cat. 83, ill. p. 144, PLATE 163

IX-3 *Pair of Small Pots*, Vienna, 1807, Georg Forgatsch (Kosice 1772-1832 Vienna-Wieden), silver, smaller pot H 9.7 x Dia 5.3 cm; larger pot 11.7 x Dia 6.2 cm, Marks SM: WIEN; MZ: GF, Asenbaum Collection, Prov. Vienna Art Market, 1970s, Lit. New York 2003, cat. 42, ill. p. 97, PLATE 164

IX-4 *Pitcher*, Vienna, 1807, Franz Ignatz Dermer (Vienna 1768-1820 Josephstadt), silver, 6.7 x 13.2 x 5.2 cm, Marks SM: WIEN; T: CA; MZ: DER MER; BS: FR, Asenbaum Collection, Prov. Vienna Art Market, 1960s, PLATE 165

IX-5 *Water Jug*, Vienna, 1814, Carl Blasius (Bratislava ca. 1771-1834 Vienna-Windmühle), silver, H 16.3 cm, Marks SM: WIEN; MZ: CB; VP; New York, Private Collection, Prov. Asenbaum Collection, 1970s, Lit. New York 2003, cat. 20, ill. p. 55

IX-6 *Water Pitcher*, Vienna, 1817, Lorenz Wieninger (Prinzendorf 1768-1828 Vienna-Laimgrube), silver, H 22 cm, Marks SM: WIEN; MZ: LW; VP; New York, Private Collection, Prov. Asenbaum Collection, 1970s, Lit. New York 2003, cat. 9, ill. p. 35, PLATE 169

IX-7 *Spicebox*, Vienna, 1821, Benedikt Nicolaus Ranninger (Eutin, Schleswig-Holstein 1782-1845 Vienna), silver, 3.5 x 8.2 x 5.3 cm, Marks SM: WIEN; MZ: BNR; VP; Asenbaum Collection, Prov. Vienna Art Market, 1970s, Lit. New York 2003, cat. 8, ill. p. 33, PLATE 171

IX-8 *Sugar Urn*, Vienna, 1814, Johann Klima (?-after 1848 Vienna?), silver, 16.5 x 12.2 x 8 cm, Marks SM: WIEN; MZ: I. K.; T, Asenbaum Collection, Prov. Private Collections since 1920s, Lit. New York 2003, cat. 6, ill. p. 29, PLATE 170

IX-9 *Table Bell*, Vienna, 1818, Jakob Krautauer (Vienna ca. 1772-1845 Vienna), silver, "15-lötig", H 8.5 x Dia 6.8 cm, Marks FG: 15-LÖTIG, SM: WIEN; T: AF; MZ: KRAUTAUER, Asenbaum Collection, Prov. Vienna Art Market, 1990s, PLATE 174

IX-10 *Tureen*, Vienna, 1814, Aloys Andreas Würth (Vienna 1718-ca. 1831 Vienna), silver, fruitwood, H 15.8 x 29.5 cm, Marks SM: WIEN; MZ: AW, Berlin, Collection of Manfred Ludewig, Prov. Vienna Art Market 2005, PLATE 172

IX-11 *Tray*, Vienna, 1819, Stephan Mayerhofer, Sr. (Székesfehérvár 1772-1852 Vienna-Leopoldstadt), silver, Dia 24.5 cm, Marks SM: WIEN; MZ: STM, New York, Private Collection, Prov. Asenbaum Collection, 1970s, Lit. New York 2003, cat. 70, ill. p. 131

IX-12 *Wine Coaster*, Vienna, 1828, Alois Würth (Vienna 1778-1833 Graz, Styria), silver, Dia 12.4 cm, Marks SM: WIEN; MZ: AW, New York, Private Collection, Prov. Asenbaum Collection, 1970s, Lit. New York 2003, cat. 49, ill. p. 107

IX-13 *Pair of Knife Rests*, Vienna, 1819, Johann Kain (? ca. 1763-1840 Vienna-Leopoldstadt), silver, each 4.1 x 10.7 x 4.1 cm, Marks SM: WIEN; MZ: K; VP; T, Asenbaum Collection, Prov. Vienna Art Market, 1970s, Lit. New York 2003, cat. 26, ill. p. 69

IX-14 *Three Pieces from a Cutlery Service (Knife, Fork, and Spoon)*, Vienna, 1817, Karl Sedelmayer (Vienna ca. 1766-1840 Vienna-Mariahilf), silver, knife L 24.5 cm, Marks SM: WIEN; MZ: KS, VP: T, Asenbaum Collection, Prov. Private Collection since 1920s, Lit. Vienna 1987B, p. 284 cat. 6/3/61; New York 2003, cat. 62, ill. p. 123

IX-15 *Travel Set (Beaker, Salt and Pepper Shaker, Spoon, Knife, and Fork)*, Vienna, 1816, silver, H 12 cm (with items in beaker), Marks SM: WIEN; MZ: [illegible (RS or RJ)], New York, Private Collection, Prov. Asenbaum Collection,

1970s, Lit. New York 2003, cat. 90, ill. p. 153, PLATE 202

IX-16   *Pair of Candelabra*, Vienna, 1804, Joseph Laubenbacher (Vienna ca. 1768–1823 Vienna), silver, each 32.5 x 28.3 x 13 cm, Marks SM: WIEN; MZ: K, Asenbaum Collection, Prov. Private Collection since 1920s, Lit. New York 2003, cat. 17, ill. p. 49, PLATE 177

IX-17   *Teapot*, Vienna, 1802, Jakob Krautauer (Vienna ca. 1772–1845 Vienna), silver, fruitwood, 14.8 x 24 x 11.5 cm, Marks SM: WIEN; MZ: K; BS; VP, Asenbaum Collection, Prov. Vienna Art Market, 1980s, Lit. New York 2003, cat. 25, ill. p. 67, PLATE 177

IX-18   *Box*, Vienna, 1822, Wenzel Massabost (active in Vienna 1790–1824), silver, parcel-gilt (interior), 2 x 8.5 x 5 cm, Marks SM: WIEN; MZ: WM; G: Monogram W.H., 10. V. 57, Austria, Private Collection, Prov. Austria, Private Collection, PLATE 200

IX-19   *Box*, Vienna, 1818, silver, "15-lötig," parcel-gilt (interior), 3 x 9 x 3 cm, Marks FG: 15-LÖTIG; MZ: [illegible], Austria, Private Collection, Prov. Austria, Private Collection, Lit. Vienna 1987B, p. 287 cat. 6/3/89, PLATE 200

IX-20   *Box*, Vienna, 1803, Wenzel Massabost (active in Vienna 1790–1824), silver, parcel-gilt (interior), 2 x 8.7 x 4.9 cm, Marks SM: WIEN; Österr. Einfuhrpunze 1902–22; MZ: WM; BS: FR, T: F, Austria, Private Collection, Prov. Austria, Private Collection, PLATE 200

IX-21   *Box*, Vienna, 1807, Wenzel Massabost (active in Vienna 1790–1824), silver, parcel-gilt (interior), 2.5 x 9.1 x 5.1 cm, Marks SM: WIEN; MZ: WM; G: Monogram F.E., Austria, Private Collection, Prov. Austria, Private Collection, PLATE 200

IX-22   *Box*, Vienna, 1813, Anton Oberhauser (? ca. 1751–1827 Vienna-Neubau), silver, parcel-gilt (interior), 2 x 9 x 5 cm, Marks SM: WIEN; MZ: AO; T: AF, Austria, Private Collection, Prov. Austria, Private Collection, Lit. Vienna 1987B, p. 287 cat. 6/3/86, PLATE 200

IX-23   *Butter Tub*, Vienna, 1802, Martin Kern (Szemet/Misérd 1758–1818 Vienna), silver, H 8.6 x Dia 9.8 cm, Marks: SM: WIEN; BS: FR; T: CA; MZ: MK, Asenbaum Collection, Prov. Dorotheum 2005, PLATE 197

IX-24   *Tray*, Vienna, 180?, Joseph Ignaz Fautz (Vienna ca. 1745–after 1812 Vienna), silver, H 4 x Dia 23.7 cm, Marks SM: WIEN; MZ: IF; T: CA; G: Monogram H.I., Asenbaum Collection, Prov. Private Collection since 1920s, PLATE 196

IX-25   *Caster*, Vienna, 1810, Karl Sedelmayer (Vienna ca. 1766–1840 Vienna-Mariahilf), silver, H 9.8 x Dia 3.5 cm, Marks SM: WIEN; MZ: KS; T. Asenbaum Collection, Prov. Vienna Art Market, 1980s, Lit. New York 2003, cat. 71, ill. p. 132, PLATE 173

IX-26   *Caster*, Vienna, 1807, silver, H 9.7 x Dia 4.4 cm, Marks SM: WIEN; MZ: [illegible]; VP. Asenbaum Collection, Prov. Vienna Art Market, 1990s, Lit. New York 2003, cat. 47, ill. p. 104, PLATE 173

IX-27   *Caster*, Vienna, 1813, Johann Wastel (? 1790/95–after 1815 ?), silver, H 9.7 x Dia 3.2 cm, Marks SM: WIEN; MZ: IW; T, Asenbaum Collection, Prov. Vienna Art Market, 1980s, Lit. New York 2003, cat. 103, ill. p. 167, PLATE 173

IX-28   *Teapot*, Vienna, 1803, Franz Würth (Vienna 1773–1831 Graz, Styria), silver, fruitwood, 15.5 x 17 x 27.2 cm, Marks SM: WIEN; MZ: FW; VP; T, Asenbaum Collection, Prov. Private Collection since 1920s, Lit. New York 2003, cat. 52, ill. p. 111, PLATE 180

IX-29   *Casserole*, Vienna, 1807, Anton Köll, Sr. (Vienna ca. 1767–1854 Vienna-Mariahilf), silver, H 11 x Dia 19.1 cm, Marks SM: WIEN; MZ: AK; VP, Asenbaum Collection, Prov. Private Collection since 1920s, Lit. New York 2003, cat. 32, ill. p. 81, PLATE 187

IX-30   *Box*, Vienna, 1807, Andreas Schill (?–1845 Vienna-Mariahilf), silver, 2.6 x 5.3 x 4.1 cm, Marks SM: WIEN; MZ: AS; T: A; VP: VR, Asenbaum Collection, Prov. Vienna Art Market, 1970s, PLATE 190

IX-31   *Pair of Candlesticks*, Vienna, 1806, Carl Scheiger (Vienna ca. 1794–1820 Vienna-Neubau), silver, each 7.6 x 4.6 x 4.5 cm, Marks SM: WIEN; MZ: CS, Asenbaum Collection, Prov. Vienna Art Market, 1990s, Lit. New York 2003, cat. 95, ill. p. 158, PLATE 188

IX-32   *Tea Kettle and Stand*, Vienna, 1816, Probably Johann Guttmann, Jr. (Vienna 1780/85–ca. 1816 ?), silver, fruitwood, zinc, brass, 26 x 11.9 x 17.3 cm, Marks SM: WIEN; MZ: IG; VP; T, Asenbaum Collection, Prov. Vienna Art Market, 1990s, Lit. New York 2003, cat. 33, ill. p. 83, PLATE 179

IX-33   *Box from a Toilette Service*, Vienna, 1807, Joseph Stelzer (? ca. 1758–1830 Vienna-Alservorstadt), silver, H 4.6 x Dia 7.7 cm, Marks SM: WIEN; MZ: IST, Asenbaum Collection, Prov. Vienna Art Market, 1980s, Lit. New York 2003, cat. 48, ill. p. 105, PLATE 192

IX-34   *Box with Handle*, Vienna, 1813, Joseph Kern (Vienna 1790–1832 Vienna), silver, H 9.5

x Dia 14 cm, Marks SM: WIEN; MZ: K, Asenbaum Collection, Prov. Private Collection since 1990s, Lit. New York 2003, cat. 67, ill. p. 127, PLATE 191

IX-35   *Coffee Pot and Percolator*, Vienna, 1818, Franz Köll (Vienna ca. 1769–1830 Vienna-Mariahilf), silver, fruitwood, 29.5 x 16.5 x Dia 8.2 cm, Marks SM: WIEN; MZ: FK; T, Asenbaum Collection, Prov. Vienna Art Market, 1960s, Lit. New York 2003, cat. 39, ill. p. 93, PLATE 184

IX-36   *Casserole*, Vienna, 1813, Jakob Krautauer (Vienna ca. 1772–1845 Vienna), silver, H 10 x Dia 21.6 cm, Marks SM: WIEN; MZ: K; VP; T, Asenbaum Collection, Prov. Vienna Art Market, 1960s, Lit. New York 2003, cat. 24, ill. p. 61, PLATE 186

IX-37   *Pair of Candlesticks*, Vienna, 1816, Georg Kohlmayer (Vienna ca. 1780–1844 Vienna), silver, each H 23.5 x Dia 12.1 cm, Marks SM: WIEN; MZ: GK; T; G: Monogram AB with count's coronet, Asenbaum Collection, Prov. Vienna Art Market, 1970s, Lit. New York 2003, cat. 22, ill. p. 59, PLATE 186

IX-38   *One of a Pair of Candlesticks*, Vienna, 1815, Benedikt Nicolaus Ranninger (Eutin, Schleswig-Holstein 1782–1845 Vienna), silver, H 15.3 x Dia 10.5 cm, Marks SM: WIEN; MZ: BR; T; VP, Asenbaum Collection, Prov. Vienna Art Market, 1970s, Lit. New York 2003, cat. 23, ill. p. 59, PLATE 186

IX-39   *Sugar Box*, Vienna, 1819, Jakob Schleicher (dates unknown), silver, parcel-gilt (interior), 7 x 14.5 x 8.5 cm, Marks SM: WIEN; MZ: IS; G: Monogram BD, Asenbaum Collection, Prov. Vienna Art Market, 1970s, Lit. Vienna 1987B, p. 231 cat. 6/3/36; New York 2003, cat. 58, ill. p. 118, PLATE 194

IX-40   *Box from a Toilette Service*, Vienna, 1828, Joseph Kern (Vienna 1790–1832 Vienna), silver, parcel-gilt (interior), 4.1 x 16 x 4.5 cm, Marks SM: WIEN; MZ: K, Asenbaum Collection, Prov. Vienna Art Market, 1980s, Lit. New York 2003, cat. 69, ill. p. 129, PLATE 195

IX-41   *Beaker*, Vienna, 1821, Michael Carl Dörfer (Würzburg 1796–1830 Vienna-Laimgrube), silver, H 10.3 x Dia 8 cm, Marks SM: WIEN; MZ: MC D, Asenbaum Collection, Prov. Vienna Art Market, 1970s

IX-42   *Caster*, Vienna, 1827, Christian Sander, Jr. (Vienna 1819–1900 Vienna-Favoriten), silver, H 6.7 x Dia 4.9 cm, Marks SM: WIEN; MZ: CS, Asenbaum Collection, Prov. Vienna Art Market, 1970s, Lit. New York 2003, cat. 61, ill. p. 121, PLATE 175

IX-43   *Bowl*, Vienna, 1826, Carl Wallnöfer (Vienna ca. 1799–1872 Vienna), silver, 6.2 x 31.5 x 23.5 cm, Marks SM: WIEN; MZ: WALLNÖFER; MP, Asenbaum Collection, Prov. Vienna Art Market, 1990s, Lit. New York 2003, cat. 64, ill. p. 125, PLATE 199

IX-44   *Brushes from a Toilette Service*, Vienna, 1821, Ludwig Bock (dates unknown), silver, bristles, bone, wood, 4 x 22.5 x 6.4 cm, Marks SM: WIEN; MZ: LB; T, Asenbaum Collection, Prov. Private Collection since 1920s, Lit. Vienna 1987B, p. 231 cat. 6/3/76; New York 2003, cat. 63, ill. p. 123, PLATE 201

IX-45   *Box from a Toilette Service*, Vienna, 1834, Stephan Mayerhofer, Sr. (Székesfehérvár 1772–1852 Vienna-Leopoldstadt), silver, H 7.3 x Dia 8.8 cm, Marks SM: WIEN; MZ: STM, Asenbaum Collection, Prov. Vienna Art Market, 1970s, Lit. Vienna 1987B, p. 286, cat. 6/3/86; New York 2003, cat. 57, ill. p. 117, PLATE 193

IX-46   *Small Tray*, Vienna, 1819, silver, 1.7 x 19.9 x 8.7 cm, Marks SM: WIEN; MZ: [illegible]; T, Asenbaum Collection, Prov. Vienna Art Market, 1990s, Lit. New York 2003, cat. 60, ill. p. 120, PLATE 198

IX-47   *Pair of Candelabra*, Vienna, ca. 1820, Stephan Mayerhofer Sr. (Székesfehérvár 1772–1852 Vienna-Leopoldstadt), silver-plated copper, each 47.8 x 27 x 13.1 cm, Marks MZ: MAYERHOFER; MP, Vienna, Collection of Christian Witt-Dörring, Prov. Vienna Art Market, 1980s, Lit. New York 2003, cat. 19, ill. p. 53, PLATE 176

IX-48   *Coffee Set*, Vienna, 1821, Jakob Krautauer (Vienna ca. 1772–1845 Vienna), silver, coffee pot 24.3 x 17.7 x 8.2 cm, Marks MZ: KRAUTAUER; T: AF; SM: WIEN, Vienna, Collection of Christian Witt-Dörring, Prov. Vienna Art Market, 1990s, PLATE 185

IX-49   *Beaker*, Vienna, 1826, Carl Wallnöfer (Vienna 1798/99–ca. 1857 Vienna), silver, H 11.5 x Dia 8.5 cm, Marks SM: WIEN; MZ: WALLNÖFER, Berlin, Collection of Manfred Ludewig, Purchased 2001, Prov. Vienna Art Market

IX-50   *Pair of Candelabra*, Vienna, 1825, Benedikt Nicolaus Ranninger (Eutin, Schleswig-Holstein 1782–1845 Vienna), silver, each 51 x 31.5 x 13.6 cm, Marks SM: WIEN; MZ: BR, Paris, Musée du Louvre (OA 12189-1/2), Prov. Vienna Art Market, 1990s; Asenbaum Collection, PLATE 178

IX-51   *Samovar*, Vienna, 1820, Lorenz Frank (Frankfurt am Main 1782–ca. 1853?), silver, 34.5 x 24.8 x 16.8 cm, Marks SM: WIEN; VP: VR; T: AF; MZ: LF, Asenbaum Collection, Prov. Vienna Art Market, 1990s, PLATE 178

IX-52 *Travel Toilette Set*, Kassel, 1802, Johannes Adam Kördel (Kassel 1741–1814 Kassel), case: mahogany, leather, silver, gilt, Rubinglass, ebony, contents: square mirror, hand mirror, jug, two wash basins, cup, two candlesticks, table bell, two trays, three pairs of boxes, clothes brush, letter-opener, ruby glass bottle, case 67 x 47.5 x 25.5 cm, Marks SM: KASSEL with O; MZ: KÖRDEL; G: CA with prince's crown, Kronberg, Hessische Hausstiftung, (FAS S 272-285, G 309, M 1692), Prov. Fürstliche Schlösser in the possession of the house of Hessen, Lit. Eichenzell 1991, cat. 55, pp. 29, 148f.; Kassel 1998, cat. 152, ill. p. 157, PLATE 203

Johannes Adam Kördel and his son Carl Heinrich Kördell departed from the French tradition in favor of objects clearly influenced by the neoclassical formal language of English silver. The bodies of the objects exhibit plain surface designs and are defined to an increasing extent by their outlines; the candlesticks are accentuated by narrow horizontal lines and friezes. Travel articles and toilette sets serve a practical purpose that is reflected in the design of space-saving cases. The items within are reduced to their basic forms. The set derives its effect of quality from gilding on the silver. The toilette case was made as a gift from the Hessian Prince Elector to his daughter, Crown Princess Caroline Amalie (1771–1848), on the occasion of her marriage to Duke August von Sachsen-Gotha (1772–1822).

IX-53 *Goblet*, Germany, 1804, Johannes Adam Kördel (Kassel 1741–1814 Kassel), silver, parcel-gilt (interior), H 12.6 cm, Marks SM: KASSEL with B; IK, Kassel, Stadtmuseum Kassel (94/949), Prov. Kassel, Private Collection, Lit. Kassel 1998, cat. 141, ill. p. 150, PLATE 167

IX-54 *Teapot*, Berlin, ca. 1805, Johann George Fournier (? before 1770 – after 1810 Berlin), silver, fruitwood, 15.3 x 21.8 x 10.2 cm, Marks SM: BEAR and G; MZ: IGF, Berlin, Deutsches Historisches Museum, Purchase, 2006 (KG 2005/85), Prov. Berlin, Private Collection, PLATE 181

A strict system of proportions influenced by French models began to emerge in the silversmith's art in Berlin around 1800. Compared to the plain designs of Vienna silver, the majority of pieces from Berlin exhibit a contrast between smoothly fashioned bodies and applied antique ornamentation. Table objects created after about 1805 are characterized by balanced forms and proportions and by the restriction of decoration to a very few elements. They reflect the new spirit of simplicity.

IX-55 *Coffee Pot*, Berlin, ca. 1805, Johann David Hertel (? before 1753–after 1805 Berlin), silver, fruitwood, 18 x 21 x 8 cm, Marks SM: BEAR and H; MZ: IDH, Berlin, Deutsches Historisches Museum,

IX-41

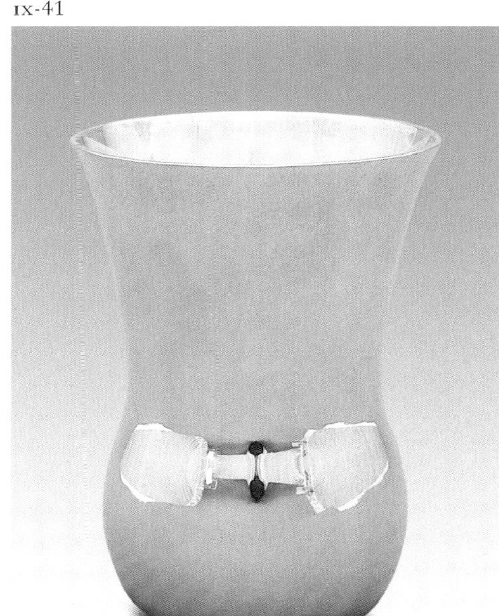

IX-49

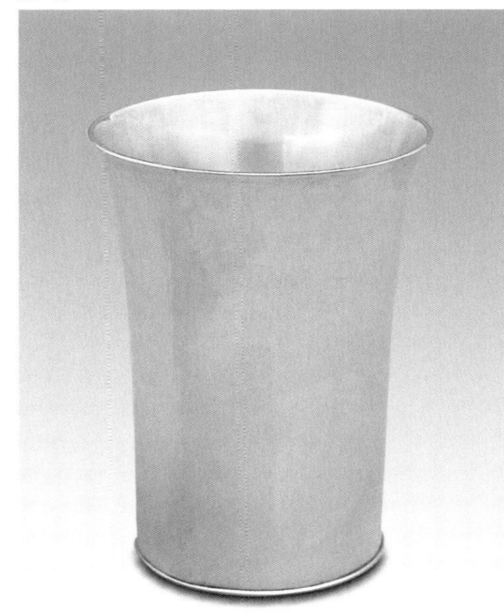

IX-59

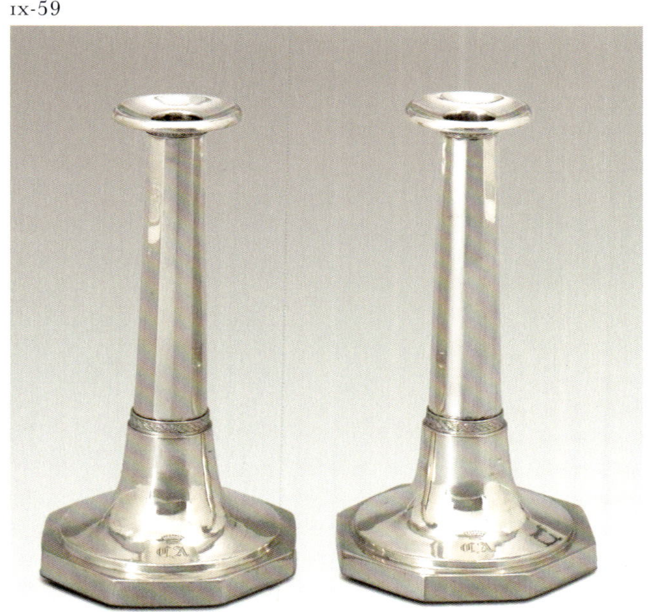

IX-62

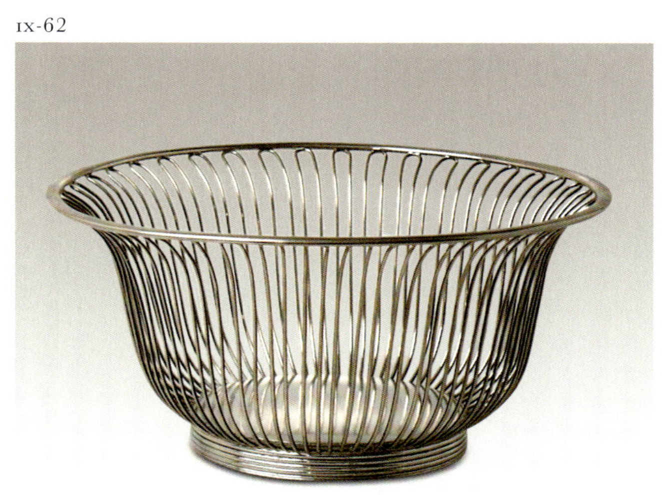

IX-60

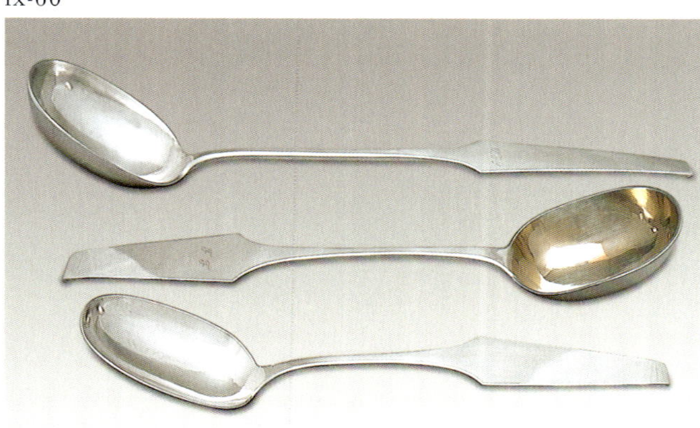

IX-64

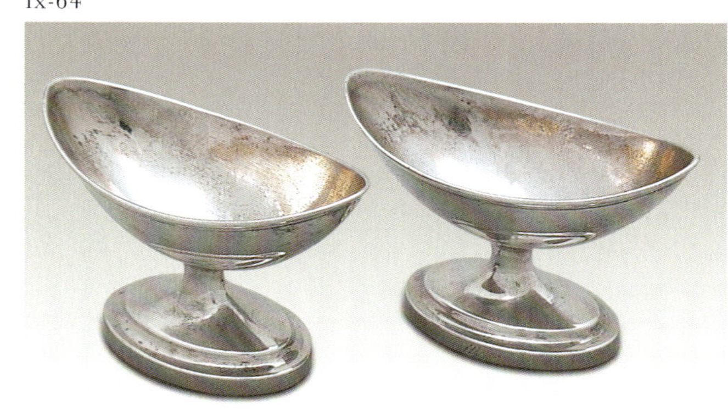

IX-66

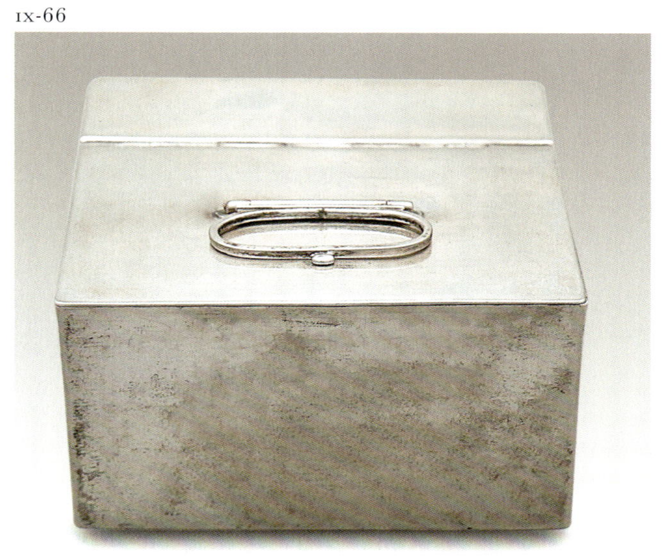

Purchase, 2006 (KG2005/86), Prov. Berlin, Private Collection, PLATE 182

IX-56 *Casserole with Lid from a Traveling Service*, Berlin, ca. 1805, Johann George Fournier (? before 1770–after 1810 Berlin), silver, gilding, fruitwood, 9.5 x 38.1 x 22.2 cm, Marks SM: BEAR and G; MZ: IGF; G: Monogram W, Berlin, Collection of Manfred Ludewig, Prov. Berlin, Art Dealer Gronert, 1987, PLATE 189

IX-57 *Milk Jug*, Germany, ca. 1810, Johannes Adam Kördel (Kassel 1741–1814 Kassel), silver, H 13 x Dia 7.2 cm, Marks SM: KASSEL with M; MZ: IK; G: Monogram A.v.S. with prince's crown, Kassel, Stadtmuseum Kassel (98/64), Prov. Kassel, Private Collection, Lit. Kassel 1998, cat. 138, ill. p. 149

IX-58 *Cream Pitcher*, Germany, ca. 1816, Carl Heinrich Kördell (Kassel 1789–1835 Kassel), silver, parcel-gilt, H 19 x Dia 15.5 cm, Marks SM: KASSEL with B; MZ: IK, Kassel, Staatliche Museen Kassel (1963/6), Prov. Munich, Private Collection, Lit. Kassel 1998, cat. 233, ill. p. 235, PLATE 166

IX-59 *Pair of Candlesticks*, Germany, 1816/20, Carl Heinrich Kördell (Kassel 1789–1835 Kassel), silver, Each H 17.3 x Dia 9.5 cm, Marks SM: KASSEL with B; MZ: KÖRDEL, Kassel, Staatliche Museen Kassel, Purchase, 1971 (1971/45a,b), Prov. Munich, Private Collection, Lit. Kassel 1998, cat. 229, ill. p. 231

IX-60 *Three Serving Spoons*, South Germany, ca. 1820, silver, two with gilding, bottom to top L 28.7 x W 5.9 cm; L 33.4 x W 7.5 cm; L 40 x W 7.7 cm, Marks MZ: NÜRNBERG; FG: 13 LOTH / MZ: HÜBSCHMAN; FG: 12 LOTH; G F.F. / G: E.L.S., Berlin, Collection of Manfred Ludewig, Prov. South German Art Market, late 1980s

IX-61 *Pair of Cups*, Munich, 1817, Anton Weishaupt (Launz 1776–1832 Munich), silver, gilded, each H 7.6 cm, Marks MZ: W: HAUPT; BZ: MÜNCHEN 1817, Munich, Bayerisches Nationalmuseum, permanent loan of the Benno and Therese Danner'schen Kunstgewerbestiftung (L86/225.1-2), Prov. Art Market, 1986, Lit. Seelig 1987, pp. 248f.; Munich 1988, cat. 3339, p. 265, PLATE 168

"Designed as companion pieces, these two cups, which widen slightly toward the top, exhibit no engraved or sculptural decoration. The smooth walls, which are round on the inside and divided into seventeen facets on the outside, are made of strong sheet silver, which is molded into a circular shape and soldered using the 'framing technique' and faceted on the outside surface by filing …. In contrast to the complex works made by Weishaupt for the silver chamber of the Munich court, which reflect the form and decoration of the Empire

style, these cups exhibit a remarkably simple, clear design" (Seelig 1987, pp. 248f.).

IX-62 *Fruit Basket*, Copenhagen, 1813, Frederik Fabritius (? 1787–1823 ?), silver, H 12.4 x Dia 25.5 cm, Marks MZ: illegible; SM: COPENHAGEN 1813; BZ: F (FREDERIK FABRITIUS); MM: CAPRICORN; FG: 56 3/4 LOTH Copenhagen, The Danish Museum of Decorative Art, Gift of the Ny Carlsberg Foundation, 1960 (20/1960), Lit. Copenhagen 2002, cat. 214, p. 144

Danish silver relies to a significant degree on geometric forms. Reduced to basic shapes – spheres, circles, arcs, cubes, and cylinders – these works define themselves through accentuation of their surfaces and outlines. The clarity of the body allows the beauty of the material to unfold to full effect. In this fruit basket made of drawn silver wire, the contour itself becomes an element of design.

IX-63 *Teapot*, Copenhagen, ca. 1800, Pierre Frontin (1758–1837, active in Copenhagen 1788–1806; 1825–37), silver, ebony, 13 x 17 x 13 cm, Marks MZ: PF; SM: COPENHAGEN; BZ: F (FREDERIK FABRITIUS); MM: CAPRICORN, Copenhagen, The Danish Museum of Decorative Art, Purchase, 1924 (A 4/1924), Prov. Copenhagen, Countess Sponnech, Lit. Lassen 1964, p. 249; Copenhagen 2002, cat. 177, p. 125, PLATE 183

IX-64 *Pair of Salt Cellars*, Copenhagen, ca. 1800, Pierre Frontin (1758–1837, active in Copenhagen 1788–1806), silver, each 7 x 10.5 x 5.5 cm, Marks MZ: PIERRE FRONTIN; BZ: F (FREDERIK FABRITIUS); G: HTB and 14 L 8 q, Copenhagen, The Danish Museum of Decorative Art, Purchase and Gift from the Ny Carlsberg Foundation, 1954 (119a-b, 1955), Prov. Hans Tobiesen Auction 111, no. 447, 1954, Lit. Copenhagen 2002, cat. 178, p. 126

IX-65 *Box*, Copenhagen, ca. 1800, silver, 1.5 x 5 cm, Copenhagen, The Danish Museum of Decorative Art, Purchase, 1902 (1651), Lit. Copenhagen 2002, cat. 180, p. 128

IX-66 *Tea Caddy*, Copenhagen, 1817, silver, H 5.8 cm, Marks SM: COPENHAGEN; BZ: F (FREDERIK FABRITIUS); MM: CANCER, Copenhagen, The Danish Museum of Decorative Art, Purchase, 1936 (B 27/1936), Prov. Copenhagen, Brdr. Berg Antiques, Lit. Copenhagen 2002, cat. 224, p. 146

IX-67 *Tea Caddy*, Aalborg, ca. 1840, Jacob Christian Smith (? ca. 1811–1876 Aalborg, active in Aalborg 1837–76), silver, H 12.5 x Dia 10.5 cm, Marks SM: AALBORG; G: 13L 4G, Copenhagen, The Danish Museum of Decorative Art, Purchase, 1993 (352 a-b/1993), Prov. Ribe, Tage Andersen, Lit. Copenhagen 2002, cat. 250, p. 164

METALWORK
SECTION X

X-1 Christian Daniel Rauch (Arolsen 1777-1857 Dresden), Model by Wilhelm August Stilarsky (Malapane near Oppeln 1780-1838 Berlin), *Bust of Queen Luise of Prussia*, ca. 1818, Königliche Eisengiesserei Berlin (1804-1873/74), cast iron, black patina, bust 41.5 x 39.5 x 25 cm; base H 12.2 x Dia 20 cm, Berlin, Stiftung Stadtmuseum Berlin (GS 98/5 SY), Prov. Berlin, Märkisches Museum Collection, Acquisition 1983, Lit. Börsch-Supan 1971, vol. 1, no. 375; Simson 1996, cat. 66, pp. 116–18; Berlin 2004, cat. 60, p. 90, PLATE 204

X-2 Christian Daniel Rauch (Arolsen 1777-1857 Dresden), Model by Wilhelm August Stilarsky (Malapane near Oppeln 1780-1838 Berlin), *Bust of Friedrich Wilhelm III of Prussia*, 1816, Königliche Eisengiesserei Berlin (1804-1873/74), cast iron, black patina, bust H 48.5 cm; base H 10 cm, Berlin, Deutsches Historisches Museum, 2001 (PI 2001/37), Prov. Ewald Barth Collection, Lit. Martins 1824, pp. 227ff.; Schmidt 1981, pp. 95ff.; Simson 1996, cat. 50.1, p. 96, PLATE 205

The iron bust of the Prussian king is listed in the index for the exhibition at the Berlin Academy in 1818. A characteristic typical of Rauch's early busts is the position of the youthful-looking king's head, which is turned slightly to one side. This figure exhibits no symbols of sovereignty. Frederick William III insisted that he not be depicted larger than life. (Leonore Koschnick)

X-3 *Jewelry Set (Parure, six pieces in original box: necklace, two bracelets, two earrings, brooch)*, Berlin, 1830/40, Eisengiesserei Siméon Pierre Devaranne Berlin (1814-ca. 1854), cast iron, black patina, necklace L 47 cm; bracelets each L 18.5 x W 5 cm; earrings each L 6.5 x W 2.2 cm; brooch L. 5.8 x W 5.6 cm; box 3 x 28.8 x 19.3 cm, Berlin, Stiftung Stadtmuseum Berlin (KH 98/4 a-g EI), Prov. Berlin Museum Collection, Lit. New York 1994, cat. 141, p. 270; Berlin 2004, cat. 658, p. 142, PLATE 207

X-4 *Necklace with Butterflies*, Berlin, ca. 1840, Eisengiesserei Siméon Pierre Devaranne Berlin (1814-ca. 1854), cast iron, black patina, L 43 x W 3.8 cm, Berlin, Stiftung Stadtmuseum Berlin

(KH 98/3 EI), Prov. Berlin Museum Collection, Lit. Clifford 1971, pl. 34; Berlin 1982, cat. 287, p. 141; Berlin 2004, cat. 657, p. 142, PLATE 209

X-5 *Purse with Belt Hook, Bracelet, Pin, and Brooch*, Berlin, ca. 1830, Königliche Eisengiesserei Berlin (1804-1873/74), ironwire and cast iron, purse L 16.9 cm; bracelet L 19.7 cm; pin L 4.1 cm; brooch L 5.5 cm, Berlin, Stiftung Stadtmuseum Berlin (KGM 83/2; KH 98/2 EI; II 72/363 E; II 66/146 E), Prov. purse: Berlin, Kunsthandel Bethmann-Hollweg 1983; bracelet: Berlin Museum Collection; pin and brooch: Märkisches Museum Collection, Lit. Berlin 2004, cat. 623-24, 632, and 634, pp. 137-38, PLATE 208

X-6 *Chair*, Gleiwitz, ca. 1830, design by Karl Friedrich Schinkel (Neuruppin 1781-1841 Berlin), Königliche Eisengiesserei Gleiwitz (1798-ca. 1945), cast iron, wrought iron, black patina, 84 x 36 x 52 cm, Berlin, Stiftung Stadtmuseum Berlin (I 50, 73 a), Prov. Berlin, Palais of Prince Carl of Prussia, Gift to the Märkisches Museum Berlin 1950, Lit. Preis-Courant Königliche Eisengiesserei Gleiwitz 1847, pl. 38, fig. 3; Himmelheber 1996, pp. 22ff.; Berlin 2004, cat. 701, p. 145, PLATE 206

X-7 *Tray for Candle Snuffer*, Austria, ca. 1819, Eisengiesserei Mariazell (1742-1898), cast iron, black patina, 1.5 x 24 x 9.5 cm, Vienna, Technisches Museum Wien (24.530), Prov. Vienna, kaiserlich-königliches National-Fabriksprodukten-Kabinett 1819, Lit. Preis-Courrant Eisengusswerk Maria Zell 1820, p. 16; Vienna 1992, cat. 39, p. 38: New York 1994, cat. 82, fig. p. 226

X-8 *Snuff Box with Woven Pattern*, Berlin, 1810/15, Königliche Eisengiesserei Berlin (1804-1873/74), cast iron, black patina, H 1.6 x Dia 8.2 cm, Berlin, Stiftung Stadtmuseum Berlin (II 83/333 E), Prov. Pirna, Collection Ewald Barth, Exchange with VEB Antique Sellers Pirna 1983, Lit. Berlin 2004, cat. 120, p. 100

X-9 *Tea Caddy*, Braunschweig/Berlin, ca. 1800, Manufaktur Stobwasser Braunschweig (1763-1856)/Berlin (1773-1910), tinplate, lacquer

painting, monochrome red, brass clasp, gilded
bronze, 14.5 x 11.6 x 6 cm, Munster, Museum für
Lackkunst, 1941 (EU-D-C-1), Prov. Bonn, Art Dealer
Wennerscheidt, PLATE 212

X-10   *Oval Tray*, Braunschweig, ca. 1825,
Manufaktur Stobwasser Braunschweig (1763-
1856)/Berlin (1773-1910), tinplate, lacquer
painting, monochrome lapis lazuli, underside black
varnish, gilde bronze handles and edging, 4.5 x
57.5 x 46.6 cm, Munich, Private Collection, 2001,
Prov. Munich Art Market, Lit. Munster 2005,
cat. 158, p. 250, PLATE 210

X-11   *Pair of Candlesticks*, Braunschweig,
ca. 1820, Manufaktur Stobwasser Braunschweig
(1763-1856)/Berlin (1773-1910), tinplate, lacquer
painting, monochrome yellow varnish, pewter
rings, each H 23 cm, Braunschweig, Private
Collection, Prov. Munich, Sammlung Detlev
Richter, Lit. Munster 2005, cat. 169, p. 253,
PLATE 211

CLOTHING

SECTION XI

XI-7

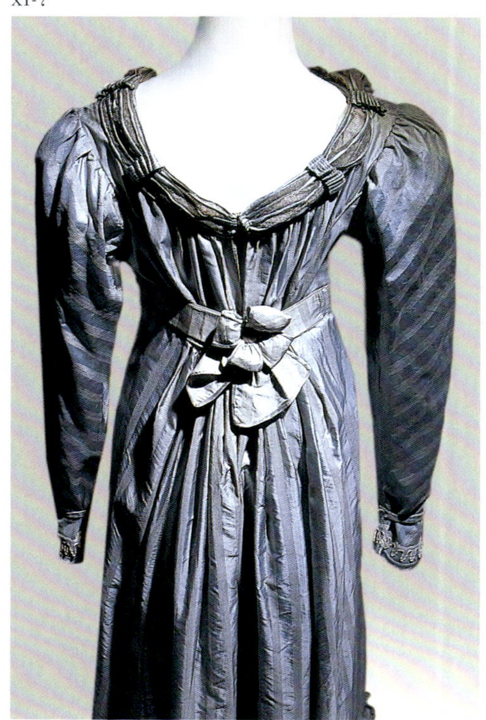

XI-17

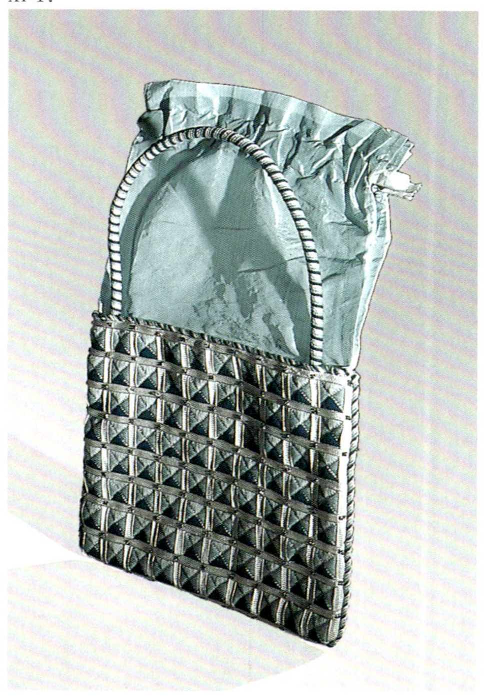

XI-1   *Summer Dress*, Bohemia, ca. 1830, white fabric, white embroidery, back L 129 cm, Prague, Museum of Decorative Arts, transferred 1964 (61.756/1964 EU), Prov. Prague, Schloss Hrubý Rohozec, Lit. Uchalová 1999, p. 38; Padua 2000, fig. 232, cat. 560, PLATE 213

XI-2   *Dress and Coat Set*, Germany, ca. 1810, cotton, linen, white linen embroidery, back L 129 cm, Berlin, Deutsches Historisches Museum, Purchase, 1996 (KT 96/190.1, 2), Prov. Beckenried, Switzerland, Galerie Ruf, PLATE 214

XI-3   *Daytime Dress*, Austria, ca. 1815/16, white linen, tulle, white embroidery, back L 137 cm, Vienna, Wien Museum (M2.281), PLATE 216

XI-4   *Woman's Dress*, Vienna, ca. 1825, white cotton, white embroidery, back L 127 cm, Vienna, Wien Museum, after 1949 (M_9), PLATE 217

XI-5   *Young Girl's Summer Dress*, Germany, ca. 1825, white "mousseline de laine," white pulled thread work, back L 119 cm, Berlin, Stiftung Stadtmuseum Berlin (KGT 93/97), Prov. Berlin Museum, purchased with funds of the Stiftung Preussische Seehandlung, Lit. Berlin 2001A, cat. 3, ill. p. 41, PLATE 218

XI-6   *Party Dress*, Austria, ca. 1820, light blue and white silk, tulle, linen, back L 128 cm, Vienna, Wien Museum, Gift of Dr. Tony Gerson, Vienna, 1981 (M15.113/3), PLATE 219

XI-7   *Party Dress*, Austria, ca. 1824, light blue silk with woven stripes, tulle, cotton, back L 136 cm, Vienna, Wien Museum (M12.034/1,2), Prov. Vienna, in honor of Dr. Heinrich Salzer, Lit. Vienna 1987B, p. 357, no. 7/6/3, PLATE 215

XI-8   *Woman's Dress*, Bohemia, Písek, ca. 1830, pale yellow batiste with white stripes, blue motifs, back L 140 cm, Prague, Museum of Decorative Arts, Purchase, 1978 (86.342), Prov. J. Kaplická, Lit. Uchalová 1999, p. 41; Padua 2000, fig. 234, PLATE 221

XI-9   *Woman's Dress*, Berlin, ca. 1837, light yellow cotton batiste, back L 128, Berlin, Stiftung

Stadtmuseum Berlin (KGT 96/122), Prov. Berlin Museum, purchased with funds of the Stiftung Preussische Seehandlung, PLATE 220

XI-10   *Bonnet*, Austria, ca. 1841/48, braided straw, blue and white checkered silk-taffeta ribbon, Depth 28 cm, Vienna, Wien Museum (M1.079), Lit. Vienna 1987B, p. 357, no. 7/6/13, ill. p. 359, PLATE 223

XI-11   *Bonnet*, Austria, ca. 1845, braided straw, white silk-taffeta lining and ribbon, Depth 24 cm, Vienna, Wien Museum (M1.259), Lit. Vienna 1987B, p. 357, ill. p. 359 (no cat. no.), PLATE 222

XI-12   *Bonnet*, Austria, ca. 1841/48, straw, Jacquard pattern, colored silk ribbons, metal fringes, Depth 28 cm, Vienna, Wien Museum, Purchase, 1942 (M1.702), Prov. Frau Friedl Hollstein, PLATE 224

XI-13   *Shawl*, Vienna, 1827, Appreturanstalt Peter Festi Wien (1814–after 1841), four-color iridescent silk crepe, 33.5 x 43 4 cm, Vienna, Technisches Museum Wien (61.928.1), Prov. Vienna, kaiserlich-königliches National-Fabriksprodukten-Kabinett Wien, PLATE 229

XI-14   *Shoes with Ribbon Ties*, Austria, ca. 1820, black silk-satin, linen, silk-taffeta ribbon, silk-satin ribbon, leather, L 23 cm, Vienna, Wien Museum (M 3.492), PLATE 225

XI-15   *Shoes with Ribbon Ties*, Berlin, ca. 1830, silk, leather, L 25.5 cm, Berlin, Stiftung Stadtmuseum Berlin, Gift of M. Weinland, 1993 (KGT 93/19)

XI-16   *Shoes*, Berlin, ca. 1830, silk, silver thread, leather, L 24 cm, Berlin, Stiftung Stadtmuseum Berlin (II 89/347 a+b K), Prov. Berlin, Märkisches Museum, PLATE 226

XI-17   *Handbag*, Austria, ca. 1840, canvas, blue wool embroidery, ecru silk ribbons, steel beads, wool and silk cord, 23 x 16 cm (with handles), Vienna, Wien Museum (M 966)

XI-18   *Man's Vest*, Austria, ca. 1830, checkered silk, linen, double-buttoned, Back L 42.5 cm, Vienna, Wien Museum (M4.907), Lit. Vienna 1987B, p. 357, no. 7/6/29, ill. p. 359, PLATE 227

XI-19   *Man's Vest*, Austria, ca. 1831, cream satin-silk with woven-in stripes, cotton, Back L 52 cm, Vienna, Wien Museum (M10.529), Lit. Vienna 1987B, p. 357, no. 7/6/28, ill. p. 359, PLATE 228

XI-20   *Walking Stick*, Austria, ca. 1830, black-lacquered wood, silver, L 94 cm, Vienna, Wien Museum (M4652/1), Lit. Vienna 1987B, p. 357, no. 7/6/31, ill. p. 361

XI-21   *Nine Satin Ribbon Pattern Samples*, Vienna, 1828, Seidenzeugfabrik Hornbostel Wien (1786–1890) (pattern book, pl. 197), silk, 33.5 x 43 cm, Vienna, Technisches Museum Wien (33.433), Prov. Vienna, kaiserlich-königliches National-Fabriksprodukten-Kabinett Wien, PLATE 230

XI-22   *Two Pattern Samples of Modern gros de tour Ribbons*, Vienna, 1828, Seidenzeugfabrik Hornbostel Wien (1786–1890) (pattern book, pl. 209), silk, 33.5 x 43.5 cm, Vienna, Technisches Museum Wien (61.705), Prov. Vienna, kaiserlich-königliches National-Fabriksprodukten-Kabinett Wien

XI-23   *Three Silk Couture Ribbon Samples*, Vienna, 1827, Bandfabrikant Franz Heller Wien (1827–ca. 1835) (pattern book, pl. 171), silk, 33.5 x 43 cm, Vienna, Technisches Museum Wien (61.903), Prov. Vienna, kaiserlich-königliches National-Fabriksprodukten-Kabinett Wien

NORTHERN EUROPEAN PAINTING AND DRAWING

SECTION XII

XII-1   Carl Gustav Carus (Leipzig 1789-1869 Dresden), *Swiss Landscape*, ca. 1822, oil on canvas, 38.5 x 47.5 cm, Halle (Saale), Stiftung Moritzburg, Kunstmuseum des Landes Sachsen-Anhalt (1/97), Prov. Dresden, Purchased from Kunsthandlung Kühl, 1927, Lit. Prause 1968, cat. 137, p. 119; Genschorek 1978, pp. 134ff., PLATE 231

Although professionally he was a doctor and a recognized scientist and naturalist, Carl Gustav Carus was an accomplished artist. Some of his paintings reveal his fascination with geology and the formation of mountain ranges. Carus was in touch with other important painters and scholars of his time; he was a lifelong friend of the Romantic painter Caspar David Friedrich, whose influence is especially evident in Carus's work from around 1817 to 1823. In 1821, Carus met Johann Wolfgang von Goethe, who admired Carus's painting as well as his scientific investigations. Carus's Swiss mountain landscapes echo Friedrich's Romantic vision of an untamed nature, but also are an important link to the Austrian mountain painters of the Biedermeier period. Carus made three journeys to Italy (1821, 1828, and 1841) and also traveled to England and Scotland, making oil studies as he went. He published his philosophy of landscape painting in *Neun Briefe über Landschaftsmalerei* (1831) and later recounted his life in *Lebenserinnerungen und Denkwürdigkeiten* (1865-66).

XII-2   Carl Gustav Carus (Leipzig 1789-1869 Dresden), *The Artist's Studio*, 1823/24, oil on canvas, 28.8 x 20.9 cm, Lübeck, Museen für Kunst und Kulturgeschichte der Hansestadt Lübeck (GK 538/1926/231), Prov. Lübeck, M. Hoffmann; Munich, Galerie Caspari; Leipzig, Pfarrer Rietschel, Lit. Prause 1968, cat. 77, p. 106, PLATE 232

XII-3   Christoffer Wilhelm Eckersberg (Blaakrog 1783-1853 Copenhagen) *Julie Eckersberg, née Juel, the Artist's Second Wife*, 1817, oil on canvas, 31.5 x 27.5 cm, Copenhagen, Statens Museum for Kunst, Bequest of the artist's daughters, 1903, (KMS1763), Lit. Washington 2003, cat. 25; Hornung and Monrad 2005, p. 176, PLATE 233

One of the most influential artists of the Danish golden age, Christoffer Wilhelm

Eckersberg began training at age twenty under Nicolai Abildgaard at the Copenhagen art academy before traveling to Paris in 1810 to study under Jacques-Louis David. After a brief stay in Rome (1813-16), Eckersberg returned to Denmark and earned his living painting portraits. He became a professor at the academy and took up residence at Charlottenborg Palace. His portraits and nudes demonstrate a close study of nature combined with the hard-edged finish of the French school. Eckersberg's precise and luminous depictions of Copenhagen and the surrounding countryside gave new direction to Danish painting, inspiring students such as Christen Købke and Wilhelm Bendz. Eckersberg's memoirs document his longstanding fascination with ships and maritime subjects; he made daily visits to Copenhagen's harbors and shipyards. Eckersberg's focus on ordinary, everyday subjects, rendered in a clear light palette, are the hallmarks of the Danish Biedermeier period.

XII-4   Christoffer Wilhelm Eckersberg (Blaakrog 1783-1853 Copenhagen), *Mendel Levin Nathanson's Eldest Daughters, Bella and Hanna*, 1820, oil on canvas, 125 x 85.5 cm, Copenhagen, Statens Museum for Kunst (KMS3498), Prov. Commissioned by Mendel Levin Nathanson; his sister Madame Rée; Hélène Rée (German, living in Paris), 1895; confiscated by the French State in 1914 but bequeathed by Rée in December 1917 to the Statens Museum for Kunst and given to the museum in 1920 following legal proceedings, Lit. Washington 2003, cat. 27; Hornung and Monrad 2005, p. 198, PLATE 235

XII-5   Christoffer Wilhelm Eckersberg (Blaakrog 1783-1853 Copenhagen), *Portrait of the Merchant Joseph Raphael*, 1824, oil on canvas, 80 x 65.1 cm, Copenhagen, The Hirschsprung Collection (113), Prov. Copenhagen, Mr. Wolf, 1824; Herman Raphael, 1872; Alfred Kaae; Heinrich Hirschsprung, 1895, Lit. Washington 2003, cat 30, ill. pp. 116-17; Hornung and Monrad 2005, cat. ill. p. 189, PLATE 234

XII-6   Christoffer Wilhelm Eckersberg (Blaakrog 1783-1853 Copenhagen), *A View toward the Wharf at Nyholm with Crane and Warships,*

1826, oil on canvas, 19.6 x 32.4 cm, Copenhagen,
The Hirschsprung Collection (114), Prov.
Purchased by Supreme Court member Poulsen
at Eckersberg's estate auction, 1854; Heinrich
Hirschsprung, 1884, Lit. Washington 2003, fig. 4,
p. 19; Hornung and Monrad 2005, cat. ill. p. 246,
PLATE 237

XII-7   Christoffer Wilhelm Eckersberg
(Blaakrog 1783-1853 Copenhagen), *The Timbers
of a Ship*, 1827, sepia on paper, 25.7 x 29.5 cm,
Copenhagen, The Hirschsprung Collection (5132),
Prov. Purchased by The Hirschsprung Collection
from Ingeborg Lund, 1937, PLATE 238

XII-8   Christoffer Wilhelm Eckersberg
(Blaakrog 1783-1853 Copenhagen), *Anchors at
Larsen's Wharf, Copenhagen*, 1838, pen, blackish
gray ink over pencil, gray watercolor, 20.1 x 20 cm,
Copenhagen, Statens Museum for Kunst (KKS417),
Lit. Hornung and Monrad 2005, pp. 332-33,
PLATE 239

XII-9   Christoffer Wilhelm Eckersberg
(Blaakrog 1783-1853 Copenhagen), *Nude Study
of a Young Woman Leaving Her Bath*, 1841, pencil, ink, watercolor, 34.8 x 24.7 cm, Copenhagen,
The Hirschsprung Collection (5137), Prov. Sold at
Eckersberg's estate auction, 1855; Purchased by
The Hirschsprung Collection in 1940 from the art
dealer J. L. Wisbech, 1940, Lit. Copenhagen 1994,
cat. 53, ill. pp. 119-20

XII-10   Christoffer Wilhelm Eckersberg
(Blaakrog 1783-1853 Copenhagen), *Nude Putting
on Her Slippers*, 1843, oil on canvas, 65.5 x 46
cm, Copenhagen, Ny Carlsberg Glyptotek, Gift
of the Ny Carlsberg Glyptotek Foundation, 1942
(MIN2062), Prov. Copenhagen, Sold to Rasmus
Borch, 1844; purchased by Dr. A. Schiøtz, 1872;
The Ny Carlsberg Foundation; Gift from the
Foundation to Ny Carlsberg Glyptotek, 1942,
Lit. Copenhagen 1994, cat. 59, p. 132, ill. p. 129;
Washington 2003, cat. 50, ill. pp. 156-57; Hornung
and Monrad 2005, cat. ill. p. 305, PLATE 236

XII-11   Christoffer Wilhelm Eckersberg
(Blaakrog 1783-1853 Copenhagen), *View from the
Domed Hall in Charlottenborg*, 1845, pen and ink,
wash, Copenhagen, Statens Museum for Kunst
(KKS4742), Lit. Washington 2003, p. 8; Hornung
and Monrad 2005, pp. 382-83

XII-12   Eduard Gaertner (Berlin 1801-1877
Zechlin, Brandenburg), *Studio of the Gropius
Brothers*, after 1832, oil on canvas, 25.5 x 35.5
cm, Berlin, Staatliche Museen zu Berlin, Alte
Nationalgalerie (IA. II 19), Lit. Berlin 2001B,
cat. 110, ill. p. 300, PLATE 250

   Eduard Gaertner was the most important
architectural painter of the Berlin school. At age

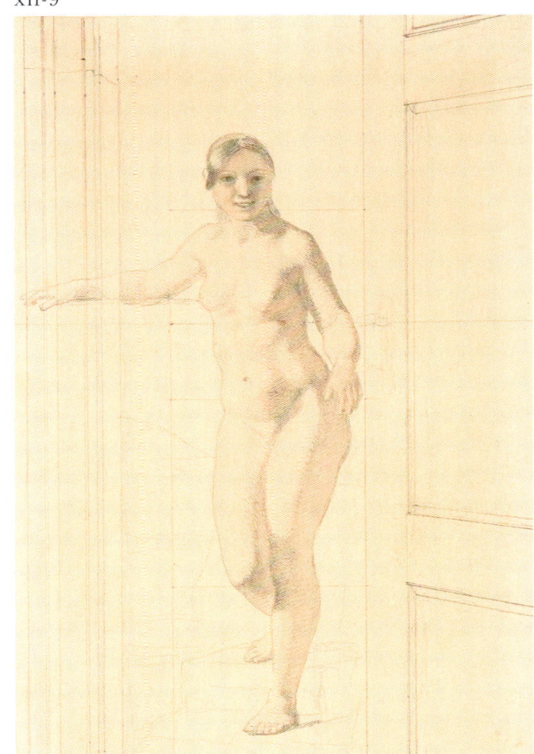

XII-9

ten, he began taking drawing lessons in Kassel, and was an apprentice painter at the Königliche Porzellanmanufaktur in Berlin from 1814 to 1821. Gaertner enrolled at the Berlin Akademie der Künste while also working with the stage designer Carl Wilhelm Gropius, who helped him hone his exceptional skills in rendering perspective. After a two-year sojourn in Paris, he settled in Berlin in 1827 and quickly became the leading painter of architectural and urban views. The surge of building in Berlin, coupled with Gaertner's great facility with architectural scenes, made this genre very popular. King Friedrich Wilhelm III became an important patron for Gaertner beginning in 1824; the artist completed his famous six-canvas panorama of Berlin for the king in 1834. In 1837, at the invitation of Czar Nicholas I, Gaertner spent two years in Russia, where he painted a large group of urban views of St. Petersburg and Moscow. After about 1840, interest in Gaertner's work began to wane, and he attempted to adapt to changing taste by adopting a looser, more painterly manner. He traveled throughout West and East Prussia, Prague, and Silesia creating landscape paintings, but never lost his passion for architecture.

XII-13   Eduard Gaertner (Berlin 1801-1877 Zechlin, Brandenburg), *View from the Roof of the Church of Friedrichswerder over the Friedrichsforum, Berlin*, 1835, oil on canvas, 93.4 x 147.3 cm, Berlin, Stiftung Stadtmuseum Berlin, purchased with funds of the Stiftung Deutsche Klassenlotterie, 1988 (GEM 88/4), Prov. Ratingen, Private Collection, Lit. Wirth 1979, p. 231; Berlin 2001B, cat. 62, p. 241, PLATE 251

XII-14   Eduard Gaertner (Berlin 1801-1877 Zechlin, Brandenburg), *The Family of the Kommerzienrat Westphal (?) in the Greenhouse*, 1836, oil on canvas, 24 x 20 cm, London, Hildegard Fritz-Denneville Fine Arts Ltd., Prov. Munich, Private Collection, Lit. Wirth 1985, fig. 2, pp. 62ff; Berlin 2001B, cat. 220, ill. p. 404, DETAIL, p. 70

XII-15   Johann Erdmann Hummel (Kassel 1769-1852 Berlin), *The Granite Basin in the Berlin Lustgarten*, 1831, oil on canvas, 65.5 x 87.5 cm, Berlin, Stiftung Stadtmuseum Berlin, Donation Erben Cantian, 1902 (VII 61/703 x), Lit. Geismeier 1979, ill. p. 190; Norman 1987, ill. pp. 74-75; Berlin 1994, p. 36, PLATE 246

As an intensely passionate professor of perspective and optics at the Akademie der Künste in Berlin, Johann Erdmann Hummel earned the nickname "Perspektivhummel." He commemorated one of the great technical feats of his day in a series of four pictures showing the grinding and polishing of a great granite bowl and its installation in the Lustgarten in front of the Altes Museum on Museuminsel. The polished exterior of the installed bowl reflects the surrounding gar-

den like a convex lens. Neatly dressed sightseers, some inverted, some foreshortened, are captured upside-down in a curved panorama on the bottom of the bowl. Hummel's art reflects his early training in that discipline as well as his scientific leanings. Born in Kassel, he attended drawing classes at the academy and went on to study architecture and later painting. He attracted the patronage of the ruling house at Hesse and a grant from the Landgraf Wilhelm IX enabled him to spend formative years in Rome where he was influenced by classical architecture and the principles of classical training.

XII-16   Johann Erdmann Hummel (Kassel 1769-1852 Berlin), *Polishing the Granite Basin for the Lustgarten*, 1831/32, oil on cardboard, 64.5 x 87 cm, Berlin, Stiftung Stadtmuseum Berlin, Donation Erben Cantian, 1902 (VII 59/926 x), Lit. Berlin 1994, p. 36; Ottawa 2000, cat. 67, ill. pp. 150-51, PLATE 247

XII-17   Georg Friedrich Kersting (Güstrow, Mecklenburg 1785-1847 Meissen), *Woman Embroidering*, 1817, oil on panel, 47.1 x 36.8 cm, Warsaw, National Museum, Purchase, 1986 (M.Ob.2073), Prov. Warsaw, Władysław Wenda; thereafter in possession of the same family; Warsaw, National Museum in Warsaw, since 1984, Lit. Schnell 1994, cat. A 79, ill. p. 314; Warsaw 2001, cat. VI-105, ill. pp. 310-11, PLATE 244

Georg Friedrich Kersting trained at the art academy in Copenhagen from 1805 to 1808, adopting a clarity and brilliance characteristic of the Danish school. In 1808, he went to Dresden, where he associated with and was inspired by Caspar David Friedrich. After 1811, Kersting became successful with interiors that included portraits. He often used the "room interiors" and suggestive windows to reflect his sitter's state of mind, but his paintings lack the complex religious and allegorical symbolism associated with the work of Friedrich. *Woman Embroidering* portrays the painter Louise Seidler, a protégée of Johann Wolfgang von Goethe, in the apartment of a mutual friend; its green walls and white curtains are characteristic of Goethe's color theory, and Goethe in turn is known to have admired Kersting's work. From 1815 to 1818, Kersting worked as a drawing master in the house of Princess Anna Sapieha in Warsaw, and subsequently became artistic director at the Meissen porcelain manufactory. His position left him little time for his art, and his painstaking execution meant that he was not very prolific. The dozen or so known works are among the earliest examples of a true Biedermeier style.

XII-18   Georg Friedrich Kersting (Güstrow, Mecklenburg 1785-1847 Meissen), *Before the Mirror*, 1827, oil on panel, 46 x 35 cm, Kiel, Kunsthalle zu Kiel, Prov. Schleswig-Holstein,

Mrs. Becker, née Binzer, 1856, given to the Kunstverein Schleswig-Holstein, Lit. Geismeier 1979, ill. 72; Vaughan 1980, ill. p. 125; Schnell 1994, cat. A 117, ill. p. 321, PLATE 245

XII-19 Wilhelm von Kobell (Mannheim 1766–1855 Munich), *Grazing Cattle with Shepherds in front of Wide Lake Landscape*, 1797, pen and black ink, watercolor, brushed white highlights, over pencil traces, 39.1 x 48.2 cm, Vienna, Albertina (14774), Prov. Albert von Sachsen-Teschen (L 174), Lit. Wichmann 1970, cat. 400, ill.; Vienna 1997, cat. 397, ill. p. 124

Wilhelm von Kobell came from a large family of painters in the Palatinate. His first teacher was his father, Ferdinand Kobell, a court painter at Mannheim. When studying at the Mannheim Kunstakademie, Kobell was strongly influenced by seventeenth-century Dutch painting. In 1792, he became court painter to Elector Karl Theodor of Bavaria, and in 1793 moved to Munich, where he received many commissions for animal paintings in the manner of Potter and Wouwerman. In 1805, after the War of the Coalition, he painted a cycle showing the victories of the Bavarian and Napoleonic armies for King Maximilian I Joseph. Among the numerous commissions that followed was a battle cycle (1807-15) for Crown Prince Ludwig of Bavaria. Despite his success with the subject, Kobell turned to small-scale rural scenes He developed a new genre of seemingly accidental "encounters" in the countryside between riders, huntsmen, animals, and people in local costume. Often there is a contrast between two social groups—peasants and gentlemen—or a physical contrast between mounted and standing figures. The participants often appear frozen in time, an effect enhanced by the cool light tones, glazed finish, and long shadows.

XII-20 Wilhelm von Kobell (Mannheim 1766–1855 Munich), *Shepherds and Herd outside a Village*, 1797, pen and black-gray ink, watercolor, brushed white highlights, over pencil, 39 x 48.6 cm, Vienna, Albertina (14775), Prov. Albert von Sachsen-Teschen (L 174), Lit. Wichmann 1970, cat. 403, ill.; Vienna 1997, cat. 398, ill. p. 125

XII-21 Wilhelm von Kobell (Mannheim 1766–1855 Munich), *Village Landscape with Goats, Shepherd, and a Horse at a Watering Place*, 1798, pen, black-gray ink, watercolor, brushed white highlights, 36.1 x 45.8 cm, Vienna, Albertina (5671), Prov. Old inventory ("de l'achat de l'Archiduc en 1856"), Lit. Wichmann 1970, cat. 420, ill.; Vienna 1997, cat. 373, ill. p. 119, PLATE 255

XII-22 Wilhelm von Kobell (Mannheim 1766–1855 Munich), *Encounter between Elegant Horsemen and a Family*, 1803, pen and black ink, watercolor, brushed white highlights, 31.5 x 43.8 cm, Vienna, Albertina (5660), Prov. Albert von

Sachsen-Teschen (L 174), Lit. Wichmann 1970, cat. 784, ill.; Vienna 1997, cat. 362, ill. p. 117, PLATE 253

XII-23 Wilhelm von Kobell (Mannheim 1766–1855 Munich), *Children and Cattle on the Bank outside a Village*, ca. 1803, pen and gray ink, watercolor, 28.8 x 38.2 cm, Vienna, Albertina (5673), Prov. Albert von Sachsen-Teschen (L 174), Lit. Wichmann 1970, cat. 709, ill.; Vienna 1997, cat. 375, ill. p. 120

XII-24 Wilhelm von Kobell (Mannheim 1766–1855 Munich), *Encounter of Riders and a Hunting Chaise Drawn by Two Horses outside Munich*, 1803, pen and black ink, watercolor, brushed white highlights, 31.1 x 44 cm, Vienna, Albertina (5661), Prov. Albert von Sachsen-Teschen (L 174), Lit. Wichmann 1970, cat. 767, ill.; Vienna 1997, cat. 363, ill. p. 117, PLATE 254

XII-25 Wilhelm von Kobell (Mannheim 1766–1855 Munich), *Peasant Woman with Children, a Goat, and Four Cows on the Country Road*, 1803, pen and black-gray ink, watercolor, 35.8 x 48.9 cm, Vienna, Albertina (5676), Prov. Albert von Sachsen-Teschen (L 174), Lit. Wichmann 1970, cat. 754, ill.; Vienna 1997, cat. 378, ill. p. 121

XII-26 Wilhelm von Kobell (Mannheim 1766–1855 Munich), *Shepherd with Three Cows and a Goat in front of a Wide River Landscape*, 1803, pen and black ink, watercolor, 35.4 x 48.6 cm, Vienna, Albertina (5677), Prov. Albert von Sachsen-Teschen (L 174), Lit. Wichmann 1970, cat. 745, ill.; Vienna 1997, cat. 379, ill. p. 121

XII-27 Wilhelm von Kobell (Mannheim 1766–1855 Munich), *Camp of the Austrian Infantry at the Neugebäude Castle between Simmering and Kaiserebersdorf*, 1805, pen and gray ink, watercolor, over pencil traces, 46.2 x 60.9 cm, Vienna, Albertina (14758), Prov. Albert von Sachsen-Teschen (L 174), Lit. Wichmann 1970, cat. 817, ill.; Vienna 1997, cat. 381, ill. p. 120

XII-28 Wilhelm von Kobell (Mannheim 1766–1855 Munich), *Austrian Infantrymen and Hussars*, ca. 1806, watercolor, over pencil traces, 23.9 x 38.1 cm, Vienna, Albertina (5655), Prov. Albert von Sachsen-Teschen (L 174), Lit. Wichmann 1970, cat. 844, ill.; Vienna 1997, cat. 357, ill. p. 116, PLATE 256

XII-29 Wilhelm von Kobell (Mannheim 1766–1855 Munich), *Cattle in the Shallow Water of the Isar River near Bogenhausen*, ca. 1806, pen and brown-gray ink, watercolor, 28.8 x 38.2 cm, Vienna, Albertina (5674), Prov. Albert von Sachsen-Teschen (L 174), Lit. Wichmann 1970, cat. 825, ill.; Vienna 1997, cat. 376, ill. p. 120

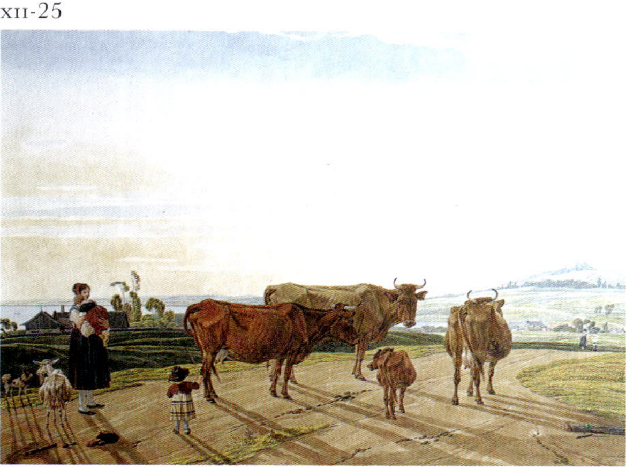

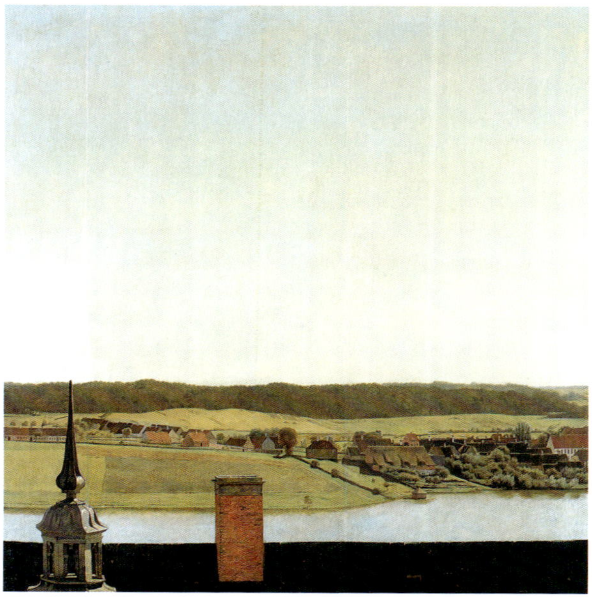

XII-30 Wilhelm von Kobell (Mannheim 1766–1855 Munich), *Württemberg Lifeguard*, ca. 1807, pen and gray ink, watercolor, over pencil, 23.3 x 37.6 cm, Vienna, Albertina (5659), Prov. Albert von Sachsen-Teschen (L 174), Lit. Wichmann 1970, cat. 881, ill., Vienna 1997, cat. 361, ill. p. 117

XII-31 Wilhelm von Kobell (Mannheim 1766–1855 Munich), *Herd at the Bank of the Traunsee*, 1813, watercolor, over pencil traces, 35.8 x 48.2 cm, Vienna, Albertina (5675), Prov. Albert von Sachsen-Teschen (L 174), Lit. Wichmann 1970, cat. 1006, ill.; Vienna 1997, cat. 377, ill. p. 120

XII-32 Wilhelm von Kobell (Mannheim 1766–1855 Munich), *Horses and Sheep on the Meadow on the Bank of a Lake*, ca. 1813, watercolor, over pencil traces, 35.5 x 48.5 cm, Vienna, Albertina (5678), Prov. Albert von Sachsen-Teschen (L 174), Lit. Wichmann 1970, cat. 1007, ill.; Vienna 1997, cat. 380, ill. p. 121

XII-33 Wilhelm von Kobell (Mannheim 1766–1855 Munich), *Cattle Market outside the Town of Constance (?) on Lake Constance*, 1820, pen and black-gray ink, watercolor, over pencil, highlights, 52.5 x 72.1 cm, Vienna, Albertina (14766), Prov. Vienna, Joseph Grünling; Albert von Sachsen-Teschen (L174), Lit. Wichmann 1970, cat. 1220, ill.; Vienna 1997, cat. 389, ill. p. 123, PLATE 257

XII-34 Wilhelm von Kobell (Mannheim 1766–1855 Munich), *Hunter and Lord at the River Isar with View of Munich*, 1823, oil on panel, 25 x 20.6 cm, Cleveland, The Cleveland Museum of Art, Mr. and Mrs. William H. Marlatt Fund, 1981 (1981.11), Prov. Montgomeryshire, Major Corbett Winder; London, Christie's, 1905; New York, Sotheby's, Parke-Bernet, 1973; New York, Ira Spanierman, and Lugano, Rudolf Heinemann, 1973; London, Artemis Fine Arts Ltd., 1980, Lit. Cleveland 1999, p. 132, PLATE 252

XII-35 Christen Købke (Copenhagen 1810–1848 Copenhagen), *View from the Grain Loft*, 1831, oil on canvas, 39 x 30.5 cm, Copenhagen, Statens Museum for Kunst (1662), Prov. Copenhagen, J. C. H. Reinhardt, 1831; Mathilde Reinhardt; Statens Museum for Kunst, since 1900, Lit. Copenhagen 1996A, cat. 34, p. 352, ill. 82, p. 139, PLATE 242

In his lifetime, Christen Købke achieved only a modest reputation, but from the later nineteenth century onward he has been seen as the greatest Danish artist of his time. The Biedermeier era in Denmark is referred to interchangeably as the "The Golden Age" or "The Age of Købke." The son of an affluent master baker, he entered the art academy in Copenhagen at age twelve and eventually became a pupil of Christoffer Wilhelm Eckersberg. Købke absorbed Eckersberg's dedication to realism, but his freer brushwork led to a more naturalistic rendering of atmospheric effects in his landscapes. Until 1833, he lived with his parents in the Citadel in Copenhagen, and his first landscapes are part of that local experience. In the 1840s, the family moved to a more rural environment near Blegdammen and Lake Sortedam, where the landscape provided Købke with endless subject matter. Some of his most beautiful paintings are of Frederiksborg Castle north of Copenhagen, which he pictured from both conventional and unusual perspectives, even from the vantage point of the rooftop. Bright summer light and a calm atmosphere contribute to a monumentality that is characteristic of the best work of the Biedermeier period.

XII-36   Christen Købke (Copenhagen 1810–1848 Copenhagen), *One of the Small Towers from Castle Frederiksborg*, ca. 1834, oil on canvas, 25.5 x 18.5 cm, Copenhagen, The David Collection (20/1969), Prov. Martinus Rørbye; Pietro Krohn; Emil Hannover; Theodor Jensen; W&M, April 1943; Agathe and Kund Neye; Auction ABR 231, 1969, C. K. David Collection, Lit. Copenhagen 1996A, cat. 75, p. 358, fig. 116, p. 188, PLATE 241

XII-37   Christen Købke (Copenhagen 1810–1848 Copenhagen), *The Rooftop of Frederiksborg Castle with a View of the Lake, Village, and Forest*, ca. 1834/35, oil on canvas, 177 x 171 cm, Copenhagen, The Danish Museum of Decorative Art, Gift of N. Petersen, 1895 (1326), Lit. Copenhagen 1996A, cat. 88, pp. 360–61, fig. 119, p. 191

XII-38   Christen Købke (Copenhagen 1810–1848 Copenhagen), *Frederiksborg Castle Seen from Jaegerbakken*, ca. 1835, oil on canvas, 75.6 x 104.1 cm, New York, Private Collection, Prov. Constantin Hansen; Miss Constantin Hansen; Mrs. Constantin Hansen (councillor of state); K. Brandt; Mrs. Gerda Brandt, 1953; London, Sotheby's, 1988; London, Sotheby's, 1989, Lit. Copenhagen 1996A, cat. 98, p. 362, fig. 122, p. 194, PLATE 240

XII-39   Martinus Rørbye (Drammen 1803–1848 Copenhagen), *Vester Edge Church with Gisselfeld Convent in the Background*, 1832, oil on paper pasted on canvas, 23.7 x 34.2 cm, Copenhagen, Ny Carlsberg Glyptotek (3249), Prov. Copenhagen, auction 1849; Kunstforningen 1905; Kunstforningen 1930; Private Collection, Lit. Copenhagen 1981, cat. 27, p. 53; Ottawa 2000, cat. 97, ill. p. 197, PLATE 243

Martinus Rørbye specialized in landscape painting and pictures of everyday life. In 1825, Rørbye became a pupil of Christoffer Wilhelm Eckersberg and in 1829 entered the Copenhagen art academy. He traveled more widely than his Danish contemporaries, visiting northern Denmark in 1833 and later Paris, Rome, and the Near East. In 1844, he became a professor at the academy in Copenhagen. Rørbye's landscapes and genre scenes capture daily life with great precision. His landscapes, like those of Eckersberg, focus on the ordinary rather than the visionary or spiritual qualities associated with the landscapes of Caspar David Friedrich and Karl Friedrich Schinkel. Even with the subject of a Danish village church, his emphasis is not on the church as a center of spiritual belief or a historical structure, but on the measure of the land and the colorful punctuation of buildings throughout.

XII-40   Julius Schoppe (Berlin 1795–1868 Berlin), *View of Salzburg*, 1817, oil on canvas, 47.5 x 60 cm, Dresden, Staatliche Kunstsammlungen Dresden, Galerie Neue Meister, 1907 (2217A), Prov. Wiesbaden, Eduard Schulz, Lit. Norman 1987, ill. pp. 80–81, PLATE 249

Although Julius Schoppe is known primarily as a portraitist, he was also a very accomplished landscapist, incorporating highly detailed panoramas into his group portraits. Schoppe first trained at the Berlin Akademie der Künste beginning in 1810, studying with the landscape draftsman Samuel Rösel. In 1816, he traveled to Vienna and then to Switzerland and Italy, where he greatly admired the work of Raphael, Correggio, and Titian. Upon his return to Berlin, Schoppe, together with the artist Carl Wilhelm Gropius, published an album of lithographs of scenery from his journey. Schoppe became a professor at the Berlin Akademie der Künste in 1836. His tidy landscapes and group portraits are characteristic of the Berlin School of Biedermeier painting.

XII-41   Julius Schoppe (Berlin 1795–1868 Berlin), *The "Emperor's Pine" in the Park of Kleinglienicke*, 1827, oil on canvas, 25 x 40 cm, Potsdam, Stiftung Preussische Schlösser und Gärten Berlin-Brandenburg (GKI 8804), Prov. Purchased by King Friedrich Wilhelm III, 1828. Lit. Potsdam 1990, cat. 4, PLATE 248

CENTRAL EUROPEAN PAINTING AND DRAWING

SECTION XIII

XIII-1   Carl Agricola (Säckingen 1779–1852 Baden near Vienna), *Interior of a Blacksmith's Shop*, 1810, gouache, 28.3 x 37.7 cm, Vienna, Albertina (4926), Prov. Vienna, Albert von Sachsen-Teschen (L 174), Lit. Hanover 1989, cat. 74, ill. p. 90, PLATE 271

Having commenced his studies in Karlsruhe, in 1793 Carl Agricola went to the Akademie der bildenden Künste Wien, where his teachers included the history painters Hubert Maurer and Friedrich Heinrich Füger. The latter proved especially influential in regard to Agricola's choice of subject matter and painting techniques, even if the student's allegorical, mythological, and religious paintings never approached the mastery of those of his teacher. While not averse to landscape painting, Agricola excelled as a painter of miniature portraits. His tiny watercolors were so popular in Vienna that he succeeded Eugène Isabey as court painter to the Duke of Reichstadt. Agricola also worked for the Wiener Porzellanmanufaktur and produced reproduction graphics.

XIII-2   Jakob Alt (Frankfurt am Main 1789–1872 Vienna), *The Palace of Duke Albert von Sachsen-Teschen*, 1816, pen and black ink, watercolor, 27.7 x 41.3 cm, Vienna, Albertina (4949), Prov. Vienna, Albert von Sachsen-Teschen (L 174), Lit. Koschatzky 1975, ill. 5, p. 18; Gmeiner-Hübel 1990, cat. 11.37, p. 317, PLATE 282

Jakob Alt received his first painting lessons from the miniaturist Johann Peter Beer of Frankfurt am Main. Alt arrived in Vienna in 1810 and like many other German artists of his generation, would have walked on to Rome, had he not decided to marry his young landlady. Although he is widely assumed to have enrolled at the Akademie der bildenden Künste Wien, his name is not listed in the archives. Alt's first success as an artist came from his work on a series of topographical prints for various Viennese publishers. The Donauansichten (a series of Danube lithographs published from 1820 onward) and countless watercolors of all the most beautiful places in Austria that he began producing for Crown Prince Ferdinand's Guckkasten in 1833 brought Alt recognition and financial security for his rapidly growing family. His two sons, Rudolf (1812–1905)

and Franz (1821–1914) learned painting from their father. Rudolf went on to become Austria's greatest watercolor landscape painter.

XIII-3   Jakob Alt (Frankfurt am Main 1789–1872 Vienna), *The Grundlsee*, 1817, watercolor, gouache, 37.2 x 54.5 cm, Vienna, Albertina (4944), Prov. Vienna, Albert von Sachsen-Teschen (L 174), Lit. Gmeiner-Hübel 1990, cat. 11.46, p. 318, PLATE 266

XIII-4   Jakob Alt (Frankfurt am Main 1789–1872 Vienna), *The Traunsee with Ort Castle*, 1817, watercolor, gouache, 36.9 x 54.6 cm, Vienna, Albertina (4942), Prov. Vienna, Albert von Sachsen-Teschen (L 174), Lit. Marks 1966, cat. 183, ill. p. 368; Vienna 1973, cat. 173; Koschatzky 1975, ill. 8, p. 21; Gmeiner-Hübel 1990, cat. 11.45, p. 318, PLATE 267

XIII-5   Jakob Alt (Frankfurt am Main 1789–1872 Vienna), *View of Vienna from "Spinnerin am Kreuz,"* 1817, watercolor, gouache, 39.7 x 57.5 cm, Vienna, Albertina (14615), Prov. Vienna, Albert von Sachsen-Teschen (L 174), Lit. Vienna 1973, cat. 35; Koschatzky 1975, cat. 6, p. 18; Pötschner 1978, cat. 134, pl. p. 286; Vienna 2005, cat. 9, ill. p. 68, PLATE 283

XIII-6   Jakob Alt (Frankfurt am Main 1789–1872 Vienna), *View to Stiebar Castle near Gresten in Lower Austria*, 1834, watercolor, gouache, 45.2 x 55.9 cm, Vienna, Österreichische Nationalbibliothek, Bildarchiv und Porträtsammlung (Pk 502/18), Prov. Vienna, Fidei-Kommiss-Sammlung, Lit. Vienna 1973, cat. 104, p. 252, ill. p. 39; Koschatzky 1975, cat. GK 9, p. 256, fig. 41, p. 53, ill.; Koschatzky 1987, cat. 46, p. 276, ill. p. 97, PLATE 295

XIII-7   Jakob Alt (Frankfurt am Main 1789–1872 Vienna), *View from the Artist's Studio in Alservorstadt toward Dornbach*, 1836, watercolor over pencil, 51.1 x 42.1 cm, Vienna, Albertina (28336), Prov. Vienna, Staatsgalerie (2247), Lit. Vienna 1973, cat. 191, p. 287, ill. p. 2; Koschatzky 1975, GK 17, p. 256, fig. 52, p. 61; Geismeier 1979, fig. 161; Gmeiner-Hübel 1990, cat. 11.124, p. 331; Koschatzky 1991, cat. GK 104, p. 74, ill. p. 14, PLATE 286

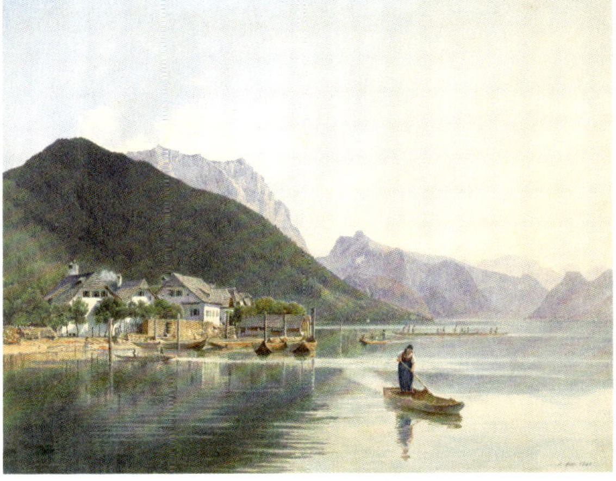

XIII-8

XIII-8   Rudolf von Alt (Vienna 1812-1905 Vienna), *The Traunsee*, 1840, watercolor, highlights scratched, 41.9 x 52.3 cm, Vienna, Albertina (22579), Prov. Vienna, Fidei-Kommiss-Sammlung, Lit. Koschatzky 1975, GK 62, p. 257; Koschatzky 1991, cat. 88, p. 74, ill. p. 60; Vienna 2005, cat. 73, p. 333, ill. p. 166

Although Rudolf von Alt attended the Akademie der bildenden Künste Wien, his experience in the workshop of his father, Jakob Alt, is more likely to have formed the cornerstone of his artistic career. Through coloring in his father's topographical prints, he acquired his mastery of watercolor technique. He discovered most of his landscapes and architectural motifs on his walks and later on his travels to Italy, Switzerland, and especially in the territories of the Austrian Empire. Alt's extraordinarily long working life of almost eighty years' duration spans that epoch of Austrian art history that began with Biedermeier. His works may be regarded as the apogee of Austrian watercolor painting in the nineteenth century.

XIII-9   Friedrich von Amerling (Vienna 1803-1887 Vienna), *Young Girl*, 1834, oil on canvas, 44.2 x 40.2 cm, Vienna, Private Collection, Prov. Vienna, Hans Piering, Lit. Probszt-Ohstorff 1927, no. 324; Feuchtmüller and Mrazek 1963, fig. II; Vienna 1993, cat. 59

The son of a drawer of gold and silver wire, Friedrich von Amerling enrolled in the engraving school of the Akademie der bildenden Künste Wien in 1815 only to switch to history painting one year later. After studying under Hubert Maurer and later Karl Gsellhofer, Amerling moved on to the Prague Academy, where in 1824-26 he was a pupil of the history painter Josef Bergler. Thanks to the patronage of Prince Paul Esterházy, he was able to spend the year 1827-28 in London, where he learned portraiture from the renowned Thomas Lawrence. After visiting Rome in 1831-32, Amerling returned to Vienna with the aim of painting a portrait of Emperor Franz I. He subsequently became the favored portraitist of the emperor, the court, and the aristocracy. Over the course of his long life, Amerling painted portraits almost exclusively (about a thousand) and was a highly regarded member of Viennese society. He traveled well into his old age, making several trips to Rome, and visiting The Netherlands, Spain, England, Germany, Scandinavia, and even Constantinople and Egypt.

XIII-10   Friedrich von Amerling (Vienna 1803-1887 Vienna), *Alexander Baron von Vesque-Püttlingen as a Child*, 1836, oil on canvas, 31.5 x 26 cm, Vienna, Österreichische Galerie Belvedere, Bequest of A. Baron von Vesque-Püttlingen, 1969 (5875), Lit. Vienna 1992-2000, vol. 1, p. 46, ill.; Vienna 2003A, cat. 27, ill. pp. 145-46, PLATE 322

XIII-14

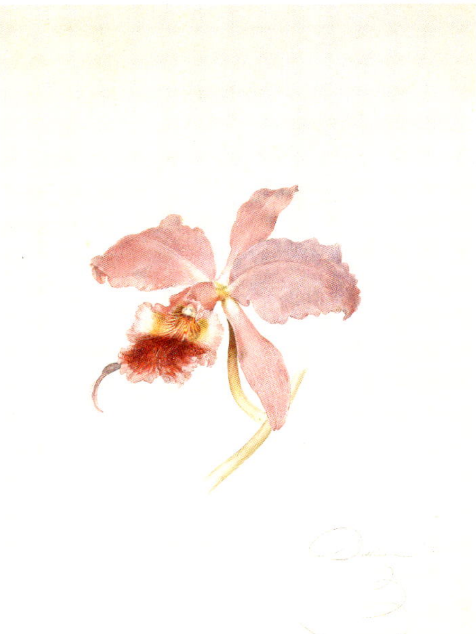

XIII-17

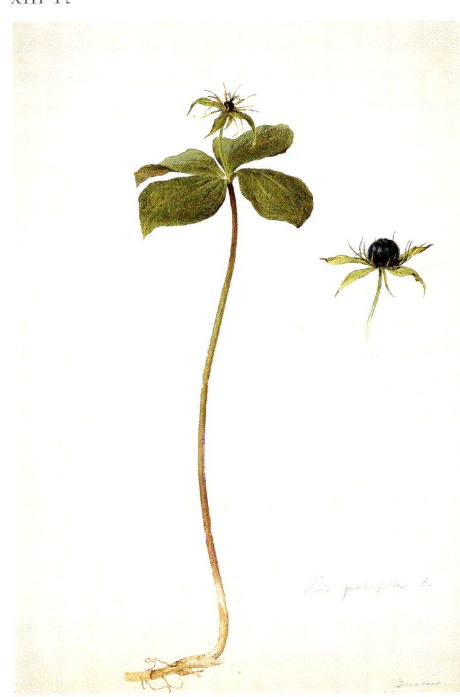

XIII-11   Friedrich von Amerling (Vienna 1803–1887 Vienna), *Prince Viktor Odescalchi in a Fancy-Dress Costume*, 1838, oil on canvas, 45 x 37 cm, Vienna, Private Collection, Prov. Vienna, Galerie Schebesta, Lit. Probzst-Ohstorff 1927, cat. 417, pp. 46, 125; Vienna 2003A, cat. 42, ill. pp. 172–73, PLATE 323

XIII-12   Moritz Michael Daffinger (Vienna 1790–1849 Vienna), *Arnica Montana L, Mountain Arnica*, 1830s/40s, watercolor, traces of pencil underdrawing, 42.4 x 27.2 cm, Vienna, Akademie der bildenden Künste Wien, Kupferstichkabinett, Purchase, 1850 (7.498), Prov. Vienna, the artist's widow, Lit. Vienna 1986, cat. 28, ill. pl. 27, pp. 107, 148, PLATE 310

Moritz Michael Daffinger's first teachers were his father followed by his stepfather, both flower painters in the Wiener Porzellanmanufaktur. Apprenticed to the factory at age eleven, Daffinger proved so talented that in 1802 the factory granted him a stipend to attend the Akademie der bildenden Künste Wien. He studied both history and portrait painting while continuing to decorate porcelain for his employer, mostly with mythological subjects or portraits. Daffinger left the academy in 1809 and the factory three years later. In 1814-15, at the time of the Congress of Vienna, he was very much in demand as a portraitist. Thomas Lawrence's visit to Vienna in 1819 was an important source of inspiration. Daffinger's own miniatures, however, were admired as masterpieces in their own right, and he soon became the most sought-after portraitist of Viennese high society. The death of his beloved daughter in 1841, however, at the height of his career, so devastated Daffinger that he turned his back on society and portraiture and henceforth dedicated himself exclusively to the study and painting of plants.

XIII-13   Moritz Michael Daffinger (Vienna 1790–1849 Vienna), *Bellis perennis L, Common Daisy*, 1830s/40s, watercolor, traces of pencil underdrawing, 35.3 x 24.2 cm, Vienna, Akademie der bildenden Künste Wien, Kupferstichkabinett, Purchase, 1850 (7.481), Prov. Vienna, the artist's widow, Lit. Vienna 1986, p. 105

XIII-14   Moritz Michael Daffinger (Vienna 1790–1849 Vienna), *Cattleya labiata Lindl, Orchid*, 1830s/40s, watercolor, traces of pencil underdrawing, 30.2 x 22 cm, Vienna, Albertina (5067), Prov. Vienna, Private Collection of Fr. Müllner, Lit. Vienna 1973, cat. 81, p. 241; Hanover 1989, cat. 21, ill. p. 31

XIII-15   Moritz Michael Daffinger (Vienna 1790–1849 Vienna), *Convallaria majalis L, Common Lily of the Valley*, 1830s/40s, watercolor, traces of pencil underdrawing, 31.5 x 20.6 cm, Vienna, Akademie der bildenden Künste Wien, Kupferstichkabinett, Purchase, 1850 (7.410), Prov. Vienna, the artist's widow, Lit. Vienna 1986, cat. 20, ill. pl. 19, pp. 99, 146, PLATE 308

XIII-16   Moritz Michael Daffinger (Vienna 1790–1849 Vienna), *Gentiana pannonica Scop., Hungarian Gentian*, 1830s/40s, watercolor, traces of pencil underdrawing, 37.9 x 24.3 cm, Vienna, Akademie der bildenden Künste Wien, Kupferstichkabinett, Purchase, 1850 (7.548), Prov. Vienna, the artist's widow, Lit. Vienna 1986, cat. 30, ill. pl. 29, pp. 111, 148

XIII-17   Moritz Michael Daffinger (Vienna 1790–1849 Vienna), *Paris quadrifolia L, Herb Paris*, 1830s/40s, watercolor, over pencil underdrawing, 37.4 x 24.5 cm, Vienna, Albertina (35533), Prov. Vienna, Auktion Lanna, Gilhofer und Ranschburg, October 1910; Vienna, Elisabeth Bondi, 1962, Lit. Hanover 1989, cat. 29, p. 30

XIII-18   Moritz Michael Daffinger (Vienna 1790–1849 Vienna), *Primula veris acaulis L, Common Primrose*, 1830s/40s, watercolor, traces of pencil underdrawing, 28.9 x 20.9 cm, Vienna, Akademie der bildenden Künste Wien, Kupferstichkabinett, Purchase, 1850 (7.622), Prov. Vienna, the artist's widow, Lit. Vienna 1986, cat. 19, ill. pl. 18, pp. 117, 146, PLATE 311

XIII-19   Moritz Michael Daffinger (Vienna 1790–1849 Vienna), *Rosa gallica L, Gallic Rose*, 1830s/40s, watercolor, traces of pencil underdrawing, 42.2 x 29.1 cm, Vienna, Akademie der bildenden Künste Wien, Kupferstichkabinett, Purchase, 1850 (7.777), Prov. Vienna, the artist's widow, Lit. Vienna 1986, cat. 22, ill. pl. 21, pp. 130, 147, PLATE 307

XIII-20   Moritz Michael Daffinger (Vienna 1790–1849 Vienna), *Var. Hepatica triloba D.C., Liverwort, variants in different colors*, 1830s/40s, watercolor, traces of pencil underdrawing, 42.4 x 29.4 cm, Vienna, Akademie der bildenden Künste Wien, Kupferstichkabinett, Purchase, 1850 (7.673), Prov. Vienna, the artist's widow, Lit. Vienna 1986, cat. 21, ill. pl. 20, pp. 121, 146, PLATE 309

XIII-21   Johann Stephan Decker (Colmar 1784–1844 Vienna), *Emperor Franz I in His Study*, after 1821, oil on canvas, 109 x 157.7 cm, Vienna, Österreichische Galerie Belvedere, Purchase, 1896, for the Kaiserliche Gemäldegalerie (2811), Prov. Vienna, Kunsthandlung Neumann, Lit. Vienna 1992-2000, vol. 1, p. 188, ill., PLATE 285

Johann Stephan Decker was the father and teacher of the genre and portrait painters Albert, Georg, and Gabriel Decker. He went to Paris at the age of twenty and studied with Jacques-Louis David, then earned his living as a portraitist before returning to Colmar in 1811/12. After spending some three years painting portraits in Pest, Decker moved on to Vienna, where he worked for both Prince Metternich and Count Sickingen. From 1827 to 1840, when he worked as a private drawing teacher in the household of Archduke Karl, he came to the attention of the court. Decker was first and foremost a portraitist, although his oeuvre includes numerous miniatures as well as genre paintings and landscapes. A copperplate engraving of his portrait of Emperor Franz I in the surprisingly unpretentious setting of his study was especially popular and widely circulated.

XIII-22 Thomas Ender (Vienna 1793–1875 Vienna), *Gate to the Graveyard*, ca. 1820, oil on canvas, 34 x 44 cm, Vienna, Österreichische Galerie Belvedere, Purchase, 1974 (6047), Prov. Vienna Art Market, Lit. Vienna 1992–2000, vol. 1, p. 223, ill., PLATE 287

The twin brother of the portrait artist Johann Ender, Thomas Ender attended the Akademie der bildenden Künste Wien from 1806 to 1813, then traveled extensively in search of subjects for his nature studies, including to the Salzkammergut (1812) and Salzburg and Tyrol (1815). After receiving the emperor's prize for landscape painting in 1817, he was charged by his patron Prince Metternich (Austrian chancellor and the curator of the Vienna Kunstakademie), with "documenting" an expedition to Brazil in 1817–18 on the occasion of the marriage of Archduchess Leopoldine of Austria to the Brazilian Crown Prince. This trip resulted in some 700 drawings and watercolors of landscapes, portraits, and depictions of indigenous flora and fauna in Brazil. In 1819, Ender accompanied Emperor Franz I to Rome and was granted a stipend that enabled him to prolong his stay. Appointed court painter to the Archduke Johann in 1828, Ender went on to paint countless views of the Alps and other Austrian landscapes. He became an examiner for the landscape drawing class in 1835, and two years later a professor of landscape painting at the Vienna academy. In 1837, he accompanied Archduke Johann to the Crimea, Turkey, and Greece. After leaving the academy in 1851, Ender continued to travel extensively, his most artistically productive trip being that to Upper Hungary and the High Tatra in 1860–62.

XIII-23 Thomas Ender (Vienna 1793–1875 Vienna), *View of the "Ausgussgletscher" in Kaprun*, 1830, watercolor, 23.3 x 37 cm, Vienna, Private Collection, Prov. Vienna, Galerie und Auktionshaus Hassfurther, Lit. Koschatzky 1982, cat. 66, p. 184, ill. p. 71; Hassfurther 1996, cat. 5, ill., p. 2, PLATE 281

XIII-24 Thomas Ender (Vienna 1793–1875 Vienna), *The Upper and Lower Pasterze with the Grossglockner and the Johannisberg near Heiligenblut*, 1834, watercolor, 40.5 x 55.5

cm, Vienna, Private Collection, Prov. Vienna, Dorotheum, Lit. Frodl 2002, vol. 5, cat. 32, ill. p. 290, PLATE 279

XIII-25 Thomas Ender (Vienna 1793–1875 Vienna), *Upper Sulzbachkees with Grossvenediger*, ca. 1834, watercolor, 33.7 x 48 cm, Vienna, Private Collection, Prov. Vienna, Kunsthandel Giese & Schweiger, PLATE 280

XIII-26 Thomas Ender (Vienna 1793–1875 Vienna), *The Vogelmaier Ochsenkar Kees in the Rauris Valley of the Hohe Tauern*, 1834, oil on canvas, 26.7 x 36.2 cm, Vaduz/Vienna, Sammlungen des Fürsten von und zu Liechtenstein (GE 2002), Prov. Acquired by Prince Franz Josef II von und zu Liechtenstein from Vienna Art Market, 1982, Lit. Vienna 2004A, cat. III.13, p. 173, ill. p. 133; Vaduz 2005, cat. 96, ill. pp. 130–31

XIII-27 Thomas Ender (Vienna 1793–1875 Vienna), *The Matterhorn Seen from Gornergrat*, 1854, watercolor, 33.3 x 50.3 cm, Vienna, Albertina (36935), Prov. Vienna, Galerie Christian M. Nebehay, Lit. Koschatzky 1982, p. 154, fig. 149

XIII-28 Erasmus von Engert (Vienna 1796–1871 Vienna), *The Big Hammerhaus in Hirschwang an der Rax*, 1825, oil on panel, 46 x 37 cm, Vienna, Österreichische Galerie Belvedere, Purchase, 1924 (2464), Prov. Austria, Private Collection, Lit. Vienna 1992–2000, vol. 1, p. 237, ill., PLATE 272

Erasmus von Engert was the son of an art dealer in Vienna's Vorstadt. As a student at the Akademie der bildenden Künste Wien (1809–23), he studied life drawing with Hubert Maurer and history painting with Anton Petter, then worked briefly as a drawing teacher at the engineering academy. From the late 1820s onward, he worked mainly as a copyist and restorer. He made a study trip to Italy in 1833 and was made custodian and restorer at the Kaiserliche Gemäldegalerie in 1840 and director in 1857; in 1860, he issued a new catalogue of the gallery's collection. His own relatively small oeuvre consists mainly of portraits and genre paintings, with the most convincing works dating from the late 1820s. Particularly charming are his depictions of people going about their humble everyday tasks in the idyllic gardens of the Vorstadt.

XIII-29 Erasmus von Engert (Vienna 1796–1871 Vienna), *Girl in an Arbor*, ca. 1828, oil on canvas, 30.3 x 37.1 cm, Germany, Private Collection, Lit. Frodl 1987, cat. 77, ill. p. 77; Vienna 1993, cat. 55, ill., PLATE 289

XIII-30 Franz Eybl (Vienna 1806–1880 Vienna), *The Landlord at the Krottensee*, 1835, oil on panel, 34.1 x 28 cm, Germany, Private Collection, Lit. Kastel 1983, cat. 92, p. 195; Frodl 1987, cat. 145, p. 247, PLATE 326

XIII-27

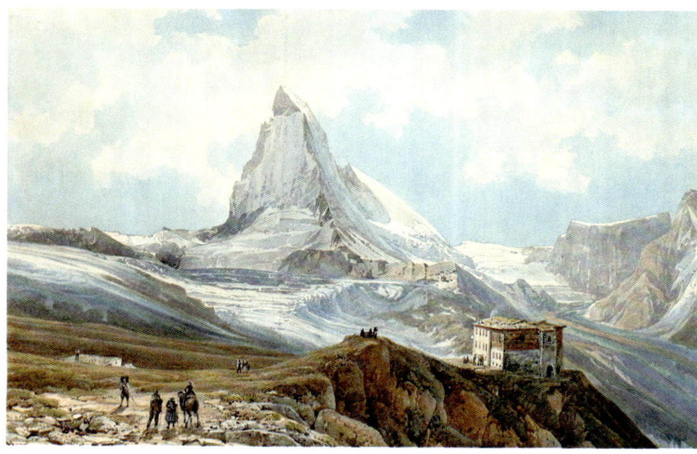

XIII-34

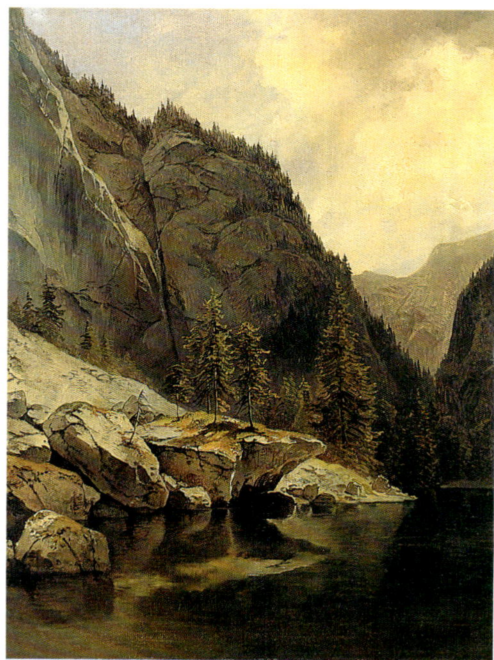

An artist of humble origins, Franz Eybl
enrolled at age ten at the Akademie der bildenden Künste Wien. After training to become an
engraver, he switched in 1817 to Josef Mössmer's
landscape class and from 1820 onward studied history painting under Johann Baptist Lampi and
Franz Caucig. His most important teacher was the
professor of history painting Johann Peter Krafft,
whose close observation of people and monumental
style had a decisive impact on his artistic development. With their extraordinary painterly quality,
Eybl's portraits soon eclipsed those of his teacher.
Eybl's more than 400 lithographic portraits made
him one of the most important portraitists of his
age. Starting in the 1830s, he turned to genre
painting, often finding his motifs in the people and
landscapes of the Salzkammergut. Eybl became a
member of the academy in 1843 and was appointed
custodian of the Kaiserliche Gemäldegalerie in 1853.
From that time on, he concentrated on the restoration of paintings and produced very few of his own.

XIII-31   Franz Eybl (Vienna 1806–1880 Vienna),
Inside of a Blacksmith's Shop, 1847, oil on canvas,
47 x 37.5 cm, Vienna, Österreichische Galerie
Belvedere, Purchase, 1907 (830), Prov. Vienna,
Auction Jauner von Schroffenegg (offered in the
Viennese Academy exhibition in 1848), Lit. Kastel
1983, cat. 195, p. 248; Vienna 1992–2000, p. 251, ill.,
PLATE 324

XIII-32   Leopold Fertbauer (Vienna 1802-1875
Vienna), *Emperor Franz I and His Family*, 1826,
oil on canvas, 63.5 x 79.2 cm, Vienna, Wien
Museum, Purchase, 1897 (16.380), Prov. Vienna,
S. Kende, Lit. Frodl 1987, pp. 15-16, fig. 7; Vienna
1987B, cat. 2/4/5, p. 70
    Leopold Fertbauer was the son of the
"bourgeois clockmaker" Philipp Fertbauer. As a
student at the Akademie der bildenden Künste Wien
(1816-1827/28), he studied landscape painting and
then history drawing. Although he painted landscapes and architecture, Fertbauer produced mainly
individual and group portraits. His works were
regularly included in the academy exhibitions of
the 1830s and he served as assistant director of the
Liechtenstein art gallery. Fertbauer is said to have
gone blind in 1844. Almost all the surviving works
by this little-known artist are still in private hands.

XIII-33   Friedrich Gauermann (Miesenbach
bei Wiener Neustadt 1807–1862 Vienna), *The
Dachstein from Plassen near Hallstatt*, ca. 1827,
oil on paper mounted on canvas, 29.5 x 40.5
cm, Vienna, Österreichische Galerie Belvedere,
Purchase, 1932 (3221), Prov. Vienna Art Market,
Lit. Vienna 1937, cat. 151, p. 27; Feuchtmüller 1987,
p. 110, ill.; Vienna 1992–2000, vol. 2, p. 65, ill.,
PLATE 296
    During his own lifetime, Friedrich Gauermann
achieved widespread renown as a landscape and

animal painter. His father, the landscapist Jakob Gauermann, was his first teacher. He emphasized the careful study of nature, a hallmark of the son's mature style. Friedrich Gauermann moved to Vienna, where he studied at the Akademie der bildenden Künste Wien. He was greatly impressed by the work of seventeenth-century Dutch landscape painters, whose realism he admired. Gauermann worked directly from nature, recording his observations in numerous oil sketches as well as studies in pencil and watercolor. His landscapes are notable for their freshness of color and the distinctive treatment of light and atmosphere. Gauermann's work was in great demand during the Biedermeier period, and prints after his paintings could be found in homes throughout Austria and Germany.

XIII-34   Friedrich Gauermann (Miesenbach near Wiener Neustadt 1807–1862 Vienna), *At the Kammersee near Aussee*, ca. 1830, oil on paper, 44.3 x 33 cm, Graz, Neue Galerie am Landesmuseum Joanneum, Purchase, 1952 (I/1123), Prov. Vienna, Dorotheum, Lit. Graz 1988, cat. 442, p. 188, ill. p. 23

XIII-35   Friedrich Gauermann (Miesenbach bei Wiener Neustadt 1807–1862 Vienna), *View from Scheuchenstein toward Gauermannhof with Schneeberg in the Background*, ca. 1835, oil on paper mounted on canvas, 28 x 40.5 cm, Vienna, Österreichische Galerie Belvedere, Purchase, 1934 (3290), Prov. Vienna, Private Collection, Lit. Feuchtmüller 1987, p. 86, ill.; Vienna 1992–2000, vol. 2, p. 67, ill., PLATE 297

XIII-36   Jakob Gauermann (Öffingen 1773–1843 Vienna), *Polsterltanz [Cushion Dance] at the Grundlsee*, 1821, oil on panel, 31.8 x 45.3 cm, Vienna, Private Collection, Prov. Private Collection, Lit. Vienna 1973, cat. 101, ill. p. 93; Marko 1980, cat. 434, p. 273, fig. 145, PLATE 269

Jakob Gauermann was apprenticed to a stonemason. When his artistic gifts were recognized, he was sent to the Hohe Carlsschule in Stuttgart (1788–92) where he studied painting and then copperplate engraving. He came to Vienna in 1798 to attend the Akademie der bildenden Künste, but his patron's bankruptcy forced him to earn a living engraving handbills and teaching drawing. Gauermann's first success, like that of many other artists of the era, came from his landscape prints, which earned him sufficient income to buy a small farm in Miesenbach in Lower Austria. It became his summer residence and yielded him an inexhaustible source of motifs. In 1818, Gauermann was appointed court painter to Archduke Johann. In his service, he produced numerous watercolors of the Styrian countryside and scenes from the life of the archduke. Gauermann taught his son, Friedrich (1807–1862), who from the late 1830s onward was Austria's best-known painter of landscapes and animals.

XIII-37   Jakob Gauermann (Öffingen 1773–1843 Vienna), *Wedding Procession to the Church of Scheuchenstein*, 1821, oil on panel, 31.5 x 45.5 cm, Private Collection, Prov. Private Collection, Lit. Marko 1980, cat. 441, p. 275, PLATE 268

XIII-38   Jakob Gauermann (Öffingen 1773–1843 Vienna), *In the Ramsau*, ca. 1820, watercolor, 36 x 121.3 cm, Vienna, Galerie und Auktionshaus Hassfurther, Prov. Private Collection, Lit. Hassfurther 1996, cat. 15, ill. pp. 50–51, PLATE 274

XIII-39   Eduard Gurk (Vienna 1801–1841 Jerusalem), *On the Embankment next to the Augarten on March 3, 1830*, 1830, watercolor, 35.5 x 54 cm, Vienna, Albertina (22611), Prov. Vienna, Fidei-Kommiss-Sammlung, Lit. Koschatzky 1991, GK 108, p. 74, ill. p. 61, PLATE 294

Eduard Gurk's father was a painter and librarian in the service of Prince Nikolaus Esterházy. The son's great gift became apparent very early, and on a trip to England, father and son are said to have produced some very accomplished watercolors. The son trained as a copperplate engraver upon returning to Vienna in 1819, yet does not appear to have attended the Akademie der bildenden Künste Wien. In 1823, he and his father published a collection of eighty colored copperplate engravings of Vienna. Having been introduced in 1827 to Crown Prince Archduke Ferdinand (who in 1835 became Emperor Ferdinand I), Gurk accompanied the court to Pressburg (now Bratislava) for Ferdinand's coronation and then to Prague in 1836. Starting in 1835, Gurk used his trips to produce large-format watercolors for the emperor's Guckkasten. Highly acclaimed in Vienna for his watercolors, in 1839 Gurk was appointed royal court painter. He died of typhus in Jerusalem journeying to Syria and Palestine.

XIII-40   Eduard Gurk (Vienna 1801–1841 Jerusalem), *Baden near Vienna*, 1833, watercolor, 44 x 56.3 cm, Vienna, Albertina (22617), Prov. Vienna, Fidei-Kommiss-Sammlung, Lit. Koschatzky 1991, GK 113, p. 74, ill. p. 62

XIII-41   Eduard Gurk (Vienna 1801–1841 Jerusalem), *The Basilica of Mariazell Seen from the Churchyard*, 1833, watercolor, 42.4 x 57.5 cm, Vienna, Albertina (22634), Prov. Vienna, Fidei-Kommiss-Sammlung, Lit. Vienna 1978, cat. 118; Koschatzky 1991, GK 130, cat. 28, ill. p. 74, PLATE 292

XIII-42   Eduard Gurk (Vienna 1801–1841 Jerusalem), *The Imperial Palace with the Ferdinand Fountain in Baden near Vienna*, 1833, watercolor, 44 x 56.3 cm, Vienna, Albertina (22613), Prov. Vienna, Fidei-Kommiss-Sammlung, Lit. Vienna 1978, cat. 109, p. 112, ill., p. 76; Koschatzky 1991, GK 113, cat. 16, ill. p. 74, PLATE 290

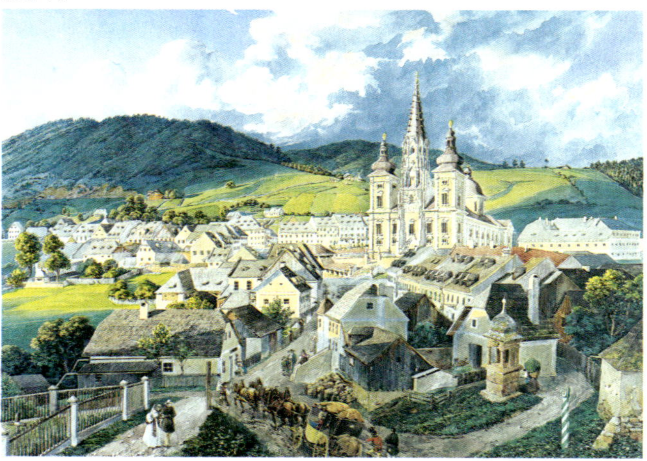

XIII-43   Eduard Gurk (Vienna 1801–1841 Jerusalem), *Mariazell from the Bürgeralpel*, 1833, watercolor, 43 x 56.5 cm, Vienna, Albertina (22630), Prov. Vienna, Fidei-Kommiss-Sammlung, Lit. Koschatzky 1991, GK 126, p. 74, ill. p. 62

XIII-44   Eduard Gurk (Vienna 1801–1841 Jerusalem), *Distant View from Grosser Höllstein toward Mariazell*, 1835, watercolor, 42.7 x 56.3 cm, Vienna, Albertina (22627), Prov. Vienna, Fidei-Kommiss-Sammlung, Lit. Vienna 1978, cat. 116, ill. p. 116; Koschatzky 1991, GK 123, cat. 27, ill. p. 74, PLATE 293

XIII-45   Eduard Gurk (Vienna 1801–1841 Jerusalem), *Mariazell from the Annaberg*, 1835, watercolor, 44 x 56.5 cm, Vienna, Albertina (22631), Prov. Vienna, Fidei-Kommiss-Sammlung, Lit. Koschatzky 1991, GK 127, p. 74, ill. p. 62

XIII-46   Eduard Gurk (Vienna 1801–1841 Jerusalem), *Mariazell from the Wienerstrasse*, 1835, watercolor, 43 x 56.5 cm, Vienna, Albertina (22633), Prov. Vienna, Fidei-Kommiss-Sammlung, Lit. Koschatzky 1991, GK 129, p. 74, ill. p. 63

XIII-47   Eduard Gurk (Vienna 1801–1841 Jerusalem), *Church and Main Square in Pilsen*, ca. 1837, watercolor, traces of pencil, 45.2 x 57.8 cm, Vienna, Albertina (22652), Prov. Vienna, Fidei-Kommiss-Sammlung, Lit. Vienna 1978, cat. 111; Koschatzky 1991, GK 148, cat. 78, p. 75

XIII-48   Eduard Gurk (Vienna 1801–1841 Jerusalem), *On the Hradschin in Prague*, 1838, watercolor, 44.6 x 58.8 cm, Vienna, Albertina (22644), Prov. Vienna, Fidei-Kommiss-Sammlung, Lit. Vienna 1973, cat. 109; Vienna 1978, cat. 123, ill. p. 123; Koschatzky 1991, GK 140, cat. 72, p. 74, PLATE 291

XIII-49   Joseph Anton Koch (Obergiblen 1768–1839 Rome), *The Hasli Valley near Meiringen*, 1817, oil on canvas, 101 x 134 cm, Innsbruck, Tiroler Landesmuseum Ferdinandeum (Gem 359), Prov. Collection of Philipp Passavant, Lit. Lutterotti 1985, G37, p. 292, pl. 9, pp. 84f., 101; Stuttgart 1989, cat. 111, ill. 184, pp. 257–59, PLATE 258

Joseph Anton Koch enrolled at the Hohe Karlsschule in Stuttgart in 1785 and six years later cast off the shackles of academia by running away to Strasbourg. Although he at first moved in Jacobin circles, he soon distanced himself from the French Revolution. After a walking tour of the Swiss Alps, during which he produced a number of nature studies, in 1795 he went on to Rome, where he had close, but not uncritical contact with the Nazarenes and helped work on the frescos of the Casino Massimo (1825–26). In 1812, Koch moved to Vienna, but found no work and returned to Rome, where he became a leading figure in a German-Roman artists' cooperative. Koch's spearheading of the revival of landscape painting in the spirit of Poussin and intensive study of nature made him a role model for several generations of Romantics and for those artists who were becoming increasingly interested in realist landscape.

XIII-50 Joseph Anton Koch (Obergiblen 1768–1839 Rome), *Mountain Landscape with Lake*, after 1830, oil on canvas, 91 x 75 cm, Basel, Kunstmuseum Basel, acquired from descendants of the artist in Rome, 1947 (2218), Lit. Lutterotti 1985, cat. G61, p. 298, pl. XIII, F. 104, Stuttgart 1989, ill. 54, p. 86, PLATE 259

XIII-51 Leopold Kupelwieser (Markt Piesting, Lower Austria 1796–1862 Vienna), *Archduke Johann Baptist of Austria*, 1828, oil on canvas, 66 x 52.8 cm, Graz, Neue Galerie am Landesmuseum Joanneum, Purchase, 1984 (I/2184), Prov. Vienna, Galerie Josefstadt, Lit. Graz 1988, cat. 827, p. 227, ill. p. 2, PLATE 270

Leopold Kupelwieser's father, an engineer, was anxious to ensure that his son had a solid education. A student of the Akademie der bildenden Künste Wien in 1809–23, Leopold studied with the history painters Franz Caucig and Johann Baptist Lampi, although his own breakthrough as an artist was as a portrait painter. Like Moritz von Schwind, he was a friend of Franz Schubert and in 1823 went to Rome, where he joined the Nazarenes and henceforth modeled his works on those of the early Italian Renaissance. After Kupelwieser became a devout Catholic, religious themes came to play an increasingly central role in his oeuvre. He also resumed portrait painting, however, and was commissioned to paint portraits of various members of the Austrian imperial family. Kupelwieser's formal language is extremely clear and his paintings are remarkable above all for their sophisticated sense of color.

XIII-52 Matthäus Loder (Vienna 1781–1828 Vordernberg), *View of Vienna*, ca. 1810, watercolor, pen and black ink, 33 x 48 cm, Vienna, Albertina (5821), Prov. Vienna, Albert von Sachsen-Teschen (L 174), Lit. Graz 1959, cat. 92; May 1965, p. 25, pl. 49; Vienna 1978, cat. 34; Wietersheim-Meran 1989, vol. 2, cat. 164, p. 56

Matthäus Loder's talents as a draftsman were recognized early and rewarded with various stipends that enabled him in 1797 to enroll at the Vienna Kunstakademie, despite his humble origins. He began by drawing flowers at the school of the Wiener Porzellanmanufaktur, then progressed to the school of architecture, to the study of anatomy, to copying from antique models, to landscapes. His first nature studies date from an 1804 walking tour in the Schneeberg region, although he also produced book illustrations, handbills, preliminary

drawings for topographical prints, and stage sets. Loder taught drawing to Archduchess Marie-Louise and in 1816 accompanied her to Parma. Unable to cope with the climate, he returned to Vienna and at the end of the year was appointed court painter to Archduke Johann. In the years following, he documented the life of the archduke and accompanied him on his travels, illustrating life in Austria and above all in Styria at that time. As almost all Loder's works remained in the collection of the archduke, he has remained virtually unknown.

XIII-53 Matthäus Loder (Vienna 1781–1828 Vordernberg), *Johann Zahlbruckner, Botanist and Private Secretary of Archduke Johann of Austria*, ca. 1820, watercolor over pencil, 33.6 x 23.7 cm, Vienna, Galerie und Auktionshaus Hassfurther, Prov. Nachkommen des Dargestellten, Lit. Wietersheim-Meran 1989, vol. 2, cat. 788, p. 378, PLATE 275

XIII-54 Matthäus Loder (Vienna 1781–1828 Vordernberg), *Sonnschienalm*, 1820/21, watercolor over pencil, white and pink highlights, 32.3 x 51 cm, Vienna, Galerie und Auktionshaus Hassfurther, Prov. Private Collection, Lit. Vienna 1978, cat. 43; Wietersheim-Meran 1989, vol. 2, cat. 714, p. 341; Hassfurther 1996, cat. 25, pp. 66–67

XIII-55 Matthäus Loder (Vienna 1781–1828 Vordernberg), *Survey on the Sonnschienalm*, 1820/21, watercolor over pencil, opaque white highlights, 26.8 x 53.3 cm, Vienna, Galerie und Auktionshaus Hassfurther, Prov. Private Collection, Lit. Vienna 1978, cat. 49; Wietersheim-Meran 1989, vol. 2, cat. 715, p. 341; Hassfurther 1996, cat. 24, ill. pp. 64–65, PLATE 276

XIII-56 Matthäus Loder (Vienna 1781–1828 Vordernberg), *View of Brandhof*, ca. 1824, watercolor, pen and black ink, pencil underdrawing, 20.7 x 24.7 cm, Vienna, Albertina (5827), Prov. Vienna, Albert von Sachsen-Teschen (L 174), Lit. Wietersheim-Meran 1989, vol. 2, p. 350, cat. 721, PLATE 277

XIII-57 Matthäus Loder (Vienna 1781–1828 Vordernberg), *Böckstein near Wildbad Gastein*, 1828, watercolor, gouache, 27.5 x 37.5 cm, Vienna, Galerie und Auktionshaus Hassfurther, Prov. Private Collection, Lit. Graz 1959, cat. 147, ill.; Vienna 1978, cat. 92; Wietersheim-Meran 1989, vol. 2, cat. 924, p. 516; Hassfurther 1996, cat. 36, ill. pp. 86–87, PLATE 278

XIII-58 Friedrich Loos (Graz 1797–1890 Kiel), *Berchtesgaden with the Watzmann*, ca. 1830, watercolor, 35 x 47 cm, Vienna, Private Collection, Prov. Karlsruhe, Collection of Dr. Wiedner, Lit. Schwarz 1977, pl. 154; Nebehay 1988, cat. 99

Friedrich Loos was a student at the Akademie der bildenden Künste Wien in 1813 and in 1816–21. His professors were Josef Mössmer for landscape drawing and Josef Fischer for painting. A walking tour in the Schneeberg mountains with Mössmer laid the groundwork for Loos's intensive study of nature. In 1825–35, Loos was a resident of Salzburg, where until 1829 he worked on Johann Michael Sattler's large city panoramas. It was here that he produced the early views of Salzburg that now rank among the incunabula of Austrian landscape painting. Leaving Salzburg, Loos lived in Vienna and Klosterneuburg until 1846 and then moved on to Rome, where he remained until 1851, creating mostly panoramic views of the city. In 1853, he decided to settle in Kiel, where he taught drawing at the university until 1883.

XIII-59   Friedrich Loos (Graz 1797–1890 Kiel), *The Ramsau near Berchtesgaden*, 1836, oil on canvas, 58 x 73.5 cm, Vienna, Österreichische Galerie Belvedere (3776), Prov. Transferred from the Kunsthistorisches Museum Wien, 1940 (purchased in the Academy exhibition for the Kaiserliche Gemäldegalerie in 1836), Lit. Vienna 1992–2000, vol. 3, p. 37, ill., PLATE 298

XIII-60   Friedrich Loos (Graz 1797–1890 Kiel), *Motif from Oberschützen*, 1838, oil on canvas, 24 x 32 cm, Vienna, Österreichische Galerie Belvedere, Purchase, 1943 (3919), Prov. Vienna, Private Collection, Lit. Vienna 1992–2000, vol. 3, p. 37, ill., PLATE 288

XIII-61   Nikolaus Moreau (Vienna 1805–1834 Vienna), *View from a Window of the Diana Bath*, 1830, oil on canvas, 39.5 x 34.5 cm, Vienna, Wien Museum (95.189), Prov. Vienna, Purchase from a private collection, 1950, Lit. Vienna 1987B, cat. 12/1/18, p. 478, ill. p. 460, PLATE 284

Very few of Nikolaus Moreau's works are known and just as little is known about the artist himself. He was probably the son of Karl von Moreau, the architect and painter who, after training in Paris, came to Vienna around 1800 and in 1801 was charged with the modernization of Schloss Eisenstadt on behalf of Prince Nikolaus Esterházy. He later made a name for himself as a history and genre painter and as such was his son's first art teacher. Moreau himself attended the Akademie der bildenden Künste Wien and right up to his premature death in 1834 had numerous portraits, genre paintings, and animal pictures included in the academy exhibitions.

XIII-62   Ferdinand Olivier (Dessau 1785–1841 Munich), *View of the Clay Pits in Matzleinsdorf and the Parish Church St. Florian*, 1814/15, pen and black and brown ink, 15.9 x 24.4 cm, Vienna, Albertina, Acquisition, 1939 Leipzig, 1939 (28272),

Prov. Leipzig, C. G. Boerner (no. 201), Lit. Boerner 1939, cat. 4, pl. II; Andrews 1964, cat. 37; Novotny 1971, cat. 2, pl. II, p. 10, PLATE 273

Johann Heinrich Ferdinand Olivier first learned drawing from the landscape artist Karl Wilhem Kolbe. In 1804, he moved to Dresden, where he was greatly influenced by Caspar David Friedrich. After a two-year sojourn in Paris, Olivier settled in Vienna and came into contact with other important artists of the period including Philipp Veit, Julius Schnorr von Carolsfeld, and Joseph Anton Koch. Together with his younger brother Friedrich, he traveled to Salzburg, making sketches of the countryside that would later form the basis for many of his paintings. Olivier's work anticipates the Biedermeier spirit in its emphasis on nature and the harmony of the natural world.

XIII-63   Ferdinand Olivier (Dessau 1785–1841 Munich), *Seven Regions / from Salzburg and Berchtesgaden. / Arranged according to the Seven Days of the Week, / Joined by Two Allegorical Sheets. / by / Ferdinand Olivier*, 1823, series of nine tinted lithographs, *Dedication*, 28 x 35.4 cm; *Sunday. Church Entry in Berchtesgaden*, 19.3 x 26.8 cm; *Monday. Roseneck Garden outside Salzburg*, 19.6 x 27.2 cm; *Tuesday. Salzburg Castle from the Noon Side*, 19.5 x 26.8 cm; *Wednesday. Footpath on the Mönchsberg near Salzburg*, 20 x 27.3 cm; *Thursday. Berchtesgaden and Watzmann*, 20.5 x 27.7 cm; *Friday. Meadow outside Aigen near Salzburg*, 19.5 x 27.1 cm; *Saturday. Graveyard of St. Peter in Salzburg*, 19.3 x 27.8 cm; *Keystone*, 27.5 x 37.4 cm, Vienna, Albertina, Acquisition, 1939 (DG 1939/3-11), Prov. Munich, W. Koeberlin, Lit. Grote 1938, cats. 126–38, pp. 212ff.; Schwarz 1977, pp. 17–20, pls. 47–55; Schwarz and Hermann-Fichtenau 1988, pp. 147–48, ill. p. 243, PLATES 263 AND 264

XIII-64   Friedrich Olivier (Dessau 1791–1859 Dessau), *Wilted Leaf*, 1817, pen and grayish-brown ink, brushed white highlights over pencil, 14.6 x 16.4 cm, Vienna, Albertina, Acquisition, 1927 (25309), Prov. Vienna, Marie Schmiedl, granddaughter of Friedrich Olivier, Lit. Grote 1938, p. 147; Bernhard 1973, ill. p. 1020; Mainz 1994, p. 50, n. 1

Like his older brother Ferdinand, Friedrich Olivier's first art instruction came from Karl Wilhelm Kolbe. He then trained at the Vienna Kunstakademie after 1811. Sketching trips to Salzburg and the Salzkammergut with his brother and other artists proved to be a turning point for the realist school of painting; Olivier, like his fellow artists, produced dense drawings full of detail. In 1817, Olivier moved to Rome, joining the Nazarene artists including Johann Friedrich Overbeck, Peter von Cornelius, Wilhelm von Schadow, and Philipp Veit. Olivier was greatly influenced by the work of Italian Renaissance masters and sought to emulate their precise drawing. His work, like that of his brother, is seen as an anticipation of the next generation of artists.

XIII-65   Johann Friedrich Overbeck (Lübeck 1789-1869 Rome), *Head of a Boy*, 1811/18, 21.4 x 18.6 cm, pencil, Frankfurt am Main, Städelsches Kunstinstitut, Gift of Dr. Hans Börner (15270), Lit. Frankfurt am Main 1977, cat. E 18, p. 192, PLATE 265

Johann Friedrich Overbeck, a founding member of the Rome-based German artists' associations the Lukasbrüder (Brotherhood of St. Luke) and the Nazarenes, was a pivotal figure in the revival of religious art in the nineteenth century. He began formal drawing lessons in 1804 with Joseph Nikolaus Peroux, and in 1806 enrolled at the Akademie der bildenden Künste Wien. There, dissatisfied with the classically oriented program, he advocated religion as the true foundation of art and with Franz Pforr, Kondard Hottinger, and Ludwig Vogel, founded the Lukasbrüder. In 1810, the group settled in Rome in the deserted monastery of S. Isidoro. Overbeck began an intensive study of Italian Renaissance art, especially the work of Bernardino Pinturicchio (ca. 1452-1513) and Pietro Perugino (ca. 1450-1523). After Pforr's death in 1812, the brotherhood broke up, but Overbeck remained in Rome and converted to Catholicism. The remainder of his long career was spent mostly in Italy, where he devoted himself to fresco, oil painting, and drawing. His work was widely known and appreciated, and its strong linearism is seen as an important precedent to the Biedermeier period.

XIII-66   Franz Pforr (Frankfurt am Main 1788-1812 Albano, Italy), *Self-Portrait*, 1810, oil on canvas, 22.7 x 17.1 cm, Frankfurt am Main, Städelsches Kunstinstitut, on loan from the Frankurter Künstlergesellschaft (4837), Lit. Frankfurt am Main 1977, cat. D 21, p. 159, PLATE 260

His father, the painter Johann Georg Pforr, and his uncle, the art professor Johann Heinrich Tischbein the younger, were Franz Pforr's first art teachers. In 1805, he enrolled at the Akademie der bildenden Künste in Vienna, where he studied under Hubert Maurer, Franz Cauzig, and Johann Martin Fischer. In 1806, Pforr, together with his friend Johann Friedrich Overbeck and other young artists, began meeting to discuss artistic ideas. The group consciously rejected the prevailing styles and instead turned to German medieval artists for inspiration. They founded the Lukasbund (later known as the Lukasbrüder or Brotherhood of St. Luke), and in 1810 moved to Rome and settled in the abandoned monastery of S. Isidoro. Pforr favored a simple, even primitive, style in his efforts to

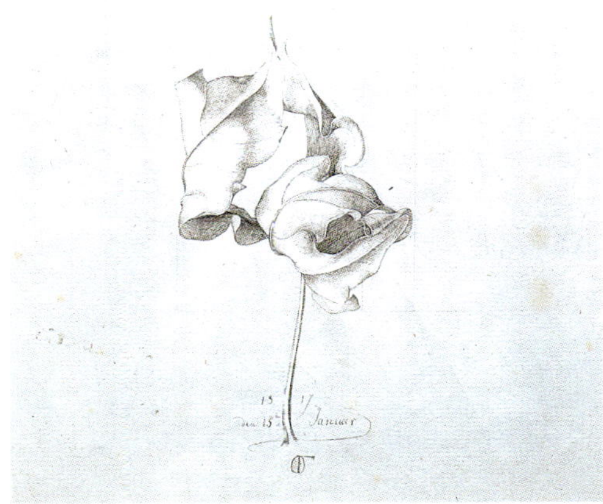

XIII-64

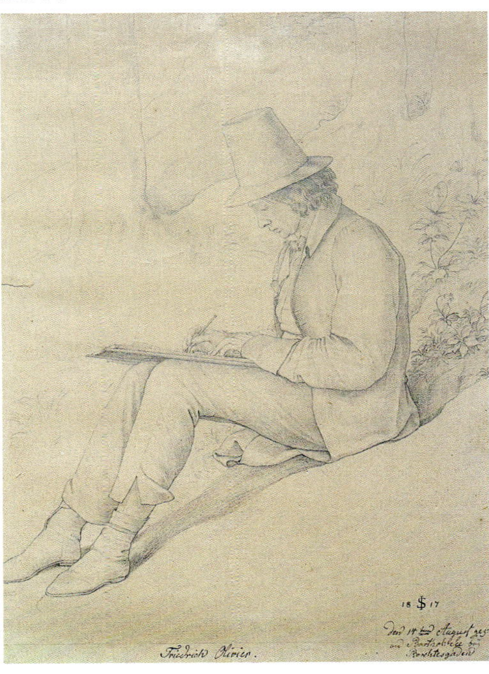

XIII-69

produce an honest and sincere art. His approach did much to influence the next generation of Biedermeier artists working in Vienna and elsewhere in Europe.

XIII-67   Johann Baptist Reiter (Linz 1813–1890 Vienna), *The Hard-Working Joiner Family*, before 1838, oil on canvas, 55.5 x 44.6 cm, Linz, Lentos Kunstmuseum Linz, donated by Walter and Uta Scherb, 1987 (790), Lit. Strobl 1963, p. 13, no. 20, ill. p. 18; Vienna 1993, cat. 80, PLATE 325

Johann Baptist Reiter was the son of a master cabinetmaker and began by learning his father's trade. As a journeyman in his father's shop, however, he spent most of his time painting signs, various pieces of furniture, and grave markers. In 1830, Reiter moved to Vienna where he enrolled in the engraving school of the Akademie der bildenden Künste Wien, but also took landscape classes and lessons in floral painting; he earned his living as a porcelain painter. In the autobiography published in 1884, he acknowledges his debt to Leopold Kupelwieser and Johann Ender, both professors of portraiture at the academy, which helps explain why Reiter's greatest achievements were in portraiture and genre painting. Reiter's portraits are distinguished for their conspicuous lack of ostentation, their intimate, close-up quality, and genrelike traits. Reiter became increasingly successful during the 1840s, but by mid-century was frequently accused of churning out pot-boilers. Nonetheless, his works still have great charm and transcend the merely anecdotal; they translate feelings and moods into paintings of great subtlety.

XIII-68   Johann Evangelist Scheffer von Leonhardshoff (Vienna 1795–1822 Vienna), *Self-Portrait*, ca. 1809, 37.1 x 28.8 cm, pencil, charcoal, blurred, Vienna, Albertina (24757), Prov. Vienna, Österreichische Galerie Belvedere, Lit. Vienna 1977, cat. 1, p. 116, ill. 1, PLATE 262

After studying at the Akademie der bildenden Künste Wien and fighting in the Napoleonic Wars, Johann Evangelist Scheffer spent the year 1812 in Venice before being appointed court painter to the Prince Bishop of Gurk, Franz Xaver Graf zu Salm-Reifferscheidt. Upon completing his academic study of painting in 1814, he traveled to Italy, where he spent a year in Rome with the Nazarenes – above all with Johann Friedrich Overbeck – although he did not became an official member of the Brotherhood of St. Luke until his return to Vienna in 1815. An exhibition of his works at the Vienna Kunstakademie in 1820 was a great success. After another trip to Italy, he returned via Salzburg to Vienna in 1821, where he died young of tuberculosis. His paintings and graphics are among the most important examples of religious art in Austria.

XIII-69   Julius Schnorr von Carolsfeld (Leipzig 1794–1872 Dresden), *Friedrich Olivier at the Königssee near Berchtesgaden*, 1817, pencil, 26.1 x 19.2 cm, Vienna, Albertina, Acquisition, 1927 (25311), Prov. Vienna, Marie Schmiedl, granddaughter of Friedrich Olivier, Lit. Grote 1938, p. 191, fig. 104; Andrews 1964, p. 111, fig. 39a; Schwarz 1977, pl. 57

Julius Schnorr von Carolsfeld hailed from a family of artists; his father, Hans Veit Schnorr, was his first art instructor. He enrolled at the Vienna Kunstakademie at age seventeen before moving to Rome in 1818 to join the Nazarenes, an artistic brotherhood of young German artists that grew out of the Lukasbund. Together with Peter von Cornelius, Johann Friedrich Overbeck, and Philipp Veit, Schnorr worked on decorating the Villa Massimo with frescoes, an art form the Nazarenes sought to revive. In 1827, he left Rome and settled in Munich, where he entered the service of King Ludwig. He created frescoes for the royal palace depicting events of German history and stories from the Nibelungenleid. Schnorr became a professor at the Akademie der Künste in Dresden in 1846, and was named the school's Gemäldegalerie director the following year.

XIII-70   Julius Schnorr von Carolsfeld (Leipzig 1794–1872 Dresden), *Portrait of Henriette Schnorr von Carolsfeld*, 1817, pencil, pen and brown ink, brown and gray washes, 20.8 x 16.9 cm, Vienna, Albertina, Acquisition, 1925 (24288), Prov. Leipzig, C. G. Boerner, Lit. Trenkmann 1985, cat. 52, PLATE 261

XIII-71   Franz Steinfeld (Vienna 1787–1868 Pisek), *The Hallstättersee in Upper Austria*, 1824, oil on panel, 59.4 x 83 cm, St. Pölten, Niederösterreichisches Landesmuseum, Purchase, 1963 (5862), Prov. Waidhofen an der Thaya, Private Collection, Lit. St. Pölten 2002, p. 68, PLATE 299

Franz Steinfeld was taught by his father, the Viennese sculptor Franz Steinfeld the Elder, famed, among other things, for the sculptures he created for the park of Schloss Schönbrunn. As a student at the Akademie der bildenden Künste Wien in 1802, Franz Steinfeld the Younger attended Laurenz Janscha's landscape classes. It was as a landscape artist that he visited The Netherlands in 1805. Impressed by the realism of Dutch landscape painting, upon his return to Vienna he began producing countless nature studies and landscapes of the surrounding countryside. He was appointed court painter to Archduke Anton in 1815, became a member of the academy in 1823, an examiner in the landscape class in 1837, and finally a professor in 1845. Steinfeld is among those artists credited with discovering the Austrian Alps; he visited the mountains at least once a year and later took his pupils with him. He is also regarded as the earliest representative of the fully developed Viennese Biedermeier landscape and he taught many of the landscape painters of the next generation.

XIII-72   Franz Steinfeld (Vienna 1787–1868 Pisek), *Torrent*, ca. 1824, oil on paper, 44 x 34 cm, Vienna, Akademie der bildenden Künste Wien, Kupferstichkabinett, Gift of the artist, 1839 (6634), Lit. Feuchtmüller and Mrazek 1963, fig. 51

XIII-73   Franz Steinfeld (Vienna 1787–1868 Pisek), *The Altausseersee with Trisselwand*, ca. 1825, oil on panel, 52.6 x 41.5 cm, Graz, Neue Galerie am Landesmuseum Joanneum, Bequest of B. Nowicky-Pernfuss, 1909 (I/433), Prov., Lit. Graz 1988, cat. 1746, p. 316, ill. p. 23

XIII-74   Franz Steinfeld (Vienna 1787–1868 Pisek), *The Hallstättersee*, before 1834, oil on canvas, 52.3 x 41.7 cm, Graz, Neue Galerie am Landesmuseum Joanneum (I/1798), Prov. Vienna, Kunsthandlung M. Suppan, Lit. Graz 1988, cat. 1747, p. 316, PLATE 301

XIII-75   Franz Steinfeld (Vienna 1787–1868 Pisek), *Landscape with Rocks*, ca. 1835, oil on paper, 35 x 27.7 cm, Vienna, Akademie der bildenden Künste, Kupferstichkabinett, Gift of the artist, 1839 (6637)

XIII-76   Franz Steinfeld (Vienna 1787–1868 Pisek), *Mountain Stream*, 1835, oil on paper, 46.6 x 36 cm, Vienna, Akademie der bildenden Künste Wien, Kupferstichkabinett, Gift of the artist, 1839 (6632), Lit. Frodl 1987, cat. 133, p. 261, ill. p. 133

XIII-77   Ferdinand Georg Waldmüller (Vienna 1793-1865 Hinterbrühl near Mödling), *Strawberry and Blue Tit*, ca. 1810, watercolor on paper, 34 x 25 cm, Private Collection, Prov. Vienna, Kunstsalon Kovacek, Lit: Grimschitz 1957, cat. 1, p. 275; Feuchtmüller 1996, cat. 1, ill. pp. 26, 418

Plunged into poverty by the premature death of his innkeeper father, Georg Waldmüller's family determined that he should become a clergyman. However, against his mother's wishes, Georg left home at age fourteen to attend the Vienna Kunstakademie. In 1813, he became a pupil of the history painters Hubert Maurer and Johann Baptist Lampi. Waldmüller earned his living during these years by painting packaging for candy, producing miniature portraits, and, beginning in 1811, teaching drawing and painting stage sets in Agram. There he met his first wife, the singer Katharina Weidner. By the time they divorced in 1822, there were four children and Waldmüller was a successful portrait artist. In 1827, he was engaged to portray various members of the imperial family, and became keeper of the art gallery of the Akademie der bildenden Künste Wien and a professor in 1829. Conflict with his fellow professors culminated in a provocative pamphlet Waldmüller published in 1845 in which he cast doubt on the value of academic art and committed himself exclusively

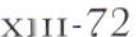

XIII-72

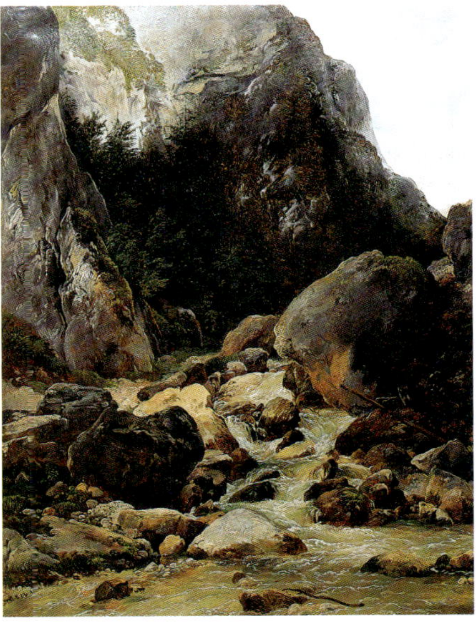

XIII-73

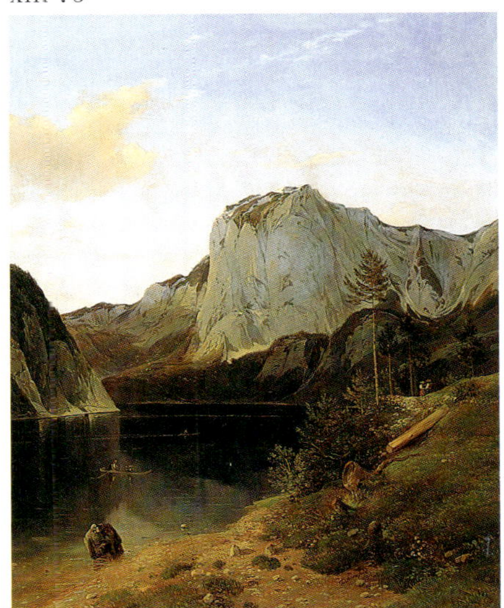

XIII-77

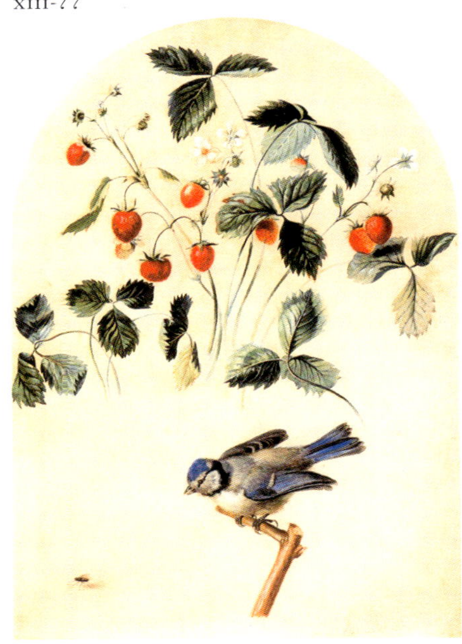

to art based solely on the study of nature. Although he was very successful up to the middle of the century, little was heard of him after he was forced to retire in 1857. Today, however, Waldmüller is widely regarded as Austria's greatest portraitist and landscape painter of the nineteenth century.

XIII-78   Ferdinand Georg Waldmüller (Vienna 1793-1865 Hinterbrühl near Mödling), *Catharina Baroness von Koudelka*, 1821/22, oil on canvas, 66 x 53 cm, Vienna, Österreichische Galerie Belvedere (5708), Prov. Acquired by exchange from the Vienna Art Market, 1964, Lit. Vienna 1992–2000, vol. 4, p. 232, ill.; Feuchtmüller 1996, cat. 90, ill. p. 426, PLATE 312

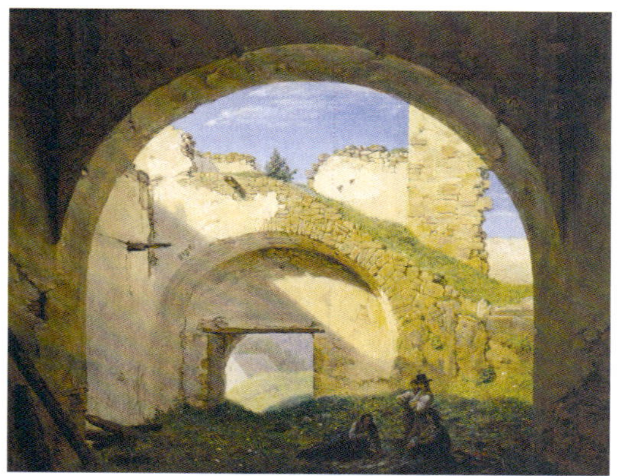

XIII-79   Ferdinand Georg Waldmüller (Vienna 1793-1865 Hinterbrühl near Mödling), *Klamm Ruin with Robbers as Staffage*, 1822/23, oil on panel, 19 x 26.5 cm, St. Pölten, Niederösterreichisches Landesmuseum (8274), Prov. Vienna, Galerie Gsell, until 1872, Lit. Vienna 1990, cat. 10, p. 238, fig. 7, p. 60; Feuchtmüller 1996, cat. 114, ill. p. 429; St. Pölten 2002, p. 72

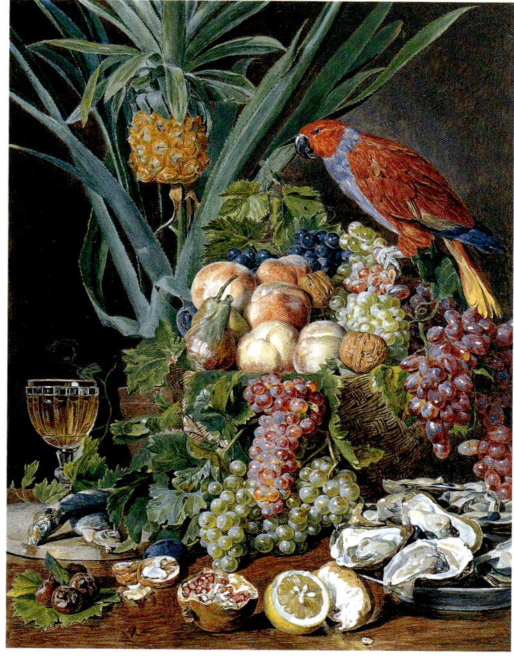

XIII-80   Ferdinand Georg Waldmüller (Vienna 1793–1865 Hinterbrühl near Mödling), *Girl with a Straw Hat (Portrait of Philippine Böhmer, Future Hofrätin Leotsch)*, ca. 1824, oil on canvas, 54 x 41 cm, Private Collection, Prov. Vienna, Galerie Maegle im Palais Harrach, Lit. Grimschitz 1957, cat. 151, p. 289; Vienna 1993, cat. 33, PLATE 316

XIII-81   Ferdinand Georg Waldmüller (Vienna 1793-1865 Hinterbrühl near Mödling), *Baron von Odkolek with His Wife and Their Two Sons*, 1826, oil on wood, 52.5 x 41.5 cm, Vienna, C. Bednarczyk, Prov. Stockholm, Thorsten Laurin Collection; Zurich, Galerie Neupert, Lit. Grimschitz 1957, cat. 439, p. 316; Feuchtmüller 1996, cat. 488, ill. p. 466, PLATE 317

XIII-82   Ferdinand Georg Waldmüller (Vienna 1793-1865 Hinterbrühl near Mödling), *Old Soldier with Three Children*, 1827, watercolor, 31.5 x 26.6 cm, Vienna, Albertina (34723), Prov. Vienna, Elisabeth M. Petznek, née Princess Windischgrätz; Vienna, Dr. Karl Ruhmann, Lit. Grimschitz 1957, cat. 212, p. 294; Hanover 1989, cat. 50, ill. p. 65; Feuchtmüller 1996, cat. 231, ill. p. 441, PLATE 318

XIII-83   Ferdinand Georg Waldmüller (Vienna 1793-1865 Hinterbrühl near Mödling), *The Burgtheater Actor Maximilian Korn (1792-1854) in a Landscape*, 1828, oil on panel, 31.5 x 26 cm, Chicago, The Art Institute of Chicago, Gift of Jane B. Gidwitz (2003.118), Prov. Vienna, Galerie Leo Schidlof, 1920; Austria, Private Collection; by descent to a brother-in-law, Bad Reichenhall, until 1974; by descent to his niece, until 2000; by descent to her son; Vienna, Dorotheum, 2001; Vienna, Private Collection; Munich, Daxer & Marschall, 2002, Lit. Grimschitz 1957, cat. 217, p. 295, pl. II; Vienna 1990, cat. 7, p. 17; Feuchtmüller 1996, cat. 237, ill., p. 441, PLATE 313

XIII-84 Ferdinand Georg Waldmüller (Vienna 1793-1865 Hinterbrühl near Mödling), *Portrait of a Gentleman in a Travel Coat*, 1829, watercolor, gouache, 18.6 x 17.4 cm. Vienna, Albertina (30638), Prov. Vienna, Schatzka Collection, Lit. Grimschitz 1957, cat. 230, p. 296; Hanover 1989, cat. 13, ill. p. 21; Feuchtmüller 1996, cat. 250, ill. pp. 60, 442, PLATE 314

XIII-85 Ferdinand Georg Waldmüller (Vienna 1793-1865 Hinterbrühl near Mödling), *Fruit Still Life with Parrot*, 1831, watercolor, gouache, 28.5 x 21.5 cm, Vienna, Albertina (34678), Prov. Vienna, Elisabeth M. Petznek–Windischgrätz, Lit. Grimschitz 1957, cat. 292, ill. p. 302, pl. 10; Hanover 1989, cat. 15, p. 25, ill.; Feuchtmüller 1996, cat. 324, ill. p. 450

XIII-86 Ferdinand Georg Waldmüller (Vienna 1793-1865 Hinterbrühl near Mödling), *The Ziemitzberg Seen from the Village Ahorn*, 1831, oil on panel, 30.5 x 24.5 cm, Cologne, Wallraf-Richartz-Museum (WRM Dep. 281), Prov. Linz, Führermuseum, Lit. Grimschitz 1957, cat. 384, p. 311; Vienna 1990, cat. 22, p. 239, fig. 18, p. 79; Feuchtmüller 1996, cat. 319, ill. p. 449, PLATE 306

XIII-87 Ferdinand Georg Waldmüller (Vienna 1793-1865 Hinterbrühl near Mödling), *Portrait of Baron von Moser in front of a Salzkammergut Landscape with Loser and Sandling*, 1833/35, oil on cardboard, 73.5 x 58.2 cm, Hanover, Niedersächsisches Landesmuseum Hannover (KA 312/1967), Prov. Berlin, Kunsthandlung Nikolai, 1928, Lit. Grimschitz 1957, cat. 405, p. 313; Vienna 1990, cat. 41, p. 241, fig. 22, pp. 86-87; Feuchtmüller 1996, cat. 450, ill. p. 463, PLATE 315

XIII-88 Ferdinand Georg Waldmüller (Vienna 1793-1865 Hinterbrühl near Mödling), *The Dachstein with the Gosausee*, 1834, oil on panel, 31.3 x 26 cm, Vienna, Leopold Museum (509), Prov. Vienna, Collection of Rudolf Leopold, 1984; Munich, Galerie Wolfgang Ketterer, Lit. Vienna 1990, cat. 37, p. 241, pl. 17, p. 78; Feuchtmüller 1996, cat. 434, ill. p. 461, PLATE 302

XIII-89 Ferdinand Georg Waldmüller (Vienna 1793-1865 Hinterbrühl near Mödling), *The Traunsee with Ort Castle*, ca. 1834/35, oil on canvas, 38 x 47 cm, Vienna, C. Bednarczyk, Lit. Vienna 1990, cat. 38, p. 241, ill. 27, p. 97; Feuchtmüller 1996, cat. 292, ill. pp. 57, 447, PLATE 304

XIII-90 Ferdinand Georg Waldmüller (Vienna 1793-1865 Hinterbrühl near Mödling), *The Dachstein from Sophien-Doppelblick near Ischl*, 1835, oil on panel, 31.5 x 26 cm, Vienna, Österreichische Galerie Belvedere (5712), Prov. Acquired by exchange from the Vienna Art Market, 1964, Lit. Grimschitz 1957, cat. 426, p. 315, pl. 51; Vienna 1992-2000, vol. 4, p. 243; Feuchtmüller 1996, cat. 476, ill. pp. 87, 465, PLATE 303

XIII-91 Ferdinand Georg Waldmüller (Vienna 1793-1865 Hinterbrühl near Mödling), *Portrait of Comtesse Julia Apraxin*, 1835, oil on panel, 38 x 32 cm, Vienna, Österreichische Galerie Belvedere (4655), Prov. Acquired by exchange from the Vienna Art Market, 1953, Lit. Grimschitz 1957, cat. 425, p. 314; Vienna 1992-2000, vol. 4, p. 243, ill.; Feuchtmüller 1996, cat. 475, ill. p. 465, PLATE 321

XIII-92 Ferdinand Georg Waldmüller (Vienna 1793-1865 Hinterbrühl near Mödling), *Portrait of the Daughter of Mr. and Mrs. Werner*, 1835, oil on canvas, 63.5 x 50 cm, Vienna, Österreichische Galerie Belvedere (3688), Prov. Vienna, Kunsthistorisches Museum, until 1939, Lit. Grimschitz 1957, cat. 413, p. 313; Vienna 1990, cat. 45, p. 241, ill. 35, p. 109; Vienna 1992-2000, vol. 4, p. 243; Feuchtmüller 1996, cat. 463, ill. pp. 103, 464, PLATE 320

XIII-93 Ferdinand Georg Waldmüller (Vienna 1793-1865 Hinterbrühl near Mödling), *Portrait of the Son of Mr. and Mrs. Werner*, 1835, oil on canvas, 63.5 x 50 cm, Vienna, Österreichische Galerie Belvedere (3687), Prov. Vienna, Kunsthistorisches Museum, until 1939, Lit. Grimschitz 1957, cat. 412, p. 313; Vienna 1990, cat. 44, p. 241, fig. 34, p. 108; Vienna 1992-2000, vol. 4, p. 242, ill.; Feuchtmüller 1996, cat. 462, ill. pp. 102, 464, PLATE 319

XIII-94 Ferdinand Georg Waldmüller (Vienna 1793-1865 Hinterbrühl near Mödling), *View of Hallstatt*, 1839, oil on panel, 45 x 58 cm, Salzburg, Salzburger Museum Carolino Augusteum (50/78), Prov. Vienna, Julius Trenkler Collection, until 1885; New York, Max Kade-Stiftung, Lit. Grimschitz 1957, cat. 537, p. 325; Vienna 1990, cat. 58, p. 242, ill. 49, pp. 132-33; Feuchtmüller 1996, cat. 592, ill. p. 477, PLATE 300

XIII-95 Ferdinand Georg Waldmüller (Vienna 1793-1865 Hinterbrühl near Mödling), *View from Höllental to the Schneeberg (Nature Study)*, ca. 1840, oil on panel, 25.5 x 31.5 cm, St. Pölten, Niederösterreichisches Landesmuseum, Purchase, 1965 (6448), Prov. Vienna, Private Collection, Lit. Grimschitz 1957, cat. 117, p. 285; Vienna 1990, cat. 18, p. 239, fig. 12, pp. 66-67; Feuchtmüller 1996, cat. 619, ill. p. 479; St. Pölten 2002, p. 76, PLATE 305

SELECTED BIBLIOGRAPHY

SALES AND
AUCTION CATALOGUES

Aukce 1945
Aukce 197., *Umĕlecka aukčni siň Zdenĕk Jeřábek*, cat. 1277. Prague, 1945.
Boerner 1939
C. G. Boerner. *Deutsche Handzeichnungen der Romantikerzeit. Deutsche Graphik des frühen XIX. Jahrhunderts. Alte Zeichnungen verschiedener Schulen*, cat. 201. Leipzig, 1939.
Hassfurther 1996
Galerie und Auktionshaus Hassfurther. *Erzherzog Johann. Die Kammermaler*, cat. 23. Vienna, 1996.
Nebehay 1988
Galerie C. M. Nebehay, cat. 9. Vienna, 1988.
Preis-Courant Königliche Eisengiesserei Gleiwitz 1847
Preis-Courant der Kunst-Gusswaren etc., welche auf der Königlichen Eisengiesserei bei Gleiwitz gefertigt und gegen bare Bezahlung für die beigesetzten Preise nach dem Stück verkauft werden, im Jahre 1847, dazu die "Abbildungen von gegossenen eisernen Kunst Erzeugnissen in der Königlichen Eisengiesserei bei Gleiwitz." Gleiwitz, 1847
Preis-Courrant Eisengusswerk Maria Zell 1820
Preis-Courrant sämmtlicher gemeiner und Kunstguss-Erzeugnisse, des kaiserlichen königlichen Eisengusswerkes nächst Maria Zell. Bruck, 1820..

BOOKS AND ARTICLES

Andrews 1964
Andrews, K. *The Nazarenes: A Brotherhood of German Painters in Rome*. Oxford, 1964.
Andrews and Andrews 1928
Andrews, E. D., and F. Andrews. "Craftsmanship of an American Religious Sect. Notes on Shaker Furniture." *The Magazine Antiques* 14, 2 (1928), pp. 132–36.
Andrews and Andrews 1937
Andrews, E. D., and F. Andrews. *Shaker Furniture. The Craftsmanship of an American Communal Sect*. New Haven, 1937.
Asenbaum and Asenbaum 1991
Asenbaum, G. S., and P. Asenbaum. "Wiener Silber 1800–1900." *Parnass* 6 (1991), pp. 74–82.

Bahr 1898
Bahr, H. "An die Secession." *Ver Sacrum* 1, 5–6 (1898).
Bartels 1898
Bartels, A. "Was ist zeitgemäss?" *Ver Sacrum* 1, 8 (1898), pp. 19–22.
Benjamin 1999
Benjamin, W. "Paris, the Capital of the Nineteenth Century: Exposé of 1935." In *The Arcades Project*, trans. H. Eiland and K. McLaughlin, pp. 3–13. Cambridge, Massachusetts, and London, 1999.
Bernhard 1973
Bernhard, M., ed. *Deutsche Romantik: Handzeichnungen*. 2 vols. Munich, 1973.
Bertuch 1786
Bertuch, F. J., and G. M. Kraus, eds. *Journal des Luxus und der Moden*. Weimar, 1786 ff.
Blumenbach 1825
Blumenbach, W. C. W. *Wiener Kunst- und Gewerbsfreund*. Vienna, 1825.
Boehmer 1968
Boehmer, G. *Die Welt des Biedermeier*. Munich, 1968.
Boehn 1908
Boehn, M. von. *Die Mode. Menschen und Moden im neunzehnten Jahrhundert 1790–1817*. Munich, 1908.
Boensch 2001
Boensch, A. *Formengeschichte europäischer Kleidung*. Vienna, 2001.
Boidi Sassone 2000
Boidi Sassone, A. *Furniture: From Rococo to Art Deco*. Cologne, 2000.
Börsch-Supan 1971
Börsch-Supan, H. *Die Kataloge der Berliner Akademie-Ausstellungen, 1786–1850*. 3 vols. Berlin, 1971.
Börsch-Supan 1976
Börsch-Supan, H. *Marmorsaal und Blaues Zimmer. So wohnten Fürsten*. Berlin, 1976.
Börsch-Supan 1988
Börsch-Supan, H. *Die deutsche Malerei von Anton Graff bis Hans von Marées: 1760–1870*. Munich, 1988.
Brockhaus 1844
Brockhaus, F. A. *Conversations-Lexikon*. Leipzig, 1844.
Brožová 1995
Brožová, J. *Empire-Biedermeier-Zweites Rokoko*. Vol. 2 of *Das Böhmische Glass 1700–1900*. Ed. G. Höltl. Passau, 1995.

Chase and Kemp 2001
    Chase, L., and K. Kemp. *The World of Biedermeier*. New York, 2001.
Clifford 1971
    Clifford, A. *Cut-Steel and Berlin Iron Jewellery*. Bath, 1971.
Eckermann 1987 (1910)
    Eckermann, J. P. *Gespräche mit Goethe in den letzten Jahren seines Lebens*. Leipzig, 1910. Reprint, ed. R. Ott, Berlin, 1987.
Eggers 1889
    Eggers, K. *Rauch und Goethe*. Berlin, 1889.
Fabian 1984
    Fabian, D. *Kinzing und Roentgen, Uhren aus Neuwied*. Neustadt, 1984.
Faÿ-Hallé and Mundt 1983
    Faÿ-Hallé, A., and B. Mundt. *Europäisches Porzellan vom Klassizismus bis zum Jugendstil*. Stuttgart, 1983.
Feuchtmüller 1987
    Feuchtmüller, R. *Friedrich Gauermann, 1807-1862*. Rosenheim, 1987.
Feuchtmüller 1996
    Feuchtmüller, R. *Ferdinand Georg Waldmüller, 1793-1865: Leben, Schriften, Werke*. Vienna, 1996.
Feuchtmüller and Mrazek 1963
    Feuchtmüller, R., and W. Mrazek. *Biedermeier in Österreich*. Vienna, 1963.
Fischel 1900
    Fischel, H. "Das Wiener Interieur von einst und jetzt." *Das Interieur* 1 (1900).
Folnesics 1903A
    Folnesics, J. *Innenräume und Hausrat der Empire- und Biedermeierziet*. Vienna, 1903.
Folnesics 1903B
    Folnesics, J. *Unser Verhältnis zum Biedermeierstil*. Vienna, 1903.
Fred 1903
    Fred, W. *Die Wohnung und ihre Ausstattung*. Bielefeld and Leipzig, 1903.
Frodl 1987
    Frodl, G. *Wiener Malerei der Biedermeierzeit*. Rosenheim, 1987.
Frodl 2002
    Frodl, G., ed. *Geschichte der bildenden Kunst in Österreich. 19. Jahrhundert*. Vol. 5. Munich, Berlin, London, and New York, 2002.
Frodl-Schneemann 1984
    Frodl-Schneemann, M. *Johann Peter Krafft, 1780-1856: Monographie und Verzeichnis der Gemälde*. Vienna, 1984.
Geismeier 1979
    Geismeier, W. *Das Bild vom Biedermeier, Zeit und Kultur des Biedermeier, Kunst und Kunstleben des Biedermeier*. Leipzig, 1979.
Gelfer-Jørgensen 1988
    Gelfer-Jørgensen, M. *Herculanum paa Sjaelland: Klassicisme og nyantik i dansk møbeltradition*. Copenhagen, 1988.
Gelfer-Jørgensen 2004
    Gelfer-Jørgensen, M. *The Dream of a Golden Age: Danish Neo-Classical Furniture 1790-1850*. Trans. W. G. Jones. Humlebaek, 2004.
Genschorek 1978
    Genschorek, W. *Carl Gustav Carus: Arzt, Künstler, Naturforscher*. Leipzig, 1978.
Gere 1989
    Gere, C. *Nineteenth-Century Decoration: The Art of the Interior*. New York, 1989.
Gere 1992
    Gere, C. *An Album of Nineteenth-Century Interiors: Watercolors from Two Private Collections*. New York, 1992.
Gmeiner-Hübel 1990
    Gmeiner-Hübel, G. "Jakob Alt (1789-1872): Leben und Werk." Ph.D. diss. Graz, 1990.
Godsey 2003
    Godsey, W. D. "'A Bourgeois Century?': Society and High Culture in Vienna, 1780-1920." In New York 2003, pp. 375-79.
Goethe 1900 (1798)
    Goethe, J. W. "Herman und Dorothea, Die Bürger." 1798. *Im Auftrage der Erzherzogin Sophie von Sachsen*. Vol. 50. Weimar, 1900.
Goethe 1984 (1805-10)
    Goethe, J. W. *Farbenlehre*. 1805-1810. 3rd ed. Ed. G. Ott and H. O. Proskauer. Vol. 1. Stuttgart, 1984.
Graf and Sangl 2004
    Graf, H., and S. Sangl. "Ein elegantes Meisterstück." *Weltkunst* 74, 11 (2004), pp. 80-81.
Greber 1980
    Greber, J. M. *Abraham und David Roentgen: Möbel für Europa: Werdegang, Kunst und Technik einer deutschen Kabinett-Manufaktur*. 2 vols. Starnberg, 1980.
Greenberg 1996
    Greenberg, C. "The Truth about Biedermeier." *Art & Antiques*, January 1996, pp. 70-75.
Grimschitz 1928
    Grimschitz, B. *Die österreichissche Zeichnung im 19. Jahrhundert*. Zurich, 1928.
Grimschitz 1957
    Grimschitz, B. *Ferdinand Georg Waldmüller*. Salzburg, 1957.
Grote 1938
    Grote, L. *Die Brüder Olivier und die deutsche Romantik*. Berlin, 1938.
Hannover 1893
    Hannover, E. *Maleren Christen Købke. En Studie i dansk Kunsthistorie*. Copenhagen, 1893.
Hannover 1898
    Hannover, E. *Maleren C. W. Eckersberg. En Studie i dansk Kunsthistorie*. Copenhagen, 1898.
Hanzl-Wachter 2002
    Hanzl-Wachter, L. "'Im Sommer auf's Land' – Kaiserliche Interieurs der Biedermeierstadt Baden." *Österreichische Zeitschrift für Denkmalpflege* 67, 2 (2002), pp. 265-76.
Hanzl-Wachter 2004
    Hanzl-Wachter, L. *Hofburg zu Innsbruck: Architektur, Möbel, Raumkunst: repräsentatives Wohnen in den Kaiserapparatements von Maria Theresia bis Kaiser Franz Joseph*. Vienna, 2004.
Heine 2000 (1835)
    Heine, H. *Historisch-kritische Gesamtausgabe der Werke, Die romantische Schule*. Paris, 1835. Ed. Manfred Windfuhr. Vol. 8/1. Dusseldorf, 2000.

Hevesi 1903
Hevesi, L. *Österreichische Kunst im 19. Jahrhundert.* 2 vols. Leipzig, 1903.

Hevesi 1906
Hevesi, L. "Biedermaier." In *Die fünfte Dimension*, pp. 164–74. Vienna, 1906.

Hevesi 1909
Hevesi, L. "Die Wiener Kongressausstellung." In *Altkunst-Neukunst: Wien, 1894–1908.* Vienna, 1909.

Heym 1990
Heym, S. *Schloss Rosenau.* Munich, 1990.

Himmelheber 1973
Himmelheber, G. *Biedermeier Furniture.* London, 1973.

Himmelheber 1996
Himmelheber, G. *Möbel aus Eisen, Geschichte, Formen, Techniken.* Munich, 1996.

Hoffmann, Moser, and Wärndorfer 1905
Hoffman, J., K. Moser, and F. Wärndorfer. *Arbeitsprogramm der Wiener Werkstätte.* Vienna, 1905.

Hölz 1999
Hölz, C., ed. *Interieurs der Goethezeit: Klassizismus, Empire, Biedermeier.* Augsburg, 1999.

Hornung and Monrad 2005
Hornung, P. M., and K. Monrad. *C. W. Eckersberg – dansk malerkunsts fader.* Copenhagen, 2005.

Hummel 1824–25
Hummel, J. E. *Die Freie Perspektive.* Berlin, 1824–25.

Hummel 1954
Hummel, G. *Der Maler Johann Erdmann Hummel.* Leipzig, 1954.

Johansson 1995
Johansson, E. *Wilhelm Bendz.* Copenhagen, 1995.

Kant 1790
Kant, I. *Kritik der Urteilskraft.* 1st section. Berlin, 1790.

Kastel 1983
Kastel, I. "Franz Eybl 1806–1880." Ph.D. diss. 3 vols. Vienna, 1983.

Kaut 1970
Kaut, H. *Modeblätter aus Wien.* Vienna, 1970.

Kessler 1978
Kessler, H. *Wiener Mode und Wiener Malerei 1800–1850.* Jena, 1978.

Koschatzky 1975
Koschatzky, W. *Rudolf von Alt, 1812–1905.* Salzburg, 1975.

Koschatzky 1982
Koschatzky, W. *Thomas Ender, 1793–1875. Kammermaler Erzherzog Johanns.* Graz, 1982.

Koschatzky 1987
Koschatzky, W. *Österreichische Aquarellmalerei 1750–1900.* Vienna, 1987.

Koschatzky 1991
Koschatzky, W. *Des Kaisers Guckkasten. Eine Sammlung alt-österreichischer Ansichten aus der Wiener Hofburg.* Salzburg and Vienna, 1991.

Koschnick 2006
Koschnick, L. Unpublished manuscript. Deutsches Historisches Museum. Berlin, 2006.

Krafft and Ransonnette 1801–12
Krafft, J. C., and N. Ransonnette. *Plans coupes et élérations des plus belles maisons et hôtels, Nachdruck der Originalausgabe.* Paris, 1801–12.

Kreisel and Himmelheber 1968–73
Kreisel, H., and G. Himmelheber. *Die Kunst des deutschen Möbels: Möbel und Vertäfelungen des deutschen Sprachraums von den Anfängen bis zum Jugendstil.* 3 vols. Munich, 1968–73.

Lassen 1964
Lassen, E. *Dansk Sølv.* Copenhagen, 1964.

Lichtwark 1899
Lichtwark, A. *Palastfenster und Flügelthür.* Berlin, 1899.

Loos 1898
Loos, A. "Die Potemkin'sche Stadt." *Ver Sacrum* 1, 7 (1898).

Loos 1962
Loos, A. *Sämtliche Schriften.* Ed. F. Glück. 2 vols. Vienna and Munich, 1962.

Loschek 1999
Loschek, I. *Reclam's Mode- und Kostümlexikon.* Stuttgart, 1999.

Luthmer and Schmidt 1922
Luthmer, F., and R. Schmidt. *Empire- und Biedermeiermöbel.* Stuttgart, 1922.

Lutterotti 1985
Lutterotti, O. R. von. *Joseph Anton Koch, 1768–1839, Leben und Werk. Mit einem vollständigen Werkverzeichnis.* Vienna and Munich, 1985.

Lux 1904–1905
Lux, A. "Biedermeier als Erzieher." *Hohe Warte* 2 (1904–1905), pp. 145ff.

Lux 1906–1907
Lux, A. "Die Werdenden." *Hohe Warte* 3 (1906–1907).

Marko 1980
Marko, E. "Jakob Gauermann (1773–1843): Leben und Werk." Ph.D. diss. Graz, 1980.

Marks 1966
Marks, A. *Oberösterreich in alten Ansichten.* Linz, 1966.

Marquardt 1984
Marquardt, B. *Eisen, Gold und bunte Steine. Bürgerlicher Schmuck zur Zeit des Klassizismus und des Biedermeier, Deutschland, Österreich, Schweiz.* Berlin, 1984.

Martins 1824
Martins, J. "Zur Geschichte der Eisengiesserei im Allgemeinen, und insbesondere der Bildgiesserei von Eisen." In *Verhandlungen des Vereins zur Beförderung des Gewerbefleisses in Preussen*, Berlin, 1824, pp. 215–310.

Matthaei 1963
Matthaei, R. *Die Zeichnungen zur Farbenlehre. Schriftenreihe: Corpus der [Johann Wolfgang von] Goethezeichnungen.* Vol. 5a. Weimar, 1963.

Matthaei 1971
Matthaei, R. *Goethes Farbenlehre.* Ravensburg, 1971.

Maul 1996
Maul, G. *Goethes Wohnhaus.* Weimar, 1996.

May 1965
May, A. *Wien in alten Ansichten*. Salzburg, 1965.

Meffert 1986
Meffert, E. *Carl Gustav Carus: Sein Leben - seine Anschauung von der Erde*. Stuttgart, 1986.

Millar 1995
Millar, D. *The Victorian Watercolours and Drawings in the Collection of Her Majesty the Queen*. London, 1995.

Muther 1909
Muther, R. *Geschichte der Malerie*. 3 vols. Leipzig, 1909.

Norman 1987
Norman, G. *Biedermeier Painting, 1815-1848. Reality Observed in Genre, Portrait and Landscape*. London, 1987.

Novotny 1960
Novotny, F. *Painting and Sculpture in Europe, 1780 to 1880*. Baltimore, 1960.

Novotny 1971
Novotny, F. *Ferdinand Oliviers Landschaftszeichnungen von Wien und Umgebung*. Graz, 1971.

Ottillinger 2003
Ottillinger, E. *Gebrüder Thonet: Möbel aus gebogenem Holz*. Vienna, 2003.

Ottillinger and Hanzl 1997
Ottillinger, E., and L. Hanzl. *Kaiserliche Interieurs: die Wohnkultur des Wiener Hofes im 19. Jahrhundert und die Wiener Kunstgewerbereform*. Vienna, 1997.

Ottomeyer 1976
Ottomeyer, H. "Das frühe Oeuvre Charles Perciers 1782-1802 - Zu den Anflägen des Historismus in Frankreich." Ph.D. diss. Munich, 1976.

Ottomeyer 1979
Ottomeyer, H., ed. *Das Wittelsbacher Album, Interieurs königlicher Wohn- und Festräume, 1799-1848*. Munich, 1979.

Ottomeyer 1994
Ottomeyer, H. "Wege zur neuen Einfachheit - Arbeiten der Münchner Hofschreinerei 1800-1817." In *Ein Jahrhundert Möbel, für den Fürstenhof: Karlsruhe, Mannheim, Sankt Petersburg 1750 bis 1850*, cat. by R. Stratmann-Döhler and W. Wiese. Karlsruhe: Badisches Landesmuseum, 1994, pp. 77-85.

Ottomeyer and Schlapka 2000
Ottomeyer, H., and A. Schlapka. *Biedermeier: Interieurs und Möbel*. Munich, 2000.

Pazaurek 1922
Pazaurek, G. E. "Zur Geschichte des Biedermeierglases." *Der Cicerone* 14 (1922).

Pazaurek and von Philippovich 1979
Pazaurek, G. E., and E. von Philippovich. *Gläser der Empire- und Biedermeierzeit*. Leipzig, 1923. Reprint, Braunschweig, 1979.

Pötschner 1978
Pötschner, P. *Wien und die Wiener Landschaft: Spätbarocke und biedermeierliche Landschaftskunst in Wien*. Salzburg, 1978.

Prause 1968
Prause, M. *Carl Gustav Carus. Leben und Werk*. Berlin, 1968.

Pressler, Döbner, and Eller 2002
Pressler, R., S. Döbner, and W. L. Eller. *Antique Biedermeier Furniture*. Atglen, Pennsylvania, 2002.

Pressler and Straub 1986
Pressler, R., and R. Straub. *Biedermeier-Möbel*. Munich, 1986.

Probszt-Ohstorff 1927
Probszt-Ohstorff, G. *Friedrich von Amerling. Der Altmeister der Wiener Porträtmalerei*. Zurich, 1927.

Quatremère de Quincy 1998 (1796)
Quatremère de Quincy, A. C. *Über den nachtheiligen Einfluss der Versetzung der Monumente aus Italien auf Künste und Wissenschaften*. Paris, 1796, 2nd letter. In *Schriften der Winckelmann-Gesellschaft*. Vol. 16. Stendal, 1998.

Rosenblum 1975
Rosenblum, R. *Modern Painting and the Northern Romantic Tradition: Friedrich to Rothko*. New York, 1975.

Rosner 1898
Rosner, K. *Die dekorative Kunst im neunzehnten Jahrhundert. Ein Stück Kunstgeschichte*. Berlin, 1898.

Sangl 1994
Sangl, S. "Empire und Biedermeiermöbel aus der Fürstlichen Sammlung Thurn und Taxis." *Weltkunst* 22 (1994), pp. 3199-3202.

Sármány-Parsons 2001
Sármány-Parsons, I. "Art Criticism and the Construction of National Heritage." In Mihály Szegedy-Maszák, ed., *National Heritage - National Canon*, pp. 36-51. Collegium Budapest Workshop Series No. 11. Budapest, 2001.

Schmidt 1923
Schmidt, P. F. *Biedermeier-Malerei*. Munich, 1923.

Schmidt 1981
Schmidt, E. *Der preussische Eisenkunstguss. Technik, Geschichte, Werke*. Berlin, 1981.

Schmitz 1920
Schmitz, H. *Vor hundert Jahren. Festräume und Wohnzimmer des deutschen Klassizismus und Biedermeier*. Berlin, 1920.

Schmitz 1923
Schmitz, H. *Deutsche Möbel des Klassizismus*. Stuttgart, 1923.

Schmuttermeier 1988
Schmuttermeier, E. "Wiener Silber, Vom Klassizismus zum Biedermeier." *Parnass* 6 (1988), pp. 58-63.

Schnell 1994
Schnell, W. *Georg Friedrich Kersting (1785-1847)*. Berlin, 1994.

Schölermann 1898
Schölermann, W. "Lieber spät als nie!" *Ver Sacrum* 1, 1 (1898).

Schwarz 1977
Schwarz, H. *Salzburg und das Salzkammergut: Eine künstlerische Entdeckung der Stadt und der Landschaft in Bildern des 19. Jahrhunderts*. 4th rev. ed. Salzburg, 1977.

Schwarz and Hermann-Fichtenau 1988
Schwarz, H., and E. Hermann-Fichtenau. *Die*

Anfänge der Lithographie in Österreich. Vienna, Cologne, and Graz, 1988.

Seelig 1981
Seelig, L. "Wiener Biedermeier in Coburg." *Alte und Moderne Kunst* 178-79, 26 (1981), pp. 2-10.

Seelig 1987
Seelig, L. "Zwei Becher." In *Münchner Jahrbuch der Bildenden Kunst*, 3rd series, 38 (1987), pp. 248f.

Semper 1834
Semper, G. *Vorläufige Bemerkungen über bemalte Architectur und Plastik bei den Alten*. Altona, 1834.

Semper 1852
Semper, G. *Wissenschaft, Industrie und Kunst, Vorschläge zur Anregung nationalen Kunstgefühls bei dem Schlusse der Londener Industrie-Ausstellung*. Braunschweig, 1852.

Sheehan 1994
Sheehan, J. J. *German History, 1770-1866*. New York, 1994.

Sievers 1950
Sievers, J. *Karl Friedrich Schinkel: Lebenswerk*. Vol. 6, *Die Möbel*. Berlin, 1950.

Simson and Ottomeyer 1994
Simson, O. von, and H. Ottomeyer. "Biedermeier – ein bürgerlicher Stil?" In M. Bockemühl, U. Miksche, and U. von Gizycki, *Das Kunstwerk und die Wissenschaften*, Ostfildern, 1994, pp. 69-87.

Simson 1996
Simson, J. von. *Christian Daniel Rauch*. Berlin, 1996.

Söntgen 2004
Söntgen, B. "Schwellenphänomen, Perspektiv-Hummels Raumkunst." In G. Brandstetter and G. Neumann, eds., *Romantische Wissenspoetik: Die Künste und die Wissenschaften um 1800*. Stiftung für Romantikforschung. Vol. 26. Würzburg, 2004.

Spiegl 1983
Spiegl, W. "Kothgasser, Mohn und die Wiener Porzellanmanufaktur." *Weltkunst* 53 (1983).

Springschitz 1949
Springschitz, L. *Wiener Mode im Wandel der Zeit*. Vienna, 1949.

Stein 2002
Stein, L. "Hermann Muthesius im deutsch-britischen Diskurs, 1896-1905." In *Hermann Muthesius and the Deutscher Werkbund*, ed. Y. Ikeda. Kyoto: National Museum of Modern Art, 2002.

Stengel 1999
Stengel, W. "Zur Geschichte der Berliner Goldschmiedekunst, Erstveröffentlichung in einer Textbearbeitung von Albrecht Pyritz und Kurt Winkler." In R. Güntzer, ed., *Jahrbuch 1997, Stadtmuseum Berlin*. Berlin, 1999, pp. 211-60.

Stephan 1993
Stephan, B. *Skulpturensammlung Dresden: Klassizistische Bildwerke*. Munich, 1993.

Stiegel 2003
Stiegel, A. *Berliner Möbelkunst vom Ende des 18. bis zur Mitte des 19. Jahrhunderts*. Berlin, 2003.

Stifter 2000 (1857)
Stifter, A. *Der Nachsommer*. Leipzig, 1857. In *Werke und Briefe*, ed. A. Doppler. Vol. 3. Stuttgart, 2000.

Strasser [1977]
Strassser, R. von. *Die Einschreibbüchlein des Glas- und Porzellanmalers Anton Kothgasser*. Karlsruhe, [1977].

Strobl 1963
Strobl, A. *Johann Baptist Reiter*. Vienna and Munich, 1963.

Suppan 1987
Suppan, M. *Biedermeier Schreibmöbel. Erlesenes Mobiliar aus der Zeit von 1810 bis 1850*. Vienna, 1987.

Thümmler 1998
Thümmler, S. *Der Tapetenfabrikant Johann Christian Arnold, 1758-1842*. Kassel, 1998.

Tieck 1966 (1836)
Tieck, J. L. *Der junge Tischlermeister*. Berlin, 1836. In *Werke in 4 Bänden*. Vol. 4, *Romane*. Ed. M. Thalmann. Munich, 1966.

Trenkmann 1985
Trenkmann, P. "Julius Schnorr von Carolsfeld. Zeichnungen bis 1827." Ph.D. diss. Greifswald, 1985.

Uchalová 1999
Uchalová, E. *Czech Fashion: For Salon and Promenade, 1780-1870*. Prague, 1999.

Vaughan 1980
Vaughan, W. *German Romantic Painting*. New Haven and London, 1980.

Völker 1996
Völker, A. *Biedermeierstoffe*. Vienna, 1996.

Vondráček 2003
Vondráček, R. *Views of Nineteenth-Century Aristocratic Interiors from the Collections of the Museum of Decorative Arts in Prague*. Prague, 2003.

Wagner 1896
Wagner, O. *Moderne Architektur*. Vienna, 1896.

Wagner 1979 (1914)
Wagner, O. *Die Baukunst unserer Zeit*. Vienna, 1914. Reprint, Vienna, 1979.

Wagner 1987 (1889)
Wagner, O. *Einige Skizzen, Projekte und ausgeführte Bauwerke von Otto Wagner*. Vienna, 1889. Reprint, Tübingen, 1987.

Waissenberger 1986
Waissenberger, R., ed. *Vienna in the Biedermeier Era, 1815-1848*. New York, 1986.

Weiglin 1941
Weiglin, P. *Berliner Biedermeier. Leben, Kunst und Kultur in alt-Berlin zwischen 1815 und 1848*. Bielefeld, 1941.

Wichmann 1970
Wichmann, S. *Wilhelm von Kobell*. Munich, 1970.

Wietersheim-Meran 1989
Wietersheim-Meran, M. T. von. *Von der Ritteridylle zum Bilddokument. Matthäus Loder (1781-1828). Ein Kammermaler des Erzherzogs Johann von Österreich*. Vienna and Cologne, 1989

Wilk 2003
Wilk, C. "Looking at the Past through Modern

Eyes." In New York 2003, pp. 375-77.

Wilkie 1987
Wilkie, A. *Biedermeier.* New York, 1987.

Winckelmann 1764
Winckelmann, J. J. *Geschichte der Kunst des Altertums.* Dresden, 1764.

Winters 2004
Winters, L. "An Introduction to the Biedermeier Period." *The Magazine Antiques* 165, 1 (January 2004), pp. 178-83.

Wirth 1979
Wirth, I. *Eduard Gaertner, der Berliner Architekturmaler.* Frankfurt am Main, 1979.

Wirth 1985
Wirth, I. "Neues von Eduard Gaertner. Nachtrag zum Werkverzeichnis des Künstlers." *Kunst & Antiquitäten* 5 (1985), pp. 60-68.

Witt-Dörring 1987
Witt-Dörring, C. "A Viennese Secretary in the Empire Style." *The Art Institute of Chicago Museum Studies* 15, 1 (1987). pp. 54-67.

Witt-Dörring 1989
Witt-Dörring, C. *Teetischmodelle der Danhauser'schen Möbelfabrik.* Vienna, 1989.

Witt-Dörring 1991
Witt-Dörring, C. "Empire oder höfisches Biedermeier?" *Kunst und Antiquitäten*, no. 11 (1991), pp. 16-20.

Witt-Dörring 1993
Witt-Dörring, C. "A Group of Early Seat Furniture with Composition Decoration, from the Danhauser Furniture Factory." *The Journal of the Furniture History Society* 29 (1993), pp. 147-53.

Witt-Dörring 1998
Witt-Dörring, C. "Auf der Suche nach den Wurzeln der Moderne. Das Wiener Empire- und Biedermeiermöbel – Zeuge einer ausgestorbenen Materialsprache." Special issue, *Parnass* 14 (1998), pp. 38-47.

Yelin 1818
Yelin, J. C. von. *Das Kaleidoscop, eine Bairische Erfindung.* Munich, 1818.

Zatschek 1958
Zatschek, H. *550 Jahre jung sein. Die Geschichte eines Handwerks.* Vienna, 1958.

Zinnkann 1985
Zinnkann, H. *Mainzer Möbelschreiner der ersten Hälfte des 19. Jahrhunderts.* Frankfurt, 1985.

Zuckerkandl 1898
Zuckerkandl, B. "Wiener Geschmacklosigkeiten." *Ver Sacrum* 1, 2 (1898).

Zuckerkandl 1908
Zuckerkandl, B. "Kunstgewerbe I." *Zeitkunst. Wien 1901-1907.* Vienna, 1908.

EXHIBITION AND
COLLECTION CATALOGUES

Baden 1988
Im Schatten der Weilburg. Baden im Biedermeier. Cat. ed. J. Kräftner. Baden: Frauenbad Baden, 1988.

Berlin 1970
Wohnen in Berlin. Berliner Innenräume der Vergangenheit. Ed. I. Wirth. Berlin: Berlin Museum, 1970.

Berlin 1979
Pflanzen auf Porzellan. Cat. by W. Baer and H. W. Lack. Berlin: Botanischer Garten und Botanisches Museum Berlin-Dahlem, 1979.

Berlin 1981A
Hegel in Berlin. Ed. O. Pöggeler. Berlin: Staatsbibliothek Preussischer Kulturbesitz, 1981.

Berlin 1981B
Karl Friedrich Schinkel: Architektur, Malerei, Kunstgewerbe. Ed. H. Börsch-Supan. Berlin: Staatliche Schlösser und Gärten Berlin; and Nationalgalerie Berlin, 1981.

Berlin 1982
Eisen statt Gold, Preussischer Eisenkunstguss aus dem Schloss Charlottenburg, dem Berlin-Museum und anderen Sammlungen. Cat. by W. Arenhövel. Berlin: Schloss Charlottenburg, 1982.

Berlin 1987
Kunsthandwerk und Kunstgewerbe vom 17. bis zum 20. Jahrhundert. Cat. by R. Altner and S. Peibst. Berlin: Märkisches Museum, 1987.

Berlin 1989
Berliner Porzellan aus dem Schloss Belvedere. Schloss Charlottenburg. Cat. by W. Baer. Berlin: Staatliche Schlösser und Gärten Berlin, 1989.

Berlin 1994
Stadtmuseum Berlin – Berlin Museum – Märkisches Museum. Gemälde I, 1, 16.-19. Jahrhundert. Cat. by S. Beneke and S. Gramlich. Berlin: Berlin Museum and Märkisches Museum, Berlin, 1994.

Berlin 1999
Das Flora Danica-Service, 1790-1802: Höhepunkt der botanischen Porzellanmalerei. Cat. by W. Baer. Berlin: Schloss Charlottenburg, 1999.

Berlin 2001A
Berliner Chic: Mode von 1820 bis 1990. Cat. by C. Waidenschlager. Berlin: Stiftung Stadtmuseum Berlin, 2001.

Berlin 2001B
Eduard Gaertner: 1801-1877. Ed. D. Bartmann and G. Ancke. Berlin: Stiftung Stadtmuseum Berlin, 2001.

Berlin 2003
Zur Zierde wie zum Nutzen des Hauses, Berliner Porzellan für den bürgerlichen Haushalt des 19. Jahrhunderts, Die Sammlung Albrecht Schütze. Cat. by D. J. Ponert. Berlin: Stiftung Stadtmuseum Berlin, 2003.

Berlin 2004
Die Königliche Eisen-Giesserei zu Berlin 1804-1874. Cat. by E. Bartel. Berlin: Stiftung Stadtmuseum Berlin, 2004.

Cambridge 1998
Fuseli to Menzel: Drawings and Watercolors in the Age of Goethe from a German Private Collection. Cat. by H. Sieveking. Cambridge, Massachusetts: Busch-Reisinger Museum, Harvard University Art Museums, 1998.

Chiavari 1985
  L'Arte della sedia a Chiavari. Ed. L. Pessa and
  C. Montagni. Chiavari: Palazzo Rocca, 1985.
Cleveland 1999
  European Paintings of the Nineteenth Century.
  Cat. by L. d'Argencourt and R. Diederen, et al.
  Cleveland: The Cleveland Museum of Art, 1999.
Copenhagen 1981
  Martinus Rørbye, 1803–1848. Cat. by D. Helsted,
  E. Henschen, B. Jørnæs, and T. Melander.
  Copenhagen: Thorvaldsens Museum, 1981.
Copenhagen 1994
  Den nøgne guldalder. Modelbilleder. C. W.
  Eckersberg og hans elever. Cat. by A. Johansen,
  E. Salling, and M. Saabye. English trans.
  and summary by W. G. Jones. Copenhagen:
  Hirschsprungske Samling, 1994.
Copenhagen 1996A
  Christian Købke, 1810–1848. Ed. H. E.
  Nørregård-Nielsen and K. Monrad.
  Copenhagen: Statens Museum for Kunst, 1996.
Copenhagen 1996B
  Wilhelm Bendz, 1804–1852: A Young Painter
  of the Danish Golden Age. Copenhagen:
  Hirschsprungske Samling, 1996.
Copenhagen 2002
  Danish Silver, 1600–2000. Cat. by Lise
  Funder. Copenhagen: The Danish Museum of
  Decorative Art, 2002.
Copenhagen 2004
  Danish Neo-Antique Furniture, From Abildgaard
  to Klaare Klint. Catalogue of the Collection.
  Cat. by M. Gelfer-Jørgensen. Copenhagen: The
  Danish Museum of Decorative Art, 2004.
Dresden 1993
  Skulpturensammlung Dresden: Klassizistische
  Bildwerke. Cat. by B. Stephan. Dresden:
  Staatliche Kunstsammlungen Dresden, 1993.
Dusseldorf 1962
  Wilhelm von Schadow, 1788–1862. Ed. I.
  Markowitz. Dusseldorf: Kunstmuseum der
  Stadt Düsseldorf, 1962.
Dusseldorf 1979
  Die Düsseldorfer Malerschule. Ed. R. Andree et
  al. Dusseldorf: Kunstmuseum Düsseldorf, 1979.
Edinburgh 1994
  The Romantic Spirit in German Art 1790–1990.
  Ed. K. Hartley, H. M. Hughes, P.-K. Schuster,
  and W. Vaughan. Edinburgh: Scottish National
  Gallery of Modern Art, 1994.
Eichenzell 1991
  Silber auf Reisen. Cat. by A. Dobler and M.
  Siemer. Eichenzell: Hessische Hausstiftung,
  Schloss Fasanerie, 1991.
Eichenzell 2004
  Interieurs der Biedermeierzeit: Zimmeraquarelle
  aus fürstlichen Schlössern im Besitz des
  Hauses Hessen. Cat. by A. Dobler. Eichenzell:
  Museum Schloss Fasanerie; Berlin:
  Deutsches Historisches Museum; Darmstadt:
  Schlossmuseum; and Kassel: Staatliche Museen
  Kassel, 2004.
Frankfurt am Main 1977
  Die Nazarener. Frankfurt am Main: Städtische
  Galerie im Städelschen Kunstinstitut, 1977.

Graz 1959
  Die Kammermaler um Erzherzog Johann. Graz:
  Neue Galerie am Landesmuseum Joanneum,
  1959.
Graz 1988
  Neue Galerie am Landesmuseum Joanneum.
  Gesamtkatalog der Gemälde. Ed. W. Skreiner.
  Graz, 1988.
Hamburg 2002
  Karl Friedrich Schinkel: Möbel und Interieur.
  Ed. B. Hedinger and J. Berger. Hamburg:
  Altonaer Museum, Jenisch Haus, München,
  2002.
Hanover 1989
  Biedermeier in Österreich: Zeichnungen und
  Aquarelle aus der Graphischen Sammlung
  Albertina Wien. Cat. by R. Bösel and C.
  Ekelhart. Hanover: Forum des Landesmuseums
  Hannover, 1989.
Kassel 1998
  Kasseler Silber aus Barock, Empire und
  Gründerzeit. Cat. by R. Neuhaus and E.
  Schmidberger. Kassel: Staatliche Museen
  Kassel, 1998.
Kassel 1999
  Geburt der Zeit: eine Geschichte der Bilder und
  Begriffe. Cat. by H. Ottomeyer, S. Lüken, and
  M. Röhring. Kassel: Staatliche Museen Kassel,
  1999.
Kiel 2005
  Die Kopenhagener Schule. Meisterwerke
  dänischer und deutscher Malerei von 1770 bis
  1850. Cat. by D. Luckow and D. Zbikowski.
  Kiel: Kunsthalle zu Kiel, 2005.
London 1959
  The Romantic Movement. London: Tate Gallery
  and the Arts Council Gallery, 1959.
London 1972
  The Age of Neo-Classicism. London: Royal
  Academy and The Victoria & Albert Museum,
  1972.
London 1979
  Vienna in the Age of Schubert: The Biedermeier
  Interior 1815–1848. Trans. Rita Moore. London:
  The Victoria & Albert Museum, 1979.
London 2001
  Spirit of an Age: Nineteenth-Century Paintings
  from the Nationalgalerie, Berlin. Cat. by F.
  Forster-Hahn, C. Keisch, P.-K. Schuster, and A.
  Wesenberg. London: National Gallery, 2001.
Los Angeles 1993
  Caspar David Friedrich to Ferdinand Hodler:
  A Romantic Tradition. Nineteenth-Century
  Paintings and Drawings from the Oskar
  Reinhart Foundation, Winterthur. Los Angeles:
  Los Angeles County Museum of Art, 1993.
Luxembourg 1995
  Collections du Prince de Liechtenstein.
  Luxembourg: Musée nationale d'histoire et
  d'art, 1995.
Mainz 1994
  Julius Schnorr von Carolsfeld: Zeichnungen.
  Mainz: Landesmuseum Mainz, 1994.
Milwaukee 2004
  Collection Guide. Milwaukee: Milwaukee Art
  Museum, 2004.

Munich 1971
*Die verborgene Vernunft, Funktionale
Gestaltung im 19. Jahrhundert.* Cat. by W.
Fischer and K.-J. Sembach. Munich: Neue
Sammlung München, 1971.

Munich 1987
*Biedermeiers Glück und Ende: die gestörte Idylle,
1815-1848.* Cat. by H. Ottomeyer, U. Laufer, and
D. Albert. Munich: Münchner Stadtmuseum,
1987.

Munich 1988
*Kunst des Biedermeier, 1815-1835: Architektur,
Malerei, Plastik, Kunsthandwerk, Musik,
Dichtung und Mode.* Cat. by G. Himmelheber.
Munich: Bayerisches Nationalmuseum
München, 1988.

Munich 1991
*Zopf- und Biedermeiermöbel: Katalog der
Möbelsammlung des Münchner Stadtmuseums.*
Cat. by H. Ottomeyer and E. Langenstein.
Munich: Münchner Stadtmuseums, 1991.

Munich 1993
*Die anständige Lust: Von Esskultur und
Tafelsitten.* Cat. by U. Zischka and H.
Ottomeyer. Munich: Münchner Stadtmuseum,
1993.

Munich 1997
*Nymphenburger Porzellan. Die Sammlung
Bäuml.* Cat. by A. Ziffer. Munich:
Nymphenburg Palace, Stuttgart, 1997.

Munster 2005
*Stobwasser: Lackkunst aus Braunschweig und
Berlin.* Cat. by D. Richter. Munster: Museum
für Lackkunst, 2005.

Neuwied 2004
*Von den Eiszeitjägern bis Munsteiner: wie der
Mensch sich schmückt.* Cat. by B. Willscheid.
Neuwied: Kreismuseum Neuwied, 2004.

New Haven 1970
German Painting of the Nineteenth Century.
Cat. by K. S. Champa with K. H. Champa. New
Haven: Yale University Art Gallery, 1970.

New York 1981
*German Masters of the Nineteenth Century:
Paintings and Drawings from the Federal
Republic of Germany.* New York: The
Metropolitan Museum of Art, 1981.

New York 1994
Cast Iron from Central Europe, 1800-1850.
Cat. by D. E. Ostergard. New York: The Bard
Graduate Center for Studies in the Decorative
Arts, 1994.

New York 2003
Viennese Silver: Modern Design 1780-1918.
Ed. and trans. Michael Huey. New York:
Neue Galerie; and Vienna: Kunsthistorisches
Museum, 2003.

Nuremberg 1995
*Mein blauer Salon: Zimmerbilder der
Biedermeierzeit.* Cat. by C. Lukatis. Nuremberg:
Germanisches Nationalmuseum Nürnberg,
1995.

Ottawa 2000
*Baltic Light: Early Open-Air Painting in
Denmark and North Germany.* Cat. by C.
Johnston, H. Börsch-Supan, H. R. Leppien,
and K. Monrad. Ottawa: National Gallery of
Canada, 2000.

Padua 2000
*Biedermeier: Arte e cultura nella Mitteleuropa
1815-1848.* Ed. R. Vondráček and V. Vinas.
Padua: Palazzo della Ragione, 2000.

Paris 1990
*Vienne 1815-1848: un nouvel art de vivre à
l'époque Biedermeier.* Paris: Château et Trianon
Bagatelle, 1990.

Paris 2003
Aux origines de l'abstraction, 1800-1914. Ed. S.
Laporte. Paris: Musée d'Orsay, 2003.

Potsdam 1990
*Blick auf Potsdam: Ansichten aus dem 18. und
19. Jahrhundert.* Cat. by G. Bartoschek, H.
Börsch-Supan, and A. Schendel. Potsdam:
Schloss Glienicke, 1990.

Prague 1976
*České sko 1800-1860. Katalog výstavy
Uměleckoprůmyslového musea v Praze.* Cat. by J.
Brožová. Prague, 1976.

Prague 2001
Buquoyské sklo v Čechách 1620-1851. Ed.
H. Brožková. Prague: Uměleckoprůmyslové
Museum, 2001.

St. Pölten 2002
*Waldmüller bis Schiele: Meisterwerke aus
dem Niederösterreichischen Landesmuseum.
Vom Biedermeier zum Expressionismus.*
Cat. by C. Aigner and W. Krug. St. Pölten:
Niederösterreichisches Landesmuseum, 2002.

Schallaburg 1997
*Zeugen der Intimität. Privaträume der
kaiserlichen Familie und des böhmischen Adels.
Aquarelle und Interieurs des 19. Jahrhunderts.*
Schallaburg: Schloss Schallaburg, 1997.

Stuttgart 1989
*Joseph Anton Koch, 1768-1839: Ansichten
der Natur.* Cat. by C. von Holst. Stuttgart:
Staatsgalerie Stuttgart, 1989.

Tulln 2005
*Biedermeier. Gemälde aus der Österreichischen
Galerie Belvedere.* Tulln: Minoritenkloster,
2005.

Vaduz 2005
*Biedermeier im Haus Liechtenstein: Die Epoche
im Licht der Fürstlichen Sammlungen.* Cat. by J.
Kräftner and T. Gabriel. Vaduz: Kunstmuseum
Liechtenstein, 2005.

Vienna 1930
Ferdinand Georg Waldmüller. Vienna:
Hagenbund–Neue Galerie, 1930.

Vienna 1937
*Gemäldekatalog der Galerie des neunzehnten
Jahrhunderts im Oberen Belvedere,* 2nd ed.
Vienna: Österreichische Galerie Belvedere,
1937.

Vienna 1969
Wien 1800-1850: Empire und Biedermeier.
Cat. by H. Bisanz et al. Vienna: Historisches
Museum der Stadt, 1969.

Vienna 1973
*Das Jahrhundert des Wiener Aquarells,
1780-1880.* Cat. by W. Koschatzky. Vienna:
Graphische Sammlung Albertina, 1973.

Vienna 1977
Johann Evangelist Scheffer von Leonhardshoff, 1795-1822. Vienna: Österreichische Galerie Belvedere, 1977.

Vienna 1978
Biedermeier und Vormärz. Die Kammermaler Matthäus Loder und Eduard Gurk. Cat. by W. Koschatzky and Maria Theresia Gräfin Meran. Vienna: Albertina, 1978.

Vienna 1981
Moderne Vergangenheit Wien 1800-1900. Cat. by P. Asenbaum, S. Asenbaum, and C. Witt-Dörring. Vienna: Gesellschaft bildender Künstler Österreichs, Künstlerhaus, 1981.

Vienna 1986
Die Blumenaquarelle des Moritz Michael Daffinger. Zur Erforschung der österreichischen Flora im Vormärz. Cat. by U. Jenni, R. Wagner, and M.-T. Winkler. Vienna: Kupferstichkabinett der Akademie der bildenden Künste, 1986.

Vienna 1987A
153 Sesselmodelle aus der Danhauser'schen Möbelfabrik. Vienna: Österreichisches Museum für angewandte Kunst, 1987.

Vienna 1987B
Bürgersinn und Aufbegehren: Biedermeier und Vormärz in Wien 1815-1848. Ed. R. Waissenberger. Vienna: Museen der Stadt Wien, 1987.

Vienna 1989
Kunst und Industrie, Aspekte einer Sammlung. Vienna: Österreichisches Museum für angewandte Kunst, 1989.

Vienna 1990
Ferdinand Georg Waldmüller. Cat. by K. A. Schröder. Vienna: Kunstforum Länderbank, 1990.

Vienna 1992
Eisenkunstguss der ersten Hälfte des 19. Jahrhunderts. Cat. by E. Schmuttermeier. Vienna: Österreichisches Museum für angewandte Kunst, 1992.

Vienna 1992-2000
Kunst des 19. Jahrhunderts. Bestandskatalog der Österreichischen Galerie des 19. Jahrhunderts. 4 vols. Vienna: Österreichische Galerie Belvedere, 1992-2000.

Vienna 1993
Wiener Biedermeier. Malerei zwischen Wiener Kongress und Revolution. Ed. G. Frodl and K. A. Schröder. Vienna: Kunstforum der Bank Austria, 1993.

Vienna 1996
Genormte Fantasie: Zeichenunterricht für Tischler, Wien 1800-1840. Cat. by G. Fabiankowitsch and C. Witt-Dörring. Vienna: Österreichisches Museum für angewandte Kunst, 1996.

Vienna 1997
Die deutschen und Schweizer Zeichnungen des späten 18. Jahrhunderts. Cat. by M. Gröning and M. L. Sternath. Vienna: Graphische Sammlung Albertina, 1997.

Vienna 2000
Glas aus 5 Jahrhunderten: Herbstausstellung 2000. Vienna: Glasgalerie Michael Kovacek, 2000.

Vienna 2003A
Friedrich von Amerling, 1803-1887. Ed. S. Grabner. Vienna: Österreichische Galerie Belvedere, 2003.

Vienna 2003B
Glasgalerie Michael Kovacek: Glas aus 5 Jahrhunderten. Vienna: Glasgalerie Michael Kovacek, 2003.

Vienna 2003C
Der Preis der Schönheit: 100 Jahre Wiener Werkstätte. Cat. by P. Noever, S. Mattl, P. Rainer, C. Witt-Dörring, and H. Zobernig. Vienna: Österreichisches Museum für angewandte Kunst, 2003.

Vienna 2004A
Klassizismus und Biedermeier. Cat. by J. Kräftner. Vienna: Liechtenstein Museum, 2004.

Vienna 2004B
Massenware Luxusgut: Technik und Design zwischen Biedermeier und Wiener Weltausstellung 1804 bis 1873. Cat. by R. Mittersteiner. Vienna: Technisches Museum Wien, 2004.

Vienna 2005
Rudolf von Alt, 1812-1905. Cat. by K. A. Schröder and M. L. Sternath. Vienna: Albertina, 2005.

Warsaw 2001
National Museum in Warsaw Guide. Ed. D. Folga-Januszewska and K. Murawska-Muthesius. Warsaw: National Museum, 2001.

Washington 2003
Christoffer Wilhelm Eckersberg, 1783-1853. Cat. by P. Conisbee, K. Monrad, and L. B. Rønberg. Washington, D.C.: National Gallery of Art, 2003.

Winterthur 1993
Faszination Glas. Historisches und modernes Glas aus der Tschechishen Republik. Cat. by F. Hobi and B. M. Bollinger. Winterthur: Gewerbemuseum, 1993.

Zaragoza 2004
Vidrio de Buquoy en Bohemia, 1620-1851: En las colecciones del Museo de Artes Decorativas de Praga. Cat. by O. Drahotová et al. Zaragoza: Fundación Centro Nacional del Vidrio, 2004.

PHOTOGRAPHY CREDITS

Photography of decorative arts is by Lois Lammerhuber, Vienna, unless noted below

John Hall © Abbeville Press: I-17, II-34. © The Art Institute of Chicago, Chicago (photography by Robert Hashimoto): I-19. © 2003 Asenbaum Photo Archive: IX-6, IX-15. Bayerisches Nationalmuseum, Munich: I-7, II-14, IX-61. D & S Antiques, Vienna: I-40. Daniel Romualdez Collection, New York: II-33. The Danish Museum of Decorative Art, Copenhagen: IX-62. Deutsches Historisches Museum, Berlin (photography by Arne Psille): II-3, XI-2. Deutsches Museum, Munich: V-14, V-15. Courtesy of Didier Aaron & Cie, Paris: I-3. Didier Aaron, Inc., and Barry Friedman, Ltd., Paris and New York: II-40. Photograph courtesy of Dorotheum, Vienna: VII-1. © Galerie Martin Suppan, Vienna, Austria: I-11. John R. Glembin: I-18, II-27, II-29. Hessische Hausstiftung, Kronberg: IX-52. © The Hirschsprung Collection, Copenhagen: II-6. Courtesy of Iliad Antik, New York: II-23, II-25. Courtesy of Iliad Antik, Prague: I-10. Kunstkammer Georg Laue München, Munich: V-21. © 1997 The Metropolitan Museum of Art, New York: II-21. Museum of Decorative Arts, Prague (photography by Miloslav Šebek): I-25, II-28, XI-1, XI-8; (photography by Gabriel Urbánek) VII-5, VII-10, VIII-6, VIII-9, VIII-13–VIII-21. Museum für Lackkunst, Münster: X-9. © Humboldt-Universität zu Berlin, Museum für Naturkunde, A. Dittmann: V-16–V-20. Private Collection, Wernberg: VIII-2. Wolfgang Pulfer: I-6, VIII-1. Schlapka KG, Axel Schlapka, Munich: II-36. © Staatliche Museen Kassel (photography by Ute Brunzel, D. Schwerdle): IX-58, IX-59. Stadtmuseum Kassel: IX-53. Stiftung Preussische Schlösser und Gärten Berlin-Brandenburg, Potsdam, (photography by Sebastian Rosenberg): II-8, II-10. Stiftung Weimarer Klassik, Goethe-Nationalmuseum, Weimar: V-6, V-9–V-12. Toledo Museum of Art, Toledo, Ohio: VIII-8. Uhrenmuseum Beyer Zürich: V-22–V-24. © 2006 Christian Wachter/VG Bild-Kunst, Bonn: VIII-3, VIII-7, VIII-11. © Wien Museum, Vienna: VIII-4, VIII-10.

Photography of paintings and works on paper is courtesy of the lenders, unless otherwise noted below

© Albertina, Vienna: XII-21, XII-22, XII-24, XII-28, XII-33, XII-34, XIII-1–XIII-5, XIII-7, XIII-39, XIII-41, XIII-42, XIII-44, XIII-48, XIII-56, XIII-62, XIII-63, XIII-68, XIII-70, XIII-82, XIII-84. © The Art Institute of Chicago, Chicago (photography by Robert Hashimoto): XIII-83. © The Cleveland Museum of Art, Cleveland: XII-34. Deutsches Historisches Museum, Berlin (photography by Sebastian Ahlers): IV-4. © Ursula Edelmann, Frankfurt am Main: XIII-65; courtesy of Artothek: XIII-66. Courtesy of Galerie und Auktionshaus Hassfurther, Vienna: XIII-23, XIII-38, XIII-53, XIII-55, XIII-57. Courtesy Galerie Maegle, Vienna: XIII-80. John R. Glembin: XII-38. © The Hirschsprung Collection, Copenhagen: XII-5–XII-7, XII-9. © Pernille Klemp: XII-36–XII-37. Kveta Krizova: IV-16–IV-18. © Kunstmuseum Basel, Martin Bühler: XIII-50. © Kunstsammlungen der Veste Coburg: IV-10–IV-12. Lois Lammerhuber: III-2–III-5, III-8–III-12, VI-1–VI-9. © Philipp Mansmann: XIII-29, XIII-30. Museum of Decorative Arts, Prague (photography by Miloslav Šebek and Ondřej Kocourek): VI-10. National Museum in Warsaw (photography by Teresa Żółtowska-Huszcza): XII-17. Niederösterreichisches Landesmuseum, St. Pölten (photography by Wolfgang Bernhard): XIII-71; (photography by Reinhard Kasper): XIII-79, XIII-95. Ny Carlsberg Glyptotek, Copenhagen (photography by Ole Woldbye): XII-39. © Österreichische Galerie Belvedere, Vienna: XIII-10, XIII-21, XIII-22, XIII-28, XIII-31, XIII-33, XIII-35, XIII-59–XIII-60, XIII-78, XIII-90–XIII-93. Rheinisches Bildarchiv Köln: XIII-86. Royal Collection © 2005 Her Majesty Queen Elizabeth II: IV-25–IV-28. © Staatliche Museen Kassel (photography by Ute Brunzel and D. Schwerdle): VI-11–VI-16. Stiftung Preussische Schlösser und Gärten Berlin-Brandenburg, Potsdam (photography by Gerhard Murza 1994): XII-41. Stiftung Stadtmuseum Berlin (photography by Hans-Joachim Bartsch): IV-3, IV-23, XII-13; (photography by Roman März): XII-15, XII-16. Tiroler Landesmuseum Ferdinandeum, Innsbruck. © Foto Linster: XIII-49. © 2006 Christian Wachter/VG Bild-Kunst, Bonn: XIII-9, XIII-11, XIII-24, XIII-58. © Wien Museum, Vienna: XIII-32.

Details

cover: XIII-7, back cover: I-16, pp. 2–3: XI-12, pp. 4–5: I-10, pp. 6–7: VII-3, pp. 8–9: II-15, pp. 10–11: XI-13, pp. 12–13: II-42, pp. 16–17, XII-19, pp. 20–21: XIII-26, p. 26: XIII-75, pp. 28–29: XIII-57, p. 30: XIII-9, p. 42: XII-21, p. 56: I-27, p. 70: XII-14

Biedermeier: The Invention of Simplicity is published
on the occasion of the exhibition of the same name organized by the Milwaukee Art Museum, the Albertina,
Vienna, and the Berlin Deutsches Historisches Museum. The exhibition is on view at the Milwaukee Art
Museum from September 16, 2006, through January 1,
2007; the Albertina, Vienna, from February 2 through
May 13, 2007; the Berlin Deutsches Historisches
Museum from June 8 through September 2, 2007; and
the Musée du Louvre, Paris, from October 15, 2007,
through January 15, 2008.

Published by the Milwaukee Art Museum in
conjunction with Hatje Cantz Verlag

Coordinator and Editor
Terry Ann R. Neff, t. a. neff associates, inc.,
Tucson, Arizona

German Editor
Karin Osbahr, Hatje Cantz

Translators
Allison Plath-Moseley
Bronwen Saunders
John Southard

Design and Typography
Studio Blue, Inc., Chicago

Photography
Lois Lammerhuber, Vienna

Paper
Profimatt, 150 g/m²

Binding
Bramscher Buchbinder Betriebe GmbH & Co.
KG, Bramsche

Reproduction
Grasl Druck und Neue Medien, Bad Vöslau

Printed by
Dr. Cantz'sche Druckerei, Ostfildern

Library of Congress
Cataloging-in-Publication Data

Winters, Laurie.
Biedermeier: The Invention of Simplicity / Hans
Ottomeyer, Klaus Albrecht Schröder, and Laurie
Winters; contributions by Albrecht Pyritz ... [et al.].
p. cm.
Catalog of an exhibition at the Milwaukee Art Museum,
Sept. 16, 2006–Jan. 1, 2007 and at three other museums.
Includes bibliographical references.

ISBN 978-3-7757-1796-0 (clothbound: alk. paper)
ISBN 978-0-944110-89-8 (softcover: alk. paper)

1. Biedermeier (Art) – Europe, Central – Exhibitions.
2. Art, European – Europe, Central – 19th century –
Exhibitions. I. Ottomeyer, Hans. II. Schröder, Klaus
Albrecht. III. Milwaukee Art Museum. IV. Title

N6465.B5W56 2006
709.43'0747755 – dc22

2006016784

Hatje Cantz books are available internationally at
selected bookstores and from the following distribution
partners:

USA/North America: D.A.P., Distributed Art
    Publishers, New York, www.artbook.com
UK: Art Books International, London,
    www.art-bks.com
Australia: Tower Books, Frenchs Forest (Sydney),
    www.towerbooks.com.au
France: Interart, Paris, www.interart.fr
Belgium: Exhibitions International, Leuven,
    www.exhibitionsinternational.be
Switzerland: Scheidegger, Affoltern am Albis,
    www.ava.ch

For Asia, Japan, South America, and Africa, as well
as for general questions, please contact Hatje Cantz
directly at sales@hatjecantz.de, or visit our homepage
at www.hatjecantz.com for further information.

Hatje Cantz Verlag
Zeppelinstrasse 32
73760 Ostfildern
Germany
Tel. +49 711 4405-200
Fax +49 711 4405-220
www.hatjecantz.com

Trade edition (clothbound with dust jacket)
ISBN 978-3-7757-1796-0 (English)
ISBN 978-3-7757-1795-3 (German)

Museum edition (softcover: alk. paper)
ISBN 978-0-944110-89-8

Printed in Germany